ENCYCLOPAEDIA OF
AVICULTURE
VOLUME 3

Lesser Double-collared Sunbird, *Nectarinia c. chalybea*

Scarlet-chested Sunbird, *Nectarinia senegalensis gutturalis*

Himalayan Yellow-backed Sunbird, *Aethopyga siparaja seheriae*

Malachite Sunbird, *Nectarinia f. famosa*

Purple Sunbird, *Nectarinia a. asiatica*

Tacazze Sunbird, *Nectarinia tacazze*

ENCYCLOPAEDIA OF
AVICULTURE

VOLUME 3

Edited by

A. RUTGERS *and* K. A. NORRIS

with
CYRIL H. ROGERS

Contributors include

J. L. Albrecht-Moller
H. J. Bates
R. L. Busenbark
Rosemary Low
K. A. Norris

BLANDFORD PRESS

POOLE   DORSET

English language edition first published in 1977
English text © 1977 Blandford Press Ltd
Link House, West Street, Poole, Dorset BH15 1LL

Original edition published in the Dutch language as
Encyclopedie voor de vogelliefhebber by A. Rutgers
© 1964–1968 by NV Uitgeverij 'Littera Scripta Manet'
Gorssel, Holland.

ISBN 0 7137 0802 6

Colour plates by J. F. van den Broecke and H. J.
Slijper, printed in Holland by Littera Scripta Manet.

Line drawings by W. J. Boer Leffef, J. F. van den
Broecke, Pieter Pouwels and Dr. A. K. Vink. Drawings
not otherwise credited are based on Gould.

Text set by Woolaston Parker Ltd., Leicester; books
printed and bound by Richard Clay (The Chaucer
Press) Ltd., Bungay, Suffolk, England.

CONTENTS

LIST OF COLOUR ILLUSTRATIONS

The complexities of preparing international editions of the Encyclopaedia, together with a further restriction of the availability of certain species to aviculturists, have necessitated that a few of the colour plates contain one or two birds which are not described in the main text of Volume 3.

LIST OF COLOUR ILLUSTRATIONS ● ix

PREFACE

The three volumes of the Encyclopaedia cover birds that are kept in aviaries and whose whole life cycles can therefore be studied and followed from first-hand observation. Some of the species dealt with are those kept in zoological gardens, since their needs cannot be adequately met in private collections. One or more representatives of every family is described and illustrated.

However, owing to present-day conditions and national conservation restrictions, etc., certain species have been omitted as examples of these birds are no longer available to aviculturists.

Where there are main articles by H. J. Bates and R. L. Busenbark, the descriptions of the selected species which follow are taken from their original material. Sexes are alike unless differences are specifically listed.

There are indexes covering the scientific and English names. A bibliography of books and magazines is given in each volume.

As far as nomenclature is concerned—especially in scientific names—we have, in general, followed those names contained in the parts already published of James Lee Peters' *Checklist of Birds of the World*.

We have followed the work of R. Mayr and D. Amadon, *A Classification of Recent Birds* wherever the names had not been included in Peters' *Checklist*.

For the many species which had already been named and are sufficiently well known by aviculturists, we have retained such names. However, in a few books published recently, the translators or compilers have given new names to birds that are already well known by other names. This naturally leads to unnecessary confusion. Only when the new names showed a definite improvement have they been listed as synonyms.

Keeping birds as a hobby is a very lively and fascinating occupation, in which both young and old may participate. The possibilities of study are so varied, that not only have biologists found in it the work of a lifetime, but thousands of amateurs have also added their contributions. Every observation of the birds' behaviour during the mating and breeding times, including nest-building, the duration of the breeding period and the food eaten at that time, is of importance in order to obtain a complete picture of the life of each individual bird.

It is important for all those keeping birds to know the conditions required by the different species so that they do not suffer any deprivations, and can quickly get accustomed to their altered way of life. Every year fresh breeding results are being obtained, and new species of birds are being included in collections. There are still a number of birds which cannot be kept in aviaries because, so far, no suitable equivalent has been found in place of their natural food. But as advances are being made, more species of birds can be kept and are able to breed. This is in the interests of the birds themselves, because should their life in the wild be threatened, aviculturists must be ready to ensure their continued existence.

In order to make foreign literature easy of access, the names of many birds are given in German, French and Dutch, where known. The English editions of Volumes 1 and 2 were edited by Kenneth Norris. While working on Volume 3, he unfortunately died. The subsequent advice of Cyril Rogers and his over-all editing has been most valuable, and we are grateful also for the help given by Rosemary Low, John Yealland and others.

PUBLISHER'S NOTE

CONTROLS ON IMPORTS OF CAPTIVE BIRDS INTO GREAT BRITAIN*

As from the 1st March, 1976, all imports of captive birds *and* hatching eggs into Great Britain are subject to licence. Each consignment of birds requires a licence, issued in advance of the importation and after approval of the proposed quarantine premises.

Quarantine requirements

A condition of the import licence is that all the birds will undergo a period of quarantine in approved premises provided by the importer. The quarantine period will normally be 35 days, subject to extension in the event of, or on suspicion of, disease.

Quarantine is on an 'all in–all out' basis. Several consignments of birds can be quarantined together, up to the maximum capacity of the premises. In such cases the quarantine period will run from the date of entry into quarantine of the last consignment, but the conditions of quarantine will be in force from the time of the first arrival.

Quarantine premises need to be approved in advance by the appropriate Agriculture Department and are specified in the import licence.

The other requirements and fuller details will not be given here, but all aviculturists and those involved in supplying or acquiring birds for breeding, or keeping in Great Britain should consult the document of the Ministry of Agriculture, Fisheries and Food.

Imports of small groups of birds

Notwithstanding the foregoing rules, licences are granted for imports into Great Britain of up to 12 non-psittacine birds from countries whose disease status and methods of disease control are considered satisfactory by the Agriculture Departments. Special conditions apply here and aviculturists should again check the detailed regulations given by the UK Ministry of Agriculture, Fisheries and Food.

WILD BIRDS AND THE LAW

As Volume 3 contains species which are found in the wild in both the British Isles and North America, the publishers feel that it is worth while drawing the attention of readers to the various laws which govern the protection, capture and captivity of birds in those areas. For example, in the UK, the legal requirements are contained within the Protection of Birds Act, 1954, as amended, and a useful summary may be found in the R.S.P.B. publication *Wild Birds and the Law*.

* See also Appendix on page 224 for details of special import controls covering some species contained in Volume 1.

DIETS FOR SOFTBILLED BIRDS

BY H. J. BATES AND R. L. BUSENBARK

(An edited version of the original article and with material added by K. A. Norris and Rosemary Low.)

Softbilled birds are so called because in the wild they eat soft foods such as fruits and insects. Some eat more fruit than animal matter, and others eat insects and small animals in far greater proportion than fruits.

Many birds depend upon flower nectar for a major portion of their foods, but most of these still consume portions of fruits and insects. These birds require a nectar diet, while others require nectar plus a standard insectivorous mixture. The great value of fortified nectar food is not generally realised for many types of birds which are not considered to be nectar feeders. It is particularly valuable during the early stages of transition for stubborn birds which are very slow to accept domestic foods.

There are several families of softbills which have always been considered delicate in aviculture in that their main problem is that they refuse to accept inert foods. These are usually highly insectivorous birds. Another group of softbills, mostly very small birds, requires a different diet again, because of delicate digestive systems.

There has been wonderful progress in recent years in the keeping of softbills but it is still a highly challenging field. Diets remain too complicated and time-consuming for some fanciers. Many birds will accept one or two items out of loose mixtures, one or two components out of a total diet, but will refuse other items. This means an incomplete diet and deterioration of health, perhaps gradual but often rapid.

The various diets listed below are rather broadly classed, and there are additions or exceptions for many of the different groups; these will be covered in the sections dealing with the families. Many will doubtless be improved as experience expands. Not everyone will agree with these diets; many will have favourites with which they have experienced success; and the fact that they are not listed here does not mean the writers disapprove of other alternatives.

Any softbilled diets should be compiled with these objectives: acceptability, simplicity, digestability and total nutrition.

GROUP A: STANDARD SOFTBILLED DIET

Suitable for the easiest birds such as bulbuls, many thrushes, starlings, mynahs, waxwings, barbets, colies, and babblers and several allies (Leiothrix, Sibias, etc.)

In Europe there are several reliable brands of insectivorous foods, such as Prosecto, 'Stimulite' and 'Sluis', which are available from most pet shops.

For those who prefer to make up their own mixture, the following recipe may be found useful. The ingredients consist of:

> 5 lb (2·3 kg) turkey-rearing pellets (without additives)
> 2 lb (0·9 kg) soya flour
> 8 oz (0·3 kg) Vionate or Vitamindif
> 1 lb (0·45 kg) clear honey
> 1 pt (0·5 l) of ground nut or maize oil.

The dry ingredients should be well mixed together then the honey should be added and thoroughly blended. Finally, the oil must be well stirred in to ensure that it is evenly distributed throughout the whole mixture.

Another recipe, used with equal success, is as follows:

> 4 lb (1·8 kg) proprietary rearing food for Canaries (such as 'Egbisco')
> 2 lb (0·9 kg) peanuts (shelled but not roasted)
> 1 lb (0·45 kg) raisins or sultanas
> 2 lb (0·9 kg) clear honey
> 1 lb (0·45 kg) castor sugar
> 1 lb (0·45 kg) self-raising flour
> 6 eggs
> a small bottle of rose-hip syrup
> 2 tablespoonfuls (60 g) of brewer's yeast.

The eggs, flour and sugar are mixed into a batter and the eggshells are added after being crushed. The mixture is baked in a slow oven until it is hard right through and is then broken up and ground into a fine flour. The nuts and raisins or sultanas are mixed with the grated cheese and the 'Egbisco'. The honey is heated until it is very hot but not boiling and added to the dry ingredients with the rose-hip syrup. All this is mixed together thoroughly with dripping and is then dried off with soya flour and egg mixture. It is then broken up finely and can be stored in an airtight container.

An alternative diet for birds in this group and the next has been used successfully for years in a large collection in Southern California. The ingredients are boiled brown rice, raisins (or grapes in season), diced banana, diced apple, other soft fruits in season and a trace of a mineral supplement mixed together in one dish. The diet is completed with live foods and a pellet form of dry dog food. Some fanciers add cooked sweet potato and grated carrot to this mixture.

Fruit and Live Foods

Fruit should be given in variety. Apples, grapes, soaked raisins and oranges are the most popular. Orange should be limited because of its acid content but it is nevertheless valuable in proper proportion. Pears, peaches, apricots, figs, berries and currants, are all good in season when they are available at reasonable prices, also nectarines and avocados. Papaya is widely used in Asia, and bananas are useful where they are grown. Unfortunately, underripe or overripe bananas are hazardous to many of the smaller or more delicate birds. To be completely safe with the questionable groups of small or delicate birds, it is best not to feed imported bananas which are harvested long before they are ripe. For other birds, bananas are safe if given in limited quantities.

Live foods in a variety are not so easily managed as fruit. Mealworms are readily available but should not be fed excessively. They are very nourishing but also rich and stimulating. An average ration for a bulbul would be about 12 mealworms per day. The delicate birds such as wrens and warblers should receive no more than 3 or 4 mealworms per day, and these can be made more digestible by soaking them for a few minutes in hot water which softens the harsh outer skin.

Fruitflies (*Drosophila*) are an excellent source of live food for many smaller, very active birds, especially nectar feeders. There are two very easy methods of developing a fruitfly culture. The first is an accumulation of overripe fruits, in any container from one to five gallons placed in the aviary or bedroom where the temperature is at least 60°F (15·5°C). The container is covered with quarter inch wire mesh to prevent the birds from getting into the rotting food. Frequent additions of fruit are necessary to continue attracting the fruitflies. Another method of breeding fruitflies is to set up a pan with red bran over which vinegar has been poured. Cover with a mesh as mentioned above. The culture develops quickly.

Gentles (maggots) can be produced in a comparatively odourless culture. Red bran soaked in water in any convenient container is placed in the sun to attract flies. After three days or so, the gentles can be harvested regularly with no additional cleaning. If the maggots are obtained from decaying meat, they should be cleaned by putting them in bran for a day before giving them to birds.

One way to attract flying insects is to use a night light of about twenty-five watts. A night light can also be placed low in the aviary over foods to attract birds which are not well. Instead of huddling away in hidden seclusion, birds needing care will benefit from the heat of the bulb, will be encouraged to eat and will be easily noticed.

GROUP B: MODIFIED STANDARD SOFTBILLED DIET FOR LARGER BIRDS

Suitable for jay thrushes, jays, magpies and allies, toucans and hornbills. This group of larger, stronger birds thirves on the standard diet with the addition of raw meat and unwanted fresh eggs from small birds in the collection. As with the diets above, this addition should be limited so that the total intake of the basic insectivorous mixture will not fall below the necessary requirements. The writers recommend that either horse meat or beef available in pet shops be used; the price is lower. Horse meat is perhaps the best because the fat content is, at least in the U.S.A. usually held at five per cent.

There is slight acid content in the horse meat, but this causes no harm if fed judiciously. The fat in beef for pets is usually held at 15 per cent which is less than that of most ground beefs available in meat markets.

The birds mentioned in this group will take mice readily and are likely to kill and eat any that enter their aviary. Young mice will be considered a great delicacy. Such birds as toucans and hornbills will also eat small birds if the opportunity arises, which is one reason why they must never be housed with such small species. Sparrows which find their way into their enclosure are likely to be killed and eaten.

GROUP C: MODIFIED STANDARD SOFTBILLED DIET FOR SLOWLY ACCLIMATISING BIRDS

These are the difficult and stubborn, often called delicate, birds which accept only live foods instead of inert domestic foods for long periods. Included are trogons, rollers, kingfishers, motmots, bee-eaters, hoopoes, pittas, fairy blue birds, and minivets. Their nutritional requirements are the same as for the second group, to lure them on to the diet. Each family in this group varies in its willingness to transfer. Fairy blue birds and motmots are perhaps the least difficult, but they are nevertheless a challenge. Hoopoes, if adult, require the oddest adaptation; but this will be mentioned in the section dealing with Hoopoes.

Rollers take quite readily to meat and live foods, but this is sustaining for only a short while. Mixing the insectivorous mixture with the meat is started with small amounts at first and gradually increased until proportions are correct. With most of the others, it is a difficult task even to lure them on to the meat; this is accomplished by sprinkling it with mealworms.

The easiest way to bring about the satisfactory transfer of wild caught adults is to house them with other birds already accepting domestic diets. The new birds learn more quickly by following the example set by other birds. The previously acclimatised companions should be as closely related in disposition and habits as possible but should not be aggressive or overbearing. Unacclimatised birds are usually more docile than acclimatised birds of the same habits, and any aggressiveness directed against them would prevent them from adapting to aviary life.

All softbilled birds must be transferred to domestic diets by gradual degrees using subterfuge, mixing ingredients, and housing them with acclimatised birds which act as teachers; but none are as slow to learn as the birds in this group.

One particularly helpful item during the transition phase is the fortified nectar described in the next section, which in itself will supply total nourishment and will help to sustain the birds during this difficult time. None of these birds are nectar feeders, and so the importance of this item as a mainstay must be considered temporary. The liquid texture is wrong for a permanent diet.

The ideal way to adapt the difficult birds to aviculture is to introduce them to a domestic life while they are youngsters and far more adaptable than adults. (At this stage they will learn to accept domestic foods quite easily but this is a task for the collectors and exporters. Not many will assume the complicated task which in many instances requires hand feeding.)

In Japan, delicate or small softbills are usually fed on a mixture composed of equal parts of rice and soya bean meal to which is added dried fish powder in approximately one half the total measure of the above two ingredients. This is for such birds as white eyes and Pekin Robins. For larger and stronger birds rice hulls are added to this mixture to provide additional vitamins. The soya powder, by the way is a very nourishing food which the writers have successfully used in place of milk in various nectar mixtures. It is also helpful in maintaining the reds on many birds which fade in aviaries although carotene is more efficient in this respect.

In Thailand, the writers saw the successful acclimatisation of many of the most difficult softbills which were taken as youngsters. They were being fed on a mixture which mostly consisted of diced fish and rice with a popular leafy green vegetable cooked with the rice. There were other ingredients, but they were minor extras as far as texture and appearance were concerned.

The birds from India are usually fed on a substance called gram powder which is a finely ground powder of a pale shade of yellowish-brown. Mynah meal (available in the USA) closely approximates this colouring, but it is not as finely ground. The birds are apparently accustomed to a mushy wet solution of gram powder.

Any of the youngsters which have been fed by hand will be delightfully tame. Handling and offering food from the fingers will be necessary to retain this tameness.

GROUP D: NECTAR FEEDERS

Suitable for hummingbirds, sunbirds, sugar birds (honeycreepers), white eyes and flower peckers, but they also require a considerable amount of fruit in their diet. Sunbirds should be offered fruit, but most pay little attention to it. Perhaps the greatest progress in aviculture during the past few years has been with birds in this group. Several species have been reared in aviaries. There are a number of nectar recipes. Minor changes can be made for the other birds in this group.

The first formula consists of:

> 5 parts water
> 1 part honey
> liquid vitamins
> 1 beef cube per quart (to supply the animal protein).

Some aviculturists add milk: but, if the birds will take it, soya powder can be substituted. If milk is added, it should be canned evaporated milk, fresh milk is too harsh. Fruitflies complete the diet for hummingbirds and sunbirds and the latter also like spiders. For honeycreepers, flower-peckers and birds of similar diets, the beef cube can enough water to make a pint (0·5 l) of mixture.

The second nectar diet, which we will call fortified, is the formula also recommended as a supplementary food during the acclimatisation of the difficult species in the previous group as well as for many other softbills. This nectar or any of the three is especially helpful to fruitsuckers and orioles both Old World and New World.

In a blender, liquify:

10 mealworms	Add: 284 fl oz (10 ml) liquid vitamins (available at
2 oz (57 g) of honey	chemists for human use)
1-in. (2·54 cm) cube of liver	1 tablespoonful of condensed milk
½-in. (1·2 cm) cube of carrot.	enough water to the mixture to total 36 oz (about 1 kg).

Fruitflies are not needed with this mixture, but many aviculturists still prefer to supply them. This mixture sours quickly.

Mr. Kenneth Sutherland using both of these formulas made the following comparisons. When placed side by side, his hummingbirds preferred the first formula as long as they had fruitflies. Denied fruitflies for a few days, the hummingbirds started taking the above formula.

Another popular and simple formula to be used along with the fruitflies consists of:

> 1 half cup sugar
> $1\frac{1}{2}$ teaspoons baby cereal food
> $1\frac{1}{2}$ teaspoons of a top grade vitamin-mineral supplement
> 8 drops liquid vitamins
> 3 teaspoons evaporated milk
> enough water to make a pint (0·5 l) of mixture.

Aviculturists using this mixture may prefer to use distilled mineral-free water which for many areas may be wise. They also caution would-be users not to store this mixture longer than three days because it can cause watery droppings.

If stored, it should be kept in a refrigerator and removed an hour before use but it is preferable to mix it fresh daily. There is at least one commercial nectar food on the market which has been successfully used by many people. Several aviculturists either add or substitute glucose or, in the USA, corn syrup to their mixtures. For honey-creepers, bananaquits, white eyes, and flower-peckers, use the nectar and add a variety of fruits, live foods, and pound cake, or use the following diet.

GROUP E: DIET FOR PARTIAL NECTAR FEEDERS

Suitable for tanagers, bananaquits, and for many small, delicate birds. Perhaps the best simple diet formula the writers have ever seen for tanagers and birds of similar requirements was given to the writers by Ron Blakely, Director of the Brookfield Zoo in Illinois. A beautiful sunbird at the zoo was also thriving on this diet.

Combine $2\frac{1}{3}$ parts of brown sugar with 5 parts of water.

To half of this amount for a morning feeding, add $\frac{1}{2}$ part of one of the top quality powdered total foods now popular with dieters.

For an afternoon feeding, add 1·2 cubic centimetres of a liquid compound beef extract instead of the dietetic powder. A variety of fruits completes the diet.

An alternative diet is the fortified nectar described above plus one of the standard diets for softbills.

The powdered dietic total food mentioned above is available in several brands. The one used by the writers has 23·5% protein, 66·5% carbohydrate, 3·5% fat, 4% minerals, and 2·5% moisture. There is a further breakdown of 16 vitamins and minerals. In a one-half cup measure as indicated above, the protein supplied is about 7 oz (between 19 and 20 g). The vitamin-mineral content is much less than that supplied by many powdered supplements for pets which can be added in small doses if the aviculturist so desires. These dietic powders, it should be emphasized, are in themselves total nutritional requirements for humans; but, since they are for dieters, the fat content is held low.

One point in reading labels should be stressed. It is not enough just to read the percentages and units of the various ingredients because some of the ingredients are measured by the pound, others by the ounce, and possibly others by different weights. Read the total label and compute accordingly.

It is possible to obtain a proprietary brand of nectar paste, known as 'Stimulite', which needs only to be diluted with water in accordance with the instructions on the tin. This is an excellent preparation on which the most delicate nectar feeders can be successfully kept in excellent condition.

Gevral Protein is a perfectly balanced 'complete' food in concentrated form, and may be used for the preparation of a nectar food in conjunction with a pure cane sugar syrup, as follows: $3\frac{1}{2}$ oz granulated sugar should be dissolved in 10 fl oz of boiling water and left until quite cold. $\frac{1}{6}$ oz Gevral Protein should be mixed into a smooth, thin cream with cold water and added to the cold syrup, and more cold water added to make up to 20 fl oz (1 pint). It is most important that the Gevral should be prepared with cold water and that the syrup should be quite cold before blending, as hot water will destroy some of the vitamins contained in the Gevral.

Tubes of nectar should always be hung in the shade in order that the mixture may remain fresh for as long as possible. Both 'Stimulite' and the Gevral mixture have the advantage that they do not sour or ferment as quickly as does a mixture containing any form of milk or milk food, but both should be renewed at least once every 24 hours, and more frequently if the temperature of the cage or aviary is high. Gevral Protein is not always readily obtainable, and in an emergency a nectar food may be made up as follows, but the mixture should only be used as temporary measure, until a more suitable mixture is available:

> 1 tablespoon clear honey
> 1 tablespoon condensed milk
> 1 tablespoon baby cereal or Horlicks.
> 6 or 8 tablespoons of hot water should be added and the mixture allowed to cool before being fed to the birds.

Plate I

Black-headed Trogon, *Trogon citreolus*

Quetzal, *Pharomachrus m. mocino*

Narina's Trogon, *Apaloderma n. narina*

Cuban Trogon, *Priotelus temnurus temnurus*

Duvaucel's Trogon, *Harpactes duvaucelii*

Plate II

Indian Trogon, *Harpactes f. fasciatus*

Kookaburra, *Dacelo n. novaeguineae*

Blue-naped Coly, *Colius macrourus*

Blue-crowned Motmot, *Momotus momota*

Banded Aracari, *Pteroglossus torquatus*

Blue-throated Barbet, *Megalaima a. asiatica*

Two or three times a week a very little meat extract and a few drops of Vitamins A and D should be added. A rather more natural and nutritious mixture may be made up as follows:

> 1 pint (0·5 l) dried ants' cocoons
> 1 pint (0·5 l) dried flies and ground silkworm pupae
> $\frac{7}{8}$ pint (0·4 l) fine-grade biscuit meal or toasted breadcrumbs
> $\frac{7}{16}$ pint (0·2 l) dried egg powder
> $\frac{1}{2}$ lb (225 g) pure lard
> 1 tablespoon clear honey.

First the lard should be grated and rubbed into the crumbs, and then the remaining ingredients added and well mixed in.

All the mixtures should be stored in air-tight tins, in a cool, dry place and before being fed to the birds sufficient for a day's supply should be moistened to a crumbly texture, with grated raw carrot.

HANDFEEDING

If it becomes necessary, most softbills can be handfed and after an initial learning period will usually cooperate. Of great importance in handfeeding is frequent small feedings rather than few and large meals. The writers start with canned apple sauce to which is added liquid vitamins, baby cereal, and a little mynah meal (a fine-grade insectivorous mixture can be substituted for the last item). This is easily digested can be fed with very little effort from an eyedropper or baby bird feeder. With mynah meal the insectivorous mixture is gradually increased and the mixture assumes a less liquid texture. Gelatine can also be added. Small mealworms will soon be accepted and soon the bird can be encouraged to probe for other foods in feeding trays. It is important that it drops an acquired dependence upon human presence in association with food supplies. Presence of a self-feeding bird is helpful in establishing its independence. Many hand-fed birds refuse to eat unless the food comes from a human hand, so strong becomes the association.

GROUP F: REFINED SOFTBILLED DIET FOR SMALL OR DELICATE SOFTBILLS

Suitable for wrens, warblers, niltavas, flycatchers, yuhinas, small robins and allies.

These birds need a mild diet because they have delicate digestive systems. In the beginning, hard boiled egg, which is usually quickly accepted by these birds, is used to attract the birds on to a fine-grade insectivorous food which is mixed sparingly at first with the egg and gradually increased. In time, the egg is discontinued or reduced to a small proportion. It should be noted that eggs spoil quickly in hot weather, also for delicate systems, they are difficult to digest.

Many successful aviculturists add grated cheese and ground nuts along with pound cake, fruits, and live foods but the latter should not be harsh or strong. Mealworms should be soaked in hot water for a few minutes before feeding to soften the skins which could cause harm. An alternative diet, also mild, would be cottage cheese, peanut butter and insectivorous mixture.

For very difficult or delicate insectivorous species a special diet has been devised and used with great success by leading aviculturists in South America and England. The ingredients are as follows:

> 8 oz (225 g) finely minced, lean ox-heart
> 8 oz (225 g) pureed carrot
> 5 oz (140 g) fine-grade sausage rusk
> 5$\frac{3}{4}$ oz (168 g) pure Edam or cottage cheese
> 2 teaspoons 'Gevral Protein'
> $\frac{1}{2}$ teaspoon 'Vionate'.

The whole is thoroughly mixed and rolled into balls, from the size of a pea to that of a hazel nut, according to the species to be fed.

Hand-feeding, until the birds learn to pick up from the food dish, may be necessary for those which habitually feed on the wing. The dish should be raised, on a hanging tray, well above the ground, for all 'in flight' feeders.

DIETS FOR SEEDEATERS

BY ROSEMARY LOW

The birds described by aviculturists as seedeaters are easy to cater for. Seed is not the only food eaten, but it is the principal item of the diet. Most species will also eat insects and many relish fresh greenfoods, wild or cultivated. The variety of foods which can be offered to any one species is, in many cases, rather limited by the birds' tastes, but everything should be done to provide as much variety as possible. Foods can be divided, broadly speaking, into four groups: seeds, fresh greenfoods, livefoods and softfood in its various forms.

Seeds

Canary seed and the various kinds of millets, are offered to almost all seedeaters. Canary seed has the highest protein content of the cereal seeds and will be preferred to millet by most species, with the exception of waxbills, whose tiny beaks can shell panicum millet more easily. Canary seed is light yellowish-brown in colour, elliptical in shape, with a brown kernel. It is grown in several countries including (in a small way) England. Morocco and Australia are two of the chief producing countries. It is a good idea to vary the type of canary seed obtained or to provide a mixture of more than one kind.

Several kinds of millet are fed to birds. Panicum millet, a round, light brown seed, is the smallest but its food value is not high. As this is the most popular seed with many small seedeaters, it is advisable to add a liquid multi-vitamin preparation to the drinking water or to sprinkle a proprietary yeast mixture for birds or brewer's yeast (obtainable from chemists) on the seed. Yeast is rich in Vitamin B which is essential for good feather growth. Lack of this vitamin may result in bare patches in the plumage, although this can also be caused by feather plucking by other birds. Incidentally, all dry seeds are deficient in Vitamins A and D, so a vitamin additive is essential for birds whose diet consists of little else.

White millet is larger than panicum and easily recognised by its colour. This will be readily eaten by all medium-sized and large seedeaters and by some of the smaller species. Japanese millet is of particular value for Australian grassfinches bred in Japan and exported from that country. Plate yellow millet is also available. Some seed merchants offer a mixture of millets containing all these types; however, feeding each kind of seed in a separate container is preferable where more than about half a dozen birds are kept together. This will prevent wastage as some birds, in their search for a favourite seed, will scatter all the others from the container.

A seed which can be eaten by the smallest birds and which will help to counteract the low food value of pancium millet, is niger—a small, long, black seed. Its high oil content will help to promote good feather condition. It can be mixed with panicum millet and is relished by many kinds of seedeaters. Other oil seeds suitable for finches, waxbills and other commonly kept species are linseed, maw (poppy seed) and hemp. The latter is a larger, round seed, with a nutty flavour, and will need to be crushed for the smaller birds. It is a great favourite with many British finches, for whom its use will need to be rationed; however, its high price means that few fanciers can feed it *ad lib*. Hemp is a particularly nourishing seed and valuable for birds rearing young and those wintering outdoors. It is unfortunate that it has become so expensive but, judged by its food value, it is no more expensive than millet.

A supply of paddy rice (obtained only from leading bird seed merchants) is necessary for some newly imported seedeaters, such as Pintailed Nonpareils, which will need to be gradually weaned on to canary and other seeds.

Millet sprays are a great favourite with seedeaters of all kinds, which derive great enjoyment from picking the seeds out of the spray. As it is more expensive than loose millet its use will be limited to once or twice a week by most fanciers.

All foreign seedeaters, except waxbills and a few other tiny species, should be offered the following seeds: canary, white millet, panicum millet, niger and one of the other oil seeds, i.e. a little hemp, maw or linseed. Some pet shops will stock mainly packeted seed and canary, millet and parrot food in a loose form but mail order bird seed merchants will stock the complete range of seeds available.

British finches require a slightly different basic diet, which varies according to the species. The basic diet will be British finch mixture, which consists of canary seed, rape, linseed and hemp, with sunflower for the larger species such as Greenfinches and Bullfinches. As each type of seed can be obtained separately, the fancier can prepare his own mixture for each species, if he wishes. Other seeds available from merchants in Britain for British finches are radish, gold of pleasure, British wildseed mixture and the more expensive teazle and white lettuce seeds.

Greenfoods

There are numerous wild and cultivated greenfoods which are eagerly eaten by seedeaters and, being a natural source of vitamins, will help to keep them in good health. Some birds are reluctant to sample certain kinds, but few will refuse seeding grasses, especially annual grass.

Numerous wild greenfoods can be offered. These include chickweed (the most popular after seeding grasses), young dandelion leaves and, for British finches, the seeding heads, sowthistle, persicaria, dock and plantain. It is becoming increasingly difficult, because of the danger of poisonous sprays, to find areas from which greenfood can be gathered with safety. It is a wise precaution to avoid collecting greenfoods from agricultural or cultivated land unless one can be certain that no spraying has taken place. All greenfood should be washed before it is offered, unless collected from one's own garden where no contamination by chemical sprays, dogs or cats could have occurred. Uneaten greenfood should be removed by the end of the day.

The only cultivated greenfoods suitable for seedeaters, with the exception of parrots, which are not discussed here, are lettuce, spinach, watercress and mustard and cress.

Live food

An important part of the diet of most seedeaters; few species available to aviculturists will refuse insects but many do so because the kinds offered are too many. Waxbills, for example, may be persuaded to sample mealworms and maggots, but they prefer much smaller insects, especially greenfly and blackfly. A greenfly-infested cutting from a rose bush or fruit tree is probably the biggest treat that one can offer a waxbill. They will eat whiteworms and tubifex worms used by aquarists.

The larger seedeaters, such as cardinals and buntings, take mealworms and gentles more readily, especially meal-worms which few seedeaters can resist. These insects present few problems—except their high price. They can be obtained by mail order and from some pet shops. Mealworms should be kept in bran in a wooden box and can be bred under these conditions, but the life cycle is a long one. Maggots, on the other hand, can be kept only a few days, unless stored in a refrigerator. It is imperative that they are cleaned thoroughly before they are offered to birds. They should be kept in sand for a few days so that their exterior is thoroughly cleaned and any undesirable matter in the gut has a chance to pass through. Most maggots are fed on rotting meat and are in no condition to feed to birds when received. Failure to clean them can and has, on many occasions, resulted in the death of the birds to whom they were offered.

A food of great value, especially for the smaller species, is live ants' eggs (*not* the dried kind obtainable from aquaria shops). The difficulties involved in locating and transporting ants' eggs are considerable for many avi-culturists but those who live in suitable areas will have a great advantage during the breeding season, for ants' eggs are an invaluable rearing food. Small spiders and some other small insects are a most useful tonic for waxbills and other small birds which are slightly off-colour.

Fruitflies will be eaten by some seedeaters but are principally used as a food for softbills. Cultures are started simply by keeping rotting fruit or banana skins in a temperature of at least 60°F (15·5°C). The fruit can be placed in jars or boxes, the top of which is covered with some material which does not allow the flies to escape until required. They breed readily but the main danger of such a culture is that of birds contracting aspergillosis, an incurable fungus disease, from the rotting fruit. For this reason, the culture should not be 'grown' where the birds are kept. A jar should be placed in the cage or aviary shelter and renewed daily with a fresh culture.

Soft foods

Some seedeaters will accept a fine insectivorous mixture as offered to softbills, especially if they are kept with birds which take this readily. Seedeaters which normally include a fair proportion of insects in their diet should be encouraged to eat an insectivorous food, especially cardinals and buntings and the larger and more delicate wax-bills, such as Violet-ears and Grenadiers.

Sweetened bread and milk is an excellent food for newly imported seedeaters such as waxbills, which may be under stress and will benefit from a softfood of some kind. It is equally valuable as a rearing food, especially when livefood and/or greenfood can be offered only in small quantities; healthy chicks are far more likely to result than when an all-seed diet is used. Some seedeaters will accept a proprietary eggfood as prepared for Canaries and this too, is highly recommended.

Grit

All birds which eat seed require grit and cuttlefish bone. Grit is essential; it is needed to grind the seed in the gizzard. Cuttlefish bone is an important source of calcium and therefore vital for breeding hens for the formation of egg-shells. For very small seedeaters, it should be scraped over the seed. The whole bone can be offered to larger species.

HINTS ON GENERAL REQUIREMENTS AND ACCLIMATISATION OF SOFTBILLED BIRDS

BY H. J. BATES AND R. L. BUSENBARK

Specialised requirements are covered in the different family sections, but a few more generalised hints will be helpful to the fancier of softbilled birds.

Softbilled birds fare better in planted aviaries than in aviaries furnished only with perches, food and water dishes, and other birds. They are much happier and will sing better in planted, semi-naturalised environments. Also, very few softbilled birds ever breed in unplanted aviaries, as they need the seclusion of shrubbery or trees.

A generous supply of water for bathing, frequently replenished and cleaned, is a necessity for nearly all softbills.

Perches are quickly and easily soiled because of loose droppings and because the birds clean soft, sticky foods from their beaks by wiping them on the perches. Therefore, perches should be of the type that permits easy cleaning, or they should be replaced frequently. Branches have the advantage of softness, a yielding springiness, and varying diameters which are restful to the feet; but they must be replaced often because they are difficult to clean. A variety of problems arise from dirty perches.

Softbills, because of their diets, have loose watery droppings. Food supplies particularly must be kept out in the open away from shrubs or perches to prevent soiling. If the floors are of concrete, they should be washed down frequently. Earth floors should be turned occasionally. Actually, the droppings in the wild state are more firm and less liquid than the droppings of most softbills in captivity, because most of the foods in captivity are softer. Mynah pellets more than any other food have helped to improve the droppings of softbills in captivity.

The enormous range in variety, size, and disposition of softbills, many of which have more individualistic behaviour patterns than any other birds in captivity, pose problems in assembling collections for community aviaries. Several factors must be considered. Size is usually the first consideration. Do not try to mix large birds with small ones unless the large birds are particularly docile. Disposition is equally important, as aggressiveness is a big problem in mixed collections. There are many suggestions given in the sections on the different families regarding suitable companions. Frequently birds, because of individual behaviour latitude, can become bullies and quite unexpectedly exert a dominance which can be very harmful.

Territorially inclined birds are most likely to become aggressive to their own kind, to close relatives, or to other territorial birds whose requirements would, in the wild state, mean competition for the same food. This characteristic is particularly pronounced among the mockingbirds, thrushes and allies, and the New World Orioles or Hangnests. The endearing songs are very often meant to warn would-be intruders that this territory is claimed and occupied. Therefore, keep out!

Another type of competition which causes aggressiveness is colour similarity. For example, many birds with red in their colouring will resent other birds with red and will be constantly sparring for dominance. Yellow is also frequently a competitive colour. Not all birds, by any means, are affected in this manner; and often the ability to maintain domination is absent. Nevertheless, this somewhat subtle aggressiveness needs to be checked.

During breeding seasons, aggressiveness is heightened, and many birds rob nests of eggs and baby birds. Live foods, by the way, become particularly important during the breeding season. They are vitally necessary for the youngsters, for the maintenance of breeding interest, and they help to fulfil the need that causes many birds to become nest robbers. Breeding information is given briefly in the sections dealing with the different families.

Temperatures for softbills are a problem in many areas. There are instances recorded where some of the most unlikely birds have withstood very low temperatures with no harmful effects; but, over the complete range of average softbills, it is unwise to allow temperatures to fall below 45 or 50°F (8–10°C) in winter. There is no need to run risks. Heated shelters are necessary for this protection. It is probably permissible to allow most softbills access to unheated flights during cold weather if there is no danger from winds or storms, but they should also be able to come inside to warmth when they desire. Food should be inside the shelter during cold weather, and all birds should be returned to the warm shelter at night. This means that a light inside the shelter should be available after dark to attract any stragglers or late outsiders.

Birds should never be treated like fragile hothouse plants. This occurs as a result of over-pampering and the maintenance of continually high temperatures. The birds never have a chance to develop any hardiness; and, during emergencies and heating failures, these birds have the least chance of survival.

Birds eat more during cold weather, and the diet must be particularly efficient if they are to withstand cold.

Ailments are difficult to treat among softbills. Most occur because of dietary deficiencies which may be slight and slow in development. Frequent observations are necessary to detect these problems. Listlessness, absence of sheen, and fluffed feathers are symptoms. The weakness may result in aggression from other birds.

For all softbills, first aid is the most important life saver in nearly all ailments. In many instances, it is the only treatment needed. First aid consists of heat, about 80°F (27°C) night and day, and foods appetizing enough to encourage the birds to eat frequently. Fortified nectar should be given instead of water, and a precautionary broad spectrum antibiotic will prevent secondary infections and help clear up any infections already present. The writers prefer to use a product containing sulphamethazine as the antibiotic. To broaden the effectiveness of this antibiotic if compounded ailments seem evident, an aureomycin product especially compounded for birds can be added to the sulphamethazine preparation.

There are specifically constructed hospital cages available in some areas; but any standard, suitably sized cage can be converted for hospital use. Cover the cage on top and three sides. Instal a light bulb for heat day and night. In most cages, a twenty-five watt bulb will be satisfactory. In larger cages, use forty watts. Some people will object to the light at night because they feel the patient will be deprived of needed rest during recuperation. There is no need for this objection. A sick bird will rest many times during the day or night with or without a light. Low points in life occur at night, and if there is no heat the chances for survival during these low ebbs are greatly reduced. A light at night encourages the bird to eat whenever it awakens, so low perches should be placed near food supplies.

Acclimatisation follows much the same procedure, but it usually occurs in heated aviaries instead of cages. The precautionary antibiotic is usually helpful. Food supplies are different, and are detailed in the section on diets. Lights should be close to food supplies which should be placed at several easily accessible levels. Incoming birds may be carrying lice or other vermin, and they should be sprayed with a safe insecticide. Respraying every day in acclimatisation aviaries is advisable.

Not all birds settle down to aviary life at the same time. Some recover from shipment shocks more quickly than others and are often helpful in leading others to the food supplies. The first examination usually reveals certain birds which require more intense care at first. These should go into hospital cages straight away. Any unusually strong or aggressive birds should be segregated from the main flock within a very short period if not at once. The writers always include a few acclimatised birds of mild disposition to act as teachers so that the new birds can be more quickly transferred to new diets. After the critical first three days the heat may gradually be turned down, but lights should be left on for a few nights longer.

Inspections and physical examination should be made very frequently for the first week; and rearranging, segregation, and adjustments to diet must be made wherever indicated. Most birds will be strong enough and will be totally on their new diets in a week's time, after which they can join other birds. The examination and observation of each bird must be particularly thorough, however, before this is possible. Any thin birds should be held back; and, should any illness be evident, the entire lot should be held back.

The delicate and stubborn groups will not, in most cases, have made the satisfactory transfers to new diets in one week's time. The writers have extended the acclimatisation period to sixty days, in rare instances, with some of the most difficult birds.

ORDER: COLIIFORMES

Colies or Mousebirds

The Colies or Mousebirds are a small group of very highly specialised birds found throughout the greater part of Africa from the Sudan and Ethiopia to Cape Province. There are six species, all of which are so similar that they have been united in a single genus, *Colius*. With the exception of the Red-backed Mousebird or Chestnut-backed Coly, *C. castanatus*, and the White-backed Coly, *C. colius*, all show minor variations. Many subspecies have been named, some of which are of doubtful validity since it appears that curious individual variations occur, notably in the colour of the eyes which may be slate grey, brown, dark straw or yellow, and the feet which are pink, red, brown, mauve or purple.

The bodies of all species are about 4¾ in. (12 cm). They have long graduated tails with very strong shafts, which may reach 10 in. (25 cm) in length, and prominent head crests. Their beaks are short, stout and curved, the feet are very strong, furnished with long, sharp claws, and are unique in that all four toes can be direct forward, enabling the birds to perch or cling on practically any position. The plumage is soft and hair-like; the feathers do not grow in bracts as is the case with the majority of birds. Structurally, they bear no close affinity to any other group of birds.

All species are grey or brown in general colour and this, combined with their habit of creeping about in dense bushes or running about on the ground, has given rise to the alternative name of Mousebirds. The sexes are alike in all species.

They are highly gregarious and flocks of 20–30 may often be seen clambering through the bushes or flying from tree to tree in search of food which consists largely of fruit, berries, buds and tender leaves. They also eat quantities of insects, and occasionally rob the nests of other small birds, carrying off the young.

They roost huddled together, usually clinging to the rough bark of a tree trunk or other vertical surface, or hanging in a horizontal position below a branch.

Nests are well concealed in thick foliage and consist of a shallow cup of fibres and rootlets, lined with grasses and green leaves which are constantly renewed. Some species construct a platform of twigs to support the more delicate materials of the cup. Two to four eggs comprise the normal clutch, either unmarked white, or speckled and scrawled with brown, and both sexes share in the 12–14 days of incubation. The young are fed by regurgitation and when only a few days old will creep about the surrounding branches, using their beak, wings, and feet, to propel themselves forward, but always returning to the nest at night until they are able to fly.

Their curious habits make them attractive aviary birds, and because of their gregarious nature they do better if kept in groups. They appear to be quite peaceable with other species but should not be included with nesting birds. They are naturally inquisitive and intelligent, always ready to sample any kind of food, and consequently are comparatively easy to accustom to a standard insectivorous mixture to which should be added soaked sultanas and currants, various berries, and finely cubed soft apple. Soft, sticky fruit such as banana should be avoided as Colies are greedy birds and quickly become over-fed. Twigs of apple, prunus and hawthorn in bud, and seeding chickweed may be offered, and they should also have a supply of maggots, mealworms and other available live insects. They cannot stand cold or wet conditions. They prefer planted aviaries but will thrive in unplanted aviaries with shady shelters. They have been successfully reared in captivity.

Genus: Colius

STRIATED COLY, SPECKLED COLY, NATAL STRIATED COLY, SPECKLED MOUSEBIRD, *Colius striatus* Gmelin
G. Braunflugelmausvogel; F. Coliou raye; D. Gevlekte Muisvogel

DISTRIBUTION: Africa; Ethiopia in the east, Nigeria and Cameroon in the west, and several areas southward on both sides of the continent.

DESCRIPTION: Sexes alike. Feet and legs red; beak black and white; blackish facial area; pale, near-white cheek area. Upper parts brownish-grey, under parts striated. The striations are narrow bars of grey on a buffish or pale background. Length: about 4¾ in. (12 cm) with tail variable between 7–8 in. (18–20 cm).

SUBSPECIES: The slight differences in the 16 races are not important to the aviculturist except that it is easy to assume wrongly that the variations could be sexual rather than racial. Variations in colours of irides as especially predominant, ranging from red to brown to grey to blue to yellow. *C. s. nigricollis* in the west has a blue spot behind the eyes. *C. s. leucotis* has a whiter cheek patch, a brownish throat and narrow striations on the mantle. *C. s. jebelensis* also has whiter cheeks. *C. s. cinerascens* has a black throat. *C. s. kiwuensis* has some black on forehead but not on lores. The chin is dusky and the brown is darker and warmer in shading. The latter characteristic also marks the subspecies *C. s. kikuyensis*. *C. s. hilgerti* has brownish cheeks and more black on the throat.

Striations may vary in intensity in many instances. A breeding record for the Natal Striated Coly is reported by Mrs. K. Draper of Basingstoke, England, in *Foreign Birds* of Sept./Oct. 1958. Two young birds were hatched and as there was an infertile egg, she assumed 3 eggs were laid. The nest was built of grass, moss, small twigs and chickweed, with no special lining, and was very small for the size of birds.

The parents used the same nest later and again laid 3 eggs, all of which hatched. Mrs. Draper tried to check the incubation period, which seemed to be about 14 days.

In *Foreign Birds* Jan./March 1973 another breeding success was reported by Mr. and Mrs. R. G. Perry of Thurmaston, Leicestershire, England. In 1972 3 chicks were hatched, but when they left the nest only 2 were observed. They looked the same as their parents except that the beaks were all silver colour and they were much smaller.

RED-BACKED MOUSEBIRD, CHESTNUT-BACKED COLY, *Colius castonatus* Verreaux and Verreaux

DISTRIBUTION: Gabon and Angola south to Mossameder.
DESCRIPTION: Upper parts mainly earth brown with bright chestnut back and rump, under parts light brown to buff, tail earth brown with cream outer vanes on the outer feathers. Face and forehead black speckled with grey, crest brown. Ear coverts and neck grey, irides yellow, upper mandible black with grey patch, lower mandible horn-coloured, legs coral red.

First breeding at Jersey Zoological Park, 1967, as reported in *Avicultural Magazine* (2) Vol. 81, April/June 1975, pp. 79–80. The following are extracts:

They were kept in a small cage (in the Tropical Bird House) only 3½×3×4 ft (1×0·9×1·2 m) this was shared by 4 Red-faced Mousebirds *C. indicus* which had to be removed due to the persistent aggression shown to them by the Red-backed. Their cage was furnished with a large wire cone filled with leaves, to which the pair were seen to add fresh green leaves from the twigs which they received daily. A clutch of four eggs was laid, two of which proved to be infertile, the remaining two hatching after 12–14 days' incubation.

On the occasion of the study the mousebirds built an entire nest for themselves, whereas previously pairs always used conical wire frames lined with hessian. The large bulky nest was constructed principally of coarse straw, lined with fine grasses and feathers. The clutch of 3 uniformly off-white eggs averaged 22×17 mm—this clutch was the only one measured. The nest was sited 54 in. (137 cm) from the ground in the centre of a dense Hebe (*Scrophulariaceae*) shrub, at which they were constantly nibbling.

A precise period of incubation was not established for this clutch, but incubation probably commenced with the laying of the first egg, as the young hatched on consecutive days. On hatching the pink-fleshed nestling could be seen to be sparsely covered with greyish down. The lower mandible was dark, upper mandible yellow as was the entire top of the head. The eyes were closed. The adults seemed to brood constantly until the young fledged—and would set up a shrill clamour when the nest was inspected, remaining only a yard or so away and complaining loudly.

At 2 days old it could be seen that the first chick was developing very rapidly with the flight feathers showing dark under the skin. At 6 days, the inch-long tail feathers were starting to open as were the flights, coverts and body tracts. The crest was noticeable and the legs were seen to be darkening; it was also noted that down (from the pheasants) had been newly added to the nest. At 9 days the chick was alert and watchful. When 11 days old the chick left the nest when it was inspected, although still unable to fly.

The birds were given a diet of ripe fruits, hard-boiled eggs and leaves (chiefly hawthorn). They occasionally ate mealworms.

BLUE-NAPED COLY, *Colius macrourus* (Linnaeus)
G. Blaunackenmausvogel; F. Coliou à nuque bleue; D. Muisvogel (Pl. II)

DISTRIBUTION: Guinea-Bissau, Sudan, Nigeria, Somali, Ethiopia.
DESCRIPTION: The most attractive features are a bright blue patch on nape and red at base of upper mandible extending through the lores and surrounding the eyes. Plumage soft in appearance with pinkish wash on the predominant greyish shading. Upper parts darker than under parts. Feet and legs purplish-red. Tail is longer than that of *C. striatus* and the hen's tail is slightly shorter than that of the cock.
SUBSPECIES: Of the three subspecies, *C. m. griseogularis* is darker than the nominate race described above; *C. m. pulcher* has a richer vinous wash on chest.

The remaining four species are:

RED-FACED COLY, *Colius indicus* (Latham), from south-eastern Africa. The red face of this species is a little more extensive than the red on *C. macrourus*, and the forehead is whitish, but there is no blue on the nape. The grey upper parts have a slight greenish wash. There are five, possibly six, subspecies.

WHITE-HEADED COLY, *Colius leucocephalus* (Reichenow), from eastern Africa in a limited range, mostly in Kenya and Tanganyika. It has a white head and crest; bold striations in dull black; white on neck, mantle and throat. Remaining upper parts grey; under parts have a vinous wash on the chest and buff on the abdominal area. Subspecies *C. l. leucocephalus* is darker.

WHITE-BACKED COLY, *Colius colius* (Linnaeus), from western part of South Africa has a white rump.

ORDER: TROGONIFORMES

Trogons and Quetzals

BY H. J. BATES AND R. L. BUSENBARK

FAMILY: TROGONIDAE

Trogons occur in Central and South America, Mexico, southwestern United States, Cuba, Africa, India, Sri Lanka, Burma, Thailand, Laos, Khmer, Vietnam, Malaysia, Borneo, the Philippines, and various parts of Indonesia. Nearly all have strong similar characteristics, so that relationships are easily detected. The Cuban Trogon and the quetzels have very different appearances because of variations in feather structure.

All trogons are characterised by the position of their toes; the first two point backwards. Their skin is very thin, and as their feathers easily fall out it is advisable not to handle these birds.

Trogons have rather long, broad tails, usually squared at the tips. The heads are comparatively large, and the thick necks are short. The short thick beaks have hooked tips surrounded by blackish bristles. The bodies are slightly heavy in appearance, but the long broad tails give them a graceful appearance. Male trogons are very colourful but females are usally less bright and less evenly coloured. Most of the dominant male colours in the American species have a brilliant metallic gloss.

The colour of most trogons is similar. All the upper parts, head and neck are one colour; this may be green, bronze, red or purplish-blue. A bold dividing band, usually white, across the middle of the chest, separates the bright red or yellow colouring of the under parts of males, which is usually glossy in an even shade through to the under tail coverts. In most trogons the under side of the tail is bodly marked with fine black and white striations, and with some species these are also on the wings. Their plumage is soft and fragile and easily damaged.

Trogons are calm in aviaries, and they may appear sluggish, but this is a natural characteristic. They put plenty of energy into their flight when disturbed or when searching for food, but it is not a nervous energy.

The ideal aviary is a large, planted, shady flight, but the birds will do well in an unplanted, shady aviary with a flight of 20 ft (6·5 m), long enough to enable them to get adequate flying exercise.

In their wild state they feed on large quantities of insects and some fruit, but the Asian species are almost completely insectivorous and therefore more difficult to acclimatise to domestic diets. When they do accept domestic foods they adapt very well to aviary life. (Group C diet is recommended.) They should always be considered as slightly delicate and must not be subjected to severe cold. The main danger from cold or from overbearing companions is that the birds will not eat. To correct this is difficult, because they are basically stubborn and, without food, they lose interest in living. It is much easier to prevent this situation than to correct it.

Most trogons are peaceful but they should not be kept with small birds which they might harm, or with such aggressive birds as jay thrushes, which might harm them. Touracos and plantain eaters are excellent companions in large aviaries; these peaceful larger birds are very active and they encourage the trogons to exercise.

Diet for trogons is the standard softbilled diet (Group A) plus additional raw minced meat, about 10 to 12 mealworms a day, and, if available, other insects, such as spiders, beetles, etc.

All the Asian species appear to feed on insects, in contrast to those from South America, which live mainly on blossoms and fruit. The South American species possess shot-metal colouring, and those from Aisa have mostly brown and black upper parts and bright red under parts, from which they get the name of Fire Trogons.

Many trogons have clear, penetrating call notes which are not unpleasant, although the sounds are bizarre and exotic. Most of the birds are very beautiful and difficult to obtain.

In the wild, the birds nest in cavities in decaying trees, and in captivity would need a large planted flight and a suitable nesting log. Disturbances or inadequate diet could cause parents to detsroy eggs or chicks.

Not all trogons are likely prospects for aviculture as some are very localised and rare in the wild. Many come from areas which are not even minor sources for local or world-wide aviculture, and the birds are not easily obtainable.

Genus: Pharomachrus

QUETZAL, RESPLENDENT TROGON, *Pharomachrus m. mocino* De la Llave (Pl. I)
G. Quetzal, Pfauentrogon; F. Quetzal, Trogon Resplendissant; D. Quetzal

DISTRIBUTION: Mountains of Chiapas, Guatemala, Honduras El Salvador and northern Nicaragua.

DESCRIPTION: *Male*. Breeding plumage: whole of head, upper parts and breast metallic golden-green, the feathers of the head and nape long and hair-like, forming a rounded crest. Wing coverts elongated, curving downwards and forward, well beyond the lower edge of the wing; flights dusky. Four of the upper tail coverts filmy in texture and greatly elongated, the central pair often more than 2 ft (60 cm) in length. Central tail feathers black, the three outer pairs pure white. Abdomen and under tail coverts bright crimson. Iris dark brown, surrounded by a white orbital ring; beak greenish-yellow; legs and feet, which have the first and second digits directed backwards, dusky. *Female*. Head and chin, lower breast and abdomen dull brown. Mantle, back and upper tail coverts shining green, the coverts extending to the tip of the tail but not beyond. Wing coverts green, under tail coverts red, iris brown with dark orbital ring, beak blackish, legs and feet dusky. Length: excluding elongated tail coverts of the male, 14–15 in. (35–38 cm).

The quetzal is dignified and graceful in stature, not only because of the long tail but also because of the full body and rather large head, which appears to be larger on account of

Quetzal, *Pharomachrus m. mocino*

the rounded crest radiating outwards and upwards from the eyes. The long feathers of the male stay for about 6 months each year and fall at the end of the breeding season.

During their acclimatisation they must have the proper diet for fruit-eating and insectivorous birds, with a little minced raw meat and 10 or 12 mealworms a day. They acclimatise more easily if the pair can be housed with touracos, who show them where to find their new food and adapt to their new conditions. Once properly acclimatised, quetzals can be kept in by aviculturists in good conditions for some years. One even lived for 22 years in the New York Zoological Gardens.

SUBSPECIES: Two other subspecies are recognised: *P. m. costaricensis* (Cabinis) from the higher mountains of Costa Rica and western Panama; and *P. m. antisianus* (d'Orbigny) which occurs in the subtropical zone of the Merida region of Venezuela, Colombia, Ecuador, Peru and Bolivia. In the

latter form the tail coverts are the same length as the tail, but the males do not develop the greatly elongated central feathers which are such a striking feature of the breeding males of the Central American birds.

Quetzals frequent the dense rain forests of altitudes up to 9,000 ft (2,707 m). They are arboreal and somewhat solitary birds, often remaining perched for long periods in an upright position, with their heads hunched down. Their food consists of fruit, insects, small frogs, lizards and snails, and they usually feed on the wing, fluttering amongst the branches, snatching fruit or insects from the twigs or foliage. They nest in holes in trees, and the male, which shares in incubation and feeding the young, sits with the long tail plumes bent forward over his back, the tips protruding from the entrance hole. To do this it is thought that the male must enter the nest hole backwards. The eggs, which are described as uniformly pale blue in colour, are about the size of a pigeon's egg, and the clutch is usually 2–3 in number. Incubation is said to last from 17–19 days.

In the *Aviculture Magazine* (Nov./Dec. 1943, Vol. VIII, No. 6, pp. 165ff.) J. Delacour published a report of the breeding results achieved in raising the quetzels *Pharomachrus m. costaricensis* by Mrs. Zeledon of Costa Rica. The birds were housed in a very large aviary with thick vegetation. We quote the following passage:

'We noticed the young bird peeping through the entrance hole on 8th August 1940, and on the 12th it left the nest.
Both male and female were feeding it as long as it was confined to the nest, but, once outside, only the mother cared for it, feeding it earthworms in the morning, and fruit. On the 16th of the same month it fed itself for the first time.
The plumage of the young bird at the moment it left the nest was uniform coffee-colour, except the wing coverts, which were green.
Both parents had been kept for three years in the big aviary and previously for two years in a much smaller aviary in which they would get very wild as soon as approached. In the big enclosure they are quite steady and take no notice of visitors. The pair was composed of a young male and an adult female purchased from the natives.'

Mrs. Zeledon commented on the importance of the condition of the tree trunk in which the quetzals nest. When, in 1942, she replaced the original old tree trunk, no attempt at breeding was made. She raid, 'I measured the old trunk and found it to have a diameter of about 12–13 in. (30–33 cm). The nesting hollow was approximately 9 in. (23 cm) in diameter. At the bottom was a shallow cup hollowed out, leaving a rim all around of a width of about 2 in. (5 cm). The lower rim of the entrance hole, almost 5 in. (13 cm) in diameter, was about 6 in. (15 cm) from the rim of the cup.
Any future attempt at breeding should take into consideration the condition of the log, which should be so well rotted throughout that bits can be pried off with the fingernail, and should have an entrance hole and nesting cavity smaller than the measurements given above. The birds will accommodate it to their liking themselves. It would also be a good plan to wet the log thoroughly from the outside with a hose daily, to reproduce natural conditions.'

WHITE-TIPPED QUETZAL, *Pharomachrus fulgidus* (Gould), lives in the subtropical mountainous areas of Venezuela. *Male*. Has broad white tips on the three black outer tail feathers. *Female*. Has a bronze sheen added to the green on the head.
There are two subspecies *P. f. fulgidus* and *P. f. festatus*.

PAVONINE QUETZAL (Peacock Quetzal), *Pharomachrus pavoninus*, Spix is from northern South America. Both sexes have a black tail, but it is not long and they do not have a frontal crest. *Female*. Has extensive reddish colouring on lower chest and abdomen, but this colour is lighter and less bright than in the *male*. There are three subspecies.

Genus: Trogon

COLLARED TROGON, BAR-TAILED TROGON, *Trogon c. collaris* Vieillot

DISTRIBUTION: Locally distributed in tropical zone of South America east of the Andes (except northern Venezuela), south to Bolivia, Matto Grosso and Rio de Janeiro; islands of Trinidad and Tobago.

DESCRIPTION: *Male.* Upper parts, head, beak and upper chest brilliant metallic green with coppery shadings. A bold white band across the chest is followed by brilliant red on the rest of the under parts. Fine white and black striations occur on wing coverts and some of the inner secondaries. The outer tail feathers are boldly barred in black and white, with broad white tips. This pattern is strongly dominant on the underside as well as the upper side. Bill yellowish-horn. *Female.* Has brown replacing the green, and the red under parts are lighter in shading. The barred tail feathers are reduced to dull striations with white tips. Bill dull horn colour. Length: about 9 in. (22 cm).

This is one of the most typical of the trogons.

SUBSPECIES: There are four similar subspecies: *T. c. puella*, *T. c. extimus*, *T. c. virginalis*, *T. c. exoptatus*. These birds can be kept very well in a well-planted aviary on the standard softbilled diet, with the addition of raw minced meat, 12 mealworms daily, and if possible other kinds of live insects. Fresh fruit must always be included in the diet.

It is recommended that Collared Trogons be kept with other peaceable birds of a similar size. The aviary should be heated in cold weather. ·

Collared Trogon, *Trogon c. collaris*

MASKED TROGON, *Trogon p. personatus* Gould
G. Maskentrogon; F. Couroucou masqué; D. Maskertrogon

DISTRIBUTION: Subtropical zone of the mountains of western Venezuela, Santa Marta Mountains, Central and Eastern Andes of Colombia, eastern Ecuador and eastern Peru.

DESCRIPTION: *Male.* Upper parts of body, with breast and central tail feathers, dark copper shot with green. Outside tail feathers black with fine white transverse lines and white tip. Face and throat black. A broad white band separates the breast from the red under parts of the body. *Female.* Slightly smaller with brown on upper parts and breast, the lower parts being pale pink. Length: 10½ in. (25 cm).

The Highland Trogon is listed as a subspecies, *T. p. temper-*

atus, by Peters, and as a separate species, *Trogon temperatus*, by de Schauensee.

The humid forestal hills in the subtropical and moderate zones of the Andes range of mountains conceal these quiet vari-coloured birds. They live in pairs and are difficult to see amid the dense foliage of the trees, as for the greater part of the day they remain sitting quite still. It is only when they are hunting for insects, or feeding on berries, blossom and other tree fruits, that they become conspicuous because of their striking colours.

WHITE-TAILED TROGON, *Trogon s. strigilatus* Linnaeus

G. Grüntrogon; F. Couroucou à queue blanche; D. Witstaarttrogon, Groene Trogon

DISTRIBUTION: Tropical South America east of the Andes south to Peru, northern Matto Grosso and Maranhão, Island of Trinidad.

DESCRIPTION: *Male.* Glossy yellowish-orange under parts from lower breast through under tail coverts with no white dividing line between the light and dark colours on the breast. The under side of the tail is entirely white. Dark upper parts highlighted by glossy purplish-blue on chest, crown and nape. Blue-green with a heavy sheen on back and central tail feathers, with a deeper shade of blue on upper tail coverts. Black outer tail feathers tipped in white. Beak dull horn colour, surrounded by short bristly hairs. *Female.* Mostly grey with some fine white striations on wing and some orange-yellow on lower abdomen and under tail coverts. Length: 9½–10 in. (23–25 cm).

The White-tailed Trogon has remarkably small feet, which are completely covered by the feathers of the lower part of the abdomen when they sit. They often sit lengthwise on a thick branch. It is their habit to remain quiet and patient until a flying beetle or butterfly passes by, when, in a fast

White-Tailed Trogon, *Trogon s. strigilatus*

flight, they seize their prey and return with it to the branch. They will also pick at fruits when on the wing. Their large eyes indicate their life in the dim light of the forests.

The nest is often placed in a termites' nest in a tree. Both male and female make the entrance passage and the breeding hollow, which takes about a week. Seven days or so after the nest is ready the first egg of a clutch of 3 is laid.

In South America some 20 species occur, which mainly have similar diversity of colour and markings.

Genus: Apaloderma

NARINA'S TROGON, *Apaloderma n. narina*
(Stephens) (Pl. I)
G. Zügeltrogon, Narina; F. Trogon narina; D. Narina-
trogon

DISTRIBUTION: Heavy woods and gallery forests of eastern
and southern Africa from Darfur and Eritrea through
Kenya, Tanganyika, the Kivu district of southern Congo,
to Angola and Cape Province.
DESCRIPTION: *Male*. Has bright red under parts from middle
of breast through under tail coverts. Upper parts, head,
neck and upper breast bright glossy green. Inner tail
feathers on upper side glossy green and blue. Outer feathers
striated and have broad white tips. Bare skin areas behind
eyes yellow in colour; similar area on chin blue. *Female*. Has
brown on sides of face, throat and breast. Colours are duller
and blend, rather than being sharply separated. Rose
replaces the red and the green is less iridescent. Length:
11½ in. (29 cm).
SUBSPECIES: Similar, but vary mainly in size and in amount of

bare skin behind eyes.
There is a romance regarding the name of these trogons:
they are said to be called after a beautiful Hottentot named
Narina. They are remarkable because of the lack of plumage
on parts of the head, round the base of the bill and eyes,
and at the throat. There are 3 species in Africa, and they can
occasionally be seen in collections.

Narina's Trogon lives in the dense forests and feeds mainly
on insects, which are caught in the tops of the trees. When
the bird sits in repose on a branch it keeps its head deep
between its shoulders and lets its tail hang downwards. It
flies quite silently and can be heard only when it utters a few
scolding noises.
At mating time the male utters a plaintive cry, and it is
possible to attract the birds by imitating their call. They nest
in hollow tree trunks, where they lay from 2–3 white eggs,
which they brood for about 20 days. When the young leave
the nest they remain in the vicinity of the older birds for
some time.

Genus: Harpactes

INDIAN TROGON, CEYLON TROGON, STRIPED TROGON,
Harpactes f. fasciatus (Pennant) (Pl. II)
G. Bindentrogon, Kurna; F. Couroucou strié de l'Inde;
D. Gestreepte Indische Trogon

DISTRIBUTION: Sri Lanka.
DESCRIPTION: Bill powerful and bent, with a smooth cutting
edge. *Male*. Upper parts chestnut brown; head and neck
black, throat and crop grey; breast and abdomen scarlet red.
Between crop and breast there is a narrow white band and
over the back of the head a red band; around the eye there is
a naked blue area. Tail reddish-brown on upper part;
exterior tail feathers black with white. Iris brown, bill dark
blue and feet greyish-blue. *Female*. Lacks the black on the
head, and lower parts ochre instead of red. Length: 12½ in.
(30 cm).
Of the 11 species that occur in Asia this is the most well
known. It is found in the darkest areas of the forest. Like
other trogons, this is a bird of the twilight, who prefers to
remain sitting at the top of a tree, flying off only to catch a
butterfly or other insect.
All Asian species seem to feed mainly on insects, by contrast
to those from South America, which feed largely on flowers
and fruits. The latter have the typical green metallic sheen,
while the Asian species mostly have brown and black upper
parts, and vivid red under parts, to which they owe the name
Fire Trogon.

coverts. Under side of tail whitish, and dark brown on upper
side. Mostly hidden by overlapping feathers, are two pairs
of black ones. *Male*. Wings black; striations, as well as
edges of primaries, white. Extremely beautiful, with pink
breast sharply separated by brilliant scarlet on remaining
under parts through under tail coverts. Facial, forehead and

Philippine Trogon, *Harpactes ardens*

PHILIPPINE TROGON, *Harpactes ardens* (Temminck)

DISTRIBUTION: Philippine Islands.
DESCRIPTION: In both sexes, bold, large, bare eye rings are
purplish. Beak mostly bright yellow with greenish base.
Striations on wings very finely drawn and cover a much
larger area than in any species previously mentioned,
extending from above the bend of wing through all the wing

throat areas blackish, blending into reddish-purple on nape
and dark reddish-brown on remaining upper parts. *Female*.
Dull brown, darker above and paler below; striations black.
Length: 15 in. (38 cm).
This is a peaceful bird. Only during mating does it utter a
sound, which is reminiscent of the miaowing of a cat. In
addition to insects, it eats berries and other fruits.

DUVAUCEL'S TROGON, *Harpactes duvaucelii* (Temminck)   (Pl. I)
G. Duvaucels Trogon; F. Couroucou de Duvaucel; D. Vuurtrogon, Trogon van Duvaucel.

DISTRIBUTION: Southern Tenasserim, Thailand, Malaysia, Sumatra, Rhio Archipelago, Banka, Billiton, Borneo, North Natuna Islands.

DESCRIPTION: *Male.* Outstanding features are the black head, red rump and pink under parts. The typical pattern of the wings in both sexes is the same as described for other trogons, and the blackish eye rings and beaks found in both sexes are darker in the male. The black of the head ends at the nape and on the throat. Remaining red under parts fade to pinkish on under tail coverts. Mantle, back and the black-tipped tail are brownish. The tail is the same as that of the Philippine Trogon. *Female.* Mostly brownish with a pinkish abdomen. Length: 13¾ in. (34 cm).

These birds will lose their bright colours if they are exposed for a considerable period to the sun's rays, and specimens kept in unplanted aviaries generally suffer in this way. They keep at their best if housed where it is both humidly warm and shady. In Borneo and Sumatra they live in the darkest mountain forests.

Genus: Priotelus

CUBAN TROGON, *Priotelus temnurus temnurus* (Temminck)   (Pl. I)
G. Kubatrogon; F. Couroucou de Cuba; D. Cuba-Trogon

DISTRIBUTION: Cuba.

DESCRIPTION: *Male.* Upper parts rich metallic green with some bluish-black on head and wings. Lower cheek area, chin, throat and chest white. Remaining under parts brilliant red. Bold and irregular white markings accent the dark wings. Central tail feathers dark greenish-blue with some black. Outer feathers, which vary in length, white with some bright green markings. Each tail feather is broad, ending in an elongated swallow-tail curve. *Female.* Slightly smaller with greyish-white chest lightly shaded with rose-pink. This rose-pink also occurs on the under parts. Length: about 11 in. (28 cm).

SUBSPECIES: *P. t. vescus*, on the Isle of Pines. A very distinctive trogon with an outstanding tail decoration.

These birds dwell in dense tropical forests, where they feed on insects and fruits. They are difficult to catch and mainly young birds are taken out of the nests and reared by hand. Such birds are naturally tame and quickly get used to aviary diet.

Trogons are of a tranquil disposition and during the day they seek a place in the shade and now and then utter their penetrating call. In Cuba the bird is called Tocororo, after its call. They fly extremely well and are at their fullest advantage in an open, unplanted, shady aviary. They are not unduly shy of human beings and can often be seen sitting quietly in a tree. The tail, with its format of half-moon-shaped under feathers, is held somewhat to the front, while the bird sits a little bent over towards its front, thus forming an arc. The Cuban Trogon has auricular feathers that are shaped like hairs. Trogons seldom alight on the ground and are hardly able to walk on their short and weak legs. The bill is toothed. In the breeding season the plumage emanates a peculiar smell of musk. The birds were first kept in the Zoological Gardens of Amsterdam.

Cuban Trogon, *Priotelus temnurus temnurus*

ORDER: CORACIIFORMES

SUBORDER: ALCEDINES

Kingfishers

BY H. J. BATES AND R. L. BUSENBARK

Kingfishers fall into two basic groups from an avicultural viewpoint. One stays near water and depends for food almost exclusively upon fish, crustaceans, and aquatic insects. The other inhabits dense forests and jungles, feeding in much the same manner as other large highly-insectivorous softbills. Their prey can include small animals, birds and reptiles. Those kingfishers which adapt well to captivity are young birds taken from the nest as fledglings. They must be hand-fed at first, and such young birds quickly learn to accept new kinds of domestic food. Adults rarely learn to accept these foods and, if they do, the acceptance is very slow. Delays are hazardous and health could be permanently impaired, even for those exceptions which manage the change-over. One way to expedite the change is to have a thoroughly domesticated kingfisher to lead others to the new foods. There is no doubt that hand-feeding young birds is the most successful way of domesticating kingfishers.

The writers noticed that young kingfishers in Thailand were being fed on a mixture of foods which consisted mostly of chopped fish and rice, which is the main diet for most difficult softbills there and in many oriental countries. American and European importers must change the birds over to other diets, but this is a relatively simple task. Higher percentage of raw meat should be added to the standard softbilled diet and young mice, when available, are very helpful. Since kingfishers regurgitate pellets of undigested food and fat, they must have considerable roughage in their diet if they are to be kept in a healthy condition.

Kingfishers usually nest in burrows which they dig out of cliff-banks, but some will best in hollow trees. Collectors usually watch nests closely so that they know at what stage to take the young birds for domestication.

Kingfishers all have large flat heads, short necks, heavy bodies, and very large, thick beaks. Most have short strong tails. Many are brilliantly and beautifully coloured. Sexes are usually alike, but in some instances the hens are more attractive than the cocks.

Genus: Alcedo

KINGFISHER, *Alcedo atthis ispida* Linnaeus
G. Eisvogel; F. Martin-chasseur vulgaire; D. Ijsvogel

DISTRIBUTION: Europe, Asia.

DESCRIPTION: Upper parts shining bluish-green; under parts chestnut-brown. Crown and neck distinguished by small sea-green horizontal stripes on a dark-green background; head feathers are elongated and form a short crest. Small chestnut-brown stripes run above cheeks and under eyes; chin and throat ochre white. A dark sea-green line runs from base of beak below ear region to sides of breast. Middle of back and tail turquoise blue. Beak black, with base of under mandible reddish. Feet and legs sealing-wax red. Length: 7 in. (18 cm).

These birds are found in pairs along streams and small rivers with clear water, in both low-lying and mountainous regions up to a height of 5,000 ft (1,800 m). As they fly like an arrow over water, the eye is caught by the light flashing from their plumage. They perch in various places along the water, between which they alternate in order to watch for their prey. They dive from their perch into the water, and not until they are under water do they use their wings. With or without their prey, they return to their perch. Pairs will lay claim to a wide territory and defend it vigorously against intruders. Apart from fish, of which they need 10 or 12 a day, they eat crayfish, snails, dragonflies and grubs. The inedible parts of what they eat are regurgitated in the form of pellets. They are found perched high in trees only in the mating season, when the fierce 'tee-eet' can be heard—the cry of the male to attract the female.

In a steep river bank they dig tunnels 23–40 in. (60–100 cm) deep, with a wider nesting chamber at the end. The eggs and young lie on regurgitated pellets, fishbones and scales. The 5–7 eggs are round in shape and shining white. The hen alone sits on the eggs for 16–17 days, and the cock brings food to her.

Attempts have for long been made to keep kingfishers in cages and aviaries. With adult specimens this does not always succeed, for they remain wild and will refuse food. Young birds allow themselves to be fed with fish and meat, and can become quite tame. In the company of young tame birds, older birds can also be accustomed to these altered conditions of life. If these birds are to be kept successfully, their aviary should be supplied with running water, into which live fish are introduced, although the birds can also be accustomed to eating fresh dead fish. Kingfishers are housed in such ideal circumstances in the Frankfurt Zoo, where they can be studied in their own element, and their movements followed even during their under-water hunting.

MALACHITE KINGFISHER, *Alcedo c. cristata* Pallas
G. Zwerghaubenfischer; F. Petit martin pêcheur huppé;
D. Malachiet-Ijsvogel

DISTRIBUTION: Africa from Senegal, Eritrea, Nubia to the Cape of Good Hope.

DESCRIPTION: Head has an attractive long crest, which is greenish-yellow with black horizontal bands. Rest of the upper parts ultramarine blue. Under parts, except the white throat, brown, as are sides of head and feathers beneath wings. Beak, legs and feet bright red. Length: 6 in. (15 cm). Outside the breeding season these charming kingfishers move about along lakes with broad banks of reeds and in swamps. In the breeding season pairs look for small streams with steep banks, where they dig their tunnels. This kingfisher is very common within its environment. It is distinguished for its rapid flight. On its perch a bird sometimes moves quickly up and down, and turns round with lightning speed. It moves its crest quickly up and down when excited or in danger. Its food consists principally of dragonflies and small fish. The nests of a number of pairs are often found close together. The eggs are shining white.

In 1957 a nest with 5 young was found in the neighbourhood of Port Elizabeth in South Africa. Three of the young were taken from the nest and raised by hand. They flourished on small pieces of fish, requiring 10–15 small fishes a day each. After eating whole fish, they later regurgitated the bones and scales. A few days after all their feathers had grown they left the nesting box in which they had been reared and flew round the room. It was a few days before they took an interest in the tank of water in which small fish were swimming. They were fed with small slices of heart, which were thrown into the water. Later they began to eat dead fish. They always took hold of the fish in such a way that the head went down first. They bathed every day. From the day they left the nest they showed the typical up and down movement of the head, but erected the crest only a few times. They were less highly coloured than their parents. The cheeks and breast dark greyish-brown; abdomen orange-brown, a shade lighter than scapulars and flanks. Beak black with white tip. Feet and legs reddish.

These kingfishers can be kept in good condition on a diet of fish and meat when taken as young birds.

NATAL PYGMY KINGFISHER, *Ispidina picta nataiensis* (A. Smith)

G. Natal Zwerg-Eisvogel; F. Martin pêcheur de Natal; Dwerg-Ijsvogel

DISTRIBUTION: South-eastern Africa from Natal and Pondoland north to Tanzania, the Kivu Highlands, Zambia and probably the Upper Katanga.

DESCRIPTION: Forehead and crown deep violet-blue with light blue cross stripes; mantle, wings, rump and tail violet-blue; under parts warm reddish-brown. A brown stripe runs from the eyebrow as far as the neck. Ear coverts and cheeks mauve on a brown patch just under the ear, and a white spot below; throat has a large white spot. Beak, feet and legs bright orange. Length: 5¼ in. (14 cm).

These Pygmy Kingfishers are found in regions to the south of the Sahara, where thorny bushes and small trees grow in the desert. They are predominantly dry-country birds, feeding mostly on grasshoppers, tiny lizards, caterpillars, beetles and the like, often very far from any water. As other kingfishers dive into the water to capture their prey, so do these Pygmy Kingfishers let themselves fall from their perches into the grass for the same purpose.

Its nest is in the typical hole in some earthy bank, and is in every respect similar to that of almost any other member of the family, but the site chosen is more often the side of a termite mound into which the bird excavates the tunnel, rather than the softer, sandier site of a river bank. The extra work involved in digging a hole through a hard sun-baked surface finds its effect in the greater wearing down of the bill, for it is very noticeable how short the beak of this bird is compared to that of a Malachite Kingfisher. In captivity, when the bird is relieved of all this hard work, the beak quickly becomes overgrown and out of character, despite the lesser work involved in smacking its bill against a perch in order to stun its food, which kingfishers always do.

On a few occasions, specimens have been imported into the United States, and in 1962, eight were brought over in good condition. They were fed on mealworms, strips of raw heart, and live whiting. The fish were put into a shallow trough of water so that the birds could dive in to seize them. Sexes can be distinguished by the beak, as the lower mandible of the hen has more the shape of a keel.

In 1963 breeding results were obtained in the zoological gardens of Trenton, USA. Together with flycatchers, tanagers and mesanges, 5 Natal Pygmy Kingfishers were put in a special aviary which was densely planted and provided with running water. An earthen wall was built and faced with cement; into this a number of holes were bored, through which the birds could see the earth. In one of these holes a pair of birds made a straight corridor, 10 in. (25 cm) long and hollowed at the end. Through this corridor their activities could be observed constantly. For 18 days both parents sat on the eggs alternately and after this they could be seen daily bringing whitebait to the nest. After 6 days the parents left the nest for periods and it was then seen that it contained 2 youngsters. They were fed eight times in every hour. After 18 days they left the nest, but both parents continued to feed them, although they had become sufficiently independent and dived after small fish. The parents then started breeding again.

Mr. D. M. Reid-Henry of Woodford Green, England, reported in the *Aviculture Magazine*, May/June 1970, his observations of the Malachite and Natal Pygmy Kingfishers. Regarding the latter he said that although it was in the main a species of the dry country, it was very keen to take several baths a day, and was always ready to retrieve any food from under water. His experience was that kingfishers were adaptable to change in dietary habits but had little stamina to withstand cold. In general they are peaceable birds and may be kept in company with other species without danger.

RED-HEADED PYGMY KINGFISHER, *Myiocegx lecomtei* (Cassin)

G. Rotkopf Zwerg-Eisvogel

DISTRIBUTION: Limited area from equatorial forests of Ivory Coast to Gabon and eastwards to Uganda.

DESCRIPTION: About the same size as *Ispidina picta* and generally similar in pattern. Head and neck rufous-orange with some bluish spots and a black forehead band. The rest of the pattern and colouring is like *I. picta*. Beak, feet and legs bright red.

Two other Pygmy Kingfishers are:

PYGMY KINGFISHER, *Chloroceryle aenea* (Pallas)

G. Zwerg-Eisvogel

DISTRIBUTION: Southern Mexico, Central America and northern South America.

DESCRIPTION: Upper parts dark iridescent green with some white spots on wings and outer tail feathers. Throat pale buff with an orange tint blending to bright rufous on chest and sides, with white on central abdominal area and under tail coverts. *Female.* Has chest-band of green, faintly and irregularly striated with white. Beak red, feet and legs dull red. Length: about 5 in. (13 cm) including long beak.

MINDANAO KINGFISHER, PHILIPPINE FOREST KINGFISHER, *Ceyx melanurus* (Kaup)

DISTRIBUTION: Philippine Islands.

DESCRIPTION: Upper parts, except for a white band across the back and sides of neck, rich rufous heavily spotted with lilac. Some black occurs on scapulars and flights; throat white; chest and sides bright lilac washed with rufous, and centre of abdomen white. Beak red; feet and legs reddish. Length: 5 in. (13 cm) including beak.

This is one of several very small forest kingfishers which are exceptionally vivid and which can be successfully kept in aviaries. Slight variations in colouring and size occur in the different races.

Genus: Dacelo

KOOKABURRA, LAUGHING JACKASS, *Dacelo n. novae-guineae* (Hermann) (Pl. II)
G. Lachender Hans, Jägerliest; F. Martin-chasseur géant; D. Australische Bosijsvogel, Lachende Hans

DISTRIBUTION: Queensland (except Cape York Peninsula), New South Wales, Victoria and South Australia.
DESCRIPTION: This is a bird of dull colouring and cluttered pattern, but it has an interesting personality. Beak brownish-black above and buff below. A broad, buffish eyebrow starts above beak and tapers off behind crown. Dark and dull brown in a long elliptical patch occurs on cheeks, surrounds eyes and lores, and tapers to lower side of neck, with a dark crescent on lower nape. Back, wings and tail dull brownish-black with buffish tips on many of the feathers and pale brownish striations on tail; wing coverts tipped with pale iridescent shades of blue and green. Remainder of plumage dusty buff with inconsistent darker feather edges in some areas. Iris light greyish brown. Beak horn-coloured, feet and legs brown. Length: a little larger than 11 in. (28 cm) not counting the beak.

Kookaburra, *Dacelo n. novae-guineae*

The Kookaburra, the one kingfisher with a long and successful avicultural history, is likely to be found only in zoos, because it is protected in its native range and therefore difficult to obtain. In the wild state it is beneficial because it destroys rodents and other harmful vermin. It even includes small snakes in its diet.
The birds make their nests in hollow trees, old tree stumps and holes in buildings, laying 3–4 white eggs. It was first bred in captivity at the London Zoo (*Zoological Society Report*, 1905).

BLUE-WINGED KOOKABURRA, *Dacelo l. leachii* Vigors and Horsfield
G. Haubenliest; F. Martin-chasseur hoppé; D. Blauwvleugel Ijsvogel

DISTRIBUTION: Queensland, except Cape York Peninsula.
DESCRIPTION: *Male.* Crown whitish-yellow, crest feathers having dark tips. Neck white; back brown; upper tail coverts and rump light blue; tail dark blue; wings blue and brown with pale yellow edges to feathers; ear coverts grey-brown. Iris white, beak dark brown on upper, dull white on lower; feet and legs grey. *Female.* Has brown tail with narrow black and cream transverse bands. Length: 16½ in. (42 cm).

SUBSPECIES: Four subspecies have been described, which show slight variations of form and colour. These are *D. l. superflua*, *D. l. intermedia*, from southern and south-eastern New Guinea respectively, and *D. l. occidentalis* and *D. l. cervina* from West Australia, the Northern Territory and some Melanesian Islands.
The habits of this Kookaburra are the same as those of the Laughing Jackass. The birds are usually seen in pairs on a dead branch high up in a tree. Their principal food consists of locusts and reptiles, but they often steal eggs and young birds from their nests. They breed in abandoned termites' nests high up in gum or eucalyptus trees. A few specimens were on show in the London Zoo as long ago as 1884.
As they spend a good deal of the day sitting quietly on a perch, it is possible to keep them in a large cage, as long as they have an opportunity to fly round the room for an hour a day. They can share a spacious aviary with pigeons, aracaris, touracos and other birds which can defend themselves. They can be kept in good condition if fed with large insects, raw meat, mice, rats, sparrows and fish. The species has not yet been known to breed in captivity.

Genus: Halcyon

BLUE-BELLIED KINGFISHER, *Halcyon cyanoventris* Vieillot
G. Bloubauchliest; F. Martin-chasseur à ventre bleu; D. Blaubuik Ijsvogel

DISTRIBUTION: Java and Bali.
DESCRIPTION: Head, wing coverts and tips of flight feathers black. Throat, breast, neck and collar brownish-red. Flight and tail feathers blue-green. Under parts, back, scapulars and a patch on neck deep shining cobalt blue. Base of large flight feathers white. Beak, feet and legs red. Length: 11 in. (28 cm).
These brilliant birds can be seen in thorn and bamboo bushes and hedges round rice fields. In shallow water and on the ground they look for crabs, fish, snails and worms. In contrast to most kingfishers, who prefer to rest on a post or a dead branch, they are just as likely to sit on the ground. In the mating season the cock sings hoarsely from the top of a tree and is answered by the hen, who flies at a great height. Together they make for their nest a hollow in a crack in rock which is filled with earth, or bore a tunnel in the steep bank of a river. The 3 or 4 white eggs are round in shape.
These birds are very rarely found in collections. Mr. K. A. Norris, in Surrey, England, obtained a specimen in 1937. The bird lived for 3 years and would certainly have lived longer if a sudden shortage of its proper food had not caused its death. A fine colour plate is given in *Foreign Birds* (1960, p. 286).
There are a large number of Asiatic species which now, as ever, find their way into collections, and can be kept in good condition on the standard diet for insectivorous birds, supplemented with pieces of raw meat and fish. The following species may be mentioned: the Black-headed Kingfisher, *Halcyon pileata* (Boddaert), from India, China and Indonesia; the Violet Kingfisher, *Halcyon coromanda* (Latham), from the same regions; the White-headed Kingfisher, *Halcyon saurophaga* (Gould), from New Guinea, the Moluccas and the Papuan Islands; and finally the Java Wood Kingfisher, *Halcyon chloris* (Boddaert), of which 47 subspecies are recorded, all of which occur in Indonesia or in the scattered archipelagoes.

WHITE-BREASTED KINGFISHER, *Halcyon s. smyrnensis* (Linnaeus)

G. Baumliest, Braunliest; F. Halcyon à poitrine blanche; D. Witborst-Ijsvogel

DISTRIBUTION: Asia Minor, Iran, Baluchistan, northern and southern India.

DESCRIPTION: Neck and breast white; back, rump and upper tail coverts light blue; remainder bright chestnut brown. Wings show patterned markings of black, light blue, white and dark blue. Tail bright blue with black markings. Irides brown, beak coral red; legs and feet brownish-red. Length: 11 in. (28 cm) including beak of about 2 in. (5 cm).

These kingfishers prefer to live along the water's edge, although they also inhabit forests far from water. Usually they live in pairs. A bird will sit on a favourite perch, which it uses as a look-out, watching for its prey. It dives swiftly on to its victim and flies with it to a place where it can beat it to death by bashing it against a perch or branch in order

Sacred Kingfisher, *Halcyon s. sancta*

White breasted Kingfisher, *Halcyon s. smyrnensis*

finally to swallow it. Its food consists of fish, tadpoles, grasshoppers and other insects. Small mammals and even young birds are taken for food. From its perch the bird utters a hard chattering call. They build their nests in earth walls of the sea shore, in which they dig deep tunnels. Four to 7 white eggs are laid. Both birds sit alternately and bring up their young between them.

The White-breasted Kingfisher belongs to the species which is most often imported and it was regularly to be seen at the London Zoo, as well as elsewhere. Of the 4 other subspecies, the Indian Kingfisher, *Halcyon s. fusca*, which occurs in great numbers in Thailand, is now the most frequently available to aviculturists.

SACRED KINGFISHER, *Halcyon s. sancta* Vigors and Horsfield

G. Götzenliest; F. Halcyon sacré; D. Heilige Ijsvogel

DISTRIBUTION: Australia, New Zealand, islands in the South Pacific, southern Philippine Islands, Indonesia and southern Borneo. The wide range is partly the result of migration.

DESCRIPTION: Under parts buffish-white; upper parts bluish-green with a lustrous sheen. Wings more blue than green. Broad buff-white collar on neck divided by narrower black band which circles the entire head, running through the lores, eyes, cheeks, and across the nape. Iris brown. Beak mostly blackish. Feet and legs brown. Length: about 8 in. (20 cm).

WHITE-COLLARED KINGFISHER, *Halcyon chloris* (Boddaert)

D. Javaanse-Ijsvogel

DISTRIBUTION: India, Burma, Thailand, Borneo, Malaysia, most of south-east Asia, the South Pacific and Australia.

DESCRIPTION: Beak mostly blackish, with some white on inner half of lower mandible. A narrow black mark runs through the eyes and borders on nape and lower boundaries of blue cap. Sides of forehead, reaching above eyes, white. A white collar around the nape connects with white under parts. Large cap on head and all upper parts below white collar, bright greenish-blue, with shading varying somewhat to greenish on back and to dark blue on flights. Sexes differ slightly in this beautiful and simply patterned species. *Female.* More green and duller in colouring. Length: about 9 in. (23 cm).

SUBSPECIES: There are 47 subspecies widely distributed as above. There are several variations because of the enormous number of these.

It has been possible for aviculturists to obtain *H. chloris* from Thailand. Hand-reared youngsters are very tame, but they may become less so as they get older.

WOODLAND KINGFISHER, *Halcyon senegalensis* (Linnaeus)

D. Bos-Ijsvogel

DISTRIBUTION: Many areas in Africa, including Senegal, Angola and Ethiopia.

DESCRIPTION: Beak red on upper mandible, black on lower mandible. Back, wings, rump and tail varying shades of blue, ranging from greenish-blue to cobalt, with some black on wings. Under parts mostly white, with grey on chest washed with faint greenish-blue. Head dull grey, with white forehead and eyebrow line. Feet and legs black. Length: about 9 in. (23 cm).

This species has been bred at the Winged World, England, and this is described, as follows, in *The Avicultural Magazine*, Vol. 77, No. 6, Nov./Dec. 1971:

'We put our two Woodland Kingfishers together for the first time in one of our larger glass-fronted compartments. They very quickly settled down together. During the following weeks they appeared to be looking for a suitable hole for nesting. She nested in a plywood nest-box approximately 8 in. square (20 cm²) with a half open front. This had been fixed near the roof of the compartment. The cock was never observed to assist in the incubation of the eggs at any time.

We do not know the incubation period owing to the fact that we were unaware of the time when the hen started to take an interest in this nest-box. After a while we heard noises coming from it, so assumed the pair must have young, and then

Plate III

Gould's Heavenly Sylph, *Aglaiocercus kingi*

Naked-throated Bellbird, *Procnias nudicollis*

Cock-of-the-Rock, *Rupicola rupicola*

Streamer-tailed Hummingbird, *Trochilus polytmus*

Hooded Pitta, *Pitta sordida cucullata*

Bengal Pitta, *Pitta brachyura*

Plate IV

Lilac-breasted Roller, *Coracias c. caudata*

Indian Blue Roller, *Coracias benghalensis*

Hoopoe, *Upupa e. epops*

Australian Bee-eater, *Merops ornatus*

Brown-headed Barbet, *Megalaima z. zeylanica*

Black-collared Barbet, *Lybius torquatus*

Plate V

Great Hornbill, *Buceros bicornis*

Pied Hornbill, *Athracoceros malabaricus leucogaster*

Red-billed Hornbill, *Tockus erythrorhynchus*

Black-backed Magpie, *Gymnorhina tibicen*

Abyssinian Ground Hornbill, *Bucorvus abyssinicus*

Plate VI

White-crested Jay Thrush, *Garrulax l. leucolophus*

Chinese Jay Thrush, *Garrulax c. chinensis*

Rufus-bellied Niltava, *Muscipa sundara*

Lesser Niltava, *Muscipa macgregoriae*

Silver-eared Mesia, *Leiotrix a. argentauris*

Pekin Robin, *Leiotrix l. lutea*

Black-headed Sibia, *Heterophasia c. capistrata*

noticed mealworms being taken to the box by the cock. We also noticed a certain amount of aggression towards the other birds in the compartment.

After a week had elapsed we started to supply half-grown locusts and day-old mice, which were quickly taken up to the nest by both parents. We continued with this method of feeding until the youngster left the nest, which was 29 days after we first assumed that it had hatched. We then cut down on the amount of mice and locusts to encourage it to partake of our normal daily diet. The young bird was noticed to be eating mealworms on its own a week after leaving the nest, and strips of beef about a week later.

There was only one youngster in the nest, and we found no signs of any other eggs. The box was completely empty and quite clean and dry. The young bird is slightly smaller than its parents, and in perfect feather. The bill blackish, and colouring somewhat paler generally, with the under parts being very finely striped horizontally in back.'

BLUE-BREASTED KINGFISHER, *Halcyon malimbica* (Shaw)

G. Blaubrustliest; F. Martin-chasseur à poitrine bleue; D. Blaauwborst-Ijsvogel

DISTRIBUTION: Africa, mostly in the west but also in the central area.

DESCRIPTION: Upper mandible bright orange-red; lower mandible black. Head greyish with paler area on forehead and above mask. A small black mask covers lores, surround eyes, and tapers to a point behind the eyes above the cheeks. Throat white. Sides of face, nape and chest soft blue with undefined gradual boundaries. Remainder of under parts soft white tinged faintly with blue and grey. Lower back, rump and upper tail coverts soft greenish-grey; tail cobalt blue. Most of the wings black with some bright blue on central areas of primary and secondary flights. Feet and legs orange. Length: about 11 in. (28 cm) including beak.

Racial differences are slight, but the beak of one has brighter shade of red, which also occurs on part of the lower mandible. Some races have more extensive and deeper shades of blue, extending in some forms on to the head.

BROWN-HEADED KINGFISHER, BROWN-HOODED KINGFISHER, *Halcyon albiventris* (Scopoli)

D. Bruinkop-Ijsvogel   G. Braunkopffliest;

DISTRIBUTION: East to west coasts of South Africa below the equator but not the Republic of South Africa.

DESCRIPTION: Head soft dull greyish-brown, except for white on throat and nuchal collar. Back and rump cobalt blue, shading to greenish-blue on tail. Wings and mantle mostly black, with pale blue on flights, particularly noticeable when wings are spread. The tips are blackish in a similar pattern as described for the White-breasted Kingfisher. Under parts buffish-white. Beak, feet and legs red. Sexes are slightly different. *Female*. Having brownish-black instead of black on wings and mantle. Length: about 9 in. (23 cm).

GREY-HEADED KINGFISHER, *Halcyon leucocephala* (P. L. S. Müller)

G. Graukopffliest; F. Martin-chasseur à tête grise; D. Griskop-Ijsvogel

DISTRIBUTION: Most of tropical Africa from east to west coasts. The wide range is partly due to migration.

DESCRIPTION: This species is more attractive than any African one so far described because of brighter shadings and chestnut under parts, starting on the lower chest and extending through the under tail coverts. Head soft grey tinged with brown. A small black mark occurs on the lores. Throat white; chest a very pale shade of grey tinged with chestnut. Lower back and tail bright cobalt blue, but back is hidden when wings are folded. A large black area covers the same area on mantle and wings as described for *H. albiventris*. Flights bright blue. Beak bright coral red. Feet and legs red. Sexes similar, but there is slightly more brown on head of female. Different races have most noticeable variations in the shading of blue on wings and tail. Length: about 8 in. (20 cm) including beak.

CHOCOLATE-BACKED KINGFISHER, *Halcyon badia* (Verreaux and Verreaux)

D. Bruinrug-Ijsvogel

DISTRIBUTION: Africa, Liberia and equatorial forest area to western and central Angola.

DESCRIPTION: This species is more attractive than *H. leucocephala* because it has reddish-chocolate on head, sides of face, neck, mantle, scapulars and wing coverts. The lower areas are shaded with black; under parts white with a tinge of buff. Some blue occurs on flights, shading to brownish-black on outer areas. Back and rump bright blue with tail paler greenish-blue. Beak dark red; feet and legs brown. Length: 8 in. (20 cm) including beak.
This is a rare deep-forest bird.

Genus: Tanysiptera

GALATEA RACKET-TAIL KINGFISHER, *Tanysiptera g. galatea* G. R. Gray

G. Seidenliest; F. Halcyon galatée; D. Galatea raketstaart, Raketstaart-Ijsvogel

DISTRIBUTION: New Guinea and western Papuan Islands.

DESCRIPTION: Crown and neck greenish-blue. Under parts dark blue; rump and tail feathers white the latter with small light blue tips, and the two elongated median tail feathers light blue with scattered white dots. Beak sealing-wax red; legs and feet grey-brown. Length: 11 in. (28 cm).

These kingfishers differ from the others in their step-like, elongated tail, and the racket-shaped median tail feathers. The latter are very narrow for part of their length and then spread out in oval discs. The birds live in the woods and feed principally upon millipedes and lizards. They are among the most handsomely coloured species, but are very rarely in aviaries and only in some zoos.

SUPERFAMILY: TODOIDEA

Genus: Todus

FAMILY: TODIDAE

BROAD-BILLED TODY, *Todus subulatus* G. R. Gray

G. Plattschnabel-Todie; F. Todier vert; D. Groene Todie

DISTRIBUTION: Haiti.

DESCRIPTION: Upper parts of body shining grass-green. Chin and throat feathers carmine red with silver-grey tips. Upper breast and sides of breast flecked with red; abdomen yellowish-white, a few feathers at the extremities being slightly tinted red. Irides grey; upper mandible dark horn colour, lower mandible reddish. The fine flat beak, with virtually no comb, is very noticeable and is surrounded by black bristles. Tail and wings are particularly short. Length: 4½ in. (11·5 cm).

Todies always live in trees and thick bushes, and are remarkably tame. In the foliage they look for all kinds of insects for their food. With their heads down and their beaks erect, they sit quietly on a branch, but with their mobile eyes they carefully follow everything going on around them. They have a somewhat quiet and mournful whistling cry.

Although they are only rarely kept in cages or aviaries, they can be maintained in good condition on a diet of mealworms, flies and small insects. They nest in holes, digging passages of 8–12 in. (20–30 cm) deep with their beaks and claws, and in a somewhat enlarged nesting hole lay 4–5 white round eggs. The nest is carefully lined with moss, vegetable wool and fine fibres.

SUPERFAMILY: MOMOTOIDEA

FAMILY: MOMOTIDAE

Motmots

BY H. J. BATES AND R. L. BUSENBARK

Motmots of eight different species in six genera are found in Mexico, throughout most of South America (except for Chile and Uruguay), and most of Argentina. Several of the species are subdivided into numerous similar subspecies. Because the subspecies do show variations, there will be many different popular names in use. Motmots are mostly attractive birds and the colour pattern is similar in most species; bright colours occur on the tails, faces and to a lesser extent on the wings. There is a similar arrangement of patterns and colours on the heads of most species, with bright blue markings heightened by black contrasts. Prominent also is a broadened apostrophe-like spot on the breast of most species. Body colouring is soft—mostly shades of olive and brown. Feet and legs are dark. Sexes are similar.

The tails are the most interesting and distinctive features. The two central tail feathers have racket-tipped ends, preceded by varying lengths of bare shaft, which extend beyond the normal long and slender tail. Two species lack the racket tips and are therefore less distinctive in appearance. All have graduated tail feathers, the shortest underneath and the upper central pair the longest.

Motmots have rather long broad beaks, large heads, and short thick necks. In the wild state they sit quietly hidden in shady trees in their lowland forest habitats while searching for food. Their tails move from side to side in a pendulum movement and may be stopped and held at seemingly off-balance angles.

Motmots prefer and thrive in planted aviaries because of their somewhat solitary, calm and retiring nature, but they cannot be easily observed in such aviaries. They will do well in unplanted aviaries if they are given shady shelters and unobtrusive companions. Although the length of the various species ranges from 7 to 17 in. (18–43 cm), even the larger ones should not be subjected to the aggressive companionship of Laughing Jay Thrushes or birds of similar disposition, unless the aviary is really large and well-planted.

Motmots require a careful acclimatisation period in order that a satisfactory transfer to domestic diets can be achieved. They eat mostly insects or other live food, and some fruit in the wild state, but the fruit or other greenstuff is negligible in comparison with their insectivorous requirements. They are not as difficult to acclimatise as rollers, but they still cannot be considered easy. Once acclimatised, they are hardy and easily managed, provided their food does not become unbalanced. The diet is the standard softbilled fare, with a little extra meat, and, when possible, extra live food.

In the wild state motmots nest in rocky crevices or long tunnels which they excavate in the sides of cliffs. They have successfully nested and reared young in aviaries. A noteable successful breeding occurred in the San Diego Zoo, California, USA, where the birds chose just such a cliff site in one of the huge planted aviaries.

TODY MOTMOT, *Hylomanes momotula* Lichtenstein
G. Zwerägeracke; F. Motmot nain; D. Kortstaart-Motmot

DISTRIBUTION: Southern Mexico, Central America, northwestern Colombia.

DESCRIPTION: This is the smallest of the motmots, and it has no racket tips to tail. Crown and nape rufous-brown, and the turquoise eyebrow is again present. The black cheek patch is enhanced by a buff-white stripe below the eyebrow. The same shade also covers the lores. White on sides of throat and abdomen are also notable differences. Pale brownish-olive on throat and breast contrasts with the green of the back, scapulars and rump. Flights and tail olive-brown. Length: about 6½ in. (17 cm).

This is one of the shyest of the motmots and is one of the less distinctive.

They inhabit regions with dense growth and live on insects and to a lesser degree on fruits. They also seize small mammals and reptiles, hacking their bodies with their tooth-edged beaks into pieces in order to be able to swallow them. They nest along quiet river banks, in which they dig corridors with their beaks and feet. They also take possession of the hollows of other animals. Their 2–4 eggs are white and are alternately incubated by both parents. Much care has to be taken in acclimatisation. In the early stages plenty of live food should be added to the other food they are being given. Pieces of raw meat and mealworms are also liked by this species.

Blue-crowned Motmot, *Momotus momota*

Tody Motmot, *Hylomanes momotula*

BLUE-CROWNED MOTMOT, BRAZILIAN MOTMOT, *Momotus momota* (Linnaeus)　　　　(Pl. II)
G. Motmot, Sägerack; F. Motmot; D. Motmot

DISTRIBUTION: Mexico, Central America, South America, southward to north-western Argentina.
DESCRIPTION: Head marked with a black mask, covering lores and cheeks, surrounding eyes, and tapering to a tip behind cheeks. Bright, glossy turquoise forms a broad brow, which is narrow on forehead and tapers off on back of crown. Crown has a black area. Wings and tail turquoise-blue mixed with green. Rest of colouring soft olive-green, upper parts darker than under parts. Length: 18 in. (45 cm). The blue-crowned Motmot was bred at Winged World, Lancashire, England, by Clive Roots, as reported in the *Avicultural Magazine*, No. 86, 1970, p. 188.

JUCATAN MOTMOT, TURQUOISE-BROWED MOTMOT, *Eumomota superciliosa* (Sandbach)
G. Tünkesbrauen Motmot; F. Motmot à sourcils bleus; D. Wenkbrauenmotmot

DISTRIBUTION: Southern Mexico and Central America.
DESCRIPTION: Broad turquoise-blue eyebrow extends in a broad even band covering lores, running slightly under but not over eye, and ending boldly and bluntly on side of neck. Cheeks are not covered, and there is no tapering tip. A trace of purplish-rufous colouring follows eye between black mask and blue brow. A distinctive difference from other motmots is the long triangular beard; narrow upper tip starts at chin and flares outwards almost to chest. Frosty turquoise-blue borders sides of beard, underlines eyes, and covers chin. Flight feathers are black on tips but are otherwise bright greenish-blue, as is the tail. Dull greenish-olive covers remaining portions of head, neck, mantle and breast. Soft rufous shades back and abdomen; remaining area of back and wings a brighter shade of green, with a slight cast of olive. Length: about 13 in. (33 cm).
This is one of the most beautiful of all motmots. The standard tail length is considerably shorter in proportion to body length than *M. motoma*, and this results in much longer bare shafts on the two central tail feathers. Nearly half the total tail length is bare shafts and racket tips of blue, broadly banded with black.
In addition to *Eumomota superciliosa*, representatives of other species are occasionally imported into Europe. Among these are the long-tailed species: the Keel-billed Motmot, *Electron carinatum*, from South Mexico; and the Broad-billed Motmot, *Electron platyrhynchus*, from Colombia, Ecuador, Peru, Bolivia and Brazil.
The Rufous Motmot, *Baryphthengus ruficapillus*, and the Blue-throated Motmot, *Asphata gularis*, both from the same habitat, also belong to these species.

SUBORDER: MEROPES

FAMILY: MEROPIDAE

Bee Eaters

BY H. J. BATES AND R. L. BUSENBARK

Bee Eaters are difficult to keep because of their highly insectivorous nature. They do not easily adapt to a domesticated diet because it is inert. A remarkable feature is their preference for stinging insects, whose stings they do not remove before swallowing them, though they seem to render the stings harmless. Even large bumble bees and horse flies are greedily snapped up as soon as they leave their nests. Bee Eaters keep careful watch beside a nest and in this way capture innumerable insects. Live food in a satisfactory variety is not available in an adequate supply to bird keepers, and so they must rely on artificially compounded diets. Bee Eaters are particularly reluctant to accept such food and because of this difficulty few have ever been kept for long periods. However, many of the most dedicated aviculturists consider them a challenge and have sought opportunities to work with them.

The writers saw the successful results of such an experiment while travelling in Thailand. In the aviaries of Swart Chantharojvong of Bangkok were many birds known to be difficult in confinement. These included Hoopoes, Pittas, Falconets, Kingfishers and Bee Eaters. Swart Chantharojvong's approach to nearly all these very difficult birds was to get young ones which had not yet become firmly entrenched in their natural tendencies, so that they would accept unfamiliar food. The large young Bee Eaters with which he was working were in excellent condition and plumage and were feeding on the standard diet he uses for all such insectivorous birds. His diet, of course, was far different from what Europeans or Americans would offer, because of differences in the availability of various dietary items. But the main point is that he had taught these birds, while they were still young, to accept inert food. Transfer to other domesticated diets is a relatively simple task after such excellent groundwork.

Bee Eaters in the wild state are gregarious by nature, but the writers cannot suggest suitable companions in aviaries. Presumably birds which are about the same size, and neither aggressive nor weak, would be most suitable. Also, because they are gregarious with their own kind, it would seem wise not to keep them singly. In the wild state bee eaters are calm and poised when perching. When flying, their easy and graceful flight is punctuated by short acrobatic excursions, which seem to be only momentary detours to catch insects. The wing span is extensive. The best housing would therefore consist of spacious flights, so that the birds would be able to exercise, and so ward off any tendency to sluggishness. As most Bee Eaters are especially beautiful when flying, large flights provide an opportunity for added appreciation of these birds.

For nests Bee Eaters excavate tunnels in the ground or in the sides of cliffs, using no nesting material. In this respect, as well as in other characteristics, their habits somewhat resemble those of motmots; but motmots are far more successfully kept in captivity.

Bee Eaters are attractive and graceful, partly because of their long and slender curved beaks, which are black in most species, and partly because most have long slender tail extensions on the two central feathers. The patterns and colour arrangements on most species give a sleek and streamlined appearance. Colours are smooth and intense and sharply divided or softly blended. The irides of most species are bright red. Many are extraordinarily beautiful. Sexes are similar, but females of most species appear to be a little smaller, and tail extensions are often slightly shorter. Immature plumage is much less colourful.

Altogether there are 24 species, distributed in 7 genera. Four genera are confined to Africa; one genus, with one species, is confined to the Celebes Islands. One genus, with 2 species, is widespread in South-east Asia; and one genus, *Merops*, with 9 species, is widespread in range, which includes Europe, Africa, India, Asia, South-east Asia, Australia, Papua–New Guinea, and almost all areas in between. Some are migratory. It is with this genus that aviculturists are most concerned.

All 9 species in the genus *Merops* are shapely and beautiful. All except one species have central tail extensions, which vary considerably in length, and all have a black mask which appears to follow the line of the long and slender curved beak through the lores, lower part of the eyes, the ear coverts, and on to the sides of the neck.

Genus: Merops

LITTLE BEE EATER, *Merops pusillus*

DISTRIBUTION: South of Sahara in West Africa, east to Ethiopia and Somaliland, and south to Natal.

DESCRIPTION: Beak slender and curved; tail more square than *M. ornatus* and yellowish on under side, with darker tip. Head and back green; wings yellowish with dark flights. Throat yellow, divided from under parts by black band extending from base of beak under eyes and down across chest, where it is wider. Under parts orange-yellow. Feet and legs dark yellowish brown. Length: about 7 in. (17·8 cm).

An account by Clive Roots of the breeding of *Merops pusillus* at the Winged World, Morecambe, England, is given in *Avicultural Magazine*, Vol. 76, No. 4, July/August 1970, p. 139–40. It is believed that this may be a first success. Here are extracts:

'An artificial wall for tunnel-nesting birds was built into a wall in which gaps, approximately 1 ft (30.5 cm) square were left.

These were later covered with a wire mesh screen in which small holes were left, and a weak plaster mixture, dyed the colour of the rocks, was trowelled over the screen. A retaining wall was then built about 6 ft (183 cm) behind this rock face and the gap between filled with soil and planted. Vines were also planted in crevices left between the rocks.

Four Little Bee Eaters were housed in this exhibit, but the first pair to come into breeding condition would not tolerate the presence of others. Their first nesting attempt, in the spring of 1969, was unsuccessful, as they chose one of the holes nearest the top of the wall. The depth of soil over their tunnel was therefore no more than a few inches and the front part collapsed soon after they started feeding their young.

Little Bee Eaters were observed excavating a new tunnel, once again near the top of the wall, in the middle of March. Towards the end of the month it became apparent that egg-laying and possibly incubation had commenced, because of the long period of absence of one of the birds. As far as we could tell, incubation started on 4th April, and on the 25th of the month the first of the many visits to the tunnel with food commenced. Both parents fed the nestlings with mealworms, mealworm pupae and blowflies. Crickets and locusts were also offered but were ignored. From entering the nest-hole with food to re-appearing again no more than 4 seconds elapsed, so we naturally assumed that the tunnel was short, possibly about 18 in. (45 cm) long, but we never took the risk of inspecting the entrance hole or tunnel during incubation and rearing, for fear of upsetting the birds.

After a rearing period of exactly 28 days, 3 nestlings appeared. One was a poor flier, another could manage reasonably well, although it could not perch, and both consequently spent most of the time on the floor. The third nestling was poorly feathered and was replaced in the tunnel. The nestlings at this stage were green above, had a black eye streak, brownish-white throat, and pale green under parts, streaked with green on the breast. They were the same size as the adults, but their bills were short and straight. Two days later the most backward of the two still out of the tunnel disappeared and we assumed it had returned to the nest. This proved to be correct, for the following day saw the reappearance of this and the third nestling. Neither could fly properly, and, as it soon became obvious that the parents were ignoring them, they were re-moved. One died within the hour, but the poorly feathered one was successfully hand-reared. This breeding attempt therefore reached a successful conclusion, as the other youngster was reared to independence by the parents.'

CARMINE BEE EATER, *Merops nubiscus* Gmelin
G. Scharlachtspint; F. Guêpier carmine; D. Schar-lakenrode Bijenter

DISTRIBUTION: Africa: north of the Equator, from Senegal on west coast to Ethiopia in east.
DESCRIPTION: The most beautiful and most distinctive of all bee eaters. Entire head greenish-blue with black mask acting as an effective accent. Blue occurs on upper tail and under tail coverts. Some olive green and black mark wings, but all these colour accents are completely subordinate to the bright carmine red which covers the rest of the plumage. Length: 13 in. (33 cm) including 3 in. (7·5 cm) tail extension.

GREEN BEE EATER, *Merops orientalis*
G. Grünspint

DISTRIBUTION: Africa, Saudi Arabia, India, Ceylon, Burma, Thailand, Cambodia, Laos and Vietnam.
DESCRIPTION: Considerably smaller than *M. apiaster* and far less colourful. Overall colour green. The narrow black mask is less prominent, but the red irides are more out-standing. A narrow black band separates throat and chest. Blue on throat, a bronze cast on wings, and a golden-brown wash on head are colour variations, but they are less vivid than the variations found on other species.
Length: 9 in. (23 cm), including the 2 in. (5 cm) central tail extension.
SUBSPECIES: There are slight variations in the different subspecies, especially in throat and head shading.

BLUE-TAILED BEE EATER, BROWN-BREASTED BEE EATER, *Merops superciliosus*

DISTRIBUTION: Africa, Saudi Arabia, India, China, Burma, Thailand, Malaysia, Borneo, Indonesia, Philippines, and many other parts of South-East Asia and the South Pacific.
DESCRIPTION: Most attractive Asian bee eater. Head, above black mask, rich chestnut, which extends down neck,

mantle and back. Wings dusky bluish-olive; lower back, rump, upper and under tail coverts light blue. Tail blue with greenish wash. Blue covers large area on chin, throat, lower cheek area, lower sides of neck, and upper breast, where it shades into a soft dull bluish-green on remaining under parts. Length: 11 in. (28 cm) including 3 in. (7·5 cm) tail extension.

EUROPEAN BEE EATER, *Merops apiaster* Linnaeus
G. Bienenfresser; F. Guêpier meridional; D. Bijeneter

DISTRIBUTION: Europe, Africa and some parts of Asia.
DESCRIPTION: Beak long, curved and slender. Tail narrow, with short central extensions. Iris red. Facial mask black; chin and throat bright yellow, bordered with black band above breast. Under parts soft, bright, smooth greenish-blue. Forehead pale whitish, changing to brown washed with lilac-purple on crown. Mantle, back and central portions of wings brown, fading to golden brown with some rust-orange on lower back. Bend of wing has more green than blue, and flights and tail feathers intermediate between green and blue-green. Length: 11 in. (28 cm) including tail extension. The beautiful European Bee Eater is migratory, with a very extensive range. It is the best known of all bee eaters.

AUSTRALIAN BEE EATER, RAINBOW BIRD, *Merops ornatus* Latham (Pl. IV)
G. Schmückspint; F. Guêpier d'Australie; D. Aus-tralische bijeneter

DISTRIBUTION: Australia.
DESCRIPTION: Upper parts grass-green; crown, neck and flight blue; lower parts darker green; throat a clearer green and separated from breast by a broad, deep black band; vent stripe blue; cheeks black, marked off from below by band of light blue. Iris brownish-red, beak black, feet and legs fleshy grey. Length: 8 in (20 cm) including tail extension.

Australian Bee Eater, *Merops ornatus*

This is the only bee eater which is native to Australia. Large groups of these birds are found in dry areas with few trees. In the daytime they live in couples, and find a place on a bare branch from which they can overlook their hunting ground, but towards evening they gather in great flocks. They hunt all kinds of beetles and large insects.

They nest in colonies and dig passages in steep banks, sometimes more than 39 in. (1 m) deep. At the end is the nesting chamber, which is 8 in. (20 cm) long and 6 in. (15 cm) wide, and usually contains 5–8 round white eggs.

SUBORDER: CORACII

FAMILY: LEPTOSOMATIDAE

Genus: Leptosomus

CUCKOO ROLLER, COUROL, *Leptosomus d. discolor* (Hermann)

G. Kurol; F. Courol malgache; D. Kurol

DISTRIBUTION: Malagasy Republic.

DESCRIPTION: *Male.* Slate-grey upper parts, with green sheen; neck light grey; crown black; lower parts light grey. The jay-like beak is black. The neck feathers point forward and cover the base of the beak. *Female.* Has red-brown and black horizontal stripes above the neck, and pale red-brown under parts with black spots. Both sexes have a short crest. Feet and legs brownish. Length: 17 in. (43 cm).

These birds are usually seen in pairs or small groups, flying above the tree tops, whistling loudly, with slow wing beats and graceful swerves. When they perch on the top of a tree or telegraph pole and utter their cry, they sit bent forward, with throat feathers puffed out. In the tops of trees the birds find numerous large insects, such as butterflies, beetles, grasshoppers and large hairy caterpillars. The gizzards of courols have been found entirely lined with the long hairs of caterpillars, in a similar way to the cuckoos' gizzards. In addition to insects they also eat small amphibians and chameleons. They seize these in their beaks and beat them against a thick branch until their prey is unconscious before they swallow them.

In common with the cuckoos, courols have the ability to turn their outermost toe in either direction. They mostly nest in tree hollows and sometimes in walls or banks.

FAMILY: CORACIIDAE

SUBFAMILY: CORACIINAE

Rollers

BY H. J. BATES AND R. L. BUSENBARK

Rollers are very beautiful birds but are seldom found in private collections. They show to best advantage in large aviaries, such as those in zoos and bird gardens. In small aviaries it is impossible to see their complicated array of beautiful colours. Large aviaries also provide them with the best of captive conditions for display, good health and needed exercise. They perch in dominant places for long periods in open areas where they may be easily observed. For the most part they are native to open field and lightly wooded areas rather than forests and are therefore less shy in aviaries than are most jungle birds.

Rollers in the wild usually feed on large insects and small animals such as rodents, salamanders and frogs. In captivity they are reluctant to change to domesticated food, which is inert, and acclimatisation periods can therefore be difficult. They will readily eat small strips of raw meat, mealworms and live insects, but to begin with will refuse softbilled mixtures for long periods, although eventually they will learn to eat these. (See Group C for diet.) The acceptance of meat and mealworms may give the keeper a mistaken confidence, for these items alone do not constitute a satisfactory diet. Mixing softbilled food, small amounts at first and then gradually increased, with meat is the best transition method, even though it is slow. Rollers do not eat fruit and the necessary vegetable matter they need in the wild state comes from insects and small animals which have, in turn, consumed vegetable matter.

In the wild state, Rollers nest in holes in trees, which are often appropriated from other birds. In captivity they would undoubtedly be among those birds which are reluctant to gain an interest in nesting activities. This is partly because of their somewhat solitary nature and of their unusual natural calmness, which can easily become sluggish in captivity. This sluggishness can be traced to the absence of challenge in the struggle for existence. This vital lack of excitement does not extend to most birds in captivity, but it does to Rollers. Live foods in as extensive a avariety as possible are recommended; small rodents, frogs, salamanders, large insects such as grasshoppers, and any other available live food, are important in meeting this challenge.

Rollers are unusually peaceful with most birds, mainly because there is no close association. They should not, of course, be housed with small birds. Excellent companions for Rollers would be Touracos, Plantain Eaters and Red-billed Blue Magpies, which are quite peaceful and yet very active. The association with such active birds is helpful in prodding Rollers into needed exercise to overcome sluggishness. In the wild state they have rather raucous voices, not frequently used.

Rollers are heavy-bodied and have very fine, almost furry, body feathers. The colours are mostly blues of various shades, with other subsidiary colours which are mostly pastels. The colours are often mixed or blended and patterns are complicated, with colour dominance often in the wrong places. Yet Rollers of the genus *Coracias* are very beautiful birds, especially when they spread their wings and tails, which are their most colourful features. The heads are rather large and somewhat flat in appearance, with the large heavy beaks also flat and hooked at the tip. The different species vary in size and the tails show considerable variation.

Rollers are rare in aviculture, but several species can become more important when their management is better understood.

Broad-billed Rollers, both the Oriental and African species, are not as attractive as the Rollers belonging to the *Coracias* genus described above. They are a little smaller in body size and have shorter tails, broader and shorter beaks, and are less colourful in plumage. The shading is generally dusky, but there are some attractive colours on the three species.

Genus: Coracias

INDIAN BLUE ROLLER, *Coracias benghalensis*
(Linnaeus)   (Pl. IV)
G. Veilchenracke, Bengalenracke, Hinduracke; F. Rollier de l'Inde; D. Indische of Aziatische Scharrelaar

DISTRIBUTION: Eastern Arabia, southern Iran, Baluchistan, the Punjab and the Indian Peninsula south to about latitude 20°N.

DESCRIPTION: Sexes alike. The wing spread is extensive, and the richest colouring is on the wings. Most of the body colours are soft, variable pastels, which are often cluttered with insignificant markings. The appearance is that of a larger bird because of the big head and heavy body. Beak blackish. The top of the flat head has a soft pastel-blue cap. The shading varies in different subspecies. Following the cap and covering the neck, back and scapular area is a dull blend of olive-greyish-blue with a lilac wash. Facial areas below the cap are soft lavender, which extends down to the chest; buffish streaks radiate downward and outward from the throat; lower chest and abdomen are lavender-brown. Under and upper tail coverts are beautiful shades of soft turquoise. Feet and legs yellowish-brown. Length: 13 in. (33 cm).

The Indian species has more of a brownish shade on the back and a vinous shade on the chest than does the Thai and

has a paler shade on a broad outer area of the tip, becoming broader on the outer feathers.

The huge wings glow in the same light and dark shades of blue found in the tail, but there is a little less green in the turquoise. A very broad band of royal blue cuts across the wings diagonally, with the paler blue banding the outer six flight feathers. A touch of dark blue tips the outer edges of the outer flights. The turquoise highlights the scapulars and the bend of the wings. These same colours are repeated on the under side of the wings.

EUROPEAN ROLLER, *Coracias g. garrulus* Linnaeus
G. Blauracke; F. Rollier d'Europe; D. Europese Scharrelaar

DISTRIBUTION: Europe, especially northern Europe and Russia for breeding. Migrates to India and tropical Africa in winter.

DESCRIPTION: Sexes alike. Head, neck and under parts light blue with a greenish wash. Wings show light and ultra-marine blue; rump royal blue; flight feathers black and tail, which is broad and squared, greenish-blue. Back browner than *C. benghalensis* and breast more blue. There is a frosty eyebrow across the forehead and over the eyes. Feet and legs dark yellowish. Length: 12½ in. (31 cm).

These birds often breed with a number of pairs very close to one another, sometimes in the company of bee eaters. The centre of the nest is covered with fine stalks, animal hairs and feathers. The 4–5 eggs are white. Both parents sit on the eggs and the young are fed on maggots and various insects. A first breeding was recorded by W. H. St. Quentin (*Avicultural Magazine*, Vol. 7, 1901, pp. 217–9).

LILAC-BREASTED ROLLER, FORK-TAILED ROLLER,
Coracias c. caudata Linnaeus   (Pl. IV)
G. Gabelracke, Gabelschwanzracke, Grunscheitelracke; F. Rollier à longue queue; D. Vorkstaart-Scharrelaar

DISTRIBUTION: Africa, major parts of the continent south of the Equator.

DESCRIPTION: This lovely species is characterised by length-ened tail feathers, which are, however, not so long as those of the Abyssinian Roller. Sexes alike. Band on forehead and stripe on eyebrow white. Lores and ear coverts brown. Area of cheek and chin white. Crown green as far as nape,

Indian Blue Roller, *Coracias benghalensis*

Burmese species, *C. affinis*, which is bluish by comparison. The upper side of the tail is vivid, except for the two central feathers, which have the same shade as the back. The other colours are mainly rich royal blue, which appears to be blended with turquoise, and a lustrous turquoise-green, which is a much lighter shade. The distribution and pattern of these blues varies in the different races. The Indian form, which the writers have owned, showed the dark blue at the base and at the tip of the tail. The Thai and Burmese race

Lilac-breasted Roller, *Coracias c. caudata*

covered with light blue cere. Upper parts purplish-red with white quill marks; lower parts light blue. Rump and upper tail coverts cobalt blue. Wings show various shades of blue. Outer flights black, others greenish-blue with brown quill stripes. Beak black, irides brown, feet and legs brown. Length: about 12 in. (30 cm).

These birds live, either in pairs or in small groups, in open woods, on lake sides and in regions where palm trees grow singly. They prefer to keep to tops of trees, from where they can chase grasshoppers and similar insects. On the ground they also catch beetles, crabs and small amphibians. They are tireless, often chasing groups of weaver birds, and constantly make a noise. They fly, rather more through the branches or along the ground. The birds mate while on the wing, at which time prolonged screeching occurs. The birds lead a wandering existence, except during the breeding period, when they remain in one place for a considerable time. Their nests have been found in the hollows of trees, sometimes as much as 18 ft (5·5 m) above ground, and are made of stalks and lined with hair and feathers. The 3–4 eggs are white.

The Lilac-breasted Roller is occasionally found in collections sometimes with other jay-like birds. They can easily be kept on insectivorous food, well mixed with small pieces of raw meat. Occasionally living insects or a young mouse should be added to their diet.

ABYSSINIAN ROLLER, *Coracias abyssinica* Hermann
G. Senegalracke, Schwalbenschwanzracke; F. Rollier
d'Abyssinie; D. Abessynse Scharralaar

DISTRIBUTION: Africa, in a broad-banded range across the continent north of the Equator.

DESCRIPTION: Sexes alike. Plumage almost identical with that of the Indian Roller, but is somewhat smaller. An important point of difference is the tail, the two outside feathers of which are considerably lengthened. The body is somewhat more blue. Back a little browner. On the forehead and chin white stripe markings are clearly visible. Has a chestnut-coloured cere. Various blue colour variations on wings and tail. Feet and legs yellowish-brown.

These rollers live in the open prairie. They congregate in dense thickets, from where they catch large flying insects such as grasshoppers. They also eat small mammals and reptiles. Their flight is swift and twisting, and they can catch their prey on the wing.

The species is only rarely imported, but they are found in zoological garden collections, such as those at Wassenaar (Netherlands). Although it is quite possible to pair a couple of these roller, they have so far not been persuaded to nest in an aviary.

A single specimen can easily be kept in a spacious cage with other birds of similar size, for instance any jay-like species. Caged birds must, however, have an opportunity every day of flying round the room. They soon learn to return to the cage, especially if a couple of mealworms are left in it. But they do themselves far more justice in a spacious aviary. It is better not to have any small birds in the same aviary, as they may be killed and eaten. The rollers love to take baths, even rolling in damp foliage like the Grass Parrakeets.

Genus: Eurystomus

ORIENTAL DOLLAR BIRD, ORIENTAL BROAD-BILLED ROLLER, *Eurystomus o. orientales* (Linnaeus)
G. Ostroller; F. Rolle à gros bec, Eurystome d'Asie; D. Oosterse Scharrelaar

DISTRIBUTION: India, South-East Asia, Burma, the Philippines, New Guinea, Thailand, Indochina, Malay States.

DESCRIPTION: Sexes alike. Head olive-brown; lores and scapulars bright sea-green. Wings and under parts greyish-sea-green. On the chin and throat is a large deep blue spot. Flights and tail feathers black with thin blue edges; wings have a blue speculum. Lower part of tail indigo blue. Beak red with a black tip. Feet and legs red, claws black. Iris brown; around the eye is a bare red orbital ring. Length: 12¾ in. (32 cm).

These birds are much less attractive than the rollers belonging to the *Coracudae* family. They differ from them in their shorter tails, cut off square, their shorter and broader bills, and their less colourful plumage. They usually keep to wooded areas, hunting insects, which form their main food, and become active only in the afternoon. During the warmest part of the day they look for a place at the top of a tree. As well as catching their prey in the air they have also been seen hanging from a branch while removing the mouldy bark of the tree with their beaks in a search for beetles. They also look on the ground for beetles, snails, ants and termites. During this operation one bird keeps watch in a tree and as soon as he senses danger he utters his hoarse cry. Their nests are built in the hollows of trees at great heights, and 3–5 snow-white eggs are laid. The birds become very aggressive during the breeding period.

A subspecies occurring in Australia is the Dollar Bird, *Eurystomus orientales pacificus* (Latham), so called because of the light spot which appears in the middle of the wings and which resembles a dollar coin. In various parts of Africa two other species occur: the African Broad-billed Roller, *Eurystomus glaucurus* (Vieillot), with six subspecies, and the Blue-throated Roller, *Eurystomus gularis* (Vieillot), with two subspecies. In their behaviours and requirements these two are identical. Only a few specimens have reached European collections. They can only be kept in the company of larger birds, and in winter must have a heated dwelling place.

FAMILY: UPUPIDAE

Genus: Upupa

HOOPOE, *Upupa e. epops* Linnaeus
G. Wiedehopf; F. Huppe puput; D. Hop   (Pl. IV)

DISTRIBUTION: Widespread in Europe, Asia, Africa, India, China.

DESCRIPTION: *Male.* Basic colouring soft orange-brown enhanced by many black and white markings. Great fan-like crest, which is frequently and nervously displayed, broadly tipped with black, narrowly preceded by a paler shade of the orange-brown. Wings and tail (which is rather long and dove-like with a squared end) black with broad, irregular whitish bands. Beak is exceptionally long and slender in a downward curve, and is used for probing for food. Feet and legs brownish-grey. Immature birds have a dusty shade on the white areas and a slightly greyer shading on the black areas. Pale fleshy areas at the corners of the beak are very noticeable in youngsters. *Female.* Duller and perhaps a little smaller. Length: about 12 in. (30 cm).

Hoopoes are very active and somewhat nervous birds. They spend more time on the ground than any of the previously-described soft-bills and have strong running legs, but they are by no means restricted to the ground. Their running is punctuated by staccato-like forward movements of the head in the manner of doves and many fowl.

Hoopoes have traditionally been notoriously difficult to transfer to domestic diets and losses have usually been high during the acclimatisation period. The customary procedure recommended during the transfer period is to cover the floor with loose soil and plant generously with earthworms and mealworms. In Bangkok hoopoes are hand-reared and are fed largely on diced fish and rice with other minor additions. Once the birds accept this food, they will readily transfer to other domesticated foods.

They nest in holes in trees, walls, old buildings, among rocks, and in banks on the ground, laying 4–5 whitish eggs. A first breeding is recorded by M. Aronstein in *Bird Notes* (2) 2, 1911, pp. 221–2, 257–9.

Hoopoe, *Upupa e. epops*

THAILAND HOOPOE, *Upupa epops longirostris* Jerdon

G. Thailand Wiedehopf; F. Huppe à long bec, Huppe de Thailande; D. Langsnavel-Hop.

DISTRIBUTION: Assam, Burma, Thailand, Indochina, Malaysia, Sumatra.

DESCRIPTION: Main colour orange-brown, with black and white markings on upper parts. Head and fan-shaped crest purplish-brown with black tips. Back and sides of neck and scapulars yellowish-dusty-grey; remainder of back and wing coverts black with yellowish-white stripes. Large flight feathers have white tips; small flight feathers have 3 or 4 white stripes. A white band runs across the black tail. Chin whitish; throat and breast pale creamy pink. Beak black; feet and legs dusty-grey; irides reddish-brown. Length: 12 in. (30 cm).

SUBSPECIES: The habits of the 9 subspecies are identical. In 1964 successful breeding of this species was recorded from Trenton and San Diego, both in the USA (*Avicultural Magazine*, Vol. 70, No. 4, July/August 1964). The birds were brought from Thailand in 1961 and were reared by hand by Mr. Swart Chantharojvong. The male began to court the female by feeding her with mealworms. He visited the nest for a full week before the female showed any interest. Later the birds spent some time on the nest every day. The incubation period lasted 18 days and only the female sat on the eggs. She left the nest twice a day to eat and drink. When the young hatched the female remained another 14 days on the nest and her food was brought by the male, although she did not allow him into the nest. The young remained in the nest for 28 days. The food on which they were reared was mainly mealworms. The parents were given earthworms and mixed food, including horse-flesh, bread, shrimps, flies, hard-boiled yolk of egg and curdled milk. Some of this was also fed to the young.

A breeding success in 1969 was reported at Winged World, Morecombe, England, by Mr. Richard Martin. In an article in *Cage and Aviary Birds*, January 1974, he refers to this and also to a later breeding in 1973 at Padstow Tropical Bird Gardens, England, when a first clutch of 6 were reared. Two other breedings by the same birds followed that year but were less successful. It is thought that this failure may have been caused by a change in the brand of vitamin/mineral supplement.

SUBORDER: BUCEROTES

FAMILY: BUCEROTIDAE

Hornbills

BY H. J. BATES AND R. L. BUSENBARK

Hornbills are bizarre and fascinating, but their great size removes most of them from the realm of private aviculturists except for those with extensive aviary space. Zoos particularly like them because they represent excellent displays and are long lived. Some of the smaller ones are less than 2 ft (61 cm) in length, and the larger ones are almost 5 ft (152 cm).

Hornbills are very heavy-bodied birds with large feet and legs, long gangling necks, and huge curved beaks. On top of the beak is usually a very large casque, variable in size, shape, colour, and design according to genus and species. Hornbills are awkward and clumsy, and their flying is heavy and laboured. It is difficult to give them a large enough flight area to ensure normal exercise, but hornbills settle down quickly to aviary life and do not seem to suffer from restricted exercise. They should, of course, be given a large aviary for ordinary movement. Though many are noisy in the wild state, most are quiet in captivity.

The unusual nesting habits of hornbills are notable. Most species use cavities in trees as nesting sites. The hen is sealed into this cavity so that only her beak can reach outside the small opening to receive food from the cock. Several materials are used to strengthen the mortar in this plastering job, but most of it is a very hard mud base. Incubation varies from four to six weeks, with various genera, and young stay in the nest from four to eight weeks.

Collectors in the wild take young birds from the sealed nests just before fledgeling age and handfeed them at first. Young birds adapt quickly to domestication and become marvelously tame pets, but mature birds are reluctant to accept confinement and domestic diets. Fortunately, most collectors know this.

The maturation and growth processes are very slow with hornbills. The dull, cluttered plumage is unattractive, and the crowning casques are undeveloped and uncoloured for a long time. They are less presentable as zoo exhibits during this period, but the reward of complete domestication is worth waiting for. The tameness of handfed fledgelings is a very wonderful experience. Not many birds can match that puppy-dog devotion which young hornbills give to their owners. If adult hornbills are clumsy and awkward, young birds are even more so. Their ludicrous appearance is exaggerated by very long down-curved eyelashes.

The diet for hornbills in captivity is the simple, standard softbilled diet with extra meat rations and an occasional mouse or small bird. Some species are more carnivorous than others.

Hornbills are found mainly in Africa, India, most countries of South-east Asia and major islands in the South Pacific. Most of those available to aviculture and zoos are from India and Thailand. Several of the most attractive and most interesting ones come from the Philippines, and these are only infrequently available. Altogether there are 45 species of hornbills distributed in 12 genera. The species are subdivided into many races which frequently show notable differences in appearance. Sexes are usually alike, but hens are mostly a little smaller.

Most species have casques which are composed of lightweight sponge-like horn on the inside. The writers once received an adult Rufous Hornbill, *Buceros hydrocorax*, with the forepart of the casque broken away during shipment; the honeycombed texture was clearly visible. Normal regrowth replaced the damaged area leaving no scar tissue or discolouration. Not all hornbills have this texture, however; the casque of the Helmeted Hornbill is described as being solid 'like ivory' and has been used for ornamental carvings.

African Hornbills

For the most part, hornbills from Africa are more bizarre than any of the Asian species and mostly less attractive. With the exception of *Aceros undulatus* Wreathed Hornbill, and its similar relatives, most of the Asian hornbills have a considerable beauty in their appearance, but most of the African species lack beauty.

There are 14 species and numerous subspecies of the African genus *Tockus*, one of which inhabits India and Ceylon and another of which inhabits India. They range in size from about 15–21 in. (33–53 cm) and show considerable variations, mostly nondescript and unspectacular. Several are lacking or almost lacking in casques. Those having casques are somewhat like Tarictic Hornbills, *Penelopides panini*, except they are less attractive. Some even have diagonal serrated sides of the lower mandible like Tarictics. The crown and nape feathers are bushy, forming a recumbent crest. Most have dull greyish, brownish or blackish plumage. Beaks vary in colouring and pattern with dull reddish dominating most.

The four species of the genus *Bycanistes* range in size from 22–30 in. (55–76 cm) with correspondingly heavier bodies and larger casques. The species *B. cylindricus* Temminck, called the Brown-cheeked Hornbill and one of the largest species in the genus, has a magnificent casque with a prominent ridge on top and deep serrations. A subspecies, *B. c. albotibialis* Cabanis and Richenow, is called the White-thighed Hornbill and has a casque almost like a downturned Rhinoceros Hornbill. The species *B. subcylindricus* has a less impressive casque than the nominate race above. It has two subspecies called the Black and White-Casqued Hornbill and the Grey-cheeked Hornbill.

The species *B. brevis* Friedmann, called the Silvery-cheeked Hornbill, has a casque almost similar to the Great Hornbill. The species *B. bucinator* Temminck, with four very different subspecies is called Trumpeter Hornbill, Laughing Hornbill, and Piping Hornbill. Casques vary, some with deeply grooved mandibles and no casques to long, slender, and low casques with or without rippling ridges.

Two species about 36 in. (90 cm) long of the genus *Ceratogymna* are the Yellow Casqued Hornbill, *Ceratogymna elata*, and the Black Casqued Hornbill, *Ceratogymna strata* (Temminck). Both have magnificent crowning casques with the names indicating two of the major differences. Other differences, such as the crests and wattles, are also highly individualistic.

The two Ground Hornbills, *Bucorvus abyssinicus* and *Bucorvus leadbeateri*, are turkey-like in many respects. They have long and strong legs for running and relatively short tails. Both have large bare blue wattle areas on the throat which form inflatable pouches. The beaks are long, the casques small, and the colours mostly dull blackish. Large bare blue skin areas surround the eyes.

Genus: Tockus

RED-BILLED HORNBILL, RED-BEAKED HORNBILL, *Tockus e. erythrorhynchus* (Temminck)   (Pl. V)
G. Rotschnabeltok; F. Calao Tock; D. Roodsnavel-Toktok

DISTRIBUTION: Senegal, Sudan, Ethiopia, Somalia, Kenya, Uganda and Tanganyika.
DESCRIPTION: *Male.* Head dark brown in centre; ear coverts brownish. A stripe runs down the neck, sometimes extending down the back. Upper parts brownish-black, with large

white spots on wings. Large flight feathers black with white tips; small flight feathers show white edges. Median tail feathers dark brown, outside ones black at base and white at tips with a black transverse stripe. Iris light brown or yellow, beak curved, blood-red without casque; legs and feet greyish-brown. *Female*. Similar but somewhat smaller. Length: 18¼ in. (47 cm).

The Red-billed Hornbill is a true tree bird, which descends to the ground only when it can no longer find in the trees any of the fruits which are its main food. These birds mostly form small groups which have selected a particular tree in a region as their roosting place. In contrast to other hornbills, who prefer seclusion, the Red-billed Hornbill likes to display itself and therefore seeks out the outside branches of high trees.

A spacious aviary is best for them in captivity; they do not often utter their loud cry and will sit for long periods on a high branch. Their behaviour does not become lively until the mating period. The cock feeds the hen, and together they build onto the entrance to the nest. They pass each other nesting material, though they may not wish to make use of it, and it seems more of a kind of game. This work precedes the actual mating.

The hen disappears into the nesting hollow as soon as the entrance has become so small that she can scarcely get through it. Only then does she begin to lay her eggs; often 4–6 in all. The entrance slit is then made even narrower so that only her beak is able to protrude in order to receive the food that the cock industrially brings her. She remains in the nest until the young are ready to fly, that is for about 2½ months.

Although these birds do not have a very attractive appearance, their habits are so interesting that they have found a place in many collections. Apart from fruit they eat the standard diet for insect-eating birds, while bread and milk, pieces of meat, various kinds of grain, boiled rice and potatoes should be given for variety.

A successful breeding result, achieved by H. A. Gerrits Curator of Birds, Wassenean Zoo, Holland, was reported by him, with illustrations, in *Birds Illustrated* (Dec. 1955), of which here are the main points:

'In April 1955 we placed in the aviary two bowls filled with water and clay. After the birds had already shown a certain amount of interest in the large nesting block which had been placed high in the aviary they soon began to spread the edges of the entrance hole with clay mixed with excrement and sand. The female bird worked on the inside of the nest, while the male bird flew continuously to and fro to keep her supplied with nesting material. By the end of April the entrance had been made so small that the female could only with difficulty enter the nest. Finally this small opening was closed by the birds, leaving only a small cleft through which she could be fed. After this the male bird kept bringing her food, and always took away her excrement, which he deposited as far away from the nest as possible.

After mid-June there were already young in the nest. This was noticeable because every now and then the male bird caught small birds and brought them to the nest so that they could be torn into pieces and fed to the youngsters. At the end of June the female herself broke the plaster and emerged from the nest, and she appeared to be wearing a renewed plumage. Her condition was perfect; not a single feather had been damaged and she was splendidly clean. She had lost no weight and nothing of her flying capacity. There was no doubt that she had completely moulted in the nest.

At first both parents fed the youngsters, although the female did not take the task seriously. At the end of June both parents closed the opening again, leaving only a feeding cleft. A week later the female lost all interest in the offspring.

On July 11th it was seen that the youngsters had broadened the cleft from inside, and later that day the first one left the nest, only a few days later to be attacked and killed by the female. The father had supplied it continuously with food, although it was immediately self-supporting. The other two youngsters were caught and kept apart when they emerged. In the wild the mother will, directly after leaving the nest, fly away and take no more notice of the youngsters. It is possible that the occupation by them of what she regards as *her* aviary might be considered by her as an intrusion. At first the youngsters showed a preference for live food, but within a few days accepted the normal basic diet.'

Genus: Anthracoceros

PIED HORNBILL, *Anthracoceros malabaricus leucogaster* (Blyth)   (Pl. V)
G. Weissbauch Malabarnashornvogel, Weissbauchspitzhornvogel; F. Calao pie; D. Witbuik-Malabarneushornvogel

DISTRIBUTION: Burma, Thailand, India, Tenasserim, Khmer, Laos, Vietnam, parts of Malaysia, south-eastern China.
DESCRIPTION: Beak mostly yellowish-horn with a narrow black rim surrounding base of beak and rear of casque. Black band broad on sides of lower mandible. Irregular black band runs diagonally from upper forward end of casque to centre of beak, spilling onto upper mandible. Casque very large in proportion to beak; its forward end connects directly to beak. Large circle of bare white flesh surrounds the eyes. Another large bare skin area of white covers lower facial area below eye, separated from eye circle by black line. Rest of head, neck, under parts down to lower chest black, also upper parts except for broad white areas on ends of flights and tail. The black on back and wings glossy with some bluish-green iridescence. Central tail feathers black, remainder slightly graduated and black with an irregular white pattern on ends. Under parts from lower chest through undertail coverts white. Iris brown. Feet and legs blackish. Length: 28–30 in. (71–74 cm) including the beak, which has considerably more downward curve than any of the other species. Sexes similar, but female a little smaller.

These smaller hornbills live in dense forests where they feed on fruits or with their long beaks seize an insect or other small animal from a branch or leaf. They also fish in

Pied Hornbill, *Anthracoceros malabaricus leucogaster*

shallow water and when they catch a fish they throw it up into the air and very deftly catch it again in their beaks.

Pied Hornbills are perhaps the most ideal of all hornbills for aviculture. They are attractive and frequently available from Thailand.

Similar to *A. malabaricus leucogaster* and also called the Pied Hornbill is *A. coronatus*. It is slightly larger; all except central part of tail feathers totally white; black on chest terminates higher on chest; forward end of longer casque angles sharply backwards before connecting to beak.

SUBSPECIES: *A. c. coronatus*, Malabar Pied Hornbill, from India and Ceylon, has black over most of the upper area of casque; this is mainly confined to inward connecting area of long casque.

A. c. convexus, Southern Pied Hornbill from Malaysia, Borneo and many areas in Indonesia, has only a small area of black on casque, mainly confined to inward connecting angle of long casque.

A. malayanus, Black Hornbill from Malaysia, Borneo and parts of Indonesia has a broad white band on all except the central feathers of the broad squared tail. There are no white areas on face, but some have white eyebrows. Beak and casque yellowish-horn with no markings. *Female*. Has blackish beak and pink or white bare skin around eyes. Feet and legs black. Length: 29 in. (73 cm).

These species are rarely seen in collections, nor are the two species from the Philippine Islands: *A. montani* Sulu or Montano's Black Hornbill which is similar in shape to *A. malayanus* but casque not quite so long. Tail white; all remaining plumage as well as beak and casque black. Back and wings glossy with slight greenish iridescence. *A. marchei* Palawan Hornbill is similar but beak and casque are yellowish-horn, and casque is larger. Bare skin around eyes; band at base of lower mandible reddish.

FAMILY: BUCEROTIDAE

SUBFAMILY: BUCEROTINAE

Genus: Buceros

GREAT HORNBILL, CONCAVE-CASQUED HORNBILL, *Buceros bicornis* Linnaeus (Pl. V)
G. Doppelhornvogel; F. Calao bicorne; Z. Dubbel-hoornvogel

DISTRIBUTION: India, Burma, Thailand, Cambodia, Laos, Vietnam, Malaysia and Sumatra.

DESCRIPTION: Sexes alike, except for the irides. *Male*. Has a red iris and the female a white iris, though there are contradictions on this point. Tail is long and each feather very broad, even at tip. Tail on both sides basically white, except for a broad black band in lower area, but it usually has a dull buffish shade because of a preening oil from the oil duct gland on rump; this applies to other white areas. Rest of body plumage from mantle and upper chest black except for broad white tips on ends of wing coverts and flights; flanks white. Neck from rear of crown and below chin white; facial areas and chin black. Huge casque and sharply-pointed beak yellowish-horn with reddish tip on upper mandible and black at base of beak and rear rim of casque. Length variable, around 50–55 in. (127–140 cm) including beak.

Great Hornbills can be kept extremely well with related birds in a large aviary, but smaller birds will be eaten by them. Young Great Hornbills are born completely without feathers. Development takes a long time and for 3 years they do not resemble their parents.

The captive breeding and nesting of this species is unusual. Mr. Ken Stott reported on the nest making of a pair at the San Diego Zoo (*Avicultural Magazine*, Vol. 57, No. 4, July/August 1951). Though this did not result in a successful breeding much useful information was obtained from the observations by members of the zoo staff.

The most attractive of all hornbills is *Buceros hydrocorax* Rufous Hornbill from the Philippine Islands. It is rarely seen in collections. The colouring and pattern are very different from *B. bicornis*. Concave casque is an integral part of the bill and extends onto the crown; all the casque and nearly half of beak near base bright rosy-red, paler on beak than casque.

Remaining beak area horn-coloured. Broad black boundary surrounds beak and casque covering part of crown, chin, and facial areas except for the upper cheeks. Pale buff occurs on the chin; remaining head and neck plumage, furry in texture, is bright warm rufous shade. Upper parts except for tail brown; chest dull blackish-brown blending to chestnut on abdomen. Flanks and under tail coverts pale buffish-chestnut and tail whitish but usually stained. Feet and legs dark red. Length: about 37 in. (94 cm) including the beak.

Great Hornbill, *Buceros bicornis*

ABYSSINIAN GROUND HORNBILL, NORTH AFRICAN GROUND HORNBILL, *Bucorvus abyssinicus* (Boddaert) (Pl. V)
G. Nord-Hornrabe; F. Bucorve d'Abyssinie; D. Abessijnse Hoornraaf of Grondneushoornvogel

DISTRIBUTION: Gambia eastward through upper Guinea to northern Cameroon and across the Sudan to Eritrea and Ethiopia, south to the edge of the Guinean forests, northern Uganda and northern Kenya.

DESCRIPTION: *Male*. Main colour black, with the exception of yellowish-white quill feathers. Iris brown; beak blackish-horn-colour. Around eyes is a broad naked ring of blue skin. Neck area also blue and naked. The lowest parts of throat and neck are bright red, and are also naked. Horn black and open in front. Feet and legs heavy and greyish-black. *Female*. Similar, but has completely blue throat and neck. Length: 46¼ in. (1·18 m).

These birds are mostly seen in pairs in prairie land with a

dense afforestation and at heights varying from 3,000–12,000 ft (900–3,600 m) above sea level. After the breeding period larger groups form. Although they will sleep in trees at night, they otherwise keep to the ground. They walk like ravens and in the event of danger try to hide behind stones or dense bushes for safety, instead of flying away. They often rest on a stone or on a low branch of a tree. They can be found on prairie lands searching for reptiles or small mammals. In addition to insects, snakes, rats and mice, they eat small birds, eggs, grain, tubers and greenstuff. As killers of snakes they are very much respected. A fight between a hornbill and a snake makes an exciting spectacle. The bird approaches the snake from the flank, with its wings outspread for protection, and unexpectedly catches the snake a heavy blow with its bill. It has, however, to pull back its head very quickly and bring it behind its wings for safety. The final killing of the snake may take quite a long time. Young birds which are brought up by hand become tame and affectionate and make pleasant domestic pets; they zealously hunt mice, rats and sparrows. In addition to the standard diet for insect-eating birds, they also need some boiled potatoes, pieces of meat, dead mice and sparrows.

In *Avicultural Magazine*, Vol. 79, No. 1, Jan./Feb. 1973, there is an account by John R. Fairfield of a breeding of the North African Ground Hornbill at the San Diego Wild Animal Park, California, USA, in August 1972. Two off-white eggs were laid, and one chick was hatched naked, with eyes closed, but died soon after. The second egg was fertile but was broken open by the female. It was the second hatching in captivity of this rare species ever recorded, the first being in Bristol, England, in 1971.

In southern and eastern Africa a still smaller species is met with. It is the Kaffir Hornbill, *Bucorvus leadbeateri*, which resembles a turkey because of its heavy feet and the shape of its body. This species has hardly a horn on the upper mandible. Face, sides of neck and gullet are red; the throat is blue. *Female*. Has red only on the face; throat and neck are blue. In contrast with the other hornbills, their breeding hollows remain completely open.

Genus: Bycanistes

BLACK AND WHITE CASQUED HORNBILL,
CASQUED HORNBILL, *Bycanistes subcylindricus* Slater

DISTRIBUTION: East and west Africa (Ashanti to southern Nigeria).

DESCRIPTION: Underwing coverts, lower abdomen and under tail coverts white; secondaries and innermost primaries almost wholly white as are the apical halves of the outer tail feathers. Length: *Male* 33 in. (83 cm), *Female* 29 in. (78 cm). The young bird has a smaller bill and casque than the adult female and some brown feathers with black centres on the head.

Their basic food in the wild, where they live in forests, is insects and fruit, particularly bananas. They have been seen catching white ants by hawking from a tree. They also eat the nestlings and eggs of smaller birds. They have a distinctive flight pattern, alternately beating their wings and gliding. They follow the usual nesting pattern of the Hornbills, the female being walled up in the nest high up in a tree. The eggs are thought to be white and 2 in number.

A pair were brought into Britain in 1959 at about 1 month old. They were naked except for a few flight and tail feathers and hand-reared on a diet of insects and fruit, mainly bananas.

They arrived at Winged World in Morcambe, England, in April 1971, and were placed in an aviary 15 × 20 × 10 ft high. The following April the birds showed signs of wanting to nest. They spent some time in mutual feeding and preening.

A barrel was erected 8 ft (2·5 m) from the ground in a far corner of the aviary away from the public. On May 5 the female entered the barrel and they started to mud up the hole. By May 17 only a small slit remained through which the female was fed by the male. The nest remained clean as the female excreted through the entrance hole. In June the feeding habits fluctuated for a couple of weeks, then they stabilised with locusts becoming a favourite food. On June 29 one chick was seen through the hole—42 days after completion of mudding up. The diet then consisted mainly of locusts, mice, young rats, mince and a small amount of fruit.

On September 17 the female broke out of the barrel. The male became very excited calling and flying around the aviary. One youngster emerged from the nest and a second 2 hours later, 123 days after mudding up. Both the young birds could fly well after leaving the nest to which they never returned.

In the autumn they had to be moved to a different aviary with a heated shelter. Next spring they showed signs of nesting, but did not in fact breed; there is a possibility that they may nest alternate years.

In May 1974 the birds began mutual feeding and preening. On May 26 the female was firmly mudded up. The male assiduously fed the female who would call for food and vibrate her bill on the side of the entrance hole. The male would then fly to the barrel and offer her a morsel of food, which she would take from his bill. The male would remain at the hole and regurgitate pieces of fruit and other food which he would pass to his mate. On July 11 live locusts were fed for the first time—this was an indication that young had been born and were old enough to take them.

It was interesting to watch the male feed his family with the locusts. He would fly down and catch one, then fly with it to the nestbox, carefully regurgitate it and pass it to his mate. He would never eat any locusts himself. He fed them 3 times a day, so in all about 50 locusts were eaten daily, until the young fledged.

July 16 the young were heard calling for food for the first time. July 29 a pale coloured bill was seen at the entrance hole. September 15 the hole was thought to be a little larger, and next day (113 days after initial mudding up) the female and one youngster were out of the nest. September 17 the second chick was seen mudding up the entrance hole from inside. This may help to substantiate the theory that young hornbills seal themselves in the nest after the mother has left to help her mate feed them. September 18 the second youngster came out. When the young flew out, the male tried to feed them, but they refused and he had to revert to the original method of feeding via the female. Within a few minutes of leaving the nest the young were able to fly and land on a perch 12 ft away.

The birds are housed in a secluded aviary, thickly hedged on the outside and south faces, with a grassed floor.

The breeding of April 1971 is believed to be a first breeding and reported in *Avicultural Magazine*, No. 79, pp. 23–5 1973. All the above information was supplied by Richard Porritt and Martyn Riley of Birdworld, Farnham, Surrey.

ORDER: PICIFORMES
SUBORDER: GALBULAE

SUBFAMILY: CAPITONOIDEA

FAMILY: CAPITONIDAE

Barbets

BY H. J. BATES AND R. L. BUSENBARK

Barbets are tropical birds which have large heads, thick necks, stocky bodies, reasonably short and broad tails, and large beaks surrounded by bristles. The beaks are in no way as large as the beaks on hornbills or toucans, but this is still the most dominant feature.

Most barbets should not be kept with birds their own size. There are exceptions, of course, but most are aggressive. The large beaks are formidable weapons in attacks against other birds. Large aviaries of uncrowded mixed collections are usually safe but not always.

In the beginning, barbets are delicate; and the transfer period is difficult because of the reluctance to accept domestic diets. They also seem to be sensitive to temperature extremes. The little Coppersmiths are particularly sensitive to cold, and the Toucan Barbets cannot stand really hot weather at any time. Otherwise, barbets settle down happily, though sometimes noisily, to aviary life.

The writers feed the standard softbilled diet (Group A) with a little extra raw meat, live foods, and fruit. Nectar, oddly enough is beneficial. The nectar in this instance should be the high protein type also offered to woodpeckers, hummingbirds, and others of similar requirements.

The late Mr. K. A. Norris, in an article in the *Avicultural Magazine* Vol. 56, No. 3, 1950, points out that these birds must not be given solely grapes and soft sweet fruits, as these contain only very little building-up material. The composition of the diet must include the insectivorous moistened with scrapings of carrot. Berries of hawthorn, rowan, privet, dried currants, raisins (soaked overnight), dates and figs cut into pieces, and, of course, apples make valuable additions. These birds are very sensitive to draughts and damp, so that an inside aviary is best for them. Barbets have short and rounded wings, which prevents them from flying over long distances. For this reason they are resident birds.

In the wild state, barbets nest in holes in trees which they excavate in much the same manner as woodpeckers. The living habits of most of the species have not yet been sufficiently investigated. It is not yet known whether the birds remain together the whole year through, though it has been decided that sometimes they use the same nests year after year, and construct a second entrance for them.

Genus: Capito

PLAINTIVE BARBET, SCARLET-CROWNED BARBET, *Capito aurovirens* (Cuvier)
G. Klagender Bartvogel; F. Barbu à poitriqe orange; D. Oranjeborst-Baardvogel

DISTRIBUTION: Columbia, Ecuador, Peru and north-western Brazil.
DESCRIPTION: *Male*. A bright red cap covers the entire top of head from forehead to lower nape, and golden-yellow extends from chin through chest. Dull olive-brown covers the central facial area and all body colouring, with a paler shade on the under parts. There is a spotty, irregular white eyebrow. *Female*. Similar but has white on the crown. Length: about 7 in. (17 cm).

Barbets from South America are not very well known to aviculture. Usually it is the Indian or African species that are found in zoological gardens or private collections. It is possible to leave these birds in an outside aviary only during the summer and, even then, there should be indoor shelter available for them, containing a heating lamp, so that the birds have an opportunity of warming themselves under it. A pair can be kept, in a spacious area, with glossy starlings, mynahs and other birds able to defend themselves.

If a nest box is provided, they promptly start using it as a sleeping place. Bananas, grapes, cherries and elderberries form their favourite food, although they soon learn to eat insectivorous food and wholemeal bread soaked in milk, as well as green food. They do not bathe often, but when they do they are very boisterous. They like sitting in the rain. Titbits like mealworms and ants' eggs help to tame these birds, who are extremely inquisitive by nature. During the winter they can also be placed in a roomy cage.

ORANGE-FRONTED BARBET, RUFOUS-FRONTED BARBET, *Capito squamatus*, Salvin
G. Orangestirn-Bartvogel; F. Barbu à front orange; D. Oranje voorhoofd Baardvogel

DISTRIBUTION: Colombia and Ecuador.
DESCRIPTION: *Male*. The forehead is orange, deepening to red-orange on the crown and then shading to white on the hind crown. The rest of the head and upper parts are glossy black, with a bluish wash and white edges on inner secondary flight feathers. Under parts are yellowish on the chest, fading to dingy white on the abdomen. *Female*. Has a scaled back because of white edges on all the feathers of back and wing coverts. Length: 6½–7 in. (16·5–17 cm).

These barbets also chiefly inhabit those tropical areas that are covered with dense brushwood and forests. They prefer fruit and, when berries are plentiful, the front of their plumage becomes sticky and dirty from the juices. In this period great numbers of them sometimes visit the fruit orchards belonging to private houses and do great damage. They nest high in the trees and, with their powerful bills, they quickly enlarge the existing hollows. They lay 3–4 eggs, which are hatched out in 14 days. Orange-fronted Barbets are only rarely imported. It takes a long time before they get used to insectivorous food and they should be given all kinds of sweet fruits, wholemeal bread with honey water, small pieces of raw meat and mealworms. It is recommended that the birds are kept indoors during the winter, at room temperature.

Orange-fronted Barbet, *Capito squamatus*

BLACK-SPOTTED BARBET, *Capito niger* (P. L. S. Müller)

DISTRIBUTION: Surinam, Guyana and north-eastern Brazil north of the Amazon.

DESCRIPTION: *Male.* Crown and under parts golden yellow paling towards the belly, with black spotted flanks. Sides of head, back and wings black with a yellow band across the wing coverts. *Female.* Is similar but the yellow under parts heavily spotted with black. Length: about 7 in. (18 cm).

What is believed to be the first breeding success occurred at Winged World, Morecambe, England, and was reported by Bryan S. Ward in *Avicultural Magazine*, Vol. 77, No. 6, Nov./Dec. 1971, pp. 194–195, as follows:

'The pair started to show an interest in a rotten log which was only 2 ft 6 in. (about 75 cm) in height. They started to tunnel downwards and continued to a depth of about 12 in. (30 cm), where the tunnel must then have widened out into the nest chamber, although this could not be seen by looking into the hole.

The first indication that they were actually nesting was when we heard the young chicks in the nest, as neither of the adult birds seemed to have been out of sight long enough to incubate any eggs. The parents seemed rather hesitant in taking food into the nest whilst we were watching, but during the 34 days nestling period they were observed to take mealworms to them and latterly fruit, mainly sultans. For the 10 days prior to the youngsters leaving the nest they were given day-old mice; these they enthusiastically picked up and took into the log.

Two young barbets left the nest, one cock and one hen, the cock leaving 2 days after its nest mate. They both have the individual markings of their parents but the colouring is slightly paler.'

Genus: Eubucco

LEMON-THROATED BARBET, *Eubucco richardsoni* (G. R. Gray)

DISTRIBUTION: Colombia, Ecuador, Peru and western Brazil.

DESCRIPTION: *Male.* Dark red on forehead, crown, sides of face and chin. Yellow on throat and sides of neck, followed by bright red on chest. Remaining under parts are dull yellowish-white with green streaks. Back green shading to olive on wings and tail. A dull bluish band crosses the nape. *Female.* Has yellow on the face, reduced to a small area near the ear coverts and to a broad chestband. Forehead and facial areas black. Length: about 6 in. (15 cm).

FLAME-HEADED BARBET, RED-HEADED BARBET, BOURCIER'S BARBET, *Eubucco bourcierii orientalis* Chapman

G. Rotbrust Buntbärtling, Scgarlachkopf Bartvogel; F. Barbu de Bourcier; D. Roodkop-Baardvogel.

DISTRIBUTION: Ecuador.

DESCRIPTION: *Male.* Entire head, neck and chest bright scarlet fading to yellowish on abdomen. Green streaks occur on the yellow and gradually overcome the yellow on the ventral area and under tail coverts. Upper parts are all green. A narrow bluish-white collar on the nape sharply divides the red from the green. *Female.* Lacks the red and instead has black on the forehead, yellow on the crown, fading to olive on the nape, pale blue on the face, green on the throat and yellow on the chest. Length: about 7 in. (17 cm).

SUBSPECIES: Of the seven subspecies, *E. orientalis* has its habitat in the eastern slopes of the Andes in Ecuador.

These multi-coloured birds dwell in the dense shrub lands and in the tropical forests. Their chief food is fruit of all

Flame-headed Barbet, *Eubucco bourcierii orientalis*

sorts, although, mainly in the breeding season, they also hunt assiduously for insects. They use their sturdy bills to hollow out dead and partly-decayed trees, where they sleep and breed. The 2–4 eggs are laid upon a few scant fibres and leaves and are incubated by both the male and female in turn for 13–15 days. They also share in bringing up the young, and keep the next scrupulously clean.

These brightly coloured birds are only very occasionally imported. They have to become acclimatised in a heated inside aviary, as they are extremely sensitive to both damp and cold. They must not be permitted to go into the outside aviary during the summer months unless they have access to a heated aviary and until they have become used to the standard diet for insect eaters, augmented by various fruits, a quantity of mealworms, and from time to time some shredded raw meat.

Genus: Semnornis

TOUCAN BARBET, TOUCAN-BILLED BARBET, *Semnornis ramphastinus* (Jardine)   (Pl. VIII)
G. Tukanbartvogel; F. Barbu Toucan; D. Toekan Baardvogel

DISTRIBUTION: Subtropical zone of the Andes of Ecuador.
DESCRIPTION: The large swollen beak is bright yellowish-horn, with a large black spot on the sides near the tip extending on to both mandibles. An extensive black facial triangle surrounds the red iris. A sharp line of silvery-white feathers extends from above the eyes to the lower sides of the nape, where the end is almost tuft-like. Black covers the forehead, the top of the crown, and broadens to form a half-collar on the lower nape, where the feathers are bristly and very glossy. All the rest of the head, throat and neck is pale silver-grey. The back and mantle are brown, and the wings and tail are slate grey. The chest is dark red, spilling irregularly on to the abdomen. The sides, lower abdomen, lower back, rump, upper tail and under tail coverts are deep golden-yellow. Sexes are alike, except that the male is reported to have longer black feathers on the nape. Length: 8 in. (20 cm).
SUBSPECIES: *S. r. caucae* differs from the nominate race, which has the red ending higher on the abdomen.
These birds live in sub-tropical forests and are to be seen alone or in pairs on the wooded slopes of the Andes Mountain Range at heights of about 8,000–10,000 ft (2,500–3,000 m) above sea level. Although the birds are very striking in their variegated colours, they are nevertheless difficult to see in their wild state as they are excellently camouflaged by the play of light on the dense foliage. They betray their whereabouts by the call of the male bird, which is immediately answered by the female.
The two different call notes of these birds are unusual. One is an imitation of a braying donkey both in sound and stance. The head is tipped upwards on an outstretched neck, the beak is opened wide, and the bray can be heard for a considerable distance. The other note is a sharp snapping sound. The writers have had groups of several of these birds, and they all utter their call at the same time. When the entire group joins the snapping chorus, one is reminded of popping popcorn.
Toucan Barbets have the most attractive colourings and the most comic personalities of all barbets, but they are not often available. The species is relatively peaceful with similar sized birds. They cannot stand hot summer weather; there have been periods in southern California when the temperature has risen to more than 100°F (38°C), with the result that several of these rare birds were lost.
Their powerful bills are provided with two teeth, the reason for which has not yet been discovered, as berries and other fruits, and various insects, form the main part of their diet. In captivity they show a great partiality for cockroaches. The birds should be kept in an inside aviary, as they are sensitive to cold and damp.
Mr. Bryan S. Ward, of Heysham, Lancashire, England, reported in *Avicultural Magazine*, Vol. 78, No. 6, Nov./Dec. 1972, a breeding of the Toucan Barbet at Winged World, Morecambe, as follows:

. . . We purchased our pair of barbets towards the end of 1970. During the following year they attempted to nest, by chipping away at a rotten log in various places, and ultimately succeeded in making a suitable nesting hole about 18 in. (49 cm) from the floor. This attempt was thwarted when one morning we found the female with a damaged wing, hopping around on the floor and unable to fly. She has never fully recovered, and can fly only very short distances, but gets around very well by jumping from perch to perch.
After a long period of convalescence, we reintroduced her to the male and within a couple of days she had started to use the hole that they had both hollowed out previously, even though, since her accident, both the male and the log had been removed to another compartment.
As with most barbets, they spent quite some time in the hole, so I am unaware of when she first started laying her eggs, and consequently of the actual incubation time. We heard sounds from the youngsters on 16th August 1972 and as they grew older they also grew considerably more noisy, in fact they were the most noisy of any young I have ever heard. The three youngsters remained in the nest, for what seemed to be a very long time, the first of them leaving 43 days from the initial time of hearing them. The other two left at further intervals of two days.
For the first half of the nestling period they were, as far as I know, fed mainly on mealworms, plus a small amount of our soft food mixture. Latterly, the parents were observed taking fruit, chiefly grapes, into the nesting hole, and for the last couple of weeks, mice two or three days old were given and quickly taken into the nest for the young birds.

Toucan Barbet, *Semnornis ramphastinus*

The young are exactly the same as their parents except that they are approximately 1 in. (2·5 cm) smaller and their colouring slightly paler. Their eyes, unlike the adults are black.
There is one other member of the genus which is similar in many respects. It is the Costa Rican or Prong-billed Barbet, *Semnornis frantzii*, and is from high mountainous areas of Costa Rica and western Panama.

Genus: Psilopogon

FIRE-TUFTED BARBET, *Psilopogon pyrolophus*, S. Müller
G. Rotbuschelbartvogel, Ohrenbartvogel, Sumatra Bartvogel; F. Barbu à plumules de feu; D. Roodbortsel-Baardvogel

DISTRIBUTION: Malaysia and Sumatra.
DESCRIPTION: Sexes similar. Except for the head and upper chest the entire colouring is green, darker above and soft below, and with some blue and black edging the wing feathers and shading the tail. The large beak is pale greenish-horn, with a dark smudge in the centre of the sides of both

Plate VII

Orange-headed Ground Thrush, *Zoothera c. citrina*   Red-legged Thrush, *Turdus plumbeus rubripes*

Eastern Bluebird, *Sialia sialis*

Dhyal Thrush, *Copsychus s. saularis*

Shama, *Copysychus malabaricus*

Plate VIII

Baillon's Toucan, *Andigena bailloni*

Spot-billed Toucanet, *Selenidera maculirostris*   Sulphur-breasted Toucan, *Ramphastos s. sulfuratus*

Toucan Barbet, *Semnornis ramphastinus*

Crimson-breasted Barbet, *Megalaima h. haemacephala*

Plate IX

Purple Sugarbird, *Cyanerpes caeraleus*   Blue Sugarbird, *Dacnis cayana*

Yellow-rumped Cassique, *Cacicus cela*

Yellow-winged Sugarbird, *Cyanerpes c. cyaneus*

Western Meadow Lark, *Sturnella neglecta*

Silky Cowbird, *Molothrus bonariensis*

Plate X

Green-headed Tanager, *Tangara seledon*   Blue Tanager, *Thraupis virens*

Blue and Black Tanager, *Tanagrella velia*

Superb Tanager, *Tangara fastuosa*

Mrs Wilson's Tanager, *Tangara nigro-cincta*   Paradise Tanager, *Tangara chilensis*

mandibles. A tuft of long, fine, bristly red feathers, fastened at the base of the upper mandible, extends forward over the beak. Forehead, crown and nape are black, shading to black mixed with a deep maroon on the hind neck. *Female*. Is more black in this area. A sharp line of bright greyish-

Fire-tufted Barbet, *Psilopogon pyrolophus*

white crosses the crown above the eyes and trails into an extended eyebrow. The cheeks are greyish and the chin is black, shading into green. A dominant feature is a broad double-coloured collar circling the lower throat and sides of the neck. Bright orange-yellow is the first colour, followed by black. The black and yellow are rather sharply divided in the centre of the collar, but both are softly blended into the green on both sides. Length: 10–11 in. (27 cm).
Like the woodpecker, Fire-tufted Barbets can be met within groups of 3–6, climbing on the trunks and branches of the trees in the mountain forests in Malacca and Sumatra. They are then obviously searching for insects, which, next to numerous fruits, form their food.
This species is very attractive, but rare in aviculture. A few specimens come to Europe, where they readily find a place in the various zoological gardens, as they are not only elegant, multi-coloured birds but very soon become tame and can be kept very easily with toucans, touracos, fruit doves and glossy starlings. Their vivacity and the beauty of their plumage do not show to good advantage in a cage, no matter how spacious; for this, an aviary is necessary. Like other barbets, they are sensitive to damp and cold, so that heated winter quarters are essential.
To the insectivorous food a mixture of apples, bananas, oranges, dates and figs, all cut into small pieces, should be added, and every now and then a little shredded meat and mealworms must also be given.

Genus: Megalaima

GIANT BARBET, GREAT HILL BARBET, *Megalaima v. virens* (Boddaert)
G. China-Grün-Bärtling, Blauköpfiger Bartvogel; F. Barbu géant; D. China-Baardvogel

DISTRIBUTION: India, China, Burma and Laos.
DESCRIPTION: Sexes alike. The beak is pale horn, dark on the ridge of the upper mandible, and the head is black with bluish and greenish highlights. The upper chest and back are olive-brown, and straw-coloured streaks on the mantle are variable with different species. Wings, rump and tail are green, with some indistinct brownish edges on wing feathers. Under parts are pale dull yellow, streaked heavily with brown and green. Green on sides and central abdominal area is variable. Under tail coverts are bright red. Length: 12 in. (30 cm).
SUBSPECIES: There are four subspecies, which show only very small differences in colouring. The one appearing in most collections is the Himalayan Barbet, *Megalaima virens marshallorum* (Swinhoe). It is found on the slopes of the Himalayas and breeds at heights of 3,000–8,000 ft (1,000–2,500 m) above sea level.
In winter the birds descend to the foot of the mountains and to the valleys. They prefer trees with a lot of foliage, and so are difficult to discover, but they are to be seen now and then along the edges of the wood. They are recognised by their call. One of them will often sit high up in a well-shaded tree and will utter his monotonous, sad call, often for hours on end. As he turns his head while calling from one side to the other it is difficult to fix his exact location.
The birds themselves carve out their nest hollows high in a tree. A narrow entrance leads to a wider breeding cavity. Four white eggs are laid. This species is large and exceptionally aggressive, and the bird has an enormous voice, which is unpleasant. It may be characteristically quiet in one location and almost constantly noisy in another. However, it is extremely hardy and easy to transfer to domestic diets. The huge beak gives it a tenacious fortitude. It will not hesitate to attack birds several sizes larger than itself. It can also inflict a fairly severe bite upon a human.

BROWN-HEADED BARBET, LINEATED BARBET, GREEN BARBET, *Megalaima z. zeylanica* (Gmelin)　　(Pl. IV)
G. Ceylon-Kupferschmied, Ceylon Grünbärtling; F. Barbu à tête grise de Ceylan; D. Ceylon-Baardvogel

DISTRIBUTION: India, Sri Lanka, Khmer Republic, Thailand, Java, Bali and southern Vietnam.
DESCRIPTION: Head, neck and chest pale dull brown with buffish streaks. Iris reddish-brown; bare skin around the eye buffish. The rest of plumage green, paler on under parts. Pale horn-coloured beak is too slender for attractive proportions, and the colouring is too dull and cluttered for an attractive appearance. Length: 11½ in. (24 cm).
The Lineated Barbet frequents mountain slopes which are covered with trees bearing dense foliage and feeds on a number of fruits, including the wild fig. Its camouflage amid the foliage is perfect and in case of danger the bird calmly remains sitting among the green leaves and is practically invisible. The breeding hollow is carefully chiselled out in a soft-wood tree. The 2–4 eggs are laid at intervals, so that the young can emerge with plenty of time between each chick.
This is the most readily available of all the barbets. The birds soon get used to the domestic diet, are strong, and can be kept with toucans and hornbills. They are, however, very noise and aggressive.

SMALL GREEN BARBET, *Megalaima viridis* (Boddaert)
G. Grünbartvogel; F. Petit barbu vert; D. Kleine Groene Baardvogel

DISTRIBUTION: Southern India.
DESCRIPTION: Similar to the Lineated Barbet, *Megalaima z. zeylanica*, in pattern and colouring, except for a darker shade of brown on the top of the head and very pale buffish-white on the throat and neck. Eyebrows and a stripe underlining the eyes are also paler. Length: 8 in. (20 cm).
These birds inhabit the dense forests in pairs or in small groups. They gather in large groups when the wild figs are

ripe. They have been found to do great damage in the coffee plantations in India, for they eat great quantities of the fruits. They also eat flying ants, butterflies and other insects. The birds themselves make nesting hollows at various heights in dead trees. Their 2–4 eggs are white in colour.

They were imported into Germany for the first time in 1894 and, after that, they became irregular imports. They can be kept in good condition with the standard insectivorous food, augmented by various soft, ripe fruits and some mealworms.

YELLOW-FRONTED BARBET, *Megalaima flavifrons* (Cuvier)

G. Goldstirnbartvogel; F. Barbu à front doré; D. Goudvoorhoofd-Baardvogel.

DISTRIBUTION: Ceylon.

DESCRIPTION: Slightly smaller than the Small Green Barbet, *M. viridis*, the Yellow-fronted Barbet is more attractive, but the colouring is still a little streaky and cluttered. Golden-yellow on the forehead and sides of the lower mandible, and a large blue facial mask, are the main variations. The brown is present on the crown and nape but not on the chest. The back and chest have a green and whitish scaled appearance.

Yellow-fronted Barbet, *Megalaima flavifrons*

The beak is less slender and better proportioned. Length: 7 in. (18 cm).

In Ceylon these birds may be met with in pairs or in groups of 4–6, in the open fields, along the waterside or edges of the woods, or in the dense mountain forests. They live mainly on fruits from trees and, when they visit orchards, they damage them considerably. During breeding time the pairs live strictly separately from the rest, and in this period they are extremely noisy. As soon as they have carved out a nesting hollow and the hen has laid her 2–3 white eggs the birds become quieter. In 1905 they appeared for the first time at the Zoological Gardens in Berlin. Since then they have been seen in numerous collections.

CRIMSON-BREASTED BARBET, COPPERSMITH

Megalaima h. haemacephala (P. L. S. Müller) (Pl. VIII)
G. Kupferschmied, Gelbkehlbartvogel, Goldbartvogel; F. Barbu à front rouge, Barbu à poitrine cramoisie; D. Roodvoorhoofd-Baardvogel.

DISTRIBUTION: The Philippines.

DESCRIPTION: Sexes alike. The beak is black; the forehead and forecrown are bright red. A crescent of red marks the upper chest. The chin and throat are bright yellow, and this colour frames the lower edge of the red crescent. The iris and a circle of bare flesh are red, surrounded by a large circle of bright yellow. A black line runs through the iris, dissecting the yellow circle. The remaining facial area and the hind-crown are black. Upper parts are green, with some brown and blue on the wings. Under parts are pale greenish white, with prominent streaks of olive-green. Feet and legs are red. Length: about 6 in. (15 cm).

These most elegant and smallest of all the barbets eat fruit

almost exclusively and it is not easy to get them used to the aviary diet. As a result of this, and because they are delicate, they are one of the less frequently imported birds. They appeared for the first time in the London Zoo in 1901. They sleep and breed in a nesting box. In the wild state the entrance to the next is always to be found under an overhanging branch of a tree. The 2–3 white eggs are incubated alternately by both parents.

Crimson-breasted Barbet, *Megalaima h. haemacephala*

BLUE-THROATED BARBET, BLUE-CHEEKED BARBET,

Megalaima a. asiatica (Latham) (Pl. II)
G. Blauwangenbartvogel; F. Barbu à gorge bleue; D. Blaauwwang-Baardvogel

DISTRIBUTION: Northern India from Mussoorie and Kashmir eastward to Assam, south to Burma and the northern Shan States.

DESCRIPTION: Sexes alike. The back of the neck and all body plumage, including wings, bright green. The tail is somewhat bright blue mixed with green. A large area on the chin, the throat, sides of the throat, and face surrounding the eyes, bright blue. Irides red, the forehead and nape are bright red. A narrow yellow band extends across the crown and connects with the blue just above the eyes. A broad black band follows the yellow band and trails backwards on the sides of the neck to the lower nape, serving to separate the blue from the red. There are traces of red at the corners of the beak and on the lower boundaries of blue on the sides of the throat. The heavy beak is pale horn, with black running irregularly along the top of the upper mandible and on to the tip of the lower mandible. Length: 8½ in. (21·5 cm).

SUBSPECIES: There are five subspecies. *M. a. monticola* (Sharpe), from Borneo, has greatly reduced areas of blue and red, so much so that it really does not even look like the same species.

This is the most frequently available and perhaps the most popular of all barbets. It is one of the most attractive of the stronger species and is of a medium size. Neunzig states that it is particularly suited to a spacious cage, where its colourful and smooth plumage is a delight to the eye. It is aggressive to most birds of its own size, or even larger, and can kill thrushes and such birds as *Chloropsis*. Suitable companions would be White-crested Laughing Jay Thrushes or slightly less aggressive birds.

Blue-throated Barbets live almost exclusively in fruit-bearing trees, even though these may be among houses. They make themselves inconspicuous, but betray their presence by their constant calls, especially in the spring. They make their breeding hollows high up in dead trees, where their 2–4 eggs lie on a thin layer of grass, bark and splinters of wood. In addition to all kinds of figs and berry fruits, these birds also eat lizards, beetles and other insects.

In the cage or aviary the birds should be able to bathe every day. Besides the insectivorous food, which should be richly fortified by fruits, mealworms should also be supplied.

In winter the birds may remain in the outside aviary, provided that heated night quarters are available. Nesting boxes should be supplied, as all barbets are in the habit of roosting in them.

RELATED SPECIES OF BARBETS

There are several species, reasonably similar, which are not well known in aviculture. They are attractive, and most are about the same size, except where noted. The body colouring is about the same as for the Blue-throated Barbet. All have black beaks.

HUME'S BLUE-THROATED BARBET, *Megalaima incognita*, Hume, with two subspecies, is from Thailand, Cambodia, Laos, Vietnam and the southernmost part of Burma. A yellow eye ring is topped by a black eyebrow. A red line crosses the forehead, connecting with darker red spots in front of the eyes. The crown is bluish-green, and a red patch on the hind crown is bright. There is a black moustache.

GAUDY BARBET, *Megalaima mystacophanos* (Temminck), with three subspecies, from southern Tenasserim southward over the Malay Peninsula and Sumatra.

Male. Has yellow covering the forehead and fore-crown, followed by a bright red patch from the centre of the crown to the hind-crown. A heavy black eyebrow with a blunt end extends from the eye to the end of the red hind-crown. A red patch covers the chin and part of the throat. A small bright red spot occurs on the side of the throat and a small yellow patch underlines the outer base of the lower mandible. Blue, less intense, surrounds the cheeks and marks the middle of the throat. *Female.* Lacks all yellow and black, but the red head-patch is present. Crown, throat and minor facial areas are dull blue. A small red patch occurs near the nostrils of both sexes.

GOLD-WHISKERED BARBET, *Megalaima chrysopogon* (Temminck), is from Borneo and Sumatra. It is very like *M. mystacophanos*, except that the eyebrow is changed to a mask, the chin and throat are greyish with a lilac cast, and a large yellow patch on the lower cheek area is one of the most prominent features.

MULLER'S BARBET, *Megalaima oorti* (S. Müller), with 5 subspecies, is from Malaysia, Laos, Vietnam, Sumatra, Hainan, Formosa and south-eastern China. The forehead is dark red and the crown is yellow, followed by more red and then blue. The chin and upper throat are yellow. A blue band crosses the brown area of the throat, followed by a red line, which divides the blue from the green chest. The sides of the face are blue, with black above and below the eye.

MANY-COLOURED BARBET, *Megalaima rafflesii* (Lesson), with 4 subspecies, is from Sumatra, Banka, Malaysia and Borneo. This species is a little larger and brighter, and the beak is larger. The top of the head, from forehead to nape, is deep crimson, and a bright yellow patch occurs on the lower side of the face. A good-sized red patch follows underneath and a

little behind the yellow patch. Blue covers the chin and throat and also forms a long trailing eyebrow. A large elliptical area of bare skin around the eye is slate blue bordered below with slight touches of yellow and red. Black in a subordinate area covers the ear coverts and borders the yellow patch on the lower face.

GOLDEN-THROATED BARBET, *Megalaima franklinii* (Blyth), with 5 subspecies, occurs in India, Malaysia, Burma, Thailand, Laos and Vietnam. The head pattern is similar to that of Müller's Barbet, except that the red patch on the hind-crown is smaller and is surrounded by a black band. The chin and upper throat are golden-yellow. Lower throat and face are grey, with a touch of orange at the base of the lower mandible.

YELLOW-CROWNED BARBET, *Megalaima henricii* (Temminck), with 2 subspecies, is from Thailand, Malaysia, Borneo and Sumatra. It is the same size as the Blue-throated Barbet and is considerably softer in colouring. A golden-yellow fore-head lengthens on the sides to form bold eyebrows. A narrow red band on the nape shows a separated red spot on the lower side of the throat. Chin and large throat areas are soft pale blue, and soft green covers the crown, nape and face. Lores are black.

GOLDEN-NAPED BARBET, *Megalaima pulcherrima* (Sharpe), from north-western Borneo, is less bright than *M. henricii*, but it has the same soft blues and greens. Yellow occurs in a narrow band on the nape, and red is absent. Soft blue covers the top of the head from forehead to nape and a large area on chin and throat. Extensive facial areas are soft green, and the lores are black.

CRIMSON-THROATED BARBET, *Megalaima rubricapilla* (Gmelin), with 2 subspecies, is from Ceylon. It is similar to the Crimson-breasted Barbet, except for the following differences. The red crescent on the upper chest is greatly reduced in size and confined to the throat. The under parts are uniform green, only slightly less vivid than the upper parts. There are no streaks. Upper parts are brighter green, the yellow areas have an orange shading, and the red has an orange tint. The Indian race, *Megalaima malabarica* (Blyth), lacks the yellow, having instead bright scarlet on forehead, face and throat.

LITTLE BARBET, *Megalaima australis* (Horsfield), with 7 sub-species, has a wide range, including India, Burma, Khmer Republic, Laos, Malaysia and Borneo. The forehead and fore-crown, and a broad crescent across the throat, are black, with pale greenish-blue on chin and upper throat, and bright blue on hind-crown. A red eyebrow and a broader red bar under the eye both extend to the sides of the neck. The lower bar is interrupted in the centre by black. A trace of red occurs below the black throat crescent. Sexes are alike.

BLACK-THROATED BARBET, *Megalaima eximia* (Sharpe), a similar species from Borneo, with two subspecies, is a little less attractive than *M. australis*. Size is the same and sexes are alike. The black forehead is smaller, and the crown is crimson instead of blue. The short eyebrows and the ear coverts are blue. A bright yellow spot occurs under the eyes, with a faint trace of red behind. A blackish area covers the chin and throat, but it is far less intense than the black throat crescent of *M. australis*. A narrow yellow band, followed by a dull red band, occurs on the lower throat.

Genus: Tricholaema

PIED BARBET, *Tricholaema l. leucomelan* (Boddaert)
G. Buntbartvogel; F. Barbu pie; D. Bonte Baardvogel

DISTRIBUTION: South Africa in southern Cape Province, the Karroo and Orange Free State.

DESCRIPTION: The top of the head has a broad red band over the forehead. Lores, the stripe under the eye, the auriculars and the cheeks and neck are light red. The eyebrow stripe is

yellow, getting whiter towards the back. The remaining upper parts are black with yellow spots. The upper tail coverts have yellow ends. The under parts are white. The thighs and wings are black and white. The quill feathers and tail are blackish-brown with pale yellow edges. Iris is brown, the bill brownish-black, and feet slate-grey. Length: about 6 in. (15 cm).

These very lively barbets dwell in acacia woods and bushes,

alone or in pairs. The 6 different races show little difference in colouration. Their main food consists of fruits, which they get in every possible position, hanging in the branches. They

Pied Barbet, *Tricholaema l. leucomelan*

also eat a good quantity of insects. They make their nests in hollow tree trunks. The entry to the nest has a diameter of 1·6 in. (4 cm) and a depth of about 6 in. (15 cm).

In 1914 the first specimens arrived in the Berlin Zoological Gardens. In later years these birds made occasional appearances in private collections. Pied Barbets tolerate an aviary extremely well, and a life of eleven years and more is no exception. The birds should not be kept with smaller ones, as they attack them and could seriously injure them with their strong bills. They can swallow great lumps of fruit whole. Like other barbets, they sleep at night in a nest box. In addition to insectivorous food, they must always get plenty of fruit, some raw meat and mealworms.

RED-FRONTED BARBET, *Tricholaema diadematum* (Heuglin)

DISTRIBUTION: Upper White Nile across central Ethiopia to northern Somalia.

DESCRIPTION: Sexes alike. Crown black. Forehead red; stripe over eye yellow; extension on sides and neck white. Stripe through eye and down sides of neck black. Nape black, speckled white; mantle black, flecked with lemon-yellow. Rump lemon-yellow; chin to chest white. Remainder of under parts buffish-yellow with a few blackish streaks on flanks. Young have black forehead.

M. D. England bred the Red-fronted Barbet at Neatishead, Norfolk, England, as reported in *Avicultural Magazine*, Vol. 79, No. 1, Jan./Feb. 1973, pp. 12–13:

'They bored a hole in a rotten stump of Silver Birch, *Betula pendula*, but this was left unused after they had broken open the nest-cavity. A second hole—in another log of rotten Silver Birch—was bored by both birds and one youngster was reared in it. This was fed by regurgitation by both parents, which also shared incubation and brooding. Incubation and fledging periods could not be ascertained, but the latter was certainly in excess of 28 days, though probably not much so. On the last day before the youngsters left the nest, the nest cavity was opened up in a similar fashion to the previous one, as also was the hen's roosting hole.'

BROWN-THROATED BARBET, *Tricholaema melanocephalum stigmatothorax* Cabanis

DISTRIBUTION: Southern Ethiopia and southern Somalia across the drier part of Kenya to northern Tanzania.

DESCRIPTION: Sexes alike. Above, black with yellow-lemon stripes, mantle, rump and wings; flight and tail feathers edged with yellow; white stripe over eye extends down nape; broad black stripe through eye joins black of nape and mantle; gape to cheeks and under parts white; chin and throat black, partly extending down to centre of abdomen. Beak black.

What is thought to be a first breeding success took place at Winged World, Morcambe, England, and was reported by Clive Roots in *Avicultural Magazine*, Vol. 76, No. 4, July/August 1970, p. 145, as follows:

'Barbets, and the other arboreal nesting species, prefer to drill their own holes into the semi-rotten tree trunks provided for this purpose, and only when these are unavailable do they resort to using nest boxes. Due to the nature of the nest-hole, which had an entrance no more than 1 in. in diameter and then appeared to drop vertically into the trunk, we were unable to ascertain how many eggs were laid, or exactly how long the incubation period was, although we consider it to have been about 12 days. Both sexes shared the incubation duties, and mealworms, maggots and house crickets were taken into the nest cavity. After 8 days our prepared insectile and minced beef mixture was taken in, and a little fruit too. Only a single nestling resulted from this breeding, and from a subsequent one also. Both adult birds fed the nestling, which appeared at the entrance of the nest hole approximately 2 weeks after hatching. They continued to feed it for several weeks, but would not tolerate its presence when they went to nest again.'

Genus: Lybius

DOUBLE-TOOTHED BARBET, *Lybius b. bidentatus* (Shaw)

G. Doppelzahnbartvogel; F. Barbu à bec dentélé; D. Dubbelgetande Baardvogel

DISTRIBUTION: West Africa from Guinea-Bissau to southern Nigeria, including southern Ethiopia, western Kenya, north-western Tanzania, and the Sudan.

DESCRIPTION: About the same size as the Flame-headed Barbet, and attractive but less distinctive in both pattern and colouring. Deep grooves in the upper mandible cause serrations which account for the name. The beak colouring varies slightly from ivory to greyish. The eye is surrounded with a large ellipse of yellowish flesh. There are white tufts on the sides. Upper parts are a very dark mixture of brown and black, with some red shaded into the head and a pinkish bar on the wings. Under parts are bright red with no black belt on lower chest or black line under the cheeks.

Because of the deep grooves in the powerful bill this species is sometimes confused with the Groove-billed Barbet, *Lybius dubius* (Gmelin). Double-toothed Barbets are frequently to be found in pairs or in family groups in areas covered with acacias. They collect together in large flights when certain fruits ripen, and make a lot of noise. Their food consists of various berries, bananas and insects. Their deep and long-maintained cry, 'Keks-keks', reminds one strongly of the call of the Tree Cuckoo, *Phoeniculus senegalensis*.

Only on very isolated occasions have specimens of these barbets been imported into Europe and kept in captivity for considerable periods in heated aviaries.

BLACK-COLLARED BARBET, *Lybius t. torquatus* (Dumont)   (Pl. IV)

G. Schwarznacken-Bartvogel, Rotkopf-Bartvogel, Halsband-Bartvogel; F. Barbu à collier; D. Halsband-Baardvogel

DISTRIBUTION: Most of southern Africa and eastern areas of Kenya and Tanzania.

DESCRIPTION: Body thick and tail very short. Beak and lores

black, and a bright red hood covers the head to the back of the crown and the lower chest. A very broad black collar surrounds the red and extends on to the mantle. The remaining upper parts are greyish-black with some pale yellowish on the edges of the wing feathers. Under parts are pale yellowish-white with dull slate on the under sides of the tail. Immature birds lack the red and have dull black as a replacement. Length: 7–8 in. (17 cm).

These decorative barbets are common on the South African veldt, around the small 'kopjes' covered with bushes and small trees. Sometimes a whole flight will seek their food on one fruit-bearing tree and the din is deafening. When feeding, their behaviour recalls that of parrots. They make holes in

Black-collared Barbet, *Lybius t. torquatus*

the trees by planing the wood off instead of chiselling it like the woodpecker. First they make a small hole in a tree and from inside outwards they then enlarge this entry. The hen worms herself through the very narrow opening and after that she will be busy for hours, with brief pauses, planing round the inside of the hole. Three white eggs are generally laid in the nest.

The Lesser Honey Guides, *Indicator minor*, often lay their eggs in the nests of the Black-collared Barbet.

The first of these barbets were kept in the Zoological Gardens of Berlin in 1911. In later years they appeared occasionally in collections. If an old tree trunk, somewhat rotten inside, is hung up in the aviary, the birds will very soon make a nesting hollow, which will have a diameter of about 2 in. (6 cm). The chips they pick off the soft wood are carefully thrown away some distance from the tree trunk. The birds obviously do this to avoid betraying the position of the nesting hollow. They take about fourteen days to construct the hollow.

These barbets hate the cold. When the temperature falls below 60°F (16°C) they become sluggish and their plumage loses its sheen. The warmer it is, the more animated they are. They do not bathe but like walking through wet undergrowth. In very dry weather they should be well sprayed daily with water. In addition to soft foods, they are fond of apples and various kinds of berry. They should be wintered in a heated inside aviary.

GROOVE-BILLED BARBET, BEARDED BARBET, *Lybius dubius* (Gmelin)

G. Senegal-Furchenschnabel; F. Barbican à poitrine rouge; D. Roodborst-Baardvogel

DISTRIBUTION: Western Africa, semi-arid belt from Senegal to the Logone River.
DESCRIPTION: Unusually coloured and patterned, this fine barbet has a strange beak, which is particularly broad and

deeply grooved on the upper mandible, causing irregular and jagged edges. A large ellipse of yellowish flesh surrounds the eye. Upper parts are all shiny black with a pale straw-coloured rump. White occurs in a small area high up on the sides of the abdomen. All other plumage is black and brilliant red. The face is mostly black, except for a long patch of red on the lower cheek area, strongly underlined in black. The very narrow chin is black, and red continues in an even brightness through the under tail coverts. Under side of tail is black. A bold black belt irregularly divides the lower chest and abdomen. The thighs are black, and the feet and legs are flesh coloured. Length: 9 in. (23 cm).

In flight these birds appear to be black and red, and contrast strongly with the green of the foliage. Sometimes they come to the ground for a moment or two. They live mostly in pairs. These rare barbets were seen for the first time at the London Zoo in 1939, where they lived for some years on the normal fruit and insectivorous diet supplied to barbets, with the addition of a few mealworms. Mr. H. A. Fooks succeeded in 1953 in taking a number of young birds out of their nests and bringing them up by hand. This proved an easy task, using milk, bread and Mellin's Food mixed with an equal quantity of mashed banana. Directly the feathers began to come through daily quantities of ants were added to the diet, and it was clear that the young birds reacted very favourably.

OTHER AFRICAN BARBETS

BROWN-BREASTED BARBET, *Lybius melanopterus* (Peters) with two subspecies, from East Africa, is similar to *L. dubius* but is less attractive. The red is less bright and ends on the upper chest. Upper parts, and a broad chest band, are brown, pale on chest and mantle and darker on wings, tail and neck. The brown is dull greyish-horn.

Another species with similar red areas is the Black-billed Barbet, *Lybius guifsobalito*, Hermann, with two subspecies, of East Africa. All colouring, except the red, is shiny blue-black, with white tips on wing coverts and yellow edges on the flights.

The red is restricted to the forehead in the BANDED BARBET, *Lybius undatus* (Rüppell) and its four subspecies, in East Africa. Under parts are barred black and white.

RED-FACED BARBET, *Lybius rubrifacies* (Reichenow), in a very limited range near Lake Victoria, is like the Black-billed Barbet, but the red is reduced to the forehead and face.

VIEILLOT'S BARBET, *Lybius vieilloti* (Leach) with three slightly varying races in East Africa, and Senegal to Nigeria and northern Cameroons, is similar to *L. rubrifacies* but has red speckles on the black nape and crown and on the yellowish-white under parts. Brown upper parts have white streaks. Rump and upper tail coverts have a yellow streak.

BLACK-BACKED BARBET, *Lybius minor* (Cuvier), with three subspecies, from the Congo, northern Angola and Zambia, has an unusual colouring—red on forehead and abdomen, bluish-black on upper parts, white on face, sides of mantle and under parts down to the red on the abdomen.

Different from all the African barbets listed above is WHITE-HEADED BARBET and its 6 subspecies, *Lybius eucocephalus* (Defilippi) from East Africa. White covers the head, neck, throat and chest. The black beak is a strong contrast. Upper tail and under tail coverts are whitish. The rest of the colouring is dark and dull brown, with large white spots.

There are altogether 41 African barbets, distributed in 7 genera, including those listed above.

Genus: Trachyphonus

YELLOW-BREASTED BARBET, ABYSSINIAN BARBET, *Trachyphonus m. margaritatus* (Cretzschmar)

G. Perlbartvogel; F. Barbu perlé, Trachyphone perlé; D. Parelbaardvogel

DISTRIBUTION: Air and extreme northern Nigeria, eastward through the semi-arid belt to western Ethiopia.
DESCRIPTION: A remarkable peculiarity is the slender bill, moderate in length and slightly bent at the crest. The upper

parts of the body are brown, covered with white bands and white drops. The back of the head, the neck and the lower parts of the body are a glossy sulphur-yellow, with a red cere on the breast. The forehead, crown, one spot on the throat and a band on the breast are black. The rump and vent area are dark scarlet red. The iris is dark red, the bill light red, and the feet grey. Length: about 7½ in. (19 cm). These birds are peaceful and mainly live in pairs among groups of trees in a permanent dwelling place. In contrast with most barbets this variety does not seek the secrecy of dense foliage. The birds industriously search for insects, seeds and fruits. Nests have been found in steep earthen walls in which holes have been dug, exactly as kingfishers do. The 4 eggs lie upon the loose earth. The birds probably nest several times in a season. In addition to insectivorous food, they eat every kind of fruit, as well as mealworms and raw meat.

At the beginning of this century they were imported into Europe, but since then only occasionally.

LEVAILLANT'S BARBET, CRESTED BARBET, *Trachyphonus v. valliantii* Ranzani

G. Levaillants Bartvogel, Schwarzruckenbartvogel; F. Barbu de Levaillant Ranzani; D. Levaillants Baardvogel, Druppelvlek Baardvogel

DISTRIBUTION: Southern Africa from about Zambesi River southward.

DESCRIPTION: *Male*. Mantle, wing coverts, tail and a broad band over the breast blue shot with black. The upper parts have white stripes and spots. The crest is black. The ends of the feathers of the band across the breast are sometimes pink. The forehead, sides of the head, throat and breast, and the rump, are a lemon-yellow colour, spotted here and there with red. The upper tail coverts are red; the iris is reddish brown; the bill is a greenish-yellow, and the feet are grey. *Female*. Somewhat duller in colouring, and also a little smaller. Length: about 8 in. (20 cm).

In areas of dry scrub and in open woodlands these birds are fairly common. They are frequently to be found in the neighbourhood of ant hills. During the hottest midday sun they shelter amid the dense foliage. They sleep in the hollows of trees, and, in addition to fruits, they eat a great quantity of insects, particularly ants.

Some barbets carve their nests out of ant hills, or even out of the ground itself. An east Indian species does the former, and this African species the second. Both male and female birds work together at this task. The young take a long time to develop.

In 1911 they arrived for the first time at the Zoological Gardens in Berlin. In England, in the same year, two hand-reared specimens, which were tame, arrived. They did well on bananas, grapes, a number of live insects and some raw meat. They were exceptionally sensitive to cold and had to be kept in a heated aviary.

In France some Levaillant's Barbets were successfully bred in 1928 (*l'Oiseau*, 1928). Mr. B. E. H. Sanders of Natal, South Africa, describes in *Foreign Birds*, June 1957 how he bred them:

'My pair of Crested Levaillant's Barbets were kept in an outdoor aviary, which they shared with Black-cheeked Lovebirds and some weavers and whydahs. A log of wood was provided, fixed some 5 ft (1·5 m) above ground.

When this was first put into the aviary there was one hole, about the size of a small apple, some half way up the log. About 8 in. (20 cm) above this I saw the barbets make another one. They bored out a vertical tunnel from one hole to the other, inside the log, and continued this downwards to a depth that it was not possible to measure. Thus I was unable to inspect the eggs or young.

I soon found the purpose of this double entrance arrangement. I put in all sorts of fruit in the aviary, cut into quarters . . . . The cock came out of the top hole and flew to the apple, while the hen went in the bottom one with a beakful of fruit. Then she emerged from the top hole, while the cock went in by the bottom one. This procedure was carried out first thing in the morning and last thing at night . . . . One young barbet left the nest about the last day of December 1956 and a second one was reared from a later nesting. Both are now fully fledged and independent . . . . Food used, in addition to the fruit, mainly apple and some orange, was bread and milk. Rearing was done entirely by the parents, and in this both shared.'

FAMILY: INDICATORIDAE

Genus: Indicator

MALAYSIAN HONEYGUIDE, *Indicator archipelagus* Temminck

G. Malaya-Honinganzeiger; F. Indicateur malais; D. Maleise Honingspeurder

DISTRIBUTION: Malaysia, Borneo, Sumatra.

DESCRIPTION: Upper parts greyish white. Breast and throat brownish. Tail brown with olive green edges to the feathers and a dirty white spot on the 3 outside pairs of tail feathers. Bill strongly developed, the upper mandible being dark and the lower one white. Length: about 7 in. (18 cm).

These birds were originally classified under cuckoos because they have two toes in front and two behind, and they deposit their eggs in the nests of other birds. Further researches led to putting these birds into a separate family, closely related to the barbets. Honeyguides owe their name to the fact that they lead human beings and animals to beehives. This bird, with his decoy call, leads natives to trees in which bees dwell. The natives carefully open the hive and let the honey run into a pot, throwing away the honeycomb, which is promptly eaten up by the honeyguides.

THE BLACK-THROATED HONEYGUIDE, *Indicator indicator* (Sparrman), which can generally be found in the whole of Africa south of the Sahara, lays its eggs in the nests of *Spreo bicolor*, which also lays white eggs. The Honeyguide, after laying her own egg, tries to break the other eggs, which the rightful owners endeavour to prevent. The young honeyguide has large hooks on its bill and with these it is able to throw the other young birds out of their nest. Later on these hooks disappear. It has not yet been ascertained whether all honeyguides perpetrate brooding parasitism, and it is no more certain that they show the same reaction as regards bee's nests.

Toucans, Toucanets and Acaris

BY K. A. NORRIS

The Family Ramphastidae comprises five genera, and four sub-genera, containing, in all, forty-one species and eighty-seven forms (Peters' *Check List of Birds of the World*, Vol. 6), all confined to tropical America. They are strikingly coloured birds, with enormous, compressed beaks, the culmen being arched, and terminating in a decurved tooth, the cutting edge being serrated or undulated.

Their tongues are long, flattened and fringed or feather-like, in some species reaching a length of 6 in. (15 cm). They have powerful legs and their feet are zygodactylous. Their wings are short and rounded and, with the exception of the species belonging to the genus *Ramphastos*, their tails are long and wedge-shaped. They are almost entirely arboreal, extremely active and restless, and in spite of their comparatively short wings, are fast and high flying, but on the rare occasions when they descend to the ground they move with awkward, clumsy hops and if fully gorged with food, they even appear to experience some difficulty in again taking flight. Their voices are exceedingly harsh but they are also capable of producing a rattling sound, somewhat like the loud purring of a cat, which appears to signify pleasure or contentment.

The chief food of all species is fruit and in a wild state they evince a decided preference for the dry and fibrous fruits of various species of *Ficus* and palms. The fruits are swallowed whole and the stones subsequently regurgitated. Roosting or nesting holes used by Toucans are often found to contain a thick layer of these discarded stones. They also consume quantities of large bodied insects and such small reptiles and other vertibrates as they are able to capture, and will rob the nests of other species of eggs and fledglings. During the early stages of development it is probable that young toucans are supplied with a high proportion of animal food.

The enormous beaks which appear to be so clumsy and heavy are in fact very light, consisting only of a thin sheath covering a network of extremely light and spongy cancellated bony tissue and it is in connection with the feeding habits of the birds that the use of these beaks becomes apparent. The serrated edges enable the bird to secure a firm hold upon the food, and the great length facilitates the plucking of fruits from the extremities of the thin twigs and branches whilst the bird can remain perched on the more substantial boughs which more readily support its weight. It is also suggested that the formidable appearance and brilliant colouring of the beak assists the bird when robbing the nests of other birds, since even the small birds of prey hesitate to attack a toucan or to come within range of its snapping beak.

Any object which is too large to be conveniently swallowed whole is skilfully manipulated in the tip of the beak until it is so crushed and moulded as to be readily gulped down the widely extended throat. Small birds are sometimes held under one foot while the flight and tail feathers are removed, but more often they also are held in the tip of the beak and vigorously rubbed against a branch until the feathers are removed and the bones broken. After some further crushing and moulding, the head is thrown back, the beak opened wide and the food allowed to slip down the throat. When drinking, water is scooped up with the lower mandible and then allowed to run back into the throat. As already mentioned, toucans seldom descend to the ground and they prefer to drink and to bathe in water which has accumulated in the fork of a tree. In times of drought however they will reach down to the surface of a pool or stream from an overhanging branch and in this also the long beak serves them well.

When roosting, the head is turned back and the beak laid along the back and enveloped in the feathers. At the same time the tail, which is capable of remarkable vertical movement, is brought upwards and forward until it also lies along the back and the bird then appears as a shapeless ball of feathers. The smaller toucans of the genus *Pteroglossus* roost in holes in trees, as many as six birds sharing one roosting hole, while other species are thought to remain on branches high above the ground and concealed among the dense foliage.

All species nest in holes in trees, choosing the highest sites they can obtain. The larger species favour the discarded nesting holes of Macaws for which they compete with trogans and other large hole-nesting species. The smaller toucans use the holes excavated by woodpeckers, sometimes even evicting the rightful owners from a freshly excavated site. If the hole is in a dead tree stump, the toucans may enlarge the cavity or entrance by removing some of the rotten wood but they are not known actually to excavate nesting holes themselves. No nesting material is used, the 2–4 white eggs being laid on the natural bed of wood chips accumulated in the bottom of the nesting hole. Both sexes incubate and during the day, change over at frequent intervals, neither remaining on the nest for periods of much more than an hour in duration. It is not known which bird covers the eggs at night but it is probable that the hen alone undertakes this period of duty.

Incubation lasts from fifteen to sixteen days so far as the smaller species are concerned but the period taken for the eggs of the larger species to hatch has not been ascertained. When first hatched, the young are naked, blind and helpless and are slow to mature, seldom leaving the nest before six weeks after hatching. Most species appear to be single brooded but the Emerald Toucanets of the genus *Aulacorhynchus* have been known to rear two broods in a season.

With the exception of the members of the genus *Selenidera*, the Spot-billed Toucanets, and a few species of *Ptero-glossus*, the Aracaris, the plumage of the sexes is alike, but in all species the sex may be fairly readily determined by the difference in shape and size of the beak. Generally speaking, that of the male is distinctly longer and frequently narrower, with the culmen less arched, while the upper mandible of the female of most species is much more abruptly terminated. In the case of the exceptions mentioned above, that part of the plumage which is glossy black in the males is replaced by warm brown in the females.

Toucans do well in confinement, but on account of their size and extremely active nature, they are not suitable subjects for keeping in a cage. Unless they have ample room to leap from perch to perch and to exercise their wings, they soon become over fat and listless, their plumage becomes dull and their condition deteriorates rapidly. In a large indoor enclosure, or better still in an aviary provided with an outdoor flight and a well lighted shelter in which some artificial heat can be provided during cold weather, they will live for years and remain in excellent condition. A minimum temperature of 45–50°C (7–10°C) should be maintained in the roosting quarters.

As it may be necessary to confine the birds to the shelter during severe weather, it is as well to accustom them to feed and drink there at all times and a wide shelf should be fitted about 4 ft. (1 m) above the ground, on which the food dishes and a large pan of water can be placed. Toucans delight in sitting out in a shower of rain, continually shaking and preening their plumage, and cleaning and polishing their beaks by rapidly scratching them with their foot; this is no doubt their normal method of bathing. If they are deprived of the opportunity to 'rain-bathe' during the winter months they will occasionally enter a bath, especially if it is raised well above the ground, and for this reason the pan of water provided in the shelter should be at least 3 in. (7·6 cm) deep, and large enough for the bird to stand in and thoroughly soak its plumage.

Perches in the shelter should be large enough to enable the bird to grasp them comfortably and far enough apart to ensure that it has to use its wings when leaping from one to another. Toucans like to roost high-up and one perch should be placed within some 18 in. (45 cm) of the roof for this purpose. The floor of the shelter is best covered with a thick layer of coarse sawdust.

For the smaller species, particularly the Aracaris, a nest box should be provided and which they will use for roosting at all times of the year. This box should be about 18 in. (45 cm) deep and with the base about 9 in. (23 cm) square, and should have an entrance hole 3 in. (7·6 cm) in diameter, about 4 in. (10 cm) from the top. Wooden slats should be nailed across the inside, below the entrance hole to act as a ladder by which the birds can easily climb out. A 2-in. (5-cm) layer of rotten wood chips and peat moss should be placed in the bottom.

The outside flight needs little furnishing and should, in fact, be kept as free as possible of obstruction so that the birds may have freedom for flight and exercise A firmly secured perch at each end of the enclosure will provide them with facilities for sunning themselves and for rain-bathing. As they are playful and agile they will also appreciate one or two branches, set upright in the centre of the aviary, or a small, growing tree in which they can clamber amongst the branches. The ground must be well drained and may be planted with turf which should be kept well cut, or covered with a layer of clean shingle

Steps must be taken to ensure that rats cannot get into the aviary but it is not necessary to exclude mice as the latter will quickly be caught by the toucans, and will provide a useful addition to their menu.

Toucans will not attack the woodwork of their aviary but even the smaller species will quickly tear holes in the ordinary light-gauge wire netting and it is therefore necessary to use a heavy gauge wire preferably of the spot-welded type, with 1 in. × ½ in. (25 × 12 mm) rectangular mesh.

Their staple food should consist of a mixture of fruit with a proportion of a good quality insectivorous mixture added. Bearing in mind their preference for the dry, fibrous types of fruit to which they have access in their wild state, the basic mixture should be made of such dried fruits as are readily available at all times of the year, dates, dried figs, raisins and sultanas, and apple. The raisins and sultanas should be soaked in water overnight but must be well drained and dried on a cloth before being added to the mixture. Dates, figs and apple should be cut into ½ in. (12 mm) cubes and the mixture should be in the approximate proportion of one part of dried fruits to four parts of apple. To this should be added one part of a dry insectivorous food and all the ingredients then well mixed together to ensure that each piece of fruit becomes well coated with the insectivorous mixture. If properly prepared, the mixture should be comparatively dry and completely free from sticky masses of fruit, which the birds cannot readily throw into the air and swallow. The use of wet, over-ripe or juicy fruit such as grapes, pear or tomato in the mixture should be avoided as, apart from the mess made by the birds shaking it off their beaks, soft fruit of this kind is very rapidly digested and is not sufficiently sustaining for birds of such a restless and active nature. Grapes are certainly greatly appreciated by Toucans, and most other species of fruit eating birds, and four or five may be given each day, as a tit-bit. The birds should be encouraged to take them from the fingers and this will help to keep them tame and steady. They are also very fond of cherries and, when available, these may be given in place of grapes. It is quite unnecessary to remove the stones as the birds are well able to deal with these and they will pass through the system or be regurgitated in due course without any ill effect.

A few mealworms or other insects such as locusts may be given daily and occasionally a mouse or small bird. Raw butchers' meat is not necessary and, in fact, is best avoided as it tends to make the birds bad tempered and savage.

A healthy Toco Toucan will consume about $\frac{1}{2}$ lb. (227 g) of the stock insectivorous mixture each day.

Many of the toucans which reach the bird market have been taken from the nest when very young and hand-reared by natives, and consequently are tame and fearless. If properly treated they will remain tame and very playful, and will make most delightful pets. On the other hand, those which have been trapped as adults are usually very nervous when first imported, and great care must be taken to avoid causing them any sudden fright or they may dash blindly about the aviary and seriously injure themselves or even break their necks.

Most of the small species will live amicably together and young birds of the genus *Ramphastos* will also agree for a time, but as the latter become fully mature they tend to become exceedingly spiteful and sooner or later serious fighting occurs even between the opposite sexes of the same species. A careful watch must therefore be kept at all times and any signs of aggressiveness must be the signal to place them in separate aviaries.

So far no species of toucan has been reared in captivity and, in fact, there are only three or four records of any attempt having been made by these birds to nest in an aviary. The nearest approach to success was achieved at the London Zoo in 1913, when a pair of Spot-billed Toucanets, *Selenidera maculirostris*, hatched a single chick. Unfortunately it did not long survive. The Toco Toucan, *Ramphastos toco*, and Swainson's Toucan, *Ramphastos swainsoni*, have both laid, at San Diego Zoo, California, USA, but in each case the eggs proved to be infertile.

Genus: Alaucorhynchus

EMERALD TOUCANET, *Alaucorhynchus p. prasinus* (Gould)

G. Lauchgrüner-Arassari; F. Toucanet vert, Toucanet émeraude; D. Groene Arassari

DISTRIBUTION: Mexico, Central America, Colombia, Ecuador, Venezuela and Peru.

DESCRIPTION: The beak is the most attractive feature. Lower mandible black; upper mandible has broad yellow stripe on the side, which almost encircles it, except for the upper rim and a small area just below the rim. The yellow flares upwards and outwards with a tapering curve. The dark upper rim tapers to a point, giving way to yellow halfway on upper ridge. Outer areas on lower side of upper mandible

Emerald Toucan, *Alaucorhynchus p. prasinus*

black. The ring around the base is formed by a thin white stripe. Iride brownish-red, the eye being encircled by dark greyish-green. A small whitish patch on the chin is connected to a very pale greenish-white line that runs in an arc to the back of the eye. This serves as a boundary for the triangular facial area. Under tail coverts red, tail dark greenish-black with traces of brown on the tips. Rest of plumage pastel green, darker above and a paler, furry texture below. Length: just over 12 in. (31 cm) including the beak.

SUBSPECIES: There are at least 15 subspecies, which differ only slightly in colour and format. The variations usually concern the throat, beak, bare eye skin and tail. Area of white on chin is variable in extent. In some, chin and part of throat may be grey, as *A. p. griseigularis*, from Colombia; or blue-grey or even blue as in the Blue-throated Toucanet, *A. p. caeruleogularis*, from highlands of Chirique and Varaques. The basal connecting line on beak is bold and white in some races. Some lower mandibles show variations between red and brown near base, and upper mandibles may show considerably less yellow both in extent and brightness, and even a different pattern. In *A. p. phaeolaemus* from Colombia the yellow is dull and shaded with green, and covers only the ridge of the upper mandible. Facial skin may vary from dark grey-green to brownish. Under tail coverts are sometimes brown, and the brown tips on the tail are brighter and broader in some races.

In the wild state these birds can be seen only when they are on the move, because when they sit still they merge completely with the foliage. The sound they utter is best compared to a kind of growl. The first specimen was imported into Germany in 1925 and was housed in the Zoological Gardens in Berlin. The bird was unusually tame and remained in the outside aviary during the day. It spent the winter in a heated inside aviary. A pair of Emerald Toucanets lived quite peaceably in the company of large parakeets, jays and magpies.

CHESTNUT-BILLED EMERALD TOUCANET, CRIMSON-RUMPED ARCARI, RED-RUMPED GREEN TOUCANET, *Alaucorhynchus h. haematopygus* Gould

G. Rotburzel-Grunarassari; F. Toucanet à croupion rouge; D. Roodstuit-Arassari

DISTRIBUTION: Subtropical zone of the western, central and eastern Andes of Colombia and Sierra de Perijá in extreme western Venezuela.

DESCRIPTION: *Male.* Almost entirely green. Plumage of head, back, wings and tail dull dark green with golden wash on nape and bluish tone on ear coverts. Under parts pale yellowish-green with bluish wash on sides of breast. Upper tail coverts crimson; under tail coverts greyish; tail tipped with dark chestnut. Beak, long and rather straight, black with reddish-chestnut stain along centre of each mandible and upper mandible tipped with same colour, broad pure white band across base. Irides dark brown; naked orbital patch dark plum red. Legs and feet blue-grey. *Female.* Similar but distinctively smaller and with much smaller beak. Length: about 16 in. (40 cm).

Emerald Toucanets inhabit much higher country than do those of the various genera already mentioned, reaching about 10,000 ft (2·88 km) in the Andes, and they are consequently less affected by cold. Nevertheless they must be protected from severe frost and they dislike the cold damp climate and the foggy atmosphere of Europe. They should be kept in an aviary provided with a well-protected shelter to which they can be confined in the winter, or brought indoors during the colder months and kept in a large enclosure or cage not less than 4 ft. (1·22 m) in length. They usually live amicably in pairs but it is best not to associate them with other species. Like most toucans, they are of a nervous disposition, but with gentle treatment and encouraged by the offer of titbits will usually become reasonably steady.

Genus: Pteroglossus

The Aracari Toucanets of this genus have pronounced jagged teeth notched into their beaks. They have long slender bodies and tails, smaller heads, and long slender beaks. The tail feathers are graduated and have rounded tips. A rather large bare facial patch covers the lores, surrounds the eyes, and tapers to a tip above the cheeks. A dark hood covers the head to the mantle and upper breast. The hood and upper parts, except the rump and upper tail coverts, are black, but traces of other dark colours sometimes appear. The base colour of the under parts is yellow, but there are many variations, with patterns of red and dark bars or broad bands. Beaks are also variably patterned and coloured. Sexes are alike, but females usually have shorter beaks and traces of brown on the black nape.

Aracaris inhabit wooded country at the lower levels. They roost in holes, and in aviaries should always have a nest box available. They appear to be particularly susceptible to cold and frost, and must have adequate protection, with artificial heat during winter months; without this they may lose their toes and even parts of their bills from frostbite. As they are nervous birds and seldom overcome their shyness in captivity, they are better suited to a large aviary where they can retire to the seclusion of the shelter when strangers are near.

They are aggressive and active birds but in aviaries settle down well with their own kind after an initial introductory period. They are not satisfactory companions for other types of bird. They easily transfer to diets in captivity and they like more live food than do toucans. Mealworms are acceptable.

BANDED ARACARI, COLLARED ARACARI, *Pteroglossus t. torquatus* (Gmelin) (Pl. II)
G. Halsband-Arassari; F. Aracari à collier; D. Halsband-Arassari

DISTRIBUTION: Tropical zone from Vera Cruz and Oxaca southward through Central America to the Panama Canal.
DESCRIPTION: *Male.* Upper parts black, shaded with inky-blue on head; chestnut nape, greenish mantle and shoulders. Rump and upper tail coverts dark red. Bare skin surrounding eyes blue; tapering triangle above ear coverts red; irides bright yellowish-straw. Under parts pale yellow and somewhat dull with smudges and fine streaks of red shading. A blackish crescent-shaped spot occurs in central upper breast area, and a black band separates breast from abdomen. Thighs and flanks brownish. Bill has whitish-yellow band at base. Lower mandible, upper ridge and tip of upper mandible black; rest of upper mandible horn-coloured with dark shadows enhancing notched teeth. *Female.* Very similar, but bill usually smaller. Brown spots can be detected on neck. Length: about 16 in. (40 cm) including the 4 in. (10 cm) bill.
These aracari can be kept very satisfactory with related species. They must have live food, so that sometimes mealworms should be given.
This subspecies is fairly often imported; the first occasion was to the London Zoo in 1807. The other subspecies are seldom imported.

RED-RUMPED ARACARI, SCARLET-RUMPED ARACARI, RED-BACKED ARACARI, *Pteroglossus erythropygius* Gould
G. Rotrücken-Arassari; F. Aracari à croupion rouge; D. Roodrug-Arassari

DISTRIBUTION: Western Ecuador from the Chandron Valley to Esmeraldas.
DESCRIPTION: Strongly resembles *Pteroglossus t. torquatus* except for the following differences: bare skin on face all red; bill mostly horn-coloured with black on a broad tip of lower mandible and in a long slender area on lower part of upper mandible. The slender stripe is broad near base and ends in an upturned flourish a little forward from centre.
Although Red-rumped Aracari were shown for the first time at the National Exhibition in London in 1859 they are now rarely seen in aviary collections.
The Stripe-billed Aracari, *Pteroglossus sanguineus* Gould, from Colombia and Ecuador, is similar to *P. erythropygius*, but slightly larger. The bare facial skin is bluish-black with red on tip following the eye. In addition to the pattern of the bill of *P. erythropygius*, there is a black rim on the top of the upper mandible and the lower mandible is all black.

MAXIMILIAN'S ARACARI, BLACK-NECKED ARACARI, *Pteroglossus a. aracari* (Linnaeus)
G. Schwarzkehl-Arassari; F. Aracari à cou noir; D. D. Zwartkeel-Arassari

DISTRIBUTION: Amazonian Brazil, south of the Amazon, west to the Rio Madeira and southward in the coastal states of Espirito Santo and probably Rio de Janeiro.
DESCRIPTION: *Male.* Head, throat and mantle glossy black, with a blue sheen and a slight wash of chestnut on ear coverts. Remainder of upper parts very dark greenish-black, with the exception of the crimson upper tail coverts. Under parts sulphur yellow, with band of scarlet, more or less edged with black, across abdomen, and a faint red wash following the black of throat. Flanks and under tail coverts brown, with olive-green intermixed. Naked orbital patch very dark leaden grey, irides dark brown. Upper mandible ivory, with a narrow band of black on culmen which does not extend to tip. Teeth white, with a slight staining between each. Lower mandible entirely black and there is a narrow but distinct band of white across the base of both. Legs and feet greenish-grey. *Female.* Rather smaller, with smaller beak, the stripe on the culmen often wider, especially at the base. Length: about 16 in. (40 cm).
SUBSPECIES: A similar subspecies, Mount Roraima Aracari, *P. a. roraimae*, from southern and eastern Venezuela, Guayana and Surinam, is distinguished only by the broad

Maximilian's Aracari, *Pteroglossus a. aracari*

black line on culmen, extending to tip of beak, and by the citron yellow under parts. These two forms are often confused. Two other subspecies, *P. a. atricollis* and *P. a. vergens* from Brazil also differ only in minor details, the latter, however, being readily identified by having the sides of the head, chin and upper throat dark chestnut-brown.

This species was first obtained by the London Zoo in 1872. Although it is common in its native country, it is not imported in very great numbers, and several other species of aracaris, such as *P. viridis inscriptus*, the Lettered Aracari, are usually more readily obtainable.

LETTERED ARACARI, *Pteroglossus viridis inscriptus* Swainson

G. Schrift-Arassari; F. Aracari écrit; D. Schrift-Arassari

DISTRIBUTION: Amazonian Brazil, south of the Amazon, from the Guaporé and the Madeira to Para, extending eastward to Maranhão and Pernambuco and south to north-west Matto Grosso.
DESCRIPTION: Bare skin on face green. Head, neck and area around upper part of breast glossy black in the male and chestnut-brown in the female. Upper parts greyish-green, with the exception of rump, which is scarlet-red. Under parts yellow, with some brown on lower breast and brownish-green on thighs. Cheeks and throat brown. Bill has slight white indentations on cutting edges and a yellow spot at base. Uppermost groove of upper mandible yellowish-horn-colour; remainder of bill almost wholly black, especially lower part. On base of lower bill there is a red triangular spot and in centre of black sides of bill there is a red sheen. Length: about 13¼ in. (33 cm).

The Lettered Aracari is probably the best known, the most frequently imported and about the smallest of all toucans. The bird is quite satisfied with a comparatively small cage, provided it can have an hour of free flying around the room every day. This species sometimes becomes quite tame but is nervous when strangers come near.
The northern subspecies, *P. v. humboldti*, also called the Lettered Aracari, is larger and has some red in the bare skin behind the eye, an all-black lower mandible, and a different pattern on the upper mandible. Dull yellowish-horn covers most of the upper mandible, except for black on the upper rim and tip and black shadows on the tooth serrations.

DOUBLE-COLLARED ARACARI, *Pteroglossus b. bitorquatus* Vigors

G. Doppelband-Schwarzarassari; F. Aracari à double bande; D. Roodnek-Arassari

DISTRIBUTION: South bank of the Amazon, east of the Tocantins and adjacent parts of northern Maranhão.
DESCRIPTION: This is perhaps the most attractive member of the genus. Bare facial area red, but eyes encircled by blue. Dark head and upper parts, more variable than those of most species, faintly shaded by blue on head, reddish-chestnut in a bold shade on nape, and dark green instead of black on wings and tail. Yellow under parts have one very bright variation: a yellow band, slightly broader in the centre, occurs just below the black hood. Whole breast is vivid red and below this the yellow recommences and continues through under tail coverts, except for a dull indeterminate band of green on flanks and across ventral area. Upper mandible yellowish-horn with ivory teeth. Lower mandible white on basal half and black on outer half. The dividing line angles outward from a point on the upper cutting rim near the base to the midway point on the lower rim. The white band at the connecting base is found

Double-collared Aracari, *Pteroglossus b. bitorquatus*

on the lower mandible only. It is preceded by a narrow curved black band. Length: about 16 in. (40 cm).
SUBSPECIES: The subspecies *P. b. sturmii*, living on the right bank of the Rio Madeira, has the lower mandible totally black, and Reichenow's Aracari, *P. b. reichenowi*, on the south bank of the Amazon, lacks the yellow band on the upper chest.

YELLOW-BILLED ARACARI, IVORY-BILLED ARACARI, *Pteroglossus f. flavirostris* Fraser

G. Elfenbeinschnabelarassari; F. Aracari à bec d'ivoire; D. Roodkop-Arassari

DISTRIBUTION: Amazonian Colombia and eastern Ecuador, eastern to southern Venezuela and north-western Brazil.
DESCRIPTION: Bill ivory-yellow with black teeth and some pale brown in the upper part of lower mandible. Bare facial area mostly red with black preceding the eye. Crown and nape glossy black and the rest of head dark chestnut with a black boundary on lower throat. The breast has two broad bands, crimson on upper breast and black on lower. Narrow and irregular crimson borders the lower boundary of black. Remaining under parts, except for olive-green flanks, yellow tinged with green, and under side of tail a dull greenish shade. Upper parts olive-green, except for a crimson sump and maroon mantle. Length: about 14 in. (35·5 cm).
This aracari is rarely kept in collections although Mr. K. A. Norris described a specimen that he saw in England in 1960.
SUBSPECIES: *P. f. azara* from western Brazil may be identified

because it lacks the black teeth and the red on the bill. *P. f. mariae*, from north-eastern Peru, does have the black teeth, but on the upper rim of the upper mandible it has dark yellow spots, as well as on the whole of the lower mandible.

Yellow-billed Aracari, *Pteroglossus f. flavirostris*

CURL-CRESTED ARACARI, *Pteroglossus beauharnaesii* Wagler

G. Beauharnais-Arassari; F. Aracari de Beauharnais; D. Krulkuif-Arassari

DISTRIBUTION: Amazonian Peru, western Brazil, east to the Rio Madeira, and northern Bolivia.

DESCRIPTION: *Male.* Crown and back of head black and white, the feathers having the appearance of glossy scales or wood chips, black in colour with a white streak in the centre of each. This effect is caused by the barbs of each feather being fused together, and with the dilated shaft, into one consolidated disc, each disc curving upwards, producing the appearance of a mass of curls Throat and cheeks pale straw, many of the cheek feathers being tipped with black; ear coverts white with a few black feathers intermixed, the feathers being elongated and sharply pointed. Mantle and rump crimson; remainder of the upper parts dark, glossy green. The under parts yellow, with crimson freely intermixed and with a broad black abdominal band edged with crimson; thighs olive and under tail coverts yellow, washed with crimson. The tail is long, wedge shaped and very dark green. Beak, upper mandible maroon-red fading into yellow towards the tip and with a broad, pale blue mark commencing from the nostril and widening towards the tip. Serrated tomium white. Lower mandible pure white with dark yellow tip and a maroon bar across the base. Irides dark rich brown; naked orbital patch bright blue; legs and feet greenish-grey. *Female.* Similar but rather smaller and with smaller beak. Length: about 17½ in. (44·5 cm).

Although this very remarkable toucan, by far the most colourful of all the species, has been well known from recorded descriptions and cabinet skins from an early period, it was not until January 1960 that the first living specimen was brought into captivity. It was purchased from a dealer in Miami, USA, and exhibited at the Bronx Zoo. Shortly after, several were imported to England, one being sent to the London Zoo and the remainder going to private collections. Very little is known of their habits but they require the same treatment as other species of toucans.

Genus: Selenidera

There are six species of toucanet in this genus, which are not outstanding in colour or in the size of the beak. Sexes are different. The main interest in these birds is in their rarity, and they are mostly seen in zoos. Most are the smallest members of the family, with the shortest beaks. In appearance they are somewhat thick-set and dumpy.

YELLOW-EARED TOUCANET, *Selenidera spectabilis* (Cassin)

G. Gelbohrarassari; F. Toucanet à oreillons jaunes; D. Cassins Arassari

DISTRIBUTION: Central America.

DESCRIPTION: *Male.* Crown and neck black. Ear coverts golden yellow. Throat, breast, middle of abdomen glossy black; sides of body orange-yellow. Flanks chestnut-brown; lower tail coverts red. Remainder of upper parts olive-green; tail grey. Skin above eyes bluish-gr en; area under eyes yellowish-green; skin just below beak yellow. Irides light red. Top part of upper mandible greenish-grey; lower part dark brownish-black. *Female.* Similar, but crown and neck chestnut-brown; ear coverts glossy black. Length: about 16 in. (40 cm).

Yellow-eared Toucanets are not regularly imported. In a collection it is quite safe to keep them together with related species as they are by nature peaceful birds. Heated winter quarters are essential.

The Lemon-collared Toucanet, *Selenidera reinwardtii* (Wagler), comes from Colombia, Ecuador and Peru. *Male.* Has a reddish-brown beak with black on the ridge and on a broad tip. Facial skin is yellowish-green. Ear coverts yellow and lengthened into tufts. A narrow yellow collar on the nape adds brightness to the black of head, nape and under parts. Lower sides mixed yellow and olive; flanks brown and under tail coverts red. Upper parts olive-green with brown covering most of the tail, except the base and tip. *Female.* Has brown instead of black, and yellow areas are less bright. The length varies from 11–13 in. (28–33 cm) including the beak, which is 2–2½ in. (5–6·5 cm).

SPOT-BILLED TOUCANET, *Selenidera maculirostris* Lichtenstein   (Pl. VIII)

G. Bindenschnabeltukan, Goulds Kurzschnabeltukan; F. Toucanet à bec tacheté; D. Vleksnavel-Arassari

DISTRIBUTION: South-eastern Brazil.

DESCRIPTION: *Male.* Head, nape, throat and breast black; ear coverts prolonged into a tuft of orange and yellow feathers; yellow half-collar at base of nape; back, rump, wings and tail dark olive-green; 6 central tail feathers tipped with dark chestnut and inner webs of flights brownish. Abdomen yellowish-green; flanks orange; thighs mingled rufous and green; under tail coverts crimson. Beak bluish-green, tipped with yellow and with both mandibles more or less heavily blotched with black. Irides orange, with split pupils; naked orbital patch bright blue; feet and legs blue-grey. *Female.* Head, nape, throat and breast warm chocolate brown; ear tufts greenish-yellow; half-collar at nape narrow, pale yellow—in some specimens almost absent; wings and tail brownish-green; 6 centre tail feathers tipped with dull chestnut; abdomen olive-brown; under tail coverts crimson. Beak similar to that of male but black markings usually less distinct. Irides, orbital patch, legs and feet as male. Length: about 13½ in. (33 cm).

Spot-billed Toucanet, *Selenidera maculirostris*

SUBSPECIES: A subspecies, *S. m. gouldii*, has the upper mandible three quarters black and the lower very pale blue-green. The iris is also green.

This little toucan makes a delightful pet and is reasonably sociable with its own kind, but, in common with all toucans, it is unsafe to keep with species smaller than itself owing to its predatory habits. It is less active than the large toucans of the genus *Ramphastos* and may be kept in a large cage of not less than 4 ft (1·22 m) in length. Being naturally tame and inquisitive, it may be allowed out into the room each day for exercise, and will usually return of its own accord. If it is desired to attempt breeding, however, the birds should be transferred to an aviary with an open flight and well protected shelter, in which artificial heat can be provided and to which they should be confined during cold weather. Nest boxes should be provided both in the shelter and in the open flight.

The species was first imported in 1874 and was exhibited at the Berlin Zoo in that year. The first to be seen in England was at the London Zoo in 1879 and, as already mentioned, a young one was hatched at the London Zoo in 1913.

Spot-billed Toucanets are imported regularly, in small numbers, and a few are obtainable both in England and on the Continent each year.

Genus: Andigena

These Mountain or Hill Toucans are unusual birds and have been making a few appearances in recent years, particularly in zoos. The genus is subdivided into two subgenera: *Baillonius*, with one species, and *Andigena*, with four species and several subspecies. Baillon's Toucanet is very different from the other members. It has been frequently available but is not very attractive.

Most members of the subgenus *Andigena* resemble large toucanets rather than small toucans. The beaks and heads of the most attractive ones are smaller and more slender in proportion to body size than those of toucans, and the tails are longer. The less attractive Black-billed Mountain Toucan is an exception, for it has a much broader beak and therefore a larger head. Mountain Toucans lack the bibs and the large areas of black found in members of the genus *Ramphastos*. The most extensive colour is a soft pastel grey, which serves as a fine base for contrasting colours.

The size range is approximately 17–21 in. (43–53 cm) including the beaks, which vary from 3 to nearly 5 in. (7·5–13 cm) in length.

LAMINATED-BILLED TOUCAN, PLATE-BILLED MOUNTAIN TOUCAN, *Andigena laminirostris* Gould
D. Plaatsnavel-Toekan

DISTRIBUTION: Subtropical and temperate zones of south-western Colombia and western Ecuador, south of the Rio Chanchan.
DESCRIPTION: Sexes are similar. Forehead, crown, nape and mantle black with dull gloss; wings golden-olive-brown; rump yellow, upper tail coverts grey-green; tail black, central feathers tipped with chestnut; ear coverts, side of neck, throat, breast and flanks clear silvery-blue with a tuft of bright yellow feathers on flanks; thighs dark chestnut; under tail coverts crimson. Irides warm dark brown. Naked orbital patch is greatly enlarged and extends from above the eye to the base of the lower mandible, the area above and in line with the eye being bright blue, the remainder clear light yellow. Upper mandible black with a horny plate, which has the appearance of being welded to the side, beginning at the base of the beak and extending for approximately half the length of the mandible. This plate is pale buff with transverse bars of chestnut, pale blue and brown. Lower mandible dark chestnut for basal half, remainder black. Legs and feet blue-grey. Length: 20 in. (50 cm).

In 1961 the first living specimen of the Laminated-billed Toucan was obtained and exhibited at the New York Zoo. At about the same time a few were offered by a German collector living in South America but there appears to be no record of these having reached Europe. In 1965, however, a few were imported by a London dealer and were the first to be seen alive in England. Having regard to the high elevation of their range, they should be reasonably hardy, but, in common with all birds coming from these high altitudes, they would probably suffer from exposure to the cold fog and dampness of the winter months in northern Europe.

BLACK-BILLED MOUNTAIN TOUCAN, *Andigena n. nigrirostris* (Waterhouse)
G. Schwarzschnabelblautukan; F. Toucan à bec noir; D. Zwartsnavel-Toekan

DISTRIBUTION: Subtropical zone of eastern Andes of Colombia.
DESCRIPTION: *Male.* Forehead, crown, nape and mantle glossy black; back and wings olive-brown; rump lemon-yellow; upper tail coverts greenish; tail greyish-black, the central feathers tipped with chestnut. Cheeks, ear coverts and chin white; remainder of under parts pale greyish-blue with flanks and thighs chestnut and under tail coverts dark crimson. Beak black. Irides dark red-brown; naked orbital patch blue below the eye and otherwise yellow. Legs and feet blue-grey. *Female.* Similar but slightly smaller, with smaller beak. Length: 20 in. (50 cm).
SUBSPECIES: The colour of the beak varies with the different

subspecies. The nominate race has an all-black beak. One subspecies has deep maroon on the base, and another subspecies has deep maroon on the base and ridge of the upper mandible.

One example of this species was imported to England in December 1960 and was probably the first species of the genus *Andigena* seen alive in this country or in Europe.

BAILLON'S TOUCAN, BANANA TOUCANET, *Andigena*
bailloni Vieillot (Pl. VIII)
G. Goudtoekan, Bergtoekan; F. Toucan de Baillon;
D. Goldbrustbergtukan

DISTRIBUTION: South-eastern Brazil in states of Espirito Santo, Rio de Janeiro, São Paulo, Parăna and Santa

Celarina.

DESCRIPTION: *Male*. Forehead, front of crown, sides of head and whole of under parts golden yellow; flanks olive-green; back of crown, nape, back, upper tail coverts, wings and tail dark olive-green; rump crimson. Beak pale olive-green, bluish at base and with pale red in centre of upper mandible, and a red mark near base of lower mandible. Irides yellow; naked orbital patch pale red; legs and feet grey-green. *Female*. Similar but slightly smaller and yellow of under parts not quite so intense. Length: about 15 in. (38 cm).

This small toucan has been known in Europe for many years and has been regularly imported, although never in great numbers. It is one of the less hardy species and requires careful acclimatisation and some heat during the winter months. In warm summer weather it benefits greatly from having access to an outdoor aviary.

Genus: Ramphastos

Toucans of this genus, with 11 species, are the largest in the family and have the most massive beaks. All the plumage on body, wings and tail is black, except in the case of two members. Colour variations occur on upper and lower tail coverts and on the bib. The black on the wings is slightly glossy. Main characteristics are colourful bare flesh around the eyes and a large bib which starts above the eyes on the sides of the forehead and includes all the face, throat, sides of neck and upper breast. This is a dominant characteristic and is always in a sharply contrasting colour. These are shapely birds, whose appearance is greatly enhanced by their huge beaks.

ARIEL TOUCAN, *Ramphastos vitellinus ariel* Vigors
G. Arieltukan; F. Toucan Ariel; D. Ariel-Toekan

DISTRIBUTION: Brazil south of the Amazon.
DESCRIPTION: Light yellow in pale margin near base of beak. Iris blue with a fine black circle surrounding the eye. Bare facial area bright orange-red. Bib vivid orange, followed by vivid scarlet on most of under parts. Rump and tail coverts scarlet; thighs black. It was first exhibited in London in 1855.
SUBSPECIES: Sulphur- or White-breasted Toucan, *R. v. vitellinus*, to be found in Trinidad, northern Venezuela, the Guinas and northern Brazil, has a bluish-grey margin near the base of the beak and a bright blue bare facial area. Irides are brown. Bib white, with large yellow area in centre and broad red band along lower boundary.
The Keel-billed or Channel-billed Toucan, *R. v. culminatus*, comes from Colombia and Bolivia. The name 'Keel-bill' is also often used by ornithologists to designate the Sulphur-breasted Toucan. The popular names refer to the high grooved ridge of the upper mandible. *R. v. culminatus*, and other species, are sometimes called 'White-breasted Tou-

cans'. *R. v. culminatus*: basal margin of the beak is bluish-grey, with pale yellow along the ridge of the upper mandible. Bare facial skin blue, and bib white with a narrow border of red on lower boundary. Rump and upper tail coverts orange. This bird first appeared in 1897 in the Berlin Zoo.

GREEN-BILLED TOUCAN, RED-BREASTED TOUCAN,
Ramphastos dicolorus Linnaeus

G. Bunttukan; F. Toucan à bec vert; D. Bonte Toekan,
Groensnavel-Toekan

DISTRIBUTION: South-eastern Brazil, Paraguay and north-eastern Argentina.
DESCRIPTION: *Male*. General colour glossy black. Cheeks, throat and breast deep yellow, suffused in centre with orange, and divided from crimson lower breast by a pale yellow pectoral band. Abdomen black; upper and under tail coverts crimson-red. Beak yellowish-green with a broad basal band of black and the tomium narrowly red. Irides pale blue;

Green-billed Toucan, *Ramphastos dicolorus*

naked orbital patch orange-red. Legs and feet blue-grey. *Female*. Similar, but may be distinguished by the more arched culmen and more abruptly truncated upper mandible and the fact that the beak is usually nearly 1 in. (2·5 cm) shorter than that of the male. Length: nearly 19 in. (46 cm). In its native country the Green-billed Toucan appears to be one of the commonest species, frequenting open woodland

Ariel Toucan, *Ramphastos vitellinus ariel*

and occasionally associating with Toco Toucans when feeding. The first specimen to be exhibited at the London Zoo arrived in 1876 and it is still the most frequently imported of the larger species.

This species is usually fully adult when importers receive it and it is difficult to tame. It is also one of the more aggressive species, even though it is smaller than all those listed above and has a smaller beak. After careful introduction it is a satisfactory companion for other toucans. This is one of the two exceptions of the genus which has a colour other than black below the bib.

SULPHUR-BREASTED TOUCAN, RAINBOW-BILLED TOUCAN, *Ramphastos s. sulfuratus* Lesson (Pl. VIII)
G. Fischer Tukan; F. Toucan à bec caréné; D. Fischer's Toekau

DISTRIBUTION: South-eastern Mexico from Puebla, Oazaca and Vera Cruz, south to northern Guatemala and Honduras.
DESCRIPTION: *Male.* General colour glossy black, the nape being washed with maroon. Sides of head, throat and upper breast sulphur yellow, divided from black under parts by a narrow crimson pectoral band. Rump white; under tail coverts scarlet. Upper mandible pale apple-green with a narrow pale yellow stripe along the culmen and a broad wedge-shaped orange-yellow mark along the cutting edge; there is also an oval deep-red mark at the tip and the teeth are marked with black. Lower mandible also apple-green but washed with bright pale blue, the tip deep red. There is a narrow black line across the base of both mandibles, followed by a broader band of very pale bluish-green. Irides deep blue-grey; naked orbital patch yellowish-green. Legs and feet blue-grey. *Female.* Similar colouring, but much smaller and with a smaller and more abruptly-terminated beak. Length: about 18 in. (45 cm).
SUBSPECIES: There is a subspecies known as the Short-billed Toucan, *R. s. brevicarinatus* (*R. s. intermedius*). It is to be found in south-eastern Guatemala to Panama, across northern Colombia to Santa Marta region and the adjacent parts of Venezuela. It is similar to the Sulphur-breasted Toucan, although smaller and with a smaller and more truncated beak. The red spot at the tip of the beak is less sharply defined and the red pectoral band more pronounced. A specimen was presented to the London Zoo in 1884. It is available occasionally but is less frequently imported than the Sulphur-breasted Toucan.
R. s. sulfuratus is by far the most colourful of the genus and is less spiteful than the Toco Toucan. Although it is not safe to associate Sulphur-breasted Toucans with other smaller species, a pair may usually be kept together without undue risk of fighting, provided they are in a spacious aviary. Their voices are high-pitched and shrill and they tend to be restless and nervous, especially when strangers approach their aviary.

SWAINSON'S TOUCAN, *Ramphastos swainsonii* Gould
G. Swainsons Tukan; F. Toucan tocard; D. Bruinrug-Toekan

DISTRIBUTION: South-eastern Honduras, western Ecuador and eastward in Colombia to the Magdalena River.
DESCRIPTION: Irides greenish, and bare skin area surrounding the eyes bright green. Bib yellow, shading to white at base, followed by a narrow red border at bottom. Upper tail coverts white, under tail coverts scarlet-red. The massive beak is diagonally divided into light and dark colours. The dividing line starts at top of the base of upper mandible and slowly stretches downward in a gently irregular line, ending at lower edge of upper mandible about one-fourth the

distance from outer end. Upper part yellow; lower area, including lower mandible, deep reddish-maroon, shading to blackish at tip of lower mandible. Length: about 22 in. (56·5 cm), beak about 6–8 in. (15·5–20·5 cm).
Swainson's Toucans are traditionally more wild than the Toco or Cuvier's Toucan and are difficult to tame. They are one of the most attractive species. They first arrived in England in 1876. Their care in the aviary is the same as for other toucans. All toucans must be kept in heated quarters throughout the winter.

CUVIER'S TOUCAN, *Ramphastos c. cuvieri* (Wagler)
G. Peru-Grosstukan; F. Toucan de Cuvier; D. Witborst-Toekan

DISTRIBUTION: Eastern Colombia, eastern Ecuador, eastern Peru and northern Bolivia eastward to southern Venezuela and the Rio Tapajoz.
DESCRIPTION: Bare skin on face bright blue with no variation in eye ring colour. Bib white with red border on chest.

Cuvier's Toucan, *Ramphastos c. cuvieri*

Upper tail coverts yellow, and a chrysanthemum-like rosette of red under tail coverts surrounds the vent. Beak mostly black with narrow yellow band on upper ridge. Wide band across base of beak yellow on upper and faint sky-blue on lower mandible. Black rim at connecting edge of beak prominent. Length: 20 in. (50 cm).
The subspecies *R. c. oblitus*, from Amazonian Brazil, is smaller and has a trace of deep red near the base of beak.

RED-BILLED TOUCAN, *Ramphastos tucanos* Linnaeus
G. Rotschnabeltukan; F. Toucan à bec rouge; D. Roodsnavel-Toekan

DISTRIBUTION: South-eastern Venezuela, Guyana, Surinam, and northern Brazil, chiefly north of the Amazon and west to Manaus, but extending into Maranhão.
DESCRIPTION: Like *R. c. cuvieri*, but with deep red in centre of outer half of both mandibles; red varies among individuals. Length: 18 in. (45 cm).
There are two other species, also similar, and too rare in a localised range to be available. The Inca Toucan, *Ramphastos inca* Gould, from eastern Bolivia, has less red on beak, more red in border on chest; upper tail coverts orange. The rank of the species *R. aurantiirostris* from Venezuela, Surinam, and Guyana, is disputed, and it may eventually be discounted as a separate species. It is apparently known only from museum skins. The red of the beak is bright and mixed with orange.
In their wild state these birds live exclusively in high trees,

where they make their nests in deep hollows. If they are kept in the company of related birds or of other large birds who are able to defend themselves, food and drinking troughs should be placed in various parts of the aviary. This helps to prevent the birds from quarrelling, which they will do if there is only one food trough.

TOCO TOUCAN, GIANT TOUCAN, *Ramphastos t. toco* Müller

G. Riesentukan; F. Toucan toco; D. Reuzen-Toekan

Toco Toucan, *Ramphastos t. toco*

DISTRIBUTION: Guyana, Surinam, northern and eastern Brazil, south of the vicinity of Belem.

DESCRIPTION: *Male*. General colour glossy black; ear coverts, side neck, throat and upper breast white, tinged with yellow and orange-red in adults. Upper tail coverts white, lower tail coverts scarlet. Irides very dark brown, with cobalt-blue orbital ring and naked orbital patch orange. Beak orange, stained with red on culmen and lower mandible; sharply defined black mark at tip of upper mandible and broad black basal band. Legs and feet blue-grey. *Female*. Similar but slightly smaller and generally more compact. Beak shorter, broader and much more abruptly terminated. Length: about 24 in. (60 cm).

The first recorded description of a toucan was made by Oviedo in his *Sumario de la Natural Historia de las Indias*, 1527. This, and subsequent early descriptions, all appear to refer to this species. Consequently the Toco is regarded as the type of the genus *Ramphastos*, and therefore of the family *Ramphastidae*. It is the largest of the toucans and is a forest dweller. It leaves the tops of the highest trees only in periods of drought, when there is a shortage of its natural food. It will then descend in flocks to the plantations bordering the forests and will cause havoc among the orange groves.

The first record of this species being exhibited alive in Europe was at the Amsterdam Zoo in 1851, and the first to reach the London Zoo was in 1863. Small consignments are usually available in the European bird markets each year.

SUBSPECIES: A southern subspecies, *Ramphastos t. albogularis* is found in southern Brazil, parts of north Argentina and Bolivia, and is distinguished by the complete absence of any yellow or red on throat and upper breast.

SUBORDER: PICI

FAMILY: PICIDAE

Genus: Jynx

SUBFAMILY: JYNGINAE

EUROPEAN WRYNECK, *Jynx t. torquilla* Linnaeus

G. Wendehals; F. Torcol ordinaire; D. Draaihals

DISTRIBUTION: Europe and western Asia.

DESCRIPTION: Upper parts dusty grey, with fine dark streaks, dots and stripes; under parts white, marked with dark triangular patches. Throat and neck have fine grey transverse lines on a yellow background. A dark line begins at top of head and runs down to end of back. Dark grey, dark brown and light brown patches are found over the whole plumage. Irides light brown. Feet, legs and beak greenish-yellow. Length: nearly 8 in. (20 cm).

Wrynecks prefer to live in areas where there are plenty of trees, but they avoid dense woods. A pair may nest in a park, an orchard or a garden where there are old trees, so long as they find a suitable nesting hole. Because of the protective colouring of their plumage they become almost invisible when they are hanging on to the trunk of a tree, but they betray themselves by their cry of 'wie-ied, wie-ied', repeated several times. When alarmed or captured, they make a snake-like hissing noise, accompanied by a curious twisting of head and neck, in an attempt to frighten the possible enemy.

They feed largely on ants, which are picked up from the ground or from trees. They also take ants' eggs, as well as grubs and insects of every kind. Their long tongues, with sticky points, enable them to pick up pupae and ants from cracks and crevices. The female lays 7–8 eggs, on which she sits for 14 days. The young are almost naked at birth and remain in the nest for a long time. Both parents look after them.

At present these birds are found only in aviaries at a few zoos. The main problem is that of their food, as a diet of ants' eggs alone is not sufficient. They may also accept mealworms, maggots, and even finely-grated raw meat. The basis of their diet should be a good insectivorous mixture, to which, however, it is necessary to accustom them. An artificial nectar mixed with a little baby food will be eagerly accepted.

SUBFAMILY: PICINAE

Woodpeckers

BY H. J. BATES AND R. L. BUSENBARK

The enormous family of woodpeckers is well scattered throughout the world. Their colours and patterns are bold and beautiful. There are thirty-three genera in the subfamily Picinae, divided into 182 species, which are further subdivided into a great many subspecies.

Plate XI

Purple-throated Euphonia, *Tanagra chlorotica*

North American Scarlet Tanager, *Piranga olivacea*

Chestnut-bellied Euphonia, *Tanagra pectoralis*

Scarlet-rumped Tanager, *Ramphocelus passerinii*

South American Scarlet Tanager, *Ramphocelus bresilius*

Crimson-backed Tanager, *Ramphocelus dimidiatus*

Plate XII

Blue-crowned Chlorophonia, *Chlorophonia occipitalis*

Yellow-winged Cassique, *Cassiculus melanicarus*

Violet Euphonia, *Tanagra violacea*

Montezuma Oropondola, *Gymnostinops montezumae*

Boat-tailed Grackle, *Cassidix mexicanus*

Swallow Tanager, *Tersina viridis*

Plate XIII

Occipital Blue Pie, *Urocissa erythrorhyncha occipitalis*

Hooked Racket-tailed Tree Pie, *Crypsirina cucullata*

Red-vented Bulbul, *Pycnonotus c. cafer*

Red-eared Bulbul, *Pycnonotus jocosus emeria*

Golden-fronted Fruitsucker, *Chloropsis ap. aurifrons*

Hardwick's Fruitsucker, *Chloropsis hardwickei*

Plate XIV

Spotted-breasted Oriole, *Icterus pectoralis*   Bullock's Oriole, *Icterus bullocki*

Baltimore Oriole, *Icterus galbula*   Purple Grackle, *Quiscalus lugubris*

Troupial, *Icterus icterus*

Bobolink, *Dolichonyx oryzivorus*

There is considerable controversy regarding care for woodpeckers. Some fanciers have reported that they are the easiest birds to maintain, and others have given up trying because they have found them too difficult. They are highly insectivorous by nature, consuming mostly grubs or larval forms of many insects, and it is not possible in captivity to supply them with the necessary live foods. Mealworms as a source of live food are helpful but not enough. The largest variety possible should be offered. In addition to giving standard soft-billed food, which is very slowly acceptable, two very important additions are recommended—peanut butter and a strong nectar. Most woodpeckers accept them readily. The nectar should be as nearly as possible a complete all-in-one food. In addition to honey, vitamins and minerals, it should contain one of several powdered or liquid supplements which are high in protein. This could be a baby food or one of the powdered dietetics which are total supplements.

If a woodpecker is to be kept in a cage, the cage must be higher than its width and the frame made of metal, for these birds rapidly destroy any woodwork. The wall at the back of the cage should be covered with bark, and two or three large branches should be fixed there.

Genus: Colaptes

GOLDEN-WINGED WOODPECKER, YELLOW-SHAFTED FLICKER, *Colaptes a. auratus* Linnaeus
G. Goudspecht; F. Colapte doré, pic doré; D. Goudspecht

DISTRIBUTION: South Carolina, USA.
DESCRIPTION: *Male.* Top of head and neck grey; line crossing eye reddish-cream; sides of head and neck reddish-cream; moustaches and a crescent across chest black. Nape with black horizontal lines; rump white and upper tail coverts have large white streaks. Upper parts whitish, with flanks and sides vinous red with large black blobs. Flight feathers black with 4 or 5 light brown patches, which together form a horizontal band. Median lines yellowish-orange. Irides light brown; upper beak brown; lower beak bluish. Legs and feet bluish-grey. *Female.* Does not have the black moustaches. Length: 13 in. (32 cm).

In the spring several males may pursue a single female, up to the moment when she chooses her mate. After selecting a suitable tree trunk, the two birds at once begin to hollow out their nest. The female lays 4–6 white eggs and as soon as the second egg is laid the parent birds sit on them in turn.

Golden-winged Woodpecker, *Colaptes a. auratus*

The young leave the nest towards the sixth day. Sometimes there is a difference of 10 days between the oldest and the youngest. These birds feed mainly on insects, but will also take berries, nuts and various kinds of fruit—apples, pears and peaches.

Unlike the nuthatches and tree-creepers, woodpeckers cannot climb head down; they always climb upwards or sideways, often making spiral movements, which enable them to escape possible pursuers who cannot follow these agile movements. As they climb these woodpeckers support themselves by their tails, for the tail feathers are very resistant and curve back slightly. When the woodpecker flies towards a tree, it lands at the bottom of the trunk and immediately begins to climb. Its cry, resembling the word 'flicker', can often be heard as it sits on a branch.

They can be tamed and may breed, even in an aviary. They like to sleep in a nesting box where they hang on to the sides. They can be kept in excellent condition on a diet of a general mash supplemented by insects, ants' eggs, mealworms and maggots.

PAMPAS FLICKER, *Colaptes c. campestris* (Vieillot)
G. Pampasspecvt; F. Colapte des Pampas; Pic des Pampas; D. Braziliaanse Zwartkeel-specht

DISTRIBUTION: Eastern Bolivia, Brazil, chiefly the centre and south-east.
DESCRIPTION: *Male.* Throat and top of head black; cheeks, neck and top of breast golden-yellow; back and wings pale yellow with blackish-brown bars. Base of breast and abdomen yellowish-white, and every feather has fine dark transverse bars. Flight feathers greyish-brown with golden yellow median lines. Tail feathers blackish-brown, with transverse yellow bars. Irides dark red; beak dark grey; legs and feet slate-grey. *Female.* Is less highly coloured, and the outlines of the colouring are less marked. Length: 13 in. (32 cm).

Unlike most other woodpeckers, the Pampas-flicker prefers non-wooded semi-desert, where little groups of these birds can be seen looking for termites and other insects. From time to time they fly towards one of the few trees, where they begin to peck with great energy. They also go to the large cacti which are numerous in these regions and which often contain termites' nests. They will hollow out their nests in a large soft-wooded tree. The female lays from 2–6 eggs, and both birds sit. This species nests twice a year.

The White-throated Flicker, *Colaptes campestroides*, from southern Brazil, Paraguay, Uruguay, the greater part of Argentina south to Rio Negro and La Pampa, is similar to the Pampas-flicker, but has a white throat.

Genus: Dinopium

GOLDEN-BACKED THREE-TOED WOOD-PECKER, *Dinopium j. javanense* (Ljungh)

G. Javanischer Stummelspecht; F. Pic tridactyle de Java, Pic Javanais; D. Javaanse Drieteenspecht.

DISTRIBUTION: Malaysia, Java, Sumatra.

DESCRIPTION: Front of scapulars and back golden-yellow; rest of back and rump ruby-red; wing coverts olive-green; rest of wings greenish-black with white patches; tail black. Upper parts black with white patches; top of head and crest red; sides of head marked with two black lines. Length: 10½ in. (27 cm).

These large woodpeckers usually live in pairs along the sides of wooded mountain slopes, Dr. Hagen has observed them in the mangrove forests on the east coast of Sumatra. A pair is very attached to each other; if one is killed, the other throws itself upon the body and does not leave its dead mate, even when approached. These birds are very rare in collections.

GOLDEN-BACKED WOODPECKER, *Dinopium b. benghalense* (Linnaeus)

G. Goldrückenspecht; F. Pic à dos orange; D. Oranje-rugspecht

DISTRIBUTION: Upper Punjab, United Provinces, Bihar and Assam, south to central India, Orissa and Bengal.

DESCRIPTION: *Male.* Top of head and crest bright ruby-red, with occasional black or white marks. Sides of head and neck white, with two black lines. Nape of neck, back and tail black. Scapulars and upper back intense golden-yellow, sometimes with an orange-red sheen. Flight feathers brownish-black with large white and olive-yellow patches, except on the outer feathers. Chin, throat and front of neck black, with numerous fine white streaks. Breast feathers yellowish-white with broad black edges; these form bars across sides and lower tail coverts. Irides reddish-brown; beak lead-grey; feet and legs greenish-grey. *Female.* Black with white marks on forehead. Length: 11 in. (28 cm).

This woodpecker does not live in the forest, but in cultivated fields, bordered by rows of old trees, or near parks and gardens. It is found alone or in pairs, climbing along the trunks of trees or branches, moving along by fits and starts. When at rest, it always keeps its head well erect. With its very strong beak it pulls off the bark of the tree to reach grubs. Its principal food consists of termites, which are picked up from the ground. Its cry is high pitched and sharp; its flight is undulating. The birds do well in a large cage and can be fed on an insectivorous mixture supplemented with ants' eggs and mealworms. They will also eat some sunflower seed and various nuts and apples. They like drinking honeydew.

Genus: Melanerpes

RED-HEADED WOODPECKER, *Melanerpes e. erythrocephalus* (Linnaeus).

G. Rotkopfspecht; F. Pic à tête rouge; D. Roodkopspecht

DISTRIBUTION: South Carolina, USA.

DESCRIPTION: *Male.* Head and neck red; back, wings and tail black; small flight feathers, rump and under parts immaculate white; outer flight feathers have white edging at ends. Irides brown; beak, feet and legs bluish-black. *Female.* Is a little smaller and her colours are less vivid. Length: 9½ in. (24 cm).

This is undoubtedly the best-known American woodpecker. In winter the birds travel in pairs through the forests, looking for a tree suitable for hollowing out their nesting hole. During this period they eat mainly fruit and insects. Before winter comes they make a store of beech-masts and nuts, which they hide in a hole in a tree and cover with a layer of pieces of bark and fragments of wood. When their normal food is not available, because of snow or ice, they open their store and eat their winter supplies. When they capture their prey alive, they pick off the indigestible parts before swallowing it. This preparation takes place on a particular tree stump, which they also use as a sleeping place. These woodpeckers are often found in zoos.

PUCHERAN'S WOODPECKER, *Melanerpes p. pucherani* (Malherbe)

G. Pucheransammelspecht; F. Pic à joues noires; D. Pucheran's Specht

DISTRIBUTION: South-eastern Honduras, Nicaragua, eastern Costa Rica, Panama, the Pacific slope and lower Cauca Valley in Colombia, western Ecuador.

DESCRIPTION: Forehead golden-yellow; crown and nape of neck red. Eyebrows and ear coverts black; there is a white line behind the eye. Back and inner flight feathers black with white transverse lines. Back and upper tail coverts white. Throat whitish, breast olive-grey; the rest of the under parts yellowish-olive-green with black transverse lines. Centre of abdomen red. The tail red, with white edges to central tail feathers. Length: about 7½ in. (20 cm).

These woodpeckers are very common in coastal tropical forests and their way of life is similar to that of *M. e. erythrocephalus.*

Pucheran's Woodpecker, *Melanerpes p. pucherani*

YELLOW-FRONTED WOODPECKER, *Melanerpes f. flavifrons* (Viellot)

DISTRIBUTION: South-central Brazil.

DESCRIPTION: Forehead, throat and sides of head yellow; top of head and abdomen red; sides yellowish to greyish-green with black streaks; back and rump white; the rest of plumage black. Length: about 8 in. (22 cm).

These woodpeckers are suitable for aviaries, and in these

several large nesting boxes should be hung. In 1961 Mr. J. E. Collins, England, succeeded in reproducing this species (*Avicultural Magazine* 67, 1961). Two of the 3 eggs which were laid were hatched after the birds had sat for about 12 days. The two birds took turns to sit and the young flew when they were a month old. They were fed on maggots, ants' eggs, soft fruit and biscuit dipped in nectar.

The Golden-crested Woodpecker, *M. c. cruentatus*, from the Guianas and the Para region of eastern Brazil, came into the collection of a German bird fancier in 1962, although these birds are very rarely imported.

The head, throat and breast of the male are midnight-blue, with a large dark red patch in the centre of the head. This patch is not found in the female. The middle of the abdomen is blood-red, surrounded by an area of black and white stripes. This same pattern is found on the vent region and under the tail. There is a yellow circle round the eyes. The neck has several yellow lines, which grow wider towards the back, where they join to form the golden-yellow crest. Rump white; tail feathers black, with white marks on outer feathers. Beak thin and black; legs bluish-grey.

As these woodpeckers do not touch vegetation, they can be kept in a planted aviary. They sleep in a nesting box. In 1963 Mr. H. Hillemacher succeeded in breeding them in an aviary. The pairs took turns to sit for 18 days in a small nest-box. Two of the 4 eggs hatched, and the young left the nest towards the fourth week. They were fed on a fine mash for insectivorous birds, mixed with white skimmed-milk cheese and mealworms.

These woodpeckers must be protected from cold in winter. The temperature of the aviary should be kept above a minimum of 50°F (10°C).

Genus: Leuconerpes

WHITE WOODPECKER, *Leuconerpes candidus* (Otto)
G. Weissspecht; F. Pic blanc; D. Witte Specht

DISTRIBUTION: Brazil, central Bolivia, Paraguay, Uruguay, northern Argentina.

DESCRIPTION: Head, rump and under parts white; cheeks and a line leading from the eye to the nape of the neck black. In the male the crown and the vent area carry a yellow sheen. Back, wings and tail black, with outer tail feathers having numerous white marks. Length: 13 in. (33 cm).

The habits of White Woodpeckers are similar to those of woodpeckers generally. Most of those imported are already tame, because they are young birds taken from the nest and raised by hand. They like to climb along the netting and peck the logs and branches, where they make small holes. They show a distinct preference for birch trunks, where they like to exercise their beaks. They sleep in large nesting boxes. They should have the diet for insectivorous birds, supplemented by mealworms and ants' eggs.

C. H. Macklin reported a successful breeding in *Avicultural Magazine*, Vol. 11, No. 9, Sept. 1937, of which the following are:

'The pair were fed on insectivorous food, "Mosquito" and fruit, banana, apple, grapes. They took quite a large quantity of fruit. They were kept in a cage in my bird-room until April. They did a good deal of damage to the woodwork but spent most of their time demolishing the natural oak bark with which the cage was lined. Owing to the large amount of fruit in their diet they were rather dirty but kept themselves quite spotless with frequent baths.

On April 19 I put them in one of my outdoor aviaries which I was able to give them to themselves. I put in a few apple branches and fir poles, both horizontal and upright for perches. The woodpeckers immediately inspected the tree trunk and the box and took to the latter for roosting purposes, having slightly enlarged the entrance hole.

On May 29 the first egg was laid in the box. They had made no nest at all and the bottom of the box contained only a few chips of bark. On June 3 there were 4 eggs in the box, but one was only half size and I removed it. They were glossy white and rather small for the size of the birds. The bottom of the box was flat, so I put a handful or so of coarse sawdust under the eggs to stop them rolling about. Both male and female took turns at sitting and did not come off when the aviary was entered for feeding, etc.

On June 15, 2 eggs hatched; the third was infertile. Next day I started a supply of ants' eggs and heard the young birds squeaking when fed. The male did most of the feeding. For the first week they were fed chiefly on mealworms and ants' eggs, but also seemed to take beakfuls of soft food into the nest. After feeding they removed the excreta and dropped it at the end of the flight. On June 21 the 2 chicks were still naked, skin pale pinkish-white, but were just showing tail quills. A week leter their bodies were darker and the wing quills showing. July 2 body feathers just showing. On July 8 one of the chicks was dying, its abdomen was swollen and inflamed.

On July 15 the second chick was well feathered and was showing the lemon-yellow male's patch on the back of the head. On July 21 at 36 days old, the young bird came out of the nest hole and sat on the top of the box for a short while before popping back into the nest. Three days later he was flying strongly about the aviary. He was nearly as big as his parents and his plumage was the same as theirs except that he had no yellow on the abdomen and the bare skin round the eyes was pale blue instead of yellow. He spent a great deal of time in the nest and roosted there at night. By August 15 he was well established and feeding himself.

ORDER: PASSERIFORMES

SUBORDER: EURYLAIMI

Broadbills

Broadbills are rare in captivity, but are very interesting birds. They are highly insectivorous, except for one genus, Calyptomena, which includes quantities of fruits and berries in its diet. Members of this genus are the most frequently available in aviculture and are more easily adapted to aviary life—but it must be emphasised that they are difficult to keep. The acclimatisation procedures described for rollers, trogons and other difficult groups should be followed.

Broadbills are often lethargic in captivity. They can fly only over short distances, and in the wild they hawk their prey. They live in swampy, shady forest areas. In many ways broadbills are like cotingas, having similar courtship displays.

Another characteristic is the elaborate construction of their nests. The teardrop-shaped nests are suspended on long woven strings, usually above water, and they have long ballast tails. The nests, with canopied side openings, are carefully and skilfully woven from many different materials and are camouflaged by bits of moss and lichen. The African species use for the walls large leaves which they fasten together with plant fibre and cobwebs. Broadbills vary in appearance, but the bodies are thick-set, the heads large, the beaks hooked, rather flat, very broad, and, in most species, short. All are unusual, and many are attractive in their colouring.

Genus: Eurylaimus

BANDED BROADBILL, *Eurylaimus j. javanicus* Horsfield

G. Hornrachen, Braunköpfbreitrachen; F. Eurylaime de Java; D. Javaanse Hapvogel

DISTRIBUTION: Indonesia.

DESCRIPTION: *Male.* Crown and throat reddish-grey, more reddish-brown behind neck and on nape. Breast and under parts pale wine red. A narrow band around the breast is black with a reddish glow. Elongated scapulars, mantle, wings and centre of rump black, with sulphur-yellow markings. Tail feathers black; with a narrow white transverse stripe near the edge. Beak broad and thick, blackish in colour, but grey along cutting edges. Feet brownish-yellow. *Female* lacks the band across the breast. Length: 8¾ in. (22·2 cm).

The Black and Yellow Broadbill, or Black-headed Broadbill, *Eurylaimus ochromalus* (Raffles), from Borneo and Sumatra, is about 2 in. (5 cm) smaller. Upper parts and head black, with yellow on wings, upper tail and under tail coverts. Breast, sides and abdomen pale pink, blending gradually with the yellow under tail coverts. A broad white band across the throat extends on to sides of neck. This is followed by a broad black band dividing the throat and upper chest, and this connects with the black upper parts. Beak broad, thick and blackish in colour. Feet and legs brownish.

Banded Broadbill, *Eurylaimus j. javanicus*

Genus: Corydon

DUSKY BROADBILL, *Corydon s. sumatranus* (Raffles)
G. Dunklesbreitmaul; F. Eurylaime sombre; D. Sumatraanse Hapvogel

DISTRIBUTION: Sumatra.

DESCRIPTION: Bill broad and thick, the noticeably curved upper mandible having side edges which are S-shaped. Main coloration black. On the throat is a leather-like shield. There is a white stripe on the wings, and also just before the end of the tail. Some reddish-yellow feathers in the middle of the back. Beak and bare skin around eyes lustrous carmine red; tip of beak blue. Feet and legs blackish. Length: 9½ in. (24 cm).

These broadbills occur in small groups in the dense humid forests, where they live mainly on insects. They are mostly found along the banks of rivers and swampy pools, where they search for worms and shellfish, which they also eat in addition to their main insect food.

The split in the beak is carried back to under the eye, so that the opening of the beak is unusually large.

Dusky Broadbill, *Corydon s. sumatranus*

SUBFAMILY: CALYPTOMENINAE

Genus: Calyptomena

GREEN BROADBILL, LESSER GREEN BROADBILL, *Calyptomena v. viridis* Raffles

G. Smaragdrake, Kleines Smaragdbreitmaul; F. Eury-laime èmeraude; D. Smaragdgroene-Hapvogel

DISTRIBUTION: Thailand, Malaysia, Borneo.
DESCRIPTION: *Male.* Very bright green with black markings on wings, cheeks and above lores. Flights and tail black. A white spot occurs above lores. An unusual crest, emanating from the forehead, extends forward over most of the beak. This crest is not large but it is very dense. *Female.* Duller and lacks the black markings. Length: about 6½ in. (16·5 cm). Female is somewhat larger than the male.

Green Broadbills are more easily adapted to aviculture than are others of the genus because they eat more fruit and are

therefore already accustomed to some inert food.

The two remaining Green Broadbills are Hose's Broadbill, *Calyptomena hosii* Sharpe, and Whitehead's Broadbill, *Calyptomena whiteheadi* Sharpe, both from the mountains of Borneo. Both are larger than *C. v. viridis,* but are similar in most characteristics. Hose's Broadbill is about 8 in. (20 cm) long. The male has a beautiful shade of bright blue extending from the upper breast through the undertail coverts. Females retain the black markings and have blue on the abdomen. Whitehead's Broadbill, in a more restricted range in the vicinity of Mount Kinabalu, is about 10 in. (25 cm) in length. Black markings are more extensive and more irregular than those of *C. v. viridis,* and the throat is black.

The Green Broadbill appeared for the first time in the Zoological Gardens of London in 1928.

SUBORDER: TYRANNI

SUPERFAMILY: FURNARIOIDEA

FAMILY: DENDROCOLAPTIDAE

Genus: Campylorhamphus

RED-BILLED SCYTHE-BILL, *Campylorhamphus trochilirostris* (Lichtenstein)

G. Sichelbaumhacker; F. Falcirostria bec en sabre; D. Kolibriesnavelige Muisspecht

DISTRIBUTION: Brazil.
DESCRIPTION: Back and abdomen reddish-brown; head, neck and breast brown with white spots. Behind and under the eye there are white stripes. Wings, upper tail coverts and tail feathers dark chestnut brown. Beak about 2½ in. (6·4 cm) long, in the shape of a sickle and reddish-brown. Length: 8½ in. (21·6 cm).

This genus has 13 species and 48 subspecies, all of which live in South America, and in their behaviour strongly recall tree-creepers and woodpeckers. In the tropical forests they

search the tree trunks for insects, which form their only food. Their pointed and curved bills enable them to pick insects out of deep crevices. The Red-billed Scythe-bills prefer to live in mountainous regions where tall palm trees grow. Like woodpeckers, they clutch the trunk, while they insert their beaks deep into holes or between the bark. They nest in tree hollows, but, as their beaks are not strong enough to excavate for themselves, they make use of those deserted by woodpeckers. They remove the old substrata and then carry in fresh leaves and bark. The 2 white eggs are incubated alternately by both parents and after about 15 days the naked young hatch. They remain for about 3 weeks in the nest, after which they are fed for another 2 weeks by the parents.

FAMILY: FURNARIIDAE

Genus: Furnarius

OVENBIRD, *Furnarius r. rufus* (Gmelin)

G. Töpfervogel; F. Fournir roux; D. Ovenvogel

DISTRIBUTION: Southern Brazil, Uruguay, central and eastern Argentina.

DESCRIPTION: Upper parts rust-brown, mantle and head lighter brown, flights grey, throat white. From the eye a rust-coloured yellow stripe runs towards the back. Under parts light brown. Beak brownish. Iris, feet and legs yellowish-brown. Length: 7½ in. (19 cm).

In their habits ovenbirds are somewhat like thrushes. They do not stay only in the trees, but often come to the ground look for food, which consists chiefly of insects. To catch these they take great leaps, and they fly only for short distances. Ovenbirds are popular with the natives, not so much because they exterminate insects as because of the ingenious nests they build in trees, on roofs, telegraph poles and fence posts. They find a place where they can first build a horizontal foundation of loam, about 3–5 in. (7·6–12·7 cm) thick. Remains of plants are often mixed into this thick layer of loam. The birds carry lumps of mud to the nest and trample these flat with their feet. When the foundation is ready they make an upright brim all round, 2 in. (5 cm) high, and on this they build more layers, which incline towards the inside; they repeat the process until the inside walls touch each other. The nest becomes as hard as stone in the sun and reaches a height of about 6 in. (15 cm). At the front an entrance is left of some 2 in. (5 cm) wide and 4 in. (10 cm) high. After this the birds construct a sort of spiral threshold transversely across the nest, behind which there is the breeding nest, which they line with grass and straw. A complete nest weighs from 11–22 lb (5–10 kg). They lay 4–6 eggs, which are incubated by both parents. A nest is used only for one season, usually for 2 clutches. They are later used by a number of other birds, usually sparrows or swallows.

Ovenbirds possess a cry which is shrill and shrieking, and frequently uttered. They seize large pieces of food in one claw and then bite bits off it. When they walk on the ground

Ovenbird, *Furnarius r. rufus*

they hold their head erect and wag their tail up and down. In Brazil they are popularly called 'Joa de bano' ('Pavement Johnnies'). They soon become tame, and, with a diet consisting of soaked bread, boiled rice, live insects and small pieces of raw meat, they can be kept in good condition in captivity.

FAMILY: FORMICARIIDAE

LINED ANT-SHRIKE, *Thamnophilus p. palliatus* (Lichtenstein)

G. Rostbrauner Bindenwollrücken; F. Thamnophile rouge; D. Miersperwer

DISTRIBUTION: Brazil.

DESCRIPTION: Crown black. Upper parts black with fine white transverse stripes; under parts black with white transverse stripes. Flanks flecked with yellowish-white. On tip of blackish beak is a small hook, bending downwards. Feet and legs brownish. *Female*. Has also on the top of her head fine white stripes. Length: 7 in. (17·8 cm).

This extensive family has 52 species and 224 subspecies, which all live in Central and South America. As the name indicates, ants form the major part of their food, and the birds spend the greater part of the day on the ground in the tropical forests. Sometimes whole armies of ants travel in formation and form an easy prey for the ant-shrikes, who travel with them.

Lined Anti-shrikes build bowl-shaped nests in bushes low above the ground. The 2–3 white eggs, marked with dark violet scribblings, are incubated alternately by both parent birds for 15 days, and the young leave the nest some 12 days later. The rump is covered with soft down-like feathers, which is how the birds get their German name of 'Wollrücken' ('woolly-back').

In 1933 these birds were seen for the first time at the Zoological Gardens in Berlin. Their behaviour is reminiscent of shrikes. They are not particularly shy, and may be seen in gardens, parks, and along the edges of woods. They live singly or in pairs. They have seldom been included in collections.

ROYAL ANT-THRUSH, ANT BIRD, *Grallaria v. varia* (Boddaert)

G. Konigsameisenstelzer; F. Fourmillier; D. Grondmiervogel

DISTRIBUTION: Guyana, Surinam, French Guiana, and probably adjacent parts of northern Brazil.

DESCRIPTION: *Male*. Main colouring brown flecked with white. Crown ash-grey down to neck, with black feathered edges. Back brown with yellow-brown shafts. Wings reddish-brown and blackish-brown, tail rusty-red. Lores, cheeks, and a stripe from chin to throat, yellowish-white with black feathered edges. Under parts yellowish-brown, upper throat feathers white with black edges. Upper mandible brown, lower mandible somewhat lighter, and near the chin reddish-white. Iris brown; feet and legs reddish-grey. *Female*. Is dark brown and has no grey on crown. Length: 8½ in. (21·6 cm).

Royal Ant-thrushes occur in 27 species in Central and South America, and are distinguished from the other members of the family by their long legs, their short stumpy tail and large head. They are widespread and live in dense jungles, where they nearly always keep to the ground, under the shade of the overhanging foliage. Because of their excellent camouflage colouring, they are seldom observed. In early morning they can often by heard uttering their luring call—a whistle. No nest is built, but the female lays her 2 eggs on dry leaves. They are whitish-green, here and there flecked with brown.

The birds live exclusively on live insects and worms. With their strong claws they scratch in the loose soil and if they get hold of a worm they pick small pieces off it. They will also eat young mice and young birds in the nest.

They were seen in the Berlin Zoological Gardens for the first time in 1902. During the daytime they kept themselves hidden, but towards evening they became lively and sprang around the branches of the trees. They were fed with worms, fresh ants' eggs and raw meat chopped up finely. At present they are rare in aviculture.

Royal Ant-thrush, *Grallaria v. varia*

FAMILY: CONOPOPHAGIDAE

Genus: Conopophaga

CHESTNUT-BELLIED GNATEATER, *Conopophaga a. aurita* (Gmelin)

G. Braunbrustmückenfresser; F. Conopophage à ceinture châtaine; D. Bruinborst-Muggeneyer

DISTRIBUTION: Guyana, Surinam, French Guiana, Brazil north of the Amazon from Manaus to the Rio Jamunda.
DESCRIPTION: *Male.* Crown dark chestnut-brown. Back olive-brown with black feathered edges. Wings and tail black. Lores, sides of head and throat black. A long silvery-white stripe runs from behind the eye to the neck. Breast bright chestnut-brown, sides of body olive-brown, centre of abdomen and under tail coverts yellowish-white. *Female.* Has white lores and a white eyebrow stripe. Sides of head and throat whitish-yellow. Length: 5 in. (12·7 cm) of which tail is 1 in. (2·5 cm) long.

Chestnut-bellied Gnateaters are similar to pittas and royal ant-thrushes in appearance and in their habits. They have short, rounded-off wings and never fly long distances. They live in the jungle or under dense scrub and are hardly ever seen during the daytime. They seek their food, which consists of worms, snails and numerous insects, on the ground. They utter a peculiar hissing sound. For a nest they form a shallow basin of branches and moss, gathered together between dry leaves. Their 2 eggs are spotted with brown.

FAMILY: TYRANNIDAE

Tyrant Flycatchers

H. J. BATES AND R. L. BUSENBARK

Tyrant Flycatchers form an enormous group of birds which are found from Canada to the southern part of South America. They are the New World counterparts of the better known family Musicapidae, the Old World Fly-catchers. Tyrant Flycatchers are not important in aviculture, partly because they are too difficult to maintain in captivity and partly because most of them are dusky and unattractive. There are exceptions, of course. Some have interesting and beautiful plumage; and one very hardy species, the Great Kiskadee, has been available from time to time. This is the only Tyrant Flycatcher the writers have ever seen mentioned on exporters' lists.

Most Tyrants are reluctant to accept artificial diets; and, even when they do, the diet must be particularly refined. The standard softbill mixture will not suffice for very long. Because of dietary deficiencies or an unbalanced food, Tyrant Flycatchers in seemingly good health will frequently drop dead for no otherwise explainable reason. Overfeeding of mealworms frequently causes trouble.

Among some of the more attractive and interesting Tyrant Flycatchers which might become popular if availability and dietary problems could be overcome are the following: Fork-tailed and Scissor-tailed Flycatchers, both with long streaming tails; Long-tailed Tyrants, which imitate some of the Long-tailed Manakins; Vermilion Flycatchers, of which there are several kinds and which fade in captivity; Royal Flycatchers, with their fine flaring, colourful lateral crests.

Most Tyrant Flycatchers have two characteristics in common: large, soft-looking eyes surrounded by bare skin, and long, slender, hooked beaks surrounded by stiff bristles. In captivity they seem relatively peaeeful, but in the wild state they are noted for their successful aggression against birds several sizes larger than themselves.

GREAT KISKADEE, KISKADEE FLYCATCHER, SULPHURY
TYRANT, *Pitangus sulphuratus* (Linnaeus)

G. Schwefelgelber Tyrann; Bentevi; F. Tyran á ventre
jaune; D. Zwartgele Tiran

DISTRIBUTION: Widespread from Texas to Brazil.

DESCRIPTION: Upper parts, from lower nape, brown. Under
parts, from throat to under tail coverts, bright yellow. A
dominant white eyebrow line covers the narrow forehead
and arches over eyes, trailing backwards to lower nape.
Thick beak is black, and a black mask covers the lores and
surrounds the eyes and cheeks, extending back to sides of
neck. A wide flaring patch of white covers chin and throat,
and tapers up the sides of neck to the end of black mask.
Black on large head extends down to white eyebrow, and a
broad band of orange-yellow extends down centre of crown
from forehead to back of crown. These feathers are bristly
and slightly erectile. Body is heavy and tail medium-short.
Feet and legs blackish. Length: about 9 in. (22 cm).

This species does not follow the information given in the
opening article. It is very hardy and easily transferred to

Great Kiskadee, *Pitangus sulphuratus*

standard softbilled diets but likes a little extra raw meat and
live food.

There are several other Tyrant Flycatchers of different sizes
which fit this general description, but most are duller in
colouring. A successful breeding reported in *Avicultural
Magazine*, Vol. 78, No. 6, Nov./Dec. 1972, is as follows:

> 'Two Great Kiskadees, *Pitangus sulphuratus*, were reared at
> Padstow Bird Gardens, Cornwall, England, from a pair bred in
> 1970 at Winged World, Morecambe. Although the parents had
> been reared in a tropical house, they adapted well to, and
> reared their youngsters in, an outdoor planted aviary, of ground
> area 200 square ft and height 7 ft, constructed against two
> Cornish stone walls. The incubation period was 14–15 days and
> the chicks left the nest when they were 25–26 days old. They
> were reared on a diet of fruit, "insectile food", maggots, meal-
> worms and strips of fish and raw meat, to which had been added
> vitamins and mineral salts.'

VERMILION FLYCATCHER, SCARLET FLYCATCHER,
Pyrocephalus r. rubinus Boddaert

G. Rubintyrann; F. Tyran rouge écarlate; D. Robijn-
tiran

DISTRIBUTION: South-west USA to northerly part of South
America.

DESCRIPTION: *Male.* Crown and under parts vermilion. Lores,
ear coverts, back, wings and tail blackish-brown. Edges of
quill feathers, wing coverts and tail white. Throat entirely
white. On the lowest part of the breast and on the remainder
of the under parts is a red cere. Beak blackish-brown; iris
light brown; legs and feet greyish brown. *Female.* Greyish-
brown on upper parts and white, with greyish brown stripes,
on under parts. Length 5½ in. (14 cm).

The Vermilion Flycatcher, *Pyrocephalus r. rubinus*, is with-

out doubt one of the most beautiful of this extensive family.
The male, when flying, gleams and glitters like a jewel. The
feathers of the crest can be set upright.

The birds live along the edges of forests, on the waterside,
and in the open fields. They sit upright high on the branch
of a tree, on the lookout for insects, which they always catch
on the wing. With their prey they then return to their perch;
with one claw they clasp the large insect, while they bite
small pieces off it.

These birds were first imported into Germany in 1951, and
were kept by Dr. J. Steinbacher, who gave a full account of
them in *Die Gefiederte Welt*, 1952, section 7. The birds
quickly get used to their new diet, which can consist of a fine
insectivorous food and mealworms. The latter must be
given twice a day, and not more than 4 or 5 for each bird.
The soft food may be dampened with carrot scraping or
shredded apple. The birds accustom themselves equally well
to a spacious cage or an outside aviary, provided this is
connected with heated night quarters. They greatly need
warmth and in periods when the sun does not provide this
they should be given the benefit of heaters. It is disappoint-
ing that the male bird loses his magnificent red colouring,
which becomes a spotty red and white. Pairs remain together
and constantly maintain contact by soft coaxing calls.

The birds are fond of being sprayed now and again. They
soon become tame and will accept mealworms out of one's
hand.

Indigestible table scraps will be regurgitated.

Although the birds will build their basin-shaped nests, in
which they lay their 3 white eggs, no breeding results have
been reported so far.

EASTERN KING BIRD, AMERICAN KING BIRD,
Tyrannus tyrannus Linnaeus

G. Königsvogel; F. Tyran royal; D. Koningsvogel

DISTRIBUTION: Temperate North America. In the winter,
Cuba, East, Central and South America.

DESCRIPTION: Head black; in centre of crown there is a large
orange-red spot; neck and back grey. Upper tail coverts
black with white tips. Cheeks and under parts white. There
is a greyish tinting over the head. Sides of breast grey. Wings
blackish-brown with light feathered borders. Tail black with
a white tip. Iris brown; bill black; legs and feet black.
Length: 8¾ in. (22·4 cm).

Although these birds live in woods, they generally visit the
outskirts because they catch their prey, which consists

Eastern King Bird, *Tyrannus tyrannus*

mainly of all kinds of flying insects, when on the wing. They often come into the vicinity of settlements, where they are regarded as guardians of the poultry, as from their high perches in a tree or a telegraph pole they spot small birds of prey; with a loud chatter, they fly down and attack them. The poultry know this and flee under carts and into sheds until the danger has passed.

Their flight is as swift as an arrow, and is also directional. They can, however, glide through the air and hover skilfully. They are less speedy on the ground. In their own hunting territory they do not tolerate other birds, and will pursue magpies and crows, and birds that are much bigger than they are themselves. The crest generally remains hidden under the grey feathers of the head, but, as soon as the birds get excited, the red feathers of the crest shoot up in the air. They serve, therefore, to avert danger, and also play a part during mating. The birds nest in high trees. On the fork of a branch they will attach their basin-shaped nests to the forks of branches with twigs and grasses; the nests are lined with hairs, plant wool and feathers. The female builds the nest by herself, and also incubates by herself the 3–4 pinkish-white eggs, which are spotted with brown. Incubation takes 13 days. The male bird guards the nest and chases away all intruders.

These birds are imported from time to time. They are not suitable for a cage as they are naturally very lively. In an aviary they do themselves justice only when they can be kept with larger birds which are able to defend themselves. They are a menace to smaller birds. If fed on universal food, dampened with scrapings of carrot or apple, some thinly sliced raw meat and plenty of living insects, they can be kept alive and well.

FAMILY: PIPRIDAE

Manakins

BY H. J. BATES AND R. L. BUSENBARK

Manakins are somewhat closely related to cotingas and have several basic characteristics of tanagers. They are rare in aviculture but have become more numerous in recent years. Many manakins are aggressive to their own kind after settling down in aviaries, which they claim as their own territories, but they live well with finches. They are very steady in aviaries and are therefore easily observed.

Manakins are relatively small, about the size of finches. They have stocky bodies with large heads and short necks and thick, broad, short beaks. Several have long tail appendages and other decorations. Their favourite habitats are dense forests or thick undergrowth. They range from Mexico to Argentina, with 59 species in the family.

Manakins in the wild have very interesting characteristics. Most seem to be polygamous, and females are very drab in colouring. They do all the incubating and rear their young with no assistance from the male. Males are usually very attractive, and many engage in complicated nuptial displays, which are usually impressive and often noisy. Some displays occur high in trees but most are centred around a small area on the ground, which is kept free from litter. In many characteristics the displays are similar to those of the Cock-of-the-Rock, with group participation and an admiring audience of females and other males awaiting their turn. The display can also consist of several males competing for one female.

The displays include elaborate stances, frequent turnings, and stiff-legged hopping, mostly to show off their colours to best advantage. Outspread wings, particularly upwards, and lowered heads, accompanied by beak snapping or odd wing slapping and rustling sounds, are particularly characteristic. Some displays include aerial acrobatics performed by pairs of well coordinated males. Unfortunately, the displays are not frequent in captivity.

Manakins are considered to be delicate, but they accept artificial diets more readily than do cotingas. Because they are rare and somewhat expensive, the writers know of no one who has taken the risk of testing their hardiness regarding temperature extremes.

The diet should be very refined. Basically it is similar to the diet for cotingas, except that the fruit ratio is higher. Nectar similar to that supplied for cotingas is also more important both during and after acclimatisation. The total dietary ingredients need not be quite so complicated as those offered to cotingas. Rice, sweet potatoes, meat and most live food can be omitted. Usually two meals a day are offered. Necessary animal protein is available in the insectivorous mixture and in the fortified nectar.

One successful diet includes grated hard-boiled egg and carrot mixed with banana and mynah meal, with grapes and diced bananas added to the top to create interest. If they can be induced to eat mynah pellets they will benefit from the total nutrition in that food substance.

Bananas are a very controversial item of diet for birds. Many bird keepers, including the writers, consider the bananas available on the market to be dangerous for many of the more delicate birds. All bananas shipped to foreign markets are harvested before they have ripened, and the unnatural ripening process causes digestive upsets to delicate systems. Moreover, if given bananas many of the fussy feeders will feast upon them to the exclusion of other more important foods.

The main parts of the diet are the variety of fruits, the insectivorous mixture, and nectar. Peanut butter and pound cake are helpful, and the supplements added to the nectar and fruit are particularly important. If milk is to be included, it should be canned evaporated milk rather than fresh milk, as the latter is particularly harsh to delicate digestive systems. Soya powder mixed with water is better than milk.

Manakins were once considered suitable only for very advanced aviculturists. However, as feeding methods, transport, and acclimatisation procedures improve, these birds are becoming available more frequently. They are very interesting birds and are well worth the extra effort required to maintain them in good condition.

BLUE-BACKED MANAKIN, SUPERB MANAKIN, *Chiroxiphia pareola* (Linnaeus)

G. Prachtschnurrvogel, Blaubrutpipra; F. Manakin tijé; D. Blauwrugmanneke

DISTRIBUTION: Colombia, Venezuela, French Guiana, Guyana, Surinam, Brazil, Bolivia and the islands of Trinidad and Tobago.

DESCRIPTION: *Male.* Has two dominant colour splashes. A large mantle area of brilliant turquoise-blue includes scapulars and upper back. A large triangular crown patch is brilliant red and partially erectile, almost like a crest. Rest of colouring black. Beak black. Feet and legs yellowish. *Female* dull greenish, paler on under parts. Immature males have the red crown patch, but are otherwise like the females. Length: about 5 in. (12·5 cm).

These birds need warmth and should be provided with a heated aviary where the temperature is kept steady at 75°F (24°C). They should also be provided with facilities for bathing, the water being luke warm. Similar to *Chiroxiphia pareola* is the Lance-tailed Manakin, *Chiroxiphia lanceolata*, from Panama, Colombia and Venezuela.

The bird is slightly larger. Central tail feathers are pointed and longer than the others. There is a paler shade of sky blue on back, and the black plumage is tinged with grey on face, head and under parts. Irides black. Feet and legs are orange. *Female.* Olive-green instead of green, and under parts have yellowish tones in the lower areas. Central tail feathers are longer and pointed, as in the male.

RED-CAPPED MANAKIN, RED-HEADED MANAKIN, YELLOW-THIGHED MANAKIN, *Pipra mentalis* (Sclater)

G. Gelbhosenpipra, Belbschenkelschnurrvogel; F. Manakin à cuisses jaunes; D. Geeldijmanneke

DISTRIBUTION: Mexico, Ecuador.

DESCRIPTION: *Male.* Has a flaming red-orange hood covering the head and nape, but not the throat. Thighs, under sides of wings, and a small chin area, pale yellow. Remaining areas, including throat, black. Has a slight crest. Iris whitish; feet and legs yellow. *Female.* Dark, dull green, paler below and mixed with yellow on throat and abdomen. Lacks the crest. Length: about 4½ in. (12·6 cm).

The subspecies, *P. m. minor*, in the more southerly range, is a little smaller and has a darker shade of red.

Red-capped Manakins live, like most of their related species, in the dense forests, where they climb through the branches, trying to clear the small beetles and insects. They are always in action in small groups. They also eat berries of all kinds. With their secondary wing feathers enlarged, twisted and stiffened, the birds are able to produce a droning and rattling noise, which they also make during their remarkable dances at mating time. With soft coaxing calls, 4 or 5 male birds lure the females to their mating territory, which is generally concentrated on a high, horizontal branch from which all the leaves have been entirely stripped. In addition to flute-like sounds, they make all kinds of other noises, which they produce with the help of their feet, wings and tail. They raise their crest feathers and lift themselves high up, so that their yellow thighs are clearly visible. They trip along over the branch, make quick turns, and fly from branch to branch. The females also utter sounds which spur the male birds on. Mating follows and then the females fly away. The females build their shallow shell-shaped nests in a fork of the branch, where they lay 2 spotted eggs, which are incubated by the female and hatched in 19–21 days. She defends her nest herself, when she reproduces the various dance movements and noises of the male bird. When the young appear she feeds them every hour with berries, centipedes and all kinds of insects, which she regurgitates from her crop. The young remain about 2 weeks in the nest. The male chicks look like their mother.

WHITE-BEARDED MANAKIN, EDWARDS'S MANAKIN, *Manacus manacus* (Linnaeus)

G. Mönchschmuckvogel, Weissäbelpipra; F. Manakin moine, Manakin barbu; D. Monnikspipra.

DISTRIBUTION: Colombia, Ecuador, Peru, Venezuela, Brazil, Paraguay, Argentina and Trinidad.

DESCRIPTION: *Male.* Main colour black and white. A black hood stretches from forehead over head as far as nape of neck and to side of head as far as eyes. Wings, from scapulars, uppermost part of back and tail, black. Lowest part of back and upper tail coverts grey. Lower parts white, as is a wide band on neck and upper mantle. The lengthened feathers on sides of throat form a kind of beard. Bill black; feet and legs yellow. *Female.* Olive-green, bright yellow on upper parts; somewhat paler on lower parts; throat greyish. Length: 4½ in. (11·3 cm).

These ornamental birds travel through the dense brushwood in small groups. They are very active and utter a typical sound with their flight feathers, recalling the noise of a spinning wheel. At times, with the help of their beaks and feet, the birds add to the noise by making sounds resembling sharp crackings and rappings, and now and then a dull buzzing or humming noise is heard. The male bird prepares a display territory on the ground between two saplings, where he clears the space of small twigs, branches and leaves. He then starts to fly backwards and forwards between the trees, to the accompaniment of the marvellous assortment of noises with which he attracts the female birds to him. He blows through the cavity in his larynx, which causes the feathers around his throat to form a voluminous beard.

These birds eat both berries and insects. The females build shallow bowl-shaped nests in trees and lay 2 whitish eggs which are covered with innumerable brown spots and stripes. Incubation lasts 3 weeks.

FAMILY: COTINGIDAE

SUBFAMILY: COTINGINAE

Cotingas, Bell Birds, Umbrella Birds

BY H. J. BATES AND R. L. BUSENBARK

The Cotinga family comprises some of the most bizarre and unusual birds ever kept in captivity. They exhibit an extraordinary diversity in colour combinations and forms. Some are very colourless and resemble several of the less attractive Tyrant Flycatchers. There are almost 90 species and among these are the particularly unusual Fruit Crows, Bell Birds and Umbrella Birds. Some authorities class Cocks-of-the-Rock in this family, but they are treated separately in this work.

Most Cotingas occur in Central America and the northern areas of South America, but one reasonably attractive species of Becard occurs as far north as Texas and Arizona. Others range as far as Argentina, and one very drab Becard occurs in Jamaica. Of the relatively few members which have been kept in captivity, all must be considered rare. Only the Bare-throated Bell Bird becomes available through commercial avicultural channels with any frequency, and even this species is not easily obtainable. It is perhaps the species most easily adapted to artificial diets, and this may partly be because many of those available are youngsters, which adapt far more successfully than adults.

If there is one common characteristic attributable to all members of the family so far as the bird keeper is concerned, it is the extreme difficulty in transferring Cotingas to avicultural diets. Once this task is accomplished, Cotingas settle down quite well to aviary life.

Not many people would venture to test their hardiness by subjecting them to overbearing companions or hazardous temperatures. The writers have seen Cotingas and Bell Birds in outdoor aviaries in Southern California doing very well in all seasons, but this could not be used as a criterion for most areas.

The diet for Cotingas in the wild state is fruit and insects in variable quantities for different species. They take to fruit in captivity reasonably well, even although it is of a different nature from that which they would find in their natural habitat. Live insects are difficult to supply, but a good portion (not exclusively mealworms) should be given during the slow transition period, when insectivorous foods can be gradually increased by mixing with fruit. During the acclimatisation period, and even beyond, a strong high-protein nectar food will help to maintain the necessary degree of nutrition. This should, however, be considered a secondary item in the diet. One successful diet includes diced fruits in variety, soaked raisins, cooked sweet potato and boiled rice, grated hard-boiled eggs, ground horse-meat or beef, ground insectivorous food, powdered bone meal, and a powdered vitamin–mineral supplement. This is all mixed together in a crumbly manner; it should not be sloppy nor too solid. At first to entice the birds to eat, more diced fruit and mynah pellets can be sprinkled on top of the mixture. Even live food can be sprinkled on top to encourage acceptance of the new diet. Eventually a greater increase of mynah pellet consumption would be desirable.

Female Cotingas are usually drably coloured, some in sooty browns and others in dusky greys or greens. Tityras, Attilas and Becards belong to the Cotinga family, but these usually hold little interest for bird keepers. They are not flamboyant or colourful enough to warrant the difficult acclimatisation process. As mentioned before, very few Cotingas have been available to bird keepers. With improvements in diet, increased knowledge, and establishment of better sources of supply, Cotingas may become better known to aviculturists. One species, the Black-throated Cotinga, *Pipreola riefferii*, successfully nested in 1962 in the aviaries of Edward Marshall Boehm in New Jersey, USA.

ORANGE-BREASTED COTINGA, ORANGE BREASTED FRUITEATER, *Pipreola jucunda* (Boissoneau)
G. Orangebrustkotinga; F. Cotinga à poitrine orange; D. Oranjeborst-Cotinga

DISTRIBUTION: Colombia and Ecuador.
DESCRIPTION: *Male.* The bright orange beak is broad and flattish and with the golden irides contrasts sharply with the shiny black head. An extensive broad bib of bright orange covers the upper breast and encircles the sides of neck in a very narrow line. An irregular black line borders the lower area of orange on upper breast. Most of the under parts are yellow, with green on the sides. The juncture of green and yellow is irregular and streaky. Lower abdomen, flanks and under tail coverts have the yellow shaded with green. Upper parts below the nape bright green. Feet and legs dark yellow. *Female.* Lacks the orange on breast and is mostly dark green, paler below and streaked with yellow on breast. Head dark greenish-black. Length: about 7½ in. (19·25 cm).

These birds live in pairs in the rain forests, both in the tops of trees and in the lower fruit-bearing bushes. They are quiet birds, whose fairly harsh voices are heard only during the breeding season, when the male birds perform their remarkable dances high in the tree-tops.
They were first imported into England, where they were kept in a tropical aviary. They arrived in Germany in 1965.

As the birds come from high mountainous regions, tropical warmth is by no means desirable. Dr. Geisler of Heidelberg, who was taking care of the birds, came to the conclusion that they were most comfortable in a temperature of about 65–68°F (18–20°C) and in a humidity of 60%. He fed the birds with a variety of chopped fruit, boiled rice and boiled mealworms, with a small quantity of 'Federvit', just enough to cover the point of a knife.
P. jucunda have bred in San Diego Zoo, USA.

GOLDEN-BREASTED COTINGA, GOLDEN-BREASTED FRUITEATER, *Pipreola aureopectus*
G. Goddenbrustkotinga

DISTRIBUTION: Colombia and Venezuela.
DESCRIPTION: Similar to *P. jucunda*, but less bright. *Male.* Yellow replaces the orange, and the head has dark green on facial areas. Bluish tinges occur on the back of head, back and upper tail coverts. *Female.* Has yellowish streaks on throat.

BLACK-THROATED COTINGA, *Pipreola riefferii*
D. Zwartkeel-Cotinga

DISTRIBUTION: Colombia, Venezuela and Bolivia.
DESCRIPTION: Strongly resembles the Orange-breasted Cotinga, *Pipreola jucunda*, but has a black front and breast.

The black on the head is covered by a green cere, and the front is black and is bordered by a yellow band, which forms a collar. Upper parts dark green, lower parts yellowish-green. Some wing coverts have white tips. Tail green with a yellow tip above, and below is greyish-black. Iris brown; bill, legs and feet brilliant red. *Female*. Greener on lower parts, with yellowish spots on wing coverts.

In January 1961 pairs of both species arrived in the New Jersey aviaries of Edward M. Boehm, where they were taken care of by Charles Everitt, who gives an extensive report in the *Avicultural Magazine*, Vol. 69, No. 4, July/August, pp. 141–4. The birds had first to pass the winter in a cage, and two did not survive. The others were later transferred to a large aviary, which they shared with Golden Orioles, Toerakos and Bell Birds, among others. The aviary was 18 yds (16·4 m) long and 6 yds (5·5 m) wide; running water and heating had been installed.

In one of the many trees that stood in the aviary the female of the Black-throated Cotinga built, out of grass, roots and horse-hair, a basin-shaped nest in a basket previously placed in position. Everything was woven together with horse-hair. Two light-brown eggs were laid. The male bird fed the female in the nest and kept all other birds away. Incubation took about 19 days. The young were provided solely with live food, consisting of flies, moths, mealworms and other insects. After 10 days their diet was augmented by fruit, minced raw meat and small fish, which the parent birds fished out of the water. The youngsters left the nest after 3 weeks.

BANDED COTINGA, BANDED CHATTERER, *Cotinga maculata* (Müller)

G. Halsbandkotinga; F. Cotinga cordon bleu, Cotinga tityre; D. Blauwe Cotinga

DISTRIBUTION: Eastern Brazil.

DESCRIPTION: *Male*. Main colour is a deep ultramarine blue, with scattered black marks. Throat, breast and upper abdomen deep purple. A narrow blue band runs across head. Flight and tail feathers black with blue outer fringes. Irides brown; the beak, legs and feet dark brown. Length: in. (21 cm). *Female*. Brown with whitish breast; feathers of abdomen have yellow edges.

The cotingas live in the depths of very humid forests, in perpetual shade. They are quiet birds, which can spend hours sitting on a branch. Their sweet call is seldom heard. The Banded Cotinga is certainly one of the finest in appearance; this is why the natives have cruelly hunted them, as well for their tasty flesh. Prince von Weid mentions that the purple colour changes into a yellowish-orange when the skins are dried near a charcoal fire. This violet colour is not the consequence of a particular structure of the feathers, producing a refraction of the light, but results from a pigment called 'cotingine'.

The mating display which takes place in the tree-tops has not yet been sufficiently studied. The female constructs a goblet-shaped nest where she lays 2–4 eggs, on which she probably sits herself.

The Banded Continga was imported for the first time to London in 1875, and shortly afterwards was also to be found in the Berlin Zoo. The birds were fed on dates and raw meat sprinkled with sugar; and they also ate insects. They very much enjoyed a bath. In winter they need a heated aviary.

The Purple-breasted Cotinga, *Cotinga cotinga*, is horizon-blue. The flight feathers and the tail feathers are black. The lower parts are a purplish-violet, except for the sides and the lower tail coverts.

PURPLE-THROATED COTINGA, SPANGLED COTINGA, *Cotinga cayana* (Linnaeus)

G. Purpurkehlkotinga, Cayenne-Kotinga; F. Cotinga de Cayenne; D. Purperkeel-Cotinga

DISTRIBUTION: Colombia, Venezuela, Ecuador, Peru, Bolivia, French Guiana, Brazil.

DESCRIPTION: *Male*. Head broad and body stocky. Head, mantle, rump and under parts iridescent turquoise-blue, sometimes shaded with a greenish cast. A glossy purplish throat patch covers a large area on chin, throat and upper breast. Blackish striations, spots and scale marks appear on upper parts and crown. Wings and tail blackish, with traces of turquoise on outer edges of many feathers. Beak black. Feet and legs blackish. *Female*. Dull brownish, thickly mottled with paler and darker areas on feather edges. Length: about 8½ in. (21·3 cm).

These cotingas are true arboreal birds, who chiefly inhabit the tops of trees. They feed almost exclusively on fruit and berries. They are generally to be observed in pairs or in small family groups, but, in the season when berries ripen, larger groups are sometimes seen. They are peaceful birds, who will remain perched on a branch for hours on end.

They can be kept very well in a spacious cage, but there their inertia becomes accentuated. Preference should therefore be given to placing them in an aviary where they are able to exhibit their magnificent colours, especially in flight.

In 1929 the Zoological Gardens in London were presented with a pair. Cotingas are among the most attractive birds for exhibition in a zoo, and they remain in good condition on a fruit diet, with the addition of raw meat and living insects.

Breeding results are extremely rare. In the New Jersey aviaries of Edward Marshall Boehm a successful breeding was achieved in 1962, with a pair of Black-throated Cotingas, *Pipreola riefferii*.

Cocks-of-the-Rock

FAMILY: RUPICOLIDAE

The two species of Cock-of-the-Rock are highly prized among aviculturists and zoological societies. They are expensive, but are more frequently available than formerly, as it has been found possible to feed them successfully.

At the beginning of acclimatisation many experienced fanciers mix the food items into a thick paste, which is rolled into small pellets. A good proportion of their diet should consist of fruit—mainly apples, pears and grapes. Banana and soaked currants can be included, but as they are fattening they should only be used sparingly. A fine-grade insectivorous mixture should be mixed into some of the pellets, and this should be persevered with in order to add important variety to the staple diet. Every other day should be finely-minced fresh, raw beef, about a teaspoonful per bird, should be included. After the birds become accustomed to aviary feeding, the pellets of food can gradually be discontinued, as they learn to accept the same textures of food as other cotingas. Fruit should always be a main part—apples, pears and grapes should be diced. Occasional baby mice are also acceptable. In the wild state these birds often eat snails, but they do not always accept them in captivity. Locusts and grasshoppers are accepted. Since the brilliant plumage of Cocks-of-the-Rock usually fade in captivity, carotene should be added to the diet to hold the colour.

Cocks-of-the-Rock should not be subjected to overbearing or aggressive companions. They are more than usually peaceful with most medium or large softbills. The scarlet species has longer legs and is more active and arboreal than the orange, but if either species is inclined to be aggressive it will probably be the Orange Cock-of-the-Rock, which spends more time on the ground and has slow-moving, skulking habits. When it does become aggressive, however, it moves very rapidly and precisely. The beak can be a formidable hammer.

In the wild state Cocks-of-the-Rock participate in elaborate displays, which are both social and nuptial in character. The social aspect is very interesting, involving many birds. Males go through odd dances, punctuated by wing-spreading and tail-fanning. The noisy, appreciative audience consists of males waiting for their turn to perform, as well as females.

Both species are heavy-bodied birds, with short broad tails and yellowish-orange fowl-like beaks. The dominant crests of very fine feathers are rounded and perpetually raised, nearly covering the beak. Males are brightly coloured, but females and immature birds are dull shades of brown.

Nests are built of mud and saliva against the wall of a ravine or cliff, usually near a stream. If a spacious aviary could be furnished to resemble as far as possible their natural surroundings, there seems no reason why Cocks-of-the-Rock should not breed. They are very fond of bathing. The aviary should be provided with a thick layer of fresh vegetable mould and dense growing cover. The soil should be kept sufficiently moist.

They can be kept in an outside aviary throughout the year, but it is essential to provide a roomy shelter for them during periods of severe cold or wet weather. Some heat should be provided, but the temperature should not be above 50°F (10°C).

COCK-OF-THE-ROCK, ORANGE COCK-OF-THE-ROCK, *Rupicola rupicola* (Linnaeus) (Pl. III)

G. Orage Felsenhahn, Guyana-Klippenvogel; F. Coq de la roche de Guyane; D. Oranje Rotshaan

DISTRIBUTION: Guyana, Surinam, French Guiana, parts of Brazil, Venezuela and eastern Colombia.

DESCRIPTION: *Male.* Under parts and most of upper parts bright orange. The wide fan-shaped crest has a chestnut-brown edging. It begins in front of the eyes and almost covers the upper mandible of the bill. Blackish wing feathers have orange-white markings in central portion of the outer flights. Inner coverts are graduated down the back and are broad blackish feathers with prominent pale greyish bands and squarely flared sides, all bordered with orange. Many

Cock-of-the-Rock, *Rupicola rupicola*

back and scapular feathers are greatly elongated and filmy, extending out to the sides. These filaments grow with age and may cover the distinctive inner coverts. Tail brownish with a reddish-orange tip. Irides golden. *Female.* Dark olive-grey with smaller crest. Tail and wings more brown; lower wing coverts light orange. Length: 14 in. (36 cm).

The Scarlet or Peruvian Cock-of-the-Rock, *Rupicola peruviana*, from Venezuela, Colombia, Ecuador, Peru and Bolivia, is now making its appearance in a number of zoological gardens. It is a little larger than *R. rupicola*, mainly because of its longer tail. *Male.* Under parts and upper parts, down to mantle, scapulars and back, brilliant scarlet. Tail and most of wings black. Inner wing coverts, grey very broad and more rounded. Crest softer and very full, and there is no change in border colouring. Irides golden-yellow. *Female.* Brownish-orange, varying to dark maroon in the different species, and the dark portions are olive-grey and brown.

ORNATE UMBRELLA BIRD, *Cephalopterus o. ornatus* (Geoffroy St. Hilaire)

G. Schirmvogel; F. Céphaloptère orné; D. Parasolvogel

DISTRIBUTION: Colombia, Venezuela, Ecuador, Peru, Bolivia, western Brazil, Guyana.

DESCRIPTION: Plumage black. Tails rather short. Upper mandible black; lower mandible dusky-horn colour. Except for two outstanding characteristics, this bird is almost crow-like. The first is a very large mushroom- or umbrella-shaped crest of hair-like feathers capping the head. These feathers are erectile and can be extended forward over the beak. The second characteristic is an inflatable appendage called a lappet, connected to the lower throat. In this species the lappet is loosely but fully feathered, with broad, rounded, pale-tipped feathers of glossy bluish-black. The reason for the lappet is unknown, but it is probably used in courtship displays. During inflation of the lappet, the feathers are somewhat upstanding. Length: variable from 16–20 in. (40–50 cm).

SUBSPECIES: The Long-wattled or Pensile Umbrella Bird, *C. o. penduliger*, from western Colombia and west Ecuador, has a round and narrow lappet, which ranges from 11–13 in. (29–32·5 cm) in length. This form is usually identified as the subspecies *C. o. penduliger*, but some authorities consider it too distinctive to be of the same species. There are other forms of Umbrella Bird, but none so outstanding as the Long-wattled.

Genus: Procnias

Bell Birds

There are four species of Bell Bird, which are noted for their loud ringing calls. These bell sounds carry in amazing clarity and volume for great distances, so that Bell Birds are unsuitable for aviaries in residential neighbourhoods The huge gape of the mouth is also astonishing. The sizes range from 10 to about 11½ in. (25–29 cm) in length, including the tails of about 3 in. (7·5 cm). They are forest-dwellers who prefer mountainous country. They live alone or in pairs and keep to the tops of trees.

They can be kept in spacious cages, as they sit tranquilly on their perches. Their diet must consist of various fruits such as dates, oranges, pears, bananas, raisins and all kinds of berry fruits. Boiled potatoes and rice, and insectivorous foods can be mixed with the fruits. It is recommended to fit into the cage a double base of gauze so that the droppings can fall through.

NAKED-THROATED BELL BIRD *Procnias nudicollis* (Vieillot)

G. Nachtkehlglockenvogel; F. Oraponga à gorge nue; D. Naakthals-Klokvogel (Pl. III)

DISTRIBUTION: Brazil.

DESCRIPTION: *Male.* White with a large area of bare bright bluish-green skin on head. The bare area covers a broad forehead, surrounds the eyes, and extends to the lower area of the throat, where it is heavily wrinkled. Beak, large eyes, feet and legs black. *Female.* Mostly olive, with very dull shadings and yellowish under parts. Length: 11¾ in. (30 cm).

Naked-throated Bell Bird, *Procnias nudicollis*

The other 3 species are interesting, but seldom seen in collections:

White Bell Bird, *Procnias alba*, from Venezuela, the Guianas and parts of Brazil, is also white, but does not have the bare facial and throat areas. Instead it has a black fleshy erectile wattle growing out of the forehead just above the base of the beak. The wattle is sparsely covered by very small white feathers. *Female.* Also soft, dull olive, with yellowish shadings underneath. Length: about 11 in. (28·5 cm).

Three-wattled Bell Bird, *Procnias tricarunculata*, from Central America, has a particularly huge gape. Three long and slender pendant wattles are very noticeable. One hangs from the forehead at the base of the upper mandible. The others occur on each side at the corners of the mouth. The head, neck, mantle and upper breast are white. Remaining plumage is reddish-brown. Length: 10¾ in. (28 cm).

The most fascinating of the Bell Birds is *Procnias averano*, the Mossy-throated Bell Bird, of Colombia, Venezuela, Trinidad, Guyana, Surinam and north-eastern Brazil. This species was first displayed by the New York Zoological Society. It was a wonderfully steady bird, in excellent condition, and it seemed to enjoy showing off to the public. Also called the Bearded Bell Bird or the Black-winged Bell Bird, this species is about 11 in. (28·5 cm) long, with black wings and a very dark brown head. The rest of the plumage is whitish. Head broad and beak especially broad, with a very wide throat. Tiny black wattles of thin flesh hang thickly from the large throat area, like string moss draping from the roof of a cave. *Female.* Olive-green above and pale yellowish below, greenish streaks. Throat greyish with pale streaks.

FAMILY: PITTIDAE

Pittas

BY H. J. BATES AND R. L. BUSENBARK

To aviculturists, Pittas are recognised particularly by two characteristics; they are difficult and they are delicate, and those most coveted have varying amounts of brilliant metallic colouring. A popular name for the Pitta is 'Jewel Thrush'.

In all species the bodies are very stocky and rounded, with short necks, large heads, and very small, rounded tails. The beaks are reasonably long and thick in much the same form as those of true thrushes. The upper mandible has a slightly hooked tip. The feet are large and the legs long. Cock and hen are usually alike. Many females are a little duller in shading, but sexing is usually very difficult. The colour variations in the 23 species are amazing.

Pittas, in a single genus, have a wide geographical range, which includes Africa, India, China, Burma, Thailand and neighbouring countries, Malaysia, Borneo, Indonesia, the Philippines, Japan, Australia, and many islands in the South Pacific. They have no close relatives, but their nearest counterparts, so far as outward appearance is concerned, are the Ant Thrushes of Mexico, Central America and South America. Ant Thrushes (or Ant Pittas) are very dull in colouring, and aviculturists are not usually interested in them.

All of the Pittas prefer terrestrial habitats in the half-light of dense, damp tropical forests which are softly carpeted with humus. When they leave the ground during the daytime they seldom go higher than low branches or into underbrush. They are very good ground runners and seem to prefer running to flying. The wings are rather short and rounded, and yet, surprisingly, many pittas are migratory. Flight is swift and direct, even though the rapid wingbeats suggest panic.

The writers have had up to a dozen Pittas at one time in the same aviary. Observation reveals unusual and very interesting behaviour. Because of their terrestrial habits and the nature of their natural habitat, their feet tend to be unusually delicate and they cannot for long endure concrete or ordinary soil floors. The writers cover the floor of their cages or aviaries with a thick layer of peat and decaying leaves, and also add natural logs with soft bark for perching. Shrubs or small trees are also essential, as Pittas perch two together in branches close to the ground. Conservatory aviaries are ideal to provide a suitable environment, and they also more closely resemble the warm and humid conditions to which Pittas are accustomed.

For the most part Pittas live peacefully with other species, and they should not be associated with aggressive companions. However, they are jealous of their own particular territory and do not tolerate others of their own kind. Once they become settled in their aviary and stake out their territories, they may badger or chase each other, which results in more turmoil than actual damage. However, this trait is one which could cause problems because of the slow intimidation and wearing-down process, such as described in the section on toucan behaviour. Gradually the weaker ones will be denied access to food, causing a slow deterioration in health. This danger can also be brought about by other aviary companions who are territorial birds, notably many members of the thrush family, which are by nature more aggressive, frequently terrestrial, and often larger than Pittas.

Pittas have a thrush-like gait which consists of short and rapid runs, punctuated by abrupt stops and frozen immobility. In an aviary they usually fly only when disturbed. Most such flights are for short distances and are close to the ground, but the birds are sometimes apt to panic and injure themselves on aviary wire.

The wings and tail are used in two very interesting displays: the tail seems to be used as an emotional indicator. It frequently wavers slowly up and down in a precise, almost stealthy, manner, while the bird stands motionless. In an unrelated gesture, the wings are frequently spread upwards in flashing movement. This could well be an act of defiance or a means of intimidation of others, but the writers have seen no other acts of aggression committed in conjunction with this display.

Both of these characteristics could be used in courting displays. Some of the brightest metallic colours occur on the long upper and lower tail coverts and on the upper sides of the wings. A broad white area occurs on the under sides of the wings of most species, and, while not colourful, the sudden flashes from upspread wings certainly attract attention.

Pittas in the wild state feed on insects, and they do not adapt themselves satisfactorily to artificial diets of inert food for long periods. Unless an unlimited supply of live food is available during the transition period there will be a high percentage of losses. If there is a plentiful supply of live food the Pittas seem even less inclined to sample other foods. The fortified nectar as used for Cotingas and Manakins helps to supply the necessary balanced nutrition during such periods.

The difficulties mentioned apply to adults. In recent years Pittas have become more frequently available and more successfully established in confinement. The reason for this is nearly always traceable to those trappers and exporters of high integrity who take only young birds. The writers were visting such an exporter in Thailand one day when a group of young Blue-winged Pittas arrived from the northern part of the country. All were in immature plumage and had the yellow skin of fledglings at the corners of the beak. They were completely steady and also gregarious. They were interested in everything around them, including their food plates, and were eating very well. Their tameness indicated that they had been hand-reared and had become accustomed to handling. With youngsters such as these the transfer to the different foodstuffs used in other countries is easily accomplished in a short time, and the risk of losses would be very greatly reduced.

Diet should consist of reasonably standard softbilled diet, but allowances must be made for the birds' extremely insectivorous nature. Mynah pellets are excellent if the birds can be induced to eat them, and youngsters will usually learn to take this food. Fruit is seldom eaten. Live food in variety is necessary. Mealworms are, of course, acceptable, but they will not suffice as the sole live food.

The Bengal Pitta, *Pitta brachyura*, successfully nested in the aviaries of Mr. Edward Marshall Boehm in 1960. A record of this achievement, written by Mr. Charles Everitt, appears in the Jan./Feb. issue of the *Avicultural Magazine*. Eggs were laid daily, and five formed the complete clutch. Incubation in this instance started with the laying of the second egg and continued for 18 days, when the first two hatched. Two others hatched on subsequent days. The four youngsters were reared exclusively on live food. They left the nest in 16 days and were independent 5 days later. The parents quickly built a new nest and successfully raised a second brood.

Not all of the 23 species of Pitta are attractive enough to be coveted by aviculturists, and many of the most beautiful do not occur in present-day collecting areas. Moreover, Pittas are very difficult to keep.

BENGAL PITTA, INDIAN PITTA, *Pitta brachyura*
(Linnaeus)   (Pl. III)
G. Neunfarbenpitta, Bengalenpitta; F. Brève du
Bengale; D. Bengaalse Pitta

DISTRIBUTION: Indonesia, India, Sri Lanka, Japan, South-
East Asia.
DESCRIPTION: *Male.* Crown light brown with stripe from
forehead to neck. Eyebrow stripe white, bordered on upper
edge by a narrow black stripe. Chin, throat and neck whitish.
Under parts yellowish-brown. Area of the crop somewhat
browner. Vent and lower tail coverts scarlet red. Upper
parts green; upper tail coverts and small wing coverts light
blue. Remainder of coverts green. Flights black with a
broad white band over the middle. Tail black with blue tip;
bill black; feet and legs yellow; iris brown. *Female.* Has a
lighter lower mandible to the bill, which is somewhat
longer and more pointed. Length: 7¼ in. (18 cm).

HOODED PITTA, GREEN-BREASTED PITTA, *Pitta
sordida cucullata* (St. Müller)   (Pl. III)
G. Schwarzkpofpitta; F. Brève sordide, Brève à
capuchon; D. Bruinkop-Pitta

DISTRIBUTION: India, Burma, Thailand, Malaysia, Philippines, Papua-New Guinea.
DESCRIPTION: Top and back of crown darkish reddish-
brown; remainder of head, throat and neck black. Under

Hooded Pitta, *Pitta sordida cucullata*

parts green, angle of wings and rump vivid cobalt-blue.
From middle of abdomen to over lower tail coverts runs a
deep black-edged red. Blue spot on wings is the same size as
that of the Bengal Pitta, *P. brachyura.* Tail black with blue
tip; the white speculum on wings is extensive. Back and
wings dark green, flights black. Bill black. Feet and legs
black. Length: about 12 in. (30 cm).
Müller's Pitta, *P. s. mulleri*, from Thailand, Borneo and
Indonesia, is somewhat larger in size and lacks the black
above the red on the under parts.

FAMILY: PHILEPITTIDAE

VELVET PITTA, *Philepitta castanea* (St. Müller)
G. Schwarzlappenpitte; F. Philépitte veloutée; D.
Fluweel Asiti

DISTRIBUTION: Madagascar.
DESCRIPTION: *Male.* Main colouring black velvet. On
forehead and above eye there is a naked light blue-grey
wattle. On bend of the wing there is a yellow spot. Feet and
legs pinkish-grey; bill pinkish-horn colour. *Female.* Green,
as is her wattle. Length: 6½ in. (16·5 cm).
This family consists of only 4 species, which are found
in Madagascar. Very little is known about them.

Velvet Pitta are fairly heavy birds, somewhat resembling
thrushes, and they have sturdy feet. They live in humid
tropical forests, sometimes at great heights. They are
arboreal birds, who seek their food (which consists mainly
of berries and fruit, and sometimes insects) in the trees or in
the undergrowth near the ground. Although not shy, they
are very quiet and have a thrush-like song. They build in a
bush a pear-shaped nest about 12 in. (30 cm) long, made of
palm fibres, mosses and leaves. Up to 3 eggs are laid. They
are hatched out in 28 days, the young remaining in the nest
for 42 days.
Velvet Pittas live alone or in pairs.

SUBORDER: SUBOSCINES

FAMILY: MENURIDAE

SUPERB LYRE BIRD, *Menura superba* (Latham)
G. Leierschwanz; F. Oiseau Lyre; D. Liervogel

DISTRIBUTION: Australia.
DESCRIPTION: *Male.* Main colouring dark greyish-brown;
lower parts of the body brownish-grey, lightest on abdomen.
Wings reddish-brown. Tail brown above and silvery-white
below. Outer feathers grey, reddish-brown and brownish,
banded against a white background. Central feathers grey.
Iris dark brown, surrounded by a naked grey wattle. Bill,
feet and legs black. Length: 52 in. (130 cm) including
28 in. (70 cm) tail. *Female.* Upper parts brown; lower parts
brownish-grey. Length: 32 in. (81 cm) with a normal tail.
Lyre Birds are shy and remain in woods and undergrowth in
dense cover. The call of the courting male, mingled with a
number of sounds that he has picked up in his territory and
cleverly imitates, is regularly heard, but the bird itself is
hardly ever seen.
The outside pair of tail feathers form the frame of the lyre;
the two centre pairs lack the actual web and are long and
narrow; the six pairs of quills lack barbules and have no

beards. They are brown above and white underneath.
During courtship the tail is spread out, and the white tail
feathers lie over the back and touch the ground in front of
the head.
The solitary male tolerates no other male bird in his large
territory. He establishes a few courtship areas, which he
visits in turn and to which he lures the females. The female
constructs her huge nest from ferns, bark, plant fibres and
moss, low above the ground, and lines it with feathers.
The work takes her about a month. The one egg, dark grey
and covered with black spots, is incubated by her alone in
35–40 days. The young are hatched naked, but after a few
days are covered with long black downy feathers. They
leave the nest after 10 weeks.
Lyre Birds were first imported to Europe in 1867, when they
were on display at the London Zoo. There is a descriptive
article in *Avicultural Magazine*, Vol. 53, No. 3, May/June
1947.
Albert's Lyre Bird, *Menura Alberti*, a somewhat smaller
species, inhabits Queensland and the north-east of New
Zealand. Upper parts are reddish-brown, lower parts

Plate XV

Red-headed Troupial, *Amblycercus holosericus*
Yellow-headed Troupial, *Xanthocephalus xanthocephalus*
Red-breasted Marsh Bird, *Pezites militaris*
Military Starling, *Leistes militaris*   Red-shouldered Marsh Bird, *Agelaius phoeniceus*

Plate XVI

Black Cuckoo Shrike, *Campephaga ph. phoenicea*

Scarlet Minivet, *Pericrocotus flammeus speciosus*

Black-naped Oriole, *Oriolus ch. chinensis*

Fairy Bluebird, *Irena p. puella*

Drongo, *Dicrurus adsimilis*

Plate XVII

Self Blue Border Canary

Yellow Border Canary

Dilute Blue Border Canary

Red Orange Canary

Yellow Canary

Green Canary

Yorkshire Canary

Lizard Canary

Gloster Fancy Canary

Ivory Canary

Plate XVIII

Linnet, *Carduelis cannabina*

Siskin, *Carduelis spinus*

Chaffinch, *Fringilla coelebs*

Hawfinch × Bullfinch

Greenfinch, *Chloris chloris*

Yellowhammer, *Emberiza citrinella*

Brambling × Bullfinch

reddish-grey, outside tail feathers black. Length: 31¼ in. (about 81 cm).
In zoological gardens success has been achieved in incubating eggs in a machine and under a broody hen. Incubation was

RUFOUS SCRUB BIRD, *Atrichornis rufescens* (Ramsay)
G. Kleiner Dickichtschlüpfer, Rotbraunerdickicht-vogel; F. Atrichorne roux; D. Roodbruine Doorn-kruiper

DISTRIBUTION: New South Wales and south-eastern Queensland.
DESCRIPTION: Upper parts dark reddish-brown, with fine black transverse stripes. Throat and breast white, with a dark grey spot. Remaining lower parts reddish-brown, brightest on vent area. *Female.* Lacks the dark spot on throat. Length: 7½ in. (19 cm).

SUBORDER: OSCINES

Minivets

FAMILY: CAMPEPHAGIDAE

Besides the ten species of minivets, this family also includes the larger and more variable groups of cuckoo-shrikes; but they are not considered avicultural subjects. Minivets, some of which are very colourful, are not standard avicultural subjects because they are very difficult to transfer to artificial diets. They are highly insectivorous in much the same manner as Rollers, Fairy Blue Birds, Trogons, and other difficult birds; and they are also more delicate. They should be given the third diet as outlined for the other difficult birds, and collectors would be well advised only to work with young birds rather than with adults.
The bright red and orange colourings which are normally so vivid, tend to fade badly in captivity. A carotene agent must therefore be included in the diet.

SUBFAMILY: CAMPEHAGINIDAE

BLACK CUCKOO SHRIKE, *Campephaga ph. phoenicea* (Latham) (Pl. XVI)
G. Mohrenraupenfresser; F. Echenilleur pourpre; D. Roodschouder-Rupsvogel
DISTRIBUTION: Africa, south of the Sahara.
DESCRIPTION: The main colouring is black. *Male.* Has a yellow-orange spot on his shoulder. The inside of its beak is orange-yellow, and forms a distinct mark of identification with regard to other black birds. *Female.* Light brown on the upper part of her body, and whitish-brown, spotted transversely, on her lower parts. The bird is about 7½ in. (19 cm) long.
These are very commonly distributed birds, which do not strike the eye, and which in open country with small woods try to live quietly next to one another endeavouring to find their food, which consists mainly of caterpillars, also hairy ones, and all kinds of other insects and fruits. Most of their time these birds spend in the dense undergrowth or on the ground under the foliage. Their flight is rather fluttery, but so directional that even during flight it is still able to grasp at insects. Its call is a quivering note. They nest in a bush or low tree. The nest is small and difficult to discover as the whole of it is covered with cobwebs. The 2 or 3 eggs are light green with a number of purple-brown spots and dots on the blunt end. The female broods by herself during 20 days. The young are fed by both parent birds, and after 3 weeks fly out of the nest.

considerably quicker than in the case of birds in the wild, where the female has to leave the nest every day to seek her own food.

FAMILY: ATRICHORNITHIDAE

This small bird is probably descended from the large Lyre Birds. It inhabits the extensive thickets on the coast. It moves over the ground with its tail stiffly upright, searching for insects, snails, worms and seeds in the undergrowth. It has a clear whistling song and also gives innumerable imitations of other birds. It builds a dome-shaped nest, low above the ground, made from grass and leaves and lined, with a layer of smooth, paper-like substance. The 2 white eggs are covered with reddish-brown spots, and are incubated only by the female. The bird is fond of taking sand baths, during which it practically covers itself with sand.
The chances of survival for all birds living on the ground is slender, and it is therefore fortunate that the habitat of this rare little bird lies inside the Lammington National Park.

SCARLET MINIVET, *Periscocotus flammeus speciosus* (Latham) (Pl. XVI)
G. Scharlachmennigvogel; F. Grand minivet écarlate; D. Oranje Rupsvogel
DISTRIBUTION: Himalayas, from east Kashmir to east Assam.
DESCRIPTION: *Male.* Glossy black covers all of head, neck, upper breast, upper back, most of wings, and central tail

Scarlet Minivet, *Periscocotus flammeus speciosus*

feathers. Bright deep red covers remaining under parts, lower back, rump, outer tail feathers, and irregular wing patches. Under wing coverts yellow. *Female.* Dusky grey on top of head, nape, back, and shoulders. The grey softly shades into slate on flights and central tail feathers. Yellow replaces red of male and is more extensive since it also covers chin, throat, and upper breast. The yellow also blends into grey on forehead and facial area.

SUBSPECIES: There are several variations. Length: varies from about 6–9 in. (15–23 cm). The pattern of red areas on wings also differs, but the relationship between the various subspecies is obvious. Shape is graceful chiefly because of long tail with its graded, rounded, and undulating taper. Full body is crowned by a well-proportioned head and neck. These birds live in the hardwood trees in the dense forests which cover the foothills of the Himalaya Mountains. They fly above the tops of the trees whilst chasing insects, but they also clamber busily from branch to branch and from leaf to leaf in order to strip them bare of caterpillars and other insects. They seldom alight on the ground.

In the beginning of the century they were imported into Germany for the first time. The birds have to be very carefully acclimatised, and it takes a considerable time before they can accustom themselves to the mixed food for fine insect-eaters. All kinds of living insects, grasshoppers, crickets and meal worms must act as medium. Ants' eggs, dried flies and water fleas should also be mixed up with the food to make it attractive to the birds. The varied mixed food should be dampened with scrapings of carrot. When the bird has to be kept in a cage the magnificent red colour soon starts to fade, which can be helped a little by a carotene preparation. If however the birds are kept during the day in a sunny outside aviary, then their colorific splendour will not only be maintained, but the faded parts will also regain their original colour once more.

Bulbuls

BY H. J. BATES AND R. L. BUSENBARK

FAMILY: PYCNONOTIDAE

The large bulbul family includes several very popular insectivorous species which are not difficult to keep. Many of these birds can be recommended to beginners, because they are very robust and do not require complicated provision.

They thrive on a normal diet for softbills. Most are peaceful and mix well, sizes and personalities ranging from Pekin Nightingale and to Old World Orioles. Bulbuls have a good reputation as singers; but they are rarely as excellent as many thrushes. Their song is similar to that of the Pekin Nightingale; melodious, though the repertoire is limited.

There are 15 genera and approximately 120 species, as well as a large number of sub-species, distributed throughout Africa and southern Asia, as far as the Philippines and Japan. Comparatively few of these species are available, and these come to us mainly from India, Thailand, Malaysia and Hong Kong. Africa, where the greatest number of these species are found, provides very few of these birds for bird-fanciers. Only the large zoos possess African bulbuls, often called green bulbuls or brown bulbuls.

Most bulbuls do not have colourful plumage; certain species display a pattern of complete contrasts, and many have a crest. They have an elegant shape, a tail of average length and very soft plumage. Both sexes usually have the same plumage. They very easily grow accustomed to artificial diet, and although very active and lively, they usually behave calmly and quietly in an aviary. A cage is not suitable for them, for they very rapidly damage their feathers by their great activity; and yet they are more adaptable to life in a cage than the Japanese Nightingale.

Several species of bulbuls have nested successfully in an aviary. The nest is usually cup-shaped; sometimes the birds accept a nesting box for canaries, but this is something of an exception. The sitting period is thirteen days. The young birds leave the nest when they are about two weeks old, and are independent at about a month.

Genus: Pycnonotus

RED-EARED BULBUL, RED-WHISKERED BULBUL, *Pycnonotus jocusus emeria* (Linnaeus)   (Pl. XIII)
G. Rotohrbulbul; F. Bulbul à oreillons rouges; D. Roodoor-Buulbuul

DISTRIBUTION: India, Burma, Thailand, Laos, Vietnam, Khmer, Malaysai, Hong Kong and China.
DESCRIPTION: Stiff erect crest, bright red cheek spots and red lower tail coverts. Upper parts dark brown, lower parts are white, and bill black. The head is brown like the crest and is almost black. Towards the sides, the white lower parts becomes somewhat browner, especially on lower abdomen and lower breast. A fine narrow black stripe runs from the base of the lower mandible of the bill, under the white cheeks to the neck. Length: about 7¼ in. (18 cm).
Bulbuls prefer to visit human habitations, gardens and orchards, and often form large groups which become very tame and trusting. Their food consists of living insects and fruit, which they eat the ripe and unripe. Large flocks can obviously cause considerable damage. They build their basin-shaped nests in dense undergrowth, about 4½ ft (1·4 m) above the ground. The bottom of the nest consists of ferns and dry leaves. The 3 or 4 eggs are rose-white and

covered with red spots and dots in every variety, especially at the blunt end. In cages they soon become used to universal food to which pieces of fruit have been added. A couple of mealworms should also be given every day. Breedings have been repeatedly obtained, but in most cases

Red-eared Bulbul, *Pycnonotus jocuses emeria*

to ensure successful breeding it was necessary to give the birds the disposal of their own, planted aviary. The male then proceeds to perform his copulatory dance, in which the tail is outspread and the head held on one side. During the brooding period, the birds become shy, and they will only feed their young when no one is near them. As rearing food, fresh ants' eggs and small mealworms must be available. Only when the youngsters have flown out of the nest should bread soaked in milk, raisins and various fruits be given. There are 9 subspecies and cross-breeding has also taken place with the Kala Bulbul, *Pycnonotus cafer*, the White-Eared Bulbul, *Pycnonotus leucotis*, and the Syrian Bulbul, *Pycnonotus xanthopygos*.

RED-VENTED BULBUL, *Pycnonotus c. cafer* (Linnaeus) (Pl. XIII)

G. Kalabülbül; F. Bulbul indien; D. Kalabuulbuul, Roodstuit-Buulbuul

DISTRIBUTION: Sri Lanka.

DESCRIPTION: Crest and head black, body flecked with brown and lower tail coverts bright vermilion. The white spot on the coccyx is only to be seen distinctly during flight. The ear coverts are brown. The tail feathers are brownish black and have white tips. The eyes are brown; the bill and the feet are black. Length: 8¾ in. (22 cm).

These birds occur pretty generally within the distribution area, except in the dense woods and over 5,350 ft (1,630 m)

Red-vented Bulbul, *Pycnonotus c. cafer*

above sea level. They eat insects and berry fruits. In addition to their friendly and melodious call, they let out a loud, harsh, screech in case of danger and during the afternoon siesta they sing a soft murmuring song. During the mating dance the male spreads his vermilion red lower tail coverts and puffs out his other feathers. The female flattens her crest, assumes an attitude of being crushed together with hanging wings and tail, quivers with her wings and makes all manner of twittering sounds.

The nest is built in a dense bush and is made of small twigs and lined with fine plant fibres. Every year the birds produce 2 or 3 batches, each of 2 or 3 eggs.

There are 9 subspecies. They were first to be seen in the Zoological Gardens in London in 1864. All the experience with these birds have led to the conclusion that a pair cannot be kept together with other birds as fatal fights are the result. They have been cross-bred with the Red-Eared Bulbul, *Pycnonotus jocosus* and with the White-Cheeked Bulbul, *Pycnonotus leucogenys*. In literature the old family name *Molpastes* is still often used. Neunzig gives the name as *Pycnonotus pygaeus*.

WHITE-CHEEKED BULBUL, *Pycnonotus l. leucogenys* (J. E. Gray)

G. Weisswangenbülbül; F. Bulbul à oreillons blancs; D. Witwang-Buulbuul

DISTRIBUTION: Himalayas.

DESCRIPTION: Forehead and the crest (curved frontwards) brown with fine white feather edges. The area around the eye, chin, throat, and parts of the sides of the neck, are black; ear coverts are white. The rest of the body and the wings are olive-brown, darker on upper parts of the body than on lower parts, which become whitish towards the abdomen. The tail is brownish-black, and middlemost

White-cheeked Bulbul, *Pycnonotus l. leucogenys*

feathers have broad white tips. The iris is brown, feet and bill black and lower tail coverts a lively yellow. Length: 8 in. (20 cm).

In their extensive distribution area, stretching from Iraq and Saudi-Arabia over Iran, Afghanistan and India, 5 subspecies occur. In hills and mountainous areas the birds appear mostly in pairs in gardens and parks, and become so tame that they sometimes search out food on the verandas of houses. Birds which breed in the higher mountains—up to heights of 4,500–6,000 ft (1,400–1,800 m) above sea level come down into the valleys in winter. They have a pleasant and melodious call, and are always active, either chasing flying termites or busy plaguing an owl blinded by the sunlight.

Their food consists of berries, fruit, larvae and insects, which they also search for on the ground. Their basin-shaped nests are usually about 4½ ft (1·4 m) above the ground. In the wild state, hybridism occurs with the Kala Bulbul. Except during the brooding season, these birds can be included in a mixed aviary, but towards pairing time the male becomes aggressive towards all other birds, whilst the female helps to disturb nests and plunder them for eggs or young.

If the birds have their own aviary, then they will proceed to brood. They take to a nest-box or build their own nest in a dense bush. The female broods the 3 or 4 eggs by herself for 12–13 days; both parents, but chiefly the male, feed the young. At first this is solely with ants' eggs and little mealworms, but later, when they have flown out of the nest, they are fed rearing food.

The older nomenclature *Otocompsa* and *Molpastes* are sometimes met in the literature.

RED-THROATED BULBUL, *Pycnonotus melanicterus gularis* (Gould)

G. Rotkehlbülbül; F. Bulbul à gorge rouge; D. Rood-keel-Buulbuul

DISTRIBUTION: South-western India.

DESCRIPTION: Head and crest black, chin and throat ruby-red, breast orange-yellow, and abdomen yellow. Upper parts of the body are olive-green. Irides yellow, the bill black and the feet are greyish-black. Length: 6½ in. (16·5 cm). This species has 10 races, which have as common mark of identification the black head and crest, even if the latter has sometimes turned out to be rather small. These birds live in pairs or in small groups in open woodland away from human habitation. They feed on berries and insects. Their song sounds rather mournful. The most beautiful variety seems to be *melanicterus johnsoni* from Thailand, and which has a bright red spot over chin and throat.

Red-throated Bulbul, *Pycnonotus melanicterus gularis*

In the aviary these birds soon become tame and even a little sluggish. They will eat from the hand and are partial to mealworms. They can become too fat as a result of over-feeding. Initially there may be some resistance to artificial food. With universal food and 5 or 6 mealworms daily, with a good nutricious nectar drink, one can keep the birds in excellent condition. In addition, all kinds of fruit must also be given to maintain plumage. A pair of birds could share a medium-sized aviary with other birds but they most definitely require flying space in order to keep them in good condition.

The subspecies *melanicterus dispar*, occurring in Java and Sumatra, is olive-green on upper parts of the body, with black head and chin and the characteristic bright red stiff throat feathers. The breast and abdomen are a golden-yellow. It is rarely seen in inhabited parts though specimens have come into the possession of fanciers on a few occasions. The song is renowned and is sometimes repeated up to 20 times.

Another subspecies, the Black-cheeked Bulbul, *Pycnonotus melanicterus flaviventris*, from the eastern Himalayas occurs at heights of 750–2,150 ft (229–645 m) above sea level. The head and throat are glossy black the lower parts greenish-yellow, with vivid yellow on the breast.

Since 1897 this race has been imported into Europe. They will peacably live with other bulbuls. Neunzig mentions that a female belonging to a fancier in Germany made a nest in a nesting basket as well as in a bush, breeding successfully with a Red-eared Bulbul. The birds are completely winter-resistant, and can go through the whole year in the outside aviary provided there is good night accommodation available.

RED-EYED BULBUL, *Pycnonotus nigrigens* (Vieillot)
G. Maskenbülbül; F. Bulbul à yeux rouges; D. Roodoog-Buulbuul

DISTRIBUTION: Namibia and South Africa.
DESCRIPTION: Head and throat are black, upper parts of the body brown, lower parts brownish-white. The abdomen is white in the centre. The flanks are greyish-brown and lower tail coverts are yellow. The tail is brownish-black.

The iris and the edge of the eyelid are red; the bill and the feet are black. Length: 7¼ in. (18 cm).
These birds live in the dry prairieland and keep to trees and bushes in the vicinity of rivulets. Larger groups can often be seen together. Fruits, especially the wild figs and a number of berries form the main part of their diet, but it appears that they also collect nectar from flowers. They are considered detrimental as they often pay visits to orchards in large numbers.

They are very lively and noisy but soon become trusting. Their call consists of a couple of flute-like notes. Nests are built in dense bushes or low trees, mostly at heights from 3–9 ft (1–3 m). The nests are basin-shaped and are made from twigs and grass stalks, lined with plant fibres. The 3 eggs are rose-white and covered with brownish-red and purple-grey spots. The female sits by herself for 12 days. Both parents feed the young, who fly out from the nest within 14 days of being hatched.

Red-eyed Bulbul, *Pycnonotus nigrigens*

YELLOW-VENTED BULBUL, *Pycnonotus au. aurigaster* (Vieillot)
F. Bulbul à ventre jaune; Bulbul Cudor; G. Kotilangbülbül, D. Kotiland Buulbuul, Geelbuik- Buulbuul

DISTRIBUTION: Java, Sumatra.
DESCRIPTION: Top of the head and chin black, face brownish-black, with cheeks and throat grey. Upper parts of the body are olive-brown; the feathers on the mantle and neck have grey edges. Upper tail coverts are white, lower parts brownish-white, vent and lower tail coverts are bright yellow. The iris is reddish-brown; the bill and feet are black. Length: 7¼ in. (18 cm).
Very common in all regions that have been brought under cultivation, and where plenty of blossoms and fruits are to be found, since these are their main food. With exception of the breeding season, they form flights of 4–8 birds, which often stay in the middle of settlements. They are not at all shy and notwithstanding the fact that they are being seriously hunted because of the damage that they can do to a plantation, they remain just as noisy and careless as ever. They will hang suspended to the outside twigs of the fruitbearing trees making their melodious call. They nest mostly in dense bushes and the nest is made of stalks and dry leaves, lined with soft plant fibres.
They were first imported to London in 1865, and in 1878 to Amsterdam.
A single specimen will always live peacably together with other birds. During mating advances the male bird spreads his wings, holds his head downwards, and lets his song be heard. As a cage bird the Yellow-vented Bulbul becomes remarkably tame, eats raisins and mealworms out of the hand, and learns to fly freely in and out of a room. In addition to his melodious flute-like notes, he gives a soft chirrup just like a hedge sparrow and especially in the evenings.

BROWN-EARED BULBUL, *Hypsipetes f. flavala* (Blyth)

G. Braunohrbülbül; F. Bulbul à oreillons bruns, Bulbul à ailes jaunes; D. Bruinoor-Buulbuul

DISTRIBUTION: Nepal, Assam, Burma.
DESCRIPTION: Top of the head and crest hairs dark grey; remaining upper parts ash-grey; the bridles (reins) and beard stripe are black. The throat, middle of the abdomen and lower tail coverts are white; lower parts are ash-grey. The wings are light and dark grey, and the outside vanes of the quill feathers are olive-green. The iris is dark reddish-brown, the bill black and the feet lead-grey. The auriculars are a glossy brown. Length: 8½ in. (21 cm).

These birds occur in small flights in the lower part of the mountainous country, at heights of 3,000–6,000 ft (900–1,830 m) above sea level. They search trees and bushes for berries and insects, making a loud twittering sound, alternated now and then by a few melodious flute-like notes. In contrast with many other bulbuls these perch horizontally. In 1877 they were first introduced to London, and later were also imported irregularly to other parts of Europe. They quickly become tamed and trusting and eat pieces of apple, raisins and mealworms out of the hand. They live peaceably together with other birds.

SUBSPECIES: The Yellow-eyebrowed Bulbul, *Hypsipetes indicus*, from Sri Lanka and India has no crest, and is differentiated by a clear yellow face, yellowish-green lower parts and olive-green upper parts. It lives in groups in the mountain woods among high trees, usually near rivers. The birds are noisy constantly making their pleasing flute-like notes while searching foliage for insects or fruit. Their nests are situated high in the fork of a branch (or at the end of a branch) hanging over the water. The basin-shaped nest is strengthened on the outside with pieces of tree bark and insect cocoon thread.

The Madagascar Bulbul, *Hypsipetes madagascariensis*, from India, China, Thailand and Madagascar, has a length of 10 in. (25 cm). The main colouring is dark grey. On the lower parts the grey vent fades to white.

FAMILY: IRENIDAE

Chloropsis and Fairy Blue Birds

The family Irenidae is composed of three different genera, all of which are notably diverse in character. One genus *Chloropsis* consists of Fruitsuckers, and another *Irena* of Fairy Blue Birds. These two groups are spectacular, and they contain some of aviculture's outstanding birds. They are totally different in character, personality, appearance and requirements.

The third genus is composed of four species and numerous subspecies of Ioras which are not well known to aviculturists. Ioras are native to Sri Lanka, India and South-East Asia. They are pleasing in appearance, but are not great beauties. In their native areas they are highly regarded for the great quantities of insects they consume.

All three genus are considered to be rather closely related to bulbuls.

Genus: Chloropsis

Chloropsis are also popularly called Fruitsuckers or Leaf Birds. There are eight species, but only one is regularly available. All are wonderful birds with delightful personalities.

They retain their naturally friendly and confiding personalities in aviaries or cages if they are given favourite food items such as mealworms, grapes, or soaked raisins from the hand. Mealworms should be limited to eight or ten per day. Few other aviary birds are as openly curious or as naturally friendly as Chloropsis. If conditions are right, the Chloropsis is also a good singer.

The birds in this genus are occasionally called Leaf Birds because of their predominant colouring of brilliant, glossy green. The black beaks are slender and curved and their natural diet contains a large percentage of nectar. The bodies are rounded but nevertheless sleek, shapely, and well-balanced by the tail and long slender beak. The head and neck add to the graceful proportions.

The diet for the different species of Chloropsis is the standard diet plus nectar. These birds acclimatise quite well, but their diet must be regulated rather strictly. They easily can, and often do, develop excessive fondnesses for certain foods. The intake of these foods can exceed the other items to such an extent that the diet will become unbalanced. Banana, in particular, is the usual source of trouble. With an unlimited supply of banana, Chloropsis tend to restrict their dietary intake to nectar, mealworms, and great quantities of banana which is certainly not a good balance. The writers exclude banana from the diet entirely to prevent this hazard.

Another occasional hazard with Chloropsis is a proneness to respiratory trouble in damp climates. They should be safeguarded against drafts even more strictly than most birds.

Despite these shortcomings, Chloropsis are among the finest birds which readily adapt themselves to aviary conditions. They mix well with tanagers, bulbuls, orioles and most other birds within these size ranges. They sometimes show animosity for other Chloropsis or bright green birds, but those owned by the writers have only rarely been pugnacious to other birds.

Genus: Chloropsis

GOLDEN-FRONTED FRUIT-SUCKER, GOLDEN-FRONTED GREEN BULBUL, *Chloropsis au. aurifrons* (Temminck)   (Pl. XIII)
G. Goldstirnblattvogel; F. Verdin à front d'or; D. Goudvoorhoofd-Bladvogel

DISTRIBUTION: Himalayan mountains and Burma.
DESCRIPTION: Plumage is largely grass-green, the lower parts being paler. Forehead, as far as middle of crown of head, lustrous orange-yellow. Lores, sides of face and upper breast velvet black. Top of throat, up to base of beak, blue. Black parts are marked off by a narrow orange band; blue mark at join of tail. Flight feathers and tail blackish-brown; median tail feathers green. Irides brown, beak black, legs and feet, lead-grey. Length:10¾ in. (28 cm). *Female.* The black is less extensive, forehead green.
The fruit-suckers remain almost entirely in the tops of trees, usually those with a dense foliage, where it is difficult to find them. They betray themselves by their pleasant call, and the

Golden-fronted Fruit-sucker, *Chloropsis au. aurifrons*

attractive flute-like sounds which they make continually. In pairs, they seek humid woods, where they find an abundance of berries, nectar and insects on which they feed; they also eat numerous caterpillars. They construct their cup-shaped nest of grass, moss, bark and fibre; it lies in the fork of a branch amongst the thick foliage, and is so well camouflaged that it is difficult to find. The 2 or 3 whitish-pink eggs have reddish-brown marks, like pencil marks, on them.
Since these birds only come to the ground to drink and to bathe, but hates to eat on the ground, the feeding dishes should be hung on the trellis or placed on a board, always below the drooping branches of a bush.
Fruit-suckers can be housed with Bulbuls, Tanagers, Orioles and Bluebirds. They will soon imitate the flute-like sounds of their companions. Fruit-suckers often imitate other less pleasant sounds, which have nothing to do with their song; but if a Shama Thrush or Japanese Nightingale lives near by, it will soon imitate their song, or certain sections of their songs. Fruit-suckers are usually housed in a planted aviary.
Mix breadcrumbs, or crumbs of stale bread or broken biscuits with the general mash, as well as dehydrated ants' eggs, dehydrated flies or sandhoppers. They should also be given minerals and charcoal. The mash should be moistened

by the addition of a solution of honey or grated carrots. Pieces of fruit can also be mixed with it, or else the fruit can be given separately, once it is seen that the birds are eating the mash. To vary the diet, they can also be given bread soaked in milk containing sugar or honey. Half an orange will be completely emptied; the birds draw out the juice with their very long tongue.
There are many records of these birds being kept by aviculturists at liberty in the garden; they return to the aviary to eat. Fruit-suckers are sensitive to damp cold; in winter they must be housed in a heated, planted and well arranged aviary.

HARDWICK'S FRUIT-SUCKER, HARDWICK'S GREEN BULBUL, *Chloropsis h. hardwickei* (Jardine and Selby)
G. Hardwick's Blattvogel; F. Verdin de Hardwick; D. Blauwvleugel-Bladvogel   (Pl. XIII)

DISTRIBUTION: India, Burma, Thailand.
DESCRIPTION: *Male.* Upper parts dark green, brighter on coccyx. Head has a golden sheen on crown. Forehead, orbital stripe and ear coverts yellowish-green. Lores, sides of head, and neck black. Across cheeks runs a wide light blue band. Under parts light green, running into orange-yellow towards vent. Primaries and coverts cobalt, remainder of wings green. Tail green with outer feathers blue. Iris brown, bill and legs black, feet blackish-grey. Length: 8 in. (20·3 cm). *Female.* Has no blue on wings, less black on throat and more yellow-green underneath.
In their habits, this Leaf Bird shows much similarity with *C. aurifrons.* The few nests that have been discovered between the dense foliage of high trees were made of twigs and stalks, covered on the outside with pieces of inner bark and cobwebs, and lined inside with soft fibre of plants.
In 1879 the first specimens came to the Zoological Gardens in London, and later to all the European countries. There are various opinions about this bird's song. It contains a number of scolding, chattering, and squeaky sounds, but also clear flute-like notes and rollers which recalls the song of the canary. It is quite certain that many bird sounds are included in their varied song repertoire.

Hardwick's Fruit-sucker, *Chloropsis h. hardwickei*

Genus: Irena

Fairy Blue Birds are quite difficult to accustom to artificial diets and should therefore be fed according to Diet C described on pages 2–3. This is the standard diet plus extra meat for difficult birds. The writers ease the acclimatisation period by housing incoming Fairy Blue Birds with mynahs which transfer easily and which are very helpful in teaching many other birds to accept foods with which they are not familiar.

Fairy Blue Birds are not completely peaceful with smaller softbills after they settle down in their aviaries. A pair owned by the writers at this moment is congenial to its other companions which include Red-breasted Marsh Birds, Gray's Thrushes, Saltators, and a few other birds of similar easy going temperament.

Fairy Blue Birds have successfully nested in the aviaries of Mr. Boehm in New Jersey. The nest is open and cup-shaped. The incubation period is thirteen days, and the young leave the nest when they are about twelve days old. They were not completely weaned for another month. This successful breeding was accomplished under ideal conditions with the right quantities and varieties of live food. The parents also fed raw meat to their young.

FAIRY BLUEBIRD, *Irena p. puella* (Latham)

SUBFAMILY: IRENINAE

G. Elfenblauvogel, Irena; F. Oiseau bleu des feés; D. Irena Buulbuul, Blauwe Feevogel   (Pl. XVI)

DISTRIBUTION: India, Burma, Thailand, Laos, Vietnam, Khmer, Malaysia, Borneo, parts of Indonesia, and some of the Philippine Islands.

DESCRIPTION: The large head, short neck, and heavy bódy are well-proportioned. An odd feature is the exceptionally small feet. The beak, feet, and legs are all black; and the eyes are bright ruby-red with black pupils.

Male. Has two colours only in his plumage. Upper parts are richly glossed blue in a very beautiful shade. Under parts are velvety black. The sharp separation lines dividing these two colours provide an interesting pattern. The blue encircles the top of the crown and becomes narrow on the nape before it broadens to include the wide shoulders. It tapers inward in the area of the secondary wing coverts and also includes the back, rump, upper tail and under tail coverts which are greatly elongated almost to the tip of the black tail. The remaining wing areas are black. The male is an extraordinarily beautiful bird. Length: about 10 in. (25 cm). *Female.* Is totally different in colour. She is a uniform shade of soft blue which seems to be combined with a trace of green all suffused by a smoky haze. The eyes are red as in the males. Young birds of both sexes are like females, but their eyes are dull coloured.

SUBSPECIES: The different subspecies show very minor variations such as slightly varying shades of blue and different lengths of the tail coverts. The subspecies *I. tweeddalei* from the Philippines is duskier and the colours are less sharply defined.

Irena cyanogaster with four subspecies, the Black-mantled or Philippine Fairy Blue Bird, has a duskier shade of blue and a broad black mantle. Dark blackish-blue extends from the lower breast through the under tail coverts.

FAMILY: BOMBYCILLIDAE

SUBFAMILY: BOMBYCILLINAE

Waxwings

The three species of Waxwings are all very similar in appearance and characteristics. The diet is the standard softbill diet plus greater quantities of fruit. Soaked raisins (or currants) and diced apple are the most suitable fruits. In the wild state, these birds consume quantities of small fruits such as pyracantha or privet berries. These items can be mixed with mynah pellets to coax them onto this more complete diet. For the most part, Waxwings do not show much of a preference for live food in captivity unless they are taught by other birds which take a more varied selection of foods. Greenfood is also important, and seeding grasses are important when they are available.

Waxwings are very beautiful birds. They adapt very well to aviary life even though at first they may show signs of panic

Waxwings are peaceful birds and mix well with bulbuls, Pekin Robins and all birds of similar size and temperament. The harmless intimidation posture includes fluffed feathers on the rump and chest, outstretched neck and open beak, and spread wings. When the black beak is open, the inside shows soft pink. Occasional beak snapping accompanies this posture.

Waxwings are softly and somberly shaded; but they have beautiful shapes and smooth, finely combed plumage. There are a few outstanding accents which characterise the genus. Each of the three species has a sharply drawn mask covering the forehead and lores, surrounding the eyes, and tapering backwards in a slender line to the back of the crown. The tapered recumbent crest is very shapely and smooth and is frequently raised. The main colouring is soft olive-brown on the head, neck, back, and chest. Variations are gradual and smooth. The back is darker and the chest is a little paler. Under parts fade to pale greyish-olive in the abdominal area. The underside of the tail is dull greyish-black.

The wings are bluish-grey slate, and the rump and tail are slate-grey becoming darker on the lower tail area.

In general, the sexes are alike. The call note is high, thin, and a little aggravating.

CEDAR WAXWING, *Bombycilla cedrorum*

D. Ceder-Pestvogel

DISTRIBUTION: Alaska, south-western Canada, north-western and central United States. Migrates southward to winter in various areas of South America and many Caribbean islands.

DESCRIPTION: In addition to the characteristics mentioned above, the Cedar Waxwing has several distinguishing features, most of which are bright and attractive. The tail is brightly tipped with yellow. The six inner flight feathers have small appendages of a bright coral shade. These waxlike appendages are stiff and shiny with no appearance of feather structure. They account for the name waxwing. They are ⅛ in. (3 mm) long and less than 1/16 in. (1·6 mm) wide. The dark brown throat is framed by a small white moustache, and a fine line of white borders the lower rim of the eye. The under tail coverts are greyish-yellow. Length: 6½ in. (16·5 cm) including the 2 in. (5 cm) tail.

WAXWING, BOHEMIAN WAXWING, *Bombycilla garrulus* (Linnaeus)

G. Seidenschwanz; F. Jaseur boréal; D. Pestvogel

DISTRIBUTION: Very widespread range includes northern Europe, Russia, Siberia, Alaska to north-western Canada, western and Rocky Mountain areas of United States. Winters in very large areas of United States from New York to Texas and California, central Europe, Japan, and southern China. Migrations show irregular choices of climate for winter environments.

DESCRIPTION: This species is slightly larger and a little more colourful than *B. cedrorum*. The flight feathers are tipped in yellow and white, and the wing coverts have white tips. Under tail coverts are rufous. The white line under the eye is longer stretching far behind the eye. The throat is much

Waxwing, *Bombycilla garrulus*

darker with a blackish shade. Length: about 8 in. (20 cm).

EASTERN WAXWING, JAPANESE WAXWING, *Bombycilla japonica*

DISTRIBUTION: Eastern Siberia, migrating in winter to Japan and the Ryukyu Islands.

DESCRIPTION: The tail is tipped with red instead of yellow, and the scapulars and under tail coverts have a reddish tinge. Flights have white tips with some red, and the waxy appendages are absent. Length: about 7 in. (18 cm).

FAMILY: MUSCICAPIDAE

SUBFAMILY: TURDINAE

Thrushes, Solitaires, Bluebirds, Robins and Allies

BY H. J. BATES AND R. L. BUSENBARK

Several members of the subfamily of thrushes and allies are excellent avicultural subjects and very popular. The huge subfamily of 49 genera and approximately 305 species includes many birds which are not ordinarily called thrushes.

Thrushes are usually popular because of their songs. Some have very attractive colouring, but the great majority are considerably less attractive than other avicultural favourites. Thrushes and allies usually have very likable personalities, which adapt well to aviary life. Since most thrushes are territorial birds, they often do not settle peacefully into aviaries with close relatives and several are very aggressive to other birds. The family runs the full gamut of personalities, however, and many are most mild-mannered and are considered to be delicate.

Not many thrushes are regularly available to aviculturists, although a great many have been successfully maintained in captivity.

Most of the popular members in aviculture thrive on the standard softbilled diet. Solitaires, bluebirds and other small members fare better on refined diets. A few species have been bred in captivity. Incubation is 13 to 14 days, and youngsters leave the nest in about 2 weeks. They are not completely self-feeding for another 2 weeks. More live food and raw meat are necessary during the breeding periods. During breeding seasons all thrushes may develop a far greater sense of aggressiveness.

The nests are usually cup shaped and are made of grasses and mud, with soft grasses for lining.

Genus: Zoothera

ORANGE-HEADED GROUND THRUSH, DAMA THRUSH, *Zoothera c. citrina* Latham (Pl. VII)
G. Damadrossel; F. Grive orangée; D. Damalijster

DISTRIBUTION: India, Sri Lanka, China, Burma, Thailand, Malaysia, Borneo, Bali, Java, Hainan, Andaman and Nicobar Islands.

DESCRIPTION: *Male.* Head and neck down to shoulder, and all under parts, rusty-orange with a bluish-grey line tapering behind the eye. Vent area usually whitish. Remaining upper parts bluish-slate-grey. A bar of white occurs on wings. Beak blackish; feet and legs flesh-coloured. Length: 8–9 in. (20·3–22·9 cm) in the various races, with rather a short broad tail. *Female.* Slightly smaller and has a dull brownish shade replacing bluish-grey areas, and rusty-orange areas are much duller. Immature birds are similar to females.

SUBSPECIES: White-throated Ground Thrush, White-masked

Ground Thrush, *Zoothera citrina cyanotus*, from southern India, has white on face, chin and throat. There are two brownish bars on sides of face.

Orange-headed Ground Thrushes live quietly in dense mountain forests, at heights from 1,200–3,600 ft (366–1,100 m) above sea level. Only in the breeding season is the male bird heard singing some stanzas of his fine and powerful song. The nest is built in the fork of a branch, 5 ft (1·5 m) above the ground. It is shaped like a cup and is loosely made of thin twigs, leaves and bark, lined with moss, hair and plant fibres. The 3 or 4 eggs are greenish-white with brown spots.

Orange-headed Ground Thrushes are excellent aviary birds. They are very attractive, quite hardy, and are easily acclimatised. A single bird can very well be kept in a spacious cage for his song alone. He will not become as tame as the Shama and will need 2 hours' flying every day. These thrushes are placid birds and learn to imitate many sounds. In addition to the insectivorous food, moistened with a little grated carrot, 5 or 6 mealworms, or pieces of raw meat, must be given every day. To this may be added pieces of apple, plenty of berries, greenstuff, salad and chickweed.

These birds were to be seen in the Zoological Gardens. London, as long ago as 1876. They can be kept with others of similar size in an aviary with sleeping quarters separated. Feeding trays should be placed at strategic points in order to prevent quarrels. The Orange-headed form was bred by H. Astley as reported in *Avicultural Magazine*, (3) 2, 1910–11, p. 368. The White-headed form was bred at the London Zoo in 1912. (*London Zoo Reports*).

There are many other species in this genus, but many are not aviary birds. Some of the more attractive are listed below.

Kuhl's Ground Thrush, *Zoothera interpres*, with 2 subspecies, from Thailand, Malaysia, Indonesia, Borneo and the Philippines. Beautiful, but rare in the wild state. Head and neck chestnut; face, throat and upper breast black; upper parts slate-grey; under parts white with black spots on lower breast and sides; two broad white wing bars and

white on face. Length: 6½ in. (16·5 cm).

Pied Ground Thrush, Ward's Ground Thrush, *Zoothera wardii*, from India. *Male*. Head, neck, upper chest and upper parts black; under parts and eyebrow white; white spots on lower back. *Female*. Olive-brown above and buff below, with dark bars.

Orange-headed Ground Thrush, *Zoothera c. citrina*

Ashy Ground Thrush, *Zoothera cinerea*, from the Philippines. Very rare. Upper parts dusky black; under parts white and pale yellow with large black spots on most areas; white wing patches; face black and white.

Siberian Ground Thrush, *Zoothera sibirica*, with 2 subspecies. Widespread in USSR, China, Korea and Japan, migrating to many areas in South-East Asia, including Malaysia and Thailand. *Male*. dark, dusky-bluish-grey, paler on under parts. Eyebrows and central abdomen white, and tips of under tail coverts whitish. *Female*. Olive-brown above mottled brown and whitish under sides; buff eyebrows. Length: 9 in. (22·9 cm).

Other species, less attractive or less distinctive, occur in many Indian and South-East Asian areas, as well as several in Africa, and 2 in North America.

Abyssinian Ground Thrush, *Zoothera piaggiae*, was bred by B. S. Ward at Winged World, Morecambe, as reported in *Avicultural Magazine*, Vol. 77, (5), Sept./Oct., p. 168.

Genus: Turdus

Black Robins or Black Thrushes

There are several species of Black Robins or those which are near black which have very interesting personalities as well as beautiful songs. Most are quite aggressive to other thrushes their own size, and several bird keepers have had unpleasant experiences with some of the largest ones because of their dominance.

On the other hand, the writers have had some of their most fascinating experiences with one species, *Turdus serranus*. This single individual became tame of his own accord and showed an unending affection for those he liked. He indulged in two favourite displays both of which were accompanied by very quiet but unbelievably sweet songs into which he had incorporated songs of other birds including an entire chorus of canaries!

One of the displays consisted of strutting along the tops of a row of bird cages with head lowered, wings half spread, and fluffed body feathers. He executed this display only at night when one of his favourite humans was close by.

The other display consisted of a very bold and active affair which started with a fast brush against the head of one of the writers. This was the signal for the writers to interrupt all activities while the bird carried out his expression of affection. He jumped into the air many times and with flapping wings, open beak, and ecstatic song pounced upon an oustretched hand held high again and again gradually settling down to his strutting display while standing on the hand. This display was executed at least once daily for many years.

This bird was the ruler of a large enclosed patio which was lined with cages and aviaries. He could not be trusted with any small birds but did allow, or at least tolerated, several birds such as macaws, cockatoos, a Cockatiel, a Half Moon Conure, Trumpeters, toucans, and Coleto Mynahs.

GLOSSY BLACK THRUSH, GIANT MOUNTAIN ROBIN, *Turdus serranus*

DISTRIBUTION: Mexico, Central America, Colombia,

Venezuela, Peru, Ecuador and Bolivia.

DESCRIPTION: *Male*. Entirely black, glossy in several areas of upper parts, dull on under parts with occasional tinges of brownish-black. Beak, feet and legs bright yellow or yellowish-orange; there is a bold fleshy yellow eye ring. *Female*. Olive-brown above and pale reddish-brown below. Length: 11 in. (28 cm).

RED-LEGGED THRUSH, *Turdus plumbeus rubriceps* (Temminck)   (Pl. VII)
G Kubadrossel; F Merle moquear à pieds rouge; D Cuba-spot Lijster

DISTRIBUTION: Cuba.
DESCRIPTION: *Male*. Slatey-grey bridles, sides of head and throat. Stripes on cheek, chin, abdomen, vent area and flanks are chestnut-brownish-yellow. Lower tail coverts white. Wings grey with white tips, central tail feathers black, outer ones slate-grey with white tips. Irides brown, edge of eyelid red, beak black. Feet and legs are reddish-orange. Length: 9½ in. (23 cm).

Genus: Cossypha

CAPE ROBIN, *Cossypha c. caffra* (Linnaeus)
G. Kaprötel; F. Cossyphe du Cap; D. Kaaps Roodborstje

DISTRIBUTION: South Africa.
DESCRIPTION: *Male*. Upper parts olive-brown, crown grey, rump and upper tail coverts reddish-brown. Has a white eyebrow stripe. Sides of head black, neck and throat light reddish-brown, breast and sides of body grey. Centre of abdomen white, anal area and lower tail coverts rust coloured. Iris brown, bill black, legs and feet brown. *Female*. Neck cream coloured, throat white, upper breast rust coloured. Length: 7¼ in. (18·4 cm).
Cape Robins live in gardens and parks where there is plenty of brushwood. They are mobile birds, which regularly

Cape Robin, *Cossypha c. caffra*

spread their wings and tails. They run quickly over the ground, sometimes with their tails standing straight up in the air. They were first imported to Germany in 1909, since when they have been irregularly brought into Europe.
These lively birds are not suitable for a cage, but they can be tolerated in a mixed aviary as long as a pair is not included. If this happens, the male will chase the female fiercely, and if she has no way of escape into dense undergrowth she may be harmed. The best method is to put the female into the aviary first, and introduce the male bird just prior to the

breeding season.
The song is varied and not too loud. The birds soon get used to universal food, mixed with fruit cut into small pieces, bread and milk, grated carrot, boiled apple and egg. In addition, 10–12 mealworms should be given each day. Breeding results were obtained in South Africa in 1954. When the young flew out of the nest the male parent bird had to be seized, as he pursued them fiercely.

NATAL ROBIN, NATAL REDBREAST, *Cossypha natalensis*
D. Natal Roodborstje

DISTRIBUTION: South Africa.
DESCRIPTION: Crown chestnut, upper parts chestnut with a touch of grey. Wings bluish-grey; sides of head, rump and lower parts warm reddish-brown. Tail black and reddish-brown.
The first breeding results were obtained in the Boehm aviaries in the USA in 1963. The nest was in a hollow tree stump, about 4 in. (10·2 cm) deep. It was basin-shaped and made from grasses. The female incubated for 14 days and 3 eggs, which were blue with brown markings. Both parents fed the young with insects and mealworms and after 12 days they left the nest. In addition to live food they avidly consumed sliced raw meat.
A few more subspecies of this family have been imported from various parts of Africa: Blue-shoulder Robin-Chat, Blue-shoulder Redbreast, *Cossypha cyanocampter*, from Ghana and Cameroon; Heuglin's Robin-Chat, Heuglin's Redbreast, *Cossypha heuglini*, from Kenya and Mozambique; White-browed Robin-Chat, White-capped Redbreast, *Cossypha niveicapilla*, from Ghana and Cameroon.
C. niveicapilla was bred at Birdland, Gloucestershire (L. Hill) as reported in *Avicultural Magazine*, Vol. 74, 1968, p. 25.
White-headed Robin-Chat, *Cossypha albicapilla*, was bred by A. Ezra as reported in *Avicultural Magazine*, Vol. (5) 4, 1939, p. 304.
They are all birds of the dense brushwood, who seek their food to a great extent on the ground. They possess varied song talent, and include many sounds from other birds.
They should be given heated winter quarters.

Genus: Sialia

American Bluebirds

BY K. A. NORRIS

The genus *Sialia* comprises three species only, all inhabiting the American continent extending as far northward as Canada. They have the rounded head and bold eyes common to most species belonging to the Turdidae family, but their wings and tail are long and their legs comparatively short. Consequently their movements on the ground are somewhat clumsy, unlike those of the true thrushes and chats. In fact, their posture and behaviour suggests a close affinity to the flycatchers and they are equally skilled at 'hawking' insects on the wing.

Their food consists mainly of insects although weed seeds are said to form an important part of their diet and they will also occasionally take soft fruit such as wild raspberries and elderberries. The young however appear to be reared exclusively on insects.

According to Taverner (*Birds of Canada*), their choice of nesting sites is very varied and they are equally content with the hollow cornices of buildings, dead tree stumps, old woodpecker holes in telegraph posts, or in open fronted or hollow log nest boxes hung about the buildings and trees of the prairie homesteads. In wild, barren country they are found nesting in crannies in the rocks and cliffs—in fact, their only requirement seems to be a suitable hole to shelter the nest, irrespective of where it may be; and like the robin, *Erithacus rubecula*, they seem to favour the vicinity of human habitation. The nest is constructed mainly of grasses, with a few dead leaves and moss in the foundation, the cup being lined with finer grasses. Some 4–6 pale blue eggs are laid which the hen alone incubates for about 14 days. The young leave the nest between two and three weeks after hatching and the parents continue to feed them for a further week or so before they learn to fend for themselves. Two, and sometimes three, broods are reared in a season.

In display, the cock assumes a stiff posture, either slightly crouching or upright, with his wings partly open and quivering, thus showing to full advantage the brilliant blue of his upper parts. He will also hover in front of the hen, holding a blade of grass in his beak, or offer her food whilst hovering directly above her and occasionally gently tapping her on the back with his feet if she does not immediately accept his offering.

In captivity bluebirds are hardy and may remain in an outdoor, unheated aviary throughout the year provided that they have access to a draught-proof shelter. They will nest freely either in an aviary or large cage but it is preferable that they should be in an outdoor enclosure where they may have the opportunity to supplement the food supplied to them with winged insects which they themselves may be able to capture. They will use any form of nest box and young have been successfully reared on maggots and mealworms alone. It is an advantage however to vary the diet with small caterpillars, spiders, moths and ant cocoons whenever possible. As many as 1,500 insects a day may be used to rear a brood of five young to maturity.

During the nesting season they become exceedingly aggressive and if breeding results are to be achieved, the pair should be given an aviary to themselves. A careful watch must be kept on the behaviour of the cock as he may persistantly drive the hen until she becomes completely exhausted, if she is not ready to go to nest. If the aviary is large and sufficient natural cover has been provided in which the hen may find shelter from his attacks, it is unlikely that she will suffer any serious harm, but if the enclosure is small, the cock may succeed in driving her into a corner from which she cannot escape. If she is not then rescued she may be seriously injured or even killed.

Bluebirds are very strictly protected in their native country and are now so rare in captivity that any aviculturist who is fortunate enough to possess a pair cannot afford to risk such losses, however anxious he may be to increase his stock. If therefore the pair do not settle down amicably together after a day or so, they should be separated and kept in a large cage, divided by a wire slide, until they are obviously on better terms with each other. After a time the cock may begin to offer insects to the hen through the partition and it is then usually safe to reintroduce them to their breeding quarters.

Their staple food should consist of a high grade insectivorous mixture moistened with grated raw carrot or apple. Water should not be used to mix the food as it tends to turn sour much too quickly in hot weather, nor has it any food value whereas the juice of carrots or apple is, in itself, a valuable food, containing several properties which assist the digestive process and improve the quality and natural colouring of the plumage. In addition, the birds should have a liberal supply of live insects at all times and, as already mentioned, the supply must be unlimited when young are being reared.

Bluebirds are migratory within the American continent and with the approach of winter it may be found that they become extremely restless, constantly flying from end to end of their aviary. At this time there may also be constant bickering between the sexes and it is then as well to separate the pairs and to keep them apart, either in separate aviaries, or in cages, until the approach of the next breeding season when they may be reintroduced to their breeding quarters. It may also be found necessary to separate the young cocks from the hens during the winter but it is usually safe to keep all the birds of the same sex together until the following spring.

It is hardly necessary to add that a brood of young birds should be separated from their parents as soon as possible after they become independent, and certainly before a second brood is hatched, otherwise they will be attacked by the old cock and seriously injured or killed.

EASTERN BLUEBIRD, *Sialia sialis*

G. Hüttensanger; F. Rouge-gorge bleu; D. Canadese Sialia (Pl. VII)

DISTRIBUTION: Temperate eastern USA and in Canada, across the southern part, commonly to Manitoba, more rarely to Saskatchewan.

DESCRIPTION: *Male*. Crown to tail, and including face, deep sky-blue; throat, breast and flanks bright chestnut. Irides very dark brown, beak and legs blackish. *Female*. Similar but blue of upper parts less intense and under parts dull brown. Length 6½–7½ in. (16·5–19 cm).

Immature birds mainly brown extensively flecked and spotted with buff-white. Only flights and tail are blue and this is usually more intense on the young males. There are 4 subspecies which vary only slightly. It was first bred, at the London Zoo, in 1860.

Eastern Bluebird, *Sialia sialis*

WESTERN BLUEBIRD, MEXICAN BLUEBIRD, *Sialia mexicana*

G. Mexicanischen Hüttensanger; F. Rouge-gorge bleu de Mexique; D. Mexicaanse Sialia

DISTRIBUTION: North-western USA and southern British Columbia.
DESCRIPTION: *Male*. Head to tail, including face and throat, deep purplish-blue with bar of deep chestnut across back and shoulders. Breast and flanks deep chestnut; abdomen pale greyish-blue. Irides very dark brown, beak, feet and legs blackish. *Female*. Much paler and duller in colour, bar across back sometimes brown but never chestnut; throat pale greyish faintly tinged with blue; breast and flanks greyish brown. Immature birds much like those of the Eastern Bluebird but the blue on flights and tail is more violaceous. Length: 6½–7 in. (16·5–18 cm).
SUBSPECIES: Six subspecies are recognised but there is little apparent difference.

MOUNTAIN BLUEBIRD, *Sialia currucoides* (Bechstein)

G. Berghüttensanger; F. Rouge-gorge bleu des montagnes; D. Berg-Sialia

DISTRIBUTION: Western North America, in Canada from the west coast east to Manitoba, north to the Yukon and Mackenzie Valley.
DESCRIPTION: *Male*. Above uniform bright cerulean-blue; throat, breast and sides pale greyish-blue, abdomen, flanks and crissum whitish faintly tinged with blue. Irides very dark brown, beak, feet and legs blackish. *Female*. Mainly dull greyish-brown, lighter below with abdomen and crissum whitish. Flights and tail dull blue. Immature birds are like female but more whitish on throat and with back and under parts heavily spangled and streaked with buff-white. Outer flights and tail washed with dull blue, slightly more intense on young males.
Although females of each species are very similar in general colouring the female Mountain Bluebird may readily be distinguished by her more elongated form and upright posture. Length: 6½–7¾ in. (16·5–18·5 cm).
This species was first bred, in England, in 1938.

Mountain Bluebird, *Sialia currucoides*

Genus: Copsychus

SHAMA, WHITE-RUMPED SHAMA, *Copsychus m. malabaricus* (Scopoli)   (Pl. VII)

G. Schamadrossel; F. Merle Schama; D. Schamalijster
DISTRIBUTION: India, Sri Lanka, Andaman Islands, Burma, Thailand, Malaysia, Indonesia, Borneo and Hainan.
DESCRIPTION: *Male*. The slender black beak is ¾ in. (1·9 cm) long. Feet and legs are dark pinkish-flesh. The longest central tail feathers are glossy black, and all remaining graduated feathers, which fit mainly underneath the central ones, have broad white tips. Upper parts and hood, which covers the head and extends on to upper breast, glossy black. Rump and upper tail coverts pure white. Under parts below the black are rich glossy chestnut. *Female*. Slightly smaller and has a much shorter tail. Colouring mainly dull brown, with shades of grey on upper parts. Young males, in addition to shorter tails, have dark slate-grey replacing the black, and pale rufous replacing the chestnut of the adults. About 11 in. (27·9 cm) in length including the beautiful tail of 7½ in. (19·1 cm). Total length varies with subspecies, as the length of the tail is different in several races and also varies with age. Immature males of the same races may have tails fully 3 in. (7·6 cm) shorter than adults. The longest-tailed races which the writers have had came from Thailand.
Shamas are wonderful aviary birds, having dominant and lively personalities, and are popular as individual caged

pets. Sleek and beautifully proportioned, they show great precision in their rapid movements and immobile pauses. Shamas flip their tails up and down and often hold them in interesting poses. Their saucy attitudes and personalities are mostly reflected in their tail movements. They are excellent song-birds and are rightly classed among the finest singers in the world. The clear liquid notes, with silvery tones, are beautifully melodious.
Because of their alertness and dominant personalities, shamas frequently become tame enough in aviaries to accept live food from the fingers.
Because shamas are dominant birds, their companions must be chosen carefully, although their domination is usually directed against their own kind. They should not be housed with small defenceless birds or with birds of aggressive personalities which could overcome them. Robust bulbuls, medium-large thrushes of the genus *Turdus*, Chloropsis, larger tanagers, and others of similar sizes, are good companions.
Caution is needed over keeping shamas and dhyals together. Shamas usually dominate dhyals, but both are strong enough in most instances to balance the scales to the point where dominance is not dangerous. In aviaries which have dhyals but not shamas, the dhyals usually dominate. Because the dominance is often subtle, these birds, if mixed should not be limited to two individuals. There is safety in

numbers.

Standard softbilled diet, with a little extra live food and raw meat, is a satisfactory diet for shamas, dhyals and allies. What is possibly a first breeding by R. Phillipps was reported in *Avicultural Magazine*, Vol. 4, 1897–98, pp. 138–42.

> 'In the first few days they were fed by the female, later by the male also. The young Shamas were reared on cockroaches, mealworms and gentles. While feeding the young, the parents refused not only to carry domestic food to them but wholly gave up domestic food themselves.'

Strickland's Shama, *Copsychus stricklandii*, with 2 subspecies, from Borneo, has a white crown but is otherwise the

Shama, *Copsychus m. malabaricus*

same as *C. malabaricas*. The smaller shorter-tailed White-eyebrowed Shama, *C. luzoniensis*, with 3 subspecies, from the Philippines, is about 7 in. (17·8 cm) long. A long white eyebrow, white wing bars, chestnut rump, white on lower breast and abdomen, are the main differences from *C. malabaricus*. Black Shama, *C. niger*, with 2 subspecies, is also from the Philippines. This rare species is all black and 8 in. (20·3 cm) long. Orange-tailed Shama, *C. pyrropygus*, from Malaysia, Borneo and Sumatra, is about 8 in. (20·3 cm) long, or a little longer, including the shorter tail. The rump and most of the tail are chestnut-orange, with a broad black terminal bar. Upper parts, head, neck and upper breast are sooty greyish-black; under parts are dull rufous with a paler central area. A slender white eyebrow stripe occurs above the lores.

DHYAL THRUSH, MAGPIE ROBIN, *Copsychus s. saularis* (Linnaeus) (Pl. VII)
G. Dajalrossel; F. Merle dial des Indes; D. Dayalijster

DISTRIBUTION: India, Sri Lanka, China, Andaman Islands, Burma, Thailand, Malaysia, Borneo, Indonesia, the Philippines.
DESCRIPTION: *Male*. Upper parts and hood covering head,

neck and upper breast glossy black with a bold white wing bar and white outer tail feathers. Remaining under parts white. Beak blackish; feet and legs flesh-coloured. *Female*. Dark greyish instead of black, and pale grey in white areas.

Dhyal Thrush, *Copsychus s. saularis*

Shades are variable in different races. Length: 7–9½ in. (17·8–24·1 cm).

SUBSPECIES: There are minor variations in the 17 subspecies. These variations include lesser amounts of white on tail, and black on abdomen. In one race all colouring is black, except for white wing bar.

Dhyals are less flamboyant in personality than shamas. The simple colouring is good, but not as outstanding as that of the shama, and the tail is much shorter. Personalities and songs, though subordinate to those of shamas, are nevertheless excellent. Requirements are the same as for shamas.

They live in dense woods where there is under-brush, both in flat country and in mountainous regions up to a height of 3,600 ft (1,100 m) above sea level. They spend the winter in flat country, always in the vicinity of water, and they often come into gardens and around houses. Their food consists of worms, caterpillars, butterflies, beetles and other insects, which they find under bushes and trees or in agricultural and pasture land. In the morning and evening, and sometimes at night, they sing from a high branch or from the edge of a roof. The song is varied and not too loud.

When dhyals are kept with other birds they behave peacefully, except when they are nesting. They must then have a separate aviary. The female builds a basin-shaped nest of straw and bark in an open nesting-box or basket. Five eggs form the clutch, incubation lasts for 13 days, and the young leave the nest after 3 weeks.

In addition to insectivorous food and mealworms, various mixed foods can be made up, in which bread and milk, hard-boiled egg, raw meat, grated carrots, currants, elderberries and ants' eggs can be mixed up together.

These birds are proof against the climate and, provided they have sleeping quarters that are damp-proof, they can safely be left in an outside aviary during the winter.

As far back as 1873 they were kept in the London Zoological Gardens, where they bred. (*Foreign Birds for Cage and Aviary*, 1, 1906, p. 146.)

Although at first they are shy, they quickly learn to recognise their keeper, and will soon eat mealworms out of his hand.

Genus: Myadestes

Solitaires

There are seven species of Solitaires ranging from Alaska to southern Brazil. These are dull birds of nondescript colouring, and they require a refined softbilled diet. They are steady and poised in aviaries and are very peaceful; they tame easily. Perhaps their main drawback is that they become too sedentary in either cage or aviary and must often be prodded into exercise. Consequently rich diet must be avoided. Mealworms in excess especially seem to cause digestive trouble, and this is perhaps a little difficult to curb since mealworms happen to be the nest means of taming these birds, and gaining their confidence.

The large heads, somewhat coarse plumage, and large, soft eyes are characteristic of most of the thrush species. Despite their total lack of beauty from the standpoint of appearance, they are very highly regarded among those who appreciate good quality in song.

TOWNSEND'S SOLITAIRE, *Myiadestes t. townsendi* (Audubon)

G. Klarinettenvogel; F. Solitaire de Townsend; D. Klarinetvogel

DISTRIBUTION: Alaska, Canada, Western USA, Mexico.
DESCRIPTION: Upper parts brownish grey; under parts grey. Wing patch pale buff. Around the eye is a narrow white feathered ring. Length 8 in. (23 cm).
In summer months these birds live in trees and feed on insects which they catch on the wing. During winter months

Townsend's Solitaire, *Myiadestes t. townsendi*

they feed mainly on all kinds of berry fruits, especially juniper-berries. In the breeding season the birds are generally seen in pairs. They nest in rock crevices, the nest is extensive, bowl-shaped and made of twigs, stalks and pieces of bark. The 3 or 4 eggs are greenish-blue, covered with reddish brown spots at the blunt end. Their song is loud and unusually beautiful, and by some people considered as superior to that of the nightingale. These birds were first introduced into Germany in 1868, and later fairly frequently. The first breeding result was obtained in Moscow in 1912 in Mrs. Prowé's aviary. The nest was built of hay and coconut fibre in an open nest box. The 3 eggs were hatched by the hen in 12 days, and both parents reared the young on ants' eggs and mealworms, and later with fruit and berries. The youngsters left the nest after 14 days.

BROWN-BACKED SOLITAIRE, JILGUERO, *Myadestes obscurus*

G. Braunrücken Klarinettenvoge; F. Solitaire à das brun; D. Bruinrug-Klarinetvogel

DISTRIBUTION: Mexico.
DESCRIPTION: Head, neck, and under parts dull grey. The large eyes have encircling narrow white feathered rings. Olive-brown in dull greyish shades covers most of the upper parts. The colouring is duskier on rump and has olive-slate in tail. Beak, feet and legs brown. The wings have more brown of brighter shades. Length: 8¼ in. (21·5 cm) including short black beak of ⅝ in. (1·6 cm) and à 3½ in. (9 cm) tail.

Genus: Garrulax

Jay Thrushes

The 43–44 species of Jay Thrush (or Laughing Jay-Thrush) which comprise the genus *Garrulax* are different from all other members of the family. They are large and audacious and should be kept with other large and aggressive birds. They will easily overpower and kill small birds; they are fond of nestlings and are excellent mousers. Some are of medium size and less pugnacious. All the popular species are very hardy and readily accept artificial diets. The standard softbill diet, with additional raw meat and live food is suitable.

Not all Jay Thrushes would prove of interest to aviculturists but some are very popular with bird keepers and zoos because they have fascinating and often comic personalities.

Jay thrushes are all heavy-bodied, with medium-long tails, large heads and strong beaks. They are very gregarious and are more entertaining in large groups.

WHITE-CRESTED JAY THRUSH, *Garrulax leucolophus* (Hardwicke)   (Pl. VI)

G. Weisshaubenhäherling; F. Garrulax à huppe blanche; D. Mitkuifgaai

DISTRIBUTION: India, South-East Asia, Sumatra.
DESCRIPTION: A very full and shapely crest is composed of very fine, soft feathers. Head and crest back to nape and under parts, with a large bib down to chest, white; brighter on forehead, throat and chest, and tinged with grey on back of crest and hind crown. Beak and a long slender facial mask black. The mask covers the lores, surrounds the eyes, and encloses part of cheek area. The rest of the colouring is dark and smooth but rather dull, with the brightest shades adjoining the white areas. Irides reddish-brown; feet and legs greyish. All the plumage, except flights and tail, is long, soft and luxurious. Sexes are very similar and usually difficult to distinguish, but females have slightly smaller crests, with a little more grey in them. Length: about 12 in. (30·5 cm) including the 4½ in. (11·4 cm) tail.

SUBSPECIES: One of the Thai subspecies is a little smaller and has a broad area of grey on the nape. The sumatran

White-crested Jay Thrush, *Garrulax leucolophus*

subspecies, *G. l. bicolor*, has shades of black in the brown. With its graceful white crest, nearly always carried erect, it is one of the most beautiful birds that can be kept with other birds of its own size in a large flight. It is exceedingly active and can easily capture and devour any small birds, but is a cheerful and inquisitive inmate of an aviary, and constantly on the move. Its song, which is powerful, consists of a variety of flute-like tones. Unfortunately, it seldom becomes tame.

It is seldom possible to breed from these birds as they have an unfortunate habit of swallowing their young when these are a week or so old.

To be seen to best advantage a pair should be kept in a small aviary by themselves. They are among the most amusing and entertaining of birds; they sleep huddled together and cover each other with their wings. During the day they play together and tumble over each other with a constant cackling, which sounds much like human laughter, but they are too noisy to be kept in the house.

HOAMI, MELODIUS JAY THRUSH, SPECTACLED JAY THRUSH, CHINESE NIGHTINGALE, *Garrulax c. canorus* (Linnaeus)

G. Augenbrauenhäherling; F. Garrulaxe à sourcils; D. Hoami, Bruine Gaailijster

DISTRIBUTION: South China, Assam.
DESCRIPTION: Over-all colouring brown, in warm, earthy, near-chestnut tones. Under parts slightly paler, with golden-brown on throat and chest. The dominant feature is the white spectacled effect which surrounds the eyes and then trails into long eyebrows behind. The white has a frosty tint of pale blue. The large beak is horn-coloured with brownish-horn along the upper mandible and the tip. Irides brown; feet and legs yellowish. Length: 8¾ in. (22·2 cm).
Hoamis are birds from wooded mountainous country, although they also make their appearance in lower regions where there is shrubbery and undergrowth. They are also seen in gardens. They are not shy birds; they move about with quick leaps through the branches of bushes and often alight upon the ground. Their song is beautiful and can be heard in the early morning and evening. The range of voice is so extensive that they are able to sing both deep and very high notes, and thus produce a really wonderful melody. The bird is very active and must be kept in a cage of at least 4 ft (1·22 m) so that it can take adequate exercise. It may be kept in a flight with other birds, provided these are large and of a quiet disposition, as the Hoami is apt to display sudden fits of bad temper.
In the wild they feed chiefly on insects, but in captivity feed on oats, hemp, canary seed, fruit, and numerous insects such as mealworms, beetles and locusts, and finely cut raw meat. Small mice and small fish are also eaten.
In a spacious and well-planted aviary these birds will soon nest. They build a bowl-shaped nest of thin twigs, leaves and grass, and line it with fir needles, and it is ready in 4 days. The 4 light-blue eggs will be incubated alternately by both parents, and the chicks will be hatched in 12 days. These are reared exclusively on ants' eggs and insects. In order to be certain of success the adult birds can be left to seek their own food among the undergrowth as soon as the youngsters arrive. The birds are fond of sunflower seeds, which they clasp in one claw against their perch and open with a powerful blow of their beaks. They are fond of bathing. They can pass the winter in an unheated room.

WHITE-THROATED LAUGHING JAY-THRUSH, *Garrulax a. albogularis* (Gould)

G. Weisskehlhäherling; F. Garrulaxe à gorge blanche; D. Witkeel-Gaailijster

DISTRIBUTION: India, China, Nepal, Formosa.
DESCRIPTION: *Male.* Upper parts olive-brown, rump orange-brown. Under parts yellowish-rust. Tail has a broad tip, which is white on the upper side and greyish on the under side. There is no crest, but a broad, flaring white throat patch is very dominant. The throat patch starts directly under the beak and spreads out under the eyes to cover the lower cheek area and sides of neck. Irides bluish-grey; beak dark brownish-horn; feet grey. Length: 10¾ in. (27·3 cm). *Female.* A little smaller.
These birds occur in large flights in woody mountain country. They are lively and noisy by nature, and often come to the ground, where, among the shrubs and in the bamboo

White-throated Laughing Jay-Thrush, *Garrulax a. albogularis*

fields, they seek their food, which consists of insects for which they search under the leaves. They also remove the moss from tree trunks in order to get at the larvae. They construct large basin-shaped nests of grass, leaves, moss and plant fibres in a fork in a branch of a tree. Three to four eggs are laid, which are blue, without spots or markings.
These birds were imported for the first time to London in 1876.

STRIATED LAUGHING JAY THRUSH, *Garrulax s. striatus* (Vigors)

G. Streifenhäherling; F. Garrulaxe strié; D. Gestreepte Gaailijster

DISTRIBUTION: India and Burma.
DESCRIPTION: This is not a colourful species, but it is robustly handsome, with a very strong appearance. The colouring is deep, rich brown, slightly paler on the under parts. Very prominent but fine pale buff striations occur everywhere, except on the tail and flights. Irides red; feet bluish-grey. The heavy body and large head appear even larger because of the long, luxurious and very bushy feathers, which are especially prominent on the head and neck. The black beak is shorter than that of most jay thrushes. Length: 11½ in. (29·2 cm).
These birds live in pairs or in small flights in lower mountainous regions. They stay in inaccessible low forest land and feed on fruit and insects. They twitter, and also make hoarse cackling noises. The birds are strong and soon get used to life in an aviary.
Also from India is the Streaked Laughing Jay Thrush, *Garrulax lineatus* (with five subspecies). It is smaller and much duller than *Garrulax s. striatus*, with no bushy feathers. The head and chest are dull greyish-brown.
Red-capped Jay Thrush, *Garrulax mitrata*, from Sumatra, Malaysia and Borneo, has white stripes on its chestnut-brown head and neck. Under parts are olive-grey, vent and lower tail coverts chestnut-brown.
White-breasted Jay Thrush, *Garrulax cachinnans jerdoni*, comes from India. It has white eyebrow stripes, edged on both sides with grey; throat and breast grey; ear coverts reddish-brown.

CHINESE JAY THRUSH, BLACK-THROATED LAUGHING JAY THRUSH, *Garrulax c. chinensis* (Scopoli)　(Pl. VI)
G. Weissohrhäherling; F. Garrulaxe de Chine; D. Witwang-Gaailijster

DISTRIBUTION: China, Burma, Thailand and neighbouring countries, Hainan.
DESCRIPTION: Upper parts dark mauve-grey with slight tints of brownish-olive on wings and tail. Under parts paler mauve-grey. Crown dark mauve-grey. The head has interesting markings. A small bristly black crest occurs on the forehead. Black on a small mask surrounds the eyes, covers a small area below the lores and a large area on the chin and throat. A large cheek patch is white. Beak black; feet blackish-brown. Length: about 11 in. (27·9 cm).
This species is a little smaller than most popular jay thrushes and has a disposition which is considerably milder than most. Although dark and sombre, it has an interesting pattern and a good song, and is a desirable aviary bird.
Chinese Jay Thrushes nest in low trees and lay 3–4 eggs.
Masked Jay Thrush, *Garrulax perspicillatus*, from South China, has a black forehead, black sides to the head and ear coverts. The remaining upper parts are greyish-brown and the under parts are rusty-brown-white. Length: 12 in. (30·5 cm).
These birds were imported for the first time in 1878, to the London Zoological Gardens, where, in 1964, the first breeding result was obtained. A pair had been living there since 1956, in an outside aviary, with White-throated Jay Thrushes. The bowl-shaped nest had been built of hay and straw, high up in a bush. As the adult birds became greatly alarmed when anyone approached the vicinity of the nest, it was impossible to keep a close watch. When the young bird left the nest it was fed by both parents, and also by the White-throated Jay Thrushes. In addition to insectivorous food, plenty of mealworms and maggots were given to them.

SUBFAMILY: TIMALIINAE

Babblers, Laughing Jay Thrushes and Allies

This subfamily contains several groups of loosely related birds. There are about 380 species in about 61 genera. The family has undergone several revisions in classification by different authorities. As far as the aviculturist is concerned, the classification will be confusing; but the bird keeper will probably not worry about the relationships. Superficially, the relationships are not readily apparent and are often very obscure and technical. Not many people would be able to see a relationship between Yuhina and a White-crested Laughing Jay Thrush. Members of the family are most numerous in Asia, but also range from Africa to Australia.
There are comparatively very few species which are readily available, but some of these are among the most important and most popular of all softbilled birds. Those called babblers are rarely of interest to bird keepers.
Most species are easily acclimatised and quickly take to artificial diets. Two exceptions are the Blue-winged Siva and the Yuhina, both of which require a more refined diet and are more delicate during the acclimatisation period. These species should be kept with smaller birds because even the Pekin Nightingale is a little overbearing towards them.
Babblers, Sibias, Mesias, and Pekin Nightingales require the simple standard softbilled diet. Jay Thrushes require the standard diet plus extra rations of raw meat and live foods.

Babblers

The large groups of babblers, scimitar babblers, tit babblers, shrike babblers, and so on, are not of interest to most bird keepers. They have poorly defined colours and patterns, and uninteresting shapes for the most part, and there is such a tremendous number that space prohibits a detailed coverage.
Their care is of the standard softbill diet, plus regular acclimatisation procedure. Large birds may tend to be quarrelsome with smaller ones but they are usually active and gregarious birds with bright personalities.

Genus: Chrysomma

GOLDEN-EYED BABBLER, *Chrysomma sinensis* (Gmelin)
G. Goldaugentimalie; F. Timalie aux yeux d'or; D. Goudoog-Timalia

DISTRIBUTION: Burma, Thailand, Laos, China.
DESCRIPTION: Upper parts reddish-brown, crown and nape lighter. Cheeks, area around eyes, lores and stripe above ear coverts white. Ear coverts brown. Throat and breast white; abdomen cream-coloured. Wings rust-brown, flights dark brown with rust-coloured edges. Tail brown with rust-coloured margins. Irides brown, yellow at edges; eye cere orange–red. Bill black with yellow nostrils; legs and feet golden-yellow. Length: 6½–7 in. (16·5–17·8 cm).
These birds are distributed widely and therefore several subspecies have been recognised, which show slight differences in depth of colour.
Usually the birds are seen in pairs or in small flights. They avoid dense woods and by preference seek out high grassland with low bushes, or gardens and parks. They rarely alight on the ground, and find their food along the twigs and leaves. Their nests are in high hedges or trees and are made of broad blades of grass and bark, which the birds stick together with cobwebs, and line with fine grasses. Sometimes nests are hung between three strong grass stalks; they are cone-shaped, the tip pointing towards the ground. The 4–5 eggs are oval in shape, pink in colour, and are covered with brick-red, violet or brown markings.

Plate XIX

Grey Zebra Finch ♂
Silver Zebra Finch
White Zebra Finch
Chestnut-flanked White Zebra Finch

Grey Zebra Finch ♀
Fawn Zebra Finch
Penguin Zebra Finch
Pied Zebra Finch

Plate XX

Fawn Canary	Dimorphic Canary	Red Cinnamon Canary

Dilute Orange Red Cinnamon Canary   Golden Green Canary

Opal Green Canary   Melanin Pastal Dilute Fawn Canary

Red-hooded Siskin × Canary (Copper Hybrid)   Orange Red Canary

Cinnamon Canary

Plate XXI

Avadavat, *Amandava a. amandava*

Green-breasted Waxbill, *Amandava s. subflava*

Green Avadavat, *Amandava formosa*

West African Quail Finch, *Ortygospiza atricollis*

South African Quail Finch, *Ortygospiza atricollis muelleri*

Plate XXII

Gouldian Finch, *Erythrura gouldiae* (*mirabilis*)

Firetailed Finch, *Stagonopleura bella*

Diamond Sparrow, *Stagonopleura guttata*

Red-eared Firetail Finch, *Stagonopleura oculata*

Painted Finch, *Emblema picta*

In 1868 *Chrysomma sinensis* was first imported into England, since when they have often been kept. These birds are suitable for an aviary and as they are lively and active they require a lot of space. Their soft song is very pleasant to hear.

They live peaceably with other birds, and are fond of bathing. In addition to universal food, they also eat egg food and a number of juicy fruits. They should be fed with some living insects and mealworms every day.

Genus: Turdoides

WHITE-RUMPED BABBLER, *Turdoides l. leucopygius* (Rüppell)
G. Weissbürzeldrossling; F. Turdoide à croupion blanc; D. Witstuit-Gaailijster

DISTRIBUTION: Ethiopia.
DESCRIPTION: Main colouring bronze-brown. Head, abdomen and rump white. Crown grey. Length about 10½ in. (26.7 cm).
These birds occur in large numbers in the wild, either in canefields or in dense brushwood. They are noisy, active birds. If they are disturbed they at once form a dense flight, which makes a loud clamour, and dissolves suddenly as the birds scatter.
Various members of this family are occasionally imported and included in aviaries. Somali Babbler, *Turdoides l. smithii*, is one of them. Upper parts are bronze-coloured with lower parts lighter. The feathers of the throat are greyish with white edges; those of the breast and abdomen are also white-edged. Rump and sides of head white. Crown brownish-grey with white-feathered edges. Length: 10½ in. (26·7 cm).
A cage does not suit these birds, as they need a great deal of room in which to move. They are vivacious, intelligent birds, whose crest is practically always erect. As well as a number of pleasant whistling sounds, they will also produce imitations of bird songs and other noises. They can be kept with other large birds who are able to defend themselves. They soon get accustomed to insectivorous food and fruit mixture, and are especially fond of mealworms and small pieces of raw meat. They should be given the opportunity or taking extensive baths daily, and they can remain in the aviary in both summer and winter. A pair will always stay together and show great mutual affection. Young birds will quickly become tame.

Genus: Dumetia

RUFOUS-BELLIED BABBLER, *Dumetia h. hyperthra* (Franklin)
G. Rotbauchtimalie; F. Dumétie à ventre roux; D. Roodbuik-Timalia

DISTRIBUTION: India and Nepal.
DESCRIPTION: Front half of crown reddish-brown. Upper parts, wings and tail olive-brown. Sides of head and lower parts bright reddish-brown. Irides light brown; bill light horn colour; feet pale flesh colour. Length: 5½ in. (14 cm).
This species dwells in dense shrubbery on the edge of forests, in open grassland where dense thorn bushes abound, or in bushes that are densely covered with spurge, which is common in South India. The birds live in small groups, mostly hidden in the green foliage. They search plants thoroughly for insects, and at the slightest sign of danger utter an alarm call and disappear into the dense undergrowth. Nests are often built on or slightly above the ground, often between the roots of bamboo plants, and are spherical and loosely woven from fresh bamboo leaves. Four white eggs are laid, which are covered with reddish-brown flecks. These birds have been imported on several occasions. They have bred with success, the first result being obtained by Capt. R. S. de Quincey in Hereford in 1960. The birds were kept in a densely-grown aviary, with spectacle birds, tanagers and humming birds. They often alighted on the ground and wore their sharply-layered tails mostly spread out. They built a number of nests, some on the ground, others in sturdy plants about 32 in. (81 cm) above the ground. They produced 3 clutches of 3 eggs, but only 1 youngster was reared. Incubation was about 13 days and the young remained 18 days in the nest. After 3 weeks the young bird was identical with the parents. Ants' eggs and the larvae of wasps formed a good rearing food. The old birds were shy during incubation; they took turns on the nest, and looked after the young extremely well.

SUBFAMILY: PICATHARTINAE

Genus: Picathartes

The two species of *Picathartes*, also called Bald Crows, are from Africa. They are unusual birds, and because they are like no other species, they have been difficult to classify. They have several of the characteristics of crows and were classified with the crows for some time; they have recently been reclassified as related to the babbler family. Picarthartes are rare in captivity, but a few zoos keep them and have been very successful. The birds thrive well on the standard softbilled diet. They are mainly terrestrial birds and like rocky habitats. They hop more than they walk, which is a little unusual for long-legged birds. In appearance they do indeed resemble a long-legged and bald-headed crow. The long legs and large feet are bluish-grey and the large beak is black. Nostrils have a peculiar position in the middle of the upper mandible instead of being located near the base. Irides are brownish, the neck is very slender, and the head appears to be quite small because it is entirely devoid of feathers. Upper parts from the mentle are slate-coloured. Under parts are all white. Length: about 14 in. (35·6 cm) including the long tail.
These birds are rare in aviculture but a few zoos keep them and have been very successful.

WHITE-NECKED GUINEAFOWL, BARE-HEADED ROCKFOWL, *Picathartes gymnocephalus* (Temminck)

G. Weisshalsstelzenkrähe, Belbkopffelschüpfer; F. Picathartes à cou blanc; D. Kaalkopkraai

DISTRIBUTION: Western Africa from Sierra Leone eastward to Togo.
DESCRIPTION: White on the neck starts on chin and base of skull. A large circular area of dull black occurs on each side of the back of the head. Remainder of head yellowish-flesh-coloured. Whole of under parts pure white, upper parts black. Beak black; legs and feet bluish-grey.

GREY-NECKED BALD CROW, GREY-NECKED ROCK-FOWL, *Picathartes oreas* Reichenow

G. Grauhalsstelzenkähe; F. Picathartes à téte grise; D. Grijskop-Kaalkopkraai

DISTRIBUTION: Cameroon.
DESCRIPTION: Back of head red, forehead blue; remainder of head, cheeks, areas around eyes and ears black. Under parts white, upper parts slate grey, wings black.
These birds need the varied diet for insect-eaters, including fruit such as grapes, bananas and apples. They need a warm humid temperature, although they can tolerate a lower temperature for a time.
First appeared in the London Zoological Gardens in 1948.

Genus: Minla

BLUE-WINGED SIVA, BLUE-WINGED MINLA, *Minla cyanouroptera* (Hodgson)

G. Blauflügelsonnenvogel; F. Siva aux ailes bleues; D. Blauwvleugel-Siva

DISTRIBUTION: India, Burma, Thailand.
DESCRIPTION: Blue flights with whitish edges and a dark bluish tail are the dominant features, but these are not really bright. A pale elliptical patch surrounds the eyes and contrasts sharp!y with a blackish eyebrow. Dull greyish head has paler narrow stripes, and facial area and nape also greyish. Remaining upper parts olive-brown with dull blue tinges. Under parts buffish-grey. Iris brown; beak dull yellowish-horn; feet flesh-coloured. The relationship to the Pekin Nightingale is rather obvious, but the Blue-winged Siva is very dull by comparison. Length: about 6 in. (15·2 cm).
SUBSPECIES: There are eight subspecies.
These Blue-winged Sivas inhabit the mountain slopes of the Himilayas up to a height of some 5,000 ft (1,500 m) above sea level. Their flight is fast and light and they clamber quickly through the trees searching for small beetles and insects. They nest between climbing plants and build basin-shaped nests of leaves, grass and moss, sometimes lined with buffalo hairs. Their 3–5 eggs are bluish-white and at the blunt end are covered with rusty-brown and violet markings. Their song is soft and melodious and when they are searching for food they utter a twittering sound.

They were introduced to London in 1877, since when they

Blue-winged Siva, *Minla cyanouroptera*

have been occasionally imported. In addition to insectivorous food they eat a variety of fruit, living insects, mealworms, and often also various seeds. They are fond of drinking honey-water. If they are kept in pairs they show themselves exceptionally affectionate and soon become tame.
In 1907 the first breeding results were obtained by Fr. Nagel. Incubation lasted for 14 days. The young birds were fed on sweetened egg food, bread, with sugar or honey, soaked in milk, mealworms chopped up small, ants' eggs and soaked minced raisins.
In 1971 it was bred by D. G. Osborne as reported in *Avicultural Magazine*, Vol. 77, 1971, pp. 73–75.

Genus: Leiothrix

PEKIN ROBIN, PEKIN NIGHTINGALE, RED-BILLED LEIOTHRIX, *Leiothrix l. lutea* (Scopoli) (Pl. VI)

G. Sonnenvogel; F. Rossignol du Japon; D. Japanse Nachtegaal

DISTRIBUTION: India, Sikkim, Burma and China.
DESCRIPTION: Beak bright red on outer half and dull brownish-black on basal half. A large area on chin and throat is bright yellow with broad lower border of dark rust-orange on breast. Outer fineline webs of primary flight feathers are edged in bright yellow. About one-third of base length has slightly longer webs of dark rest-orange. Secondary flights have small yellowish bar near secondary coverts. When wings are folded, the pattern is very colourful and prominent; when open, however, only small areas of colour are visible and these are dominated by larger areas of dull olive-slate. A pale olive-buff colour covers the facial area before and behind the eyes with rather sharp dividing eyebrow line separating the dark, soft olive of top of head. Olive colour of head fades to greyish-olive over most remaining upper

parts, except for the bright wing colours described already and slate tips to the tail. Remaining under parts are pale olive, fading in the abdominal area. The females are similar,

Pekin Robin, *Leiothrix l. lutea*

but yellow on throat and red-orange on beak and are less bright than in the male. Intensity of colour can be misleading, however, as the yellow fades appreciably in many birds after a time in captivity. Females have a dark greyish tone in the loreal area which is fairly constant. Length: 6 in. (15 cm) including the 2 in. (5 cm) tail, which is forked and slightly spread at tips.

In the wild these birds live in the undergrowth of forests. Their flight is speedy and they dive to the lower part of the trees, especially fir and spruce, which they search along the twigs and branches for insects and small beetles. These birds are lively, and except during the breeding season are to be found in large groups.

In the breeding season the male can be heard singing his magnificent rich and varied song. The nests are basin-shaped and made of leaves and moss and lined with soft material. The 3 to 4 eggs are light greenish-blue, covered with spots and stripes in brown and purple, especially at the blunt end.

The eggs hatch after 14 days, with both parents sharing incubation and the feeding of the young. At least two clutches of eggs are laid each season.

This species cannot be kept with small finches as they will steal eggs and young out of the nests. In a well-planted aviary a pair will usually commence breeding. They build a nest in a bush or will make use of a breeding box. They are strong birds, which can live in an aviary for ten years or more, but during the winter must be kept in frost-free quarters.

In addition to insectivorous and egg food, they also eat small quantities of all kinds of seeds and soft fruits. They are fond of nectar and should have some mealworms every day, which they will quickly learn to eat from the hand. While the young are being reared mealworms and other small insects are indispensable, and up to forty should be given daily.

SILVER-EARED MESIA, *Leiothrix a. argentauris* (Hodgson) (Pl. VI)
G. Silberohrsonnenvogel; F. Mésia à joues argentées; D. Zilveroor-Nachtegaal

DISTRIBUTION: Himalayas area of Nepal, Sikkim, Bhutan, Assam.
DESCRIPTION: Beak and forehead bright yellow. A very large cheek patch behind eye is silvery-white. Crown and sides of face (except cheek patches), down to lower sides of neck are black. A collar across nape and an extensive chin and throat patch is rust-orange, brighter on throat; these colours shade into soft olive and then grey. Rump and tail coverts are brilliant red on male and duller on female. The long square tail is dull black. The wing pattern is similar to that of *L. lutea* but is much more vivid. A large deep red area starts below the bend of wing. Narrow outer rims of flights are yellowish-orange. The rest of wing colouring is greyish-olive, except the shoulders, which are more grey. Length: 6½–7 in. (16·5–17·8 cm).

The relationship to the Pekin Robin, *L. lutea*, is quite obvious, but this is a much more aristocratic cousin. It is larger, more colourful, and rarer. There are several slight colour variations in the 9 different subspecies. The song is similar to that of the Pekin Robin, but is somewhat stronger. *L. a. tahanensis*, from Thailand and Malaysia, has an orange forehead instead of yellow. Other variations in different subspecies involve the size and deeper and more extensive shades of red.

The Silver-eared Mesia is an exceptionally delightful bird and can be highly recommended. It requires the same care as does *L. lutea*.

Genus: Heterophasia

BLACK-HEADED SIBIA, *Heterophasia c. capistrata* (Vigors) (Pl. VI)
G. Schwarzkappentimalie; F. Sibia à tête noire; D. Swartkop-Timalia

DISTRIBUTION: India and adjoining areas in the Himalayas.
DESCRIPTION: This slender, long-tailed species has a straggly and not fully developed recumbent crest which is often raised, but only partially. Head, down to the throat, is black, as is also the slightly curved beak. A diagonal line from nape to throat is a sharp dividing line separating the black from chestnut colouring which follows. This line is broken by the black encircling cheeks. Basic colouring of all other plumage rich chestnut, brighter on rump.

Wings and tail have soft colour variations which are very attractive.

The tail has a pale frosty band of bluish-grey on the ends, preceded by a broad black band, which also forms a narrow border to the sides up to the base. The wings have the same frosty shades of bluish-grey and slate-black in variable and dominant accent markings. Bluish-grey occurs mostly on the secondary flights and shoulder areas and is more extensive than the slate markings. Iris brown; bill black; feet yellowish. Length: 9 in. (22·9 cm).

The Black-headed Sibia is an extremely handsome species,

Black-headed Sibia, *Heterophasia c. capistrata*

with a robust masculine appearance. It is very hardy and adapts itself quickly to the simple standard softbilled diet. It likes to perch in exposed positions from which it has a good view of its surroundings. It is peaceful in most instances, but is well able to be aggressive and assert its rights over many larger birds. It is not a talented songbird, but its different notes and calls are quite pleasant.

Genus: Yuhina

BLACK-CHINNED YUHINA, BLACK-CHINNED FLOWER PECKER, *Yuhina n. nigramenta* Blyth
G. Meisentimalie; F. Yuhina à menton noir, Timalie à menton noir; D. Zwartkop-Timalia

DISTRIBUTION: India, China, Burma, Laos.
DESCRIPTION: Colouring dusky greyish-brown with black on crest and on a small chin patch. Upper parts dark olive-brown, under parts greyish white, tinged with buff on

abdomen. Lower mandible red. Sexes alike but *female* has slightly shorter crest and often more red on beak. *Male* has a melodious call note which is distinctive. Length: about 4 in. (10 cm).

Yuhinas are not very colourful, but they have delightful personalities and use their crests frequently in all kinds of displays. They do well in planted aviaries with small, mild-mannered softbills or finches, but are aggressive to related birds. They should be kept in pairs because they are very affectionate to their partners. Once acclimatized they do not mind low temperature but must have a dry and frost-free shelter for the winter.

In the wild they live in mountainous country and on high plateaux, where they keep to the low forests. They wander around in large flocks and towards winter migrate to more southerly parts. Their crests are constantly in movement as they search for their food among foliage. They find insects in the large blooms of rhododendrons and as their heads get covered with pollen, they aid the fertilization of the plants. They also eat juicy, soft fruits. Their call is soft and monotonous.

The acclimatisation period may be prolonged, as the change-over to artificial foods is difficult. The diet must be the refined softbill misture recommended for delicate birds. Fortified nectar is necessary and they like small live insects such as fruitflies. A variety of soft fruits must also be given. Mealworms and maggots seem to be too tough-skinned for them, but small young mealworms or scalded adults are more digestible.

Yuhinas have been bred in captivity, but success is difficult. For breeding purposes they should be kept in a small planted aviary on their own and be provided with plenty of fine grass and rootlets for building a nest. Their nest is cup-shaped and usually they prefer to build it in a well-leafed shrub or climbing plant. Plenty of live insects are essential for rearing purposes—fruitflies, small spiders, aphides, blackfly and the like.

Both sexes share in the 13-day incubation period and in feeding the chicks. Youngsters usually leave the nest when just over 2 weeks old and require at least 2 more weeks of parental care before they start to feed themselves.

They were first imported into Germany in 1904 and were kept successfully in heated vitrines in the Berlin Zoo, together with the Yellow-naped Yuhina, *Yuhina flavicollis*.

Breeding results have been obtained several times. A detailed account of a breeding which took place in a heated inside aviary is given in *Die Gefederte Welt*, 1963, No. 6. A nest was built in the branch of a fir tree, out of coconut fibres. It took the birds 3 days to complete. Three eggs were laid and incubated for 12 days almost entirely by the hen, who was relieved by the male for short periods so that she could eat and drink. Besides the fine, fat-free soft food for insect-eaters (Aleckwa) they were given meatfly maggots, banana

maggots and nectar with milk. When the young were 5 days old the first young mealworms were given. It was interesting to note that the birds preferred to drink the water in which clusters of millet had been soaked; this water was especially rich in infusoria. The young left the nest after 13 days; they were paler in colour and markings than the parent birds.

The pairing dance by the male was performed on a branch, during which he spread his tail and wings; the crest lay flat on his head and feathers on his flanks stood out. As he did this, he made a hissing sound. Then he let himself fall over frontwards with wings and tail outspread and hung himself upside down from the branch; after this he went round in a circle and sat down on the branch.

There are 9 species of Yuhinas and numerous subspecies. Yellow-naped Yuhina, *Yuhina flavicollis* (with 7 subspecies) has range including India, Burma, Laos and one subspecies in northern Thailand.

Crest dark brown, moustache streaks black. White eye ring and white on cheeks as well as throat is reasonably prominent. Nape particularly variable, but usually pale buff. The subspecies *Y. f. humilis* and *Y. f. clarki* have fine brown streaks on the underparts.

Stripe-throated Yuhina, *Yuhina gularis* (with 3 subspecies) from India. China and Burma, has pale, dull orange legs and maroon-brown stripes on white throat. Upper parts greenish-olive, lower parts olive-yellow.

Black-chinned Yuhina, *Yuhina n. nigramenta*

White-Bellied Yuhina, *Yuhina zantholeuca* (with 8 subspecies) has a widespread range from India, China, Burma, Thailand and neighbouring countries, Malaysia, Borneo and Sumatra. Under parts white, upper parts yellowish-green, undertail coverts yellow, crest pale. Length: 5 in. (12·5 cm).

Old World Flycatchers
SUBFAMILY: MUSCAPINAE

Old World Flycatchers are very delicate when first obtained, and the acclimatisation period is particularly difficult owing to the fact that most species are very reluctant to accept domestic diets. All the birds in this group require the Refined Diet (Group F). Fortified nectar is especially useful in the beginning. After the dietetic transfer is accomplished, the birds are still only half-hardy. They should be protected from overbearing and aggressive birds as well as temperature extremes. It would also be wise if a reasonably high humidity could be maintained as all the birds in this group which are popular with bird keepers are from humid climates. Those from Japan are accustomed to some cold, but most species migrate from cold areas when winter approaches.

The Musciapidae family consists of 378 species excluding thrushes, babblers, warblers, and a few other groups. Only a comparatively few species ever become available to aviculturists, and only the very experienced bird keepers are successful with them.

NOTE: Several changes in ornithological classification have occurred, and not all authorities have accepted them. The trend is towards simplification, which seems to be a very good idea. The members of the genus *Niltava* have now been absorbed into the large genus *Muscicapa* (see below), but the popular name Niltava will probably continue with aviculturists for some time to come.

SUBFAMILY: RHIPIDURINAE

Fantail Flycatchers

Fantail Flycatchers have rather long tails which are easily fanned out in frequent side to side and perpendicular movements as well as opening and closing movements. There are some very attractive species in the group. A few of the more attractive members will be very briefly described.

Several members resemble, with slight variations the 7 in. (18 cm) White-browed Fantail Flycatcher (*Rhipidura aureola*) of Sri Lanka, India, Burma and Thailand. Colouring above is dusky brownish-grey, under parts white, throat grey. A broad white eyebrow stripe covers forehead and extends onto nape. Tail feathers, except for central pair, have broad white ends. Dull white spots occur on wings. A moustache is also dull greyish-white. Sexes are alike. The White-throated Fantail Flycatcher, *Rhipidura albicollis*, from the same areas has a white throat and brown underparts. The Malaysian Fantail, *Rhipidura javanica*, has a black collar across the white throat. The Perlated Fantail, *Rhipidura perlata*, has black on throat and breast. Large white spots occur on these areas and on the wing coverts.

One of the more attractive species is the 5½ in. (13·5) Blue Fantail Flycatcher, *Rhipidura superciliaris*, from the Philippines. This species is soft, dark blue above, paler below to breast. Remaining under parts shade to white. The Blue-headed or Rufous-bellied Fantail, *Rhipidura cyaniceps*, also from the Philippines, has greyish-blue on head, throat, breast, and mantle. Wings, lower back, and outer tail feathers chestnut. Central tail feathers blackish. Under parts below breast vary with different subspecies from whitish to pale rufous to deep chestnut. The Black and Cinnamon Fantail, *Rhipidura nigrocinnamomea*, another Philippine species, is more boldly coloured than the previous species. Head, nape, and chin black with a bold white eyebrow stripe which extends across forehead. Throat whitish; remaining colouring is same as in above species except the two central tail feathers are chestnut (or rufous) instead of black.

Frum Australia and Papua–New Guinea comes the Black-and-White Fantail Flycatcher, *Rhipidura tricolor*, Vieillot. Length: 7¾ in. (20 cm)

Blue Flycatchers

There are several beautiful blue flycatchers of the genus *Muscicapa*. Sexes differ in colour. Most females are brown in various shades. This grouping does not include all the attractive members of the genus, nor does it include all of those with blue. We have details of the breeding of *Muscicapa tickelliae* which are given here. Other species will be described briefly with notations of the major differences.

TICKELL'S BLUE FLYCATCHER, *Muscicapa tickelliae* (Blyth)

G. Braunbrüstiger Blauschnäpper; F. Niltava de Tickell; D. Tickell's Vliegenvanger

DISTRIBUTION: India, China, Burma and Thailand.

DESCRIPTION: *Male.* Upper parts blue; forehead and stripe above eyes lighter blue, also fold of the wing. Lores bluish-black. Sides of head dark blue; throat and breast orange-brown; abdomen and lower tail coverts white. Wings brownish-grey with blue edges. Irides legs, and feet brown; beak blackish brown. *Female.* Paler blue on upper parts and duller on under parts. Length: 5½ in. (13 cm).

These Flycatchers live in the higher mountainous regions, mostly in pairs, high up in the trees, but they also seek insects on the ground, where they move forward in little jumps. They nest in the hollows of trees or banks, and construct their nests of grass and leaves.

They were imported for the first time into Berlin in 1907, and placed in a glass cage. Their song is not loud and reminds one of the Redbreast's, but sometimes they include couplets of other birds' songs. They move their tails constantly from left to right at the same time making all kinds of curious bows.

In 1964, in the aviaries of the Max Planck Institute in Munich, Germany, the first breeding results were obtained. One strange fact is that the female sang more than the male, though somewhat softer. On the floor of the 12×9¼ ft. (4×3·25 m) aviary a thick layer of dead leaves had been scattered, which had been collected from the woods and in which the birds found plenty of live food. In a half-opened concrete nest box the birds built a nest of moss, and lined it with soft plant fibres; the underlay consisted of a layer of leaves. Four brownish eggs were laid, on which the female

sat from the time the fourth egg was laid. She regularly left the nest to eat and drink and to bathe. The incubating period was about 12 days. The birds were fed with ants' eggs, to which were added the larvae of wasps, grasshoppers and moths, scattered on the ground. In order to be certain that the young were getting sufficient vitamins and calcium during the first few days, they were given some wasp larvae upon which was sprinkled some 'Federvit' and calcium vitamins. These details were taken from a report by Dr. H. Löhr in *Die Gefederte Welt*, 1966, No. 6.

In England a first breeding result was obtained in the aviary of the Rev. J. R. Lowe, as reported in *Avicultural Magazine*, Vol. 72, 1966, pp. 115–117.

'In the spring, in a corner of a well-planted aviary, a small heap of pig manure was put down in order to attract insects, and towards the time when the birds showed a desire to breed, the aviary had been transformed into a small thicket. The birds built a nest out of grass, moss and plant fibres above a thick branch which leant against the back of the aviary. The hen sang enticingly to the cock, spreading out her tail in the form of a fan, and quivering her wings, upon which the cock flew towards her and they mated. Immediately afterwards he sat in front of her in an attitude of pride for 15 seconds. After the female sat on the eggs for 12 days, they hatched and both parents began to feed the young. Maggots and mealworms formed the basis of the food the young received, while the older birds had in addition all the kinds of live insects which they could catch in the dense vegetation in the aviary. From the fifth day the hen only sat on the fledglings at night. From the sixth day she began to carry the droppings away from the nest to a large stone which lay a long way from the nest. When the youngsters had flown out of the nest they were caught and put into the inside aviary which is only connected with the outside aviary by an opening high up, so that the older birds could continue to feed the young ones without the risk that they might get lost among the thick vegetation. These birds are remarkably quiet in aviaries, which is not really so strange when one considers that birds in their wild life are also used to sitting for long periods quite still on a branch jutting out of a tree, and darting out just now and then to pursue a passing insect. In the aviary they dive as quick as lightning on to the feeding tray or onto the ground to seize a mealworm, which they promptly take back to their perch to kill and then swallow. They will also fly to the perch with a piece of apple, where they will bite little pieces out of it.

To keep the bird in good condition, it is necessary to vary the food. Fine insectivorous mixture should form the basis into which the following may be introduced: apples, carrots, egg, rusk or cake, finely ground nuts, and a nectar food such as is prepared for the Humming Birds. Every day each bird requires from 6 to 8 mealworms and in the summer some fresh ants' eggs. They are not able to withstand cold or draught. With exception of the breeding season, it is sometimes necessary to keep the pairs separated, as they find it difficult to tolerate each other.'

BLUE-THROATED FLYCATCHER, *Muscicapa rubicoloides*

DISTRIBUTION: South-east Asia on the southerly hills of the Himalayas.

DESCRIPTION: Main colouring blue and there is a large blue patch on throat. *Female*. Brown where the male is blue.

JAPANESE BLUE FLYCATCHER, BLUE-AND-WHITE FLYCATCHER, *Muscicapa cyanomelana* (Hay)

G. Japanischer Blauschnäpper; F. Niltava bleu du Japon; D. Japanse Blauwe Vliegenvanger

DISTRIBUTION: Burma, Thailand, Malaysia, China, Korea, Japan.

DESCRIPTION: *Male*. Upper parts blue; on top of head, shoulders, rump and tail, blue is lighter. Narrow forehead band, sides of head, chin and throat, black. Under parts white. Beak black; feet and legs brownish-black; irides dark brown. *Female*. Olive-brown with white lower parts. Length: 6 in. (15 cm).

The birds migrate within their own distribution territories, and pass the winter in Japan and Borneo. They live in forests, feeding on insects, and in spring return to their nesting territories. Their sweet song reminds one of the Pekin Robin and the Redbreast. They are very lively birds who quickly become tame. In Japan they are kept as cage birds. They were imported for the first time in 1885, in Germany; since then they have appeared occasionally in several countries. It is important to give them an insectivorous mixture, supplemented with fresh or dried ants' eggs and some mealworms—but not many of the last. A little white cheese may occasionally be added to the food. These birds are very fond of bathing.

RUFOUS-BELLIED NILTAVA, RED-BELLIED NILTAVA, *Muscicapa sundara* Hodgson (Pl. VI)

G. Rotbauchfliegenschnäpper; F. Niltava à ventre rouge; D. Oranjebuik-Vliegenvanger

DISTRIBUTION: Himalayas, from Murree to the extreme east of Assam; Manipur and Lushai Hills; Chin and Kachin Hills, and down through the hills of Central Burma to Tenasserim, South-East Asia and Western China. In summer at elevations from 5,000 to 8,000 ft. (1,500–2,500 m) descending in the winter to lower levels and into the foothills.

DESCRIPTION: *Male*. Crown and rump shining cobalt blue as also are a spot on either side of the neck. Nape, back and tail deep violet-blue; forehead, face, ear coverts, side of neck and throat velvety-black; shoulders shining violet blue, coverts and secondaries black with outer webs violet-blue, flights dark brown with deep blue on the outer webs; breast and abdomen rich chestnut, paler towards the vent. Irides very dark brown, beak, feet and legs black. *Female*. Olive-brown on the upper parts with the tail chestnut. Brilliant sapphire blue spot on either side of the neck, concealed except when the head is raised and the neck extended. Under parts more olive-brown, lighter on the chin and belly, and with a whitish crescent on the throat. Irides dark brown, beak, feet and legs dark blackish-brown. Length: 6½ in. (16·5 cm).

SUBSPECIES: Three races are recognised but there is only very slight variation, the chief differences being in size.

This, the most beautiful of all flycatchers, frequents high forest, usually in the close vicinity of rock-strewn water courses where the vegetation is dense and insect life abundant. Unlike the familiar Spotted Flycatcher of Europe, it is seldom seen at any great height above the ground, preferring to perch on some moss-covered rock or tree root in the deep shade of the moisture-laden undergrowth, making short flights in pursuit of winged insects or, more frequently, darting on those moving on the ground.

Rufous-bellied Niltava, *Muscicapa sundara*

Although insects form its main diet they are sometimes supplemented by berries and other small fruit.

The nest is a very shallow, loosely made pad of moss, usually placed on a hollow ledge or in a rock crevice in the close vicinity of water. The eggs, normally 4 in number, are pinkish or buff, thickly freckled with reddish brown. Incubation period of 14 days is carried out solely by the female, the young leaving the nest about 10 to 14 days after hatching. They quickly begin to feed themselves and are independent in a very short time although the male continues to feed them for a week or so, or until such time as his female is again nesting.

The Rufous-bellied Niltava was first imported to England in 1901 but it was not until 1961 that the species was first successfully bred (by K. A. Norris) in captivity, as reported in *Avicultural Magazine*, 67, 1961, pp. 175–181. Nests were then built by three different hens and in each case were placed high up on rafters or in open-fronted nest boxes. An untidy mass of materials, grasses, rushes and moss formed the foundation, the ends being left trailing from the rafter on which the nest was placed, but in the centre a deep cup was formed of fine grasses and moss. As soon as incubation commenced, the hens occupied their time in tidying up the foundations of the nests, each trailing strand being drawn up and carefully woven into the sides of the nest thus increasing the depth of the cup until only the top of the sitting bird's head could be seen. The adult birds kept in excellent condition on a fine grade insectivorous mixture, moistened with grated carrot or apple, with the addition of a liberal supply of maggots and mealworms, together with such spiders, fruit flies and other insects as they were able to capture. The young however, were reared entirely on live insects and it was not until some time after they had left the nests that they learnt to eat the mixture supplied to the adults. They also discovered and gorged on ripe pear which was provided for some of the small tanagers which shared their aviary, but showed no inclination to take elder berries or soaked currants which were also available. Wood lice proved irresistible and they spent much of their time searching the corners of the aviary and round flower pots for these crustaceans.

Once acclimatised, these niltavas prove to be hardy and can be left in an outdoor aviary throughout the year, provided they have access to a well-built shelter which will protect them from draughts, dampness and severe frosts. It may however be found that the sexes become quarrelsome during the winter months in which case it is better that they should be separated until the following spring. They may be safely associated with other small insect eating birds such as Tanagers, other species of Flycatchers and Zosterops, in a large and well-planted aviary, but not with others of their own species.

GREATER NILTAVA, LARGE NILTAVA, *Muscicapa grandis* (Blyth)
G. Grossniltava; F. Grand Niltava; D. Grote Niltava

DISTRIBUTION: Widespread in the oriental region, Central Nepal, Sikkim, Bhutan, Assam hills north and south of the Bramhaputra, Manipur, Burma, Thailand and extending to Yunnan and the Indochinese and Malaysian subregions.
DESCRIPTION: *Male*. Top of the head, rump, wing coverts, and a spot on either side of the neck shining deep cobalt blue; lores, forehead and sides of head black; tail and flights black edged with deep blue; chin, throat and upper breast black shading into blue-black on lower breast and to ashy blue on abdomen and under tail coverts. *Female*. Above fulvous brown; tail and flights edged with deep rufous. Chin, throat and upper breast pale buff with patch of bright blue on either side of neck; remainder of under parts olive brown. Beak, feet and legs black in male, brownish in female. Irides very dark brown in both sexes. Length: 8 in. (20 cm).
This species inhabits the thick undergrowth of the evergreen forests at elevations between 4,000 to 8,000 ft. (1,200–2,500 m). It is a somewhat sluggish bird, unlike most of the Flycatchers, spending much of its time perched in the dense bushes in deep shade. Its food consists mainly of insects but it is said also to eat fruit in the form of berries.

Greater Niltava, *Muscicapa grandis*

The nest, formed largely of green moss, lined with moss roots and fine grasses, is placed in any convenient crevice in rocks or banks, or between the exposed roots of trees. The eggs, usually 4 in number, are creamy-white thickly speckled with reddish-brown.
In confinement it is said to live well and should be provided

with a good quality insectivorous mixture together with a liberal supply of live insects such as maggots and mealworms. Sweet grapes, cut in half, or ripe pear may also be offered.
During the summer months it may, with advantage, be kept in a planted, outdoor aviary but during the winter months, should be given the protection of an indoor enclosure, where artificial heat can be provided and the temperature maintained at not less than 45°F (7°C).
It was first imported to England in 1913, when a pair was brought over by Major Perreau. These were said to be the only pair in Europe at the time and there appears to be no record of the species having again been imported. Certainly it has not been seen in England for very many years, nor, as far as is known, bred in captivity.

LESSER NILTAVA, SMALL NILTAVA, *Muscicapa macgregoriae* (Burton) (Pl. VI)
G. Kleiner Niltava; F. Petit Niltava; D. Kleine Blauwe Vliegenvanger

DISTRIBUTION: Himalayas, from Garhwal to Assam, at an elevation of 3,000 to 5,000 ft. (900–1,500 m).
DESCRIPTION: *Male*. Forehead, sides of crown, rump, upper tail coverts and a patch on either side of the neck brilliant cobalt blue; remainder of upper parts purple-blue except crown, lores and around eyes black. Under parts, chin, throat, sides of neck and upper breast deep purple blue, shading to ashy grey on lower breast and to pale ashy on abdomen, flanks and under tail coverst. Beak, feet and leg blackish, irides very dark brown, almost black. *Female*.

Upper parts warm olive-brown, the rump and upper tail coverts being rufous; tail olive-brown edged with rufous and the central pair of retrices entirely rufous. Chin pale rufous, a patch of bright blue on either side of neck. Remainder of under parts ashy yellow, shading on abdomen and inder tail coverts to ashy-grey. Length: 5 in. (12·5 cm).
The Lesser Niltava is more active than either of the other species, and in typical Flycatcher style, takes much of its food on the wing, hawking flying insects from some vantage post, usually the upper branches of a bush. It seldom descends to the ground.
The nest, which is similar to that of the Greater Niltava, is usually placed in a hollow in a bank or amongst the roots of a tree or clump of bamboo, often near water. The eggs are also very similar to those of the Greater Niltava, being cream coloured, very thickly speckled with reddish-brown.
This species was first imported in 1923, when a male was presented to the London Zoo. Since then it has been frequently offered on the market and in recent years has become comparatively common. It needs very careful acclimatisation but once established it lives well on a fine grade insectivorous mixture moistened with grated raw carrot, to which must be added a daily supply of live insects. Although able to withstand quite low temperatures, it is sensitive to damp and foggy conditions and is best given the protection of indoor accommodation during the winter months. In the spring and summer it should be transferred to a well-planted outdoor aviary provided with a dry and draught-proof shelter. It has not yet been bred in captivity but there appears to be no reason why it should not nest if given an aviary to itself. A nest box with part open front would probably be the most acceptable and this should be either fixed to a wall, about 4 ft (1·23 m) from the ground, and well screened with bunches of heather or pine branches, or wedged firmly into the base of some thick shrub. The disadvantage of the latter position is that the sitting bird might be disturbed by mice if these pests should gain access to the aviary.
It is almost certain that the young would be reared on live insects only, and mealworms or maggots would be too large

for such tiny young birds when first hatched. Live ants cocoons would undoubtedly be the most suitable food during the first week after hatching, together with small moth larvae and fruit flies. Later very small mealworms or larger mealworms chopped up could be added. Mosquito larvae, which can be easily collected from any stagnant pool or water tank, can be put in a shallow pan of water in the flight and will prove a useful addition to the diet.

Paradise Flycatchers

BY H. J. BATES AND R. L. BUSENBARK

Genus: Tersiphone

Very few birds can surpass the elegance of Paradise Flycatchers. The main characteristics are the full crest and two long central tail feathers which may reach up to 17 in. (43 cm) in length in adult males. Even without the two long feathers, Paradise Flycatchers are graceful birds. Their slender bodies and slightly fan-shaped tapering tails total 7–8 in. (18–20 cm). Females and sub-adults of both sexes are totally different in colouring from fully adult males. To call all of those younger birds immature is not quite correct because in the wild state young males still in sub-adult plumage often rear young.

Paradise Flycatchers are very difficult to get and even more difficult to transfer to domestic diets. Even after the transfer has been successfully completed, they are still not hardy. The writers once received a shipment of several 'pairs' of these rare birds from India. Sex could not be determined because all were in juvenile plumage. Youngsters adapt more readily than do adults, but the maturation process of developing full tails and colour transformation in the males is very slow. The adaptation to domestic foods was very time consuming because the birds showed no interest in inert foods. By mixing live foods with the mynah pellets, the birds gradually accepted the pellets; but they still received quantities of live food and fortified nectar. Those which the writers have had were calm and well poised in their aviaries. They seemed to enjoy hovering in flight in the way hummingbirds do; but, of course, they were far less efficient than the hummingbirds. Companions had been chosen for congeniality or for unobtrusiveness. Pittas, White-cheeked and Black-crested Bulbuls, and several small tanagers shared the aviaries.

African Paradise Flycatchers

There are several species of Paradise Flycatchers in Africa. The long tailed varieties are generally shaped like the first species described, and most of them are coloured more or less like the sub-adult phase of *Tersophone paradisii*. Shades of brown vary to some extent, and underparts vary from pale grey to dark grey. The lengths of tails vary considerably, and the black of the head may shade from glossy black to grey. Crests also vary in shapeliness. The Blue Flycatcher is shaped just like the Paradise Flycatchers, but the central tail feathers are only slightly elongated. The colour is pale blue above and soft, pale grey below.

Another group of similarly shaped crested flycatchers from Africa lacks the long tail feathers. They are dark on the head and upper parts and dull greyish-white on the under parts. The dark areas on some are black, with or without gloss. Some are highly iridescent with blue reflections. Variations are minor. These birds will probably not be popular with bird keepers because they are equally as difficult as the more beautiful species.

SUBFAMILY: MONARCHINAE

PARADISE FLYCATCHER, *Tersiphone p. paradisi* (Linnaeus)

G. Indien-paradiesschnäppen; F. Gobe-mouches paradisier; D. Indische Paradijsvliegenvanger

DISTRIBUTION: India, South-east Asia, Indonesia.

DESCRIPTION: *Male*. Has glossy black covering entire head, crest, and neck. Remaining areas white with many fine black lines on the upper parts mainly marking the feather shafts. When the wings are folded, they appear to be blackish. Beak, feet, legs, and bare eye ring blue-grey. Inside of mouth bright greenish-yellow. Standard tail and body length varies from 7–8 in. (18–20 cm). The full grown tail feathers are 15–17 in. (38–43 cm). *Female*. Lacks the long central tail feathers. Upper parts and tail are rich chestnut. Under parts basically white with a dull shade of grey on chest and sides.

Young males are like females, chestnut-brown, and retain this colouring into their third year. The central tail feathers may be only slightly elongated during the second year, but they are fully grown before they attain their adult colouring. These birds live in pairs in light wooded areas, in orchards and gardens. They build their conically shaped nest in the fork of a branch, using grass, moss, plant fibres and cobwebs for it. The 3–5 eggs are speckled with cream and reddish brown. Both birds incubate and rear the young. Incubation period is about 16 days, and the young leave the nest within 14 days. Their food consists of insects. The birds migrate within their habitat, and spend part of the year in the high mountains.

This species is the best known in the Philippines and Japan; related species occur but they are rare in aviculture.

FAMILY: PARIDAE

SUBFAMILY: PARINAE

Tits

BY H. J. BATES AND R. L. BUSENBARK

The large family of tits has several members which are adaptable to aviculture and the Japanese Tumbler is the best known. It has one of the most intriguing personalities in the bird world. All tits are intelligent, active and very alert birds with friendly dispositions. They are curious about everything and are always probing into crevices and any likely place for insects or other items of food.

Tits are small stocky birds with large heads, thick necks, short tails, and short, blunt beaks which are often used as hammers in woodpecker fashion.

The omnivorous diet of Japanese Tumblers includes a wide array of items. It can be successfully used as a basis to establish the diets of other tits, but most other species must be considered mote delicate and less adaptable. The diet should therefore be somewhat more refined for the other members and usually should not include seeds.

The writers have had hundreds of Japanese Tumblers but only a relatively few varieties of other tits. The Japanese Tumblers, as with most Japanese importations, always arrive in excellent condition and are already accustomed to artificial diets. Their acclimatisation is very simple. The other varieties which the writers have received were all very delicate and difficult to transfer to artificial diets.

The diet which the writers offer to Japanese Tumblers (or Varied Tits) includes the standard softbill diet plus finely minced raw meat, peanut butter, parrakeet mixture, health grit, and cuttlebone. Raw meat is particularly important especially in large incoming shipments. If the Tumblers do not have this extra food, the stronger birds will attack and eat any weaker companions.

Other tits which the writers have received were given the same diet, but they paid no attention to any of the items which seedeaters usually prefer. Fortified nectar was added instead, and it proved to be very helpful. All purpose food was also offered along with the other items.

JAPANESE TUMBLER, VARIED TIT, BUCKET BIRD, *Parus varius* Temminck and Schlegel

G. Rotbauchmeise; F. Mésange brune du Japon; D. Japanse Mees

DISTRIBUTION: Japan, Korea and China.

DESCRIPTION: The sturdy and bluntly pointed blackish beak ⅜ in. (1 cm) long. Large, alert eyes black. Pale tan encircles crown, covers lores, excludes eyes, flares backwards to include cheeks, and tapers off at lower end of neck. A darker irregular tan stripe starts at centre of hind-crown, becomes very broad on nape, and ends at lower nape. Remaining head colouring black including a narrow black cap which extends to nape and a broad throat bib which extends onto upper breast.

Mantle brown, and remaining upper parts grey with slight blend of brown. Under parts dusky tan with brown on sides nearly covering breast. Under side of tail grey. Feet and legs grey. Length: about 5 in. (13 cm) including a slightly forked tail of 1¾ in. (4·5 cm). Sexes are alike.

The Japanese Tumbler is very well known in aviculture. A specially designed cage enables it to perform its somersaults and to pull up a small bamboo bucket. The cage, which is manufactured in bamboo or metal, is tall and rectangular. A small enclosed balcony at the top of one side acts as a springboard for the backward somersaults onto the perch near the bottom. A small bucket is tied to a string on the underside of the balcony.

Tumblers quickly learn the bucket retrieving trick, often within ten minutes. The bucket is at first tied a short distance below the small opening in the balcony. A mealworm is placed in the bucket, and this is temptation enough for the bird to put its intelligence to work so that it can obtain the choice morsel hanging just out of reach. It grasps the string with its beak, pulls it up, and holds it fast with its foot. As soon as the first mealworm is retrieved in this manner, the string may be lengthened a little. It may gradually be lengthened after each success until the usual maximum of 15 in. (38 cm) is attained.

In Japan, Tumblers are used by fortune tellers on the streets to select little fortune cards. This short entertainment is a favourite with tourists.

As aviary birds, Japanese Tumblers display spectacular activity. They are less colourful than most of the popular aviary birds; but their ceaseless speedy flights and amazing precision easily divert attention from all other birds. Their aviaries must have safety doors to prevent escapes. Tumblers are companionable to most softbills ranging in size from Pekin Nightingales to Orioles. Their highly active nature enables them to escape the onslaughts of the more aggressive birds; but Tumblers are themselves much too aggressive for finches or small, peaceful birds.

Nuthatches

FAMILY: SITTIDAE

Nuthatches are not well known in aviculture because they are seldom available, somewhat expensive, and are difficult for importers to handle. They are rather small and shy, and most people consider them delicate. However as soon as the unusual diet is mastered and the acclimatisation period is accomplished, nuthatches surprise everyone with their really fascinating personalities.

They are completely inoffensive in every way and should be housed with small tits, Pekin Nightingales, bulbuls, and birds of similar size and temperament. The aviary must be heated in winter. The personalities are rather slow to emerge and, because the birds are so furtive, they must be studied in order to gain an insight into their unique characteristics. They have comic personalities and acrobatic movements. They spend almost as much time hanging upside down as they do perching upright, and they can be at their happiest if they have a tree trunk or large branch with rough bark in their aviary. They spend much time probing and inspecting the bark for hidden insects and grubs.

Their long, strong claws and sturdy, large feet make them far more agile than woodpeckers; and they descend trees with their heads downwards. They do not have their tail feathers developed into stiff supporting props as the woodpeckers do, nor do they need this additional means of support.

Nuthatches are so intent in their meticulous searching and probing that they can be quite closely approached in the wild without disturbing their labours. They seem to be unafraid of human beings. If they feel a sense of intrusion they quietly move to another spot with scarcely an interruption in their ceaseless searching. The American nuthatches which have been observed in the wild absentmindedly warble their soft little songs while searching tree bark crevices. The song is frequently interrupted by louder call notes which are less musical and somewhat monotonous.

In aviaries, nuthatches display an acquisitive nature. They collect whole sunflower and safflower seeds and store them away in hidden crevices for future use if necessary. They also store away shelled peanuts, walnuts, and other nuts. They can frequently be heard pounding open thin-shelled nuts using their beaks as battering rams. In this characteristic, however, they are far less pugilistic than many of the tits, and do not attack the nuts with the same gusto and fervour employed by the tits.

The omnivorous diet of nuthatches is much the same as given to the more delicate tits. The writers include perhaps more variety than is necessary; but, since little is known about nuthatches in captivity, the extra dietary items have been experimentally utilised as a precaution as well as urgent daily requirements.

The food caches provide a sense of future security for them. Most of the caches have consisted of various seeds as well as nutmeats, but one surprising dietary item hidden away was peanut butter which did not seem very practical to the writers. Nuthatches are very industrious and thrifty and seem to be equipped with a high degree of intelligence, but the writers question their good sense in storing peanut butter. Admittedly, it is less perishable than many food items; but the transporting and plastering work must have involved a considerable amount of effort. This strange behaviour, which incidentally entailed a considerable amount of cleaning effort to remove, cannot be attributed solely to the nuthatches. They could have been assisted or led by various species of tits which were also housed with them.

Nuthatches have been successfully fed the standard diet plus nectar. Also included is plenty of peanut butter, a little extra raw meat, live food in as big a variety as possible, a variety of seeds, and a variety of shelled nuts. Very few seeds are actually consumed. During the acclimatisation process, a fortified nectar is very important because most of the different items will be foreign to these birds; and they will not consume correct ratios of any of the various items to insure a balanced diet.

Nuthatches resemble kingfishers in miniature. Their thick, sharply pointed and slightly uplifted beaks dominate their physical appearance. The very stocky body, short and thick neck, and broad, flat head are further characteristics. The tails are short and broad and rounded at the ends.

There are fifteen or sixteen species of nuthatches, but only two are of interest to aviculturists. Others are either unavailable or lacking in colourful plumage. Closely allied Creepers, Treecreepers, and Wallcreepers have no avicultural status.

American nuthatches are not very colourful. The Pigmy Nuthatch, *Sitta pygmaea*, is 4 in. (10 cm) in length and has dusky bluish-grey upper parts with a sooty brownish-black cap and dusky white under parts. The White-breasted Nuthatch, *Sitta carolinensis*, of 5½ in. (14 cm) also has a black cap extending down to the mantle. Under parts are white, and upper parts are grey with many blackish areas on the wings and tail. The Red-breasted Nuthatch, *Sitta canadensis*, some 4½ in. (11 cm) in length is very much like the Eurasian Nuthatch, *Sitta europaia*, of 5 in. (13 cm) length and which is very widespread over Europe to China, South-East Asia, and Japan. The Red-breasted Nuthatch has a large black cap with a bold whitish dividing line covering the forehead and running above the eyes back to the mantle. Another black line follows below running through the lores and eyes back to the lower sides of the neck. Upper parts are dusky grey, and under parts are dusky white on the throat shading to dusky, dull reddish on the breast and remaining under parts. The Eurasian Nuthatch lacks the black cap but has the black line running through the eyes. Only the lower under parts show the dull reddish shading. There are minor variations in the different subspecies.

CHESTNUT-BELLIED NUTHATCH, DWARF NUT-HATCH, *Sitta castanea* (Lesson)
G. Kastanienkleiber; F. Sitelle à ventre marron; D. Kastanje Bruine Boomklever

DISTRIBUTION: India and Burma.
DESCRIPTION: *Male*. Beak blackish with pale greyish-horn on underside of lower mandible at base. This forms a blackish line which runs through eyes and sides of neck to sides of mantle. Eyebrows and forehead pale buffish-white. Chin and throat area dull buffish-white. Under parts from lower throat deep but bright chestnut. Upper parts greyish with tinges of dull blue. *Female*. Is much paler and duller on the parts. Subspecies variations show lower and more gradual starting points for chestnut colouring on under parts, and some are a little larger. Length: 5 in. (12·5 cm).
The habitat of these splendid birds, lies in hilly country and low-lying plains of India. These birds are more often imported than the other varieties. They need a great deal of warmth and should be acclimatised under a heating lamp. They can become very upset with incorrect feeding or transportation in an unheated container.
Dr. Löhr of Germany succeeded in getting a pair to breed in an outside aviary. This was generously supplied with old oak trunks and branches of various other trees were introduced; the hen very soon commenced to build a nest in a former nesting hollow made by a woodpecker. The entry was narrowed with loam. The hollow was filled with pieces of decaying wood and bark of a pine tree. Three eggs were laid, which were hatched after 16 days incubation. As the parent birds did not rear the first young of the clutch properly, the eggs were put in nest of Coal Tits, who brought the young up satisfactorily. One young bird was replaced in its original nest, and then the parent birds took good care of it. These birds can only be kept in pairs, as the males cannot tolerate each other when there is a female among them.

VELVET-FRONTED NUTHATCH, *Sitta frontalis* (Swainson)
G. Brillenkleiber; F. Sitelle à front noir; D. Brilboom-klever

DISTRIBUTION: Extensive range includes Ceylon, India, Burma, Thailand, Malaysia, Borneo, Indonesia and the Philippines.
DESCRIPTION: Upper parts bright and glossy cobalt-blue, under parts mostly soft lavender with whitish on chin and throat areas. Beak bright red-orange usually with black tip. Irides yellowish-straw with sharp black pupils. Black covers a broad area on lores, forehead, and part of forecrown. A long, trailing eyebrow strip is prominent in male and absent in female. Length about 5 in. (12·5 cm). Subspecies *S. f. corallipes* has a red orbital ring.
This very lovely species is by far the most beautiful of all the nuthatches. It is very rare in captivity. It was imported into Germany for the first time in 1914.

FAMILY: DICAEIDAE

RED-BACKED FLOWER-PECKER, *Dicaeum c. cruentatum* (Linnaeus)
G. Scharlachroter Blütenpicker; F. Grimperau à Dos Rouge; Dicée à Dos Rouge; D. Roodrug-Bastaard-honingvogel

DISTRIBUTION: From India towards southern China and Indonesia.
DESCRIPTION: Under parts bright red with a few black marks on back; shoulder feathers bright pale blue; lores, feathers above eyes, cheeks, ear region and sides of neck black with green and violet sheen. Lower parts yellowish-cream, and sides grey. Wings have black and blue feathers. Tail black. *Female*. Less brilliant; upper parts olive-brown, rump and upper tail coverts scarlet; chin, breast and abdomen whitish with faint wash of ochre yellow. Length: about 3 in. (8 cm).
These very lively birds haunt gardens and woods, preferring the tops of trees, where they amuse themselves by flying from branch to branch making a high pitched and rapidly repeated 'chick-chick-chick' call. As with other members of this family, their feeding habit is closely linked with the presence of the mistletoe, *Loranthus longiflorus*, they spread its seeds everywhere.
Like the colibris and nectar-eaters, the flower-peckers feed on insects and nectar of flowers, but they prefer above all the sticky berries of the mistletoe. The birds' behaviour is strange: each berry is tested before being picked and eaten whole. When the bird has gorged itself, it rests on a branch to digest its food. It then presents an unattractive spectacle, and seems to feel some discomfort in eliminating the seeds, which are covered with sticky matter. The seeds fall on the branch, because the bird perches length-wise there, and remain stuck to it. As these seeds are laxative, the berries pass rapidly through the digestive tract, and are not delayed in the stomach. Insects and spiders, on the other hand, undergo the action of the digestive juices in the stomach before the digestible parts can be assimilated.
The purse-shaped nest is ingeniously hidden under a tattered mango leaf, at a great height; entrance is from the side, fairly high on the nest. The nest is very small and made of various vegetable fibres, joined with spider webs and other soft materials; the whole hung from a branch by means of blades of grass and roots. Two or 3 white eggs are laid.
These birds are sedentary and live in family groups or in pairs. Various species are imported, such as Tickel's Flower-pecker, *Dicaeum erythrorhynchos*, the Red-breasted Flower-pecker, *D. ignipectus*, the Orange-bellied Flower-pecker, *D. trigonostigma*, and the Australian Flower-pecker, *D. hirundinaceum*.
It is a little difficult to acclimatise these birds, though they are delightful to keep, dazzling beauty and friendly behaviour, active and charming. Their diet consists of nectar, biscuit soaked in honey, various soft and juicy fruits, soaked currants, and plenty of berries, such as raspberries, bilberries etc., and a large quantity of fruit flies.

FAMILY: NECTARINIIDAE

Sunbirds

According to the classification by J. Delacour (*Zoologica*, 1944) the great Nectariniidae family consist of 106 species, divided into 5 genera: *Arachnothera*, *Aethopyga*, *Anthreptes*, *Nectarinia* and *Neodrepanis*. Since then this last genus has been classified as a family: Philepittidae. These magnificent birds, whose plumage is often enhanced by metallic sheens, and which vary in size from 3¾ in. (9·5 cm) to 10 in. (25 cm), have a distinctive appearance, emphasised by a beak which is almost always long, narrow, pointed and more or less curved, with fine serrations on the tip. The tubular and forked tongue can be projected at great distance. The rather short and rounded wings have 10 large flight feathers. The tail is sometimes short, sometimes very long, and sometimes of average length. The legs are fairly long and more robust than those of the Colibris. The mating plumage of the males is usually iridescent. They differ greatly from the females, whose plumage is quiet and more subdued. Sometimes the mating plumage is worn only during the breeding period.

Genus: Nectarinia

MALACHITE SUNBIRD, *Nectarinia f. famosa* (Linnaeus) (Frontispiece)
G. Malachitennektarvogel, Langschwanznektarvogel; F. Souï-manga malachite; D. Emerald-Honingvogel
DISTRIBUTION: Eastern mountains of Rhodesia, Transvaal and Natal, south to Cape Province.
DESCRIPTION: *Male*. Dark green with golden sheen on back; lores black; breast feathers light yellow; wings and tail black with bright green tips. Irides dark brown; beak, feet and legs black. *Female*. Olive-brown above and yellowish-grey below. Winter plumage of male similar to that of

Malachite Sunbird, *Nectarinia f. famosa*

female, but he keeps the black flight and tail feathers, as well as the two elongated central tail feathers. Length: 6 in. (15·2 cm).
These sunbirds live on vast heaths and in bamboo forests. They are often seen in pairs or in little groups amongst clumps of flowers, thistles, heathers, *leonotis* and *knipholia*, etc. They do not seem to be affected by the cold and violent winds which often blow through these mountainous regions at an altitude which varies between 5,900–13,776 ft (1,800–4,700 m). There is no true migration, but the birds travel great distances in search of their food, which consists of small insects and the nectar of flowers. The female constructs the large, oval, purse-shaped nest. It is made of moss, vegetable wool, feathers and spiders' webs, and hung at a height of about 5 ft (1·5 m) in a tree or a bush on the edge of a wood, often hidden by high grasses and bushes in flower. One egg is laid, occasionally 2, pale cream-coloured with small grey or brown dots.
The Malachite Sunbird is one of the best-known of the Nectariniidae and also the most robust of the African species. The best-known subspecies is *N. f. cupreonitens*, from Ethiopia and south-eastern Sudan.
In 1954 Mrs. K. M. Scamell of England succeeded in breeding *Nectarina famosa* (*Avicultural Magazine*, Vol. 79, 1964,

p. 169). The birds had been placed in a small outside aviary, 6·5 × 6·5 × 3 ft (2 × 2 × 1 m) and had a heated shelter. The female constructed the nest in a clump of bamboo in the outside section, using blades of grass, pieces of straw, moss, kapok and even pieces of string. The one young bird was raised on fruitflies, greenflies and houseflies. It left the nest after 14 days, and 3 days later began to drink nectar. By then he was almost as large as his mother, except that his beak was only two-thirds of the normal length.

TACAZZE SUNBIRD, *Nectarinia tacazze* (Stanley)
G. Tacazzenektarvogel; F. Souï manga tacazza; D. Tacazze-Honingsvogel (Frontispiece)
DISTRIBUTION: East Africa, southern Sudan, Ethiopia, Kenya, north-east Tanzania.
DESCRIPTION: *Male*. Head and neck verdigris green; upper parts reddish-violet; wings and tail black; central flights lengthened. Breast reddish-violet; remaining lower parts black. *Female*. Olive-brown on upper parts and grey on lower parts. Length: 6 in. (15·2 cm).
N. tacazze live in mountainous districts and are common in the Ethiopian Highlands. They are often seen in the company of other honey-eating species, and in the cold weather they are to be found in the most exposed parts of the country.
The first breeding result was obtained in 1960 in the Zoological Gardens in New York. The male had already been there since 1953, the female since 1958. In order to get the birds to breed, an artificial nest was brought in and soon the female began bringing grass stalks to build the nest, and later lined it with kapok. The male began to court her. Although these birds in their wild state lay only one egg, this female laid 4. One fell out of the nest and, of the 3 remaining, 2 young were successfully reared. Incubation lasted 15 days and the young remained 20 days in the nest. They were fed on bananaflies and numerous other insects, which had to be caught three times a day with a drag-net. The female always took a large number of flies in her beak and stuffed them into the wide open bills of the youngsters with the speed of a machine gun. A few hours after they had flown out of the nest the young birds were drinking honey out of their glass drink containers.
Their winter quarters must be heated.

SCARLET-CHESTED SUNBIRD, *Nectarinia (Chalmitra) senegalensis gutturalis* (Linnaeus) (Frontispiece)
G. Rotkehlnektarvogel; F. Souï manga à poitrine écarlate; D. Roodborst-Honingvogel
DISTRIBUTION: Coastal Kenya, Tanzania, southern Congo, Angola south to eastern Cape Province, Rhodesia, northern Botswana and north-west South Africa.
DESCRIPTION: *Male*. Crown, forehead and beard stripe shiny golden-green, throat shining verdigris green, breast carmine-red with blue tips to feathers. Upper parts brown, under parts black. Wings and tail bronzish-brown. Irides dark brown; legs and feet black. *Female*. Upper parts olive-grey, under parts olive-yellow striped with grey. Length: 5¾ in. (14·6 cm).

In some regions these birds occur in great numbers in all kinds of vegetation and apparently prefer the vicinity of settlements. It is not unusual to find nests on the inside of verandas, but they are also to be found in banana plantations gardens and lanes, and the birds often build close to hornets' nests. They feed on flying ants and numerous other large insects.

In 1965, B. E. Reed and A. Homes achieved a successful breeding. It took place in a small inside aviary measuring only $3 \times 3 \times 5\frac{1}{2}$ ft (about $1 \times 1 \times 1.6$ m) in a conservatory. The female built a nest of grass stalks, moss and pieces of paper, which had been dipped either in water or in nectar. The nest was built in an ordinary nest-box. The one egg was incubated by the female and hatched after 13 days. The chick was fed bananaflies and a large quantity of spiders—as many as 100 a day. The latter had to be collected every day with a great deal of trouble from between the wall of an old ruined building. From the 12th day the male parent helped with the feeding. He then brought maggots, as the spiders were becoming scarce. When the young bird was 24 days old, it was completely independent (*Avicultural Magazine*, 1965, No. 4). A later breeding was achieved by them in 1969 and described in *Foreign Birds* Vol. 35, No. 6, Nov./Dec. 1969. Spiders are essential for the young birds.

LESSER DOUBLE-COLLARED SUNBIRD, *Nectarinia c. chalybea* (Linnaeus) (Frontispiece)
G. Blaurotnektarvogel; F. Souï manga acier; D. Dubbele Halsband Honingsvogel

DISTRIBUTION: South Africa, Rhodesia, Tanzania, south-east Zaire and Angola.
DESCRIPTION: *Male*. Upper parts bronze-yellow, shot with copper-red. Breast steel-blue on under parts; remaining under parts greyish-brown. A narrow red band runs over breast. *Female*. Greyish-brown. Tail shows white edges on outside feathers. Under parts pale yellowish. Length: $4\frac{1}{2}$ in. (11·4 cm).

This species is generally to be found in evergreen bushes but also visits gardens in the company of other honey-eaters. The birds are sometimes to be found in very dry areas, and also at heights of 6,000 ft (1,829 m) above sea level. They fly swiftly and are also able to remain hovering in front of a flower. They become aggressive in the breeding season. In 1914 the first specimen came into the possession of an aviculturist in Paris.

PURPLE SUNBIRD, *Nectarinia a. asiatica* (Latham)
G. Purpernektarvogel; F. Soui manga pourpré; D. Purper-Honingvogel (Frontispiece)

DISTRIBUTION: India, Nepal, Sikkim, Sri Lanka.
DESCRIPTION: *Male*. Head, neck, breast and upper parts shiny dark green, shot with purple. Abdomen black with blue sheen. The small bushy feathers at axillaries yellow and orange-red. Wings and tail black, the tail showing white outside edges. Iris reddish-brown; beak, legs and feet black. *Female*. Reddish-brown on upper parts, shot with olive colour. Under parts yellow, white towards back. Sides have a greenish tinting. Wings greyish-brown, tail black with white edges. Length: $4\frac{1}{2}$ in. (11·4 cm).

The species from Asia is generally known to aviculturists, as is also the Ceylon Sunbird, *Nectarinia z. zeylonica*. Both birds inhabit the forests, sometimes at heights of from 3,600–6,000 ft (1,097–1,829 m) above sea level. Small groups will visit gardens where luxurious flowers are blooming. Here they find nectar and numerous flies and insects. They make a pleasant chirping sound.

These birds are easy to keep in an inside aviary, and in the summer in an outside aviary, provided they remain indoors

Purple Sunbird, *Nectarinia a. asiatica*

at night. In addition to a good nectar mixture, they eat bananas, oranges, grapes and other sweet soft fruit.

Genus: Aethopyga

This genus occupies a prominent place among the honey-eaters of Asia, for it accounts for 15 species, in whose plumage a vivid red predominates amid a mixture of optical colours without the metallic sheen. The colour of the rump is yellow and the central quill feathers of the tail of the male birds are elongated.

HIMALAYAN YELLOW-BACKED SUNBIRD,
Aethopyga siparaja seheriae (Tickell) (Frontispiece)
G. Gelbrückennektarvogel; F. Souï manga rouge; D. D. Geelrug-Nektarvogel

DISTRIBUTION: The Himalayas.
DESCRIPTION: *Male*. Forehead and crown brilliant dark green with a blue sheen; back and sides of head, shoulders and back dark red. Rump light yellow; upper tail coverts dark green; neck and breast brilliant scarlet-red. A blue line runs from base of beak to neck. Under parts light greenish-brown. Small wing coverts red, remainder brownish-green. Tail blackish-grey. The elongated central feathers show both green and blue; tail feathers scarlet-red. Irides brown; beak horn-coloured; feet and legs brown. *Female*. Olive-grey. After the breeding season the male loses many of his fine

feathers. Length: 6 in. (15·2 cm).

Yellow-backed Sunbirds dwell in large numbers in the green and humid forests at an altitude of 4,900 ft (1,500 m). They extract nectar from the profusion of flowers, and in this way also take the insects attracted by the sweet smell. The birds build pear-shaped nests, hanging beneath a large leaf at the end of a branch. The entrance at the side is usually hidden by a kind of canopy. The female lays 2 or 3 eggs, on which she alone sits. Properly acclimatised, this sunbird behaves quietly in a cage or aviary.

The Marquis of Ségur, in 1914, was the first in France to succeed in perfectly acclimatising hummingbirds and sunbirds. At the same time an English aviculturist, Mr. A. Ezra, was experimenting with a 'miraculous' mixture, meant for a certain species of nectar-eaters and hummingbirds, which until then had been considered unsuitable for the aviary.

These birds can now be regarded as relatively easy to keep, combining, in addition, a number of qualities appreciated in aviary birds—good temper, a fine song, and, above all, their graceful movements and the prodigious beauty of their colours.

After acclimatisation they can live throughout the year in an outdoor aviary which is connected with a heated shelter. In these conditions almost all the sunbirds, even those which come from tropical regions, can adapt to the rigours of winter. As well as fruitflies, they capture many other insects, and also eat soft fruit and a good nectar which contains vitamins and other elements indispensable for keeping them in good condition. Several mixtures are known which allow these birds to live to a good age. A Purple Sunbird belonging to the Duchess of Bedford lived 21 years in captivity.

The following are some of the more usual mixtures:

The Ezra formula: One part of honey, one part of sweetened condensed milk, one part of phosphated baby cereal. Mix all ingredients in 10 parts of boiled, tepid water. Vitamins and a drop of meat extract can also be added. At 4 p.m. this mixture can be replaced by water and honey.

Stimulite: An English commercial product based on soluble malto-dextrine.

Beraut's formula: A solution of 20% of fine suger and 80% of water, to which must be added 1–2% of protein for human consumption, containing vitamins, mineral salts and trace elements.

Care must be taken to ensure that these mixtures do not ferment when they are set out for the birds. For this reason it is best to give them to the birds in small quantities and to keep the stock in a refrigerator. If the containers are properly cleaned and left to soak in disinfected water for 6–8 hours fermentation of the mixture can be avoided. The containers must of course be well rinsed before they are used.

These birds have only one disadvantage—their aggressiveness—which means that they cannot always be kept in a group, or with other species. In any case, 2 males of the same species must never be kept together. In a very large aviary a collection will live in comparative peace if care is taken to hang a large number of food containers at a sufficient distance from each other. Only birds in excellent condition can be added to a collection which already exists, and it is essential to keep a close watch on them.

FAMILY: ZOSTEROPIDAE

Zosterops: White Eyes

The unusual family of White Eyes contains about 85 species. The number of species varies from time to time because most of them are so similar that they have kept many ornithologists guessing. The aviculturist will be less concerned with minor variations when they are so alike in general appearance.

White Eyes occur in a very widespread range which includes Africa, India, South-East Asia, China, Japan, Indonesia, Borneo, the Philippines, Australia, New Zealand, and many islands in the South Pacific. They have been introduced into many of the islands in the South Pacific and in Hawaii. They have also migrated from island to island in some of these areas.

The dominant feature is a bright white feathered ring around the eyes. There are slight variations among the species. Some have very extensive eye rings, and one race in the Lesser Sunda islands has a yellow ring. Some have the eye ring missing. White Eyes in certain areas are called Spectacle Birds, and in Australia they are known as Silver Eyes. Of the same family is the Black Eye which is a very rare species from Borneo with a black eye ring and a yellow eyebrow strip. Another variant is the Cinnamon White Eye of the Philippines which has cinnamon rufous above and pale cinnamon below. The white eye ring is absent.

Zosterops are small, always alert, and very active birds with small slender beaks. Though they are far less colourful than most of the popular avicultural favourites, they never fail to attract admirers because of their delightful personalities. They are completely inoffensive to other birds in every way. Though they are not primarily noted as songbirds, they have quiet songs which are really very pleasant.

The appearance of White Eyes suggests that they are delicate, but actually they are very hardy and easily maintained. They are certainly the easiest of all the nectar feeders. They mix well with finches and small softbills such as Pekin Nightingales and even some of the larger tanagers, most of which are peaceful. Because of their quickly adaptable and inquisitive natures, they are used to help train other more difficult softbills and nectarine birds to accept artificial diets.

The Oriental or Indian White Eyes are easily acclimatised. They have a high degree of intelligence and show an incessant curiosity which helps immeasurably in a rapid acceptance of the food mixtures provided.

The diet is the simple standard softbill diet plus nectar. In this respect, they are much the same as tanagers. Since they are small birds, they may be fed mynah meal as well as mynah pellets. There is perhaps a slight problem here. Mynah pellets are a little large, and the meal is perhaps not completely appealing. The main fear is they will not consume enough meal or pellets to balance the diet. Most White Eyes thrive on mynah pellets, but it is wise to watch the intake rather closely in the beginning.

Fruit, nectar, peanut butter, cake, and a few mealworms are very important items of their diet. Also helpful, but not really necessary, is a fruitfly culture. Soya flour is very nourishing and is usually one of the items quickly accepted by the birds. It may be fed dry in a side dish. Milk will not be necessary in the nectar if soya powder is added to the diet.

The colour of White Eyes sometimes fades in captivity. The yellow drains from their plumage leaving under parts greyish-white with yellowish-white on the throat and chest. Upper parts fade to greyish-green. The soya meal helps to prevent the fading and to restore the colour. Also, properly planted aviaries attract a variety of small insects which are similarly helpful. These birds are very adept at hawking small insects.

White Eyes have been bred in captivity but not at all frequently. They build very small nests which are suspended usually from little forked branches. Both parents build the nest out of spider webs, soft fibres, hairs, and similar materials. The incubation period is eleven to twelve days, and the young leave the nest between nine and thirteen days of age. Both parents co-operate in the incubation and rearing routines and continue feeding the young birds for a period of two to three weeks after they leave the nest. Extra small live food in variety must be given during the breeding season. Zosterops are especially fond of small spiders during nesting periods.

It is difficult to distinguish between the sexes. Males sing, and this is the most accurate distinction. Males also have a slightly more extensive and brighter shading of yellow on the throat and upper chest.

INDIAN WHITE EYE, ORIENTAL WHITE EYE, *Zosterops palpebrosa* (Temminck)

G. Gangesbrillenvogel; F. Zostérops des Indes, Zostérops and lunettes; D. Ganges-Brilvogel

DISTRIBUTION: Bengal, Assam, Nepal, Sikkim, Bhutan.
DESCRIPTION: Upper parts dull olive-green. Throat and central area of upper breast yellow. Remaining under parts dusky grey. White eye ring bright and bold. Beak blackish slender, pointed, and slightly curved. Japanese White eye, *Z. p. japonica*, is slightly more green, and the Chinese White eye, *Z. p. siamensis*, has more yellow on under parts. Length: from tip of beak to tip of tail averages from 4¼–4¾ in. (10·8–12·1 cm) in the different races. Beak and tail about ½ in. (1·25 cm).

There are several other species occurring in the East and a few may show slight differences. *Zosterops erythropleura*, the Chestnut-flanked White Eye, from Burma and Thailand has chestnut patches on the flanks. *Zosterops everetti*, Everett's White Eye, from Thailand, Malaysia, and Borneo is just a little more grey than the Indian or Oriental White Eye. *Zosterops atricapilla*, the Black-capped White Eye, from

Indian White Eye, *Zosterops palpebrosa*

Malaysia, Borneo, and Sumatra, has a tinge of black on the forehead and crown. *Zosterops flava*, the Javan White Eye, recorded as a subspecies of the Mangrove White Eye by some authorities, is from Borneo and Java. It is a golden olive-yellow all over with a darker shade above and more yellow below. A trace of black occurs on the lores and behind the eye. *Zosterops lutea* or *chloris*, the Mangrove White Eye, of the Celebes, Moluccan Islands, Lessa Sunda Islands, and parts of Borneo and Indonesia is a little larger, heavier, and more greenish-yellow.

GREY-BACKED WHITE-EYE, *Zosterops l. lateralis* (Latham)

G. Australischenbrillrogel; F. Zostérops des Australie; D. Australish Brilvogel

DISTRIBUTION: Australia, Tasmania.
DESCRIPTION: Grey on upper parts and breast; chin, throat and sides of head sulphur-yellow; middle lower parts are whitish and rest is olive-yellow. Eyes are grey and beak brown; feet and legs grey-brown.

Mr. R. A. Richardson of Norfolk, England kept 3 White Eyes in a small planted aviary with heated shelter attached. They fed on ripe fruit, insects and a constant supply of nectar, given in tubes. In an apple tree, the pair built a cocoon-shaped nest; it was hung from the fork of a branch and made with blades of grass and fibres, firmly packed together with spiders' webs. The 2 parents took turn to sit. One day the male had disappeared, and the female was left alone to feed the young, who in the meanwhile had been hatched. And Mr. Richardson's third bird was a male, he put him in with the female, and against all expectations, he took the place of the father who had disappeared. Only one of the young was raised. (*Avicultural Magazine*, Vol. 68, No. 2, March/April, 1962.)

FAMILY: MELIPHAGIDAE

Honey-eaters

SUBFAMILY: MELIPHAGINAE

YELLOW-TUFTED HONEY-EATER, *Meliphaga auricomis* (Latham)

G. Gelbohrbüschler; F. Méliphage à touffes jaunes; D. Geeloor-Honingvogel

DISTRIBUTION: Australia.
DESCRIPTION: *Male.* Crown and neck olive-yellow; sides of head black. Ear coverts are lengthened and are golden-yellow. Upper parts olive-brown; sides of neck golden-yellow; throat yellow on a black background. Lower parts warm yellow. On breast and flanks there is olive-grey tinting. Flights and tail light brown with lighter edges to the feathers. Irides reddish-brown; bill and feet black. Length: 6¾ in. (17 cm). *Female.* Similar but a little smaller.

Honey-eaters occur chiefly in Australia, New Guinea and on a few islands of Polynesia, where they live near special trees such as eucalyptus, because they need their nectar and pollen for food. Their tongues are shaped like paint burshes.

They are typical tree birds, who are able to suspend themselves in unusual attitudes from the thinnest twigs in order to reach the blossoms.

In 1894 a specimen arrived at the Zoological Gardens in Berlin, and since then these birds have been irregularly imported. Other members of this family also appear in collections on rare occasions. The best-known species are *Meliphaga phrygra*, which was in the Zoological Gardens, London, as far back as 1882; the Black-cheeked Honey-eater, *Meliphaga chrysops*, which made its appearance for the first time in 1875 at the Zoological Gardens in Berlin; and the White-eared Honey-eater, *Meliphaga leucotis*, which in 1881 could be seen at the Zoological Gardens in Hamburg. They are all lively birds, which should be kept in a large heated inside aviary, and during summer months in a nearby outside aviary. They should be given a good nectar mixture and a fine insect mixture, with small pieces of soft fruit sprinkled with sugar, and live insects.

WHITE-NAPED HONEY-EATER, *Melithreptus lunatus* (Latham)

G. Schwarzkopfhonigschmecker; F. Méliphage à tête noire; D. Zwartkop-honingvogel

DISTRIBUTION: Australia.

DESCRIPTION: Head black down to neck. Over crown runs a

White-naped Honey-eater, *Melithreptus lunatus*

narrow white band; remainder of upper parts olive-yellow; lower parts white. Wings brown and grey, tail olive-yellow. Irides brown; above the eyes is a naked red patch. Beak brownish-black; feet and legs olive. Length: 5 in. (12·7 cm). The Honey-eaters of this family occur in 7 subspecies in various parts of Australia. They lead a wandering existence and appear in small groups where eucalyptus trees are in full bloom. They are to be found in coastal districts and along hills, where they can be heard chattering away loudly as they clamber through the branches. They build their nests at the very end of a high branch which is hanging downwards. The nest is basin-shaped and made of fine strips of inner bark, which are attached to one another by cobwebs. The nest is lined with grass, fur and hair. The 2 or 3 eggs, dirty yellow in colour, are marked with reddish-brown and purplish-grey stripes.

About 1900 these birds were already being imported irregularly and included in zoological gardens, but now they are only rarely seen. They may be kept together with bulbuls, cardinals and thrushes, and they eat insectivorous food, fruit, insects and mealworms. Heated winter quarters are essential.

FAMILY: EMBERIZIDAE

Genus: Sporophila

SUBFAMILY: EMBEREZINAE

BY J. L. ALBRECHT-MOLLER

This genus includes some 90 species or sub-species of small, active seed-eating finches, indigenous to America and the adjacent islands, especially Tobago and Trinidad. They are found especially in the northern part of South America and in Central America, while two varieties also live in the southern-most portion of North America.

They occur mainly in bushes and small trees in damp or marshy areas, near lakes or rivers, in clearings and open spaces of great forests and are also found in gardens.

The beak is short and massive, both upper and lower mandibles are fairly deep at the base, very wide and the top of the beak markedly curved, but for a genus which includes so many sub-varieties, this naturally varies to some extent.

Total length of the finches is between 3½–7 in. (9–14 cm). The wings are of average length, and pointed. They cover the lower portion of the back and about a third of the length of the tail, which is rounded and with somewhat abbreviated side feathers. In the wing, the first digital flight feather is short, the second and third are the longest, and on almost all varieties the wing feathers (except for the outer digital flight feather) near the base on both vanes are white, and when only the outermost feather of the folded wing is visible it forms a small white patch visible over feathers 5–6. The legs are of normal length, but the rear toe is relatively long. Certain species have very extended claws and because of their marked curve they often get caught in netting, gratings, or in twigs. The birds' temperament is very variable. Towards other species of birds they are generally friendly; single birds invariably so. They can show some hostility to drive away another bird, especially in the breeding season, but they seldom harm other birds in their cage. Otherwise, they associate with birds of their own genus. When the breeding season approaches the cocks fight, generally to the death. The weakest is pursued and pecked to death unless someone intervenes. Not more than a single pair of these finches should be kept in one aviary, if the peace is to be maintained. There is nothing against breeding in a spacious cage, provided the conditions are reasonably quiet.

These finches are seed-eaters and if it is desired to breed from them it is particularly important to use germinated seeds and semi-mature seed, for instance of bird-grass (*Stellaria media*) or rye-grass (*Lolium perennes*), and green-stuff such as lettuce, spinach, chicory, dandelion or chickweed, as well as the usual varieties of millet, canary seed, seeding grasses hemp and mealworms.

All these finches have an attractive little song which varies considerably in the different species. The white-throated ones are generally the most industrious songsters, and if one has a number of pairs they provide a veritable concert. The hens sing too, but very softly. Development of colouring lasts almost 3 years, but the cock-birds, however, mature during their first year, although they may not necessarily develop to the point of fertility. The problem is to obtain a pair that get on well together. Also an immature cock can be mistaken for a female.

These finches readily build in hedges or among branches, using coconut fibre, cowhair, etc. They lay 2–3 eggs of a whitish colour, with brown or violet spots. It is generally the hens that build and sit; the cock feeds her, and sings almost unceasingly from a branch in the vicinity. When the young arrive they are fed by both parents. As nestlings

Plate XXIII

Crimson Finch, *Neochmia ph. phaeton*

Star Finch, *Bathilda ruficauda*

Cherry Finch, *Aidemosyna modesta*

Bicheno's Finch, *Stizoptera b. bichenovii*

Zebra Finch, *Taeniopygia guttata castanotis*

Plate XXIV

Sydney Waxbill, *Aegintha t. temporalis*

Pin-tailed Nonpareil, *Erythrura p. prasina*

Blue-faced Parrot Finch, *Erythrura t. trichroa*

Red-headed Parrot Finch, *Erythrura psittacea*

Royal Parrot Finch, *Erythrura cyanofrans regia*

Plate XXV

Yellow-bellied Waxbill, *Estrilda melanotis quartinia*

Orange-cheeked Waxbill, *Estrilda melpoda*

Sundevall's Waxbill, *Estrilda rhodopyga*

Red-eared Waxbill, *Estrilda t. troglodytes*

St. Helena Waxbill, *Estrilda astrild*

Plate XXVI

Bar-breasted Fire-Finch, *Lagonosticta r. rufopicta*

Peter's Twinspot, *Hypargos n. niveoguttatus*
Green-backed Twinspot, *Mandigoa n. nitidula*

Cordon Bleu, *Uraeginthus b. bengalus*
Blue-breasted Waxbill, *Ureaginthus a. angolensis*
Blue-headed Waxbill, *Uraeginthus c. cyanocephalus*

they are mouse-coloured. After 2–3 weeks, small and short-tailed, they quit the nest, cheeping, and are fed for a time mainly by the cock-bird.

CAYENNE SEED-EATER, EULER'S SEED-EATER, *Sporophila frontalis*

G. Brauenpfäffchen; F. Grosbec géant; D. Reuzen-paapje, Riesenpfäffchen

DISTRIBUTION: South-east Brazil.
DESCRIPTION: Head, crown, nape, greenish-grey to olive-brownish; over brow and eye runs a wide, pale yellow eye-brow-stripe terminating well back by the ear; flight and tail feathers dark brown with a very indistinct, somewhat paler edge. Large wing and digital feathers end in an orange-yellow spot, which forms two wing bands; wing-patches invisible. Throat and underside olive-grey with greenish sheen; middle of abdomen yellowish-white; under-tail contour feathers yellow-green with a pale brown transverse band; sometimes throat of male is rather lighter in colour than that of female; beak of male pale horn, female, dark horn; feet and legs yellowish; irides dark brown. This species has a thinner upper mandible than other species, and brow and top of head are very flat. Apart from the more marked colour contrasts in male, the sexes are identical. Length: 4–5 in. (10·5–12·5 cm).

A successful breeding was reported by W. R. Partridge in *Avicultural Magazine*, Vol. 70, 1964, pp. 111–3 and in *Foreign Birds*, Vol. 32, No. 3, 1966, pp. 93–5.

GREY SEED-EATER, *Sporophila intermedia intermedia* (Gmelin)

G. Graupfäffchen; F. Grosbec bleuâtre; D.

DISTRIBUTION: Guyana, Venezuela, Trinidad, Colombia.
DESCRIPTION: *Male.* Upper parts ash-grey; tail and wings dark brown, with pale-grey feathering; small patch on wings; the virtually white throat forms a small definite spot; breast and abdomen pale grey to biscuit; beak horn-grey; legs black; iris dark brown. *Female.* Upper parts grey-brown; wings and tail brownish, feathers edged with pale brown; wing patches not visible. Under parts biscuit, palest at middle of abdomen. Beak and legs, dark; iris dark brown. Length: 4½ in. (11 cm).
A successful breeding was reported by W. T. Page in *Bird Notes* (2) 3, 1912, p. 338.

LAVENDER-BACKED FINCH, *Sporophila castanei-ventris* Cabanis

G. Graurückiges Zwergpfäffchen; F. Sporophile à ventre rouge; D. Grijsrug-Dwergpaapje

DISTRIBUTION: Guyana, Colombia, Eastern Ecuador, Brazil, Peru.
DESCRIPTION: *Male.* Front and crown of head, rear neck and sides blue-grey; throat, front of neck, breast, abdomen and rump dark chestnut-brown; tail and wings dark brown with slightly paler edges; small white wing-patches. Beak dark horn, feet and legs dark brown; iris dark-brown. *Female.* Upper sides greyish olive brown; lower sides yellow ochre; wings and tail greyish brown with slightly lighter edges; a small white wing patch, beak, feet and legs horn; eyes dark brown. Length: 3½ in. (8 cm).
This little bird was introduced by the London Zoo in 1906. It came to Denmark in 1932. The first breeding is recorded in *Die Gefiederte Welt* by R. Neunzig and there were further breedings in 1938, 1940–3.

HICK'S SEED-EATER, *Sporophila aurita* (Bonaparte)
G. Hicks Pfäffchen; F. Sporophile de Hick; D. Hick's Paapje

DISTRIBUTION: Guatamala, Costa Rica, Ecuador.
DESCRIPTION: Chapman investigated 33 males of this species and states that they differ considerably; nevertheless in *Catalogue of Birds*, he gives a description in which the males have black throats and 'chin' areas, and in which the white neck-patches are lunate and in several specimens combined with a narrow white band across the front of the neck (looking very much like half of a pair of spectacles). It is very evident that such a specimen was in Sclater's mind when *S. a. opthalmica* was named, while the species actually described under *opthalmica* was in fact *S. a. aurita*.
Young have been bred at the San Diego Zoo, USA.

Hick's Seed-eater, *Sporophila aurita*

GUTTERAL FINCH, *Sporophila nigricollis* (Vieillot)
G. Schwarzkappenpfäffchen; F. Grosbec à calotte noire, Sporophile à calotte noire; D. Zwartkap-Paapje

DISTRIBUTION: Eastern Brazil, Guyana, Venezuela, Colombia, Tobago and Trinidad.
DESCRIPTION: *Male.* Head, neck, throat, front and sides of neck, dull black. At back of neck, black colour merges into more olive-brownish back and wings. Large wing feathers greenish-black, with paler edges, and a pale yellow wing-patch. Tail black, with yellow-green edges. Breast, abdomen and rump yellowish-white; sometimes sides of crop grubby, including dirty black feathers. Beak, whitish-grey, legs blue-grey, iris brown. *Female.* Olive-grey, darkest on top; sides of neck grey-brown; under side, greyish-yellow; abdomen virtually biscuit, beak straw colour and legs grey-blue; iris brown. Length: 4 in. (10 cm).

Burmeister states that their habitat is open plains, and that they are proficient on the wing. G. Konigswalk considers them relatively rare. Introduced to Germany in 1876. In England, bred by W. T. Page as reported in *Bird Notes* (2) 3, 1912, p. 338. Young have been raised by Albrecht-Müller, Denmark, 1935, 1937–8.

WHITE-THROATED FINCH, WHITE-THROATED SEED-EATER, *Sporophila albigularis* (Spix)
G. Weisskehlpfäffchen; F. Grosbec à gorge blanche; D. Witkeel-Paapje

DISTRIBUTION: East Brazil.
DESCRIPTION: *Male.* Forehead, crown, nape, rear part of neck and sides of head black; rear of neck shading evenly into blue-grey of back; throat and upper part of front of neck, lower sides of neck, white; with black breast band below; a very small white spot near eyes. Wings dark slate-

grey, with pale grey edges on both flight-feathers and wing contour-feathers; a marked white wing-patch on digital flight feathers; tail slate-grey and entire underside white; beak pale yellow, feet and legs grey; irides dark brown. *Female.* Upper parts grey-brown; wings and tail dark brown, with wide, pale grey edges and outer edges. Throat and forepart of neck, breast, abdomen and under-tail contour feathers white; sides of body pale grey; beak dark horn-coloured; feet and legs grey; irides dark brown.

Three eggs is the usual number, but there are seldom more than 2 young. The nestlings are grey; 10–14 days after they are fledged, the young birds resemble the hen, and at one year old they have the hen's grey-brown reflection in their plumage, and the first signs of the breast band makes its appearance. The males can already be distinguished by their song; they may also be attacked by the parent male. At 2 years the brown tinge on upper part of bird disappears, being replaced by dark-grey; breast band and neck markings soon appear; throat becomes white, and upper part of head darker.

At three years old, the young have their permanent full colours. The markings are clear and well defined; beak colour straw-coloured. The nest may be used several times; it is always clean. When the female sits only her beak and tip of tail is visible above the edge of the nest, meanwhile the male sings a great deal. It is not unusual for these birds to

White-Throated Finch, *Sporophila albigularis*

raise three broods in succession in a single season. The white-throated finch is the easiest to breed from. First record from Dr. Franken, Orn. Monatschrift, 1885.

Karl Neunzig stated in 1907 that they raised several broods. In 1915 C. D. Farrar described a controlled breeding in *Avicultural Magazine* (2), 3, 1904–5, pp. 358–62. In Denmark, Albrecht-Müller raised 81 fledged young birds, and in one year (1935) raised 23 from 7 pairs. His oldest male lived to 17 years old, but Prof. O. Radish stated in 1924 that he had one in captivity for 24 years.

LINED SEED-EATER, *Sporophila lineola* (Linnaeus)
G. Leiss-stirnpfäffchen; F. Grosbec à. front blanc; D. Witvoorhoofd-Paapje

DISTRIBUTION: Eastern Brazil, Guyana, Venezuela, Peru, Bolivia and Argentina.

DESCRIPTION: *Male.* Entire upper part black, with blue-greenish reflection. Head black with white band extending from back of beak rearwards over crown and ending in a point in the neck; 2 wide white pear-shaped cheek-stripes. Throat, forepart of neck, breast and sides of neck black; lower tail contour feathers, abdomen and flanks white; tail and wings black, the latter with a small white patch; beak shiny black; feet and legs black horn-coloured. Irides blackish-brown. *Female.* Yellowish-grey, darkest on back, wings and tail; large flight feathers have narrow paler edges on the visible edge; underside, especially the abdomen biscuit or orange; beak, feet and legs yellowish; irides dark brown. Length: about 4 in. (10·2 cm).

Compared with the other hawfinches, this species is more elegant and slight in build. The beak is not so deep as in the more typical species, which is a helpful feature when distinguishing between the females. In the wild they occupy damp regions with low scrub, in which the males sing vigorously while the female sits. Apparently they move southwards to breed, building a very small neat open nest between branches. They lay 2–3 eggs, and incubate them for 12 days. The nestlings are mouse-coloured and leave the nest when 18–26 days old. They are generally fed primarily by the male.

Bred by Albrecht-Möller, Denmark, 1933, 1935–40.

Cardinal Grosbeaks

Genus: Pheucticus　　　　　　　　　　　SUBFAMILY: CARDINALINAE

ROSE-BREASTED GROSBEAK, *Pheucticus lusovianus* (Linnaeus)
G. Rosenbrustkernbeisser; F. Gros-bec à poitrine rose; D. Rozeborst-Kernbijter

DISTRIBUTION: Eastern Canada, eastern United States to Georgia; winters from Mexico through northern South America.

DESCRIPTION: *Male.* Black on the throat, head, neck, back, wings and tail, with two white bars and one cream bar on the wing; white on the lower half of the back and rump, and white tips on the outer three pairs of tail feathers. The chest and underparts are white, except for a brilliant red triangular patch extending from the throat over the breast. The under surface of the wing is also red. The male has a duller winter plumage. *Female.* Brown except for white stripes on the head and neck, two light wing bars (duller than the male's) and off-white underparts lightly streaked with brown. The underwing feathers are red in the male and commonly yellow in the female, although they may be red or intermediate in colour. Beak is a greyish horn colour, somewhat lighter in the male than in the female, and is large

in comparison with other finches. Albinos are known to occur. Legs are blue-grey and irides black, Length: 7–8 in. (17·5–21 cm).

A woodland species which associates in pairs during the breeding season. A territory is defended by the pair against other conspecifics. In the wild this species east adult and larval insects, a variety of seeds and tree blossoms, and a wide range of fleshy fruits such as berries. Most foraging is done in the tree tops or in the shrubby understory, although individuals are sometimes encountered on the ground. Progress in foraging is by hopping or short flights. The commonest call is a sharp, metallic 'chink'; the commonest song during the breeding season is a beautiful phrased warble which alone would make this species worth keeping. The male warbles more frequently than the female. A nest of fine twigs, vines, and rootlets is built in a bush, or less commonly, in a tree. The nest is normally built by the female, but some males also do a great deal of nest building. The 3–5 eggs are bluish-white with brown markings. Both sexes incubate the eggs, brood and feed the young, and warble while on the nest.

This species is not common in captivity, although a number

of zoos and private individuals have kept specimens with success. It has been bred successfully several times in captivity. It bites with vigour, and thus the beak is best avoided in any but hand-reared individuals! A good staple diet is a mixture of small seeds with sunflower seeds and unsalted peanuts, such as commercial parrot food. Cuttlebone and gravel must also be provided. Almost any kind of fruit or beans is welcomed, but larger fruit such as apples, pears and bananas should be cut into small pieces. In addition sprouted grain, whole maize ears, insectivorous food, and live insects may be given. A few drops of liquid vitamin supplement should be added to the drinking water occasionally, but cod liver oil or its deivatives should not be given. Housing should be spacious enough to provide adequate room for at least short flights. This species does well in a mixed collection since it is relatively peaceful; females may be kept together in reproductive condition, but males in breeding condition should not be housed together. When males begin warbling they should be separated. For breeding success a well-planted flight is important, and should include tall, well-leaved bushes which are partly shaded. Live insects must be provided when the young hatch. Many will winter peaceably together. This species is remarkably hardy and will tolerate winter temperatures if sufficient shelter is provided from the wind; open water and abundant food must be available. However, in regions where the temperature drops below 40°F (20°C)

it is better to bring the birds indoors.

BLACK-HEADED GROSBEAK, *Pheucticus melanocephalus* (Swainsòn)
G. Schwarzkopfkernbeiser; F. Gros-bec du Mexique; D. Zwartko-Kernbijter

DISTRIBUTION: Western North America from Canada to Mexico; winters in Mexico.
DESCRIPTION: *Male.* Similar to *P. ludovicianus* except that the rump and lower part of the back are rusty yellow with black streaks; back is streaked with rusty yellow; there is a collar of the same colour around the back of the neck which is continuous with the rusty yellow throat, chest and flanks, and a yellow abdomen. There are large white tips on only the outer two pairs of tail feathers. The underwing feathers are yellow in both sexes. The female is similar to the female *P. ludovicianus,* except that there is a prominent white streak below the eye, a uniform light rusty yellow on the throat and chest, grading off to a lighter colour on the abdomen, and a light yellow tinge to the stripes of the head and back. The male melanocephalus does not have a pronounced winter plumage. Length: 6¼–7½ in. (16–19·5 cm).
Care, breeding techniques, habitat and dietfor *P. ludovicianus* also apply to this species.

Genus: Guiraca

BLUE GROSBEAK, *Guiraca caerulea* (Linnaeus)
G. Blankardinal; F. Gros-bec bleu; D. Noord-amerikunsc Blaue Bisschep

DISTRIBUTION: Southern United States south through to Central America; winters in Mexico, Central America and Cuba.
DESCRIPTION: *Male.* Blue with brownish-black wings and tail; there are two prominent tan wing bars. The large bill is grey and there is a black mask around the base of the bill which is not obvious because of his dark blue colour. *Female.* Brown, and slightly darker on the back than on the undersurface. Her bill is dark brown and she has two tan wing bars. The feet are dark and the eye is black in both sexes. The tail is flicked frequently and the careful observer will note that the end often describes an ellipse. This species appears to be quite nervous in its actions. It lacks a placid demeanor and is flighty even in large planted aviaries. Length 6½–7 in. (16·5–17·8 cm).

Prefers bushy hedges and thickets. A breeding territory is defended by the pair against conspecifics. Seeds of many kinds and insects are eaten. The commonest call is an explosive, sharp 'spink', and the song is a soft, rapid warble. A nest of grass stems, rootlets and hair is built is a shrub or low tree. A snake skin may be incorporated into the nest. Three or four pale bluish-white eggs are laid.
Commoner in zoos than private collections. It is easily kept and directions on the care of *Pheucticus* apply equally well here. This species also bites with enthusiasm. Males at least are aggressive toward each other all year, but not found dangerous to keep males together as they lack the 'determination' with which *Richmondena* fights, and seldom if ever harm each other. Remarkably hardy and can survive rather severe winter weather if well sheltered from the wind and given a good diet. Open water should be provided all year, although the species will eat snow when necessary. In regions where the winter becomes very cold it is safer to keep the birds indoors.

Genus: Richmondena

VIRGINIAN CARDINAL, CARDINAL, REDBIRD, CARDINAL GROSBEAK, *Richmondena cardinalis* (Linnaeus)
G. Roter Kardinal, Blut Kardinal; F. Cardinal rouge; D. Rode Kardinal

DISTRIBUTION: Eastern North America from southern Canada to Florida; western North America from Texas and Southern California to Belize; introduced to Hawaii and Bermuda.
DESCRIPTION: *Male.* Brilliant red all over, excepting a large orange bill, a black mask about the base of the bill, the black eyes and the pinkish-brown legs. Prominent crest and long tail, flicked frequently by the bird. *Female.* Rather uniform yellowish-brown with an orange bill, a red tip to the crest, and traces of red in the wings and tail. Her black mask is slightly less intense than that of the male. Plumage colouration does not change with the season. Length 7–9 in. (18–22·5 cm).

A woodland and garden species which associates in pairs throughout the year. A breeding territory is defended by the pair against conspecifics, but in winter over a dozen individuals may congregate at a feeding station. Diet and foraging are similar to *Pheucticus* except that cardinalis tends to forage lower more frequently. The commonest call is a sharp 'kik' and bird also has a series of loud, clear whistles which is highly variable and most pleasing to the ear. Both sexes whistle, and males can be heard to do so in almost any month of the year. A nest of fine twigs and rootlets is built in a bush or a vine, such as grape, by the female, who also incubates the 3–4 brown-spotted white eggs. The female alone broods but both sexes feed the young. The male feeds the female frequently throughout the breeding cycle, and the female sometimes feeds the male.
Common in collections and has been bred in captivity. Most of the directions for keeping and feeding the Red-breasted Grosbeak apply equally well here, as do the same precautions

for handling. It is probably wise to segregate both sexes into male–female pairs when they come into reproductive condition.

It is not advisable to keep more than one pair together in an aviary at any season, unless the flight is very large. For breeding success a flight well-planted with shrubs is important, and a tangle of sturdy vines should be provided in a secluded corner for nesting. Freshly cut vines function well if they are tied at several points to nearby vegetation. Live insects must be provided when the young hatch. If breeding is successful, bodies of open water in the aviary should be covered before the young fledglings, as they easily drown themselves. Does very well in an outdoor aviary all winter if shelter is provided against the wind. It is well to provide open water in winter but this is not essential where snow is available. The addition of seeds with a high oil content (such as niger and hemp) to the staple seed mixture is advisable in winter.

Virginian Cardinal, *Richmondena cardinalis*

SUBFAMILY: THRAUPINAE

Tanagers

BY H. J. BATES AND R. L. BUSENBARK

The large family of Tanagers includes many of the world's most beautiful coloured birds. They come mostly from South America but also from Central America, Mexico and the United States. There are relatively few with any additional ornamentation other than colours. Several are lightly crested; and, at the moment of writing, the writers do not recall ever seeing any long tailed tanagers except the Magpie Tanager which is not much out of standard proportions.

As far as aviculturists are concerned, tanagers do not need any extra attractions. The vivid colours and patterns found on many species are almost unbelievable. Textures of feathers are often variable. Very often bright metallic glosses and velvety soft feathers occur in vivid contrasts in individual colour schemes.

Not all tanagers are bright and colourful, and therefore many will hold little interest for the aviculturists. There are also several beautiful species which are not likely to become available because of rarity. Happily for the aviculturist, there are many exceptionally beautiful members of this family which have become available with increasing frequency in the past few years.

Tanagers show a broad variation in requirements. The larger species such as those in the genera *Ramphocelus*, *Piranga*, and *Thraupis* are usually very hardy, quickly adaptable to domestic diets, and require a very simple standard diet plus extra fruit and simple nectar. Seed is unnatural to the diet and undoubtedly is of no help whatsoever; even when tanagers are housed with seedeating birds, they do not have the slightest interest for any kind of seed.

Some species of large tanagers require greater amounts of live food than the average. Examples of those requiring more live foods are the Magpie Tanager and the Swallow Tanager, both of which are considerably more active. It can be reasonably safely assumed that any tanager which is particularly alert and active as a natural characteristic accustomed to catching live foods. This may be a little difficult to ascertain as well as a little difficult to explain. Lethargy is, of course, a danger signal and is not to be confused with the calm, peaceful, easygoing manner which is characteristic of the average tanager. Highly insectivorous tanagers usually have a thrush-like alertness as if they are always expecting an insect to fly past. The Magpie Tanager has this characteristic extremely well-developed. The Swallow Tanager, which is usually classed in a separate family or in a subfamily by itself, has this characteristic in a less pronounced manner.

The very important Calliste Tanagers of the genus *Tanagra* are often delicate at first. These birds are smaller than average tanagers and require the fortified nectar for best results. They also need a variety of fruits which should be least in the early stages of acclimatisation be grated and blended to insure a good proportionate intake of the right foods. Mynah meal or all-purpose food can be mixed with the blend and after a while mynah pellets can be sprinkled on top. When they are selected instead of accidentally eaten, the mynah pellets can be fed in a separate dish. Heavy, oily mockingbird foods should at all costs be avoided. Calliste Tanagers as a rule do not require, or voluntarily eat, large quantities of live foods. Too many mealworms can cause digestive trouble. Among the notable exceptions is the Black-eared Tanager (*Tangara perzudakii*) which spends a great amount of time probing into old logs in search of small grubs or hiding insects.

After acclimatisation, most Callistes settle very well into domestication on their rather specialised diet. Some are hardier than others and do not need the refinements, but it is wiser to offer the refined diet if there is any question of hardiness whatsoever. Many of the Callistes, particularly the smaller ones, are excellent companions to honey-creepers and hummingbirds. Planted aviaries, if not too dense, serve as excellent habitats. Despite their vivid colours, they become lost in dense foliage and cannot be seen to best advantage. Callistes are usually very peaceful birds which rarely exhibit aggressive tendencies.

Very few tanagers are known as songbirds. Those which do sing well could not be favourable compared to thrushes in quality of song. The few singers must be regarded as exceptions.

Several tanagers have been successfully reared in captivity. Nests are mostly cup-shaped and are often of flimsy construction. Some species build dome-like nests or use nest boxes. Incubation periods are usually twelve to fourteen days. The young remain in the nests for variable lengths of time depending on the genus to which they belong. The young of some genera leave the nest in as short a period as thirteen days. Others are variable up to twenty-four days. Live food intake is greatly increased during nestling stages. Aggressiveness, if present at all, is likely to become more pronounced during the breeding season.

As far as was possible at the time of publication, the order of species follows that in the standard reference for nomenclature, Peters' *Check List of Birds of the World.* There are at present several divergent opinions among noted ornithologists regarding the status of certain genera, species and subspecies. The writers have used many different ornithological reference works to try to update and correct the nomenclature wherever possible. It is an unfortunate fact that many avicultural scientific identifications have long been outdated. The writers have spent considerable time examining museum skins as well as tracing down all members of this interesting family which have never had sufficient coverage in avicultural literature. Thus, while coverage for several species is perhaps brief, this chapter represents the most complete avicultural data ever assembled for this family. Of course, popular names seem to be impossible to standardise and are too often duplicated; but the writers and publishers have tried to list the most acceptable or widely used names hoping that some of the extraneous and confusing ones can now be discarded.

Genus: Tanagra

Euphonias

There are twenty-four species of Euphonias ranging southward from Mexico. These are short, heavy-set but usually small birds, with thick, short beaks and short tails. In proportion they are much like smaller Chlorophonias except the necks are less thick.

Males are usually bright with deep, glossy purples and blues and bright yellows. Many of the different species are very similarly patterned and coloured. Beaks, feet and legs are black in many species. In others, the lower mandible is silvery-grey, and feet and legs are grey. Females are usually dull shades of olive.

Euphonias of different species are quite often available and are usually very inexpensive. A few are pleasant songsters. Immature birds are the ones most likely to be imported, and adult plumage is attained very slowly.

Euphonia, like Chlorophonias, are difficult when first imported. They should be given a fortified nectar as well as a variety of fruits. Mynah meal mixed with the fruits and a few mealworms along with the nectar are a good beginning diet. Mynah pellets should be sprinkled on top of the mixture until the birds accept them readily. They are too fond of bananas and will ignore other foods if this fruit is allowed in any quantity. The writers omit it entirely.

When they settle to a good artificial diet, they do very well and are usually very hardy.

YELLOW-THROATED EUPHONIA, BONAPARTE'S EUPHONIA, *Tanagra lauta*

DISTRIBUTION: Mexico and Central America.
DESCRIPTION: Notably distinctive in this and the next two species is that *all* the under parts including the throat are yellow. This species has yellow also on the forehead. The remaining plumage is black with purple and blue glosses. White is concealed on outer tail feathers. The female is olive above and olive yellow in a bright shade on under parts mixed with minor areas of white. Length 4 in. (10 cm).

VIOLET EUPHONIA, VIOLET TANAGER, *Tanagra violacea* (Linnaeus) (Pl. XII)

G. Violettblauer Organist; F. Euphone violet; D. Violetblauwe Organist

DISTRIBUTION: Venezuela, French Guiana, Guyana, Surinam, Brazil, Trinidad and Tobago.
DESCRIPTION: The pattern and colouring are like the Yellow-throated Euphonia. The black areas are more heavily glossed in purples and blues. Yellow covers throat and chin as well as all under parts and the forehead and forecrown. A white wing bar is concealed except when wings are spread. Under wing coverts are also whitish. A little white on the tail is also usually hidden. These very subordinate features in varying degrees are characteristic of many species. *Female.* Olive-green above and greenish-yellow on under parts shading to yellowish on the abdomen. Beak, feet and legs dark. Length: about 4 in. (10 cm).

SCRUB EUPHONIA, LESSON'S EUPHONIA, *Tanagra affinis*

DISTRIBUTION: Mexico and Central America.
DESCRIPTION: *Male*. Bright yellow on forehead and fore-crown and all under parts from upper chest. The remaining plumage including the throat from chin to upper chest is black with purple and blue glosses and white patches on the tail. *Female*. Greyish-olive, brighter above and paler below. Olive-green is brighter on forehead, rump, and upper tail coverts. Length: about 4 in. (10 cm).

YELLOW-CROWNED EUPHONIA, *Tanagra lutei-capilla*

DISTRIBUTION: Central America.
DESCRIPTION: *Male*. This species is like the Scrub Euphonia except the yellow on the head covers a more extensive area reaching almost to the nape. Upper parts are glossy bluish-black. The shiny bluish-black throat and chin are present. Under wing coverts and inner webs of wing feathers are white. *Female*. Is dull in much the same manner as the female of the Scrub Euphonia: olive-green above and yellowish below with brighter yellow in the central area. Under wing coverts are white. Beak, feet and legs are black. Length: 4 in. (10 cm).

ORANGE-CROWNED EUPHONIA, *Tanagra saturata*

DISTRIBUTION: Colombia, Ecuador and Peru.
DESCRIPTION: *Male*. The pattern is about the same as the above species, but the colouring is slightly different. Yellow areas are shaded with orange on the crown and buffish-orange on under parts with more yellow on the sides. The black areas are glossed in purplish in most areas with blue glosses more prominent in wings, tail and rump. This species has no white on the wings or tail. *Female*. Is bright olive above and olive-yellow below shading to yellow in central abdominal area. Length: about 4 in. (10 cm).

TRINIDAD EUPHONIA, *Tanagra trinitas*

DISTRIBUTION: Colombia, Venezuela and Trinidad.
DESCRIPTION: *Male*. The yellow cap is more extensive on the crown than on the preceding species, and a narrow forehead is black. Small areas of hidden white occur on inner webs of two pairs of outer tail feathers and on wing feathers. The yellow areas are bright with slight tinges of orange, and the black areas are glossed in blue. Under tail coverts are whitish-yellow. of olive in upper *Female*. Is a paler shade parts than preceding species and pale yellowish below with greyish shades in central area and whitish shades on abdomen. Under tail coverts are yellow. Length: 4 in. (10 cm).

OLIVE-BACKED EUPHONIA, GOULD'S EUPHONIA, *Tanagra gouldi*

DISTRIBUTION: Southern Mexico and Central America.
DESCRIPTION: *Male*. Bright yellow forehead and bronzed-olive upper parts with traces of blue gloss. Under parts are mostly dull olive with yellowish shading on sides and flanks and brownish shades on abdomen and under tail coverts. *Female*. Is similar to the male but has a brownish shade replacing the yellow forehead. The olive colouring above is deep and mostly without gloss. Under parts are dull for the most part but bright olive-yellow in central areas. Under tail coverts are dull brownish-olive. Black beak with grey at base; feet and legs black. Length: 4–4½ in. (10·5 cm) including 1¼ in. (2 cm) tail.

TAWNY-BELLIED EUPHONIA, SPOT-CROWNED EUPHONIA, *Tanagra imitans*

DISTRIBUTION: Central America.
DESCRIPTION: Like Gould's Euphonia but upper parts and throat are glossy bluish-black. The crown and under parts are rich yellow. In the female the forehead is chestnut instead of yellow. A bluish gloss occurs on the crown and nape. Under parts are paler than those of the female Gould's.

Genus: Lanio

BLACK-THROATED SHRIKE TANAGER, GREAT SHRIKE TANAGER, *Lanio aurantius*

DISTRIBUTOR: Mexico and Central America.
DESCRIPTION: Shrike Tanagers have shrike-like hooks on the ends of the upper mandibles. *Male*. Hood is black, covering the head and neck to lower nape and upper chest. Tail and wings are black with a small white wing bar. All body plumage is bright yellow with brownish tinges on the middle chest. *Female*. Is mostly variable shades of olive mixed with grey on the head and brown on the wings. Beak hooked and black, feet and legs blackish. Length: about 8 in (21 cm), including long rounded tail of 3 in. (7·5 cm).
The White-throated Shrike Tanager of Central America is treated as a subspecies of the above by some authorities and as a separate species by others (*leucothorax*).

Genus: Heterospringus

SCARLET-BROWED TANAGER, *Heterospingus xanthopygius*

DISTRIBUTION: Colombia and Ecuador.
DESCRIPTION: This is a rather large, robust tanager which is quite attractive in its unusual and simple pattern. It has a white line above the eye changing to scarlet and becoming very broad behind the eye; this line continues as a band across the nape. Under parts are dusky slate with white on the sides of the chest and under wing coverts. Upper parts are mostly glossy black with yellow on the wing coverts and rump. The female is duskier above and paler below.
The Sulphur-rumped Tanager (subspecies *rubrifrons*) from Central America lacks the eyebrow marks and the yellow on the wing coverts. It retains the yellow rump, but it is altogether less attractive than the nominate race. It is also smaller. Females are darker grey on the under parts with more yellow on the lower tail coverts. Length, about 7 in. (18 cm) including 2¼ in. (6 cm) tail.

Genus: Piranga

The nine species of this genus are also reasonably large as are those of the previous genus. The beaks are long, somewhat bold, and are less well-proportioned. The eyes are large, soft and dark. Sexes are different. These birds, for the most part, are less shapely than those of the preceding or the following genera. The necks are thinner and longer; and the heads are, in proportion, larger. Bodies are slender, and tails are longer.

NORTH AMERICAN SCARLET TANAGER, *Piranga olivacea* (Gmelin)   (Pl. XI)
G. Scharlachtangare; F. Tangara éclarate; D. Karmijnrode Tangara

DISTRIBUTION: Eastern and central North America migrating through Mexico and Central America to Colombia, Ecuador, Peru and Bolivia for the winter.
DESCRIPTION: *Male.* Undergoes a seasonal colour change and is patterned like the species above when 'in-colour'. The red is a little less intense but more uniform, and the black in the wings is slightly less extensive. In the winter 'out-of-colour' phase, the red is replaced by dull pale olive-green with yellow on the central abdominal area and under tail coverts. The black areas are of a much less intense shade. The transition phase is not soft or gradual, but the colouring becomes splotchy. *Female.* dull olive-green on upper parts and paler, softer green with a blend of yellow on under parts. Wings and tail are shaded with slate. Beak is orange-horn with black along upper ridge. Length: 6–7 in. (15·5–18 cm), including 2 in. (5 cm) tail.
This species is out of colour when it migrates and so probably escapes most of the attention of trappers for foreign markets. While resident in the United States, it is illegal to trap the species for avicultural purposes.
Also subject to fading in captivity, this species should be given a colour holding agent as a regular part of the diet.

WHITE-WINGED TANAGER, *Piranga leucoptera*

DISTRIBUTION: Mexico, Central America, Colombia, Venezuela, Ecuador, Peru and Bolivia.
DESCRIPTION: *Male.* Has two bold white bars and a black mask which narrowly covers the forehead and lores and surrounds the eyes extending slightly behind to a blunt point. Otherwise it is like the above species in pattern and colour and is very attractive. *Female.* Is like the above female with brown on the wings and tail and white wing bars as in the male. Length about 6 in. (15·5 cm) including 1¾ in. (4·5 cm) tail.

RED-HEADED TANAGER, *Piranga erythrocephala* with two subspecies
G. Rotkopftanager
DISTRIBUTION: Mexico.
DESCRIPTION: *Male.* Of this rare species has a bright red head mostly similar to the Western Tanager in the transition area on the neck. Under parts are bright yellow becoming pale on abdomen and shaded with olive on the flanks. Upper parts are yellowish-olive. Length: 6 in. (15 cm). *Female.* Lacks the red on the head which is replaced by the body colours (yellow on the throat, olive-green on top and greyish on the face). Upper parts are dull olive-green, and under parts are mostly dull yellow.

ROSE-THROATED TANAGER, *Piranga roseo-gularis*

DISTRIBUTION: Mexico and Guatemala.
DESCRIPTION: *Male.* Has dull red on the wings, tail, and crown. The throat, chest and under tail coverts are pinkish-rose. Remaining plumage is grey, darker above and paler below. The beak is brownish-horn, feet and legs brownish. *Female.* Has dull olive replacing the red on the male and pale yellow on the throat. Length: about 6 in. (15 cm).

FLAME-COLOURED TANAGER, SWAINSON'S TANAGER, *Piranga bidentata*

DISTRIBUTION: Mexico and Central America.
DESCRIPTION: *Male.* Is much brighter than the preceding species; the beak is black. Bright flame-red, variable in the different races, covers neck and entire under parts except for the ear coverts which are dull red bordered on the lower areas by dull black. Two whitish wing bars are sometimes tinged with pink. Upper parts are striated with dull buffish-orange and black. Tail and wings are dusky-black with white tips on outer tail feathers. Feet and legs are blackish. *Female.* Has white wing bars and a dull bill. Under parts are bright yellow, and upper parts are yellowish-olive above with fine streaks on head and nape. Length about 7 in. (18 cm) including 2¾ in. (7 cm) tail.

RED-HOODED TANAGER, *Piranga rubriceps*

DISTRIBUTION: Colombia, Ecuador and Peru.
DESCRIPTION: *Male.* Scarlet on head, neck, mantle and chest and bright yellow on the remaining under parts. The lores are reddish-brown. Remaining upper parts are much duller in colour with the only brightness occurring on the wing coverts which are yellow. Back, yellowish-olive and wings and tail blackish with pale olive edges on many of the feathers. *Female.* Has the scarlet restricted to the head. Length about 8 in. (23 cm) including 2½ in. (6·5 cm) tail.

Genus: Calochaetes

MASKED VERMILION TANAGER, *Calochaetes coccineus*

DISTRIBUTION: Colombia, Ecuador and Peru.
DESCRIPTION: Sexes differ with the female being slightly less brilliant. Mostly brilliant and uniform scarlet with black wings, tail, throat and a facial mask. Length: about 7 in. (18 cm) including 2 in (5 cm) tail.

Genus: Ramphocelus

The eight species of the genus *Ramphocelus* are all about 7 in. (18 cm) long including the tails of about 2½ in. (6·5 cm). They are strong, hardy and very attractive. The black areas which occur on the males of most species are, except for wings and tail, soft and velvety in texture. The bold ½ in. (1·8 cm) beaks characteristcally have a broad silvery-grey area near the base of the lower mandible with the remaining areas black. They do not all have this feature, but most do. Feet and legs of males are greyish-black, and eyes are burgundy-brown.

Members of this genus are among the larger tanagers which mix well with many average softbills such as bulbuls, thrushes, babblers and allied species and birds of similar disposition. They are also peaceful with most smaller birds.

Genus: Ramphocelus

SCARLET-RUMPED TANAGER, *Ramphocelus p. passerinii* Bonoparte (Pl. XI)
G. Rotbürzeltängare; F. ˙Rhamphocèle à croupion rouge; D. Roadstuit-Tangara

DISTRIBUTION: Mexico and Central America.

DESCRIPTION: *Male.* Jet black on all plumage except for a brilliant scarlet area covering the lower back, rump, and upper tail coverts. The beak is mostly silvery-grey with black on the tip and along most of the cutting edges. Feet and legs are black. *Females* of the two subspecies vary slightly. *Costaricensis* is usually a little brighter than the females of the nominate race. Chests and rumps are dull yellow to bright orange. Most of the remaining plumage is dull brown on upper parts and yellowish-buff on under parts. Length about 7 in. (18 cm).

This species is known as a songbird among tanagers in the wild state, but it rarely sings in captivity. It is often available and is an excellent subject for both beginners and experienced aviculturists.

ORANGE-RUMPED TANAGER, *Ramphocelus flammigerus* D. Oranjestuit-Tangara

D. Oranjestuit

DISTRIBUTION: Colombia.

DESCRIPTION: The tail is nearly 3 in. (7·5 cm) and the beak is ⅝ in. (2·6 cm). This species is slightly larger than the previous species and is patterned exactly the same. Instead of red, however, the colouring is bright orange. Black areas are the same. *Female.* Has dark brownish-black upper parts in all areas except for orange in the same areas as male. Under parts have bright orange on the chest, yellow-orange below the chest, and dull whitish-buff on the throat. Under tail coverts are dull burnt-orange.

The same remarks for the Scarlet-rumped Tanager apply here. Length: about 8 in. (21 cm) including 3 in. (7·5 cm) tail.

SILVER-BEAKED TANAGER, MAROON TANAGER, *Ramphocelus carbo* with seven subspecies

D. Kastanjerode Tangara

DISTRIBUTION: Colombia, Ecuador, Peru, Bolivia, Venezuela, Surinam, Guyana, Brazil, Paraguay and Trinidad.

DESCRIPTION: There are several colour variations especially in intensity in the different subspecies, and sizes are also variable.

Male. Has deep blackish-brown wings and tail and blackish on the abdomen. Wings and tail are nearly black in some races. The remaining plumage is deep velvety maroon-brown, brighter in some races. The lower under parts are paler in various shades according to race. The throat and upper chest are usually deep maroon. *Females* have dull blackish beaks and are dull brownish-red in most areas. The rump is

brighter, and slightly different shadings on the under parts mark the different races. Feet and legs are black. Length: about 7 in. (18 cm), including 2½ in. (6·5 cm) tail. The silver-grey patch on the base of the lower mandible of the black beak is very prominent.

This species is frequently available at very reasonable prices. It is also, like all the above species, hardy and ideal for beginners. Red colourings in this species sometimes fade in captivity leaving dull brownish shades instead. The Silver-beaked Tanager is not as vivid as most members of this genus due to the lack of bright contrasts, but it is a beautiful bird with its deeply glowing maroon blends.

CRIMSON-BACKED TANAGER, *Ramphocelus dimidiatus* Lafresnaye (Pl. XI)
G. Rotrückentangare; F. Tanagre à dos rouge; D. Roadrug-Tangara

DISTRIBUTION: Panama, Colombia, Venezuela.

DESCRIPTION: This species is mostly like the previous species except it is smaller and much more vivid; and the distribution of maroon is slightly different. Vivid, deep blood-crimson glows on the lower back, rump, upper tail coverts and most of the under parts. A less vivid and deeper shade occurs on the head, upper back and upper chest. Wings and tail are blackish-brown, and black occurs on the central abdmonial areas.

Females are much duller and also somewhat paler with brownish instead of blackish areas. Throat and upper chest are dark maroon-brown. Lower back, rump, upper tail coverts and most of the under parts are dull crimson-brown. Lower back, rump, upper tail coverts and most of the under parts are dull crimson-brown. Length: 7 in. (18 cm), including 2¼ in. (6 cm) tail.

This species is somewhat more delicate during acclimatization than most members of this genus, but not as delicate as many in other genera. It is more insectivorous than average tanagers and therefore does not adapt quite so easily to artificial diets. Increased supplies of mealworms provide the additional insectivorous requirement.

Many of these birds lose colour to some extent, but usually it returns. If it does not, a colour holding agent will restore the natural brilliance during the next moult.

BLACK-BELLIED TANAGER, *Ramphocelus melanogaster* with two subspecies

DISTRIBUTION: Peru.

DESCRIPTION: Much like the male Crimson-backed Tanager except that it has a longer tail, is duller and darker red on the head, and has a less extensive colouring on the rump and upper tail coverts. The subspecies *transitus* has a paler throat and chest which becomes brighter on the lower chest and flanks. *Female.* Is mostly like the female of the Silver-beaked

Tanager with the reddish on under parts and upper tail coverts, but the forehead and sides of the face are also red. The female Crimson-backed Tanager has a dusky blackish shade on the head, throat and chest. Length: about 7 in. (18 cm) including 2¼ in. (6 cm) tail.

SOUTH AMERICAN SCARLET TANAGER, *Ramphocelus bresilius* (Pl. XI)

G. Purpurtangare; F. Tangare rouge de Brésil; D. Rode Purpurtangara

DISTRIBUTION: Eastern South America, Brazil.

DESCRIPTION: *Male*. This species is much like the male North American Scarlet Tanager in pattern and colouring. However, this one is available to aviculturists whereas the other is not except perhaps during the winter migration. This species is non-migratory.

Has vivid black and brilliant red in its simple colour scheme. Black covers the wings and tail; and all the other plumage is a most intense shade of scarlet-red, dark across the back and lighter and brighter on the lower back and rump. *Female*. Is dull reddish-brown, darker and more greyish above especially on the wings and tail. Beak is black with silver-grey patch on lower base. Length: about 7 in. (18 cm), including 2½ in. (6·5 cm) tail.

This species fades drastically in captivity. It is less likely to fade in planted aviaries where natural live food is more likely to be found in variety. Colour holding agents help to maintain colour and to restore lost colour.

South American Scarlet Tanager, *Ramphocelus bresilius*

Genus: Thraupis

The eight species of the genus *Thraupis* are all about the same size, and there is not a great variation in colour in the various species. Most are very handsome and are characterised by soft shades in their plumage. They are robust, strong birds and are among the easiest of all tanagers to maintain. Sexes are alike, but females are sometimes a little duller in shading.

BLUE TANAGER, BLUE-GREY TANAGER, *Thraupis virens* (formerly *episcopus*) (Linnaeus) (Pl. X)

G. Blaugraue Tanagare; F. Tanagra gris-bleu; D. Blauwgrijze Tangara

DISTRIBUTION: Mexico, Central America, Colombia, Ecuador, Peru, Bolivia, Venezuela, Guyana, Surinam, French Guiana, Brazil, Tobago and Trinidad.

DESCRIPTION: The beak is black with dark grey on the base of the lower mandible. Feet and legs are grey, and eyes are brownish.

Blue Tanagers have three shades of blue. The major area of blue is soft pastel greyish-blue covering the head and entire under parts. Soft greenish-grey occurs on the back and rump and is brighter on the upper tail coverts. Wings and tail are glossy blue with a tinge of green. The third shade of blue is the rich and glossy near-cobalt on a large wing patch extending from the base around the bend of the wing. *Female*. Is duller and has a slightly smaller head. The beak is quite as dark as the beak of the male. Sexes, however, are quite difficult to distinguish. Young birds are like females but have less colourful shades in the glossy areas, and the plumage looks less soft. Length: 6–7½ in. (14–18 cm) according to race including the broad beak of ½ in. (1·3 cm) and the tail of about 2¼ in. (6 cm).

There are several differences in races; but the most noticeable are the *leucoptera*, *major*, *coelestes*, and possibly others which are becoming increasingly popular under the generalized name of White-winged Blue Tanagers. These races have white on the shoulders and on a wing bar. The greenish tinges are absent from the wings and tail, and the cobalt area is also absent. Edges of the flights are richer blue, and under parts are soft blue without the blend of grey.

Blue Tanagers are the most frequently available and the least expensive of all tanagers. They are excellent aviary birds, and are among the hardiest. The soft blue colouring is a welcome and attractive contrast to the colours of most other birds.

SAYACA TANAGER, *Thraupis sayaca* (Linnaeus)

G. Meerblaue Tanagare; F. Tangara sayaca; D. Sayaca Tangara

DISTRIBUTION: Colombia, Venezuela, Brazil, Bolivia, Uruguay, Paraguay and Argentina.

DESCRIPTION: Similar in general appearance to the above species but very dull and more greenish-grey than blue. The tail is 2 in. (5 cm) long, and the dull beak is ½ in. (1·3 cm). The shoulders are greenish-blue like the rest of the wings and tail instead of cobalt. The throat is greyish, and under tail coverts are dull whitish-grey. The female is duller. Length: about 7 in. (17 cm); variable in 3 subspecies.

PALM TANAGER, BLACK-WINGED TANAGER, OLIVE TANAGER, GREY TANAGER, *Thraupis palmarum*

D. Palmtangara

DISTRIBUTION: Central America, Colombia, Ecuador, Peru, Bolivia, Venezuela, French Guiana, Surinam, Guyana, Brazil, Paraguay and Trinidad.

DESCRIPTION: The race reaching aviculturists is usually a little larger than the Blue Tanager. This is not a very attractive species, but it continues to be substituted for other birds in many importations.

The flights are black, also variable in the different races. Remaining plumage is dusky olive-grey with subordinate and elusive hints of purple, blue and green haphazardly mixed in the sheen. Beak, feet and legs blackish. *Female*. Has a slightly smaller head, duller plumage and less lavender-blue sheen. It is a pleasant, hardy bird with unusual lavender-blue sheens. There are 4 subspecies showing variations in the elusive shadings to be found in the sheens mentioned above. Length: 7 in. (18 cm) including 2¼ in. (6 cm) tail and ½ in. (1·3 cm) beak.

STRIATED TANAGER, BLUE AND YELLOW TANAGER, *Thraupis bonariensis* (Gmelin)

D. Blauwgele Tangara

DISTRIBUTION: South America from Ecuador to Argentina.
DESCRIPTION: *Male.* Has yellow and blue as the bright, dominant colours. The silvery-grey beak has black on the upper mandible. A small black facial mask covers lores and chin, surrounds the eyes, and forms a narrow forehead band. Bright blue covers the head, nape and throat. Black covers the shoulders, back, a narrow band at the lower border of blue on the throat and most of the wings and tail. Most of the tail and wing feathers, except the primary flights, have blue edges.
Bright yellow covers the rump and all under parts with traces of orange centred in the chest and rump. Upper tail coverts are dark bluish-grey. Eyes are brown, and feet and legs are grey. *Female.* Is dull greyish-olive brown, darker above and pale dusky below. Length: 6½ in. (16·5 cm) including 2½ in. (6 cm) tail.
The subspecies *darwini* is smaller and has a greenish back. Called Darwin's Tanager, this race is more likely to become available to American fanciers since it is exported from Ecuador.

Striated Tanager, *Thraupis bonariensis*

BLUE-WINGED TANAGER, *Thraupis cyanoptera*

DISTRIBUTION: Brazil and Paraguay.
DESCRIPTION: This species is a littler larger and darker than the Blue Tanager. Dusky blue covers the head with a slightly brighter shade on the collar. The back and rump are dull greenish-blue, and under parts are darker than on the Blue Tanager with tinges of dull green and soft, dull olive on the sides.
The wings are bright like those of the Blue Tanager with more of a greenish tint. Epaulettes are deep cobalt. *Female.* is similar but a little duskier, particularly on the head. Length: 7 in. (18 cm), including 2¼ in. (6 cm) tail.

BLUE-WINGED MOUNTAIN TANAGER, *Compsocoma flavinucha*

DISTRIBUTION: Colombia, Venezuela, Ecuador, Peru, Bolivia.
DESCRIPTION: Brilliant contrasts, beautiful patterns, and vivid colours combine to make this one of the showiest of the large tanagers. The 3 colours are velvet-black, brilliant and lustrous cobalt-blue, and vivid golden-yellow which fades slightly after a time in captivity. The yellow covers all under parts and an extensive cap on the crown and nape. The blue occurs on a large shoulder patch in a slightly deeper shade of cobalt than the blue on the wings and tail which is a little more turquoise in colour. The blue on the wings and tail occurs mainly on the outer webs of the feathers which show up as bold lines of blue alternating with fine lines of black. Black covers the forehead, face, sides of the neck, back, rump, upper tail coverts, a V-shaped area on the flanks, and those areas of the wings not covered by blue. The beak is glossy black, and the feet and legs are greyish. Irides deep reddish. Traces of olive occur on the rump. The beak is glossy black, and the feet and legs are greyish. Sexes are very difficult to distinguish; but males are very slightly larger, a little bolder in temperament, and even a little more vivid in colour brilliance. There are several minor variations in the subspecies.
Mountain Tanagers are bold, aggressive, and exceptionally beautiful. They are poised and usually quite tame in aviaries. They should not be housed with most other species of tanagers because of their aggressiveness unless they are in large aviaries preferably planted. Even then, the dangers are imminent. A seemingly peaceful nature may exist for a long period; but a sudden temperamental outburst at any time may wreak havoc among peaceful, defenceless birds. The race described is *T. cyanoptera.* Length: 8 in. (21 cm) including 2½ in. (6·5 cm) tail.
Among the 8 subspecies, the race *T. sumptuosa* is very similar and is called the Blue-shouldered Mountain Tanager. The Green-backed Mountain Tanager (subspecies *victorini*) has dull mossy green on the back and a decidedly turquoise shading on the flights and tail. Another race, *T. antioquiae*, has black and green on the back. The race *T. baezae* is called the Light Blue-winged Mountain Tanager.

BLACK-CHESTED MOUNTAIN TANAGER, *Buthraupis eximia*

DISTRIBUTION: Colombia, Venezuela and Ecuador.
DESCRIPTION: Black covers face, throat and chest as well as wings and tail. Remaining under parts are bright yellow. Bright blue covers the crown and nape as well as lower back, rump and lesser wing coverts.
Deep, dark green occurs on the mantle and is variable in the different races. In the 2 subspecies *zimmeri* and *chloronota*, both of which are popularly called the Green-backed Mountain Tanager, green replaces the blue on the lower back and rump. Beak, feet and legs black. Length: about 9 in. (23 cm), including 3 in. (7·5 cm) tail.

Genus: Anisognathus

BLACK-CHEEKED TANAGER, *Anisognathus melanogenys*

DISTRIBUTION: Colombia.
DESCRIPTION: Upper parts are dull bluish-green, and under parts including throat are bright yellow except for black on thighs. Bright cobalt blue covers the crown and nape, and the face and sides of the neck are black. A small yellow spot occurs under the eye. Length: about 8 in. (21 cm) including 2 in. (5 cm) tail.

LACHRYMOSE TANAGER, GOLD TANAGER, BLUE TANAGER, *Anisognathus lacrymosus*

DISTRIBUTION: Venezuela, Colombia, Ecuador and Peru.
DESCRIPTION: The black sides of the head and yellow spot below the eys are the same as in the preceding species, but a yellow ear patch is added. Under parts are dull rufous-yellow. Upper parts are mostly dusky black with dull variations. Tail coverts and rump are dusky cobalt blue, and the wings and tail are blackish with dull blue-green edging on nearly all the feathers. Wing coverts are bright cobalt. Beak black, feet and legs dark. Length: about 7 in (18 cm) including 2¼ in. (6 cm) tail.
The race *pallididorsalis* has yellow-olive on the forehead, face and sides of the neck and blue-grey from the top of the head through the back.

CRIMSON-COLLARED TANAGER, *Phlogothraupis sanguinolenta*

DISTRIBUTION: Central America and Mexico.
DESCRIPTION: Most of the colouring is glossy black with bright, deep crimson on a very broad collar which extends from the forecrown to the mantle on top and from the upper throat to middle chest on the lower side. The collar is much less broad on the sides of the neck. The same colour occurs on upper tail and under tail coverts. Face, forehead and broad chin area are black. Irides are red, and the beak is pale bluish-grey with darker areas towards the tip. Feet and legs are grey. This is a vivid and beautiful species with sharp colour separations. Sexes are alike. Length: about 7 in. (18 cm) including 2¼ in. (6 cm) tail.

Genus: Inidosornis

YELLOW-THROATED TANAGER, *Iridosornis analis*

DISTRIBUTION: Colombia, Ecuador, Peru, Bolivia.
DESCRIPTION: Black covers the forehead and forms a mask over the lores and eyes. The throat is bright yellow, and this is the dominant feature. The rest of the head, chest, mantle and upper back are rich, deep, dusky blue as in the species above with purplish on the lower nape. The central abdominal area is pale buff shading to rufous on under tail coverts. Lower chest and sides are dull greyish-blue. Remaining upper parts, wings and tail are the same as in the above species. The wings, however, have dull bluish instead of greenish-blue edges. Length about 6 in. (15 cm), including 2 in. (5 cm) tail.

JELSKI'S TANAGER, *Iridosornis jelkskii*

DISTRIBUTION: Peru and Bolivia.
DESCRIPTION: *Male.* Most of the upper parts are black with rather bold purple on the wing areas. The lower back and edges of the wing and tail feathers are greenish-blue. The back of the head and sides of the neck have a bright golden-yellow patch with black on the face, throat and beak. Under parts are chestnut. *Female.* Similar. Length: 5 in. (13 cm) including 2½ in. (6 cm) tail.

Genus: Dubusia

BUFF-BREASTED MOUNTAIN TANAGER, *Dubusia taeniata*

DISTRIBUTION: Venezuela, Colombia, Ecuador and Peru.
DESCRIPTION: This species is very different from most Mountain Tanagers, and there are also variations in subspecies. Pale blue spots on the forehead and a very long pale blue eyebrow dominate the black of head and upper chest. Upper parts are dark blue with lustrous pale blue on the wing coverts. Lower chest and under parts are bright yellow fading to buffish on under tail coverts. Variations in the different races involve mainly the throat and chest. A soft buff band crosses the chest of one race; and, on another race, a pale brown shade marks the throat and chest, with traces of black on the throat. Length: about 8 in. (21 cm) including 3 in. (7·5 cm) tail.

Genus: Chlorochrysa

GLISTENING GREEN TANAGER, BROWN-EARED EMERALD TANAGER, *Chlorochrysa phoenicotis*

DISTRIBUTION: Colombia and Ecuador.
DESCRIPTION: Major colouring is rich grass-green with a brown and orange patch behind the eye. The rump is pale green, and yellowish-grey occurs on a large shoulder area and on thighs of some individuals. Wings and tail are black and green. Beak, feet and legs blackish. Sexes are alike. Length: 5 in. (13 cm).

ORANGE-EARED TANAGER, *Chlorochrysa calliparea*

DISTRIBUTION: Colombia, Ecuador, and Peru.
DESCRIPTION: *Male.* Is mostly bright shiny green with bluish-black spangles on the face, forehead, under tail coverts and abdomen. The chin, throat, and upper breast are covered by a handsome black bib flanked on the sides of the neck by a large rust-orange patch. A small orange spot occurs on the crown. The rump is also orange, and the beak is black. *Female.* Is duller and has grey instead of black on the throat. Beak, feet and legs black. Length, about 5 in. (13 cm).

MULTICOLOURED TANAGER, *Chlorochrysa nitidissima*

DISTRIBUTION: Colombia.
DESCRIPTION: *Male.* Has bright golden yellow on the back, head, and lower sides of the neck. A squarish black patch occurs on the ear coverts followed by brownish-orange which shades into bright yellowish-orange on the throat. Green covers the nape, wings, and lower back where it

shades into blue on rump and upper tail coverts. The tail is slate and blue. The green areas have thickly shaded dusky blackish on many feathers which are also usually tipped in pale buffish-green. Under parts are blue. The beak is grey and black, and feet and legs are grey. *Female.* Is duller in colour and has green on most of the body areas. Length: about 5 in. (13 cm).

OPAL-RUMPED TANAGER, *Tanagrella velia*

D. Roodbuik Tangara

DISTRIBUTION: Brazil, Bolivia, Peru, Ecuador, Colombia, Venezuela, Guyana, Surinam.

DESCRIPTION: *Male.* Yellowish opalescent rump patch followed by blue on lower upper tail coverts as in the above species. Crown, nape, and upper parts black. Forehead and face are bright blue. Under parts bright purple with bright blue on lower sides. Abdomen and under tail coverts chestnut. Underside of tail dull black. Most of wing feathers black boldly edged in bright blue. An irregular band of concentrated black spots occurs across throat and sides of neck forming a rather shapeless collar. Underside of tail dull black. Length: 6 in. (15 cm) including 1¾ in. (4·5 cm) tail and ½ in. (12 mm) blackish beak; feet and legs black. *Female.* Green, yellowish below and olive above.

BLUE AND BLACK TANAGER, *Tanagrella velia cyanomelaena* (Wied) (Pl. XX)

G. Schwarzblaue-Tangare; F. Tanagrelle bleue et noire; D. Zwartblauwe Tangara

DISTRIBUTION: Brazil.

DESCRIPTION: *Male.* Forehead blue, crown and lower back silver green, upper tail coverts, wing and tail feathers dark blue. Sides of head and throat bright blue, remainder of head and collar black, under parts greyish blue, centre of abdomen and under tail coverts chestnut. Under wing coverts white.

Better known than any of the other races and, aviculturally, is usually listed as a separate species. It differs by having a pale bluish-grey on the breast and sides and a silvery greenish spot behind the blue forehead. *Female.* Iridescent greenish-tinges instead of blue on lower facial areas, wing coverts, and on edges of many wing feathers. Length: about 5½ in. (13 cm).

Genus: Tangara

Formerly *Calliste* and *Calospiza* and not to be confused with the genus *Tanagra* (see above) which is a group of Euphonias, the real jewels of the tanager family are the Callistes, most of which are reasonably small. They run the full gamut of colours, often enhanced by velvety black. Not all are beautiful, but most are at least attractive, and many are outstanding in their beauty.

Of the approximately forty-eight known species, several are unknown to aviculture. Some, such as *Tangara gouldi*, Gould's, and *Tangara arnaulti*, Arnault's, are known only from museum skins.

MRS. WILSON'S TANAGER, MASKED TANAGER, GOLDEN-MASKED TANAGER, *Tangara n. nigro-cincta* (Bonaparte) (Pl. X)

G. Masken-Tangare; F. Tangara masqué; D. Masken-Tangara

DISTRIBUTION: Southern Mexico, Central America, Colombia, Ecuador, Peru, Bolivia, Venezuela, Guyana, Western Brazil.

DESCRIPTION: Black covers the beak and a small facial area which includes the lores, forehead, chin, and a small mask surrounding the eyes. The black is followed by glossy silvery-turquoise which quickly shades into metallic cobalt on the cheeks and forecrown. The rest of the head and neck is a glossy metallic colour which is changeable according to viewing angle. From one angle it may appear to be brassy, and from a different angle it shows a mellowed burnished shade approaching copper. In photographs the brassy shade usually predominates. The throat area darkens almost to chestnut. Irides black, and feet and legs are bluish-grey.

Most of the remaining plumage is velvety black which effectively highlights the brilliant iridescent exceptions and contrasts with the dull white on the lower under parts. The white area covers the under tail coverts and ventral area and wedges to a point in the central area of the lower breast. The lower sides, lower back, rump, and upper tail coverts are brilliant cobalt-turquoise. A very dominant glossy turquoise patch at the bend of the wing is variable in size with different subspecies. The outer webs of most of the wing feathers are edged in bright glossy green or turquoise and cobalt in the different races. *Female.* A little duller in colouring. Length: about 5 in. (13 cm) including 1½ in. (4 cm) tail.

PARADISE TANAGER, *Tangara ch. chilensis* (Vigors) (Pl. X)

G. Rotbürzel-Tangare; F. Tangara du paradis; D. Paradijstangara

DISTRIBUTION: Colombia, Ecuador, Peru, Bolivia, Venezuela, Guyana, Surinam, French Guiana and Brazil.

DESCRIPTION: The top of the head to the nape and most of the facial areas are brilliant light green with a heavy almost unreal overlay of iridescence which adds a scaly stiffness to the feathers. A narrow forehead band and an eye ring are black. A large throat patch of soft violet blue extends from the chin to the upper breast. The central abdominal area and under tail coverts are black. Remaining under parts are brilliant turquoise. A large area on the lower back and rump is bright scarlet. The outer edges of the flights and outer wing coverts are a vivid shade of violet blue, and a large patch at the bend of the wing is vivid turquoise. Remaining upper parts, beak, feet and legs are black. Irides are dark brown. The subspecies *coelicolor*, called the Seven-coloured Tanager, has a different colouring on the lower back and rump starting with red-orange shading to bright yellow. Sexes are alike. The race *chlorocorys* is smaller, has more violet blue on the throat, and only a small area of red-orange on the lower back, the remaining part of the area being bright yellow. The green of the head is absent on the nape and is replaced by black. The sides of the face remain green. Length: about 6 in. (15 cm).

SUPERB TANAGER, *Tangara f. fastuosa* (Lesson) (Pl. X)

G. Vielfarbentangare; F. Tangara fastueux; D. Veelkleurige Tangara

DISTRIBUTION: Brazil.

DESCRIPTION: This exquisite species has a rich bluish-green colouring on the head, less scaly and stiff than the above species but more extensive. It occurs on all of the nape as well as the lower sides of the face and a narrow band across the throat. The shading is duller in the female and has a faint blend of silvery-turquoise. Beak, a narrow area adjacent to the beak on forehead, chin and lores, and an eye ring are black. A narrow bluish-green collar across the lower chin and lower sides of the neck are adjacent to the broad black throat area which connects to the mantle, shoulders, upper and middle back, and most of the tertials. The lower back, rump, and upper tail coverts are bright orange-yellow and more yellow with only traces of orange in the lower areas on the female. The tail is deep bluish-black with paler and brighter blue in central areas of the outer feathers. Wings

Green-headed Tanager, *Tangara seledon*

RED-NECKED TANAGER, FESTIVE TANAGER, *Tangara cyanocephala* (Sclater)
G. Blau Kappentangare; F. Tangara à tête bleue; D. Blauwkap-Tangara

DISTRIBUTION: Brazil and Argentina.
DESCRIPTION: This is another of the most beautiful of the Calliste Tanagers. A bright cobalt blue cap is fringed with turquoise on the forehead. There is also a turquoise eye ring. Plush black feathers cover the forehead, lores, and chin. Bright coral-red covers the nape, sides of the neck, and face; throat blue. All under parts are bright green. The lower back, rump, and upper tail coverts are bright green. The back is mostly black with greenish edges on several feathers. The tail is mostly bright green, and all the wing feathers are broadly edged in bright green hiding the blackish inner areas. The bend of the wing is black followed by a bright orange wing bar preceding the primary coverts. Iris brown; beak, feet and legs black. Sexes alike with females duller. Length: $5\frac{1}{2}$ in. (14·5 cm).

Superb Tanager, *Tangara fastuosa*

are brilliant turquoise-green in a large patch at the bend of the wing and deep purplish-blue with some black in most of the remaining areas; bright yellow marks the edges of the inner wing feathers. Under parts below the black throat bib start with soft light blue on the chest shading to deep cobalt on the lower breast and deepening to blackish-ultramarine on the remaining under parts. Irides brown, beak thick and black; feet and legs slate black. Length: $5\frac{1}{2}$ in. (13 cm), including $1\frac{1}{2}$ in. (4 cm) tail.
This dazzling species is one of the loveliest of all the Callistes.

GREEN-HEADED TANAGER, THREE-COLOURED TANAGER, *Tangara seledon* (P. L. S. Müller)
G. Derifarbentangare; F. Tangara tricoloré; D. Driekleuren-Tangara

DISTRIBUTION: Brazil, Argentina, and Paraguay.
DESCRIPTION: Head, neck, and a small chin area are brilliant turquoise-green. Brilliant metallic yellowish-green broadly covers the mantle, the upper back, and the lower sides of the neck. The inner areas of most of the iridescent feathers are black which show as small blackish scales in many areas. The middle back and most of the wings and tail are velvety black. Vivid orange covers the lower back and rump shading to bright chartreuse-green on the upper tail coverts. A bright cobalt patch forms large epaulettes on the bend of the wing. Secondary flights are broadly and brilliantly edged in bright chartreuse-green with bright bluish-green edging the primary flights and tail feathers. Under parts are vivid turquoise-blue shading to green on the flanks, lower abdomen, and under tail coverts. The female is slightly duller in most of the iridescent areas. Beak black, feet and legs slate black. Length: about 5 in. (13 cm) including $1\frac{1}{2}$ in. (4 cm) tail.

Red-necked Tanager, *Tangara cyanocephala*

SILVER-THROATED TANAGER, *Tangara icterocephala*

DISTRIBUTION: Central America, Colombia, and Ecuador.
DESCRIPTION: A very narrow line across the forehead, part of the lores, a small chin line, and a line from the beak stretching to the lower side of the neck underlining the lower cheek

are black. The head to the lower nape and facial areas down to the black line are bright golden yellow. Greenish-white extends from the chin to the upper breast and forms a collar across the lower nape. Remaining under parts and rump are bright golden yellow.

The back and shoulders have golden yellow as a base, but there are bold black markings on these areas. The wings and tail are black with greenish outer edges. Irides dark brown and beak blackish to silver-grey; the feet and legs are grey; and the eyes are brown. Sexes are very similar, but females are often somewhat duller with traces of green on the head and throat. Length: about 5½ in. (14·5 cm).

BLACK-EARED GOLDEN TANAGER, GOLDEN TANAGER, *Tangara arthus*

DISTRIBUTION: Venezuela, Colombia, Ecuador, Peru, and Bolivia.

DESCRIPTION: This very handsome species has variations on under parts in the different races. The overall colouring is rich golden-yellow with black contrasts. A very small black triangle behind the eye is followed by a large black spot on the ear coverts. Tail and wings are mostly black with golden-yellow edges on wing coverts and inner flights. The black back has bright golden streaks on the edges of the feathers. Under parts vary from race to race by showing darker shades of yellow to golden brown. The race *aequatorialis* is called the Red Gleaming Golden Tanager.

This species, particularly glowing and beautifully marked, is much more attractive than the Silver-throated Tanager. Irides, beak, feet and legs black. Length: 5½ in. (14·5 cm).

BAY-HEADED TANAGER, CHESTNUT-HEADED TANAGER, COPPER-HEADED TANAGER, and one or more races are popularly called BLUE-RUMPED GREEN TANAGER. Another race is called DESMEREST'S TANAGER. BAY-HEADED TANAGER should be used instead of the other popular names. *Tangara gyrola*

DISTRIBUTION: Costa Rica, Panama, Colombia, Ecuador, Peru, Bolivia, Venezuela, Surinam, French Guiana, Guyana, Brazil, and Trinidad.

DESCRIPTION:
The several different subspecies vary considerably in shading, but the pattern is basically the same. The head, excluding throat, is chestnut; and the remaining plumage is green or green on upper parts and blue on under parts; thighs are chestnut. Concealed parts of wing and tail feathers when folded are brownish, but they usually show only the green on the outer webs. On some races there are vivid lemon-yellow epaulettes. The shape is slender and well-proportioned. In many ways, it appears to have a close relationship to the Black-headed Sugar Bird, but is more heavily built. The beak is black or greyish-black; irides reddish-brown; and feet and legs are bluish-grey. Sexes are alike, but the females in some races are paler. Length: about 6 in. (15 cm). This species is often available and is one of the hardier Callistes after a touchy acclimatization. It is a beautiful bird, but it lacks the metallic iridescence which is characteristic of the most beautiful members of the genus.

Since the variations within the different races are often pronounced, a listing of the subspecies, ranges, and their major differences may be helpful. In addition to the nominate race from French Guiana, Guyana and Surinam, the other subspecies are as follows:

deletica from Colombia, Panama, and Canal Zone; slender shape, very rich cobalt blue rump and under parts, under tail coverts green, darker green on wings, darker reddish rufous or chestnut head followed by a yellow collar on the nape, yellow epaulettes.

nupera from Ecuador and Colombia; rump and under parts green with a turquoise line down the throat to the upper breast and a broad turquoise area on abdomen, bright glossy chestnut on head, paler wings and shoulders, golden-copper gloss on nape and mantle.

viridissima from Venezuela and Trinidad; popular name is Desmarest's Tanager; blue absent except for a slight bluish gloss on under parts, golden sheen on wings, yellow collar on nape, and a little smaller than most races.

toddi from Colombia and Venezuela; paler golden-rufous head, golden collar on nape, wings yellowish-green, under parts bright green.

bangsi from Costa Rica and Panama; popular name Copper-headed Tanager; yellow collar on nape, yellow wing patch, blue under parts and green under tail coverts.

catherinae from Colombia, Ecuador, Peru, Bolivia, and Brazil; popular name also Copper-headed Tanager but head is deeper; under parts and rump blue, under tail coverts green, head dark chestnut, yellow epaulettes, and wide yellow collar.

albertinae from Brazil; like *catharinae* but head and a chin spot lighter in colour, no yellow collar but nape and upper back more yellowish-green, wings and tail a lighter shade of yellowish-green, rufous epaulettes instead of yellow.

YELLOW-BROWED TANAGER, SPECKLED TANAGER, *Tangara chrysophrys* (Sclater)

G. Tropfengare; F. Tangara tacheté; D. Druppel-tangara

DISTRIBUTION: Central America, Colombia, Venezuela, Ecuador, and Trinidad.

DESCRIPTION: Body is a little more stout than is characteristic of most Callistes. This is an unusually patterned tanager which would be considered as badly cluttered if it were not for the finely etched and orderly distribution of the precise colour separations. Because of these characteristics, this is one of the brightest and most attractive members of the genus.

Most of the plumage above appears as bright, light green with large black spots on upper sides and smaller ones on under parts down to the sides and upper breast. Actually, the black and green areas are black with bold and broad green edges on nearly all the feathers giving a scaled appearance. The small black mask covering lores and narrowly

Yellow-browed Tanager, *Tangara chrysophrys*

surrounding the eyes is outlined in yellow, boldly on the eyebrow and a little less prominently on the underside. The yellow shades softly into green. Flights and tail feathers have green on outer webs. There are traces of blue blended into the green on most of the wing feathers. Upper tail coverts and most of the rump are green on the under parts below the spotted upper breast and sides, green with traces of yellow on the sides, flanks, and under tail coverts dominates over the white in the central area of the breast and abdomen. In some races, especially in *bogotensis*, the dusky white extends up onto the throat, upper breast, and upper sides, replacing the green and serving as a ground colour for the black spots. Subspecies variations also show differences in the size and boldness of the black spots. Beak blackish, irides brown, feet and legs dark brown. Length: 5½ in. (14·5 cm) including 1½ in. (4 cm) tail.

This species in the past few years has frequently been available at reasonably moderate prices. After the acclimatization period it becomes one of the hardier members of the genus.

SPANGLED-CHEEKED TANAGER, *Tangara dowii*

DISTRIBUTION: Central America.
DESCRIPTION: Velvety black background spangled with dominant and outstanding iridescent coppery-green spots on the head, sides of the neck, and sides of the upper breast in a very attractive and unusual manner. A touch of red occurs on the back of crown, and wing and tail feathers are black with blue edges. The back is black, and the rump is soft green. The chest is black and greenish-buff, and remaining under parts are buffish-brown. Beak black, irides dark brown; feet and legs dark brown. Length: 5¾ in. (15 cm), including 1¾ in. (4·5 cm) tail.

This species has become increasingly available in the past few years and is relatively easy to acclimatize. Incoming shipments from Costa Rica usually arrive in very good shape, at least in Southern California which is the closest of the foreign markets. The Spangle-cheeked Tanager usually arrives in better condition than most birds in the same shipments.

BLACK AND GREEN TANAGER, SCALY-BREASTED TANAGER, TIGER TANAGER, *Tangara nigroviridis* with four subspecies

DISTRIBUTION: Venezuela, Colombia, Ecuador, Peru, and Bolivia.
DESCRIPTION: The beak is black with a grey base on the lower mandible. The mask extending far behind the eyes, and the forehead, chin, mantle, back, wings and tail are all black. The feathers of the tail and wings are edged in bright, glossy cobalt and bluish-green. The rump and upper tail coverts are brilliant glossy turquoise-green. The head and entire under parts have a black ground or base with large, bold iridescent spangles on the tips of all the feathers. The spangles on the head are turquoise-green; on the throat they are brilliant purplish cobalt; on the sides they are greenish-turquoise; and on the central under parts they are blended between cobalt and turquoise-green. Length: about 5½ in. (14·5 cm), including 1¾ in. (4·5 cm) tail.

SPOTTED TANAGER, *Tangara punctuata*

DISTRIBUTION: Venezuela, French Guiana, Surinam, Guyana, Brazil, Ecuador, Peru, and Bolivia.
DESCRIPTION: The major colouring is bright green with most of the black feathers of the head, upper back, and wing coverts boldly tipped with green scalelike marks which leave black spots on most of these feathers. Under parts are greenish tinged white with bold, round black spots down to the abdomen. The centre of the abdomen is white and unspotted, surrounded by greenish-white which is slightly spotted. Green is prominent on the flanks. The under wing coverts are white. Irides dark brown. Beak, feet and legs are black. The female is similar but slightly smaller and with smaller and slightly less bold spots. Length: 4½ in. (12 cm), including 1½ in. (4 cm) tail.

METALLIC GREEN TANAGER, *Tangara labradorides*

DISTRIBUTION: Colombia, Ecuador, Peru.
DESCRIPTION: Black covers the forehead, a small facial mask, and a broad chin patch. More black on the head is narrow on the central hindcrown and broad on the nape. Rich cobalt and green occur on the wing coverts. The tail and remaining wing feathers are black with blue edges. The remaining plumage is bright turquoise-green, paler and frosty on the forecrown and cobalt on the lower sides of the neck. The central abdominal area is grey shading to brown on under tail coverts. The brilliance of the iridescence is difficult to describe. Reflected light glances off with brassy highlights. Beak, feet and legs black. Length, 5 in. (13 cm), including 1¼ in. (3 cm) tail.

BLUE-WINGED TANAGER, BLACK-HEADED TANAGER, *Tangara cyanoptera*

DISTRIBUTION: Colombia, Venezuela, and Guyana.
DESCRIPTION: Head, wings, and tail are blackish with broad bluish edges on the wing feathers. Remaining plumage is glossy straw colour with a greenish wash. The female has greenish-grey on the head instead of black, and upper parts are mainly dull olive-green. Under parts are greyish with a dull shade of greenish-yellow on abdominal areas. Beak black, feet and legs dark slate. Length: 5½ in. (14·5 cm).

BLACK-CAPPED TANAGER, *Tangara heinei*

DISTRIBUTION: Venezuela, Colombia, and Ecuador.
DESCRIPTION: *Male.* Has a black cap and shiny but dusky blue on upper parts, lighter and glossier on back. Under parts, also glossy, are more silvery turquoise-greeen on the face, throat, and breast, shading then to dusky greyish-blue. Black occurs on the bases of the green areas showing triangular tipped green spangles. Beak, feet and legs black. Length: 5½ in. (14·5 cm). *Female* lacks the black cap and has dark greyish-olive above shading to bright green on the back and rump and dull greenish and grey on the under parts.

SILVERY TANAGER, *Tangara viridicollis*

DISTRIBUTION: Peru and Ecuador.
DESCRIPTION: Closely allied to the Black-capped Tanager above but with notable differences. Striking silvery-blue on the back and flanks. A peculiar shining ochraceous-yellow colours the throat, cheeks, and an ear patch. Black occurs on the breast and upper abdomen.
Female. Has brown instead of green on the top of the head and a dull yellowish-orange on the throat and face. Length: about 5½ in. (14·5 cm).
The subspecies *fulvigula* has more silvery-green margins on the back, wings, and tail and reddish on the throat and face. Female has a shade of reddish-brown on the crown.

TURQUOISE TANAGER, *Tangara mexicana*

DISTRIBUTION: Colombia, Venezuela, French Guiana, Surinam, Guyana, Brazil, Peru, Bolivia, and Trinidad.
DESCRIPTION: Forehead and chin areas are black. A broad forecrown, face, sides of neck, throat, upper breast, sides, lower back, and rump are purplish-cobalt. Most of these areas show black scaly areas because the bases of the feathers are all black. Broad central areas on breast through under tail coverts are yellow, yellowish-white, or near white according to subspecies. There is considerable variation in this feature, and the boundaries are irregular. The subspecies *boliviana* has a pleasing shade of yellow on the under parts. The hindcrown, nape, back, wings, and tail are black with cobalt and blue edges on most of the wing and tail feathers. Bright turquoise-blue epaulettes occur on the wing coverts. Beak, feet and legs blackish. Length: about 5½ in. (14·5 cm).

Genus Bangsia

BLACK AND GOLD MOUNTAIN TANAGER, *Bangsia melanochlamys*

DISTRIBUTION: Colombia.
DESCRIPTION: The chest patch is orange-yellow shading to yellow on remaining central under parts. Most of the remaining plumage is black with bright blue highlights, slightly variable in shading, on the tail, tail coverts, and wing coverts. Length: about 6 in. (15 cm).

GOLDEN-CHESTED MOUNTAIN TANAGER, *Bangsia rothschildi*

DISTRIBUTION: Colombia and Ecuador.
DESCRIPTION: Yellow forms a broad bold patch on the chest and neck with another paler patch on under tail coverts. Under wing coverts are a paler shade of yellow. Remaining plumage is black with slight bluish tinges on outer edges of the flights. Beak, feet and legs black. Length: about 6½ in. (16·5 cm) including 1¾ in. (4·5 cm) tail. This is a very attractive species with a very simple colour scheme.

Honeycreepers or Sugar Birds

Honeycreepers are rather closely related to tanagers; but, when most people see a Yellow-winged Honeycreeper, they are reminded of hummingbirds because of the size, the brilliant colours, and the long slender beaks. Not all of the Honeycreepers (more commonly known as Sugar Birds) share the superficial resemblance to hummingbirds, but those of the genus *Cyanerpes* do.

The genera *Cyanerpes*, *Chlorophanes* and *Dacnis* are each listed here as a genus of the Thraupinae, according to Volume XIII of Peters' *Check List of Birds of the World*.

Honeycreepers occur in Mexico, Cuba, Central America, and South America. Nearly all are exceptionally beautiful birds holding a very high place in aviculture. They are small birds and, for the most part, usually peaceful and can be housed with finches, Calliste tanagers, wrens, warblers or even hummingbirds.

Some of the Honeycreepers must be considered delicate and difficult to acclimatise. These delicate species do not travel easily nor do they transfer easily to artificial diets. The hardiest, most readily available, and certainly one of the most beautiful members of this family is the Yellow-winged Honeycreeper (Sugar Bird). It thrives on the standard nectar diet. Some of the more rare and delicate species do much better on the fortified nectar as given to hummingbirds and sunbirds.

In addition to nectar, the writers feed pound cake, peanut butter and a variety of fruits such as soaked raisins, apple, grapes, a little orange and other fruits in season. If bananas are offered, they are given only in the early stages of acclimatisation; and they must be very ripe. Commercial bananas cause many troubles as mentioned in the chapter in diet. For a choice, the writers also offer insectiverous food, mynah pellets, and all-purpose food. Mealworms (preferably small ones or those which have just shed their skins) are also offered. In addition, a fruitfly culture is really the best source of live food.

A few youngsters have been successfully reared in captivity. The cup-shaped nest is composed of very fine fibres, soft feathers and soft grasses. In some species, the nests are purse-shaped. Incubation usually continues for about twelve to thirteen days, and the young leave the nest in about two weeks and are fed by the parents for at least two more weeks but more often for nearly a month. The male usually does not help in incubation or in feeding the young. Near fledgling age, the male usually starts to feed youngsters. The young are fed almost entirely on live foods.

Genus: Dacnis

BLUE SUGAR BIRD, BLUE DACNIS, BLACK-THROATED HONEYCREEPER, *Dacnis cayana* (Pl. IX)

G. Pitpit; F. Dacnis bleu; D. Blauwe Pitpit

DISTRIBUTION: Central America, Trinidad, and South America from Colombia to Argentina.
DESCRIPTION: *Male*. The black on the head has much the same pattern as that of the Yellow-legged Honeycreeper. It comprises a small forehead band and a mask through the lores and behind the eyes. A long black patch covers the chin and throat. Black also occurs on tail, wings and centre of the back. The rest of the colouring is variable with the different races. It can be turquoise or light or dark purplish-blue. This same colouring occurs on the upper wing coverts. Under parts may be a little paler on the abdominal area.

Plate XXVII

Violet-eared Waxbill, *Uraeginthus g. granatinus*

Melba Finch, *Pytilia m. melba*

Aurora Waxbill, *Pytilia phoenicoptera*

Cut-throat Finch, *Amadina f. fasciata*

Red-headed Finch, *Amadina erythrocephala*

Plate XXVIII

Black-cheeked Waxbill, *Estrilda e. erythronotus*

Lavender Finch, *Estrilda caerulescens*

Vinaceous Fire-Finch, *Lagonosticta larvata vinacea*

Black-bellied Fire-Finch, *Lagonosticta r. rara*

Blue-billed Fire-Finch, *Lagonosticta r. rubricata*

Plate XXIX

Thick-billed Weaver, *Amblyospiza a. albifrons*   Spectacled Weaver, *Ploceus ocularis crocatus*

Smith's Golden Weaver, *Ploceus subaureus aureoflavus*   Black-fronted Weaver, *Ploceus v. velatus*

Mombasa Golden Weaver, *Ploceus bojeri*   Cuckoo Weaver, *Anomalospiza imberbis*

Plate XXX

White-rumped Mannikin, *Lonchura str. striata*

Bengalese, *Lonchura domestica*

Magpie Mannikin, *Spermestes fringilloides*

Bronze-winged Mannikin, *Spermestes cucullatus*

African Silverbill, *Euodice m. cantans*

Indian Silverbill, *Euodice m. malabarica*

Female. Green with blue on the head and sometimes on the back and greyish on the chin and throat; lower abdomen usually shades to dull yellowish. Irides dark, beak blackish; feet and legs dark grey. Length: about 5½ in. (14·5 cm) including 1 in. (2·5 cm) tail.

BLACK-FACED SUGAR BIRD, BLACK-FACED DACNIS,

EGREGIA'S HONEYCREEPER, *Dacnis lineata*

DISTRIBUTION: Colombia, Ecuador, Peru, Bolivia, Guyana, Surinam and parts of Brazil.

DESCRIPTION: *Male.* Has most of the upper parts jet black except for a brilliant turquoise-green cap. Black also covers the facial areas and the nape. The lower back, rump, upper tail coverts, a band across the inner wing coverts, and the edges of many wing feathers are brilliant greenish-turquoise. Otherwise the wings and tail are black. Under parts are the same shade of brilliant greenish-turquoise with a large patch of bright yellow on the central area of the lower chest

and abdomen and on the under tail coverts. The under wing coverts and the sides of the chest are also bright yellow. The under sides of the flights are dull black. Feet and legs are also black. Irides bright golden straw with sharp black pupils which contrast strongly with the black face. Length: 4¼ in. (10·5 cm) including 1 in. (2·5 cm) tail. *Female.* Has a paler beak. Upper parts are dull greyish-green with brownish slate on the wings and tail. Under parts are pale yellowish-olive shading to yellow in the central area of the chest extending through the under tail coverts. The under wing coverts show traces of dull yellow.

The subspecies *egregia* (called Egregia's Honeycreeper or Yellow-vented Dacnis) is the most likely to become available to aviculture. This is a very beautiful bird with a somewhat heavy body and large head. The subspecies *lineata* is called the White-vented Dacnis or Black-faced Dacnis. It has white instead of yellow and more of a blue shade than turquoise-green. The female is more greenish with dusky white in the central under parts. The Equatorial Dacnis (subspecies *aequatorialis*) is like Egregia's Honeycreeper, but under parts are more greenish and the yellow is richer.

Genus: Chorphanes

BLACK-HEADED SUGAR BIRD, GREEN HONEY-CREEPER, *Chlorophanes s. spiza* (Linnaeus)

G. Kappensai; F. Sucrier à tête noire; D. Zwartkop-Pitpit

DISTRIBUTION: Southern Mexico, Central America, Colombia, Ecuador, Venezuela, French Guiana, Guyana, Surinam, Brazil and Trinidad.

DESCRIPTION: *Male.* Has a sharply defined black mask. The black extends to the hindcrown and down to the lower sides of the neck in a graceful curve and then angles sharply up to the lower mandible. All the remaining colouring is smooth and lustrous turquoise-bluish-green including the chin and throat. Flights and some areas of the tail are darkened somewhat by blackish shades as well as blue-green. Some areas tend to show more green and others more blue. Upper

part of beak black, lower part pale yellow. Irides reddish-brown, feet and legs greyish. Length: about 6 in. (15 cm) varies with subspecies. *Female.* Lacks the black on the head and has more grass-green in general colour with traces of yellow on the throat and central abdominal area.

There are several variations in subspecies mainly in the shadings of body colouring. The green is emerald in shading with some races including *exsul* and bluish-green in *subtropicalis* and perhaps others. The Guatemalan Green Sugarbird (subspecies *guatemalensis*) has less black on the head of the male, a deeper green coloration and a long heavy beak. Female shows more of a yellowish shading in the green especially on the under parts.

This species is less peaceful than most Honeycreepers. It adapts itself quickly to captivity and is one of the hardier species.

Genus: Cyanerpes

YELLOW-WINGED SUGAR BIRD, RED-LEGGED HONEYCREEPER (SUGAR BIRD), *Cyanerpes c. cyaneus* (Linnaeus)   (Pl. IX)

G. Türkisvogel; F. Guit-guit saï; D. Geelvleugel-Honingzuiger

DISTRIBUTION: Mexico, Central America, Colombia, Ecuador, Bolivia, Venezuela, Surinam, Guyana, Brazil, Trinidad, Tobago and Cuba.

Yellow-winged Sugarbird, *Cyanerpes c. cyaneus*

DESCRIPTION: Males undergo a seasonal colour change. When 'in colour', during spring and summer, they are brilliant and unbelievably beautiful. A large lustrous metallic turquoise cap is the most dominant feature. Deep royal-blue on the head ends in a sharp dividing line cutting diagonally from the hindcrown across the rear facial area to the sides of the neck. Behind this is velvet-black. The royal-blue also occurs on the throat and all under parts to the vent as well as sides, lower back, rump, upper tail coverts and on a band between the bend of the wing and the base stretching down to the sides. Nearly all other areas are vevlet-black. Most of the under side of the wings is yellow except the black outer webs of the flights. The upper sides of the wings are black with yellow on the inner webs of the central flight feathers. The yellow does not show except in flight. Length: 4 in. (10 cm) including 1¼ in. (3 cm) tail. Sizes slightly variable in different subspecies. The legs are bright red in the male and duller red in the female; irides black.

Males and females out of colour are similar except for the difference in the legs. Dull, soft green predominates. There are traces of greyfrost on the head and a dull frosty white eyebrow stripe. Under parts are softer with dusky streaks becoming paler on the abdomen, vent and under tail coverts. The wings are the same as for the male in colour, but both the black and the yellow are duller.

This species is an ideal nectar feeding bird for beginners and is also popular with advanced fanciers. It has been successfully bred in captivity a few times.

PURPLE SUGAR BIRD, YELLOW-LEGGED HONEY-
CREEPER, *Cyanerpes caeruleus* (Linnaeus)　　(Pl. IX)
G. Purpurhonigsauger; F. Guit-guit bleu; D. Purper-
honigzuiger

DISTRIBUTION: Colombia, Ecuador, Peru, Bolivia, Venezuela,
Guyana, French Guiana, Surinam, Brazil and Trinidad.
DESCRIPTION: *Male.* Has very bright yellow feet and legs with
very black claws. The major colouring is a glowing shade of
a nearly violet royal-blue, but this shade is not purple.
There is no turquoise cap. A narrow black mask covers the
lores and extends slightly behind the eyes and there is a
small black bib on the throat. Wings, tail and vent are also
black. *Female.* Have pale rusty-orange patches covering the
forehead, sides of the face, and throat, bright pale blue
moustache marks and some yellow on the under parts.
Remaining areas green; feet and legs greyish. Length:
3¼ in. (8 cm) including tail which is slightly less than 1 in.
(2·5 cm) but not including the black beak which is about
½ in. (2 cm). Subspecies vary slightly in size.
This species are not as often available as the Red-legged
Honeycreeper. It also is delicate and is difficult to accustom
to artificial diets. But it is a very lovely bird; and, after the
acclimatisation period and somewhat specialised requirements are met, it does quite well. A conservatory aviary is
ideal. The nectar should be fortified, and mealworms
should not be given unless they are soaked awhile in scalding
water or are very young.
A successful breeding after 3 previous failures was reported
by E. Davison in *Cage and Aviary Birds* (9th October, 1975)
as follows:

> 'The adult pair of birds are kept in a 9 × 9 ft (2.7 × 2.7 m) flight
> inside a shed. The female made each nest in a tree-bark box.
> Nesting material consisted of pieces of string which I had cut
> into 2 in. (5 cm) lengths.
> Two eggs were laid in each round. One chick did hatch out in
> the first nest and it was fed for 7 days. Unfortunately, a supply
> of maggots that I had obtained at about that time proved to be
> contaminated, and the female fell ill and stopped feeding. I
> lost the chick and also several birds of other species which had
> eaten these maggots.
> Two young hatched out in the second nest and disappeared.
> The eggs produced in the third round were incubated for 12
> days and hatched on August 24. The female fed the chicks
> well but one day, when I inspected the nest, I discovered that
> there was only one baby inside it. I made a search and found
> the other dead on the floor.
> The female remained in the box with the chick at nights for
> 18 days. The latter left the nest on the 19th day and did not
> return to it again. The male played no part in the rearing.
> The diet provided was very much trial and error because I was
> unable to find much information about breeding Purple Sugar-
> birds in my reference books. They appeared to like fruitflies,
> maggots, mealworms, fingers of sponge soaked in nectar and
> fruit.'

FAMILY: PARULIDAE

Genus: Coebra　　　　　　　　　　SUBFAMILY: COEREBINAE

BANANAQUIT, QUIT, JAMAICAN BANANAQUIT, *Coereba
f. flaveola* (Linné)
G. Bananaquit; F. Sucrier flavéole; D. Suikerdiefje

DISTRIBUTION: Mexico, southward to Argentina, most of the
Caribbean Islands, and the Bahamas.
DESCRIPTION: Not a brightly coloured or sharply patterned
bird compared to all those previously described for the
family. Sexes are alike. The most dominant characteristics

Bananaquit, *Coereba f. flaveola*

are the bold white eyebrows and yellow extending from the
chest through most of the under parts. The head is dull
slate. The throat is particularly variable in subspecies not
only in shading which is usually pale grey or sooty black
but also in the extent of this colouring which may extend to
the lower part of the throat or even midway through the
upper chest. Blackish beak is slightly curved, sharply
pointed, and somewhat stout at the base more closely
resembling the beaks of the members of the genus *Dacnis*
than those in *Cyanerpes*. The body is also similar in shape
as the members of the genus *Dacnis*.
The remaining upper parts are dull greyish or greyish-brown
according to subspecies. In many races a white wing patch
and yellow or greenish-yellow rump relieve the dullness of
the upper parts. Length: about 4 in. (10 cm).
Bananaquits are not great avicultural favourites because
most people prefer the brighter members of the family.
Many inexperienced importers bring them to the United
States from export points in Central America, Colombia,
and Ecuador; but, when they find a general lack of interest
(in the United States at least), they seldom try a second
shipment.
Bananaquits are easily kept on a standard honeycreeper
diet; but, often, the bird fancier may have a few problems in
the beginning. Many inexperienced importers do not easily
recognise Bananaquits as nectar feeders, and they may try
to feed them only on bananas. Health deteriorates quickly
on such a limited diet, and digestive problemsc an easily
arise because of previously mentioned differences in ware-
house ripened and tree ripened bananas. Bananaquits seem
to be more appreciated in Britain than in the United States,
and so it is quite possible that more experienced dealers
may be involved with them in Britain which would certainly
eliminate the initial problems.
Though Bananaquits are not dazzling in colour or pattern,
they should not be dismissed as unworthy because they
have fine personalities. They are intelligent, curious, and
very alert in much the same manner as *Zosterops*. They are
very amusing to observe because of their acrobatic explor-
ations, the surprisingly intense and determined concentration
in their activities, and their courtship performances which

involve bowing and head swaying.

Their innate lack of fear of humans helps in accomplishing semi-tameness provided the bird fancier is willing to extend a little effort in this direction. Perhaps they will not become as tame and fearless as the hummingbird who sits on the writer's shoulder as this is being written, but they will learn to accept favoured bits of food from their owner's hand if the bird fancier will spend a little time and patience with them.

ORANGE QUIT, *Euneornis campestris*

DISTRIBUTION: Jamaica.

DESCRIPTION: *Male*. Soft and smooth greyish-blue in all areas except for a bright chestnut throat patch. Black covers a small forehead band, the lores, a very limited chin area, and very narrowly surrounds the eyes. *Female*. Dull by comparison. Olive-grey occurs on the crown and neck shading to dull olive on the remaining upper parts. Under parts are mostly dusty greyish-white with ill-defined streakiness on the throat and abdominal area. Beak and body shape are similar to those of the Bananaquit. Length: about 5½ in. (14 cm).

Orange Quits have not been available to American aviculturists, but K. A. Norris mentioned having received a consignment in Great Britain. The care is the same as for Honeycreepers and Bananaquits. Orange Quits would in the United States generate more enthusiasm than Bananaquits on the basis of rarity alone. However, they are more handsome than Bananaquits even though they lack the brightness of the yellow on the under parts.

American Orioles or Hangnests, Troupials, Cassiques, Oropendolas, Meadowlarks, Marsh Birds and Blackbirds

The family Icteridae comprises about ninety species (more or less) of New World birds. This family has several very diverse groups of birds which show considerable variation in diet, outward physical characteristics, and habits. From an avicultural standpoint, there are many differences in colour and desirability. All of these birds adapt easily to artificial diets and are very hardy and long lived. They are also very alert and intelligent and most intersting in their habits and behaviour. Many are quite aggressive, and many are fine songbirds.

The simple standard diet is satisfactory for most of the birds in this group. Mynah pellets are quickly and easily accepted. Orioles and Cassiques enjoy nectar and derive considerable benefit from it. The writers offer fortified nectar to newly imported members of this family; but, after the acclimatisation period and transfer to new foods is accomplished, the simple nectar is very adequate.

Marsh Birds require a totally different diet from the other members of this family. The Marsh Bird diet probably also applied to Bobolinks, but the writers have never kept any Bobolinks and cannot verify this. All of the Marsh Birds the writers have had thrived on only two components: plain canary seed and mealworms. This does not seem like an adequate diet, but all of those which the writers have owned were put through acclimatisation procedures with other varieties of softbilled birds and with all the transitory foods. Red-breasted Marsh Birds seem to probe through the other foods more than the Yellow-headed species. They may exist for awhile on other foods, but they do not thrive if they are denied canary seed. Other seeds are no substitute.

Not all of the birds in this family are good avicultural subjects. Most aviculturists are not interested in the American Blackbirds or Cowbirds. Blackbirds in the Americas have bold and swaggering personalities, but they do not have the melodious voices of the European or Old World Blackbirds which belong to the thrush family. Cowbirds really should be avoided, but they are occasionally included as substitutes in shipments from South America. They are unattractive, uninteresting, aggressive, and completely hardy; and they thrive on an omnivorous diet. American Blackbirds and Grackles are more attractive and slightly more interesting, but other characteristics are about the same. Grackles have fine iridescence in their glossy starling-like plumage, but they do not command much interest from bird fanciers.

Several members of this family have been given popular names of Old World birds which are totally unrelated. This appropriation of names has caused some confusion among bird keepers. Blackbirds have already been mentioned. Orioles, named for the colour yellow, are more properly called icterids, a name which is also derived from a word meaning yellow. There is no connection with the genus *Oriolus* of the Old World. Military Starlings are not starlings, and Meadow Larks are not larks. The grackles of the New World belong to this group instead of the Old World mynahs and starlings.

New World Orioles have certain characteristics general to most species. The powerful beaks are long and very sharply pointed. Black and yellow or orange are the predominant colours. The colouring is usually sharply divided and very bright. Because they are very alert and active, orioles are recognised in the wild by their bright flashes of colour and they are equally admired in aviaries for the same reasons. Most are slender and very pleasingly proportioned with strong legs and feet. Dominance varies among the different species, but most should be considered too aggressive to associate with small or gentle softbills. Several are also too strong and dominant for the medium-sized softbills.

TROUPIAL, BUGLE BIRD, COMMON HANGNEST, *Icterus icterus* (Linnaeus) (Pl. XIV)
G. Gewöhnlicher; F. Troupial commun; D. Oranje Troepiaal

DISTRIBUTION: Northern South America and the West Indies.
DESCRIPTION: The dominant colouring is black and deep yellow-orange, but the latter colour fades to an equally attractive bright yellow after a time in captivity.
A black hood covers the head and throat extending onto the upper breast. The lower boundary is jagged and irregular, but the colour separations are very sharply defined with no tendency to blend. The wings, back, and tail are black except for a broad irregular bar of white slashing across the scapulars into the secondary flights. Subordinate yellow occurs on the lesser wing coverts. Under parts below the hood and a very broad collar across the nape are bright

Troupial, *Icterus icterus*

yellow (or yellow-orange in newly trapped birds). The formidable piercing beak is black with a pale bluish-grey patch on the sides of the lower mandible near the base. A prominent bluish-grey bare skin area surrounds the eyes and forms a triangle behind the eyes. Irides are bright golden-yellow with sharp black pupils, feet and legs dark grey. Length: about 10 in. (25 cm).
Troupials are perhaps the most aggressive members of this large genus. Their sharp beaks are used as efficient weapons in subordinating any adversary.
These birds are frequently called Bugle Birds in the pet industry. Tame youngsters not only become excellent pets, but they can also be taught to whistle tunes. Unfortunately, tame youngsters are very seldom available; and so much of the legendary reputation is rather misleading since adults rarely become tame or talented pets regardless of the amount of training given.

YELLOW ORIOLE, *Icterus nigrogularis*

DISTRIBUTION: Northern South America to Brazil and Caribbean area.
DESCRIPTION: Smaller and far less aggressive than the Troupial. Black is far less extensive than on the previous species. The beak is black with a bluish-grey base. On the

head, black is limited to a slight area surrounding the eyes, a narrow border near the base of the lower mandible, and a long throat patch with an irregular outline.
The black wings have an irregular white bar across the outer margins of many feathers. The under sides of the wings are pale silvery-grey. The black tail has a few pale scallops on the under side.
The rest of the plumage is bright yellow, brightest on the cheeks and chest. Fine yellow feathers occur on the wings to shoulders and on the upper tail and under tail coverts. Feet and legs are grey. Length: about 8½ in. (22 cm) including the 3 in. (7·5 cm) tail.

BLACK-THROATED ORIOLE, LICHTENSTEIN'S ORIOLE, *Icterus gularis*

DISTRIBUTION: Texas, Mexico and Central America.
DESCRIPTION: Colour varies from bright orange to yellow in different races. *Female*. Slightly less colourful. This species is very similar to the Yellow Oriole in pattern. The black is a little more extensive on the throat, and the back is also black. The wings have a prominent yellow bar and a white bar. Feet and legs grey. Length: 8½–10 in. (22–25 cm).

SPOTTED-BREASTED ORIOLE, *Icterus pectoralis* (Wagler) (Pl. XIV)
G. Schwarz brusttrupial; F. Troupiale tâcheté; D. Zwartborst-Troepiaal

DISTRIBUTION: Mexico and Central America.
DESCRIPTION: Tail and wings are black, but there is a broad area of white in the wings and a smaller shoulder bar of yellow. The black frontal areas are limited on the face to the lores, a minor area around the eyes, and a rather narrow chin patch. The black broadens on the throat and extends to the

Spotted-breasted Oriole, *Icterus pectoralis*

upper chest. Its breast is irregularly marked with prominent black spots. Feet and legs are grey and a spot of grey occurs at the base of the lower mandible. Remaining areas are yellow or orange-yellow. The deeper shades of orange-yellow fade to bright yellow after a time in captivity. Length: 9 in. (23 cm) with 3 in. (7·5 cm) tail.
Young birds are usually more frequently available than adults. Immature birds have most of the black missing on the head but show a blackish smudge on the chest. Other black areas lack the gloss of adults.

Most imported birds arrive with clipped wings as do many of the Troupials. This very unfortunate condition requires a prolonged acclimatisation period because the clipped flights must be extracted and replaced with full strong flights. About three flight feathers on each side can be removed at intervals of 4 weeks. The regrowth of each feather requires about 6 weeks. During this period, the birds should be closely confined as flying must be discouraged to prevent breakage of growing pinfeathers. Rich foodstuffs must also be avoided. The birds cannot exercise as much as they should, and the system easily becomes unbalanced. One of the sideline problems is bumblefoot which is difficult to correct.

BULLOCK'S ORIOLE, *Icterus bullockii* (Swainson)
G. Goldstirntrupial; F. Troupiale de Bullock; D. Bullock's Troepiaal (Pl. XIV)

DISTRIBUTION: Western United States, Mexico and Central America.
DESCRIPTION: Sexes are very different. *Male.* Distinctively different from other orioles because of the head markings. Golden-orange boldly covers the forehead and a broad eyebrow which is separated from the orange cheeks by a slender black mask covering the lores and tapering behind the eyes. The black throat patch extends to the upper breast. A black cap extends onto the nape and covers the back almost to the rump. The black wings have a particularly broad white wing bar. Many of the flight feathers have white edges. The tail is black with orange-yellow on the sides. Under parts, rump and tail, golden-orange. *Female.* Full greyish-green, dusky above and paler below with yellowish tinges. The white wing bars are present but greatly reduced. Length: about 7–8½ in. (18–22 cm).
There are several subspecies, some with rather prominent variations.

BALTIMORE ORIOLE, *Icterus galbula* (Linnaeus)
G. Baltimoretrupial; F. Troupiale de Baltimore; D. Baltimore Troepiaal (Pl. XIV)

DISTRIBUTION: United States, Mexico, Central America and Colombia.
DESCRIPTION: One of America's most cherished native species of songbirds. *Male.* Has a black hood forming a bold V extending to the centre of the upper breast. The black cap

Baltimore Oriole, *Icterus galbula*

continues onto the mantle down to the lower back. The black wings have two orange-yellow bars near the shoulders, a white wing bar, and white edges on many of the inner wing feathers. The black tail has orange-yellow on the tips of the outer feathers. Bright orange-yellow covers all the remaining under parts as well as the rump and tail coverts. *Female.* Dusky-olive above and paler dusky olive-orange below. White wing bars are prominent. Blackish spots occur on the upper parts and occasionally on the throat. She is brighter than the female Bullock's Oriole. Length: 7–8 in. (18–20 cm).

YELLOW-WINGED CASSIQUE, MEXICAN CASSIQUE, CRESTED CASSIQUE, *Cassiculus melanicterus* (Pl. XII)
G. Haubenstirnvogel; F. Cassique du Mexique; D. Mexicaanse Cassique

DISTRIBUTION: Mexico.
DESCRIPTION: Most of the colouring is deep velvety-black with very attractive bright yellow accents. The yellow occurs on the rump, sides of the back, upper tail coverts, wing coverts, scapulars and under wing coverts. Irides pale brown with black pupils; beak greenish-ivory, feet and legs greyish-black. Length: 10–11 in. (25–27·5 cm) including broad 4 in. (10 cm) tail and long, sharply pointed greenish-ivory beak of 1⅜ in. (4·5 cm).
A flamboyant lateral crest of long, slender, and very flexible feathers form a distinctive feature. The crest feathers, limited in number, stem from the forehead and forecrown. At rest, the feathers lie backwards toward the nape. When fully raised, which is frequent, these feathers curve gracefully outwards and downwards towards the cheeks in an exotic flair. Females are a duller shade of black as well as being smaller.
Males engage in frequent lavish displays which are both nuptial and aggressive. During the displays they raise their crests as well as the feathers on their backs and rumps and emit ratchety, harsh squeals. The displays can quickly turn into very damaging attacks against any birds which cannot defend themselves. Cassiques should therefore be housed with bold, strong birds which are only slightly less aggressive than White-crested Jay Thrushes.
These Cassiques have an odd powdery-musk odour.
Cassiques require the same diet as outlined for New World Orioles. Nectar is very important for them. Nest-building, as with some orioles, is a highly developed skill. Nests are long pendulous pear-shaped baskets.

YELLOW-RUMPED CASSIQUE, *Cacicus c. cela* (Linnaeus) (Pl. IX)
G. Gelbrücken-Stirnvogel; F. Cassique à dos jaune; D. Geelrug-Buidelspreeuw

DISTRIBUTION: Central America, Trinidad and northern South America.
DESCRIPTION: Marked very much like the species above, but it lacks the crest, and the black is glossy. Yellow on the wing coverts is less extensive than on the above, and it is variable in subspecies. Yellow occurs on the under tail coverts as well as upper tail coverts. *Female.* Duller and shows an olive shade on the breast. Iris black pointed beak yellowish-green. Length: about 11 in. (28 cm).

Oropendolas

The Oropendolas are sometimes called Giant Cassiques. Their enormous beaks are similarly shaped, but the upper mandibles are extended in a flat casquelike development onto the crown. The shape of the bird appears strange on account of these beaks. The shapes appear as if a very modern designer had attempted to overcome an ungainly heavy-bodied, short-tailed shape by adding excessive streamlining. Oropendolas easily command attention not only because of their large sizes and unusual heads but also because of their wonderful and bold personalities and, in some species, because of their unique colour combinations.

Oropendolas are large birds with dominant personalities. Males are larger than females. Most should be housed only with larger birds of equally aggressive natures. They are very sociable birds and build their extraordinary nests in colonies often with dozens hanging like long sleeves from large trees. The nests are similar in shape to those of cassiques, but they are much larger.

The diet is the same as for Orioles and Cassiques.

Oropendolas indulge in elaborate displays rather similar to those of cassiques, but they pose their heads in unusual positions, apparently using their colours or impressive beaks to command attention. The displays are enacted during courting, in a show of aggression, and, in many instances, just because they seem to enjoy the performance They emit very strange sounds during these performances.

MONTEZUMA OROPENDOLA, *Gymnostinops montezuma* (Lesson) (Pl. XII)
G. Montezuma-Stirnvogel; F. Grand Cassique de Montezuma; D. Montezuma Oropendola

DISTRIBUTION: Mexico and Central America.
DESCRIPTION: A large bare cheek patch below the eye is mostly white with pinkish-orange in the lower area. There is a very slight crest composed of a few sparse, hair-like feathers. Black covers the remaining area of the head, nape, and breast. The body plumage is deep chestnut. The central tail feathers are chestnut, and all the outer tail feathers as well as the under side of the tail are vivid golden-yellow. The shiny black beak has a bright, sharply divided orange on nearly one-third of the outer area. Feet and legs black.

Length about 20 in. (51 cm) with female 3 in. (7·5 cm) smaller. This is the largest member of the family.

BLACK OROPENDOLA, *Gymnostinops guatimozinus*
G. Schwarzsternvogel

DISTRIBUTION: Panama and Colombia.
DESCRIPTION: The bare cheek patch is pinkish-flesh. The crest is hair-like. Glossy black covers the remaining areas of the head, under parts, mantle and central tail feathers. The back, wing coverts, and tail coverts are deep maroon. Outer tail feathers and under side of tail are rich golden-yellow. Beak is black with red tip; feet and legs black. Length: about 18 in. (47 cm) with the female about 3 in. (7·5 cm) smaller.

Marsh Birds and other Icterids

Two species of Marsh Birds are frequently available and are very pleasant aviary birds. They are very hardy if given the simple diet described at the beginning of this chapter. They are usually very peaceful and also inexpensive. The genus *Agelaius* also includes Red-winged Blackbirds, Tricoloured Blackbirds, and a few others which are not important to aviculture.

YELLOW-HEADED MARSH BIRD, *Agelaius icterocephalus* (Linnaeus)
G. Geld Kopf Stärling; F. Carouge à tête jaune; D. Geelkopspreeuw

DISTRIBUTION: All of South America.
DESCRIPTION: *Male.* Have bright yellow forming a hood covering the entire head, neck and upper chest. All the remaining plumage is glossy-black. Beak and lores are black;

feet and legs are black. *Female.* Dull brownish with olive tinges above the dull yellow eyebrow stripes. Under parts are brownish-yellow. Length: varies with subspecies, and famales are slightly smaller than males. Generally, the males are about 8 in. (20 cm).

The Yellow-headed Blackbird, *Xanthocephalus xanthocephalus*, of United States, Mexico, and Central America has a very similar pattern; but the yellow has a duller and dusky shading and extends down onto the mantle and shoulders and lower on the chest. The black is a little more extensive in the facial area, and a white bar occurs on the wings. The size is about 11 in. (28 cm). The female is dusky-brown with yellowish streaks on eyebrows and under parts. This species is not at all popular in aviculture.

Yellow-headed Marsh Bird, *Agelaius icterocephalus*

RED-BREASTED MARSH BIRD, CAYENNE RED-BREASTED MARSH BIRD, *Leistes militaris* (Pl. XV)
D. Kleine Soldatenspreeuw

DISTRIBUTION: Brazil, Guyana, Surinam, French Guiana, Trinidad and Tobago, Venezuela, Colombia, Panama, Peru, Bolivia, Argentina and Paraguay.
DESCRIPTION: The dominant colouring is a very bright and large patch of red which extends from the chin to the abdominal area. The red is very broad on the breast and has

irregular boundaries. The remaining plumage is dark brown except for a deep shade of pinkish-red about ⅜ in. (3·2 cm) wide running from the base to the bend of the wing. Variations of brown shading occur seasonally. Most of the brown feathers have buffish margins which gradually wear off leaving dark brownish-black several months before the moult.

A long trailing eyebrow stripe is buffish in the subspecies *militaris* and white in the more southerly racè *superciliaris*. A pale stripe runs down the centre of the head. The tail shows very faint narrow bars of lighter and darker shades of blackish and dark brown. Beak, feet and legs are dull horn colour. Length: 7 in. (18 cm) including short, broad tail of 1¾ in. (4·5 cm) and ¾ in. (2 cm) beak. *Female*. About ½ in. (1·25 cm) shortèr and has a less heavy body. Red on the breast is absent, but faint traces may be detected on close scrutiny. Under parts are dull brown. Upper parts have more prominent buffish edges to the feathers, and the narrow bars on the tail are more distinct. The red edge to the wing is paler and more pinkish.

MILITARY STARLING, RED-BREASTED STARLING, *Pezites m. militaris* (formerly *Sturnella*) (Linnaeus)
G. Soldatenstärlinge; F. Grand Etourneau militaire; D. Soldatenspreeuw (Pl. XV)

DISTRIBUTION: Brazil, Uruguay, Argentina, Chile and the Falkland Islands.
DESCRIPTION: This species is a larger version of the Red-

Military Starling, *Pezites m. militaris*

breasted Marsh Bird and is practically identical in colouring and pattern. The long, slender and very pointed beak indicates a close alignment with Meadowlarks, and the diet is the same; some seeds but generally more insectivorous than Marsh Birds.

Male. The red under parts are slightly more pinkish and slightly less broad. The long trailing eyebrow stripe is whitish with red on a band above the lores extending from the nostrils to above the eyes. *Female*. Has considerable traces of red on the central under parts and is a little smaller. Red above the lores is absent. The throat is buff, and buff edges on the other feathers are more pronounced. Length: 10½ in. (27 cm) including tail of 3 in. (7·5 cm) and 1⅛ in. (3 cm) beak.

The other member of this genus is Filippi's Red-breasted Starling, *Pezites defilippi*, from Brazil, Uruguay and northern Argentina. This species also has the same colouring and pattern as the Red-breasted Marsh Bird and the Military Starling, but the size is between the two. Length: about 7½ in. (19 cm) including the 2 in. (5 cm) tail and the ⅞ in. (2 cm) beak. The red areas are slightly less extensive and somewhat paler.

Red-breasted Marsh Bird, *Leistes militaris*

Two species of Marsh Birds occur in the genus *Pseudoleistes*. They are not very important in aviculture, nor are they particularly attractive. The Yellow-rumped Marsh Bird, *Pseudoleistes guiraburo*, is from Brazil, Uruguay, Paraguay and Argentina. The Brown-rumped Marsh Bird, *Pseudoleistes virescens*, from Brazil and Argentina has a brown rump and yellow on shoulders and chest.

Meadowlarks

The Meadowlarks occur in Canada, the United States, Mexico and Central America. The Eastern Meadowlark also occurs in northern South America. The wide range is due to sporadic migration. Meadowlarks are heavy bodied and short tailed. They spend much of their time on the ground and have large feet and long legs. They are among the most highly regarded of native American birds, not only because they are valuable destroyers of insects but also because they are wonderful songbirds.

The size varies from 9–10 in. (23–25 cm). Upper parts are various shades of mottled and striated browns, buffs and blackish colouring. An eyebrow stripe and a strip down the centre of the crown are prominently buff bordered by very dark bands; lores are yellowish.

The Eastern Meadowlark (*Sturnella magna*) has a bright yellow on under parts with a bold black V-shaped collar on the breast and blackish spots on the sides.

The Western Meadowlark (*Sturnella neglecta*) is nearly identical but the song is different. (See Pl. IX)
Meadowlarks thrive on the standard softbill diet. They are very hardy and are completely delightful birds. American fanciers have very little chance of working with these birds since they are strictly protected. They are insectivorous but nevertheless consume quantities of seed. Like the Marsh Birds, they prefer plain canary seed.

FAMILY: FRINGILLIDAE

SUBFAMILY: CARDUELINAE

MEXICAN ROSE FINCH, *Carpodacus m. mexicanus*
(St. Müller)   (Pl. XL)
G. Mexikanischer Karmingimpel; F. Carpodaque du Mexique (Bouvreuil du Mexique); D. Mexicaanse Roodmus

DISTRIBUTION: West coast of North America from southern British Columbia to southern Mexico.
DESCRIPTION: Face, a broad line on parotic region, front of neck and rump are red; rest of the upper parts brown with a vague dark streaky pattern. Lower parts are whitish with dark streaks, and rest carries a red sheen. The wings and tail are dark brown with light edges to the feathers. Iris brown, the beak horn-coloured and the feet and legs also horn-coloured. Length: about 5¾ in. (14 cm). There is no red on the female.

Mexican Rose Finch, *Carpodacus m. mexicanus*

These birds live mainly in dry and barren regions. They feed on seeds, berries and sometimes on aphids which they find on the ground and on bushes. The females invite the males to mate by adopting a crouching position, the wings hanging down and the tail erect, imitating the cry of the young birds calling for food. A male which has already mated will still carry out his display for other females, but mating is then prevented by the other males. In the wild, the females dominate the males only during the breeding period, but in aviaries they do so throughout the year, which is an odd fact.
The song of the male is somewhat reminiscent of that of the canary. These birds have deliberately been introduced into a number of countries, e.g. Hawaii, where they are firmly established. Unlike many other *Fringillidae*, the Mexican Rose Finch builds a covered nest. These birds are never wild; they often nest close to houses and even under roofs. They have long been kept in aviaries. The first recorded successful breeding in captivity was achieved in 1913 by M. Decoux in France. The pair accepted an open nesting-

box, which was filled with vegetable fibres and lined with horse hair. The female alone sat for 30 days on the 4 white eggs, with black dots. For the first week, the young were fed on aphides, and later on egg mash and soaked seeds. The Purple Rose Finch, *Carpodacus purpureus* (Gmelin), lives in the United States and nests in north-eastern and south-eastern Canada. It is distinguished from the Mexican Rose Finch largely by its white belly and by the more winy-red of the red parts. At the present day these birds are rarely imported, but some collectors have succeeded in breeding them, e.g. Mr. Lynch in England (*Foreign Birds*, 1959, No.1). The pair built an open nest in a thick bush and the single young bird was raised on egg mash and germinated seeds. Unfortunately the fine red colour of these birds has a tendency to lose its intensity after each moult; for this reason, grated carrot or synthetic carotin should be added to their food.
At the present day it is forbidden to export birds from the United States, and therefore the Purple Rose Finch is rarely found in European aviaries.

ROSE FINCH, SCARLET GROSBEAK, *Carpodacus e. erythrinus* (Pallas)
G. Karmingimpel; F. Carpodaque, Roselin cramoisi; D. Roodmus

DISTRIBUTION: Asia Minor, northern Europe.
DESCRIPTION: The head, neck and breast are of a fine deep carmine; on the upper part of the body towards the rear, the colour grows paler, abdomen is whitish, clouded with pink. The back is carmine-brown. The flight feathers and tail feathers are greyish brown with pink outer edges. In the female, the upper parts are olive-brown with dark rachis; the lower parts are whitish, but the breast is streaked with greyish-brown. Length: 5½ in. (14·5 cm).

These birds settle in damp grassland where there are numerous bushes and marsh trees; they are also found in coniferous woods and even in parks and gardens. But they always keep close to water. The nest is built in a thick bush 1½–2 yd (1·4–1·8 m) above the ground. They feed almost entirely on seeds.
The Rose Finch is protected by law in numerous European countries, and *in these countries it is forbidden to keep them in an aviary.* Where this is permitted, they have regularly reproduced. The autumn is the best period for familiarising these wild caught birds with aviary life, since they move about a great deal at this season. They will remain in good condition on a mixture of rape, chickweed, hemp and lettuce seeds, supplemented with rowan berries; they find the seeds of fir cones a real delicacy. In the springtime, they must be given plenty of wild plants, as well as budding branches of fruit trees and conifers. From the month of May, they should be given soft food, fresh ants' eggs and mealworms. In order to breed, the pair must have a well planted aviary of their own. The female will build her nest in a thick bush; this cup-shaped nest is built of twigs, blades of grass and feathers. The female sits for 12 days on the 4 or 5 eggs. The male helps to feed the young, which fly at 14 days. At first, the young birds are fed mainly on ants' eggs, chopped

mealworms and soft food.
They have been crossed with canaries and with various European *Fringillidae*.

Rose Finch, *Carpodacus e. erythrinus*

GOLDFINCH, *Carduelis c. carduelis* (Linnaeus)
G. Stieglitz; F. Chardonneret; D. Putter, Distelvink
(Pl. XXXVIII)

DISTRIBUTION: Europe.
DESCRIPTION: The mask is bright red, with black on the top of the head, nape of the neck and at the base of the beak. The parotic region, the throat and the breast are white, the latter being marked with a typical brownish pattern. The back is brown; the black wings are dappled yellow, and the ends of the flight feathers are white. The tail is black with white marks. The whitish beak has a dark point. *Female*. Has brownish rectal bristles; the fold of the wings is not deep black, but brownish-black. Length: 5 in. (13 cm).
These birds live in pairs or in small groups in parks, gardens, orchards and at the edge of thick woods; they do not settle in extended woodland. They prefer to nest in chestnut trees, fruit trees and maples. The nest is set high on a platform of thin leafy branches. The thick walls are constructed of fine grasses, moss, roots, and lichens and lined with soft vegetable wool. Although it lives on seeds, the Goldfinch raises its young on a diet of live insects, particularly aphids, and also on seeds pre-soaked in the parents' crop.
After the young have flown, the family remains united for a long time, during which these groups can be noticed on thistles and other wild plants, picking out the seeds with their pointed beaks. The Goldfinch has been a favourite amongst bird fanciers for a long time because of its fine colours and marvellous song. A caged bird will rapidly become tame; and a pair which is well cared for will breed readily in an aviary.
Several Goldfinches can live together in a large aviary, accompanied by other birds of the same size; but it is best to provide a separate aviary for breeding. The basis of the diet consists of a mixture of canary seeds, poppy (maw) seed, niger, thistle seeds, lettuce, burdock, linseed and hemp. Green food and a piece of sweet apple should be added everyday. In general, a pair in an aviary will build an open nest of branches, blades of grass, moss, vegetable fibre and hair. The female builds, while the male sings. It is also the female who sits on the 4 or 5 eggs for 13 days. These birds will often nest twice in a season. The young birds are raised on aphids, small mealworms, ants' eggs, egg mash and wild seeds, as well as germinated seeds.

Goldfinch, *Carduelis c. carduelis*

LINNET, *Carduelis c. cannabina* (Linnaeus)
G. Hänfling, Bluthänfling; F. Linotte mélodieuse; D. Kneu
(Pl. XVIII)

DISTRIBUTION: Europe, Asia.
DESCRIPTION: During the breeding period, the forehead and breast are blood-red. The head and neck are greyish-brown with dark streaks. The whitish throat also has dark streaks. The back and the wing coverts are chestnut coloured and the rump is whitish. The greyish-white abdomen becomes red-brown towards the flanks. The wings are brown with lighter edges to the feathers. The eyes are dark brown, the beak brownish (in winter it is lead-grey) and the feet are brown. Length: 5¼ in. (13·5 cm). *Female*. Has only a trace of red, the rump is duller and the plumage is more streaky.
These birds are common in countryside where there are many thickets and copses, as well as in cemeteries, parks and large gardens. In small groups, they go into fields, taking every kind of seed. They like to perch on gates, fences and posts. Their call can be rendered 'kek-kek-kek'; the song of the male is very tuneful and can be heard almost throughout the year. A pair will be satisfied with a small nesting territory, and the nests are often close together. Pairs are usually kept in an aviary, where they live peaceably with other birds of the same size. The mixture described, which must always contain plenty of sweet rape, should be supplemented by plenty of green food. If these birds are given a diet rich in carotenes, as well as a varied mixture of wild seeds, the fine

Linnet, *Carduelis c. cannabina*

red colours of the plumage will be preserved after the moult. They will reproduce readily in a flighted aviary, particularly if it is planted with a few small fir trees, in which they will build an open nest. This cup-shaped nest is made of twigs, grass stalks and vegetable fibres; the same nest is used for both clutches of eggs, each of which contain 4–6 eggs. The female sits for 12–14 days, and the young birds fly after about 2 weeks. On rare occasions the parents will take aphids to feed their young; they feed them mainly on regurgitated seeds, preferably half ripe fresh seeds and germinated seeds.

In a number of European countries, collectors also possess the Twite, *Carduelis flavirostris*. These birds nest in northern Britain and the far north, and winter further south in Europe. The males have no red in their plumage; they are distinguished by their yellow beak, and their plumage is dark brown with darker streaks on the upper parts, and yellowish-brown on the lower parts, the throat, breast and sides being marked with dark streaks. These birds are more ready to eat insects and ants' eggs, and also breed regularly in aviaries.

SISKIN, *Carduelis* (*Spinus*) *s. spinus* (Linnaeus)

G Zeisig; F. Tarin des aulnes; D. Sijs, Elsijs (Pl. XVIII)

DISTRIBUTION: Northern Europe, Asia.

DESCRIPTION: The chin and crown are black. The breast, throat, the sides of the neck and the head are light greenish

Siskin, *Carduelis* (*Spinus*) *s. spinus*

yellow. The upper parts are dark greenish-yellow, with a greener rump and upper tail coverts of the same colour. The belly is greyish-white with dark streaks. The black wings have two yellow stripes, and the end of the yellow tail is black. The feet and legs are brown; the irides dark brown; the beak is flesh-coloured with a dark point. Length: 4½ in. (12 cm). *Female*. Has no black on the chin and the head; her plumage has darker streaks on a grey background, instead of yellow.

Siskins like to nest in areas where there are tall conifers. After breeding, they move around in large flocks towards areas where there is plenty of food. They feed on the seeds of conifers, birch trees and elders, as well as on buds and young shoots, and various kinds of insect. The song of the male is sweet but not loud, though during the breeding period it is uttered with great fervour. The mating call can be rendered by 'tettertet' and by 'dieh'.

These birds usually nest at a great height, near the end of a branch. The pair carry out a nuptial flight, unfolding their tails, and they touch the point of each others beak. The female builds the cup-shaped nest, carefully camouflaging it with fibres.

These birds have long been found in cage and aviary, being easy to tame and their sweet murmuring song is often heard, encouraging other birds in the aviary to sing. They should be given a mixture of poppy (maw) seed, rape, niger, lettuce seed, thistle seed, burdock seed and the seeds from fir cones; they find the seeds of elder and birch a particular delicacy. Hemp seed and other oily seeds should be strictly rationed, because Siskins, especially those living in a cage, are inclined to grow fat. During the late spring and summer they must be given plenty of green food, and from time to time small mealworms and aphids as well.

A pair will reproduce even in a large cage provided that they have a nest-box somewhat camouflaged with fir branches. But success is easy to achieve in an aviary, even a small aviary where the pair can be on their own. They must have as building materials various kinds of hair, spiders' webs, soft hay, vegetable wool and feathers. The female will often accept an open nesting-box. Two clutches of eggs are usually laid every season, each containing 4 or 5 eggs, on which the female alone sits for 12 days, while the male feeds her on the nest. The young birds fly after 12 days. The two parents feed them, mainly with aphids, mealworms, ants' eggs, mash and germinated seeds.

AMERICAN GOLDFINCH, *Spinus tristis* (Linnaeus)

G. Trauerzeisig, Goldzeisig; F. Tarin triste, Tarin d'Amérique; D. Amerikaanse Sijs, Treursijs (Pl. XL)

DISTRIBUTION: U.S.A. and Canada.

DESCRIPTION: Forehead, crown of the head, lores and the eye region are black. The thighs and the tail coverts are white. The rest of the plumage is lemon-yellow. The wing coverts are yellow and black with white edges; otherwise, the wings are black with white edges and the fold of the wing is black. The feathers beneath the wing are brown. The black tail ends with a white tip. Irides are dark brown and the beak and feet yellowish-brown. Length: 4½ in. (12 cm). *Female*. Upper parts are rusty-yellow with a lemon-yellow rump; the top of the head is more or less olive, eye region yellowish-brown and the parotic region olive-brown; lores, cheeks and the patch below the eye are bright yellow.

American Goldfinch, *Spinus tristis*

In summer these birds live in the northern States of the United States and southern Canada. They are mainly to be found on the edge of woods and in areas rich in brushwood and wild plants. They feed on various kinds of seed and on green buds, also destroying many insects on Acacia flowers and fruit trees. When autumn comes, they form large flights which wander far afield, often visiting settlements, where they know they can find ample food. The song of the male is somewhat reminiscent of the European Goldfinch. They are tree dwelling birds, always looking for food amongst branches and twigs. If the winter is mild, they stay near the nesting territory; in cold weather, they emigrate towards the south and return in the spring. They nest very high in leafy trees, preferably in the fork of a branch, very close to the trunk. The nest is built of very fine pieces of grass and bark, the cup being lined with vegetable wool and fibres. The 3–5 light green eggs are laid and the female sits for 13 days. The young fly at about 15 days.

These birds are strictly protected in their own country, where it is forbidden to keep them in a cage or an aviary. Sometimes occasional specimens are exported from Mexico where they winter, and it is from there that European collectors obtain them from time to time.

BLACK-HEADED SISKIN, *Spinus i. icterus* (Lichtenstein)

G. Magellanzeisig; F. Tarin de Magellaen, Tarin à tête noire; D. Zwartkopsijs

DISTRIBUTION: South America.

DESCRIPTION: Head and nesk are black; the nape of the neck, sides of the neck, rump, upper tail coverts and lower tail coverts are light yellow. The back, scapulars and small

Black-headed Siskin, *Spinus i. icterus*

wing coverts are olive-green. The tail is black. Irides are brown, the beak lead grey, the feet brownish black. Length: 4¼ in. (11 cm). *Female*. Upper parts are olive-brown; the rump and the forehead are more yellowish, and the lower parts more greyish, with white on abdomen and lower tail coverts.

The Black-headed Siskin differs from its European relative in its entirely black head and lighter yellow lower parts. It is also more slender, and the tail longer. The song of the male is more tuneful.

From 1818 on these birds were imported into Germany, and have bred fairly easily. During the breeding period, the parents must have aphids and small beetles available. The mixture of seeds must include niger, canary seed, sweet rape, and groats, supplemented by fresh wild seeds, a little hemp or crushed sunflower seeds; and there must be no lack of green food.

When the Black-headed Siskin is compared with its European relative, one is immediately struck by the fact that the latter are real acrobats, whereas the former are far from sharing the same skill. Unlike the European Siskin, the Black-headed Siskin never takes hold of a fir cone with both feet, but holds it with one foot when picking out the seeds. The plumage is a little more loose than that of the European Siskin; they wag their tail more and also let their wings drag. Because of their slightly greater length, and stronger beak,

they rapidly establish a dominant role when they share an aviary. These birds like to bathe at length, making themselves so wet that they can no longer fly. They do not eat the whole of a mealworm, but take out the inside and leave the skin. They will breed in an inside aviary, and often accept the cage of a Roller Canary as a nest-box.

RED-HOODED SISKIN, HOODED SISKIN, *Spinus cucullatus* (Swainson)

G. Kapuzenzeisig; F. Tarin rouge du Vénézuela; D. Rode Zwartkopsijs, Kapoetsensijs   (Pl. XX)

Red-hooded Siskin, *Spinus cucullatus*

DISTRIBUTION: Venezuela, Trinidad.

DESCRIPTION: *Male*. The head and the throat are black. The sides of the neck and the lower parts are bright scarlet, and the belly and thighs white. The back and the scapulars are brownish-scarlet, with orange-red on the rump and the upper tail coverts. The wings are black, the wing coverts showing red edges and tips. The flight feathers and tail feathers have a black base. The eyes are brown, the beak a dark horn colour, and the feet and legs brownish-white. Length: about 4 in. (10·5 cm). *Female*. Has scarlet on the upper wing coverts, the rump and the lower back; the chin and lores are white; the crop and breast are orange-red; abdomen and the thighs are white and the flanks grey clouded with brown.

These brilliantly coloured Siskins live in the arid north of Venezuela and in the regions bordering on Colombia. They live on the edges of the forest, feeding on all kinds of grass and wild plant seeds, as well as small insects. At the present day, they are also to be found in Trinidad, Cuba and Puerto Rico, where they are firmly established as descendants of birds escaped from aviaries. They are strictly protected in Venezuela, and the few that arrive in Europe come from Colombia. The wild populations seem to be showing a tendency to diminish, and in the more or less immediate future, European collectors will have to be satisfied with specimens bred in their aviaries.

The original, fairly numerous, pairs were imported into Europe in 1900. They are difficult to acclimatise, and the newcomers should not be given dry seeds alone, for this will cause fatal digestive trouble. The diet must include niger, canary seeds, thistle seeds, linseed, lettuce seed, poppy seed, plantains and grass seeds; they should also be given supplements of other seeds: spinach, maple, birch, clover, groats and millet. All these seeds must be given both dry and germinated. In addition, the birds must have access to plenty of green food, soft food, grit and minerals. The insides of a dozen mealworms can be added to the mash. In addition to a varied diet, a suitable temperature is essential for keeping these birds in good condition.

When they have become accustomed to their food, the new specimens can be placed in summer in an aviary which receives plenty of sunshine, provided they are shut into the shelter at night. But it is better to keep them throughout the year in an inside aviary, facing the right way to catch plenty of sun, and heated in winter. They will always go to a sunny spot, and are only active at a temperature of 23°C as above. A number of pairs can share a large aviary. The females will quarrel during the breeding period, but these disputes are never serious. They prefer to nest in a dark place, often in a corner. They will accept a nest-box, a flower pot or half a coconut shell. The female uses coconut fibres, teased out hemp, blades of grass and moss, brought to her by the male, to build a nest in 2 or 3 days. She generally lays 4 bluish-white eggs with small red dots, on which she sits for 12 days, while the male feeds her upon the nest. But several times a day the sitting female will leave the nest to eat some more or to drink. When the eggs have hatched, the young birds can be fed at the beginning on insectivorous food and the inside of mealworms, while the female will also take plenty of chickweed and other green foods. After a week, the male will also help to feed the young, which fly towards the age of 2 weeks. They do not begin to feed themselves until they are a month old, and they are independent only at the age of 1½ months. The parents will often begin a fresh brood immediately. When they are 4 months old, the young birds begin their first moult and have their full colouring at 6 months.

These birds can also nest in a breeding cage, but in this case, the male is best removed as soon as the female has begun to sit. The female will be obliged to leave the nest more often to eat, which will lengthen the incubation period by 1 or 2 days. It is important to maintain a constant temperature of 23°C in the cage.

With the aid of the Hooded Siskin, Canary breeders have succeeded in creating an orange to orange-red Canary. By crossing a male Hooded Siskin with a female Canary, fertile male hybrids were obtained through whom the red factor was introduced to the Canary breed—the 'new' whole range being the Coloured Canaries.

YARRELL'S SISKIN, YARRELL'S GOLDFINCH, *Spinus yarrelli* (Audubon)
G. Yarrellzeisig; F. Tarin de Yarrell; D. Yarrells Sijs
(Pl. XL)

Yarrell's Siskin, *Spinus yarrelli*

DISTRIBUTION: Eastern Brazil.
DESCRIPTION: The top of the head, lores and edges of the eye rings are black. The rest of the plumage is yellow, clouded olive on the back. The middle wing coverts are black with yellow tips; the other coverts are black; the flight feathers have white edges. The tail is black. The eyes are dark brown; the feet, legs and beak are a pink horn colour. Length: 4 in. (10 cm). *Female*. Has no black on the head; her wings and tail are brownish.

We know little of the life of these birds in the wild. They feed mainly on seeds, like related species, but experience obtained since the beginning of the century has shown that they also need live food and oily seeds. These Siskins will remain in good condition on a diet of poppy (maw) seed, niger, and the seeds of lettuce and wild plants with oily seeds; this diet must be supplemented by fresh ants' eggs, insectivorous food and various kinds of green food, such as chickweed, seeding grasses and groundsel; they will also readily take the seeds of wild chicory.

GREENFINCH, *Chloris chl. chloris* (Linnaeus)
G. Grünfink, Grünling; F. Verdier; D. Groenvink, Groenling
(Pl. XVIII)

DISTRIBUTION: Europe.
DESCRIPTION: *Male*. Yellowish-green with grey and brownish-grey marks. The outer vexilla of the large flight feathers, the base of the tail feathers and the upper belly are light yellow. Length: about 6 in. (15 cm). *Female*. Lower parts are more grey and the upper parts more brown, and the yellow on her large flight feathers is less extensive.

The Greenfinch is common in areas where there are no

Greenfinch, *Chloris chl. chloris*

extensive woodlands, and his call, 'chi-chi-chi', can often be heard. Greenfinches often visit parks and gardens, nesting in thick bushes, hedges or conifers and leafy trees. The female builds a fairly loose and voluminous nest of blades of grass; she lays 4–6 whitish eggs with dots and marks of brown and black. She alone sits, while the male feeds her. The young birds hatch out after about 12–14 days and remain in the nest for 2 weeks. When they first fly, they are clumsy, and their parents take care of them and guide them. The female usually builds a new nest for her second clutch of eggs.

They will eat ripening sunflower seeds immediately and will gradually become used to taking hemp, oats, canary seed, lettuce seed, poppy (maw) seed and linseed, as well as all kinds of wild seeds. Besides these seeds, they need plenty of green food and rowan berries and sweet apple. When the sunflowers begin to ripen, their large heads filled with tender seeds are very welcome in the aviary. Oily seeds must always be rationed, because Greenfinches rapidly grow fat and then become inactive.

These birds easily breed in an aviary and even in a large cage. They usually prefer to build an open nest in a conifer, but will also accept a Roller Canary's cage as a nest-box. The female will make in it a nest lined with moss, vegetable wool and fine blades of grass. After the young are born, the parents will also accept soft foods.

HAWFINCH, *Coccothraustes c. coccothraustes* (Linnaeus)
G. Kernbeisser; F. Gros-bec casse-noyaux; D. Appelvink

DISTRIBUTION: Spain, Southern Scandinavia, Scotland, western Russia, northern Persia and the Ural Mountains.
DESCRIPTION: *Male*. The throat is red; the lower part, head and rump are a soft winy-red to brownish colour. The nape of the neck is grey, and the back is dark brown. The dark wings carry a heavy white dapple and the large wing coverts are greyish-white; in several of the flight feathers, the tips are broad, with wavy edges. The blackish tail has white tips. Thick and heavy beak is bluish-grey in the spring, but a light corn colour in winter. Iris and feet are light brown. Length: 7 in. (17 cm). *Female*. Plumage is less bright, and has less red colour on the head.

Hawfinch, *Coccothraustes c. coccothraustes*

In their nesting areas, Hawfinches often stick to the top of trees, where they are invisible amongst the foliage. They are stocky birds, with a very heavy head and neck and a short tail. The powerfully muscled jaws are capable of breaking cherry and olive stones; their muscles enable them to develop a force of 55–132 lb (25–60 kg). After the breeding period, small groups of these birds move about looking for food amongst bushes and on the ground. They walk with a lurching gait and can hop quite a distance in one bound. They feed on the contents of hips, rowan berries and the seeds of various trees. In the springtime, they eat buds and young shoots, but during the breeding period, they prefer insects. They feed very high up in trees, often forming small colonies of 4–10 pairs, each with their own small territory inside the colony. They eat rowan berries and a mixture of seeds including rape, canary seed, poppy (maw) seed and linseed; a small amount of oats and some cherry stones can be added. They should also have green food, branches with buds, mealworms and fresh ants' eggs. At the end of summer and in autumn, they find berries in season a particular delicacy.

They will also accept pieces of apple. They usually behave well in a mixed aviary, but some Hawfinches have a tendency to attack smaller birds in the same aviary, and therefore a close watch must always be kept upon them.

For breeding, a pair needs an outside aviary, planted with conifers and bushes. Nest-boxes can be hung from a bush, and in it the female will build a nest of twigs and fairly large blades of grass. She sits for 14 days on 4 or 5 bluish eggs, marked with grey and brown. The young birds leave the nest 14 days later. They are fed with soft food, mealworms, ants' eggs and soaked seeds.

BULLFINCH, *Pyrrhula p. pyrrhula* (Linnaeus)
G. Dompfaff, Gimpel; F. Bouvreuil; D. Goudvink

(Pl. XXXVIII)

DISTRIBUTION: Europe.
DESCRIPTION: *Male*. Mask and the top of the head are black. The breast is of a fine pink colour; abdomen and lower tail coverts are white. The back is ash-grey, with a white rump. The tail is midnight-blue, while the black wings have a white band. The short arrowhead-shaped beak is black, and the iris and feet are brown. Length: 6 in. (15 cm). *Female*. Breast is grey, sometimes faintly clouded with pink; the back is more brownish.

Bullfinch, *Pyrrhula p. pyrrhula*

These birds prefer areas with ample woodland in the form of copses. In northern Europe, the larger poppy-coloured subspecies, *Pyrrhula p. pyrrhula*, is found; the red is less bright, and it does not nest in western Europe, but is a winter visitor. The bird which nests here is the peony-coloured Bullfinch, *Pyrrhula p. coccinea*; this subspecies is smaller.

These birds can be seen in parks and gardens, in orchards and nurseries, but far less frequently in thick conifer woods; they prefer woods of leafy trees in thick coppices. They feed on the buds of leaves and flowers, various wild seeds, rowan berries and other wild berries. Their song is very soft and almost inaudible; it is a weak melancholy 'diu' uttered by the female as well. They also have the gift of imitation; they borrow the calls of other birds and learn to imitate other sounds and even tunes that are whistled. It is interesting to note that birds which in this way have learned to imitate a popular song never forget it.

In autumn and winter captured Bullfinches rapidly grow accustomed to life in an aviary, particularly if they are placed with other Bullfinches that have already been acclimatised. Their basic diet is a mixture of seeds which at first should include poppy (maw) seed, rape, canary seed, a little hemp, supplemented with rowan berries. Later, they should be given sunflower seeds, a large variety of wild seeds, a few mealworms, as much green food as they want and the budding branches of fruit trees, as well as any berries that are in season. Most Bullfinches will also accept soft food, particularly if it is enriched with ants' eggs.

For breeding to succeed, the pair must be placed alone in an aviary planted with conifers and other bushes and shrubs. The nest-boxes should be hidden amongst the fir branches or in thickets of broom. The female often prefers to build a free-standing nest in a conifer or a thicket of broom, using a foundation of fine twigs, and lining the cup with rootlets,

hair and vegetable wool. The male takes great care of his mate, feeding her even before the eggs are laid and throughout the time when she is sitting, which lasts for 13 days. 4 – 5 eggs are laid. The young are fed on food disgorged by their parents, who during this period like to have the ripening seeds of plantain, nettles, antirrhinums, as well as half ripe oats. They will also take fresh ants' eggs and small mealworms, and will actively hunt spiders. The pair need a breeding diet of considerable variety and will choose from it.

Canaries

WILD CANARY, *Serinus c. canarius* (Linnaeus)
G. Kanarienvogel; F. Canari sauvage, Serin des Canaries; D. Wilde Kanarie   (Pl. XXXVIII)

DISTRIBUTION: Canary Islands and Azores; has been introduced into Spain and Italy; can now be found throughout Europe.

DESCRIPTION: The plumage is principally greyish-green, with black streaks on the upper parts; the rump and forehead are

Wild Canary, *Serinus c. canarius*

greenish yellow. The eyebrows, throat and breast are yellow; the abdomen is also yellowish. The short arrowhead-shaped beak is dark. Length: about 4½ in. (11·5 cm). Streaks on the female are heavier; her upper parts are more brownish and her lower parts more grey.

The Wild Canary lives in open country, with small woods and many thickets of brushwood. These birds often form small flocks, flying through the air on an undulating course and landing in the fields. They nest amongst trees and bushes and sometimes in vineyards. Their song consists of rapid and somewhat high pitched trills and metallic sounds; it is somewhat reminiscent of the song of the Corn Bunting, *Emberiza calandra*, and has no resemblance to the sophisticated song of the Roller Canary.

The Serin, *Serinus c. serinus*, also originating in southern Europe, now nests much further north. This bird is mainly Canary yellow, with greenish-yellow on the forehead and the nape; the back and scapulars are brownish-green with broad brown streaks; the greenish-yellow of the throat changes into grey on the abdomen; the wings are brownish-grey, and

the tail is brownish-black with light edges. They build their meticulously constructed nest in the form of a cup, of stalks, fibres, moss, lichen, threads and feathers. The 4 eggs are bluish-white, with numerous small marks and streaks. The female alone sits for 12 days, while the male feeds her on the nest. The young are raised by both parents and leave the nest after more than 2 weeks.

Since 1478, the wild Canary has been imported into Spain. It soon became a favourite of collectors, who specialised at first in teaching it to sing. In this way Roller Canaries became celebrated, and in Germany, the Netherlands and Belgium in particular, this speciality became extremely popular; but fanciers at the present day take more interest in types and coloured Canaries.

In England, bird fanciers specialised in breeding type and crested Canaries, but in France, Spain and Italy several breeds of frilled Canaries have been produced. By crossing with the Hooded Siskin, *Spinus cucullatus*, the red factor has been introduced amongst coloured Canaries, which almost everywhere have become great favourites. It is undeniable that in its numerous forms the Canary is at the present day the most frequently found bird in cages and aviaries.

They should also be given soft food, rape and lettuce seed, as well as a variety of wild seeds and grass seeds. Their diet should consist larely of starchy seeds, and these should also be given in the germinated state. Various kinds of green food should also be provided.

They breed best in the aviary, and these wild birds can be crossed with the domestic Canary. Breeding is similar to that of domestic Canaries, and the offspring are obviously fertile.

DOMESTIC CANARY, *Serinus canarius domesticus*
G. Kanarienvogel; F. Serin; D. Kanarie   (Pl. XX)

The domestic Canary is a close relation of the Serin, *Serinus canarius serinus*, and the genus includes many other well-known birds, such as the Green Singing Finch, *Serinus mozambicus*. It is descended from the Wild Canary, which has greenish-yellow plumage, with grey and brown marks. By controlled breeding and selection, bird fanciers have brought into being a large number of subspecies and varieties, and more and more are being developed. The subspecies and varieties of the domestic Canary are found throughout the world, and in many countries it is the most popular cage bird.

The German miners of the Harz Mountains played a very important role in the domestication and distribution of the Canary. At first, these birds had the same plumage as their wild ancestors, and efforts were concentrated on improving their song. But as early as the 18th century, different coloured varieties were known. It has mainly been English breeders who have tried to produce Canaries of a different build by selective breeding; while in western Europe, the beginning of the 20th century saw the beginning of the remarkable development of different coloured Canaries.

At the present day, we can divide the different sub-species into three principle groups:

A. Canaries bred for their song, the main ones being the Roller, the Timbrado and the Malinois or Waterslager.
B. Canaries bred for colour: in the Netherlands, these are mainly of the Roller type; in Belgium and further south, the influence of the Mallinois is greater. In this group, we must distinguish between Canaries with a yellow or white background, and reliable hybrids derived from the Hooded Siskin, *Spinus cucullatus*, with an orange to red background.
C. Type Canaries, bred for build and shape, distinguished by their unusual build or by the typical patterns of their plumage. Within this group, there are the English Canaries, e.g. the Yorkshire, the Border, the Gloucester Fancy, the Norwich, etc.; the Frilled Canaries, e.g. the Paris Curled, the Dutch Frilled, the Paduan, the Gibber Italicus, etc.; and Canaries with a typical pattern, e.g. the Lizard.

In recent years, there has been a tendency to combine these two principal groups, and we therefore find:

A. Song and colour. In general, it is difficult to combine these two very different characteristics satisfactorily. Often, either the quality of the song or the intensity of the colour are more or less lost, because the breeding pair are the offspring of long lines specially adapted for one or other of these qualities.
B. Shape and colour. The same difficulties are found, but it is easier to maintain intact the typical qualities of these two specialised groups, so long as a rigorous selection is carried out.

Care and feeding

Canaries are granivorous. Their basic diet consists of a mixture of good quality sweet rape and the high grade canary seed, with the addition of small quantities of dehusked oats, niger, linseed, hemp, lettuce and other small seeds. Specially prepared mixtures can be bought but the birds must also have fresh wild plants, given when in season: e.g. dandelion, shepherd's purse, chickweed, groundsel, sow-thistle, various plantains, coltsfoot, etc. All these plants can be given with the seeds at various stages of maturity. The birds will also eat the leaves of these plants, and when they are not available, they can be replaced by lettuce, endives, cabbage, spinach, water-cress, etc. It is difficult to give them animal food, but this can be replaced by bread dipped in milk, and soft food. The drinking water should be changed every day, and the birds should also have minerals and special grit.

Breeding

As Canaries have long been domesticated, there are innumerable examples of successful breeding. But it is wrong to suppose that one has only to put a male and a female together and several broods of young birds will result! Depending upon the facilities available and the purpose one has in mind, breeding can be carried out in different ways. Breeding in a large aviary housing several pairs requires less constant care, but the results are usually less successful. Canaries will breed well in single breeding cages of about 24 in. (60 cm) long, 14 in. (35 cm) high and 10 in. (25 cm) deep where mating can be controlled. Many breeders leave the female to raise the brood herself, because this method requires fewer males. When this is done, a male will be put with two or even several females in turn to fertilise the eggs.

It is usually better for breeding to be done by pairs, since both birds will remain together to feed the young; when the female starts laying again, the male will continue to feed the young birds.

Canaries build a nest in an open nesting box hung on the side of the cage. But it must be placed where the nest can be examined without disturbing the birds too much. The building materials required are dry grasses, moss, cowhair, unravelled and cut hemp, and unravelled and cut jute sacking.

A few days after mating, the female will begin to lay; she lays an egg every day, mostly about 7 or 8 a.m. There are usually 4–6 eggs, on which she begins to sit at once so they hatch over a period, therefore breeders usually take out the first three eggs after they have been laid, putting them back into the nest when the fourth egg is laid. In the meantime, the eggs are replaced by imitations.

The period of incubation is normally 13 days. While the young birds are being raised, a good soft food should be given. It is advisable to give germinated seeds as well; sweet rape is seed which germinates easily, but other seeds can be germinated as well.

Towards the eighth or tenth day, the young birds can be ringed, if so desired. Ornithological societies sell closed rings for this purpose, bearing the initials of the society, the breeder's stamp a number, the year and a further number. All these details should be copied into the breeding register, to be completed later by the sex of the young bird, its colour, its song, its show points and other remarks.

Towards the age of three weeks, the young birds leave the nest but are still fed by their parents; at the same time, the mother is preparing for her second brood. It is recommended that not more than two broods, or three at the most, should be raised in a season. The normal breeding period in Europe begins towards the end of March and ends at the beginning of July.

Once the young birds are independent, they are best housed in a large well ventilated aviary, where the juvenile moult will take place. This first moult, which lasts about six weeks, is tiring for the young birds, so that they must have a very varied diet, rich in vitamins. The adults also moult every year. At this period they are less active, and the males do not sing. The moulting birds must be carefully watched. After the moult, the birds can remain in the aviary, but the sexes should be separated.

If they are shown, however, they have to be put in a cage to train them either for singing competitions or for showing.

Buying Canaries

The price of the various varieties is determined by the law of supply and demand. Breeders usually try to sell their superfluous young birds directly to other breeders; those which are not sold in this way will be taken up by dealers. Many Canaries raised in Western Europe are exported to the USA, where it is the type Canaries, which are mainly imported. Special care must be taken in buying to choose healthy birds. The Canary should be lively and active, its plummage smooth and shiny, and its eyes wide open and sparkling. The bird should be picked up, and the base of the belly examined: the skin there should have a fine pink flesh colour, and the breastbone should not be prominent. It is difficult to sex young birds, particularly in the autumn; the well developed song of the male is for practical purposes the best way to tell the sexes apart. In the springtime, when the birds are taking on their breeding plummage, they are easier to sex. There is no absolutely certain outward mark.

New birds should be placed in a quarantine cage. Canaries can carry parasites, particularly lice. This pest can be picked up by the whole breeding colony, and it is therefore essential to make sure whether or not the new birds have lice. If they have, the lice must be destroyed with an insecticide manufactured specially for birds.

Shows and competitions

Wherever Canaries are bred, local or national bird societies also organise exhibitions and competitions.

Singing competitions are of course the oldest, but the general public takes little interest in them; only a limited group of bird fanciers attend them to hear the finest singers. When the birds have been put in the cage, a jury judges the quality of the song of each separate bird or of a team of four birds. The champion birds and their offspring are often sold for considerable prices; the seller usually includes the singing certificate which testifies to the bird's quality.

In Belgium, France and the Netherlands the main interest at the present day is in shows of coloured and singing Canaries, while the main shows in Great Britain are of type Canaries, bred for their shape. The large national exhibitions always attract great public interest, and there are many visitors to the shows organised by the Belgian Association (AOB), the Netherlands Association (NBvV), or the British National Exhibition of Cage and Aviary Birds.

Varieties of colour

The original colouring of the wild Canary can be broken down into black and brown pigments, mixed with the basic yellow lipochrome colour.

Thus the varieties of colouring can be divided into two principal groups, depending upon whether or not the dark pigments (black and/or brown) are present. We give the name 'pigmented' or 'melanine' to the birds who show something of these dark pigments in their back pattern. The other group, which shows only the light background colour, is called 'lipochrome'.

In some cases, the original yellow background colouring has been lost by mutation, and the plumage of these birds has a white background. In the second decade of this century, the original yellow lipochrome of the Canary was also mixed with red, through crossing with the Hooded Siskin, *Spinus cuculiatus*, and it is this that has given orange or orange-red background colours in the canary.

Lipochromes

Taking account of the different possibilities, the following classical colours can be distinguished:

1. *The Yellow* This is the best known colour and is very widespread. Most birds kept in the home are yellow Canaries, sometimes with dark variegations. But a yellow show Canary must have an unmarked plumage, and not even the beak or the feet should show the least dark marking. Some judges even follow the practice of taking hold of each specimen, to check the under-plummage as well. Breeders also distinguish between the golden yellow (buff) and the straw yellow (yellow); there is a difference of colouring produced by the length of the feathers, and by whether or not the colour appears at the ends of the barbs of the feathers.

2. *White* Normally, a white Canary (German white or dominant) has lost every trace of yellow lipochrome in the body feathers, but the yellow is found in the narrow vexillae of the flight feathers and tail feathers. This light shading must be very indistinct; the whitest birds are regarded as the best.

The recessive white (English white) is rarer; these Canaries do not show the least trace of yellow. This variety is formed by an absolutely different mutation, and its heredity is quite distinct.

3. *Orange to Orange-red* The very intense colouring of these birds must be completely uniform, with no veining or marking. In young specimens, the flight feathers and tail feathers are lighter, while in adult specimens, these feathers should be as intense as the rest.

Care should be taken not to mate two deeply coloured (yellow) birds, it is better to mate a specimen with very intense (yellow) colour to a bird with a lighter (buff) colouring.

The salmon pink Canary is at first sight a buff (frosted) with orange-red colouring. The judges look in the main for the frosting to be equally spread, to give a light coating without hiding the colour, and for the colour to be uniform.

Plate XXXI

Chestnut-breasted Finch, *Lonchura c. castaneothorax*

Pectorella Finch, *Lonchura pectoralis*

White-headed Mannikin, *Lonchura m. maja*

Spice Finch, *Lonchura punctulata*

Three-coloured Mannikin, *Lonchura m. malacca*

Plate XXXII

Spotted-backed Weaver, *Ploceus c. cucullatus*   Layard's Weaver, *Ploceus cucullatus nigriceps*

Chestnut Weaver, *Ploceus r. rubiginosus*

                                       Baya Weaver, *Ploceus manyar philippinus*

Congo Crested Weaver, *Malimbus malimbicus*   Red-headed Weaver, *Malimbus leuconotus*

Plate XXXIII

Masked Grass Finch, *Poephila p. personata*

Parson Finch, *Poephila c. cincta*

Long-tailed Grass Finch, *Poephila a. acuticauda*

White Java Sparrow, *Padda oryzivora var. alba*

Java Sparrow, *Padda oryzivora*

Plate XXXIV

South African Buffalo Weaver, *Bubalornis a. niger*   Racket-tailed Drongo, *Dicrurus paradiseus*

Buffalo Weaver, *Bubalornis a. albirostris*

Dinemelli's Weaver, *Dinemellia d. dinemelli*

Social Weaver, *Philetairus socius*

Mahali Weaver Bird, *Plocepasser m. mahali*

Pigmented Canaries

All pigmented (or melanine) Canaries possess either black and brown pigments, or brown alone. When the dark melanines go right to the end of the barbs, we have the green Canary (black and brown pigment) or the cinnamon Canary (brown pigment alone). These birds can be found with the three basic colours we have mentioned, giving six different varieties:

A. Green=brown and black pigments on a yellow background.
B. Blue=brown and black pigments, with a white background (the yellow is absent).
C. Bronze=brown and black pigments, with an orange to orange-red background.
D. Golden Cinnamon=brown pigment, with a yellow background.
E. Silver Cinnamon=brown pigment, with a white background.
F. Orange Cinnamon=brown pigment, with an orange background.

Each of these varieties can also vary in shade under the influence of the diluting factor. This factor occurred for the first time at the beginning of the present century, in a Canary which showed the presence of the dark pigments only partially in its plumage. The extremities of the barbs were virtually uncoloured, which produced a more greyish colour. This variety was called 'agate' and is found when the brown and black pigments are diluted.

By crossing this agate with cinnamon Canaries, the diluting factor was passed on to birds of the cinnamon series; these diluted cinnamon are called 'Fawns'.

This diluting factor has given rise to six new varieties:

A. Golden agate=brown and black diluted, with a yellow background.
B. Silver agate=brown and black diluted, with a white background.
C. Orange agate=brown and black diluted, with an orange background.
D. Golden fawn=brown diluted, with a yellow background.
E. Silver fawn=brown diluted, with a white background.
F. Orange fawn=brown diluted, with an orange background.

All these varieties form the classical coloured Canaries. They are all listed in the table that follows.

CLASSICAL COLOURS

Basic Colour	PIGMENTED CANARIES				LIPOCHROMES
	Intensity of pigmentation				
	I Green Series	II Agate Series	III Cinnamon Series	IV Fawn Series	Absence of Dark Pigments
PALE YELLOW	Buff green	Agate	Brown	Fawn	Straw yellow
GOLDEN YELLOW	Yellow green	Golden agate	Buff cinnamon	Golden fawn	Buff yellow
LEMON YELLOW (blue optical factor)	Lemon green (moss green)	Lemon agate	Lemon cinnamon	Lemon fawn	Lemon yellow
DOMINANT WHITE	Blue	Silver agate	Silver cinnamon	Silver fawn	Dominant white
ORANGE	Bronze	Orange agate	Orange	Orange fawn	Orange
ORANGE-RED	Bronze orange-red	Agate orange-red	Orange-red	Fawn orange-red	Orange-red
NON-INTENSIVE	Bronze orange-red buff	Agate orange-red buff	Orange-red schimmel	Fawn orange-red buff	Salmon

New Colours

In addition to these various 'classical' colours other varieties, called 'new colours' have appeared in recent years. They can be classified in four principal series:

the ivory colourings; the pastel colourings; the opal colourings; the mosaics. These are described below.

Ivory The ivory and pink-ivory Canaries are lipochromes, i.e. without dark pigmentation. Some enterprising breeders have also succeeded in introducing this factor into the series of pigmented Canaries, and have obtained pink-ivory agates, ivory fawns, etc.

The ivory factor is recessive with regard to the classical lipochrome colours, red-orange, yellow and red. The heredity of this factor is sex-linked, like that of the mosaic factor. An ivory lipochrome specimen resembles at first sight a white with cream plumage. The best specimens possess a very moderate schimmel, with very soft silky plumage.

The ivory-pink is a combination of the ivory factor with a very intense red factor. It is an odd fact that in this series sexual dimorphisme is never observed, though it is in the mosaics; both male and female pink-ivory Canaries are similar.

Pastel The pastel factor effects the dark pigments of the Canary; its effect is to introduce an extreme dilution into these pigments, but unlike the diluting factor of the agate (also introduced into the fawn) a whole pattern is modified by the pastel factor.

The finest effect of this factor is produced in birds of the fawn series, the pastel fawn, the pastel silver fawn, the pastel golden fawn and the pastel orange-red fawn. The pattern of the typical fawn, already very diluted, becomes virtually imperceptible in the pastel; it exists only in the form of an extremely light clouding which over lays a very fine and pure background colouring.

Although the pastel factor has been introduced into the brown, agate and green series, it is impossible to see much value in it in these varieties, for they lose their complete pigmentation which is the typical characteristic of the variety. The pastel factor is likewise sex-linked and recessive with respect to the classical colours.

Opal As a result of a new mutation, the development of the brown pigment of the Canary has been completely modified. In the classical pigmentations, the pattern of the plumage virtually always carries the brown, but the opal mutants have for practical purposes completely lost this same brown. Even the black pigment is modified, so that an opal green specimen seems to possess a light greyish plumage. The best effect of this factor is found in the green series, i.e. in the opal green, the opal blue and the opal brown.

Even in the agate series, the opal factor can play a significant role, but if this same factor is introduced into the brown (opal brown) or fawn (opal fawn) we obtain birds whose plumage seems to be absolutely without pigmentation and in whom the presence of the pigmentation is noticeable only in the down (the under feathers).

A curious fact is that the opal factor, unlike the other factors which effect pigmentation, is not sex-linked. Experimental matings have shown that the opal factor is recessive with regard to all other colourings, both the classical colourings and the pastels.

Thus this latter mutation seems to have given rise to the more profound modification at present known. As in the case of the classical varieties, breeders must make their own choice of colours, and these should be encouraged, for they can extend what is already a wide variety of coloured Canaries.

Mosaic Any mosaic bird must have a plumage in which two colours are clearly separated; one of these colours is always white. The other colour is that found on the points which form the mosaic pattern, and may vary from red through orange-red to yellow. The standard description requires that the white parts should be clearly marked off and that the mosaic pattern should be complete.

TYPE CANARIES, BRED FOR SHAPE AND FEATHER PATTERN

These various sub-species have been bred with the aim of stressing various characteristics of shape or feather pattern. Colour plays a negligible role in these Canaries.

Frilled Canaries

All these Canaries have extremely long plumage and share certain main characteristics. They all have frills on the breast, back and sides. In addition, each variety displays certain typical details.

Parisian Frill The largest and the most impressive. With its extremely long plumage and magnificent curls, it is a true aristocrat. On the judge's card, priority is given to the frills on the back. These frills should be voluminous and as symmetrical as possible. In general, the frill on the breast does not present any problem, although the 'shell' curl on the crop is imperfect in sub-specimens. The frilled 'fins' on the sides must curl towards the wings, and it is difficult to do much about downward pointing feathers of the sides. Finally, adult specimens also possess 'cock feathers', narrow feathers protruding on each side of the base of the tail. The head and neck are somewhat squat, and also carry thick curls.

The best specimens, even amongst young birds, also have claws curled like a corkscrew. The tarsus seems quite short, but the best specimens have a proud upstanding appearance. Length: 8–9 in. (20–22 cm) from the point of the beak to the end of the tail.

The Dutch Frill This Frilled Canary is more common in Belgium and the Netherlands. It is about 6½ in. (17 cm) long, has smaller curls and is more elegant than the Parisian Curled.

Here again, the frills must be as symmetrical as possible, but the head and neck have a smooth plumage, while the feet are a little longer. The most highly valued are birds of intense colouring, whose plumage is accordingly shorter; schimmel specimens, on the other hand, often show details which suggest hybridisation with the Parisian Frill.

The South Holland Curled In this bird, the curls are much lighter than in the previous varieties and it is about 2⅝ in. (16 cm) in length. But its deportment is much modified; the bird adopts a curved posture, forming a kind of curved figure seven. Its long and lightly feathered thighs give it something of the appearance of a wader. This variety is much sought after in Southern Europe, because it forms the stock from which the pretty variety that follows is bred.

Gibber Italicus This small Frilled Canary is about 6 in. (15 cm) in length. It has short, scanty plumage, and the long thighs are almost naked. It forms a striking contrast with the robust Parisian Frill. Like the South Holland (Dutch) Frill, the Gibber Italicus stands curved forward, an attitude exaggerated by the shape of the feet, on which the claws are curled in the opposite to the normal direction.

The Paduan and the Milanese Frill These two varieties originate in Italy, from the neighbourhoods of Padua and Milan, respectively. They are large sturdy specimens, somewhat reminiscent of the Parisian Frill, from whom they are in fact descended. Their posture, however, is reminiscent of that of the Yorkshire.

The Milanese Frill, somewhat smaller than the Parisian, is about 7½ in. (19 cm) in length. Different colours are found: white, orange, green, etc. It is therefore a coloured Curled, and with its haughty posture, its voluminous curls and its fine and uniform colouring, it is a very beautiful bird.

The Paduan differs from the Milanese in possessing a crest. Unfortunately we rarely see a crest of the ideal shape, which is difficult to achieve, because the other characteristics of the plumage must be taken into account as well.

British Canaries

The varieties that follow originate in Great Britain, where breeders have specialised in the shape and posture of the birds. The Yorkshire and the Norwich are undoubtedly the finest creations of this kind.

The Yorkshire   This elegant and haughty Canary, about 6½–7 in. (17–18 cm) in length, also has a very upright posture. The smooth outline of its body, its fine rounded head, its wings held close to the body and the long tight tail make it the aristocrat of type canaries.

Norwich   This somewhat heavily built Canary is in complete contrast to the Yorkshire. The Norwich has short legs, a broad, rounded breast with heavy plumage, a large and chubby head and short wings. Good show specimens have extremely silky and soft plumage.

In addition to the smooth headed Norwich, there is also a Crested Norwich. The crest must be very thick and symmetrical, with the feathers ranged in good order round the exact centre of the top of the head; the extremities of the feathers of the crest should reach the eyes, which increases its heavily built appearance.

Yorkshire   Norwich   Border

Border   This is the most common variety in Great Britain. It has the appearance of a larger version of the Continental Coloured Canary; but its shape is slightly different, principally in the more rounded line of the abdomen (Pl. XX). The back also forms a pretty and slightly rounded line, while the closely held wings touch at the ends; the tail is quite short and tight. These harmonious lines make it one of the prettiest type canaries.

Gloster Fancy   This small posture canary occurs in two varieties: the Crested (Gloster Corona) and the Smooth-headed (Gloster Consort). The most sought after are the Crested, but the Consorts are indispensable for breeding. This Canary is about 4½ in. (12 cm) in length. Its smooth tight plumage and its liveliness make it a favourite with collectors. In the Crested variety, the crest must fall in an attractive round shape over the relatively flat head.

Gloster Crested Canaries are too often confused with ordinary Crested Canaries; and there also exist the products of crossings which lack the typical characteristics of this fine English variety.

Gloster Fancy   Lizard

Lizard This is a variety bearing a characteristic pattern with a typical pattern of scales on the back and a light cap on the top of the head. The cap may form a fine oval shape, but is sometimes found in an incomplete form (broken cap); and in addition there are fine Lizards which have no cap at all.

The basic colour of the original English Lizard was yellow, but in recent years breeders have introduced other colours into this variety, and from time to time blue and even bronze Lizards are shown. In Belgium, these colours and the agate, brown and fawn, have been recognised for the show Lizard since 1963.

The plumage of the Lizard is usually silky; good specimens also have a haughty erect posture and a calm attitude. The fine characteristic design loses its clarity and outline after the first complete moult, when the tail feathers and flight feathers often show whitish patches.

In addition to these Posture Canaries, we should also mention the Belgian Hunchback Canary. This variety had virtually disappeared after the First World War, but thanks to the indefatigable experiments of a handful of breeders, several good quality stocks have been built up, and at the present day Belgian Hunchbacks can be seen at shows. This is a very elegant Canary with smooth plumage, a small throroughbred head and fine long feet. In its 'working' attitude which it takes up when presented to the judge, it bends its neck, as it moves its head forward; thus it has the shape of a figure seven, but the line of the back and of the nape of the neck is straight, not sloping.

The care and breeding of Canaries bred for shape and posture corresponds largely to that of Canaries bred for colour and song. But the breeder must remember that successful breeding is less common, mainly because breeders have a much more limited choice. Moreover, the breeder is often obliged to begin with specimens which lack typical characteristics or with birds in poor health, sometimes lacking vitality. Thus his task is not merely to improve the health and vitality of his stocks, but also to practice rigorous selection, in order to emphasise the typical characteristics of the variety as much as possible.

The study of the heredity of the different factors is very important, and has recently been made more complicated by the appearance of the pastel and opal factors, which have been added to the numerous varieties of existing colours. Breeders who have the patience, the opportunity and the time to acquaint themselves with the necessary knowledge for the well informed breeding of Coloured Canaries are few and far between. Fortunately, there are a few very simple rules which any breeder can understand and follow. The most important are:

1. Do not cross an intensive (yellow) with an intensive (yellow) or a buff with a buff;
2. Do not mix background colours at mating. In addition, in order to mate birds with some chance of success, it is essential to know the latent factors which are hidden, and are not found in the outward appearance of the birds; in other words, it is necessary to know the hereditary pattern of each bird.

To achieve this aim, it is essential to keep full breeding records, and to have a card for every breeding bird, noting on it not only visible factors, but also the various latent factors. With these data, an experienced breeder can mate a pair after mature deliberation on what may often be very complicated hereditary formulae; he will also be able to calculate the appearance and the genetic pattern of the offspring. But a beginner must not shrink from this task, even if it seems difficult and complicated. He can begin with fairly easy colours found amongst birds with a simple genetic pattern. If he uses a good handbook, a beginner can succeed in mastering the first difficulties. Later, having learned from experience and by reading a more advanced handbook, he will gradually come to understand the genetic laws of the different factors, and will have no difficulty in mating his birds and calculating the results. At this point a breeder will decide the direction in which he wishes to specialise.

Breeding Canaries can be an amusing and satisfying pastime provided one has the patience to learn how to set about it. If all one wishes is to produce young without regard for their quality, one can proceed blindly without a very specialised knowledge. But anyone who is looking for specimens suitable for showing, and Canaries which will win prizes in competitions, must begin with good quality specimens, whose colouring fulfils the requirements laid down, and which also possess a series of other essential qualities such as good health, good shape, and the patience to sit and raise their young. By selection, all these good qualities can be maintained, and faults progressively eliminated. This selection is not only a long drawn out process, but also demands on the part of the breeder the gifts of observation and good judgment. Thanks to the theoreticians, breeders now have a choice of good advice and counsel, enabling them to breed with considerable success.

CITRIL FINCH, *Serinus citrinelia* (Pallas)
G. Zitronzeisig; F. Venturon montagnard; D. Citroen-Cini (Citroen-Sijs)

DISTRIBUTION: The Western Alps, the Jura, the Vosges, the Black Forest; in Sardinia and Corsica (as subspecies).
DESCRIPTION: The top of the head and the nape of the neck are bluish grey; the forehead, the rump and the lower parts are lemon yellow; the flight feathers and tail feathers are blackish brown, and the wing-coverts have light brown edging. *Female* Less vivid. Length about 5 in. (13 cm).
As its french name indicates, the Citril Finch is a mountain dweller, which is rarely found in the plains and hardly ever leaves its wooded mountainsides. In spite of this, they have frequently been on sale in Germany in recent years. As it is a bird accustomed to humid heat and quite high altitudes, it must be carefully acclimatized. Its beautiful, soft-coloured plumage, its charming song and its interesting behaviour

make it very popular with bird keepers.
If the bird has been taken during the summer, it should be given various kinds of wild seed in a semi-ripe state (e.g. chickweed, *Stellaria media*). Once acclimatized, it can be housed in a well planted outside aviary, where it can withdraw into the shade of the vegetation. Two cases of successful breeding under these conditions have been recorded in Germany; when the young birds were in the nest, the parents were given large quantities of ants' eggs.
Its diet is similar to that of the Serin, but the mixture of seeds should also include the seeds of conifers.

CAPE CANARY, GREY-NECKED SERIN, *Serinus c. canicollis* (Swainson)
G. Graunackengirlitz; F. Serin du Cap; D. Kaapse Kanarie
DISTRIBUTION: Cape Province of South Africa.

DESCRIPTION: The forehead and the top of the head are golden yellow, turning to golden olive green towards the rear; the nape and sides of the neck are ash grey; the upper parts are golden green. The lores are dark grey, the sides of the head greyish golden yellow, the parotic regions grey, clouded with gold, and the cheeks and the neck brownish golden yellow. The lower parts are golden yellow at the front, and white at the rear, with yellow on the lower tail coverts. The primary wing coverts are black, the flight feathers black with yellow edging and the small wing coverts olive yellow. On the tail there is brown and brownish yellow, while beneath it is greenish yellow clouded with grey. The irides are brown, the beak the colour of grey horn and the feet brown. Length: 5 in. (13 cm). *Female*. Duller and more brownish, and plumage is streaked on the upper parts and greyish yellow-green on lower parts.

The specific variety of this Serin is found in a restricted area of Cape Province, but several subspecies live in the mountainous regions of Ethiopia and East Africa as far as Angola; the species seems to be completely absent from South Western Africa. These birds prefer to settle in the areas at the foot of mountain slopes where there are ample woodlands and bushes; in winter they also move to open country, orchards and cultivated fields, most often in a small mixed flock including Weaver Birds and other Fringillidae. During the day, the males perch in the top of trees singing their charming, somewhat high pitched song; in the evening, when thousands of these birds gather in trees to sleep, the sound of all their voices can be deafening. These nightly gatherings take place only outside the breeding season, for when this period approaches they form pairs, and each pair go their own way. The female then builds her isolated cup-shaped nest fairly high in a tree or a bush; it is built of fine vegetable fibres and blades of grass, the cup being lined with vegetable wool. It takes about two weeks to build. She then lays 3–4 greenish white eggs streaked and spotted with red-brown and purplish grey, on which she sits for 14 days, while the male feeds her on the nest. After a good two weeks, the young birds fly. These birds feed on various kinds of seed, which they prefer to seek in the semi-ripe state on wild and cultivated plants; during the nesting season they also take insects.

Cape Canary, *Serinus c. canicollis*

These birds were imported in large numbers for the first time in 1910 and since then there have been sporadic consignments. A fancier in Port Elizabeth, South Africa housed a small group of these birds in a large aviary, from which they could fly freely in the garden; they returned to the aviary each evening. When the time came for the females to build their nest, the pairs no longer returned, and never came back to the aviary.

GREY SINGING-FINCH, *Serinus leucopygia* (Sundevall)
G. Grauedelsänger; F. Chanteur d'Afrique; D. Grijze Edelzanger   (Pl. XXXVIII)

DISTRIBUTION: North-western and North-eastern Africa.
DESCRIPTION: Upper parts greyish brown, the light grey head having pale brown median lines; rump is white. The lower parts are grey, with white on the middle. The wings are dark brown with dirty white edging, irides brown and feet and beak are a pink horn colour. Length: 4 in. (10 cm). *Female*. has rather heavier streaks on the sides.

These small birds, with their sober plumage, are quite

Grey Singing-finch, *Serinus leucopygia*

common close to water. They can be seen in small flights both in bushes and in trees near settlements, but they also live in desert regions, where they can be found in tall palm trees. They are always on the move, and their butterfly-like flight is typical. The males sing their pretty high pitched song with great enthusiasm; it is reminiscent of the song of the Canary. They prefer to perch very high up to sing.

They are amongst the most frequently imported birds and are very popular with bird keepers. If there is the opportunity to form a true pair, they will breed in a large cage or in an aviary. They must be acclimatized in a cage and be given millet on the ear, linseed, niger, canary seed, poppy seed and rape. It is important to give them clean water every day for drinking and bathing. They also like green food such as chickweed or lettuce, and will accept a little soft food and soaked seeds. If several males are housed together, they will immediately begin to squabble, for they are quarrelsome birds which must be kept in pairs.

A pair will readily accept a basketwork or wooden nest box, which they will line with coconut fibres and unpicked hemp. The male will come and inspect the work, and if he is satisfied, he will encourage the female, flying busily round the nesting place and uttering his finest song. The female lays 3–4 eggs, on which she sits alone while the male feeds her on the nest. The eggs hatch after 13 days; the female feeds the young birds, but the male will also help her when they fly. The young birds leave the nest towards the age of three weeks and are quite independent in another 6–7 weeks.

The father will often pursue his young sons fiercely, sometimes even killing them. If they have bred in an aviary, the aggressiveness of the male is less of a nuisance; but he will always keep a close guard upon the nest and will chase any other birds in the aviary who come too close to it. Grey Singing finches adapt very well to our climate, and can spend the entire year in an outside aviary, so long as it is partially covered and has a good shelter.

YELLOW-RUMPED SERIN, *Serinus a. atrogularis*
(A. Smith)
G. Gelbbürzelgirlitz, Angola-Girlitz; F. Chanteur d'Afrique à croupion jaune; D. Geelstuit Edelzanger

DISTRIBUTION: Eritrea, Angola, Ethiopia

DESCRIPTION: Upper parts are greyish brown with black median lines. The forehead is brownish white; the rump is light yellow; the upper tail-coverts have yellowish black edging. There is also a white eyelid. Lower parts are fawn white; the chin and abdomen brownish black with whitish edgings to feathers. Length: 4½ in. (11·5 cm). The sexes are alike.

These birds were once imported in large numbers, and in recent years, they have begun to be imported again. Many subspecies live within a large area over which they are found in Africa; they show only slight variations in colour and feather pattern.

FAMILY: ESTRILDIDAE

SUBFAMILY: ESTRILDINAE

KEEPING SMALL TROPICAL FINCHES

These attractive birds are by far the most popular with foreign bird keepers. Scientific study has kept pace with this growing interest, and there have been repeated changes in their systematic classification. Almost all genera and a very large number of species are available to aviculture, and will be dealt with in this work. Although tropical finch-like birds are regularly sold by importers, pet-shops and breeders, it must always be remembered that they come from tropical countries. Anyone who decides to buy a pair or sets out to keep a few together in a cage or an aviary, so that they breed there, must realise that our climate is only suitable to a limited degree. The problem is not one of just trying to keep the birds alive in our climate, but to give the birds a home which satisfies their needs. Tropical birds are not used to temperatures of 10°C (50°F) and below, which are not good for their health. Only a few varieties come from areas where it can be very cold at night. If these are birds which sleep in their nest at night, it does not matter even if there are large variations in temperature. Thanks to the better nourishment that the birds enjoy in aviaries, where they are always surrounded by plenty, they are rather more tolerant, but if they always have to live 'below normal', it is bound to have a harmful influence on their powers of resistance and on that of their young.

Of course a certain amount of adaption has already taken place, and with some varieties it is already possible to speak of them as 'domesticated'. There are many vigorous birds which have been kept through the winter in unheated aviaries and only have to be brought indoors during periods of severe frost. Nothing suggests that their fertility has suffered from this, on the contrary, it often seems as though strains with a greater resistance have been produced.

The popularity of these birds is due above all to the fact they are not difficult to feed. Many species in nature live almost exclusively from unripe and ripe seeds, and the latter can always be obtained. And during the summer months anyone can gather unripe grasses and give them to the birds. It is harder to provide animal food for those birds who need it. It is all too easy to give a diet of seeds only, because it does not immediately seem inadequate for the birds. For some species it is in fact sufficient. But while there are a good many birds which raise their young on green foods and seeds, they all need varying amounts of insectiverous food.

Almost all tropical finches build nests which are covered over and a few lay their eggs in holes and need very little nesting material. The incubation period is from 12–16 days, and is influenced by all kinds of factors. Some birds sit continuously, while others occasionally let the eggs cool a little by leaving the nest, the weather conditions also play a part. Most young birds remain in the nest for about three weeks, and are then fed by their parents for a further period up to 14 days.

Housing Tropical Finches
Tropical finches can be housed in various ways, depending upon whether one wants to keep a single pair or several species together.

For a single pair a cage will do perfectly well. If you have a well-lit, draught-free place for the cage, it can consist of wire all round, like most fancy cages. Even with a single pair of small finches, the rule is that the largest cage is the best. It is obvious that these extremely lively birds need room to hop and fly, and the smaller cages have far too little space.

A cage should be not less than 24–28 in. (60–70 cm) long, and at least 16–18 in. (40–45 cm) in width and height. If the room is too small to allow for a cage of this size, it is better not to keep birds. For some birds a cage with a floor area of 16–18 in. (40–45 cm) square and a height of 28 in. (70 cm) can be just as good. Bird keepers are very inventive in this field, and when the aim is the welfare of the birds, something practical can naturally be worked out.

A number of species of tropical finches spend the night in a nest; this must be taken into account in arranging the cage and a place for a nest box must be provided high up in the cage. It is always best to attach drink and food boxes to the outside, where they cannot be fouled, and can be filled without having to reach into the cage. A quiet corner of the room, but one where there is sunlight, must be set aside for the birds, so that they are not always being disturbed. A quieter home can be made for them by covering one of the wire sides with hardboard. This principle has led to the so-called 'box-cage', in which only the front is wire. Since a cage of this kind still has to be placed beside a window to give the birds some sunlight, it cannot always be reconciled with keeping them in the living room, since the birds want to be seen by the owner. The box-cage is the ideal home for single breeding pairs. The nest box should be hung against the back wall and to give the birds the quiet they need.

An outside aviary for tropical finches must always be provided with a well-insulted inside aviary, which can be heated in winter, and is big enough to provide winter accommodation. Part of the outside aviary should be completely covered, while the wall most exposed to the wind needs to be protected with rush mats or plastic sheet. The sleeping quarters should have lighting connected to an automatic timer and dimmer, making it possible to lengthen the short winter days and shorten the long nights. The latter is the most important, and can be sufficient on its own. The great advantage of the morning light is that the birds that are sleeping in their nests start eating earlier. It is more difficult to regulate the evening light so that the birds have gone to their nests or sleeping places when the light goes out. The light should never be turned out suddenly, because the birds fly round in the dark, and can easily hurt themselves. An automatic dimmer lowers the light gradually.

The formation of true pairs is not always particularly easy as some species show no outward distinctions of sex and a good deal of patience is usually needed. The partners may not always be suited to each other but it is not often possible to give the birds a free choice of mates. The nesting places must be numerous and of various kinds, and suited to the birds. In order to keep birds successfully, it is necessary for the owner to become acquainted with the demands that they are going to make. When the different species are discussed, this will be dealt with as necessary.

Genus: Estrilda

BLACK-TAILED LAVENDER FINCH, *Estrilda perreini* Vieillot
G. Schwarzschwanzschönbürzel; F. Astrild de Perrein; D. Blauwgrijs-Zwartstaartje

DISTRIBUTION: Angola to South-East Africa.
DESCRIPTION: The Black-tailed Lavender Finch is very similar in appearance to the common Lavender Finch *E. caerulescens* and may often be confused with it. It is darker grey and has a black patch on chin. Upper tail feathers are mostly darker red than those of *E. caerulescens*, whilst the tail is black and the under tail coverts grey-black. Length: about 4¼ in. (11 cm).

Black-tailed Lavender Finch, *Estrilda perreini*

The behaviour of this species is very similar to that of its close relative but our knowledge of its natural life is somewhat limited and there is no detailed record of its behaviour in the mating season or how it rears its young. Its call is a very soft 'Tsiu', whilst its song consists of a soft, long-drawn-out almost melancholy 'dee-ee-dew-ew'. This very active bird whose movements remind one of the titmice is best kept in an aviary where it can get adequate exercise. It associates well with most other species of its own size and disposition. In addition to the usual seed mixture the birds like a daily ration of soft food and live insects as well as greenstuff.

DUFRESNE'S WAXBILL, *Estrilda m. melanotis* (Temminck)
G. Schwarzbackchen; F. Astrild de Dufresne, Joue-noir; D. Dufresnes Astrild (Zwartbekje)

DISTRIBUTION: South and south-east Africa.
DESCRIPTION: Top of head bluish-grey; back and wings olive-green with a fine wavy pattern. Rump and upper tail coverts red; there is black on tail, lores, sides of head and cheeks. Breast light grey, centre of abdomen yellow-ochre, and sides grey-green. Upper mandible black, and lower red; feet and legs black and eyes brown. Length: 4 in. (10 cm). *Female.* Has no black on head.
These birds are very often imported, but many bird keepers have them in their stocks. They feed on millet sprays, mixed

Dufresne's Waxbill, *Estrilda m. melanotis*

millet seeds and the seeds of various grasses. In 1934, Miss Elsie Robinson of England succeeded in raising four young birds, the offspring of a single pair.

The account (*Avicultural Magazine* (4), Vol. 11, No. 10, p. 19) illustrates the well-known fact that a young beginner can often have birds that breed successfully, whereas experienced breeders do not. In fact everything depends upon one's aptitude for keeping and breeding birds.

Dufresne's Waxbill is peaceable and quiet. A pair is more spectacular if it is housed in a large cage, rather than in a large aviary with numerous other birds. The successful breeding mentioned above was obtained in an aviary which the pair shared with two pairs of Bicheno Finches, who also raised four young.

YELLOW-BELLIED WAXBILL, *Estrilda melanotis quartinia* (Bonaparte)

G. Abessinische Grünastrild; F. Astrild vert; D. Groene astrild   (Pl. XXV)

DISTRIBUTION: Ethiopia.

DESCRIPTION: Top of head and nape of neck greyish blue; back and wings olive-green; tail black, with red on upper tail coverts and rump; chin, neck and breast greyish white; abdomen yellow-ochre. Upper mandible black, and the lower mandible red. Length: 3¾ in. (9 cm). *Female.* Colouring a little less bright. This is one of the most charming of the Estrildinae; it is friendly and does not fly away when the

Yellow-bellied Waxbill, *Estrilda melanotis quartinia*

owner goes into the aviary. Both sexes construct the open round nest in a thick bush, using blades of grass, coconut fibre and small feathers. The female lays 4 eggs, which hatch in 14 days. The parents cram their young with small insects and ants' eggs for the first week; then they also feed with millet sprays both dry and soaked. They like fruit and other small flies. When they are 21 days old the young leave the nest; they look like their parents, but their beak is blackish-grey and their feet grey.

These birds must be kept in a heated aviary in the winter. During the last few years, they have quite often been imported, and have also been bred in captivity a number of times.

DISTRIBUTION: West and central Africa.

DESCRIPTION: *Male* and *female* have dark bluish-grey heads; back and wings rosy-brown; rump and upper tail coverts red; tail black; there is orange-red on lores and sides of head, this colour becoming almost red round eyes. Lower body bluish grey, with ochre-yellow in centre of abdomen. Iris

ORANGE-CHEEKED WAXBILL, *Estrilda melpoda* (Vieillot)

G. Orangebackchen; F. Bengali a Joues Oranges, Joue-Orange; D. Orangekaakje   (Pl. XXV)

brown, beak red and feet and legs brown. Length: 4 in. (10 cm).

In the wild state, these birds live near water, flitting among the tall reeds and picking up seeds from the ground. The pair live in isolation during the nesting period; the rest of the year these birds gather in large groups. They nest during the rainy season. The male carries out a hopping display, swinging his tail from side to side, he also sings in a loud voice and carries a blade of brass in his beak, which he points upwards. The nest, quite large, bottle-shaped and lined with fine grass and built on the ground, amongst the grass and wild plants.

Sometimes there is also a sleeping nest attached to the other. The female builds, but the male brings the material, 5 or 6 eggs are laid, which hatch after 12 days. The young leave the nest after about 21 days, but return in the evening for the first few days, spending the night under their parents supervision. Their beak and legs are black, and the marks on

Orange-cheeked Waxbill, *Estrilda melpoda*

their cheeks are scarcely visible; their colour develops at the age of six weeks.

The pair are very attached to each other, but sometimes two females may caress each other, which makes sexing difficult. The display of the male has to be seen and his song heard for the sex to be certain.

These birds nest quite readily in a large planted aviary, so long as the building materials are available: principally fine blades of grass. They are very shy during the nesting period and abandon the nest at the least disturbance. They feed on Penicum millet, millet sprays granised millets, poppy seeds, grass seeds, and germinated grain, and take a good deal of green food when breeding; ants eggs, fruit flies and insectivorous are indispensable during this period. Several crossings have been noted, e.g. with the St. Helena Waxbill and with the Red-billed Fire-finch.

SUNDEVALL'S WAXBILL, CRIMSON-WINGED WAXBILL, *Estrilda rhodopyga* (Sundevall)

G. Zügelastrild; F. Astrild à croupion rouge; D. Teugelastrild   (Pl. XXV)

DISTRIBUTION: North-eastern and east Africa, Ethiopia.

DESCRIPTION: Both sexes upper body fawn-brown with fine wavy pattern; crown grey; rump and upper tail coverts wine red. Lores red, wings brown with red edges, cheeks and throat white. Lower body pale brownish yellow with fine brown wavy lines. The same pattern in dark brown adorns lower tail coverts, with a pink sheen. Iris brown, beak black with a little red on each side, and at base, and feet and legs brown. Length: 4¼ in. (10·5 cm). In the male, lower tail coverts are darker.

These birds breed rather more easily than their close relations, the Grey Waxbill. They feed largely on millet

Sundevall's Waxbill, *Estrilda rhodopyga*

seeds, and show a preference for dry and germinated grass seeds. The young are crammed with small seeds, small meal worms and ants' eggs. They must have plenty of green food. The pair is shy during the breeding period and the nest is always built in a well hidden place, sometimes accepting a nest box.

Besides crossings with the Grey Waxbill, there have also been hybrids with the Orange-cheeked Waxbill and with the St. Helena Waxbill. For success in breeding, they must be housed in a large well planted aviary.

RED-EARED WAXBILL, GREY WAXBILL, COMMON WAXBILL, *Estrilda t. troglodytes* (Lichtenstein)

G. Grauastrild; F. Astrild cendré, Astrild ordinaire Bec de corail; D. Napoleonnetje   (Pl. XXV)

DISTRIBUTION: Arid steppe of north-east and west Africa.
DESCRIPTION: Upper body greyish-brown with a fine transverse pattern. Tail and upper tail coverts black, outer tail feathers having white fringes. Lower body light grey, turning to pink towards vent, while centre of abdomen is pink. Sides of head greyish white, with red on lores, forming a line which runs across the eye. Beak red, iris red-brown and feet and legs brown. Length: 3¼ in (9 cm).

Red-eared Waxbill *Estrilda t. troglodytes*

These very popular little waxbills live for the most part in regions where there is high grass, in marshy areas, or in the drier hills, but always close to water. They nest in the rainy season, and build their large, domed nest, which includes a sleeping nest amongst the grass or in a thorny bush.

Red-eared Waxbills are imported in large numbers and acclimatisation does not present any problem; these birds show considerable resistance, their plumage always being thick and firm. They are particularly difficult to sex. The deeper pink of the abdomen suggests a male; the display and song are quiet, and they can be kept either with birds of the same species or with other small exotic birds. By marking different specimens with split rings in different colours, it is easy to distinguish the pairs which form and begin to build

a nest. The males carry out their display with a blade of grass in their beak. At this point, unmated birds can be removed. The aviary should be well planted, and have plenty of clumps of tall grass, where the birds prefer to best; it is only with difficulty that they will tolerate a nesting box. If the planting also includes box, they build an open nest using blades of grass, coconut fibres, pieces of bark and feathers. Male and female build the nest together, and they usually add a sleeping nest. Three–six eggs are laid, the male and the female taking turns in incubating for 11 days and the young leave the nest at the age of about 20 days.

Although the Grey Waxbill feeds largely on various kinds of small millet, and canary seed they especially like mealworms, ants' eggs and green food. If an attempt is made to breed, the pair must be housed in a well planted aviary, where there are plenty of small insects, for the young are fed entirely upon live food for the first two weeks. Sometimes some birds accept egg and insectivorous foods. They should certainly be offered germinated seeds, pre-soaked ants' eggs, small mealworms and flies.

Crossings have been obtained with several other Estrildae, including the Sundevall's Waxbill, *Estrilda rhodopyga*, the St. Helena Waxbill, *Estrilda astrild*, the Orange-cheeked Waxbill, *Estrilda melpoda*, the Black-bellied Fire-finch, *Lagonosticta senegala*, the Cordon Bleu, *Granatina bengala*, the Golden-breasted Waxbill, *Estrilda subflava*, the Black-headed Waxbill, *Estrilda atricapilla* and Sidney Waxbill *Aegintha temporalis* the male hybrid derived from the Grey Waxbill and the Orange-cheeked Waxbill seems to be fertile. We have also found a mention of a crossing with the African Silverbill *Euodice malabarica cantans*, and even with the wild canary, *Serinus canarius* (in 1953, in Bloemfontein Zoo). The Grey Waxbill is one of the most hardy of small exotic birds, but in winter it should be housed in a lightly heated aviary.

ST· HELENA WAXBILL, RED-BELLIED WAXBILL, *Estrilda astrild* (Linnaeus)

G. Wellenastrild, Helenafasänchen; F. Astrild ondulé, Astrild de Ste Hélène; D. Sint Helena-Fazantje

(Pl. XXV)

DISTRIBUTION: South Africa.
DESCRIPTION: Both male and female have the same fawn-grey plumage on upper part with a little pink on rump and upper tail coverts, the whole body being marked with a fine wavy pattern. Tail dark grey-brown. The red lores continue in a line which goes beyond eyes, sides of head and neck greyish-white. Lower body light grey-brown with a fine wavy pattern, touched with a very delicate pink; middle of abdomen is intensely pink in male, and a paler pink in female. Beak red, iris brown, feet and legs brown. Length: 4¼ in (11 cm.)
SUBSPECIES: Eighteen subspecies have been described. They live in different regions, but show only slight variations in depth and area of colourings. The range and distribution of this species extends from tropical west coast across centre of Africa as far as east coast and Cape Province.

These charming little birds have been found in European collections since the second half of the last century. In the wild, they live in regions rich in grass, usually close to water. They look mainly on the ground for their food, consisting of various grass seeds, and also small insects, including flying ants. The round nest with tunnel entrance is built on the ground amongst the tall grass, or very low in a thick thorny bush. These nests have often been found to contain the eggs of the Pintailed Whydah, *Vidua macroura*, which is almost exclusively a parasite on the nests of these waxbills.

The song is insignificant and is composed of twittering sounds uttered in flight; the male sings the most vigorously.

These birds are regularly imported in small numbers and are

St. Helena Waxbill, *Estrilda astrild*

quite expensive. They are among the most hardy of the wax-bills and adapt well to captivity, quite often nesting. Breeding will not succeed if they are not given living food, such as ants' eggs, mealworms, mud worms and fruit flies, grass seeds in the ear are much appreciated. To encourage them to nest, they must be housed in a large well-planted aviary, where they can find a thick bush to construct their nest. Both male and female build, but the female lines the nest. Both parents sit, changing every two hours and spending the night together on the nest. The 4–6 eggs hatch after 11 days, and the young take flight after 15 days. They then resemble their parents, but their beak is black and they have no red on the lores. The colour comes at the age of two months, and at this moment they must be separated from their parents. Duting the nesting period, the birds should not be disturbed nor the nest examined, for the parents may abandon the young.

BLACK-CROWNED WAXBILL, *Estrilda nonnula* (Hartlaub)

G. Nonneastrild, Weissbrüstiger Kappenastrild; F. Astrild Nonnette, A Cape Noire; D. Non-Astrild

DISTRIBUTION: The mountainous regions of tropical North Africa.
DESCRIPTION: Top of head as far as lores black; black grey with a fine transverse pattern; rump and upper tail coverts red; tail black. Lower body and side of head white, but lower abdomen more greyish in colour. Sides, hidden by wings, red.

Black-crowned Waxbill, *Estrilda nonnula*

Black beak has red marks on sides, feet and lets black and iris brown. Length: 4¼ in (11 cm). *Female*. Distinguished by a more brownish back and dirty white on front of abdomen; while red on sides is less extensive.
These birds, which are very rarely imported, live in large groups, generally close to settlements, in coffee plantations or near cultivated fields. The pairs also nest close to each other. The nest constructed with blades of grass has a tunnel entry, is placed very low in bushes or trees, often at the height of about 39 in. (1 metre). The sleeping nests are built separately. Mrs. Wharton-Tigar, of England, obtained some of these birds from Cameroons in 1935, and was the first to succeed in breeding them. Details of her breeding report are given in the *Avicultural Magazine* (5), Vol. 1, pp. 323–5.

BLACK-CAPPED WAXBILL, BLACK-HEADED WAXBILL, *Estrilda a. atricapilla* (J. and E. Verreaux)

G. Schwarzköpfchen, Kappenastrild; F. Astrild a Tête Noir; D. Zwartkopje, Zwartkop-Astrild

DISTRIBUTION: Tropical central Africa.
DESCRIPTION: Resembles the Black-crowned Waxbill *Estrilda nonnula*, but throat and lower body are ash-grey, while red on flanks is more extensive and not completely hidden by wings. Rump red and tail and upper tail coverts black. Beak black, with a little red at base of lower mandible. Length: 4 in. (10 cm).
SUBSPECIES: The subspecies *Estrilda a. graueri*, which lives in Zaire, Uganda and Kenya, has white on throat and sides of head.
The birds live in open forests, in grassy clearings, and near plantations and bamboo woods. They form large flocks and nest in trees or in the top of bushes. The nest is bottle-shaped and there is often a sleeping nest as well. Four or 5 eggs are laid. These birds have been found sleeping in nests left by Weavers.

Black-capped Waxbill, *Estrilda a. atricapilla*

The first importation in England and Germany was in 1874, when Dr. Russ succeeded in crossing this waxbill with a female Grey Waxbill. There was another importation in 1935, and shortly afterwards breeding succeeded.
It is quite difficult to acclimatise these birds, which at first refuse all food except grass seeds, which they eat in the wild state. Several weeks pass before they acquire the taste for millets and canary seeds. However, when they have adapted to the new food, they are very hardy.

BLACK-CHEEKED WAXBILL, *Estrilda e. erythronotus* (Vieillot)

G. Elfenastrild, Rotrückenastrild; F Astrild a Moustaches Noires; D. Elfenastrild   (Pl. XXVIII)

DISTRIBUTION: South-western and southern Africa.
DESCRIPTION: Upper body ash-grey with a fine transverse pattern; back shaded red; upper tail coverts and rump red and tail black. Chin and front of head black, top of head grey. Lower body grey, with black in middle of abdomen and red on sides; lower tail coverts black. Iris red-brown, beak bluish-black and feet and legs black. Length: 4¾ in (13 cm).

Male and female have same plumage, but abdomen of female is more greyish.

SUBSPECIES: Five subspecies have been identified. They live in the regions bordering on East Africa as far as the south of Ethiopia.

These birds live in arid regions, where there are still thickly leaved trees and bushes. They like to hide in vegetation near the ground, looking for insects and seeds. They can be observed in dozens outside the nesting period, but while they are breeding, the pairs live in isolation. The nest is built in trees at a height of 12–25 ft (4–8 m); it is quite large bottle-shaped and has a tunnel-shaped entry. Sometimes the nest is surrounded by little sleeping nests, which also have a tunnel entry. Four to 6 eggs are laid. The Black-cheeked Waxbill is one of the 'difficult' species, and its acclimatisation is particularly difficult. These birds do not seem to succeed in cages, even if they are very large; on the other hand, there are risks in putting them in an aviary, unless the weather is very mild. A covered aviary, connected with a good shelter, is most suitable for these very lively specimens; the aviary should be well planted, because they like to hide. Their food should consist of germinated seeds, green food, insectivorous food, fresh ants' eggs and mealworms; ants' eggs are essential.

When the long acclimatisation period has passed, these wax-bills are as hardy as other small exotic birds. Successful breeding is rare, the parents often abandon the young, for lack of adequate breeding food. The first few days after hatching, the parents like to gather greenfly, and thereafter ants' eggs, mealworms and insectivorous food. Professor Steiner of Zurich gave some young Black-cheeked Waxbills to a pair of Java Sparrows, who raised two of them.

These birds should spend the winter indoors in a large cage or aviary which they can share with other unaggressive species. Their behaviour is similar to that of the Lavender Finch.

LAVENDER FINCH, *Estrilda caerulescens* (Vieillot)
G. Schöhbürzel, Blaugraues Rotschwänzchen; F. Astrild Queue de Vinaigre, Astrild Lavande, Gris-bleu; D. Blauwgrijs Roodstartje (Pl. XXVIII)
DISTRIBUTION: Tropical West Africa.
DESCRIPTION: General colour bluish-grey, with red on rump, upper tail coverts and central tail feathers. Lores and beak black, but base of beak has a red mark. Feet and legs black, iris brown. There are a few white dots on the base of flanks. Length: 4¼ in. (11 cm).
These birds prefer to live in grassy regions on edges of woods or near scrub. They are not shy and can often be seen in the company of Cordon Bleus and Grey Waxbills, picking up insects and seeds from the ground. The Lavender Finch needs more animal food than other waxbills; if they do not have it, they die soon after they are imported. With the aid of ants' eggs and mealworms they can gradually be acclimatised and taught little by little to eat other small seeds. Once

Lavender Finch, *Estrilda caerulescens*

they have been well adapted, they are hardy and need the same diet as the other species of waxbills. They make a charming sight in a large cage but if one wishes to attempt to breed, they need an aviary. They are difficult to sex; the male usually has darker plumage, with more intense red on lower tail coverts, but the song of the male is a better indication. As the males generally fight, only a single pair should be kept in each aviary which they can share with other small exotic birds.

These birds construct an open round nest mostly with a tunnel entry, in bushes in the aviary, sometimes they will use a nest box. The material used consists of blades of grass and coconut fibres, the inside is lined with a very fine grass and feathers. Four eggs are laid, on which the parents take turn to sit. They do not tolerate interference with the nest and sit for 12 days. If the breeding is to be brought to a successful conclusion, the birds need greenfly and other small insects; without this food, they will throw the young out. Ants' eggs can also be used.

The Marquis of Tavistock has made numerous experiments with various species of Estrildinae, which lived at liberty in the neighbourhood of aviaries. In winter the birds came out during the day and went into the shelter at night. Lavender Finches, living in controlled freedom in this way, raised young every year.

FAWN-BREASTED WAXBILL, *Estrilda paludicola* Heuglin
G. Sumpfastrild; F. Astrild de marais; D. Moerasastrild
DISTRIBUTION: Central tropical Africa.
DESCRIPTION: This bird looks very much like its close relative the Orange-cheeked Waxbill, *E. melpoda* but is readily distinguished by the absence of orange patches on cheeks. Depending on the race, sides of head are light grey, whitish

Fawn-breasted Waxbill, *Estrilda paludicola*

or yellowish. Iris red brown and beak red. Upper part of head brown to grey, back and wings brown, tail brownish-black and underparts ochre yellow to grey white, flanks being reddish pink. Length: 4–4¼ in. (10–11 cm). There are several races, differing only slightly in depth of colouring.

Its behaviour is very similar to that of the related Orange-cheeked Waxbill but pairs are perhaps not quite so affectionate and do not preen each other so often. They are good climbers and fly well. In the natural state they live in seed beds and a few clumps of reeds in the aviary are an advantage as they like to scramble up and down the stems. They call 'Veb-veeb-veb' both on the ground and when in flight, repeating it rapidly and often. Mating mostly takes place on the bough of a tree, but now and again on the ground. The male's display dance consists of jumping up and down on the perch, whilst it continually calls 'Teck-teck-teck' but unlike other grey waxbills it does not hold a blade of grass in its beak at the same time. Most grey waxbills make their nests among the reeds on the ground or just above and is made in the form of a ball with a tube-like entrance. In an aviary they will sometimes choose a nest box in which they will construct a dome-shaped nest which, however, will lack the entrance tube. The young are as difficult to rear as the Orange-cheeked waxbill. Among others Schertenleib of Switzerland was successful in breeding them in a thickly-planted open aviary.

They prefer small seeds, dry or sprouted, especially panicum millet and millet sprays. They also greatly appreciate fresh seeding grasses and seeding chickweed and small live insects and most forms of green foods.

They may be successfully kept in a cage where they will live contentedly for some years but if it is the intention to breed these, or any of the other waxbills, it is essential to provide them with a large, well planted aviary where they may find a natural supply of tiny insects in addition to the food supplied.

Genus: Lagonosticta

BLACK-THROATED FIRE-FINCH, MASKED WAXBILL, *Lagonosticta l. larvata* (Rüppell)

G. Larvenastrild; F. Amaranthe Masquée d'Abyssinie; D. Zwartkeel-Vuurvink, Zwartmasker-Vuurvink

DISTRIBUTION: Ethiopia.

DESCRIPTION: Upper parts brownish-grey, shading towards red on top of head and wing coverts; sides of head black. Under parts winey-red, but middle of abdomen as far as lower tail coverts black. Iris brown, beak blackish-grey and feet and legs grey. Length: 4¼ in. (11 cm). Male distinguished by black mask.

SUBSPECIES: Other subspecies have been described, including *Lagonosticta l. nigricollis*, Black-masked Waxbill and *Lagonosticta l. vinacea*, the Vinaceous Waxbill. These birds live in bamboo forests and in the grass along water-

Black-throated Fire-finch, *Lagonosticta l. larvata*

courses, where they find bushes to build their nests. They are shy and silent, and feed on insects and seeds.

As it is easy to confuse the Black-throated Fire-finch with the Vinaceous Waxbill, it is not certain whether the first subspecies has yet been imported. This bird would no doubt take a long time to acclimatise. It would be necessary to give them a temperature of at least 68°F (20°C), to get them fresh ants' eggs, boiled and cut mealworms, Senegal millet and fresh seeding heads of various grass seeds. It would be interesting to try and get them used to insectivorous food. Often, the acclimatisation of waxbills is very easy, and in contrast this has given the Fire-finches the reputation of being delicate.

VINACEOUS FIRE-FINCH, VINACEOUS WAXBILL, *Lagonosticta larvata vinacea* Hartlaub

G. Weinroter Amarant; F. Amaranthe Vineuse, Bengali Vineux; D. Wijnrode Amarant (Pl. XXVIII)

DISTRIBUTION: Senegal.

DESCRIPTION: Sides of head and a narrow band on forehead black. Top of head grey; back and wing coverts vinaceous reddish-grey; upper tail coverts red; tail winy-red and black and under parts winy-red, with little white dots; and under

tail coverts black. Iris brown with a bluish orbital ring; beak grey with black point; and feet and legs grey. *Female.* No black on head; winy-red is replaced by brown or by greyish-yellow on front of abdomen. Length: 4¼ in. (11 cm). (11 cm).

Batches of birds occasionally include a number of specimens of this subspecies. They can be kept together with other species of the Estrildae family. They must be carefully acclimatised, but once they have adapted themselves, they

Vinaceous Fire-finch, *Lagonosticta larvata vinacea*

are robust, with a good colour, and breed quite well in a large planted aviary, so long as they are given suitable food. Although they often build a free-standing nest in a thick bush, they sometimes accept a nest-box, provided with a little hay. The round nest is build from coconut fibres and blades of grass. Several attempts to breed them have succeeded. Details are given in a report by Mrs. Wharton-Tigar, in England, which appears in the *Avicultural Magazine*, (4) Vol. 11, 1933, pp. 437–9.

'The young resemble their mother, but the males soon acquire the black mask. The young birds have their full colour towards the age of three months. It is very improbable that these birds would reproduce in a cage, where it would not be possible to provide sufficient live food. In a planted aviary they would find not only the food given to them but also ample supplies of spiders, ants, small flies and greenfly, which are indispensable during the first ten days of the young birds' life.'

BLACK-BELLIED FIRE-FINCH, *Lagonosticta r. rara* (Antonori)

F. Sénégali à ventre noire; D. Zwartbuik-Vuurvink, Zeldzame Vuurvink (Pl. XXVIII)

DISTRIBUTION: Sierra Leone, Zaire, Cameroon.

DESCRIPTION: Upper body wine-red, with winy-red on rump, upper tail coverts and lores; brown wings are shaded with winy-red and tail black. Lower body paler winy-red, and middle of abdomen, from the base of breast as far as lower tail coverts black. Iris brown with grey circle round them; beak black, with red on sides of lower mandible, feet and legs greyish-brown. Length: 4¼ in. (11 cm). *Female.* Has brownish-grey back, with blackish-brown in centre of abdomen and black on lower tail coverts.

SUBSPECIES: A second subspecies, *Lagonosticta r. forbesi*, lives in Nigeria. Outside the breeding period these birds live in small flocks close to settlements, picking up insects and seeds from the ground. They build their nest low in bushes or trees, or even on the roof of huts. Three or 4 eggs are laid. The Black-bellied Fire-finch is imported only occasionally;

Black-bellied Fire-finch, *Lagonosticta r. rara*

these birds are delicate when they arrive and must be carefully acclimatised; the temperature of the environment is of great importance. This species, like the other fire-finches and waxbills must be housed in a temperature of at least 68°F (20°C); they cannot be kept in an outside aviary in the winter, even if it has a shelter. They should be given greenfly, fresh ants' eggs, mealworms and chickweed, as well as millet sprays and grass seeds; on this diet, the birds will soon pass the danger point and will also get used to accepting insectivorous food. They can be kept in a large cage, but will not breed there. They will live in peace with waxbills, but they are often aggressive towards other fire-finches.

They spend a great deal of time on the ground, and at the least sign of danger hide in the vegetation. That is why they should have low, thick planted bushes, while the ground in the aviary should also include a grassed section, since they like to build their nest amongst grass. The round nest is lined with feathers inside.

For breeding to succeed, the pair should be housed on their own in a separate aviary. All the insects which are indispensable for breeding the young must be obtainable there. Outside the breeding period, they are content with various kinds of millet and grass seed, but refuse this diet during the breeding period, when it is replaced with ants' eggs, flying ants, mealworms and greenfly. They should also be made accustomed to an insectivorous food. They are very shy birds, and do not tolerate the nest being examined. Sir Richard Cotterell, of England, succeeded with two consecutive broods from a single pair in 1961. The birds were by themselves in a planted aviary with a grass floor. The female began to lay at the end of July, and 4 young flew on 21st August. At the beginning of September, the pair began a new brood, and 3 young left the nest on 1st October. Ants' eggs were no longer available, and they could not be given any other insects apart from the mealworms. Some bird fanciers have reported that the parents ejected the young from the nest; this behaviour is always a consequence of an inadequate diet when breeding.

BLUE-BILLED FIRE-FINCH, DARK FIRE-FINCH, BLACK-VENTED CRIMSON FIRE-FINCH, *Lagonosticta r. rubricata*(Lichtenstein) (Pl. XXVIII)
G. Dunkelroter Amarant; F. Amaranthe Foncée, Sénégali à bec bleu; D. Donkerrode Vuurvink
DISTRIBUTION: Northern Transvaal, Zululand, Natal.
DESCRIPTION: Upper body brownish-grey with red shading; there is red on lores, cheeks and eyebrows; and ear region is

dark red. Wings brown; rump and lower tail coverts an intense red; tail and lower tail coverts black. Under parts pinkish-red; sides of breast have small white dots; centre of abdomen brownish-black. Iris red, beak blackish-blue, and base of lower mandible tends faintly towards red. *Female*. Has red on lores, while her lower body is a pink to yellowish-brown. Length: 4¼ in. (11 cm).
SUBSPECIES: There are 9 subspecies distributed across the centre of Africa; they are distinguished by slight variations, and are imported from time to time with other fire-finches. In general, this species avoids settlements, preferring to settle in regions which are rich in grass and thick bushes. The birds can be seen on the ground, looking for seeds and insects, but as soon as the slightest alarm occurs they hide beneath the vegetation. They have the habit of swinging their tail rapidly from side to side. The male has a very pleasant varied and melodious song. The round nest is built in a tuft of grass or very low, lower than 3–4½ ft (1·5 m) in a thick bush, and has a side entrance hidden by a few blades of grass which protrude from the structure. Three to 5 eggs are laid.

Blue-billed Fire-finch, *Lagonosticta r. rubricata*

It is probable that these birds occurred in batches sent from Africa, but they were considered as ordinary fire-finches rather larger than usual, and there is no mention of them in the literature. Like the other fire-finches, they need to be kept very warm while they are acclimatising. During this period they should be given greenfly, ants' eggs and mealworms, as well as millet on the ear. It is a good thing to boil the mealworms and cut them in small pieces. It is best to keep them with others of the Estrildinae family. They are more suitable for a cage.

Successful breeding has taken place, the young were raised almost exclusively on a live diet. The Blue-billed Fire-finch prefers to build an open nest in a thick bush, but some pairs have accepted a nest-box. Male and female take turns to sit, the male remaining largely on the nest during the day.

They have an alarm call, which is similar to that of the Cordon Bleu, particularly when their nest is approached. The call is repeated long after all danger has passed. The place where these birds spend the winter should be heated.

JAMESON'S FIRE-FINCH, ABYSSINIAN FIRE-FINCH, *Lagonosticta r. rhodopareia* (Heuglin)
G. Rosenamarant, Jameson's Amarant; F. Amaranthe de Jameson; D. Jamesons Vuurvink, Rose Vuurvink
DISTRIBUTION: Ethiopia.
DESCRIPTION: *Male*. Similar to the Blue-billed Fire-finch, *Lagonosticta r. rubricata*, which is often confused with it. Lores and side of forehead pinkish-red; top of head and nape of neck brownish-grey; back fawn-brown; cheeks and lower parts brighter red. *Female*. Similar, but colours are very slightly less vivid. In both sexes the upper part of flanks have a few white dots. Iris brown, with a pink circle

around them; beak bluish-grey with a black tip, and feet an legs reddish-grey. Length: 4¼ in. (11 cm).

SUBSPECIES: The subspecies, *Lagonosticta r. ansorgei*, is found in Angola, while the true Jameson's Fire-finch, *Lagonosticta r. jamesoni*, in which the upper body is strongly pink shaded, inhabits a region ranging from Kenya as far as Transvaal and Zululand.

Jameson's Fire-finch has the same habits as the Blue-billed Fire-finch. It also lives in arid grassland where there are thorny bushes, but it can be found as well on the banks of water-courses, generally in pairs. It feeds on insects and seeds, and constructs its nest low in a thick bush. If they are not provided with a suitable bush in an aviary, they are sometimes content with a nest-box.

Unlike the other fire-finches, this species seems to have less need of live insects. According to a report in the *Avicultural Magazine*, (5) Vol. 1, 1936, pp. 50–1 by Mr. F. Johnson, of England, who supplied ants' eggs and germinated seed during the breeding period, the ants' eggs were never touched and the youngsters were fed entirely on soaked seed. However, other breeders say that live food is absolutely indispensable and that the parents often throw their young on to the ground because they lack this food. Mr. Johnson's birds, however, had access to a planted outside aviary, so that we can assume that they found other insects there.

Jameson's Fire-finch, *Lagonosticta r. rhodopareia*

To have any chance of success, it is necessary to house the pair alone in an aviary with bushes and grass. The two sexes take turns to sit and they seem to tolerate the examination of the nest. The female lays 3 or 4 eggs, which hatch after 12 days, the young leave the nest at the age of 19 days. Young males can quite soon be recognised, because of the bright pink which lightens their brownish-grey back (Jameson's Fire-finch).

As has already been said of other fire-finches, great care must be taken with their acclimatisation. The bird keeper who has an outside flighted aviary which catches the full sunlight will do best. In the shaded part of the aviary there should be a feeding dish near a heating lamp; the birds will be glad of the heat when they feel the need of it, while the space that they have at their disposal will help to improve their condition; and they will also find plenty of insects.

Like other fire-finches, these birds should spend the winter in a heated aviary.

FIRE-FINCH, RED-BILLED FIRE-FINCH, COMMON FIRE-FINCH, *Lagonosticta s. senegala* (Linnaeus)

G. Amarant, Kleiner Amarant, Senegalamarant; F. Amaranthe Ordinaire, Sénégali Rouge; D. (Gewone) Vuurvink

DISTRIBUTION: Senegal, Gambia.

DESCRIPTION: *Male.* Head pinkish-red; nape of neck and back are brown shaded with red; rump and upper tail coverts red; and tail shows black and red. Lower body red,

changing to greyish-brown towards rear; and there are a number of white dots on sides of breast. *Female.* Back is more brownish and lower body yellowish-grey. Length: 4 in. (10 cm). Beak red with black on sides; iris red with a light circle around them; feet and legs flesh-coloured.

SUBSPECIES: Eight other subspecies, mostly displaying only slight differences in colour, are found throughout the main regions of central and southern Africa.

In all the regions of Africa where common fire-finches are found, they live in small groups in the immediate neighbourhood of settlements. They like to settle in grassy regions with thick brushwood, where they can take refuge when danger threatens them. They feed principally upon grass seeds and small insects.

Fire-finch, *Lagonostica s. senegala*

Outside the breeding period, large flocks often wander towards regions where they are normally not found; they also form mixed flocks with other species. The nest is found in high grass, low down in a bush or even under the roof of buildings. The 3 or 4 eggs hatch after 11–12 days, and the young leave the nest towards the 18th day. The Combassou, *Hypochera chalybeata*, is a nesting parasite, using almost exclusively the nests of these fire-finches. The female combassou lays her egg amongst those of the fire-finches while the latter is on the nest.

The females seem to be more delicate than the males and are only rarely found in shipments. Acclimatisation must be carried out with great care: plenty of warmth and flying room are indispensable during this critical period. The young fire-finches resemble the female, but the white dots on the sides of the breast are totally lacking. When these birds have been carefully acclimatised, they can live for several years in an aviary, so long as they are housed in a heated aviary in the winter.

These fire-finches will live together with other birds of the same size in large well planted aviaries. They become tame, and feed largely on millet sprays and panicum millet, ears of grass, ants' eggs and mealworms, and insectivorous foods are appreciated as supplements.

A pair will often show an inclination to breed, sometimes choosing a nest-box or constructing a fairly loose nest from blades of grass, coconut fibres and mosses; the inside cup is lined with soft material: hairs, feathers, etc. The 4 eggs hatch after 12 days, the parents sitting in turn. The breeding diet consists of ants' eggs, mealworms and insectivorous food, as well as germinated seeds. If all these forms of food are available, the parents will mostly raise their young, and often start a second brood about 10 days after the first has flown. Usually, the young start to fly at the age of 18 days. Unlike many other small exotic birds, the young fire-finches do not return to their nest at night, which may be harmful to them in bad weather. That is why at least part of the roof of the aviary should be covered, so that the young do not get wet.

The plumage of the young bird is light greyish-brown with a rump and a black back and tail. Moulting begins towards the age of 6 weeks and the young are soon similar to the parents.

Many crossings have been obtained, amongst others with the Red Avadevat, *Amandava amandava*, the Lavender Waxbill, the Orange-cheeked Waxbill, *E. melpoda*, the Grey Waxbill, *E. troglodytes*, and the Bar-breasted Fire-finch, *Lagonosticta rufopicta*.

BAR-BREASTED FIRE-FINCH, *Lagonosticta r. rufopicta* (Fraser)

G. Pünktchenamarant; F. Amaranthe pointillé, Sénégali à Poitrine Barrée; D. Puntjes-Vuurvink (Puntastrild) (Pl. XXVI)

DISTRIBUTION: Gambia, Cameroon, Ghana.

DESCRIPTION: Sides of head, lores and a small frontal band rosy-red; top of head and nape of neck brownish-grey; back brown; lower tail coverts red; tail black. Wings show black and red. Lower parts are a pale rosy-red, changing to yellowish-brown towards back of body. Breast marked with white dots in a crescent shape. Iris brownish-grey with a bluish-grey circle around them; beak pinkish-red with black edges; feet and legs dark brown. Length: 4 in. (10 cm). *Female*. Plumage less vivid.

SUBSPECIES: A second subspecies, *Lagonosticta r. lateritia*, with more grey plumage and a breast marked with little white transverse lines, lives in southern Sudan and northern Zaire.

The Bar-breasted Fire-finch is found in the grassy plains but prefers more humid spots, along rivers and creeks. Like the Common or Red-billed Fire-finch, these birds do not avoid settlements or their inhabitants. Outside the breeding period, they can be found in flocks of 20, but the pairs live apart during the breeding season. The nest is constructed in bushes, and also in low trees. It is built with blades of grass, and lined with fine blades and feathers. The female usually lays 4 eggs.

Dr. J. C. O. Harrison, of England, published in *Avicultural Magazine*, Vol. 62, pp. 128–141, 1956, an article on the behaviour of these birds, which seem to need refuges on the floor of their aviary or cage; in fact, when danger threatens, they do not fly away, but try to hide on the ground. The Bar-breasted Fire-finch likes to sleep in a nest, whereas the Common Fire-finch spends the night on a perch. The Bar-breasted Fire-finch gives a metallic cry as it flies. The display of the male consists of raising a blade of grass in its upward pointing beak, with its wings open, and wagging its tail up and down; always carrying its blade of grass, he flies backwards and forwards making all his feathers tremble. Breeding has been successful several times; success seems to depend upon an adequate diet when breeding.

When the female wishes to begin a new brood, the male will continue to look after the young. They take on adult plumage towards the age of 2 months.

BROWN FIRE-FINCH, *Lagonosticta nitidula* Hartlaub

G. Schwarzschwanzschönbürzel; F. Astrild de Perrein; D. Blauwgrijs-zwartstaartje

DISTRIBUTION: Northern Angola, northern Rhodesia, southern Zaire as far as Lake Tanganyika.

DESCRIPTION: Head and upper parts including wings, rump and upper tail coverts grey-brown. Side of head faded red. Eyelids bluish-white. Dark vinaceous breast with numerous round white spots, each distinctly outlined with black. Abdomen grey-brown. Vent and under tail coverts dusky yellowish-white; tail grey-black. *Female*. Similar, but side of head grey-brown with less red. Length: about 4¼ in. (11 cm).

Until a few years ago very little was known about this bird. Fitting it into any classification was therefore a matter for dispute. Sometimes it was described as a Twinspot, *Hypargos*, species; at others as a subspecies or race of the ordinary Bar-breasted Fire-finch, *Lagonosticta rufopicta*. As so little is known of its life in the wild, the matter was only settled in 1960 with the help of close observation of specimens in captivity. It must form a connecting link between *Lagonosticta* and *Hypargos*.

The call of the Brown Fire-finch is similar to the chirruping of the Common Fire-finch or sparrows, and sounds like 'Whit' or 'Whit-whit'. The song of the male often consists of one short line which is at first broken and abrupt but gradually develops into a rhythmical song.

The display of the male at mating times has not yet been described and as far as we know there has only been one recorded breeding, by Professor Steiner, of Switzerland. It may well be, however, that there have been other successful breedings as the Brown Fire-finch is more often imported than is generally realised, for it is not always recognised by amateurs and dealers, who occasionally call it Common or Bar-breasted Fire-finch.

The birds should be given seed mixture such as is given to small foreign finches; fresh ants' eggs, insects, such as fruit-flies, together with sprouded seeds and greenstuff.

Their behaviour in captivity is largely similar to that of the Common Fire-finch and Bar-breasted Fire-finches. They prefer large aviaries where they are less likely to be disturbed and mostly keep in thick cover, coming out into the open part of the aviary only in search of food. They prefer hopping about among the bushes to taking long flights and at any sign of danger they run along the ground and take shelter in some dark remote corner.

The Brown Fire-finch can be kept in the same way as the Senegal Fire-finch or Bar-breasted Fire-finch. A well planted aviary is preferable though less will be seen of them under such conditions because of their habit of remaining hidden in the bushes. Their natural charm can be appreciated more readily in a roomy cage where their soft song can also be heard to advantage.

Genus: Euschistospiza

GREY TWINSPOT, *Euschistospiza c. cinerovinacea* (Sousa)

G. Schiefgrauer Astrild; F. Astrild Tachete Cendré, Astrild Tacheté Gris Ardoise; D. Leigrijze Druppelastrild

DISTRIBUTION: Angola.

DESCRIPTION: Head, neck, back and wings slate-grey; back and wings are shaded brown, lower parts and rump dark red. Tail red above and black below, lower parts grey, with black in middle, from breast to tail. Sides wine-red dotted with white. Beak black, iris red-brown, and feet and legs brown. Length: 4½ in. (11·5 cm).

This species, which was imported into Europe for the first time in 1963, is rather similar to the Black-tailed Lavender Finch, *Estrilda perreini*, but the grey of the plumage is darker and the wings have a fine wavy pattern, while the Grey Twinspot is distinguished chiefly by the red sides with white dots. It lives mainly in mountainous regions, in high grass, the seeds of which provide its food. No nest has yet been found, and no success in breeding has been obtained in the aviary. But in Angola a nest has been found containing the young of the darker subspecies, *Euschistospiza c. graueri*.

Genus: Hypargos

DYBOWSKI'S TWIN-SPOT, *Euschistospiza dybowskii* (Oustalet)

G. Dybowski's Tropfenastrild; F. Bengali Tâcheté à Ventre Noir; D. Dybowski's Druppelastrild

DISTRIBUTION: Sierra Leone, Nigeria, north-east Zaire and the uplands of the African interior.

DESCRIPTION: Head, neck and breast dark grey, back, shoulders, rump and upper tail coverts red. The abdomen and lower tail coverts on male, dark grey on female. On flanks there are numerous white spots in a more or less regular pattern. Iris vary from dark red to black with red eyelids. Beak black and feet and legs black. Length: about 4¼–4½ in. (11–12 cm).

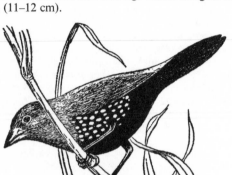

Dybowski's Twin-spot, *Euschistospiza dybowskii*

As only a few examples have so far been caught and brought to Europe alive, we know very little about their habits. They are lively birds and should be most like the Thorn-billed Weaver birds, though their tail movements remind one of the . Red Avadavat. They like living in bushes and on the ground where they pick up insects and small seeds. They have a soft, rich song with countless variations and as many alternations as that of the Brown Twinspot, but softer and more melodious. The order of the variations changes continually. Whistling, trilling, fluting notes follow each other in gay succession, male and female singing together. The soft 'wee-heet' or 'tsee-eet' which is sung with varying similar modulations may well be the contact call of these birds. When they are excited they give a sharp 'tseet-tseet-tseet'.

They are not more fussy about their food than other weaver birds. They will eat various kinds of millet, preferably green seeds, ants' eggs and green food.

PETERS' TWINSPOT, *Hypargos n. niveoguttatus* (Peters)

G. Roter Tropfenastrild; F. Amaranthe Enflammée; D. Peters Drupperlastrild   (Pl. XXVI)

DISTRIBUTION: East Africa.

DESCRIPTION: Top of head and nape of neck greyish-olive-brown; back and wings brown; rump and upper tail coverts red; tail black. Lores, sides of head and back, as well as throat carmine red. Lower body black, with a large number of white dots on sides. Iris dark brown, with light blue eyelids; beak bluish-grey. Length: 4¾ in. (12 cm). *Female.* Sides of head are greenish-brown and has less red on throat and breast.

These birds live in pairs or in a small family group in low-lying plains, on the banks of watercourses and lakes. They hide in thick vegetation, but they can be seen in the evening and in the morning, when they look for food along the paths. They eat seeds, also insects. They nest low down in the brush; the nest is round with an entrance at the side. It is built from grass, vegetable fibres and moss, the inside being lined with feathers.

Neunzig notes that they were first imported into Germany in 1902, by Hagenbeck. The first successful breeding was in 1920. Acclimatisation requires great care, and the newly arrived birds require a temperature which must not fall below 70°F (20°C). They should be housed in an inside aviary, and not in a cage, because an aviary allows the birds to get a certain amount of live food. The aviary should receive plenty of sunlight, because these birds delight in sunbathing. They find their food on the ground, beneath the vegetation.

Peter's Twin-spot, *Hypargos n. niveoguttatus*

They can live in a spacious aviary with other small species, but the pair vigorously defend their nesting territory, which causes enraged pursuits. If breeding is to succeed, the pair should be housed alone in an aviary.

In addition to various kinds of birdseed and the seeds of weeds, their food should also include mealworms, maggots, ants' eggs and various insects. Germinated seeds and green food are indispensable. If one takes care to spread a mixture of seeds amongst the vegetation every day, the birds will be kept busy.

The open nest is built low down in a thick bush, but some pairs also accept a nest-box. The two sexes take turns to sit on the 3–6 eggs, which hatch after 12 days. The young leave the nest at the age of 3 weeks. The breeding diet must include ants' eggs, live insects, maggots and germinated and dry seeds. They do not usually accept insectivorous food but it should always be offered.

ROSY TWIN-SPOT, VERREAUX' TWIN-SPOT, *Hypargos margaritatus* (Strickland)

G. Perlastrild; F. Astrild tacheté de Verreaux; D. Parel-Druppelastrild

DISTRIBUTION: Zululand, Mozambique.

DESCRIPTION: Top of head and back brown, with pinkish-red on sides of head, chin and top of breast. Front of abdomen black, sides have a large number of white dots shaded pink. Iris dark brown with light blue eyelids; beak, feet and legs slate-grey. *Female.* Grey on side of head, chin and breast. Length: 4¾ in. (12 cm).

These birds were described by Strickland in 1844, and as early as 1832 there was a specimen in the collection of Prince Esslingen; nevertheless, it was only in 1933 that we obtained some details about this fine species. Towards this period, Verreaux' Twinspot began to be imported in quantity into England. Their acclimatisation requires great care, and the birds must be housed in a well-heated large cage. They

Plate XXXV

Cape Sparrow, *Passer m. melanurus*   Arabian Golden Sparrow, *Passer luteus euchlorus*

Sudan Golden Sparrow, *Passer l. luteus*

Speckle–fronted Weaver, *Sporopipes frontalis*

Yellow-throated Sparrow, *Petronia superciliaris*

Scaly-crowned Weaver, *Sporopipes squamifrons*

Plate XXXVI

Superb Starling, *Spreo superbus*   Long-tailed Purple Starling, *Lamprotornis mevesii*

Purple-headed Glossy Starling, *Lamprotornis p. purpureiceps*

Royal Starling, *Cosmopsarus regius*

White-bellied Amethyst Starling, *Cinnyricinclus l. leucogaster*

Splendid Glossy Starling, *Lamprotornis splendidus*

should be given mixed millet seeds, live insects, ants' eggs and small mealworms. Their behaviour is similar to that of Peter's Twinspot which are close relatives of theirs. The birds like to hide in the vegetation and find their food on the ground, in clearings or along paths.

It is possible that Peter's Twinspot and Verreaux' Twinspot once formed a single species, but at the present day the former live largely in arid regions, whereas the latter prefer to settle along and on the banks of watercourses. This difference in the natural habitat has brought modifications in the pattern and colours of the plumage: usually, birds living in more humid regions showing a more intense red. Verreaux' Twinspots have been quite often found and saved during the last few years, and we can expect that bird fanciers will soon succeed in breeding them in the aviary.

Rosy-Twin-spot, *Hypargos margaritatus*

Genus: Mandingoa

GREEN-BACKED TWIN-SPOT, *Mandingoa n. nitidula* (Hartlaub)

G. Grüner Tropfenastrild; F. Astrild tacheté vert, Bengali Vert Pointillé; D. Groene Druppelastrild, Groene Robijntje (Pl. XXVI)

DISTRIBUTION: The eastern region of South Africa.

DESCRIPTION: Lower parts olive-green, with a light orange-yellow shading on rump and upper tail coverts. The olive-green wings have greyish-brown flight feathers; tail black and olive-green. There is red on lores, cheeks and chin; upper breast olive-green. Lower front of abdomen has black and olive-green and displays a large number of white

Green-backed Twin-spot, *Mandingoa n. nitidula*

pearl-shaped dots. Iris dark brown, eyelids having red edging; beak black and feet and legs brown. Length: 4¼ in. (11 cm).

SUBSPECIES: Four subspecies, in which the colours vary distinctly, have been described: *Mandingoa nitidula virginiae* on the island of Fernando Po and on the coast of west Africa, *Mandingo n. schlegeli* in Sierra Leone, Liberia and Nigeria, *Mandingoa n. schubbi* in east Africa and *Mandingoa n. nitidula* in the eastern regions of South Africa.

Twinspots live amongst the high grass of regions rich in

brushwood, and also on the edges of woods. They find their food in clearings, along paths and rice fields, feeding principally upon seeds, but also taking insects, especially in the breeding period. The nest is constructed at a height of 10–15 ft (3–5 m) and it is round, has a side entrance and is built of grass. In Zanzibar, this species is often kept as a house bird. The first specimens were imported into Europe in 1935.

The acclimatisation of these birds demands constant care, quite a high temperature and suitable food, but once they are acclimatised, the Green-backed Twinspot is one of the most robust species. It likes to live in the company of other birds, and keeps up constant contact with birds of the same species by a sweet-sounding call; they also seem to greet each other by caressing each other's plumage. If a pair is separated, the birds do not survive long. From the very beginning of acclimatisation, they should be given ants' eggs and mealworms. In addition to dry seeds, they should also be given germinated seeds. A well-planted outside aviary is best for them; and it is necessary that the topsoil should be clean and regularly renewed. These birds can share accommodation with other peaceful species.

The male builds the large open nest in a high and sheltered place, close to the roof of the aviary. The materials used are hay, coconut fibres, and other vegetable fibres; the birds also add particles of compost, especially round the entrance. The female lays 3–6 eggs, which both birds take turns in incubating for 13 days. The parents will raise the young successfully so long as they have suitable food. The young fly at the age of 3 weeks and soon begin eating millet sprays. In order to get Green-backed Twinspots accustomed to the breeding soft food, it is recommended that they should be housed in a mixed aviary, where they will imitate the other birds who eat this mash. To be successful with these Twinspots and to keep them for several years in an aviary, they must have live food throughout the year; and it is therefore beneficial for the bird keeper to learn how to breed fruitflies and mealworms himself.

The first successful breeding, with the subspecies, *Mandingoa n. schlegeli*, was obtained in 1961 by F. Karl, in Germany; the subspecies, *Mandingoa n. schubbi*, was bred in 1964, also in Germany, by R. Neff. These first successes were followed by others.

Genus: Spermophaga

GRANT'S BLUE-BILL, *Spermophaga poliogenys* (Ogilvie-Grant)

G. Grant's Samenknacher, Grant's Perlschnabel; F. Gros-bec de Grant, Loxie de Grant; D. Grant's Blausnavelastrild, Grant's Kernbijter

DISTRIBUTION: Interior of eastern Zaire and western Uganda.

DESCRIPTION: This fine representative of the genus *Spermophaga* has a splendid lustrous red and black plumage. Forehead, sides of head, throat, upper breast, sides and upper tail coverts scarlet, remainder black. Iris brown with pale blue eyelids. Beak steel-blue with mother-of-pearl reflections, tip and sides of mandibles lustrous bright red. Length: about 5 in. (13 cm). *Female*. Head and back blackish-grey; throat and upper breast red, while the lower parts are greyish-black with numerous white dots.

The behaviour of Grant's Blue-bill is very different from that of the other species of the genus *Spermophaga*. It is an inhabitant of the jungle, and shows a clear preference for perpetual half-light, and also looks for the darkest corner of the aviary, where there is little opportunity of admiring it.

The pair remain together, which is not the case for other species of the same genus. In spite of their attachment, mutual caressing of the plumage is infrequent, and this ritual behaviour exists only in the preliminary stages. The attractive call is a very melodious 'jeh-ju' but there is no true song.

These birds feed on various kinds of seeds dry and germinated, ripe grass seeds, green food, ants' eggs and mealworms. The pair feed together and stay together when they bathe. Nothing is known about their behaviour in the nesting period. The first specimens were imported in 1963 by the Swiss importer Cordier, and were obtained by Dr. Burkard.

Grant's Blue-bill, *Spermophaga poliogenys*

RED-HEADED BLUE-BILL, *Spermophaga ruficapilla* (Shelly)

G. Rotköpfiger Perlschnabel, Rotköpfsamenknacker; F. Gros-bec à tête rouge, Loxie à tête rouge; D. Roodkop-Blauwsnavelastrild, Roodkop-Kernbijter

DISTRIBUTION: East Africa as far as Lake Tanganyika.
DESCRIPTION: Entire head, neck, breast and sides of body intense red. The rump and longer upper tail coverts red; rest of plumage black. Iris red-brown, with blue edging to eyelids; beak steel-blue, with red on top and sides of mandibles; feet and legs dark greyish-green. Length: 5 in. (13 cm). *Female*. Base of breast, abdomen and lower tail coverts have a white dotted pattern; red on head and rump.

This species, which is only occasionally imported, lives in the heart of the virgin forests, on the banks of watercourses and in clearings where there is tall grass. They can be observed in pairs or in small family groups, looking for their food on the ground. They feed largely on grass seeds, and also take termites. Their nest a loose construction of fine grass has been found in trees, at a height of 10–12 ft (3·5 m). Three or 4 white eggs are laid.

The Red-headed Blue-bill is similar to the Blue-billed Crimson-breasted Weaver, but is quieter and sings less often. Its song is reminiscent of that of the Brown Twinspot, but is less varied. These Blue-bills are in general peaceful birds,

although the females often squabble when they are in breeding condition; males are less aggressive. At first, these birds are very shy and hide at the slightest sound; later they become a little more tame. So far, no success has been obtained in breeding them.

Red-headed Blue-bill, *Spermophaga ruficapilla*

BLUE-BILLED WEAVER, CRIMSON BREASTED WEAVER, *Spermophaga haematina* (Vieillot)

G. Rotbrüstiger Perlschnabel; F. Astrilde à Gros Bec Bleu, Rouge-Noire; D. Roodborst-Blauws navelast

DISTRIBUTION: West Africa.
DESCRIPTION: *Male*. Top of the head, neck, back, wings, lower breast, belly and tail are shiny black. The breast, throat and flanks are a brilliant red. The eyes are brown with a bluish rim and the feet are blackish. The colour of the beak is striking. It looks as if it was coated with a layer of mother-of-pearl and gives a bluish shine. The tip and edges of the beak are red. *Female*. Is strikingly different from the male. The black belly is dotted with numerous white spots which turn to white cross stripes on the lower tail coverts. All the colours are furthermore dull rather than shiny. Length: about 5 in. (13 cm).
SUBSPECIES: *S. h. togoensis, S. h. haematina, S. h. pustulata*. They are distinguished by the extent of red colouring on the head and upper tail coverts.

Blue-billed Weaver, *Spermophaga Haematina*

The young are more a slate-grey and reddish-brown on the belly. The markings on the jaws consist of 5 (in few a cases of 3) black spots arranged in a semicircle on a yellow background. On the lower beak there is a black marking arranged

like a half moon. The swellings on the beak are yellowish with a yellow papilla on the upper beak and a papilla-like thickening of the swelling on the lower beak.
The Blue-billed Crimson-breasted Weaver makes a very lively, but thoroughly peaceful foster child which should be kept in an aviary where it displays its habits best. The frequent fluttering of its wings makes it appear to have super-abundant energy which expresses itself in every movement.

Genus: Cryptospiza

SALVADORI'S CRIMSON WING, *Cryptospiza salvadorii*
G. Salvadori's Bergastrild; F. Bengali vert; D. Berkvink

DISTRIBUTION: North-east Africa.
DESCRIPTION: Outwardly the male and female look the same. The head and under parts are a grey-olive-green, the throat yellow-olive-green and the back, flanks, rump and edges of the otherwise black wings are a dark crimson. Iris brown, eyelids are reddish-pink, the beak black and the feet and legs brown. Length: 4¾ in. (12 cm).
The Salvadori Crimson Wing first appeared in the London Zoo after 1933. Since 1960 a limited number of amateurs have kept a few in Germany and Switzerland among other countries. It is a lively bird, not too difficult to acclimatise and will live for years either in a cage or an aviary. It likes hiding places and bushes in which it climbs with short, skilful hops. Its brief song consists of 4 soft, long-drawn-out notes followed by a final short chirrup. The couples do not keep closely together and are often found far apart. They soon return to each other, however, and stroke each other's plumage.
Nothing is as yet known about successful breedings. They eat the usual exotic mixture of foodstuffs to which African millet, fresh ants' eggs and greenstuff should be added.

Salvadori's Crimson Wing, *Cryptospiza salvadorii*

JACKSON CRIMSON WING, *Cryptospiza jacksoni* Sharpe
G. Jackson's Bergastrild; F. Bengali de Jackson; D. Jackson's Bergastrild

DISTRIBUTION: Lake Kiru region of Zaire and Ruanda.
DESCRIPTION: The head, back, rump, flanks and pinions of the arms are crimson. The neck, throat, breast and belly are a dark slate-grey. The other wing feathers, the tail and beak are black. The black eyes have a yellowish ring round them. *Female*. Has less red on the head and the other red parts are dusky. Length: about 4¾ in. (12 cm).
The first Jackson Crimson Wings came to England in 1960. The behaviour of these birds in the aviary reminds one mostly of tits. They climb and fly, head upwards or downwards, with the greatest skill through the branches and are remarkable for their curiosity. In spite of their energetic temperament they are among the most confiding of the weaver birds. The couples do not keep closely together even when, here and there, they sit side by side for a moment. The call consists of a sharp 'tseet' or 'tsip'. The male's song

Jackson Crimson Wing, *Cryptospiza Jacksoni*

is a combination of this call, a high pitched, long-drawn-out 'pee-ee-ee' and a rather deep, soft 'gai', and often a 'goo-ai-oo'. The call is often repeated but never rhythmically. On rare occasions you hear a high, trilling sound, 'guee-guee-guee-guee-guee'. The mating dance is executed with as long a stalk in the beak as possible while see-sawing up and down majestically. In addition to the usual dry sprouted and semi-ripe grass seeds, Jackson Crimson Wings like a large quantity of insect food such as ants' eggs, mealworms and especially the vinegarfly and fruitfly.

BROWN TWIN-SPOT, *Cryptospiza monteiri* Hartlaub
G. Monteiro's Tropfenastrild; F. Bengali tàcheté à ventre roux; D. Monteiro's Truplevink

DISTRIBUTION: Central and west Africa.
DESCRIPTION: *Male*. Has a slate-grey head and neck with a brown back. The upper tail coverts are red and the tail is a washy reddish-black. The throat is grey and has a perpendicular red line down it. The under side is a light brown with numerous white spots which become white cross lines on the lower tail coverts. The long beak is black, the iris brown and the feet brown. *Female*. Is the same as the male except for the red line down the throat.
A few couples of this rare and beautiful weaver bird have only in the last few years been introduced into Europe. Its behaviour differs in many respects from that of the others. Except when it wants food, it remains nearly all the time hidden in the thickest bushes of the aviary and its where-abouts is only discovered by its sharp, rather hoarse guttural cry of 'tic' or 'tec'. It's constricted guttural song is unique.
The Brown Twinspot flies out of the bushes on to the ground to pick up its food, taking long hops towards it and keeping its body horizontal. It picks up the food in quick, jerky movements and swallows grain after grain. What is remarkable is that the grains have not been husked at all. Soft foods, and greenstuff are nearly always refused. Formerly it was asserted that the Brown Twinspot did not build its own

nest. This is only partly true. The author and other amateurs have had cases where the bird has built a bell-shaped nest with a large hole at the side to go in by, in a nesting-box.

The inside is remarkably roomy and oval-shaped. Both the male and the female incubate.

Genus: Stagonopleura

DIAMOND SPARROW, *Stagonopleura guttata* (Shaw)
G. Diamantfink; F. Diamant à gouttelettes; D. Diamantfink   (Pl. XXII)

DISTRIBUTION: South and south-eastern Australia.
DESCRIPTION: Top of head and nape of neck silvery-grey; back and wings dark brown; rump and upper tail coverts bright red. Lores form a black line, sides of head are white turning to grey towards rear. A black line crosses the breast and continues along sides, where it is spotted with large white dots; lower body white. Iris brown, orbital ring red, beak red and feet and legs brownish-grey. Length: 5 in. (12 cm). *Female*. Is difficult to distinguish; may be a little smaller and black of lores duller.

Of all the Australian finches of this genus, this species is that most often found close to human beings. Its original habitat was the regions of low bushes and Eucalyptus trees, where their food was provided by grass seeds. They are not at all shy and can be found in city parks and gardens; they even nest close to human beings. The male carries out his display perched on a branch; he raises his whole plumage and begins to dance, singing, and making the branch swing up and down. The two partners then fly to the nesting place where copulation takes place. Their nests are often in groups and found in the huge heaps of branches beneath the eyrie of a bird of prey. The round nest has a side entrance and is made of fresh and dead stalks, and is lined with vegetable wool and feathers. The parents take turn to incubate the 4–8 eggs, for 12 days; the young leave the nest when they are 24–26 days old.

Diamond Sparrows were imported into Germany for the first time in 1870 by Hagenbeck; being already known in France and England before that date. At the present time they are well-known world-wide, and raised in large numbers by aviculturists.

Since these birds are calm and peaceable, they can be allowed to nest in a mixed aviary, so long as it has plenty of thick bushes. For they prefer to build a free-standing nest, although they do equally well in a large nest-box.

If breeding is to be successfully concluded, an adequate breeding diet is indispensable. During the first 10 days, this should consist of ants' eggs, small mealworms, maggots, greenfly, fruitflies and other insects, supplemented by soft food, germinated seeds and green food. It is true that some pairs have raised their young on unsupplemented insectivorous food, but this is exceptional. On the other hand, many young have been raised which only took insectivorous food and seeds.

If Diamond Sparrows are kept in a cage, they tend to get excessively fat, especially if they are given too large a ration of hemp seed and mealworms. In fact these birds are much more suitable for a large aviary, because they like to come down to the ground and also to fly. If they have plenty of exercise, they will remain in excellent condition for a long time. Some pairs are inclined to continue breeding indefinitely; one must take care to allow them to lay no more than 3 times each season. In order to stop them breeding excessively, the sexes should be separated in the winter, but each pair should be marked with an open ring and care should be taken to mate them together the following season.

A mutation has already been obtained in the domesticated birds: the Fawn Diamond Sparrow, in which all the black has been replaced by brown.

RED-EARED FIRETAIL FINCH, *Stagonopleura oculata* (Quoy and Gaimard)
G. Rotohramadine; F. Diamant (Astrild) à oreillons rouges; D. Roodoor-Amadine   (Pl. XXII)

DISTRIBUTION: South-western Australia.
DESCRIPTION: Narrow black band on forehead, lores and around eyes. Behind eyes there is a red-scarlet mark. Rump and upper tail coverts bright red. Upper body olive-grey-brown with slight dark brown horizontal lines; throat and upper breast yellowish-olive-brown with light black horizontal marks. Lower body black with horizontal white lines,

Red-eared Firetail Finch, *Stagonopleura oculata*

which are very wide on the sides and form large dots. Iris red, with greenish-blue on the edges of orbital ring, beak red and feet and legs horn colour. Length: 4¾ in. (12 cm). *Female*. Less vivid in colour.

The distribution of these birds is very restricted; they live in dense undergrowth of eucalyptus forests along the south-western coast of Australia, where there are also plenty of bushes, heaths and marshes. They live in pairs and never seem to leave this somewhat specialised habitat. Up to the present time, no one has succeeded in importing them live into Europe, but some Australian bird fanciers keep them in aviaries and have even succeeded in breeding them. The species is becoming rare in its original country, partly as a result of deforestation and clearing, which reduces their natural habitat.

Mr. Pepper, of Australia, was the first to succeed in breeding these birds, in a large well-planted aviary. He gave them various kinds of millet seeds, seeds of weeds and live insects. The birds greedily ate the greenfly which infected the plants, and also pecked on the ground; and they also learned to eat soft food.

FIRETAILED FINCH, *Stagonopleura bella* (Latham)
G. Feuerschwanzamadine; F. Diamant à queue de feu; D. Vuurstaartamadine   (Pl. XXII)

DISTRIBUTION: Tasmania and south-eastern Australia.
DESCRIPTION: Forehead band around eyes and on lores black. Rump and upper tail coverts scarlet-red; upper body olive-brown and grey, and is covered in its entirety with fine black lines. Tail dark brown with black lines. Lower body brownish-grey, and also marked with black lines, which are wider than upper body. Centre of abdomen black; eyes brown, with light blue edge to orbital ring, beak red and feet and legs flesh-coloured. Length: 4¾ in. (12 cm). *Female*. Centre of abdomen grey with black lines.

The way of life of these Firetailed Finches is very similar to that of the Red-eared Firetailed Finches, but in this case they feed largely on grass seeds. They also gather greenfly and other small insects on the leaves, and even seem to eat small snails. Their voluminous nests have been found in the dense bushes or beneath the eyries of birds of prey. They consist of a long entrance tunnel and the nesting chamber is lined with hair and feathers.

Like other Estrildinae, these birds also build sleeping nests, which are not lined. Both parents take turns to incubate the 4–6 eggs for 13 days and the young leave the nest when 24–28 days old.

The first specimens came to England in 1870, and a few years later to Europe. Neuzig tells us that this bird was very tame, which may have been due to its poor state of health. A thickly planted aviary is the ideal place to house these very wild birds, which like to hide amongst the foliage. Like the Red-eared Firetailed Finch, the Firetailed Finch also likes to bathe. When the birds begin to build sleeping nests, it can be assumed that they have adapted to their housing.

The only successful breeding has been in Australia, in Hobart Zoo in Tasmania, and later at Sydney, where Mr.

Firetailed Finch, *Stagonopleura bella*

Peir raised 20 young from 3 pairs in one year.

The wild populations of these birds seem to be seriously threatened by the clearing of the regions which form their natural habitat.

Genus: Aidemosyna

CHERRY FINCH, PLUM-HEADED FINCH, *Aidemosyna modesta* (Gould)

G. Zeresfink; F. Diamant modeste, Diamant cérès; D. Ceresamadine, Ceresastrild   (Pl. XXIII)

Cherry Finch, *Aidemosyna modesta*

DISTRIBUTION: Eastern Australia.

DESCRIPTION: Forehead purplish-red, lores red, and rest of head and upper body brown. Rump and upper tail coverts are marked with white lines; tail blackish with white tips. Chin reddish-black, sides of head white with brown wavy pattern. Iris brown, beak black, and feet and legs brown flesh-colour. Length: 4½ in. (11·5 cm). *Female*. Has white on chin and throat; and little red on forehead.

These birds usually live in the company of Diamond Sparrows in meadows where there are scattered bushes,

along watercourses or roads. They find their food on the ground, and it consists of the seeds of grasses and weeds. The nest is built on the ground amongst the high grass, or low down in a bush. It is round, with a short entrance tunnel, and carelessly constructed with grass, lined within with feathers. The parents take turns to sit on 3–7 eggs for 13 days and the young leave their nest when 21–24 days old. These birds were brought to Europe for the first time in 1872, since when they have been regularly imported, although in limited numbers. In the winter, they must be kept in a warm room, for they are certainly less birds of the wild than the members of the genus *Poëphila*.

They live peaceably with other birds of the same size, and are quite lazy. The song of the male is insignificant. Cases of breeding were noted shortly after they were first imported. A pair which gets on together will decide to nest in a large breeding cage or a mixed aviary, but the other birds must be able to defend themselves, since the modest Cherry Finch can be aggressive during nesting.

They accept a nest-box, but the pair will often build a free-standing nest in a low bush or a small fir. They use various materials; grass, coconut or hemp fibres, bark and feathers. The parents take turns to sit on the 3–4 eggs for 12 days, and the young remain in the nest for 21 days, and are fed for a further 14 days after flying. For the first few days, the parents bring them back to the nest for the night. During breeding, the parents must be given mealworms and ants' eggs, for certain birds abandon their young if they have no live food. Thus it has often been known for the young to be raised solely on seeds, soft food, green food and soaked whole meal bread.

Genus: Taeniopygia

ZEBRA FINCH, CHESTNUT-EARED FINCH, *Taeniopygia guttata castanotis* (Vieillot)

G. Zebrafink; F. Diamant Mandarin; D. Zebravink
(Pl. XIX and XXIII)

DISTRIBUTION: Most of Australia, specially the interior but not in north-east Queensland or in the south-west and south-east coastal regions, Flores Islands, Sumba and Timor.

DESCRIPTION: Top of head, neck and pronotum light grey; wing coverts and back grey; the flights a dark grey. Upper tail coverts black with large white bars at tips and so long

that they almost reach tip of blackish-brown tail. Front part of cheeks white, the latter being marked off by a thin black vertical line. Each side of head is a large chestnut-brown ear patch; sides of neck silvery-grey as are the throat and upper chest which have black horizontal stripes like the markings of the zebra, hence the name. The stripes terminate in a broad black horizontal band running across the breast. Flanks chestnut-brown with numerous round white spots; under parts white with fawn tinting towards vent. Beak coral-red, legs and feet flesh-coloured. Length: about 4 in. (10 cm). *Female*. Has no brown ear patches or no flank or chest markings; cheeks, throat and upper breast are a uniform grey. Top of head and back is a duskier grey than on male and is more fawn tinted underneath; beak orange-red.

Young resemble female and have no vertical black stripes on the cheek and black beaks. The colourings begin to appear when chicks are 5–6 weeks old and are complete in about 2 months.

SPECIES: There are 2 species of the Zebra Finch. The widely-known one described above (*Taenippygia guttata castanotis*) is found all over Australia, there are some 12 subspecies. The other (*Taenippygia guttata guttata*), is found in the Flores Islands, Sumba and Timor. Formerly this species was called *Taenippygia guttata insuralis*. Unlike *T. g. canotis*, male is silvery-grey on throat and upper breast, sides of neck have only faintly marked cross stripes and only a few thin lines on upper breast. Female is like the other species but is said to be somewhat browner.

Zebra Finch, *Taeniopygia guttata castanotis*

The Zebra Finch prefers living in open grassland with trees and low bushes, or near human settlements. On account of its liking for water it chooses the neighbourhood of small rivers, ponds and streams, even cattle and sheep troughs. It is a very sociable bird even at the time of breeding, and keeps together in flocks. It chooses various places for building its nest, but preferably a thorn bush. It often builds many nests close together or even adjacent to one another. They are untidily made with dry grass in the form of a retort. Under favourable climatic conditions, it will nest all the year round. In a drought it only stays to breed once. The natural life of the Zebra Finch has been thoroughly studied by a German scientist, Prof. Klaus Immelmann who spent a year observing and describing it in Australia.

It is not known when and by whom the first Zebra Finches were brought to Europe or who reared the first birds in captivity. Dr. Karl Russ clearly says that Vieillot reared them, but this seems due to a misunderstanding. It is true that Vieillot gives in his *Histoire naturelle des plus beaux oiseaux chanteurs de zone torride*, (1805), a fairly accurate description of the Zebra Finch, which he calls the 'Bengali

mouchet锓', but he places it wrongly in the Moluccas. It is not clear from the description whether he possessed living birds or only stuffed ones. He only says he got the bird from M. Becaeur ('Cet oiseau m'a été communiqué par M. Becaeur'). However, the Zebra Finch was probably imported about the middle of the last century and bred soon after. By 1872, when *The Feathered World* first appeared, breeding was regarded as a matter of course. As far as I know there are no reports on the introduction of the island species *T. g. guttata*. The Zebra Finch has always been a popular pet and when, in this century, new colour mutations turned up, fresh interest in their breeding was aroused.

Zebra Finches are very lively birds, on the move nearly all the time and can be kept in a cage with other birds of like size provided no nesting facilities are given. When they are nesting many pairs are very bad tempered to other birds, so it is best to keep them in a cage by themselves. They have a characteristic call which resembles the sound of a toy trumpet and the male's song consists polysyllabic trumpet notes repeated several times.

Zebra Finches are unassuming hardy birds modest in their requirements which does not mean that one can neglect them. The cage for one pair must not be less than 24 in. (60 cm) long with correspondingly large other dimensions; the larger the cage the better. Several pairs can be kept together in a large aviary or indoor flight and this suits their natural inclination best. Where colour crossing is wanted, pairs must always be kept singly. They should be given half-open nest-boxes about 4½–6 in. (12–15 cm) long, deep and high, like a budgerigar's. One nest is enough in each cage, but in an aviary 2–3 boxes are required for each pair so as to give the birds a choice and avoid quarrelling. The boxes should be hung at different heights and not too close together. Nesting material such as soft hay, soft moss, feathers and animals' hair, should be given.

Zebra Finches eat the usual mixed millet seeds such as senegal, white and Japanese millet and small canary seeds. Germinated seeds are also to be recommended strongly. For rearing give germinated seeds and soft food. Greenstuffs, specially chickweed (*Stellaria media*) and meadow grass (*Posa annua*). Good sea sand and minerals, dry eggshells, but not from preserved eggs, and small mollusc shells finely crushed should always be provided.

Zebra Finches are among the best and most reliable of the cage birds for rearing young but of course not all couples are equally reliable. Many build a nest, lay eggs and incubate for a short while, then build another nest on top of that and lay again. But most pairs are good breeders and rear one clutch after another. So after two or at most three clutches they should be given at least 6 months' rest. The nest-boxes should be taken away from cages and aviaries, and the sexes are best kept apart. Only good, strong birds and their offspring should be used for breeding. Any unreliable or poor quality birds should be removed. Incubation lasts 12–13 days and both parents share the duty. Inbreeding must be avoided. When about 3 weeks old, the young leave the nest and are still fed by the parents for another 10–15 days. As already mentioned the young have all their colours at the end of 3 months. In every case it is as well to distinguish the parents and also the young by attaching an open aluminium ring with a number on it, some distinguishing mark is essential for colour breeding. It is best to keep the young birds separated according to sex in large cages or aviaries where there are no nesting facilities. In the course of time a number of colour mutations have appeared in Zebra Finches and have been established. All the changes we know of have taken place in this century, since the First World War. It is true Dr. Karl Russ mentioned in 1887 cases where the colour change had been bred, but unfortunately did not say what colours appeared and then disappeared. Changes occur in the wild state but they die out because no choice is made in pairing. The oldest mutation recorded is the white Zebra Finch at the beginning of the nineteen twenties in Australia. Not all the birds are pure white, some have larger or smaller patches of grey flecking on the back. The Fawn Zebra Finches were first found wild in Australia and were reared in captivity by birds that had been caught. Their colour is cinnamon-brown, and lighter and darker shades can be distinguished. Silver Zebra Finches of which two kinds exist one from Europe and the other from Australia. They are a light grey and there are different shades, the darkest are hardly distinguishable from the grey of the wild bird. The colour of the patches on the cheeks varies correspondingly from the rear normal colour of the darkest to the yellowish-white of the light ones. In Europe the darker coloured ones are called blues, but they are not the blue shade of Budgerigars.

Penguin, often called Silverwing in Europe, is one of the more recent colour mutations. The upper part is a very light grey and the throat, breast and underneath part are pure white. The males have white cheek patches and they can be faintly seen on the females.

Marmoset or Chestnut-flanked White was first known as a change in Europe at the beginning of the fifties, although it had occurred wild as a mutation in Australia in 1938. The colour of the male is near white but with all the typical markings but fainter than on the dark mutations. The females are white but they keep the tail barrings and the black eye stripes and top of the head is lightly marked with grey.

Pied Zebra Finches first appeared in Denmark and there are various arrangements of colour, some in which the dark colour preponderates, others where the white is the main colour.

Cream is a combination of Fawn and Silver.

In addition to the above mutations there are a few others less well-known but worth mentioning. For example birds with a yellow instead of a red beak, Black-breasted, Grizzled, Saddle-backed and the latest Light-backed ones which obviously originated in Holland but were discovered by Professor H. Steiner, in Zurich.

There is also a crested mutation available in all colours. These birds have a small crest on their heads similar to that of the Gloster Fancy Canary.

Only a short mention need be made here of the inheritance of the various mutations. Silver (Cream) is the one dominant colour on the grey and its other mutations. There is however a silver variety that is recessive. All the other changes of colour in the wild state tend to be recessive or sex-linked.

A great deal has been written about inherited characteristics of the Zebra Finch, mostly in periodicals though there are now books devoted entirely to the culture of zebra finches.

Genus: Stizoptera

BICHENO'S FINCH, *Stizoptera b. bichenovii* (Vigors and Horsfield)

G. Weissburzeliger Ringelastrild; F. Diamant de Bicheno; D. Bicheno-Astrild   (Pl. XXIII)

DISTRIBUTION: Eastern and north-eastern Australia.

DESCRIPTION: Forehead, and a stripe leaving the forehead, passing above the eyes and falling to cheeks forming a black collar on chest and also a second collar on the breast. Top of head, neck and back are a brownish-grey with very fine black wavy markings. The dark grey wings have a chequered pattern. Rump white, marked off by a black stripe on lower back; tail brownish-black. Eye and ear

Bicheno's Finch, *Stizoptera b. bichenovii*

regions and throat white; breast and abdomen yellowish-white; lower tail coverts black. Iris brown, beak lead-grey and feet and legs grey. Length: 4 in. (10 cm). *Female.* Has yellowish-white eyebrows; and collars on chest and breast are narrower.

Bicheno's Finch is found in pairs, or, outside the breeding period, in small flocks on grassy riverside plains. They are not timid, and feed on the ground on small seeds and if they sense danger, they fly off to the nearest bush or tree. They nest in thick bushes or bunches of tall grass, and even in holes in trees or beneath the roofs of farm buildings. The nest is round and bottle-shaped; it is built from blades of grass and vegetable fibre, and lined with small feathers and wool. The female lays 3–8 eggs depending upon whether the weather conditions are favourable.

The first Bicheno Finches arrived in London Zoo in 1850, and in France shortly afterwards; by 1874 they were imported into Germany in large numbers by Hagenbeck. Sucecss in breeding is recorded many times, sometimes for several successive generations. They can be kept in company with other small birds, but no more than a single pair should be kept in each aviary, because they will not tolerate the company of their fellows. Their cry is a little reminiscent of the trumpeting sounds of the Zebra Finch, but is softer; the song of the male is unremarkable.

Bicheno's Finches are best housed in a planted aviary, since they like to stay amongst bushes, but they are lively and mobile. They breed better in an aviary than in a cage, where they are extremely sensitive to disturbances and movements. Ordinarily, they are satisfied with various kinds of birdseed, canary seed and green food, but while raising their young they eagerly take greenfly, spiders, mealworms and other live food. They accept soft food and germinated seeds. As soon as the young are a week old, their parents cram them with seed.

It is interesting to note that young Bicheno's Finches and the Double-bar Finch, which differs from them only by its black rump, both have a white rump in the juvenile plumage. In an aviary they build their nests in bushes, small evergreens and also in nest-boxes, using hay, coconut fibre, narrow leaves and pieces of bark, whilst the inside is lined with hair and feathers. The male brings the material and the female constructs the nest.

The pair sit in turn on the 4–8 eggs for 11 days. The young remain in the nest for more than 3 weeks and are fed after that for a further 2 weeks. By the time they are 3 months old, they look like their parents.

DOUBLE-BAR FINCH, BLACK-RINGED FINCH,
Stizoptera bichenovii annulosa (Gould)
G. Gitterflügelastrild, Schwarzbürzeliger Ringelastrild;
F. Diamant de Bicheno à croupion noir; D. Godel-
astrild, Ringastrild, Zwarstuit Bicheno

DISTRIBUTION: North-western Australia.
DESCRIPTION: Plumage similar to that of Bicheno's Finch,
but with a black rump. Length: about 4 in. (10 cm).
These birds live largely in grassy tropical swamps, but also
visit farm gardens and cultivated areas. Both breeds follow
a similar way of life. They drink in a remarkable way; dip
their beak in the water and suck, as do pigeons. In Australia,
Double-bar Finches have the reputation of being more
hardy, but in Europe both breeds should be cared for in an
identical way, since they both dislike cold and damp. Even
birds which are well acclimatised, should have heated
accommodation in winter.
The nuptial dance of the male takes place on the ground; he
dances around the female carrying a long blade of grass in
his raised beak. He bows low to her, giving his quiet murmuring song. The male can be recognised by this song.
Sometimes the pair do not sit upon the first clutch of eggs.
On the other hand, good breeders may produce 4–5 broods
a year and raise their young very well.
If these birds are to be kept in good condition, it is advisable
to give them not only a mixture of seeds but also green food
and from time to time ants' eggs, greenfly and mealworms.

Genus: Bathilda

STAR FINCH, RED-TAILED GRASS-FINCH, *Bathilda r.*
ruficauda (Gould)
G. Binsenastrild; F. Diamant ruficauda, Diamant à
queue rousse; D. Biezenastrild, Binzenastrild
Ruficauda   (Pl. XXIII)

DISTRIBUTION: Australia from eastern Queensland to New
South Wales.
DESCRIPTION: Forehead, lores, area round eyes, sides of head
and top of throat are red. Around eyes and on sides of neck
the plumage is covered with small white dots. Upper parts
are brownish-green, with red on the upper tail coverts; tail
brown and red. Lower parts greenish-grey, with yellow on
abdomen and lower tail coverts. Beak and iris red and feet
and legs yellow. Length: 4¼ in. (11 cm). *Female.* Plumage is
less bright; there is either no red on forehead or it is less
extensive.
SUBSPECIES: The subspecies *Bathilda ruficauda clarescens*
lives throughout northern Australia. It is distinguished by a
more vivid plumage and in particular by the more extensive
red colouring on head and more green tint of the upper
parts.
Star Finches are always to be seen in pairs, and only during
the breeding period or during periods of drought can small
groups be found near waterholes. They prefer to settle near
the mouths of rivers and in swampy regions. Their nest is
often built amongst reeds, but nests have also been found
amongst tall grass, in bushes or low trees. The nest is round
or in bottle form; it is built of grass and lined with vegetable
wool and feathers. They feed on the seeds of grass and weeds,
picking up the seeds from the ground while hanging on to
the stalks of the plants. The song of the male is a murmured
twittering; he sings constantly with his head held back.
His nuptial dance is performed perching on a branch with a
blade of grass in his beak; hopping slowly, he turns his red
rump and his white spotted side towards the female. The
latter seems to pay no attention to his assiduous courtship,
but after some time she accepts the homage of the male by
touching him with her beak and tail. Mating follows
immediately, after which the female squats down, vibrating
her tail and the pair immediately begin to build their nest.
If they are in a cage, they will be satisfied with a nest-box,
but in an outside aviary they like to build a freely constructed
nest in a thick bush, small evergreen or bunch of broom.
They use hay, green grass, fibres, and line the inside with
feathers, hair and vegetable wool. The female sits on the
3–6 eggs for 12–13 days; from time to time the male comes
to keep her company or to take her place for a short time.
When the young are hatched, the male helps to feed them;
the young leave the nest towards the third week.
If the female lays more than 4 eggs, it is wise to give the
later eggs to Zebra Finches or Bengalese. The young birds,
when they have just left the nest, closely resemble young
Gouldian Finches; like the latter, they take on their colouring very slowly, and do not display full plumage until they
are about 8 months old. The young males in the juvenile
plumage can be told apart by their song. Star Finches take
all kinds of bird-seed and canary seed, as well as all sorts of
weed and grass seeds; they need a good deal of green food.
In order to avoid egg binding in the female, it is advisable to
mix with the seed a little cod liver oil and to make a mixture
of minerals and a good grit constantly available. These
birds will also learn to eat soft food and delight in eating
germinated millet and live food, such as ants' eggs, mealworms and greenfly.
They adore the direct sunlight, and although they are
regarded as very hardy birds, they should be wintered with
heat.

Star Finch, *Bathilda r. ruficauda*

Genera: Neochmia and Aegintha

CRIMSON FINCH, BLOOD FINCH, *Neochmia ph.*
phaeton (Hombron and Jaquinot)
G. Sonnenastrild; F. Diamant Phaéton, Rubin
d'Australie; D. Zonastrild   (Pl. XXIII)
DISTRIBUTION: Northern Australia.

DESCRIPTION: Forehead red, top of head blackish-brown,
nape of neck and neck itself reddish-grey, upper parts have
red sheen, and upper tail coverts brighter red. There is
brown and red on tail. Area round eyes, sides of head, lores,
throat, breast and sides are bright red; sides are covered
with small white dots. Lower parts black. Iris brown, beak

red, and feet and legs yellowish. Length: 5 in. (12·5 cm). *Female*. Has red line on forehead, rest of head having a red sheen; her lower parts are brownish-yellow.

SUBSPECIES: Three other subspecies have been described, two of which, *Neochmia ph. iredalei* and *Nochmia ph. albiventer*, live in the areas bordering upon tropical northern Australia. The third, *Neochmia ph. evangelinae*, lives in southern New

Crimson Finch, *Neochmia ph. phaeton*

Guinea. The two latter subspecies are distinguished by a white abdomen and lighter upper parts.

Die Gefiederte Welt, 1958, pp. 61 ff, has published a detailed report on a number of successes in breeding obtained by R. Vir, of Dvur Kralové in Czechoslovakia. We reproduce here several passages which will be of interest to owners of Crimson Finches:

'For a pair of Crimson Finches I set up an aviary 2·5 × 1 × 2·2 m (1¾ × 1 × 1½ yds). The base of the aviary was covered partly with sand and partly with earth. In the earth I formed a hole where I placed a dish full of water into which fresh willow branches were dipped; they later budded. I also fixed willow branches along the sides, so that the centre of the aviary was entirely open. In one corner, a large bunch of reeds formed an attractive planted area.

4 Nesting boxes painted dark green, measuring 12 × 12 × 15 cm (30½ × 30½ × 38 in.) were hung from one side. The birds seemed to like this setting, for from the third day after being installed there, they began to build a nest in a nesting box hung at a height of 2 m. The outside of the nest consisted of thick stalks of grass, and the inside of finer grass, particularly *Agrostis vulgaris*. An enormous quantity of hens' feathers were used to line the bowl. In all there were 5 eggs. During the day, the pair took turns to sit. 2 young birds hatched after 16 days. With every subsequent brood, the period of incubation, 16 days, remained virtually the same.

(Editor's note: it may be that this breeder did not take into account the fact that the birds do not begin to sit until the 4th or 5th egg has been paid, because it seems well established that the incubation period is 12 days).

The parents then sat on their completely naked young for another 10 days; after that, they did not return to the nest even at night. When they first flew, the plumage of the young birds was grey, with a red sheen on the wings; the tail was red and the beak black. The first few days after flight, the parents took them back to the nest for the night. Once the female had begun to lay again, she ceased to feed the young and even chased them from the nest. When I captured the young birds, about 2 weeks later, I could clearly distinguish the males from the females: the tail of the former was a much brighter red.

I gave these birds various kinds of birdseed, both dry and germinated, as well as soft food to which I added chickweed chopped small. Every day, the pair were given 15 mealworms throughout the period in which the young were in the nest. They consumed considerable quantities of minerals before and after laying. The birds showed a preference for fresh egg-shells which still contained a little white. They also accepted ants' eggs, but preferred mealworms. They also consumed the young willow buds. I set Bengalese on some clutches of eggs from other pairs, and they sat and raised the young birds. The young males had some red feathers on the breast, while the breast of the young females was marked with grey, with white dots, and there was a little red on the side of the head. The black of the beak changed into a clear carmine red. Unlike a number of fanciers who claim that to raise Crimson Finches an inside aviary with an abnorm-

ally high temperature is essential, I believe I can state that these birds can reproduce perfectly in an outside aviary where the temperature varies between 16 and 20°C (60–68°F).'

SIDNEY WAXBILL, RED-BROWED FINCH, *Aegintha t. temporalis* (Latham)

G. Dormastrild; F. Astrild de Sydney, Astrild à cinq couleurs; D. Sydney-Astrild, Doorn-(Dorn) Astrild

(Pl. XXIV)

DISTRIBUTION: Eastern and south-eastern Australia.

DESCRIPTION: *Male* and *female* have bright red eye rings, rump and upper tail coverts. Top of head grey; back and wings greyish-olive-green; flight feathers grey with greenish edges; tail dark brown. Sides of head and throat light grey; lower parts bluish-grey with yellowish-grey in middle of abdomen. Beak and iris red and feet and legs yellowish-brown. Length: 4½ in. (11·5 cm).

SUBSPECIES: Two other subspecies with slight variations live in the adjacent regions; *Aegintha temporalis minor*, in northern Queensland, and *Aegintha temporalis loftyi*, in the Kangaroo Islands and the Lofty mountains.

These birds, which resemble the African Estrildinae, live in considerable numbers throughout the regions mentioned, especially on the edges of woods, parks, gardens, meadows and along rivers, and even in towns. They seek out human settlements, like our sparrows, because they know that they can find food there. During the mating period, they live in pairs, but several pairs form a group. These groups nest in a small colony, and outside the breeding period all the birds form a flock often sleeping together in sleeping nests. Their gentle song consists of no more than a simple phrase. The birds also make a low contact call, which becomes louder and more penetrating when one of them has lost sight of his partner.

Sidney Waxbill, *Aegintha t. temporalis*

The male carries out his nuptial display with a long blade of grass in his beak. In the wild, the nest is built in spiny bushes and trees covered with creepers. When they nest in gardens and parks, the birds often choose bush or rambler roses. The round or purse-shaped nest has a long entrance tunnel. It is made of vegetable fibre, fresh or dry blades of grass, and ferns, lined with soft grass, hair or feathers, with a preference for white feathers. The same nest may be used for several broods. A brush or a tree will house several nests about a yard (metre) apart.

Towards the middle of the last century, the first Sidney Waxbills were imported into England and shortly afterwards into other European countries. Dr. Russ bred them for the first time in Germany. Later, breeding was regularly successful, but as these birds have to be carefully acclimatised and since it is quite difficult to form true pairs, the species has never been really domesticated. They dislike cold and humidity and must winter in a heated aviary. They live peaceably with other species; several fanciers have observed them helping to feed young Gouldian Finches or Star Finches which have just flown, and even taking sole charge of them.

In *Die Gefiederte Welt*, 1957, p. 95, G. Overdijkink of

Bilthoven, an experienced breeder of Australian Finches, has given an account of the breeding of this species. He writes amongst other things:

> 'It was difficult for me to form a true pair by choosing from a group of birds imported in 1953. I had no success from 1953 to 1955, but in 1956 the only pair that I had left decided to nest in a coconut shell placed in a sheltered glass aviary. The 5 eggs hatched and the young left the nest towards the age of 3 weeks. They had their full colouring after 2 months. One of the young was backward and was still being fed while the others were independent; later, this small bird died. A curious fact is that a number of small Bicheno's Finches, which were already eating by themselves, started to cadge from the beakfuls of food while the Sidney Waxbills were near the food dish. When a second clutch of eggs was started, the young of the first brood tried to get back at any cost into the nest. In order to avoid accidents, the eggs of this second clutch were set under Bengalese, which hatched. The latter raised two young Sidney Waxbills together with their own young. In spite of these statements of Cayley and

Mamlok, who tell us that Sidney Waxbills cannot survive more than 2 years in the cage or the aviary, I can state as a fact that my birds, imported in 1953, are at the present time in excellent condition and are once again nesting. During the breeding period, the parents take egg mash, white bread dipped in milk, germinated seed and corn, and sometimes a few mealworms and a good deal of green food. Outside this period, they take very little live food.'

Sidney Waxbills are calm, quiet birds, easy-going and long-suffering. They must therefore be housed in the company of other birds of a similar temperament. If squabbles arise at the feeding dish, they will not have serious consequences. During the summer, grass seeds on the ear, e.g. *Poa annua*, will provide a good supplement to their diet. During the breeding period, ants' eggs and greenfly are recommended. Sometimes young birds will leave the nest before 3 weeks, when they still cannot fly. In a heated aviary, they are less likely to die as a result. A little more heat is essential before and during the first juvenile moult.

Genus: Poephila

LONG-TAILED GRASS FINCH, *Poephila a. acuticauda* (Gould)

G. Spitzschwanzamadine; F. Diamant a Longue Queue; D. Spitsstaartamadine, Pijlstaartamadine (Pl. XXXIII)

DISTRIBUTION: North-eastern Australia.

DESCRIPTION: Top and sides of head and neck bluish light grey; lores, chin, crop and throat black. Upper parts creamy-brown, with fine white edging on large outer flight feathers. Lower parts winy-brown, with white on vent region and lower tail coverts, as well as on rump and upper tail coverts. White of rump is marked off at base of back by a black stripe which continues to sides. Tail black; central tail feathers end in lengthy bristles. Iris red-brown, beak yellow and feet and legs flesh-coloured. Length: 6½ in. (17 cm) including tail. *Female*. A little smaller and mark on throat is less extensive.

SUBSPECIES: The subspecies, *Poëphila acuticauda hecki*, or Heck's Grass Finch, lives in an adjacent region of northern Australia; it differs in having a red beak and rather darker plumage.

These elegant and lively finches prefer open grassland, but can also be found in trees along watercourses, usually in large flocks. They have a melodious call, with a somewhat trumpeting song. Since they feed largely on grass seeds, they are often to be found on the ground or perched at the top of grass stalks. Their nest has been observed amongst tall grass, but also in thick bushes and low trees. The bottle-shaped nest is built of grass stalks, and the inside is lined with fine grass and some feathers. Amongst the 4–6 eggs, small pieces of charcoal have often been found. They sit for 13 days. The nesting season depends largely upon the rainy season, because the parents need grass seeds to feed their young, although they also take flying ants. During the breeding season the flock breaks up, and each pair marks out a small territory of its own.

In 1880 the first Long-tailed Grass Finches were imported into England and the Netherlands, and in 1897 into Germany, by Hagenbeck. These birds were first bred in England in 1897 and a year later in Germany. The yellow-beaked subspecies seems to be more hardy than the red-beaked, but both need a constant temperature, seed on the ear and germinated seeds as well as canary and millet seeds. When they are sharing an aviary with other birds, their aggressiveness to their own and related species, such as the Masked Grass Finch and the Parson Finch, must be remembered. They are hardy and can winter in an outside aviary, provided they have a moderately heated shelter. But they like to sleep in a nest-box, which sometimes causes difficulties: the

females begin to lay and are then often subject to egg binding provoked by the cold. These birds also breed well in a breeding cage at least 30 in. (80 cm) long, and 15–19 in. (40–50 cm) high and wide. It is sometimes difficult to select true pairs, because the distinction between the sexes is not always very clear. The best indication is always the song and seductive calls of the male.

Long-tailed Grass Finch, *Peophila a. acuticauda*

To avoid their laying too early, the pairs should be separated in winter and the females receive a ration of cod liver oil mixed with their seeds. Grass Finches need plenty of mixed grits, cuttle fish bone and minerals. They will learn to eat soft food, ants' eggs and mealworms, and this is a great help during the breeding period.

When birds breed in a cage, all they need is a sufficiently large nesting-box stuffed with hay, moss and fibre. The female likes to build a large, tightly-woven nest. When more than 5 eggs have been laid, the other eggs should be put under Bengalese, which will raise the young satisfactorily. The young remain for 3 weeks in the nest, and after they fly, they are still fed for a month or more by their parents. Like Gouldian Finches, the young birds become attached to a particular place; when their parents begin to lay again, the first brood can be housed in a compartment separated from the breeding cage by a wire slide. In this way their parents can continue to look after them. The juvenile moult takes 3–4 months, and the birds must never be moved until they have their full colours; and indeed they should not be sold or given to other bird keepers before they are at least 6 months old. Mortality is high amongst young birds who have not put on their adult plumage if their aviary is changed or they are moved. A good breeding couple can raise 3 broods of 5–6 young birds every year.

These birds seem to prefer light material for building their nest; they like to line the inside with cotton wool, kapok and white feathers. If they live in a large aviary and have no nest-box, they build a very ingenious large free-standing purse-shaped nest, and often with an entrance tunnel over which there is a door, as well as sleeping and nesting chamber.

A fawn mutation is currently being bred in Europe.

PARSON FINCH, *Poephila c. cincta* (Gould)
G. Gürtelgrasfink; F. Diamant à bavette; D. Gordel-grasfink, Kortstaartbaardvink   (Pl. XXXIII)

DISTRIBUTION: North-eastern Australia.
DESCRIPTION: Head and neck ash-grey, with light grey on sides of head, and black on chin, throat and chest. Rump and upper tail coverts white, defined by a black band which continues to sides of body. Vent region, lower tail feathers and thighs white. The black tail has two very slightly elongated central bristles. Iris dark brown, beak black, and feet and legs flesh-coloured. Length: 4¼ in. (11 cm). *Female*. Has smaller bib.
SUBSPECIES: In north-eastern Australia and north-eastern Queensland, the Black-rumped Parson Finch, *Poëphila cincta atropygialis*, is found. It has occasionally been imported into England since 1956. This subspecies is distinguished by its black rump and upper tail feathers, and also by the more brown colour of back and warmer colouring of lower parts.
The habits of the Parson Finch are basically similar to those of the Long-tailed Grass Finch. They were first imported into Europe at the same time as the Long-tailed Grass Finches. Like the latter, they were very popular, in spite of their rather severe colouring, which gave them the English name of Parson Finch and the German name *Pfaffenfink*. They breed better than the Long-tailed Grass Finch, and may have 3–4 broods in a season. They like to sleep in a nest-box, though this always brings the risk of too early laying. To avoid this danger, it is best to separate the pairs in winter. They live quietly in the company of other birds of the same size, but there are exceptions. When they are housed with other birds, the aviary must be sufficiently spacious, for Parson Finches hate intruders coming close to their nest and sleeping box. They are most suitable for a large breeding cage.
Their diet should contain plenty of grass food, soaked seeds, soft food, ants' eggs and mealworms from time to time, crushed dried eggshells, with which Vitacalcium should be mixed and cuttle fish bone. If they have a nest-box, they will quickly build a nest there, which they will use both for breeding and sleeping. They use various kinds of material, and like to have some charcoal. They sit for 13 days or a little longer. The young remain in the nest for more than 3 weeks and are fed for a long time after they have flown. When the young have been raised and the parents show signs of beginning a new brood, the first brood must be housed in a compartment next to the breeding cage. It is always dangerous to re-house these young birds before they have completely finished the juvenile moult, that is, before the age of 6 months.

MASKED GRASS FINCH, *Poephila p. personata* (Gould)
G. Maskenamadine; F. Diamant à masque; D. Maskeramadine   (Pl. XXXIII)

DISTRIBUTION: Northern Australia.
DESCRIPTION: Lores, a narrow band across forehead, face, chin and top of throat black. A large black band crosses top of rump and is continued down to sides of body. Rump and upper tail coverts, lower tail coverts and middle of abdomen white. Back brown, with a lighter brown on sides of head; lower parts winy-brown. Beak yellowish-orange; iris brown and feet and legs flesh-coloured. Length: 4¾ in. (12 cm). *Female*. Has same plumage, and the best indication of sex is the song; but 2 males housed together hardly sing at all.
SUBSPECIES: In northern Queensland the subspecies, *Poephila personata leucotis*, or White-eared Grass Finch, is found; it is distinguished by its white cheeks and yellow beak.
These birds have the same habitat as other species of the genus *Poephila*; outside the breeding period they are also found in large flocks, usually on the ground, looking for grass seeds and other food. These flocks break up at the beginning of the mating season, when each pair builds its nest in tufts of grass or thick bushes. The nest is bottle-shaped with an entrance at the side; it is built of grass and lined with fine grass and feathers; pieces of charcoal have been found in the nests. Five or 6 eggs are laid.
They were first imported into Germany in 1899 by Hagenbeck; a few years later, these birds bred in captivity.
These very lively birds must have plenty of room, and are not very suitable for cages. But they can be housed with other birds, since they are peaceable in nature. They sometimes fight with Long-tailed Grass Finches during the breeding period.

Masked Grass Finch, *Poephila p. personata*

The best results in breeding are found with a large interior aviary with a well chosen mixed collection of plants. It is difficult to form real pairs; only the song and the nuptial display of the male give any indication of sex.
Once a true pair has been formed, they nest very quickly. Some pairs accept a nest-box, but others prefer to build an open nest, close to the ground, amongst heather plants or low bushes. The nest is spacious and the inside lined with soft material; the entrance is at the side. Care must be taken not to peer at the nest, for the parents often dislike this violently and show their dislike by abandoning their eggs or their young. They sit for 2 weeks on the 5–6 eggs, and the young birds remain in the nest for more than 3 weeks. After flight, the parents feed them for at least another month, and the young birds usually return to the nest in the evening to spend the night there. They have their colouring by the age of 6 months, and care must be taken not to move young birds which have not yet entirely completed their first moult. They have been crossed with the Long-tailed Grass Finch and the Zebra Finch.

Genus: Padda

JAVA SPARROW, *Padda oryzivora* (Linnaeus)
G. Reisfink, Reisvogel; F. Padda, Calfat; D. Rijstvogel,
Padda   (Pl. XXXIII)

DISTRIBUTION: Probably lived originally in Java and Bali, but introduced by man into numerous tropical regions, where the species is firmly established and is numbered amongst the bird population of all these regions: Sumatra, Borneo and Lombok, the Malaysian peninsula, Moluccas, south Celebes, South-East Asia, southern China, Taiwan and Philippines. (Also settled in Zanzibar, Pemba, east African coasts; even in the island of St. Helena.)

DESCRIPTION: Top of head, lores, eye region, nape of neck and throat black. Sides of head white, marked off below by a narrow black stripe. Rump, upper tail coverts, tail and flight feathers black. Upper parts and breast light bluish-grey; lower parts soft pinkish-grey, with the exception of lower tail coverts and thighs, which are white. Beak red, point and edges being lighter. Feet and legs flesh-coloured, iris reddish-brown with pink edged orbital ring. Length: approximately 5½ in. (14 cm). *Female*. Beak usually a little larger. Young birds upper parts dark grey, and lower parts

Java Sparrow, *Padda oryzivora*

lighter, with yellowish white cheeks; at the time they first fly they have black beaks. Variants with a black head, and without white cheeks, are quite common. Such variants probably developed as a result of deficiencies in feeding and in other matters such as light. There is no infallible way to sex these birds. It is said that the beak of the male is larger, particularly at the base, but this is not always the case; moreover, the development of the beak is connected with the age of the bird. The only way to recognise a male is by its song, which it always sings when it is cheerful. The rather monotonous song is somewhat reminiscent of the tinkling of small bells.

MUTATIONS: Despite its very widespread distribution, there are no subspecies. However, 2 mutations have appeared in birds in captivity. The White Java Sparrow is very common and often kept by bird fanciers. However, birds with pure white plumage are quite rare; often white birds have a few grey feathers on the back, an odd or dark flight feather. Often, the bird is simply particoloured or even greyish throughout. The young of white parents are not completely white when they leave the nest; they always have grey on the back. Nevertheless, white or largely white birds leave the nest with a red beak, while pied and normal grey birds have black beaks when they leave the nest. White Java Sparrows have been kept for centuries, first in China and later in Japan as well.

The second mutation, the Cinnamon (Fawn) Java Sparrow, appeared in the aviaries of Mr. Burfield of Adelaide, Australia. According to a communication from Mr. A. Jackson, editor of the *Review of the Finch Society of Australia* (reprinted in *Cage and Aviary Birds*, 10th June, 1965), the Cinnamon (Fawn) Java Sparrow has greatly increased in numbers during the last 5 years. There is no

example of this mutation in Europe. The Cinnamon (Fawn) Java Sparrow has a dark yellowish-brown back and a belly of the same colour, but lighter. All the black parts of the wild Java Sparrow are replaced by brown. There can be a cinnamon (fawn) pied form specimens of which have been bred within the last year or so.

Java Sparrows like to live close to men, but they also live far from human beings in the grassy steppe covered with shrub and occasional trees. When the rice ripens, these birds invade the rice fields in enormous flocks, which do great damage. During this period they seem to live solely upon rice (paddi rice from which the husk has not been removed). They build a round nest of fairly coarse material but line the inside with hair, feathers, vegetable wool and other soft material. The nest is often sheltered by the edge of a roof, but can also be found amongst bushes, in a tree or even in a hole in a tree or building. The female lays 4–7 eggs.

The Grey Java Sparrow has been imported from time immemorial; Vieillot mentions it as early as 1870. In *Naturgeschichte der Stubenvogel*, 1795, Bechstein gives a detailed description. The Java Sparrow is a very pleasant cage bird, and when it is well cared for, its plumage is always faultless. Their temperament is peaceful, provided they have plenty of room. They can be kept with Weaver birds and even with Budgerigars but not with Waxbills or other small species. A pair can be housed in a cage, but it must be at least 30 in. (80 cm) in length, particularly if one wishes to breed. Success in breeding, however, is best obtained in an aviary. The first success in Europe was in Switzerland in 1890 but since then they have bred more or less everywhere. The white, pied or grey varieties, the off-spring of white parents, reproduce much more easily and raise their young better.

A Budgerigar box, with a floor surface of 8 × 8 in. (20 × 20 cm) and a height of 12 in. (30 cm) is quite suitable for Java Sparrows. The entrance to the box can be round, 2 in. (5 cm) in diameter or else the front can be half open. The birds sit for about 13 days and the young leave the nest towards the age of 4 weeks and then remain about 3 weeks in the company of their parents. The juvenile moult finishes towards the age of 3 months.

The diet of Java Sparrows includes canary seed, white and Senegal millet. They particularly like unhusked rice (Paddi), but this supplement is not indispensable. They must also be given plenty of green food, particularly chickweed (*Stellaria media*) and meadow grass (*Poa annua*) in seed. During breeding, they must be given germinated seeds: canary seed, white millet and oats, as well as soft food and where possible ants' eggs. The breeding birds must have been given ample time to get used to soft food. After they have been separated from their parents, the young birds must be given soft food, 2–3 times a week. Germinated seeds, valuable nourishment for all seed eating birds, should also be given at all times. It is obvious that both young and old birds must have clean water, grit and minerals available to them at all times.

The heredity of the mutations has not yet been seriously studied. Here is what we know:

1) The white is dominant over the grey (the wild colour). If a white bird is paired with a grey, all the offspring will be more or less white, although certain of the young may be entirely grey. The white does not seem to be a constant hereditary factor. Even if 2 pure white birds are paired for several generations, a number of parti-coloured or even completely grey birds will always be found amongst the offspring.

2) Grey birds, the offspring of white parents, crossed between themselves, can never give white offspring. For

the recessive colour cannot give rise to the dominant colour.

3) The new cinnamon (fawn) mutation is recessive with regard to the grey (the wild colour). This seems to contradict the usual rules, since the cinnamon colour is generally sex-linked.

Genus: Pirenestes

BLACK-BELLIED SEED-CRACKER, THICK-BILLED FOREST WEAVER, *Pirenestes o. ostrinus* (Vieillot)

G. Purpurastrild, Purpurweber; F. Gros-bec ponceau, Pyreneste ponceau à ventre noir; D. Purpurastrild, Pupurwever

DISTRIBUTION: Central Africa.

DESCRIPTION: Head, neck, breast and upper tail coverts red. Tail dark red, rest of plumage black, with reddish shading towards lower tail coverts. Iris red-brown with bluish

Black-bellied Seed-cracker, *Pirenestes o. ostrinus*

eyelids. Beak steel-blue with black tip, feet and legs brownish-yellow. Length: 5 in. (13 cm). *Female.* Forehead, top of head, sides of head, throat and upper tail coverts red, tail darker red. The rest of plumage brownish-grey with a few scattered red marks.

SUBSPECIES: Other subspecies, differing in shape of beak, colours or in length have been described: *Pirenestes o. sanguineus*, from the west coast of Africa and *Pirenestes o. minor*, which lives on the east coast; as well as a number of localised subspecies.

The Black-bellied Seed-cracker prefers humid regions, but also lives in the savannah on the edge of the forests. It seems that the subspecies with smaller beaks are found largely in marshy regions, while those with larger beaks live principally in the savannah and feed on hard dry seeds. All these birds also eat insects. The nest is built in a tree, is large, and is made of leaves, twigs and grass, the interior lined with fine grass. The female lays 3–5 eggs, on which both birds take turns to incubate.

Neunzig mentions that this species was imported for the first time in 1908 to the Berlin and Hamburg Zoos. These birds are shy, and hide amongst the vegetation. They become more calm and tame in the cage, but since they are very lively, they are more suitable for a large aviary.

The male carries out his nuptial dance with a blade of grass in his beak. A nuptial flight has been observed in the wild, the female going in front of the male and flying at a great height; during this nuptial flight, the male's song is heard. After flying in circles, the two birds descend amongst the brush.

At the present time this species is only rarely imported. No successful breeding has been reported. The diet consists of alpist, various kinds of seeds, live and green foods. These birds like to bathe.

Genus: Nigrita

CHESTNUT-BREASTED NEGRO-FINCH, *Nigrita b. bicolor* (Hartlaub)

G. Zweifarbenschwarzling; F. Négrette à dessous châtain, Négrette bicolor, Bengali brun à ventre roux; D. Bruinborstastrild

DISTRIBUTION: Central and west Africa, Zaire, Cameroon, Uganda.

DESCRIPTION: Forehead and lores dark chestnut; upperbody slate-grey. The flight feathers dark brown, and tail feathers black. The sides of head and lower body dark winy-chestnut. Iris dark brown, with eyelids edged with bluish-grey; beak blackish, feet and legs dark brown. Length: approximately 4¼ in. (11 cm).

Little is known about the life of these birds in the wild. They have been observed as isolated specimens or in pairs, in the company of other *Estrildinae* in clearings in the virgin forest. They seem to live mainly in the half-light of the underwood, and come on to the ground to look for their food, which seems mainly to consist of live insects, fruit and seeds. The nest of grass, leaves and moss is made in bushes or thick trees, always close to a termites nest. Four to 5 eggs are laid and are incubated in 11–12 days.

In 1934 the first specimens were imported into England, but these birds do not seem to have survived for long, for there is no mention in the literature of any details about their life in the aviary.

Chestnut-breasted Negro-finch, *Nigrita b. bicolor*

Genus: Amadina

CUT-THROAT FINCH, RIBBON FINCH, *Amadina f. fasciata* (Gmelin) (Pl. XXVII)

G. Bandfink; F. Cou-coupé; D. Bandvink

DISTRIBUTION: Senegal, Eritrea.

DESCRIPTION: Upper body yellowish-brown with a grey sheen, and has small dark brown horizontal marks. Rump and upper tail coverts light brown with pale extremities. Wings greyish-brown streaked with black, with yellow dots. Tail black marked with white. Throat and sides of head are white. In the male, neck distinguished by large band of carmine-red. Lower body yellowish-brown, with chestnut mark in centre of chest and abdomen; vent region white. Breast and sides have a pattern of black dots. Iris brown, beak slate-grey, and feet and legs flesh-coloured. Length: 5 in. (13 cm). *Female*. Distinguished by absence of red collar and the chestnut mark on abdomen and is lighter in colour.

SUBSPECIES: Two other subspecies with darker colours have been described: *Amadina f. alexanderi* in east Africa, and *Amadina f. meridionalis* in the Transvaal.

Cut-throats live in the arid steppe, where they feed largely on grass seeds. They would not have been observed, except for their liking for paying visits, often in large flocks, to settlements. They like dust baths. They will nest either high up in trees or very low in thick bushes. They often take over the abandoned nests of weaver birds, but are also perfectly capable of constructing a solid round nest with a small entrance tunnel. The female lays 4–5 eggs, on which both sexes incubate in turn for 12 days and the young leave the nest when about 21 days old.

Cut-throat, *Amadina f. fasciata*

The Cut-throats are amongst the most frequently imported exotic birds, and since 1770 they have been bred successfully in France. These birds are bred everywhere in Europe, it is found that pairs are very aggressive during the nesting period, even to destroying the nests and young of smaller birds who share quarters with them. Thus a breeding pair must be housed with birds capable of defending their brood, such as Java Sparrows and other strong Mannikins.

They are very lively birds, the male vigorously sings his somewhat raucous and warbling song, raising his feathers to show the patch on his abdomen. He gives a proud display before the female, tossing his head and stretching himself, at the same time raising his feathers. Even in a cage, a pair would breed so long as they are kept long enough before they are supplied with nesting materials.

When they are ready to breed, they will construct a nest in a nest-box filled with soft hay; the male bringing other materials, while the female forms the nest. A pair will quite readily breed 3 times in a season. Their diet consists of mixed millet and canary seeds, green food and ripe grass seeds.

Some birds will accept mealworms and soft food, but a pair will raise their young on a seed diet supplemented by germinated seeds.

Hatching takes place after 12 days and the young birds can soon be heard chirping. If their parents do not find the breeding diet which suits them, or if the female wants to lay another clutch of eggs, the young are sometimes thrown out of the nest after a few days. In nest feather young males already have the red collar on their neck and both sexes will breed when 1 year old.

The different subspecies can easily be crossed if they are kept together, and their young are fertile. Hybrids have also been obtained with the closely related species, the Red-headed Finch, *Amadina erythrocephala*, and these hybrids are also fertile. Other crossings have been obtained with the Parson Finch, *Poephila cincta*, the African Silverbill, *Euodice cantans*, the Indian Silverbill, *Euodice malabarica*, and the Java Sparrow, *Padda oryzivora*.

RED-HEADED FINCH, PARADISE SPARROW, *Amadina erythrocephela* (Linnaeus)
G. Rotkopfamadine; F. Amadine à tête rouge, Moineau du Paradis; D. Roodkopamadine   (Pl. XXVII)

DISTRIBUTION: South Africa.

DESCRIPTION: Top and sides of head and throat scarlet-red; lores whitish grey. Upper body greyish-brown; wing coverts greyish-brown bearing cream marks and black streaks. Back has pattern of black streaks, throat greyish-white, and breast white with brown and black marks. Abdomen reddish-brown, and vent region white; tail brownish-black with white tips. Iris brown, beak light steel-blue-grey and feet and legs flesh-coloured. Length: 5 in. (13 cm). *Female*. Has no red on head, and lower body is lighter.

These birds live in almost all the regions of South Africa where they are as common as house sparrows in Europe, nesting below the roofs of houses and flats. Sometimes they nest in a colony of about 30 nests; all nests are large, round and have an entrance at the side. They are constructed of grasses, and the interior is lined with soft vegetable fibres and feathers. They also like to sleep in a nest. They often use the abandoned nests of weaver birds and after it has been used for one brood, the nest is abandoned.

Red-headed Finch, *Amadina erythrocephela*

As in the case of the Cut-throat, the Red-headed Finch have been imported into Europe since the beginning of the 18th century. It even seems that Vieillot succeeded in getting a pair to breed. However, it was not until the beginning of the 20th century that these birds were imported in any number, when they became very popular. They are calmer and more peaceable in nature than the Cut-throat, particularly during the breeding period. They are less lively, often seeking out a quiet corner where they are not disturbed by their companions.

They should always be supplied with plenty of nesting-boxes and building materials, otherwise they take away the material of other nests. Red-headed Finches will often breed well in a cage. The female lays 3–6 eggs, on which both parents incubate for 13 days. Birds in an aviary breed assiduously and are quite tolerant of examination of the nest. But a breeding bird adopts a defensive attitude, turning its head from left to right, opening its beak and emitting whistling sounds. The same behaviour has been observed in the Cut-throat. Its song also consists of warbling and murmuring sounds. Their diet consists of mixed millet and canary seed, millet sprays and a regular supply of weed seeds. All dried seeds should be given in the germinated state, especially during breeding. During the winter months it is a good thing to give them a little cod liver oil, soft food and Vitacalcium, supplements which are appreciated by all small seed-eating exotic birds. During breeding, Red-headed Finches will also accept insectivorous food, ants' eggs and small mealworms.

They prefer to build their nests in an obscure corner, and a pair will gladly accept a nest-box or a basket. The nest is somewhat clumsy, made of leaves and blades of grass, lined with many feathers. Even during sitting, feathers continue to be added, when the male comes to take turn on the nest. The incubation period is 13 days and the young fly, at about 23 days, young males can already be recognised by the red which is beginning to adorn their heads. After 6 months, the young are able to reproduce, but breeding should be restricted until they are a year old.

The crossing of a Red-headed Finch with a Cut-throat gives male hybrids which are fertile; and if these are mated with Cut-throat or Red-headed Finch females, young fertile females can also be obtained. They have also been crossed with the Java Sparrow, *Padda oryzivora*.

Genus: Ortygospiza

SOUTH AFRICAN QUAIL-FINCH, *Ortygospiza atricollis muelleri* (Zedlitz)

G. Wachtelastrild; F. Astrild-caille à lunettes; D. Kwartelastrild (Pl. XXI)

DISTRIBUTION: South Africa, west Africa.

DESCRIPTION: Forehead and lores black; eyes encircled by large white band. Upper body greyish-brown with black streaks, tail black with a white tip. Throat and front of cheeks black; chin has a white bit. Sides of head and neck greyish-brown; breast and sides have horizontal black and white lines against a brownish-grey background. Abdomen chestnut, and lower tail coverts whitish and marked. Iris reddish-brown; upper mandible black and lower mandible

South African Quail-finch, *Ortygospiza atricollis muelleri*

red; feet and legs are flesh-coloured. Length: 3½ in. (8·5 cm). *Female.* Distinguished by absence of black on head; her colours are duller and their pattern less pronounced.

These birds live on the ground, in regions with abundant grass, especially close to water. They are numerous in regions which are temporarily inundated after heavy rain. They proceed along the ground, running rapidly or hopping. Their diet consists largely of grass seeds. They take to the air in an almost vertical flight, giving a sharp 'tic-pic, pic, tic' call. They nest on the ground, and the nest is usually well camouflaged below tufts of grass. Often several nests are found close together. They are built of grasses, and lined with fine grass and feathers. The entrance tunnel is covered with grass stalks. Both birds take turns to incubate the 4–6 eggs.

These curious Estrildinae always go on the ground, like the Gallinaceae, moving in short hops when they are followed. After flying, they generally land on the ground, and very rarely on a branch or in a bush. They seem to have difficulty

in moving in these high situations, squatting there without moving until they have the opportunity to return to the ground. However, they like to stand on some raised point, such as on a large stone or a protruding root. The males like to stand there to sing; they make great efforts with their neck and beak, but the result is no more than a murmur, alternating with the high pitched call already described. These birds like sunbathing, but also bathe at length in the water, allowing themselves to be soaked to the skin.

The acclimatisation of these birds requires much care. On arrival in our cold climate, they must be placed in a cage with a soft, loose cloth under the ceiling, for like small quails, these birds have a habit of flying vertically, and can easily damage their skulls if the top of the cage is solid. They begin by eating on the bottom of the cage, and they have to be patiently taught to eat from a seed pot. Thus at first the seeds have to be spread on the bottom of the cage. Millet sprays and other kinds of small millet seeds should form the first diet, supplemented by ants' eggs, small mealworms and greenfly. They adore germinated bird-seed and take a lot to feed their young, though at first the latter are fed exclusively on live food.

These birds cannot live for a very long period in the restricted space of a cage, they like to run, and also ought to be able to fly morning and evening. An outside aviary is not vey suitable for them, unless it has a heated shelter where the birds can sleep at night. Part of the outside aviary flight must be completely covered, so that the wind and the rain cannot get in. It is much better to keep these birds in an interior aviary where the floor is divided into damp and dry parts, for these birds like both. In winter the temperature must not drop below 65°F (18°C).

Since 1874 South African Quail Finches have been imported into Germany and even earlier than that into England. Their way of life was not well-known, which explains why breeding was not successful until much later. It is easy to form a pair, since the sexes are easily distinguished; but successful breeding has been rare. The birds must have the opportunity to choose their partner, and therefore it is necessary to keep numbers of both sexes together, until the pairs form naturally. During the display period, males fight, and it is necessary to separate the pairs and to house them in a separate aviary.

One of the successes was published in *Die Gefiedert Welt*, 1964, which tells how Mr. Ocko of Vienna succeeded in raising 3 generations of Quail Finches in an inside aviary. The dimensions of this aviary were 5½ × 11 ft (1·7 × 3·3 m), with a height of 6½ ft (2 m); the floor of the aviary was raised 1½ ft (50 cm) above the floor of the room. Part of the floor is covered with coarse river sand, while the other part is covered with turf. There are also sods of turf on a raised platform where the birds like to spend the night. They shared the aviary with Australian Diamond Finches, several pairs of South African Quail Finches and a pair of west African Quail Finches. In the morning, the male South African Quail Finch sought and gathered blades of grass, which were used by the female to build the nest.

The nest is built in a hidden corner, and the nesting birds must not be disturbed. Live insects are indispensable for successful breeding, which takes place during the winter months. The birds sit for 14 days. The young birds leave the nest at 3 weeks, but the parents continue to feed them for some time afterwards.

In the literature, these birds are often mentioned under their old name *Ortygospiza atricollis polizoma*.

WEST AFRICAN QUAIL-FINCH, *Ortygospiza a. atricollis* (Vieillot)

G. Rebhuhnastrild; F. Astrild caille du Gabon; D. Patrijsastrild   (Pl. XXI)

DISTRIBUTION: West Africa.

DESCRIPTION: Forehead and lores black; throat is adorned with a black mark, going down as far as the crop, while the white bib on chin is very small or even non-existant. A narrow white circle surrounds the eyes, and sometimes the outline of the eyes is marked by a few small white feathers. Breast brownish-grey; centre of abdomen reddish-brown. The horizontal white and black pattern does not extend far.

Black of lores is underlined by a thin white line. Beak red, and feet and legs brownish-flesh-colour. Lower body whitish-brown; lower tail coverts white with brown fringes. Length: 3½ in. (8·5 cm). *Female*. Has no black on head or throat.

These birds have the same habits and need the same treatment as described for the South African Quail Finch.

Several subspecies have been described, but it is difficult to distinguish them, for the plumage is similar in each case.

West African Quail-Finch, *Ortygospiza a. atricollis*

Genus: Amandava

AVADAVAT, RED AVADAVAT, BOMBAY AVADAVAT, TIGER FINCH, *Amandava a. amandava* (Linnaeus)   (Pl. XXI)

G. Tigerfink; F. Bengali piqueté, Bengali moucheté, Bengali rouge; D. Tijgerfink

DISTRIBUTION: India and Burma.

DESCRIPTION: Head and neck red with black lores and a white line beneath eyes. Back dark brown, each feather tipped with red. Upper tail coverts red. Wings dark brown with small white dots. Tail black, lower body red, with black on abdomen and lower tail coverts; sides covered with small white dots. Iris and beak red, and feet and legs brown. When not in breeding plumage coloured like female. *Female*. Upper body greyish-brown, rump and upper tail coverts red, sides of head brownish-grey, lower body whitish-yellow and sides more brownish, with a more widely spread pattern. Length: 4 in. (10 cm)

SUBSPECIES: Two other subspecies have been described, differing in colour and length: *Amadava a. punicea*, known in the trade as the Chinese Avadavat, although it lives in Indonesia and Thailand, and *Amandava a. flavidiventris*, which lives in northern China and the Sunda Islands.

These birds live wherever they can find plenty of grass, even in the immediate neighbourhood of villages and farms. Outside the breeding period, they can be seen in large flocks, but during the nesting period, a number of pairs keep company and nests are often found together in dense bushes. Nests are constructed of blades of grass, and lined with fine vegetable matter and feathers; 4–7 eggs are laid and are incubated for 10–11 days and the young fly when about 18 days old.

In the countries of their origin, these birds have been kept in cages from time immemorial. They were brought to Europe very early, and for a long time have been amongst the most popular cage birds. They easily adapt to our climate, are hardy, and have a charming song. They breed successfully, although not as well in cages as in fairly spacious and well-planted aviaries. They can be kept with their own and other species, but the males become somewhat aggressive during

the breeding period. They must have direct sunlight, and if they live in too dark a cage, their plumage soon becomes greyish and black and very patchy.

Although these birds can live on a diet of round bird seed, for raising their young they need ants' eggs, green food and small mealworms cut into tiny pieces. A pair feeding young can be allowed without risk to. leave the aviary to find suitable live food in the garden.

The male brings the nesting material which the female arranges and plaits; they take turns to incubate and have often been observed together on the nest.

Avadavat, *Amandava a. amandava*

GREEN AVADAVAT, *Amandava formosa* (Latham)

G. Olivgrüner Astrild; F. Bengali vert, Bengali vert des Indes; D. Groene Tijgerfink   (Pl. XXI)

DISTRIBUTION: Central India.

DESCRIPTION: Upper body olive-green, tail black, sides of head and upper tail coverts a more yellowish colour. Lower body yellow, sides marked with horizontal white lines on an

Plate XXXVII

Pagoda Starling, *Sturnus pagodarum*

Common Mynah, *Acridotheres t. tristis*

Bank Mynah, *Acridotheres ginginianus*

Pied Mynah, *Sturnus c. contra*

Grey-headed Mynah, *Sturnus m. malabaricus*

Plate XXXVIII

Alario Finch, *Alario alario* ♂ upper ♀ lower

Wild Canary, *Serinus c. canarius*

Goldfinch, *Carduelis c. carduelis*

Bullfinch, *Pyrrhula p. pyrrhula* ♀ left ♂ right

Green Singing Finch, *Serinus m. mozambicus*

Grey Singing Finch, *Serinus leucopygia*

olive-green background. Iris brown, beak red, feet and legs brownish. Length: 4¼ in. (11 cm). *Female*. Duller and more greyish and her abdomen paler yellow.

Green Avadavat, *Amandava formosa*

These birds are often found in sugar cane plantations, rice paddies and meadows, feeding largely on grain and seeds. The nest is solidly built from leaves and reed and grass stalks, lined inside with fine grass and often hangs from the stalks of sugar canes or amongst tall grass.

These birds were brought to England for the first time in 1873, and a few years later to other European countries. In their native country, they had already been kept in cages. In the aviary, they are much less spectacular than the Red Avadavat; they are quieter, less lively and very silent. They live in peace with the small birds who share their aviary, but during the breeding period they chase away any intruder who approaches the nest. They often go on the ground, looking for small insects under bushes and amongst dead leaves. In general, their acclimatisation is uneventful. At first they must be housed in a cage, until they have become thoroughly accustomed to bird-seed. When they are later housed in an aviary, they tolerate our climate quite happily; but they must be brought indoors in winter. The seed mixture should include millet on the ear and mixed millet seeds; they eat plenty of green food, small mealworms and ants' eggs. This supplementary diet is essential during the breeding period, because they will not accept soft food.

Females are somewhat subject to egg binding and to try to avoid these misfortunes, a little cod liver oil should be mixed with the seeds. Vitacalcium or other minerals for birds which are on sale should always be available. The nest is often built in a nest-box; the materials used are coconut fibres, feathers and grass and has an entrance at the side. Five eggs are usually laid and they sit for 12 days, the young leaving the nest when about 3 weeks old and the male continues feeding them for about 10 days. In the young

birds, the back is greyish-green, front of abdomen greyish-green, and tail and beak black. Like the Red Avadavat, these birds can live 10 years or longer in an aviary.

GOLDEN-BREASTED WAXBILL, *Amandava s. subflava* (Vieillot)

G. Goldbrüstchen; F. Centre-orange, Bengali zebré, Astrild à flancs rayés; D. Goudbuikje

DISTRIBUTION: The steppe of central Africa.

DESCRIPTION: Upper body greenish-grey, beak black, with a little white at tip. Lores black; rump, upper tail feathers and a line over eyes red; sides of head greyish with a more yellowish throat. Sides of body greenish-grey with yellow horizontal lines. Lower tail coverts orange-red, lower body golden-yellow, with an orange-red sheen in parts. Iris red, and beak red with black line on upper mandible, feet and legs reddish. Length: 3¼ in. (8 cm). *Female*. Duller, without red eyebrow.

These birds live in regions of plentiful grass, where the soil is not too dry, and prefer banks of watercourses or districts which have been flooded. There, great flights of these Estrildinae are found, but during the display period small groups formed by a few pairs. Although they will perch in trees, they live for preference amongst reeds of river banks and amongst high grass. They climb with agility along the narrow stalks, and look for grains and seeds which have fallen to the ground from the ears. The nest is usually found amongst the grass, sometimes several together. These birds also take over the abandoned nests of weaver birds.

These Estrildinae have been imported for a long time. They must be carefully acclimatised in a cage, but once they have become used to a diet of dry seeds, they can be housed in an outside aviary, with the flight made of small mesh wire netting. They are equally suitable for a cage in a flat wher they will sometimes even nest, so long as they have been accustomed previously to soft food. They live peacefully with other small birds. Their diet should consist of small dry and germinated millet seed, grass carrying its seeds and millet sprays, which they eat greedily. If this diet is supplemented by ants' eggs during the breeding period, the chances of success are increased; if they have only soft food, the young are often neglected. They must have an ample supply of fresh green food.

They usually nest in a high position, readily accepting a nesting-box or a small basket. If there are thick bushes within their aviary, they will construct a somewhat loose and careless nest, using grass stalks, coconut fibre and other materials. The male brings the materials, and the female builds the nest which is lined with soft material and feathers. Both parents sit on the 4–6 eggs, which hatch after 12 days. The young fly at the age of 3 weeks, but still return to the nest at night for some 7–10 days. Like the Red Avadavat, the Golden-breasted Waxbill loses its fine colours if it does not have sufficient direct sunlight and cannot bathe every day. A larger species *A. s. clarkei* comes from South Africa.

Genus: Pytilia

MELBA FINCH, *Pytilia m. melba* (Linnaeus)

G. Buntasrtild; F. Bleu-marquet, Astrild Melba; D. Bonte Astrild, Melba Astrild   (Pl. XXVII)

DISTRIBUTION: Angola, Zaire, Zambia.

DESCRIPTION: Forehead, cheeks and throat red; rest of head grey. Upper body olive-yellowish-green, with red on upper tail coverts and central tail feathers, other tail feathers dark brown and red. Lower body greyish-brown with white stripes; breast spotted with white. Centre of abdomen white; lower tail feathers off-white with a very vague horizontal pattern. Iris reddish-brown; beak sealing-wax

red with a black line on upper mandible; feet and legs brownish-grey. Length: about 5 in. (12 cm). *Female*. Has no red on head; her colours and markings are duller all through.

SUBSPECIES: Twelve subspecies have been described, differing only slightly in size and colour. The birds live in the north of the area of distribution and are distinguished by their red lores; those in the south have grey lores.

Outside the breeding period Melba Finches live in small groups like most other finches. In regions with plenty of grass and dry ground, with thick bushes here and there, they seek seeds and insects on the ground. They build their round nest lined with blades of grass and down in low trees or spiny bushes. From 3–5 eggs have been found. The first Melba Finches were imported into Europe in 1874, since when they have been found regularly, though in small numbers. They must be carefully acclimatised, and the birds require a constant temperature. After acclimatisation, they usually take fairly easily to breeding in an inside aviary,

Melba Finch, *Pytilia m. melba*

provided the flight has a few plants and bushes. An outside aviary is suitable for them only during the hottest summer months. More than one pair must never be kept together, males are extremely aggressive especially in the breeding period, they even attack different bur related species.

Their diet should consist not only of various kinds of mixed bird-seed, but also millet sprays, mealworms, maggots and ants' eggs. This live food is indispensable during the breeding period, and the parents also take greenflies, gnats and spiders. They do not seem to accept soft foods, but will feed germinated seeds to their young shortly before they fly.

The first successful breeding took place in 1936 in England. The breeder was not successful in getting Bengalese to raise the young, because the young Melba Finches did not seem to be able to take soft food, and seemed to need live food during the first 10 days. These birds prefer to build an open nest in a thick bush, but will sometimes use an open nest-box, building a somewhat careless nest with grass. During the day, the birds take turns to sit on the 3–4 eggs, which hatch after 13 days. The newly hatched birds are covered with grey down; they remain about 3 weeks in the nest, and are then fed for quite sometime by their parents.

AURORA WAXBILL, *Pytilia ph. phoenicopters* (Swainson)

G. Auroraastrild; F. Diamant aurore, Pytilie à ailes rouges; D. Aurora-Astrild   (Pl. XXVII)

DISTRIBUTION: Central Africa.
DESCRIPTION: Main colour grey, with a little red on shoulders and rump; upper tail coverts and central tail feathers brighter red, other tail feathers blackish with a little red. Wings reddish-brown, head and lower body are grey with a fine white horizontal pattern, heavier towards the lower abdomen. Lower tail coverts grey with white horizontal lines. Iris red, beak black, and feet and legs reddish-grey. Length: about 4¾ in. (12 cm). *Female*. Less vivid, and red is replaced by brown.
SUBSPECIES: Two other subspecies have been described: *Pytilia ph. emini* and *Pytilia ph. lineata*, or Striped Waxbill. The latter is a more greyish colour, and the pattern on the front of the abdomen is more pronounced.
In general, these waxbills are found in pairs, often in the company of other small Estrildinae. They live in the dry steppe, open woodland, and in cultivated fields, remaining

in the trees or bushes, which they leave only to seek food. They feed on grass seeds, and many insects, preferring termites. Their round careless nest of leaves, lined with feathers, is built in a bush or a low tree.

The first specimens of this species were imported into Germany in 1870. Great care is needed in acclimatising them; they require warmth, which is indispensable at first. In the summer, they can be housed in an outside flighted aviary. A well-planted aviary is recommended, for they only come to the ground to eat. They will live peaceably with other small species, but the male becomes aggressive during the breeding period, and chases all birds which venture too close to the nest. Although the young are fed mainly on insects during the first few days, several bird fanciers have succeeded in getting Bangalese to raise their young, which were fed by them largely on soft food. When the Aurora Waxbills decide to build an open nest in a bush or to nest in a nest-box, the pair will sit in turn on the 3–5 eggs. They are apparently indifferent to anyone checking the nest. When the young hatch, after 13 days, one must do all one can to give the parents suitable breeding food: i.e. fresh ants' eggs, greenfly, fruitfly, small mealworms cut in tiny pieces and various

Aurora Waxbill, *Pytilia ph. phoenicopters*

other kinds of small live insects. If the parents do not have live food, they throw their young out, however, if they decide to feed their young, they usually raise them well. The young leave the nest at the age of 3 weeks, but the parents continue to feed them for 2–3 weeks. The first successful results were obtained in 1872 in Germany, by Dr. Russ. Since then, these birds have bred almost everywhere in the world.

RED-FACED WAXBILL, *Pytilia afra* (Gmelin)

G. Wienerastrild; F. Astrild de Wiener, Pytilie à dos jaune; D. Wienerastrild

DISTRIBUTION: East Africa and Abyssinia, as far as Mozambique.
DESCRIPTION: Forehead and the area surrounding eyes, sides of head and throat red. Top of head grey; back and wings olive-yellow, rump and upper tail coverts red. Flight feathers olive-brown, tail feathers brown and red, central tail feathers red. Front of abdomen grey and olive-brown, breast and abdomen have a horizontal pattern of fine yellowish-white lines, growing wider lower down. Iris and beak red, base of beak dark brown; feet and legs flesh-coloured. Length: about 4¾ in. (12 cm). *Female*. Has no red on head, and is more greyish, with less vivid colours.
These birds usually live in pairs in dry steppe, with a few bushes, after the breeding season, several family groups

gather together. They are often found in the company of Cordon Bleus or other small Estrildinae. They generally keep to the bushes and trees, and land only to look for the grass seeds on which they feed. They also take small insects, for the most part during the breeding season.

The nest has been found in thick bushes and low trees. It is round and somewhat carelessly built, of blades of grass lined with feathers. Three or 4 eggs are laid, but sometimes the nests which have been found contained more eggs, the extra eggs being those of a Whydah with parasite nesting habits.

The first Red-faced Waxbills came to London in 1877. Later, they were imported only occasionally and in small numbers.

After the Second World War, several bird keepers neverthe-less succeeded in breeding these birds, and thanks to their observations, we know that live food and germinated seeds are indispensable during breeding; parents which do not have this diet available have thrown their young out. Other keepers have succeeded in getting Bengalese to sit on the eggs and raise the young, even though they did not have live food. The birds sit for 13 days, and the young fly at the age of 3 weeks, but are fed for a further 2 weeks by their parents.

YELLOW-WINGED PYTILIA, RED-FACED AURORA WAXBILL, *Pytilia hypogrammica* (Sharpe)

G. Rotmaskenastrild; F. Astrild à ailes jaunes, Pytilie à ailes jaunes; D. Roodmaskerastrild

DISTRIBUTION: Sierra Leone, Ghana, Togo, and Nigeria as far as central Africa.

DESCRIPTION: Forehead, behind eyes; sides of head and throat red. Top of head, neck and back brownish-grey; rump and upper tail coverts red; tail black with a few red marks. Wings brown with yellow edges; lower body grey with white horizontal lines. Iris red, beak black and feet and legs flesh-coloured. Length: about 4¾ in. (12 cm). *Female.* Has no red on head, and her lower body is more brownish.

These Pytiliae live in pairs or in small groups in the more humid regions of West Africa, particularly in the savannah, where there is abundant grass. They keep largely to trees

Yellow-winged Pytilia, *Pytilia hypogrammica*

and bushes, but feed on the ground on grass seeds and insects. Their round nest with a side entrance are made in a thicket at a height of about 39 in. (1 m). The nest itself is woven of grass stalks, lined with fine grass and feathers resting on a layer of leaves.

In 1879, Dr. Russ mentioned this species for the first time, stating that King Ferdinand of Bulgaria had kept the first bird in an aviary since 1872. It is likely that a few Yellow-winged Pytiliae have been included from time to time in shipments of Melba Finches and the Red-faced Waxbills and that neither the merchants nor the bird keepers recognised them. In 1963, Dr. Burkard received a pair which, however, had red wings and belonged to a subspecies, *Pytilia hypogrammica lopez*. The first successful breeding was obtained by M. Arbeiter, who had confused these birds with Aurora Waxbills. The pair nested in a nest-box, and the young birds died shortly after they had flown. The male was then replaced by a male Aurora Waxbill, and a year later young birds were obtained from this crossing. They should be housed and fed in the way described for the Aurora Waxbill.

Genus: Uraeginthus

CORDON BLEU, RED-CHEEKED CORDON BLEU, *Uraeginthus b. bengalus* (Linnaeus)

G. Schmetterlingsfink; F. Cordon bleu; D. Blauw-fazantje   (Pl. XXVI)

DISTRIBUTION: West Africa, Senegal, Ghana, Nigeria.

DESCRIPTION: Blue around eyes and a lighter blue on rump and tail coverts; tail darker blue. Upper body fawn grey, sides of head, throat, breast and sides pale blue. Ear patches winy red, lower body light grey, with pink sheen in middle. Iris brown, beak reddish grey with black tip, feet and legs brown. Length: about 4¾ in. (12 cm). *Female.* Lacks red ear patches her blue colouring is paler and less extensive.

These charming bires live in the arid steppe, with a few spiny bushes, but are always to be found close to water, in pairs, or small family groups. They are often observed in larger flocks at water holes and where their food is to be found. They also live close to settlements and even amongst human beings. They feed on the ground, their food consisting mainly of grass seeds, termites and other insects. They nest in thick spiny bushes or a low tree. The round nest is made of grass stalks, lined with fine grass and feathers. The female lays 3–6 eggs, on which the pair take turns to sit for 11 days and the young leave the nest when about 18 days old.

From well before any first records Cordons Bleus have been imported into Europe, and many have bred successfully. Success always depends upon the quantity of live food given

Cordon Bleu, *Uraeginthus b. bengalus*

to the parents during breeding.

They must be acclimatised with considerable care. They must never be placed in an outside aviary if they have not learnt where the feeding troughs are. It is recommended that a few millet sprays should be hung in various places, so that the birds can always find something to eat. These birds usually flourish when they are housed indoors, but will not reproduce there unless they are given plenty of live food, which is indispensable for raising the young. On the other hand, if they are housed in a well planted outside flighted aviary, they reproduce quite easily.

They should in the main be given various kinds of millet seeds, which they also like germinated, they should be given green food, fresh ants' eggs and small mealworms. In an aviary, they will also find plenty of small insects, spiders and greenfly. They like to fly after gnats, which they find on leaves and flowers.

SUBSPECIES: Seven subspecies live in various regions in Central and Southern Africa; the colours and patterns of these subspecies resemble each other closely.

BLUE-BREASTED WAXBILL, *Uraeginthus a. angolensis* (Linnaeus)

G. Angolaschmetterlingsfink; F. Cordon bleu d'Angola; D. Angola-Blauwfazantje   (Pl. XXVI)

DISTRIBUTION: Angola, Namibia, San Thomé.
DESCRIPTION: Around eyes, sides of head, throat, breast, abdomen, rump and upper tail coverts bright pale blue. Tail midnight blue, upper body fawn-grey, lower body grey.

Blue-breasted Waxbill, *Uraeginthus a. angolensis*

Iris brownish red, beak reddish grey with black tip, feet and legs brown. *Female.* Lower body light brown and her blue colouring is less vivid and less extensive. It is difficult to distinguish female Blue-breasted Waxbills. Length: 4¾ in. (12 cm).

These birds have the same habits as the Cordon Bleu; they also have a soft melodious song.

They were first imported into Germany in 1910; at the present day, and since the end of the last war, they are regularly imported. When they first arrive, if the weather is cold, they must be housed in a heated room, although they seem more hardy than the Cordon Bleu.

Mr. Goodwin of London has published in the *Avicultural Magazine*, Vol. 65, No. 6 a very thorough study of this species. He succeeded in breeding them on several occasions in his bird-room, which faces south and south-east, is moderately heated and lit by electric light 12 hours during the winter.

The basic diet consists of mixed millet seeds and poppy (maw) seeds. They must also regularly be given live food such as maggots, ants' eggs, green fly and small mealworms. A box filled with clean earth a mixture of poppy seed, mixed seed, and lawn grass seed can also regularly be sown. The birds will eat the young shoots and in this way will obtain

from the ground substances indispensable to their health. They will also remove in a very short time greenfly given on 2 branch. Once a week, a little soft food should be added to their mixture of seeds. During breeding, it is essential to give them mealworms, ants' eggs, green caterpillars, and plenty of other insects. If they do not have this live food, the parents will not raise their young. The incubation period is 11 days and the young remain in the nest until the 18th day, and are then fed by both parents for a further 2 or 3 weeks.

BLUE-HEADED WAXBILL, *Uraeginthus c. cyanocephalus* (Richmond)

G. Blaukopfschmetterlingsfink; F. Cordon bleu à tête bleue, Astrild à tête bleue; D. Blauwkop-Blauwfazantje, Blauwkopastrild   (Pl. XXVI)

DISTRIBUTION: Tanzania, Kenya, East Africa.
DESCRIPTION: The whole head, throat and sides of body vivid pale blue. Upper body light brown, with yellowish brown lower tail coverts. Iris and beak red and feet and legs brown. Length: about 5 in. (13 cm). *Female.* Blue colouring is less extensive and less bright.

These birds prefer to live in pairs or small family groups, in the arid steppe with a few bushes and trees. They feed on seeds and insects on the ground, and prefer to build their nest near a wasp's nest. The nest is oblong and has a side entrance and is somewhat carelessly built of straw.

They were first imported into England in 1927, and in 1930 M. Decoux of France was the first to succeed in breeding them. Since the Second World War, they have been imported more frequently, and at the present day successful breeding is no longer uncommon. Mr. D. Goodwin of London has published in the *Avicultural Magazine*, Vol. 68, No. 4, a lengthy account of his experiences with this species.

It seems that of the three species of Cordon Bleu, the Blue-headed Waxbill is the most hardy. It must obviously spend the winter in a heated aviary, and during the short days, the day must be artificially lengthened to 12 hours. In a nest box they build a nest of blades of grass and the female lays 3–5 eggs; two birds take turns to sit. For the first week after hatching, the young are fed on mealworms, grubs, and other insects and from then on the parents give them germinated seeds. When the young fly, on the 17th–18th day, they are

Blue-headed Waxbill, *Uraeginthus c. cyanocephalus*

very shy and wild, and bump into the netting and windows; but they soon settle down.

All small *Estrildinae* must be provided continually with good grit, minerals and sea-sand. Supplementary food is of great importance, and gives variety to the diet. These supplements will consist largely of grass seeds, which can be given on pieces of turf which are frequently renewed. Pre-germinated millet on the ear, as well as various kinds of bird seeds and grass seeds sown in the aviary are also appreciated. Once a week, they should be given a little soft food; and they should also have green food, such as chickweed, lettuce, etc.

VIOLET-EARED WAXBILL, *Uraeginthus g. grantinus*
(Linnaeus)

G. Granatastrild; F. Grenadin à oreillons violets, Astrild grenadin; D. Granaatasrild (Pl. XXVII)

DISTRIBUTION: South Africa, Angola, Rhodesia, Natal and the Transvaal.

DESCRIPTION: Head cobalt blue, with violet on eyebrows, sides of head and the parotic regions, while the lores are black. Upper body chestnut red, wings brown, rump and upper tail coverts blue and tail black. Lower body brown, with black on chin and in middle of abdomen, lower tail coverts dark blue. Beak and Iris red, and feet and legs reddish grey. Length: 5½ in. (14 cm). The colours of the female less vivid with no black on chin; lower body lighter, more creamy with faint brown sheen.

The Violet-eared Waxbills live in arid steppe with a scattering of spiny bushes. In pairs of small family groups they visit water holes, where they can be seen in the company of Melba finches and Blue-breasted Waxbills feeding on grass seeds and insects. In spiny bushes they build a round nest of grass lined with feathers. They sit on the 3–4 eggs for 13 days, and the young leave the nest some 16 days after hatching. In their nest the eggs of the Paradise Whydah, *Steganura p. paradisea*, have been found. Violet-eared Waxbills were already in possession of Dr. Russ of Germany in 1874.

Since the end of the Second World War, they have been imported fairly regularly. Their acclimatisation is tricky, particularly as these birds do not seem to flourish in a cage needing direct sunlight. At first they must be kept in a constant temperature of 70°F (21°C); when they have become accustomed to their food and seem in good condition, they can be placed in the summer months in an outside aviary which receives plenty of sunlight.

It is impossible to house them in the company of their near relatives. They must be given various kinds of bird seed, as well as live food in the form of mealworms, ants' eggs and all kinds of insects. They will also learn to take soft food especially when ants' eggs and boiled mealworms cut into tiny pieces are given on top of it. If they are kept in the company of Bengalese, Violet-eared Waxbills will also learn to eat eggs food. Their supplementary food should consist of grass and weed seeds. In 1927, Professor Steiner of Zurich succeeded in breeding them for the first time; since then, occasional success has been achieved, but the reason why this has been rare is probably the lack of live food. In a well planted aviary, the birds will build an open nest in a thick bush, but they will also accept a nest box. They must be given plenty of feathers, for even while they are sitting, the birds go on additing them to their nest.

PURPLE GRENADIER, PURPLE-BELLIED WAXBILL, *Uraeginthus i. ianthinogaster* (Reichenow)

G. Veilchenastrild; F. Grenadin pourpre, Grenadin à poitrine bleue; D. Puprpergranaatastrild, Blauwbuik-Granaatastrild, Grote Granaatastrild

DISTRIBUTION: Kenya.

DESCRIPTION: Cheeks, a circle surrounding eyes, forehead and lores are blue, rest of head and neck brown. Upper body reddish brown, with blue on upper tail coverts; tail black The lower body reddish brown with blue marks; breast has blue band across it. Iris and beak red and feet and legs black. Length: about 5½ in. (14 cm). *Female*. Blue is lighter and less extensive, with all colours less vivid.

Purple Grenadier, *Uraeginthus i. ianthinogaster*

Their way of life is similar to that of the Violet-eared Waxbill. These birds have been observed on the ground or amongst spiny bushes feeding on grass seeds and insects. In a thick bush they build a round nest somewhat carelessly made of grass, and thickly lined with feathers continuing to add feathers while they are sitting. In addition to their own 3 or 4 eggs, the eggs of Fischer's Whydah, *Tetranura fischeri* have also been found in them.

The first Purple Grenadiers were imported into Europe in 1928, and it was not until long after the last World War that they first begun to be imported in any number, enabling bird keepers to breed them. The first successful breeding was registered at Keston Bird Farm, England, in 1957. More recent successes have been noted in Germany (*Die Gefiederte Welt*, 1964, Nos. 3 and 11). Two accounts are given there, from which we learn that the birds sat and raised their young in an inside aviary. Nevertheless, it is recommended that they should be housed in an outside planted aviary with plenty of sunlight during the summer months.

Their animal food should consist of ants' eggs, flies and maggots, as well as mealworms cut into small pieces. They should also be given small germinated seed, and they also need grass seeds and green food. Sometimes a pair will wait a long time before deciding to breed, constructing several nests and then demolishing them. The male usually sits on the 4–5 eggs during the day, while the female replaces him at night.

The birds feed their young with ants' eggs, grubs, millet sprays and green food. The young fly at the age of 3 weeks and are independent a fortnight later. Their black beak begins to turn red 2 weeks later, and the young males soon sing and display.

Genus: Emblema

PAINTED FINCH, *Emblema picta* (Gould)

G. Gemalter Astrild; F. Emblème peint; D. Geschilderde Astrild (Pl. XXII)

DISTRIBUTION: Australia.

DESCRIPTION: Forehead red, rump and upper tail coverts; tail brownish black, and rest of upper body brown. Lores, eye region, chin and throat red; sides of head brown. Lower body black covered with large white dots, middle of the breast has red band. Iris light yellow, beak black and red, and feet and legs flesh coloured. *Female*. Less vivid, and red on head less extensive; white dots on lower body are more thickly scattered. Length: 4¼ in. (10·5 cm).

These birds are very numerous in certain localities in northwest of Australia and the interior of Queensland, where the climate is very warm and dry. They settle near a spring or on the bank of a small watercourse, and do not avoid the presence of humans. As artificial watering points have become more numerous in order to irrigate the desert regions, the Painted Finch has found a more favourable habitat as the result of the colonisation of his home country. In the past, these birds were obliged to live a nomadic life when the springs dried up during the long periods of drought. They feed on grass seeds, but also eat insects, which form the breeding diet during the first days of the young bird's life.

The round nest is built of grass, vegetable fibre and bark, lined with hair and very fine fibres, close to the ground in thick bushes. The bottom of the nest is often made firm with a layer of earth mixed with small pebbles, pieces of wood and bark. The two birds take turns to sit for 15–18 days. At birth, the young are completely naked, ane the parents must sit for a further 10 days; then their eyes open. Once they fly, they only return to the nest to sleep. In Australia, the breeding period of these birds depends upon the seather conditions. They begin to nest aftet the rains, when there is plenty of food available.

In 1869, these birds were imported into England for the first time, and shortly afterwards to other European countries.

Painted Finch, *Emblema picta*

Occasional specimens were reported from time to time later. The first successful breeding was obtained in 1910 by Mr. H. Wilford in England, and there is a more recent report from 1935. In the latter case, the birds were housed in a box-type cage 6 ft. (1·8 m) long. The birds sat for 17 days. Before hatching, the parents fed exclusively on mixed seed and showed no interest either in green food or soft food. Once the young had hatched, they greedily accepted mealworms and maggots, but still did not touch the soft food. The temperature during the breeding period was 60–65°F (15–16°C).

The report by Mr. Sweetman, who succeeded in raising 7 young birds in 3 hatchings during a single season, seems very different. He gave the 6 eggs to 2 pairs of Bengalese, who hatched them, and who also raised the birds with the aid of soft food and germinated seeds, but without any live food being supplied. A later clutch was hatched by the parents themselves, who accepted millet sprays and ants' eggs, but not mealworms. They sat for 15 days. Painted Finches have the habit or sleeping on the floor of their cage or aviary, and the young sleep in this way once they have flown. The young birds that were raised by the Bengalese had the habit of sleeping on the roof of a nesting box.

If Painted Finches are housed in an outside aviary, part of this aviary must be completely covered and they should be provided with perches close to the floor. These birds cannot stand the damp cold of our climate, although they are perfectly tolerant of dry cold. During the day they must have the opportunity of taking long sun baths, and in the winter months they need some heat. In the outside aviary where they live in the summer, thick bushes should be planted, since they like to nest in them. The floor of the aviary should consist of sand and earth scattered with large pebbles, on which the birds like to rest. In the nests of these birds in the wild, pieces of charcoal and bark have been found, as well as small pebbles.

Genus: Erythrura

GOULDIAN FINCH *Erythrura gouldiae* (Gould)
G. Gouldamadine; F. Diamant de Gould; D. Gould-amadine
(Pl. XXII)

DISTRIBUTION: North Australia.

DESCRIPTION: Top of head and cheeks black; this black region is marked off by a narrow light blue stripe changing on top of head and on throat to yellowish-green. Back grass green, rump and upper tail coverts varying from greenish-blue to blue. Throat violet blue, marked off by an orange line which separates this colour from yellow on abdomen. Wings have both green and brownish green, tail black; two central tail feathers are elongated and pointed. Beak pinkish white with red point; feet and legs flesh coloured and iris brown. Length: 4¾ in. (12 cm). Plumage of female is lighter. The Red-headed Gouldian Finch (*mirabilis*) and the Yellow-headed Gouldian Finch (*armitiana*) are distinguished by the deep red or orange yellow on top of head and cheeks.

In recent years, ornithologists have been divided about the classification of Gouldian Finches. The species was first assigned to the genus *Poëphila*, but science has shown that it is very close to the *Erythrurae*, the genus *Erythrura;* this thesis is based on hybrids obtained by crossing Gouldian Finches and *Erythrurae*.

Although these brilliantly coloured birds are amongst the most attractive cage and aviary birds, many bird keepers do not dare take the risk of attempting to breed them, becaus their price is quite high. Yet there are cases where Gouldian Finches have bred with the same ease as Zebra Finches. On the other hand, there have been cases where experienced

breeders have run into trouble after considerable success. In the wild state they live in the open savannah, preferably along water courses, and find their food amongst the tall grass. They like to nest in the scrub and eucalyptus trees scattered along the banks. In the region where they nest,

Gouldian Finch, *Erythrura gouldiae*

the summers are extremely hot, the daytime temperature sometimes rising to 105–115°F (40–45°C), while the night temperature does not fall below 65°F (20°C), although in the interior of the country the nights can often be very cold. During the nesting season, which coincides with the rainy season, the degree of humidity is about 70%. When the eggs have hatched, the grass seeds are beginning to ripen, and the young birds are fed on these tender fresh seeds. Most nests have been found either in trees or in termite mounds where other birds have made holes. The construction of the nest is simple, and when a pair nests in a hole in a tree, no material is used.

In 1887, the first Gouldian Finches arrived in England. They had been discovered by John Gould, who gave them the name of *Amadina gouldiae* in honour of his wife, who had accompanied him on this extremely strenuous expedition. In 1896, the first Gouldian Finches appeared in Germany. Mr. P. W. Teague, in England, was the first to obtain, over 20 years, a total of 24 generations of stock raised in captivity. The experiences and conclusions of this expert were published in the *Avicultural Magazine* from 1931 to 1946. These publications reveal a rather curious fact: these birds, housed in winter in small wooden unheated aviaries, where they were sheltered from damp and draughts, remained in excellent condition. Breeders in the Netherlands have not followed this method: their Gouldian Finches winter in a heated room. Nevertheless, nothing seems more harmful to them than winter quarters which are too warm; this seems to weaken the birds. On the other hand, in the breeding season it appears that they should be housed in a quite high and more or less constant temperature, and the attempt should be made to maintain humidity at 70%. In Australia, wild Gouldian Finches like to sunbathe in the middle of the day, while the majority of other birds seek the protection of foliage. Moreover, Gouldian Finches seem more lively and cheerful when the ambient temperature is very high. In Europe, these birds do not have enough sun in the summer, and in addition the humidity is too high in the cold weather, which seems to be very harmful to them. Young specimens which have not yet acquired their adult plumage seem particularly to dislike low temperature and cold humidity; in these conditions, their juvenile moult is brought to a halt and the young birds die quite suddenly without having shown the slightest symptom of illness. It is recommended that these young birds should be placed in a constant temperature of 70°F (23°C). Thus these young birds are best housed in a heated inside aviary, where the day and night temperatures vary between 72° and 65°F (24° and 20°C), while the humidity should be increased when the temperature rises.

There has also been considerable discussion of their feeding. Some writers advise that they should be given dry seeds in winter, and during the breeding period should recceive a diet consisting principally of ripening seeds on the ear and of germinated seeds. This mixture of seeds should consist of canary seed, millet, grass seeds and niger. The birds will show a preference for one seed or the other depending on the period of the year. In order to learn their preference, they the different kinds of seed in separate dishes. Green food should be given every day. Chickweed (*Stellaria media*) lettuce and spinach are particularly recommended. It is easy to sow chickweed in a number of boxes or pots, so that the birds can have it throughout the year.

Germinated seeds are preferable to soaked seeds. In order to soak the seeds, they should be left in water over night, and given the next day after they have been dried. To get the seeds to germinate, they should be soaked for 3 nights, being drained every morning and hung up during the day, and soaked again during the night. At the end of the 3rd day, the young shoots will already be visible. It is important to have small quantities of seeds germinating in succession, so that sufficient are available every day. The birds can also be given longer green shoots, by spreading the germinated seeds on a layer of potting compost; the green shoots will appear after a few days. In addition to canary seed, millet seeds and niger, millet on the ear can also be germinated, following the same procedure. Care must always be taken in providing green food. Chickweed gathered in gardens or in the fields has sometimes been treated with chemicals and is then very dangerous to the birds; the same is true of spinach and lettuce bought in the shops. Those who have a garden can easily sow these various seeds in the springtime, and if there is a good summer, valuable fresh seeds can be gathered. Millet on the ear can also be sown, either in the open air or in a greenhouse; the heads will be smaller than those bought in the shops, but will have quite plentiful seeds.

It seems that a vitamin supplement is indispensable for Gouldian Finches; the deficiency of certain vitamins is the cause of inexplacable sudden death. Preparations are on sale which can be mixed with the soft food, for example *Federvit* and *Pastavit*. G. Ziegler's *Die Gouldamadine* contains an easy recipe for preparing the mixture. White millet is husked in a kitchen mixer, the seeds are then mixed with the yolk of an egg. This mixture is put to dry in the sun, and is then kept in the refrigerator in a hermetically sealed pot. Even Gouldian Finches which have become used to mealworms disdain them when they have the chance to eat this soft food.

Mr. Teague believed that his success was due to the use of the English product Virol, which includes glucose (grape sugar), egg, orange juice, vegetable fat, various minerals and vitamins. Similar preparations were mentioned in the chapter on the feeding of frugivorous and insectivorous birds. When these preparations are used, care must be taken not to give excessive amounts, and it is wise to give them only once or twice a week. Some breaders give only distilled water, while others consider it enough to boil the drinking water.

Gouldian Finches raise their young better in a common aviary than in a separate cage.

The nest boxes should not be placed in position until the beak of the females becomes dark in colour, which indicates that they are in breeding condition. In the case of males who are ready to breed, the point of their beak is bright red. Birds in this condition will soon get ready for nesting, a process which begins with a display consisting of dances, bowing and singing. Then each pair inspects the nesting boxes and begins to fill the one chosen with blades of grass, pieces of bark, leaves and fibres.

The floor of each nest box should be covered with a layer of damp moss. The female lays 5 or 6 white eggs, on which both birds sit in turn for 14 days. The birds will tolerate a discreet inspection of the nest.

Gouldian Finches should never be over-crowded in the aviary, they like a calm environment and prefer to live with birds of the same species.

Heredity of the different colour varieties. In the wild, it seems that Black-headed Gouldian Finches are about three times as numerous as the Red-headed variety. Both head colours are sex-linked and the Red-headed are dominant to the Black-headed.

Birds of the two varieties can be crossed, and it is clear that the majority of Red-headed males are carriers of the Black-headed factor. We now know for certain that the colour of the head is sex linked. Thus a Red-headed female is never a carrier of the Black-headed factor, even if her mask is wholly black with a few scattered red feathers. The phenomenon is often found and has confused numerous breeders. Only by mating a Black-headed male which is a carrier of the Red-headed factor with a red-headed female can we be sure of red-headed male offspring with pure heredity (homozygote).

The appearance of a red-headed male never reveals whether he is of pure heredity (homozygote) or impure (heterozygote). In order to be sure whether or not he carries the other factor, trial matings have to be made: when a homozygote red-headed male is crossed with a red-headed female, all the offspring are bound to be red-headed; even if there is only a single black-headed young bird amongst them, this proves that the father was not homozygote.

There is nothing to show that a black-headed female has any preference for red-headed males. Moreover, professional breeders in Japan and Australia always mate red-headed males with females of either variety. In this way a certain percentage of the young will always have a red head. Some breeders claim that the offspring of a pure red-headed line are less hardy than the offspring of a heterozygote line, but there is nothing to support this assertion. If infertility occurs, the reason may be no more than inbreeding.

The outcome of any mating can be forecast, but it must be remembered that these forecasts are purely theoretical, and hold good only for a very large number of offspring. Thus a brood of 4–6 young birds may give results which are not in accordance with theoretical forecasts. Here are the forecasts for any given mating:

1) Black-headed male × Black-headed female: 100% black-headed offspring; in theory, half the offspring would be male and the other half female;
2) Black-headed male × Red-headed female: 50% black-headed females and 50% heterozygote black-headed males (i.e. carriers of the black-headed gene);
3) Red-headed heterozygote male × Black-headed female: 25 heterozygote red-headed males, 25% black-headed males, 25% red-headed females and 25% red-headed females;
4) Red-headed heterozygote male × Red-head female: 25% red-homozygote males, 25% red-headed heterozygote males, 25% red-headed females and 25% black-headed females. Thus all the young males will be red-headed, and only trial matings will show which of them are homozygote and which are heterozygote;
5) Red-headed homozygote male × Red-headed female: 50% red-headed heterozygote males and 50% red-headed females;
6) Homozygote red-headed male × Black-headed female: 50% heterozygote red-headed males and 50% red-headed females.

Thus matings 4 and 5 are test matings, to demonstrate whether or not a male is heterozygote; nevertheless, in both cases the majority of the offspring will be red-headed, and it is possible for mating 4 to give a first brood consisting solely of red-headed offspring, which may give rise to over-hasty and mistaken conclusions. Thus matings 4 and 6 are to be recommended.

The yellow-headed variety is 'accidental' mutation provoked by a factor which prevents the red from coming out. This factor is not constant, and the head colour is never truly yellow, but rather a diluted red. This factor can also be seen in the point of the beak, which is not red, but yellowish brown.

These 'accidental' mutations are generally recessive with regard to the corresponding wild factors, which here are the red or black colour of the head. It therefore follows that where a normal bird is crossed with a yellow-headed bird, the offspring, regardless of the sex of the birds, will be bearers of the latent yellow-headed factor.

Since the yellow-headed factor prevents the development of the red but no influence upon the black (melanine) black-headed birds possessing the yellow factor in the heterozygote state, or even in the homozygote state, are virtually indistinguishable from normal black-headed birds, except with regard to the point of the beak, which will not be red.

In red-headed birds, this factor is clearly manifested in the colour of the head and beak. Thus in order to breed yellow-headed Gouldian Finches, it is necessary to begin with red-headed birds.

In many cases, the yellow factor seems to be present in the latent state but without ever having had the opportunity to come out. In the wild state, a 'defect' mutation usually disappears rapidly, but in breeders' aviaries special attention is paid to every defect, even if it leads to smaller and weaker specimens. Here are the possible matings and the forecast outcome (/ =carrier of, split):

1) Yellow-head × normal: 100% normal offspring, carriers or split for yellow-headed; These offspring are normal in appearance, and when they are crossed with normal birds, the yellow-headed factor will never come out;
2) Normal × Normal/Yellow-headed carrier: 50% of normal offspring and 50% of normal offspring, yellow-headed carriers; the appearance of all these birds is similar;
3) Normal/Yellow-headed × Normal/Yellow-headed: 50% normal/yellow-headed, 25% normal and 25% yellow-headed; the normal offspring and those which are yellow-headed carriers have the same appearance;
4) Yellow-headed/ × Normal: 100% normal/yellow-headed;
5) Yellow-headed × Normal/Yellow-headed: 50% normal/yellow-headed and 50% yellow-headed;
6) Yellow-head × Yellow-headed: 100% yellow-headed.

It is clear that the black-headed × yellow-headed matings will follow the sex linked heredity, as it has been explained. Moreover, black-headed birds have no part to play in the breeding of Yellow-headed Gouldian Finches.

There is also a White-breasted variety where the usual purple on the breast is replaced by white. This mutation was first bred in South Africa and is now breeding freely in many countries. A White variety has been raised in America where the main colour is white but the red and yellow areas still remain.

Few birds have been the object of so much study: their behaviour is described in detail in many articles and books. Even the diseases which they may contract have been studied, because there is often a high and inexplicable rate of mortality. The most frequent mishaps consist of infections of the alimentary tract, the symptoms of which are not always easy to recognise, but which can now be resisted with antibiotics. A vitamin supplement is indispensable, particularly during the winter season. If effective treatment is required for sick birds, it is worthwhile turning for advice either to an experienced breeder or to a veterinary surgeon who has specialised in the treatment of small birds.

However, an amateur may avoid illness by giving his birds a very varied diet and by housing them under good conditions both in summer and winter.

PIN-TAILED NONPAREIL, PIN-TAILED PARROT FINCH, *Erythrura p. prasina* (Sparrmann)
G. Lauchgrüne Papageiamedine; F. Diamant quadricolore, Pape des prairies; D. Indische Nonpareil

(Pl. XXIV)

DISTRIBUTION: India, Malaysia, Indonesia.
DESCRIPTION: Sides of head, forehead and throat blue, with black lores; upper tail-coverts bright red. Upper parts grass green, with green and brownish black on wings. Tail brownish black, but central tail feathers red and elongated, ending in a fine point. Lower parts are light cinnamon, with red in middle of abdomen. Iris brown, beak black and feet and legs brown horn coloured. Length: about 5½ in. (14 cm). Head of female is wholly green, with no blue; lower parts are brownish grey; central tail feathers are much shorter.

Throughout the large area in which they are distributed, Pin-tailed Nonpareils live in small groups, often in the company of Munias, preferring to settle on the edge of woods adjacent to rice fields. They feed on grass and rice seeds and nest in the undergrowth or creepers. The voluminous nest, of coarse material, is round with an entrance at the side.

This species has been known since the end of the seventeenth century and was described and imported about 1870; but few details are known about it. At the present day, these birds are regularly found on sale, but only experienced bird fanciers have succeeded in accustoming them to a diet of seeds. In general, imported birds have adjusted to eating rice with the husks still on, and this must always be given to them, some soaked and the rest dry. They will also take millet sprays, either dry or soaked. As long as they have germinated or soaked seeds, they will not touch seeds. A week after their arrival, they can be given a little clean green food.

When the birds are placed in a common aviary, they must still be given soaked seeds. They will gradually learn to take millet and other seeds, oats (groats) without the husk, poppy seeds, and niger. In the spring and summer ripening seeds of grass and oats are appreciated and during the nesting period they must regularly be given soft food and ants' eggs.

They are lively and active, and the ideal place for them is a large well planted aviary, where they have the opportunity to fly and use their claws normally. When they are housed in a cage, their claws do not wear down, become too long and must regularly be cut.

Pin-tailed Nonpareil, *Eruthrura p. prasina*

The nest must be hung very high up, in a calm corner of the aviary. The materials that should be supplied are hay, vegetable fibres, moss and bark. The male gives his nuptial display on the ground or a branch, holding a long blade of grass in his beak, with his head raised. As soon as the female joins him, he drops the blade of grass which he was holding by the middle, and begins to sing, drawing his head back into his neck and making jerky movements of the tail in the direction of the female. Mating takes place afterwards in the nest. The female lays 3–6 eggs, on which the two birds sit in turn, the female sitting alone during the night. The young are entirely naked at birth, and their parents sit on them for another 8 or 9 days. Although they are usually well fed, the young birds cannot survive if they are not kept warm at night, and this is the cause of considerable mortality in the nest. In an inside aviary, where there is a constant temperature of 76°F (25°C), the young birds will remain alive, so long as there is artificial light so that the nights do not last more than 6 or 7 hours. If a pair beginw to nest early in the spring, this artificial lighting is indispensable.

In addition to germinated seeds and green food, the parents need plenty of ripening grass seeds available. Where these cannot be had, breeders can use sprouted seeds in dishes. When the young leave the nest, towards the age of 22 days, they go on demanding to be fed for a long time. But they begin to forage after a few days and are usually independent at about 5 weeks. By the time they are 6 weeks old, the males can already be recognised by the first red feathers on the belly. When they are 6 months old, the young birds take on their colour.

BLUE-FACED PARROT FINCH, *Erythrura t. trichroa* (Kittlitz)

G. Dreifarbage Papageiamadine; F. Diamant de Kittlitz, Diamant tricolore; D. Driekleurige Papa-goaimadine (Pl. XXIV)

DISTRIBUTION: Indonesia, New Guinea, North-Eastern Australia and some archipeligos in the Indian Ocean.
DESCRIPTION: Sides of head and forehead blue, with blackish lores. Upper parts dark green, with brown and green on wings, and red on rump and upper tail-coverts. Tail blackish brown with dark red edging, lower parts brownish grey. Beak black, iris dark brown and feet and legs brown. Length: about 5¼ in. (13 cm). *Female*. Less highly coloured and blue on head less extensive.

SUBSPECIES: 10 subspecies have been described, but the differences in colour and size are minimal. Amateurs do not usually succeed in identifying them and cross different subspecies, which consequently lose their characteristics. Here is a list of subspecies: *Erythrura t. sandfordi, Erythrura t. modesta, Erythrura t. pinaise, Erythrura t. sigillifera, Erythrura t. trichoa, Erythrura t. pelewensis, Erythrura t. clara, Erythrura t. woodfordi* and *Erythrura t. cyaneifrons.*

Blue-faced Parrot Finches live along the coast and in the forst, where they can be seen in pairs or in small flocks. They also visit the plantations and gardens, where they find plenty of grass, grass seeds form their main food. At the present day they are tending to settle in deforested areas where open meadows have replaced the forest and they are in fact even more abundant there than elsewhere.

The large oval nest is built in a well shaded position amongst the foliage or in a crack hidden by creepers, usually at a height of about 65 ft (20 m). The material used consists of blades of grass, leaves, ferns and root hairs, while the breeding chamber is lined with soft grass.

In recent years, birds of the subspecies *cyaneifrons*, which is smaller, have been imported from the New Hebrides. The blue on their head is very extensive. Acclimatisation is said to be easy, and these birds accept canary seed and millet immediately.

In 1886 the first Blue-faced Parrot Finches were imported into Germany, and the first successful breeding took place the following year. Since this date 8 generations have been successfully obtained; they seem to breed very easily. Where possible, breeders like to cross birds raised in captivity with imported specimens, but there are accounts of a recently imported pair nesting and raising their young after 2 weeks in the aviary.

Blue-faced Parrot Finch, *Erythrura t. trichroa*

The two partners build the nest, but the male brings all the material. During his display he holds a blade of grass in his beak and generally pursues the female with ardour, mating takes place, and the 4–6 eggs are laid in very rapid succession. The two birds take turn to incubate and the young are hatched, completely naked, after 13–14 days. They develop very slowly; their eyes open after 8 days and the first green feathers begin to grow after about 12 days. They leave the nest at the age of 3 weeks and look very awkward for the first few days.

The parents must obviously have access to germinated seeds, soft foods, ants' eggs and aphides, as well as to green food and plenty of grass seed in the heads. They are usually very fond of mealworms and should have a small ration every day. It is not unusual for a good pair to raise 2 or even 3 broods in a season. When the birds have a heated shelter in winter, they can be allowed to fly during the day in an open aviary, for they can stand cold. They live in harmony with most other small *Estrildinae*, but only one pair of Parrot Finches should be placed in a shared aviary, because the males are very aggressive during the nesting period. They also need plenty of minerals, and they will go every day to a dish filled with crushed, dried egg-shells sprinkled with Vitacalcium.

The young birds can remain with their parents if the aviary is quite large; in a smaller aviary, the father soon begins to chase the young males.

PEALE'S PARROT FINCH, FIJIAN PARROT FINCH, *Erythrura cyaneifrons pealii* (Hartlaub)

G. Peale's Papageiamadine; F. Diamant de Peale; D. Peales Papegaaiamadine

DISTRIBUTION: Fiji.

DESCRIPTION: Top and sides of head red; this red is separated by a fine line from the blue stripe behind it. Back and wings green; breast and lower parts blue. Rump and upper tail-coverts red, throat black. Length: about 4 in. (10 cm). *Female*. Abdomen more yellow in colour while blue on breast and black on throat are less extensive.

The plumage pattern of this Parrot Finch is very similar to that of the Gouldian Finch, and even more to that of the Red-headed Parrot Finch, with which it has been successfully crossed. The bird-catcher H. Bregulla published in *Die Gefiederte Welt*, 1962, pp. 123 ff, a detailed description of their life in the wild, which we reproduce:

'The island of Fiji-Levu contains large stretches of grassland covered with low scrub. The creeks and the low hills towards the interior offer a landscape of scattered bushes, and the tropical forest decends to the coast only at a very few points. Peale's Parrot Finches live in this savanna country, generally at the edge of the forest; they live in pairs or sometimes in small flocks. They feed largely on grass and flower seeds. They are lively and skilful both on the ground and in the branches, and sometimes visit the fields and gardens of large settlements. When the rice begins to ripen, flights consisting of 100 birds visit the rice fields, often accompanied by Java Sparrows; these flocks of birds do great damage there. At the end of the day, the birds return to sleep in the forest, returning the next day. They nest throughout the year in the crub and the mango trees.'

In 1912 they were first bred successfully in London Zoo, and later throughout the world. Only a few specimens were imported up to 1960 when a large number of these Parrot Finches were imported, and breeders have succeeded in raising them in their aviaries since then. A successful breeding was described by W. A. S. Gates of New South Wales in *Foreign Birds*, Vol. 37, No. 1, p. 13:

'When all birds were fully coloured, applying the principle that those with brighter plumage were cocks and that with duller plumage was a hen. I deduced I had five cocks and one hen. During the winter of 1964, first one young cock, then a second, died. This left one hen and three cocks which shared a fully planted aviary 25 ft × 25ft × 9 ft (7·6 × 7·6 × 2·7 m) with a mixed collection of birds. In August 1964, the hen and one cock started building in a finch nest box, high up at the front of the aviary, the entrance hole facing west. Efforts died away and a check revealed one egg. The nest was interesting, the box being filled with grass, feathers, leaves and pieces of banana frond inside of which was an inner nest, tightly woven of coconut fibre. In October, following frantic activity and a period of sitting, the birds again left the nest and again one egg was found. Early in January 1965, the effort was repeated and a check revealed two eggs with fully formed chicks dead in the eggs. One had broken the shell and ants had invaded the nest and this egg. The ants were destroyed and the nest box cleaned and replaced with a little grass inside.

Nesting activity started again in April and two eggs were laid on consecutive days. After fourteen days, there was one young and one egg which did not hatch. As the days passed, feeding the young one proceeded and the noise was very great for one so small. Then, after a week, activity and noise ceased and examination of the nest showed a fully formed dead chick in the egg and a dead chick quite large but obviously starved to death. The chick and the egg were preserved in methylated spirits for examination. The irridescent spots on each side of the beak were most brilliant. The beak was yellow with a black tip. The egg, similar to those earlier laid, was large, some 16 cms long by 12 cms diameter. It did not have a "sharp" end, being almost spherical in shape. The surface of the shell could be described as semi-matt and the colour the palest pink.

This was early April 1965, and notwithstanding daily supplies of hard boiled eggs, mealworms, termites, plain cake, soaked bread and the insects in a large planted aviary, the hope of a successful breeding of these birds was not achieved.

Wednesday the 19th May was a fine warm late autumn morning and we took time out to leisurely watch the antics of all the birds in the large aviary. Cursorily glancing at the furthermost nest which had never been used since being installed, we caught a glimpse of a flash of green and red dart into the nest hole. There was the noise of young chicks being fed and a flash of green and red darting out again. This called for the binoculars and an hour later, it was plain to see one of the Fijian parrot finch "cocks" half in and half out of the nest hole obviously regurgitating and feeding young. Five days later, so much activity was occurring in the nest that the lid was partly lifted off, and almost immediately, a pair of Cordon Blues commenced robbing the top of the nest of its grass. The cover was replaced hard down. As each Fijian had a distinctive colour leg ring it was soon noted that only one parent did all the feeding and at no time was the other parent involved. This may be an exception limited to this pair but further breeding will be necessary to clarify the point. As the days went by, the parent could no longer enter the nest, for as soon as it came near, the nest hole was full of yellow beaks on olive green heads. An interesting feature of the feeding was that, unlike most birds, the parent never fed the chicks directly after completing feeding itself but frolicked around the aviary for some time. The implication is that the time so taken is to ensure some form of proper mixing with salica in the crop.

On the 4th June, one fledgeling was more in than out and at noon left the nest, flew two feet to a branch and just as quickly made up its mind it didn't like the outside world, turned round and flew straight in the nest hole again without alighting on the perch in front of the nest box.

On the 5th June, a fledgeling, possibly the same one, left the nest in the morning and, in stages, flew all over the aviary. At noon, a second fledgeling flew out, but at 3.30 p.m. as the sun was slanting, each returned to the nest. Homing pigeons had nothing on these fledgelings, this returning to the nest at night by the young being another interesting feature. The fledgelings, on emerging, were olive green, the cheeks below the eyes having a tinge of blue. There was red in a tail that was so short as to be almost non existent. As with the parent birds, the underside of the wing is grey.

On the 6th June, three fledgelings left the nest, and in due course, were found side by side on a perch at the other end of the aviary. However, the surprises were not finished, for close by, having a little more difficulty, was a fourth, identical in all respects except for two little tufts of red on the top of its head. Since various periods of time apply to colouring of identical birds, one can only assume that the baby is also the one which will reach full colour first. Within a week, traces of red could be discerned in the heads of two other finches.

On the 8th June, three fledgelings were introduced to the running water trough in which they stood while the parent bathed. This was the first time that the other parent could be identified because he shepherded the three youngsters but this was the biggest surprise of all as he was one of the pair which made all the earlier nests.

The youngsters continued to grow and on the 10th one was eating freely, i.e. five days out of the nest. This youngster was devoid of fear which allowed close examination. There are two irridescent dots either side below the centre line of the beak. The beak was turning black but the bottom was still yellow and would take some time to colour. The green changed daily to a brighter hue. Combining the knowledge gained from the earlier nests and this last and very successful nest, and knowledge of how long it took one of the parents to colour up the following time cycle would appear to apply. Eggs laid one daily, hatching

14 days after sitting, leave nest 20 to 22 days after hatching depending on advancement. Red in head can be observed in a few birds on leaving the nest but it can take two to three months for red to appear in some birds. Full colouring achieved over wide period which could be between three months and a year.'

ROYAL PARROT FINCH, BLUE-BELLIED PARROT FINCH, *Erythrura cyaneifrons regia* (Sclater)

G. Königs-Papageiamadine; F. Diamant royal; D. Konings-Papegaaiamadine

DISTRIBUTION: Northern Islands of the New Hebrides.
DESCRIPTION: Head red, marked off by a large blue stripe; back darker blue with a green sheen. Rump red; central tail feathers, which are very pointed, dark reddish brown; others blackish brown with dark red outside edges. Lores and throat black; neck and breast cobalt blue, and abdomen blue with a green sheen. Wings contain both greenish blue and blackish brown feathers, with blue in fold of wing. Beak black, iris brown and feet and legs dark flesh coloured. Length: 4¼ in. (11 cm). *Female*. More green in colour, and her plumage is less bright.
The Royal Parrot Finch lives principally in the mountains, up to a height of 6,500 ft (2,000 m). They seem to be rarer than the other *Erythrurae*. They are tree dwelling birds, feeding mainly upon wild figs. Sometimes a flock gathers in a tree, but after a meal each pair leaves the flock and flies off in a different direction. They descend to the ground to drink and to bathe.
Royal Parrot Finches were first described in 1881 by Dr. Sclater, who had received skins. In 1934 a number of these birds were imported into England by W. Goodfellow and S. Mayer. Young have blue heads and yellow beaks.
Mr. Goodfellow succeeded in raising 15 young birds taken from the nest, which he fed on pre-soaked figs, hard boiled egg and confectioner's flour, and when about 6 months old the blue head plumage of the young birds was replaced by a bright red. A year later, in 1935, C. H. Macklin of England was the first to succeed in breeding them, with a pair from Mr. Goodfellow's importation. In the *Avicultural Magazine* (September 1935) he describes his experiences.
In 1963 these birds were imported in large numbers, and there are specimens at the moment in the possession of several serious collectors. Dr. R. Burkard of Switzerland gave them 20 mealworms a day for the first 20 days, and then gradually reduced this ration when the birds had put on weight again. He also gave them pre-soaked figs, and the birds ate only these seeds and the tender pulp. Soaked seeds were mixed with ants' eggs and soft food, sweeten the mixture with honey in water. The birds also took oranges. Twice, after an interval of 4 days, he gave aureomycin in the drinking water (0·5 g/litre) for 3 days. When the Finches were in excellent condition, they were housed with other *Erythrurae* and the Royal Parrot Finches soon imitated them, accepting every kind of food. Dr. Burkard's Gouldian Finches also accepted ants' eggs, mealworms, egg mash and oranges.

RED-HEADED PARROT FINCH, PARROT FINCH, *Erythrura psittacea* (Gmelin)

G. Rotköpfige Papageiamadine; F. Pape de Nouméa, Diamant psittaculaire, Diamant à tête rouge; D. Roedkop-Papegaaiamadine   (Pl. XXIV)

DISTRIBUTION: New Caledonia.
DESCRIPTION: Forehead, top and sides of head and throat red; lores black. Rump, upper tail coverts and central tail feathers red. Upper and lower parts grass green, with green and dark brown on wings. Iris brown, beak black, and feet and legs horn-coloured. Length, 4¾ in. (12 cm). *Female*. Is

less bright; red on head is paler and less extensive.
These birds live in pairs during the nesting season and in small groups outside this period. They live in grassland with scrub and feed on grass seeds. They nest in cracks in rocks, under roofs, but even more in trees. The voluminous nest is built of straw and leaves, lined with feathers. Five–7 eggs are laid, and there is no particular nesting season.
In 1877 Red-headed Parrot Finches had come into the

Red-headed Parrot Finch, *Erythrura psittacea*

possession of Mr. Wiener of England, who succeeded in getting them to breed in his spacious aviary. But these birds seem to have been brought to Paris as early as 1873, and to have reproduced there in 1886. The same year the first birds arrived in Germany and were bred shortly afterwards.
As they are lively and active, they must be housed in a large inside or outside aviary. They do not easily tolerate temperatures which fall below 60°F (15°C), and must therefore spend the winter in a moderately heated aviary. They should not be given too many mealworms, but should regularly have various kinds of fruit: figs, oranges, apples, as well as green food and soaked or germinated seeds. Soft food, ripening grass seeds, frash ants' eggs and a varied mixture of seeds are indispensable.

MANY-COLOURED PARROT FINCH, *Erythrura coloris* (Beale)

G. Vielfarben-Papageiamadine; F. Diamant des montagnes, Diamant multicolore; D. Veelkleuren-Papegaaeamadine

DISTRIBUTION: New Hebrides, New Caledonia, Philippines.
DESCRIPTION: Largely green with a blue face and red around ears. The flight feathers black with green outside edges. Rump, upper tail-coverts and central tail feathers red; other tail feathers black with a red stripe. Beak black and feet and legs horn coloured. Length: about 4 in. (10 cm). *Female*. Less bright, particularly red on ears and green on abdomen.
These birds were discovered in 1960 by an American expedition in the mountains of the Philippines. A few years later the first live specimens arrived in Europe. Dr. R. Burkard received several, thanks to the bird-catcher H. Bregulla, who had tried for a long time to capture some. The consignment also contained young specimens which had not reached full plumage, and which died fairly quickly. The other specimens adapted well, behaved calmly and tolerated quiet observation while they were at the feeding dish.
They fed largely on canary and millet seeds and millet sprays. Dr. Burkard does not advise fruit, which produced intestinal infections. The birds willingly take mealworms and ants' eggs. From the very first year of their stay in Switzerland, the birds raised some young. They are the smallest of the *Erythrurae*; they are less timid than other species of this genus.

Genus: Lonchura

BENGALESE, SOCIETY FINCH, *Lonchura domestica*

G. Japanisches Mövchen; F. Moineau du Japon; D. Japanse Meeuwtje   (Pl. XXX)

The Bengalese is a cultivated variety which is therefore not found in the natural state. It probably came from China and into Japan about 1700, so the well-known Japanese ornithologist, Prince N. Taka-Tsukasa, thinks. The first specimens to be brought to the London Zoo arrived in 1860, two pure white birds. There they were thought to be a domesticated form of the Nutmeg Finch. Only later on, in 1871, were they introduced into Germany from Japan: first the bright brown and following them the pure White and Fawn varieties. The birds have gained very wide distribution in all the countries where birds are kept and reared on bindrooms. They must surely be among the easiest birds to breed, ideal for beginners, like the Zebra Finch.

The Bengalese is a cultivated form of the Striated Mannikin —*Lonchura str. striata*—which is found in a great number of species spread over Ceylon, India, the Andaman and Nicobar Islands, Northern Sumatra, Vietnam, Laos, Cambodia, Taiwan and South China. The Chinese species—*L. striata swinhoei* (Cab)—and/or the Indochinese species— *L. str. subsquamicolis* (Baker)—is probably the progenitor of the cultivated bird.

Bengalese, *Lonchura domestica*

The present day thinking is that the Bengalese was evolved from the crossing together of several species of the *Lonchura* family which gave fertile hybrids.

The Bengalese is found in various colours, the pied being the commonest. Of this kind there are fawn/whites and grey-brown/whites which are usually described as chocolate/whites. The white patches are generally distributed unevenly, but by careful breeding, birds can be produced with evenly-placed patches.

Bengalese of one colour only have been produced and are known as Selfs. By one colour only is meant birds which show no white markings. Professor H. Steiner (Zurich) and Herr W. Langberg (Copenhagen) among others have bred almost pure black Bengalese by crossing them with Bronze-winged Mannikins, *L. fascums*.

Pure white Bengalese are rarer than pied ones and through continual in-breeding they often become rather smaller than the pied or self varieties.

Crested Bengalese have been bred and the first specimens came to England in the nineteen thirties. It is not known how old this mutation is in Japan. Later Frilled Bengalese have been produced in Japan with curly feathers on the breast, shoulders and back like the Frilled Canaries. As far as it is known these birds have not been introduced into Europe.

The most recent colour mutation is the Dilute, which causes the chocolate and fawn colours to appear at about half the normal depth of shade.

As regards the inheritance of colour, the following points should be noted. Three distinct main colours can be distinguished: Chocolate, Fawn and pure White. The main features of their inheritance are already known but not yet in all details. Dark colours are dominant over the light ones. Crests are dominant over normals and birds with crests crossed with normals of any colour gives half crest, half normal young. The crested birds are always heterozygote (recessive for smooth headed). There are no homozygotes among crested birds as such birds cannot maintain life and die in the egg. This lethal factor is known in certain breeds of canaries. One should therefore never pair two crested birds. The shape of the crest varies a good deal. By selection you can breed birds with a large round crest or a triangular one shaped like a shovel. There are even birds with two crests, one on the head and one on the neck. As already mentioned, in Japan frilled Bengalese are bred. Though crested birds are dominant over smooth headed ones, I have nevertheless found out by experiment that the quality of the crest can be improved by using smooth headed birds which had one crested parent and are known as crest-breds. Perhaps factors of mutation come into play here that are as yet unknown.

Bengalese are accommodating and hardy when properly treated, it is lively and active and must therefore not be kept in too small a cage. For a breeding pair, the cage should not be less than 24 in. (60 cm) long with correspondingly large measurements for the other dimensions, of course a larger cage is better.

Being peaceful birds several of them can be kept together, except at breeding time. They like a box to sleep in for which a box half open at the front and measuring 5 in. (12 cm) cube is suitable. As they like to bathe, a container of water should be placed for a few hours each day in the cage. Small branches cut from bushes or fruit trees are better than smooth wood perches.

They feed on the usual kinds of millet and small canary seeds. They are very fond of Italian millet. Sprouted seeds and millet sprays are an excellent additional diet which should be given daily. It is good for feeding the young. They will also eat soft food, bread soaked in milk and ants' eggs.

Green food such as chickweed, meadow grass, lettuce, etc. should be given daily.

Bengalese are most reliable breeders providing they are fit healthy birds. The sexes show no external signs of difference, males can only be distinguished by their song which it repeats often and vigorously. Soon after they leave the nest young males atart practising their song and can be identified. Breeding birds should be as large and strong as possible, unrelated and not less than eight months old. Each pair should be given their own cage supplied with a nest box, soft hay and a few feathers. The eggs are pure white and number 4–8 per clutch and they hatch out in about 12–13 days.

The young leave the nest after three weeks and are fed by the parents for another two weeks. They should be separated from the adults three weeks after they have left the nest; otherwise they will keep pushing into it, thereby upsetting the next clutch which mostly follows quickly on the first. Young birds should be accommodated in a roomy cage with a sleeping box; young from several pairs can be housed together as they do not fight. It is useful to make the birds with coloured rings as soon as their sex has been discovered. Breeding pairs should not be allowed to have more than three broods per year.

THREE-COLOURED MANNIKIN, TRI-COLOURED MANNIKIN, TRI-COLOURED NUN, *Lonchura m. malacca* (Linnaeus)

G. Dreifarbennonne; F. Jacobin, Capucin tricolore; D. Briekleurennon (Pl. XXXI)

DISTRIBUTION: Western India, Sri Lanka.

DESCRIPTION: Head and neck intensely black, upper parts dark chestnut, with reddish brown on rump and upper tail coverts. The base of abdomen, vent region and lower tail coverts black, rest of abdomen area in front white. Iris brown, beak light grey and feet and legs dark grey. Length: 4½–5 in. (11–12 cm). *Female.* A little less bright.

These birds have been observed in large flights above fields, rice paddies or rush beds; they prefer to nest in the latter. The round large nest, hung amongst the reeds or some time in a bush or a tree, is built of soft leaves and straws; lined with fine grass. It usually contains 4–7 eggs and are incubated by the parents for 13 days.

The first three-coloured Mannikins were imported into Germany during the first half of the nineteenth century; later, regular small consignments arrived in Europe. They are quiet birds, suitable for indoor or inside aviaries, though they do not breed easily there. If breeding is to be attempted, they should be housed in an outside aviary planted with reeds and bushes, where they like to hide. When they climb the stalks of reeds, they use their claws, which rapidly grow long in a cage, where they must be regularly trimmed. As the sexes resemble each other closely, it is difficult to form a true pair, and this is no doubt the reason why few successes in breeding have been noted. The male gives a sharp, penetrating call, while the voice of the female is much more gentle.

These birds feed on seed and green food, but during the breeding season they must have mealworms, soft food, germinated and soaked seeds. At first, the young birds are fed almost exclusively with these soft seeds, which their parents pre-digest in their crops.

The pair much prefer to construct an open nest, for which the male brings the material while the female arranges it, often helped by her mate. They use straw, a lot of blades of green grass, hairs and feathers.

The young remained for 23–24 days in the nest. When they fly, their abdomen is brownish grey, their back brown and their beak black; the adult plumage appears after 3 or 4 months. After flight, they usually return to the nest at night; their parents, the father in particular, continue to care for them for another 3 weeks. A warm and humid atmosphere helps both incubation and juvenile moult of the young birds. In other respects these birds are easy to acclimatise, and can remain in an outside aviary all the year round, so long as they have comfortable shelter.

BLACK-HEADED MANNIKIN, BLACK-HEADED MUNIA, BLACK-HEADED NUN, *Lonchura malacca atricapilla* (Vieillot)

G. Schwarzkopfnonne; F. Capucin à tête noire, Mungal; D. Zwartkopnon

DISTRIBUTION: Southern India, Malacca, South-East Asia.

DESCRIPTION: Head and neck lustrous black; lower parts red-brown, with black in middle of abdomen, thighs, vent region and lower tail coverts. The red-brown wings have greyish brown flight feathers. Tail brown, iris dark brown, beak grey and feet and legs bluish grey. Length: 4¼ in. (11 cm). *Female.* Somewhat less bright.

SUBSPECIES: The species *Lonchura malacca* is sub-divided into several subspecies, which differ slightly in colour or pattern. In addition to the Black-headed Mannikin, *Lonchura m. atricapilla*, we may also mention *Lonchura m. formosana*, *Lonchura m. brunneicops*, from Borneo and Celebes, *Lonchura m. gregalis*, from Borneo and the Philippines, *Lonchura m. jagori*, from Luzon, *Lonchura m. orientalis*, from Central India, which resembles the main breed of the species, *Lonchura m. sinensis*, from Malaysia, and *Lonchura m. batakana*, from Sumatra. The two last subspecies resemble the Black-headed Mannikin, but are smaller. Several of these subspecies have been imported from time to time.

These Mannikins live in small groups in the marshy rush beds or sugar plantations. They nest in the rainy season and build their round and quite voluminous nests amongst the tall grass or the reeds. The 4–8 eggs hatch after an incubation period of 13 days, and the young are fed largely upon ripening grass seeds.

Although their colours are sober, their plumage always glossy, these very quiet birds, are found in many collections. It is virtually impossible to distinguish the male and the female, which is no doubt why there are very few reports of successful breeding. When their aviary is being set out, it must be remembered that their claws grow rapidly and must

Black-headed Mannikin, *Lonchura malacca atricapilla*

be allowed to wear down; if they have a planted corner of reeds this will take place naturally. When it is necessary to cut claws that have grown too long, the bird must be held in the hand against the light, so that the small blood vessel in the nail can be seen, and the cuts do not go beyond this vein. These Mannikins live in harmony with other birds, they are used to a humid climate and like to bathe every day. During the breeding period the male can be recognised from his song: a few almost inaudible flute like sounds, which he often utters for hours on end.

These birds like to build an open nest in a thick bush or a

Three-coloured Mannikin, *Lonchura m. malacca*

clump of reeds. The eggs may be taken out to be given to Bengalese, which will hatch them and raise the young. When the young leave the nest and fly in the aviary, the Mannikins will be more inclined to nest. But if the female lays, the birds show no intention of sitting on them; if the eggs happen to hatch, the parents often abandon their young. It is probable that the fault lies in an inadequate diet: the parents must have ripening and germinated seeds and plenty of different kinds of green food. Mannikins can live throughout the year in an unheated aviary; they often live to a considerable age in captivity.

JAVAN MAJA FINCH, *Lonchura ferruginosa* (Sparman)

G. Schildnonne; F. Capucin à bavette, Nonnette à poitrine noire; D. Zwartkeelnon

DISTRIBUTION: Java, Bali.
DESCRIPTION: Head and nape of neck white; throat and front of neck black. Upper parts dark chestnut, with a lighter chestnut on rump and upper tail coverts. Lower parts dark chestnut with black in middle of abdomen. Iris brown, beak whitish-grey and feet and legs slate grey. *Female*. Similar in colour. Length: 4¼ in. (11 cm).
These birds can be seen in small groups in fields of rice and other crops. When the rice begins to ripen, they form large flocks and devastate the fields. When the rice fields are flooded, they return to the meadows, establish themselves in the nearby forests, where they nest in bushes and trees. They have a high pitched call, 'wit-wit-wit'. The song of the male is muffled, and he utters it hopping about with his feathers raised, and interrupting his song with slight snappings of his

Javan Maja Finch, *Lonchura ferruginosa*

beak. The natives like to keep these birds in cages, as they do with the Java Sparrow and other Mannikins. The nest has been discovered low down amongst the tall grass or in a thick bush; the round nest has an entry at the side. Females lay 3–6 eggs and the incubation period is 12–13 days.
In 1869 these birds were in the possession of Dr. Russ; they were the first of their species to live in captivity; later, they were very occasionally imported. Like other Mannikins, they live in harmony with *Estrildinae*, and can be housed in cage or aviary; but breeding has only been successful in well planted aviaries. The breeding diet must include ripening and germinated seeds; a little soft food and few insects.

WHITE-HEADED MANNIKIN, WHITE-HEADED NUN, *Lonchura m. maja* (Linnaeus)

G. Weisskopfnonne; F. Capucin à tête blanche, Nonnette à tête blanche; D. Witkopnon   (Pl. XXXI)
DISTRIBUTION: Malaysia.
DESCRIPTION: Head, throat and nape of neck white, nape and throat carrying a brown sheen. Upper parts chestnut; rump and upper tail coverts are lighter reddish chestnut. Breast, abdomen, thighs and lower tail coverts black; sides dark chestnut. The brown wings have blackish brown flight feathers. Iris dark brown and beak slate grey, feet and legs

brownish grey. Length: 4¼ in. (11 cm). *Female*. Less pure white on head.
SUBSPECIES: A second subspecies lives in Sumatra and Java; this is the subspecies *Lonchura maja leucocephala*, distinguished by its dark brown breast.
These birds normally live in grassland, either in the plains or on mountain slopes. Once the rice begins to ripen, they form large flocks and, accompanied by other Mannikins and Java Sparrows, invade the rice fields, where they cause enormous damage. As early as the first half of the eighteenth century they were exported to Europe, where they rapidly became accustomed to the new environment, and where they may live 15 years or more in captivity.

White-headed Mannikin, *Lonchura m. maja*

Towards 1870, Dr. Russ succeeded in breeding them in Germany, since then, however, success has been rare. The male sings during his display, but his voice is scarcely audible; he utters no more than a murmuring phrase. In a well planted aviary or a large bird room, a pair may decide to nest either in a bush or in a large nest box. Fairly coarse material is used: strips of paper, grass and moss, to build a voluminous nest with a dome and a side entry. These birds like to nest in dark corners, and it is therefore wise to camouflage the nesting box with the aid of branches of fir. Females lay 3–5 eggs, on which both birds sit for 13 days. The young leave the nest at the age of 25 days, but are still very awkward, and are cared for by their parents for a further fortnight. Their juvenile plumage is dark brown in upper parts, and brownish white in lower parts, with a black beak. Their colour comes after 4 months.
These birds can winter in an unheated aviary with a good sleeping place, and will live in harmony with other Estrildinae.

YELLOW-TAILED FINCH, YELLOW-RUMPED FINCH, *Lonchura flaviprymna* (Gould)

G. Gelber Schilffink; F. Donacole à tête grise; D. Gele Rietfink, Grijskoprietfink

DISTRIBUTION: North Western and Northern Australia.
DESCRIPTION: Head and neck whitish grey, with even lighter grey on throat. Upper parts chestnut, with very bright ochre yellow on upper tail coverts. Lower parts yellowish white, breast carrying an ochre yellow sheen. The chestnut wings have greyish brown flight feathers. Tail brown with yellow edges, iris brown, beak grey and feet and legs slate grey. Length: about 4¼ in. (11 cm).
These birds live in marshy regions and along the banks of water courses. They can be seen in pairs or in small flocks, often accompanied by the Chestnut-breasted Finch, *Lonchura castaneothorax*. At certain periods, they are also to be found in the more arid interior, but during dry seasons, return to coasts and mouths of rivers. They prefer to nest close to the water and even make their nest above the water, in bushes or in low trees. Nests are bottle-shaped and made of grass and leaves of the Pendanus palm; lined with fine grass and feathers. Females lay 4–6 eggs, generally at the

beginning of the rainy season; both share the incubation period of 12–13 days. Young leave the nest when they are 24–28 days old.

The exact classification of this species has given rise to some dispute. Since it interbreeds in the wild with the Chestnut-breasted Finch, *Lonchura castaneothorax* one may deduce that these two species are very close, but some writers prefer to classify the Yellow-tailed Finch with the White-headed Mannikin, *Lonchura maja*.

Yellow-tailed Finch, *Lonchura flaviprymna*

The first Yellow-tailed Finches were imported into England in 1904, and a few years later these birds bred. Birds living in an aviary have a tendency to develop a more brownish plumage on the breast, thus coming to resemble the Chestnut-breasted Finch.

The acclimatisation of imported birds demands a great deal of attention, but thereafter they are hardy, though they must winter indoors. Little success has been obtained with breeding in captivity. The two birds build the nest, but the male gathers the material. They take turns to sit on the 4 eggs; the female sits at night. The incubation period is 13 days, and the young remain in the nest for 20–24 days. After they fly, they return to the nest at nights, and are fed for some further weeks by their parents.

CHESTNUT-BREASTED FINCH, *Lonchura c. casta-neothorax* (Gould)

G. Braunburstschilffink; F. Donacole commun, Donacole à poitrine châtaine; D. Bruinborst-Rietfink
(Pl. XXXI)

DISTRIBUTION: Northern coast of Australia.

DESCRIPTION: Top of head and nape of neck cinnamon, each feather being grey at tip. Upper parts somewhat lighter, with rump and upper tail-coverts straw yellow. Lores, eyebrows, sides of head, region round ears, cheeks and throat black with brown lines down middle. Sides of neck, and upper breast light cinnamon, marked off by a narrow black stripe. Sides, thighs and lower tail coverts black; rest of abdomen white. Sides are marked with black and white lines. The cinnamon coloured wings have greyish brown flight feathers with cinnamon edges; central tail feathers yellow, and others greyish brown with yellowish edges. Iris brown, beak bluish grey and feet and legs brownish grey. Length: about 3 in. (7·5 cm). *Female*. Is less bright, and colour outlines are less pronounced.

SUBSPECIES: Four other subspecies, living in different regions of Papua—New Guinea, have never, or virtually never, been imported: *Lonchura c. uropygialis*, *Lonchura c. sharpei*, *Lonchura c. nigriceps* and *Lonchura c. boschmai*.

This species lives in the immense reed beds of the marshy regions, usually near coast, and very rarely in inland plains. They feed on seeds of grasses and reeds and climb with great agility along the stalks to peck at the grains in the ear. During the nesting season, the large flocks break up and the pairs look for a nesting place, close to the ground, amongst the scrub or the tall grass. The purse-shaped nest is built with stalks, reed leaves and other vegetable material; lined with fine grass and feathers.

The first Chestnut-breasted Finches were brought to London Zoo in 1860 and shortly afterwards they were imported into other European countries, and became the favourite of bird fanciers. They are very hardy and can spend the winter in an unheated aviary with a good shelter. The Chestnut-breasted Finch sings better than the other members of the genus *Lonchura*; the song resembles the sounding of a small bell and is somewhat reminiscent of the Java Sparrow. These birds can share an aviary with other Estrildinae. They like to bathe, and are very lively and active in an outside aviary. If they are in a cage, this liveliness disappears, because they are bored. They take various kinds of birdseed, and a few small insects, which are indispensable during the breeding period. A pair with young birds is glad to have mealworms, ants' eggs and maggots.

They are difficult to sex; the white on belly is somewhat less immaculate, and grey pattern on head and nape of neck is more pronounced in the female, but the song of the male is the only certain indication. In addition to this melodious song, males sometimes emit duller sounds terminating in a sharp 'tieh' which is so soft that it is scarcely audible.

If Chestnut-breasted Finches are kept in a cage, they must be given a mixture of seeds including canary, millet and oats, also plenty of green food. Kept in a cage, they rapidly grow fat. A spacious aviary is much better for them, particularly if breeding is to be attempted as they soon get fat in a cage. The display of the male is reminiscent of that of the Bengalese. A pair will accept a nesting box or a basket, but prefer to build a large free open nest, where the birds will also sleep. The two birds take turns to sit on the 3–6 eggs, which hatch in about 13 days. At first, the young birds are fed with germinated seeds, soft food, maggots, mealworms and various insects. After flight, which takes place at the age of about 3 weeks, young birds are very wild; their parents continue to feed them for 3 further weeks. In the evening, the young birds return to the nest to sleep. The juvenile plumage

Chestnut-breasted Finch, *Lonchura c. casta-neothorax*

is dark brown in upper parts, and cream on lower parts, they get their full colour after the age of 4 months.

A breeding was described in *Foreign Birds*, 1971, Vol. 37, No. 5, p. 165, by F. Holbeck of Denmark:

'My first pair built their nest in a common basket-nest, while my second pair preferred to build in a low bush. The nests were built of coconut-fibres and dried grass. No feathers were used. Both pairs had 5 eggs, and the first pair got five lovely youngsters "on twig". The feed was grass-seed, dry and half-ripe millet spray and canary-seeds, and the usual blend of seed that all my birds get every day. I mixed a special blend of hard-boiled eggs, sand-cake, Biosorbin, glucose and biscuits—a very popular blend. I also offered some green-feed, some mealworms and a "soft-bill-blend", but the half riped grass-seed was preferred.

Incubation behaviour is the same as that of the other birds in the aviary—about 13 days, and the young stay in the nest for three weeks. When they have left the nest, the female still feeds them for a short time.'

PECTORELLA FINCH, PECTORAL FINCH, WHITE-BREASTED FINCH, *Lonchura pectoralis* (Gould)
G. Weissbrustschilffink; F. Donacole à Poitrine blanche; D. Witborst-Rietfink   (Pl. XXXI)
DISTRIBUTION: North-western and north-eastern Australia.
DESCRIPTION: Upper parts silver grey with dark grey upper tail coverts, lores, sides of head, ear region, chin and throat black. A brownish red line, beginning at base of beak, forms and eyebrow, and carries on over the ear region round to the back on throat. On the top, black feathers have broad white edges, so that black forms a light scale pattern. Lower parts winy grey; sides carry a scale pattern in black and white, similar to the pattern on upper chest, but more distinct. The winy grey lower tail coverts have black and white lines across them. The brownish grey wings have small white dots at the ends of the feathers. Tail brownish black, iris brown, beak bluish grey, and feet and legs flesh coloured. Length: about 4¾ in. (12 cm). Upper parts of females is somewhat more brownish.
These Finches have been observed in large mixed flocks, consisting of several species, at the season when the fruit ripens. In the dry season they are found near the coast and near the remaining water-holes.
Towards the end of the last century, they were imported into Europe for the first time. In 1892 they were first bred successfully in Germany, and in 1905, in England. Imported birds require very careful acclimatization, and need plenty of heat. If they can winter in a heated room, they live for 10 years and more. They can be housed with other Estrildinae in a large inside aviary, and even if several pairs share the same aviary, they will live and breed in peace together.

Pectorella Finch, *Lonchura pectoralis*

They will accept a nest box, where they like to build a round nest with dry and green grass; it is largely the male who builds, but the female finishes off the place for the eggs, which she lines with fine grass. The incubation period is 13 days; the female sits at night, while the male replaces her during the day. In general, pairs raise their young well, provided that in addition to the normal mixture of seeds, they can have plenty of ripening grass seeds, mealworms and ants' eggs. The young will leave the nest when they are 22–24 days old. They have greyish brown plumage, with lower parts somewhat more brown, and beak blackish brown. Sometimes they are more than a year old before they have adult plumage. At first, the young birds return to the nest for the night; about a fortnight after flying, they are independent. There is a greater chance of successful breeding if the parents are housed alone and they often produce several consecutive broods.
The song of the male is insignificant; it resembles a soft gurgling 'Tsip-tsip'. The display of the male is interesting: it takes place on the ground, where he goes round the female stretching out his tail and dragging his wings; he makes profound bows, then goes to touch the beak of the female

with the point of his own beak.
Le Mond des Oiseaux, 1958, No. 8, published a report by L. Huysmans of a successful attempt to breed. The pair built their round, free standing nest at a hight of about 14 in. (13 cm) in a bush in a sunny corner of the aviary. The writer draws attention to the face that these birds dislike cold humidity. Most Australian Estrildinae must in fact be housed in a covered and very sunny aviary, or in an inside aviary which receives the sun.

BROWN MANNIKIN, *Lonchura fuscata* (Cassin)
G. Braunes Bronzemännchen; F. Capucin brun, Domino brun; D. Bruin Bronzemannetje
DISTRIBUTION: Timor.
DESCRIPTION: The upper parts light chocolate brown, with top of head blackish. Ear region and cheeks white; throat black. Light brown of breast is separated from white of abdomen by a thin black stripe. Tail blackish, iris brown, the beak red and feet and legs grey. Length: 5 in. (12·5 cm). The sexes are alike.
The first specimens of this species were included in the collection of Mr. G. H. Gurney of England in 1928. In Timor these birds live in grassland regions; they can be seen along paths looking for seeds and small insects.
An account of a successful attempt to breed has been published in the *Avicultural Magazine,* 1951, No. 3. Mr. Martin of England possessed a pair of these birds in a mixed aviary, in the company of budgerigars and other seed eating birds. The Brown Mannikins built a nest of blades of grass in a budgerigar box. The first clutch of 4 eggs were infertile, but after the box had been emptied, the birds began to build again in the same nesting place. Besides blades of grass, they also used strips of paper, moss and small feathers. They took regular turns in sitting, and after 16 days, the parents fed their own young. They took no interest in live food (mealworms and ants' eggs); on the other hand, they ate a great deal of seeds and green food, particularly germinated grass seeds. Two of the young flew and became independent.

BROWN MUNIA, DUSKY MANNIKIN, *Lonchura fuscans* (Cassin)
G. Borneo-Bronzemännchen; F. Munie de Bornéo, Capucin de Bornéo; D. Borneo-Bronzemannetje
DISTRIBUTION: Borneo.
DESCRIPTION: Principally blackish brown, with black on flight feathers, tail feathers and face; the rachis are lighter. Iris and beak brown; feet and legs reddish brown. Length: 4½ in. (11 cm). Sexes are alike.
The life of these birds in the wild is little known, but we do know that they live in small flocks in the fields and invade the rice fields when the rice is ripening. They are not timid, and also visit settlements.
A pair reproduced in an inside aviary, accepting a basket where within a few days they built a nest of very fine hay and coconut fibres. The nest was never checked, in order not to disturb the pair. After 4 weeks, 4 young birds flew; they resembled their parents, but had black beaks. 15 days later they were independent.
These birds accept various kinds of birdseed; soft food and germinated seeds are indispensable during the breeding season. In winter it is recommended that they be housed in a heated aviary.

JAVANESE MANNIKIN, BLACK-BEAKED BRONZE MANNIKIN, *Lonchura leucogastroides* (Horsfield and Moore)
G. Schwarzbürzelbronzemännchen; F. Capucin de Java; D. Zwartstuit-Bronzemannetje
DISTRIBUTION: Java, Sumatra.

Plate XXXIX

Long-tailed Glossy Starling, *Lamprotornis caudatus*

Coleto Mynah, *Sarcops c. calvus*

Bali Mynah, *Leucopsar rothschildii*

Rosy Pastor, *Sturnus roseus*

Wattled Starling, *Creatophora cinerea* ♂ left ♀ right

Plate XL

Greater Hill Mynah, *Gracula r. religiosa*

Yarrell's Siskin, *Spinus yarrelli*

American Goldfinch, *Spinus tristis*

Mexican Rose Finch, *Carpodacus m. mexicanus*

Hooded Siskin, *Spinus cucullatus*

Mexican Goldfinch, *Spinus mexicanus*

DESCRIPTION: Head, neck and throat black. Brown upper parts carry fine yellow lines; lower parts black, with brown at vent region and in lower tail coverts. Wings brown and tail black. Iris brown; upper mandible greyish black and lower mandible lead grey; feet and lets bluish grey. Length: 4¼ in. (11 cm). Sexes are alike.

Javanese Mannikin, *Lonchura leucogastroides*

The native name of these birds is 'Priet'. They are quite common near settlements, and also visit clearing, fields and gardens, where they look for their food of seeds on the ground. Outside the breeding period, they form small flocks. The fairly large round nest is built amongst climbing plants or reeds, or in a thick bush and has a side entrance in the middle.

The first specimens of this species were imported into Germany as early as 1879. They were imported several times after 1930, to a number of European countries.

The habits of these birds are very similar to those of the Bengalese. The song is an insignificant humming, but the male sings continually; this song is the best means of sexing.

SHARP-TAILED MUNIA, HODGSON'S MUNIA, *Lonchura striata acuticauda* (Hodgson)

G. Spitzschwanzbronzemännchen; F. Domino à longue queue; D. Spitsstaart-Bronzemannetje

DISTRIBUTION: The Himalayas, Burma, Malaysia.

DESCRIPTION: Top of head blackish brown and back chocolate brown; rump and upper tail coverts reddish brown with a white stripe across rump. Back marked with fine white lines produced by light coloured rachis. The parotic region and the

Sharp-tailed Munia, *Lonchura striata acuticauda*

sides of the head and of the neck are black, turning to brown towards the sides. The flanks, thighs and lower tail coverts are rusty yellow with white rachis; the rest of the belly is white with dark rachis. Tail is black. Iris brown, upper mandible black, lower mandible lead grey and feet and legs bluish grey. Length: 4¼ in. (11 cm). Sexes are alike.

SUBSPECIES: There are 8 subspecies, displaying only slight differences in colour or length: *Lonchura str. striata, str. acuticauda, L. str. fumigata, L. str. semistriata, L. str.*

explita, L. str. subsquamicollis, L. str. swinhoei, and *L. str. phaëtonoptilla.*

All these Munias are granivorous, but take live food during the breeding period. They live in small family groups or in pairs in the fields, visiting rice fields and gardens at the time when the seeds are ripening. Hodgson's Munia lives in mountainous country up to heights of 5,000 ft (1,500 m). It nests in small trees, where it builds a round nest of leaves and blades of grass; the nest is solidly built and possesses very thick walls and a side entrance.

These birds have been imported since the seventeenth century, and seem to have reproduced as early as that. Some of the subspecies mentioned above were the ancestors of the Bengalese. However, the behaviour or these Munias is different from that of domesticated birds, for they are not happy nesting in a breeding cage; they detest any examination of their nest, and may abandon their brood if the breeder disturbs them.

WHITE-RUMPED MANNIKIN, STRIATED MANNIKIN, *Lonchura str. striata* (Pl. XXX)

G. Weissbürzeligerbronzemännchen; F. Damier à grosse maille, Capucin Domino; D. Gestreept Bronzemannetje

DISTRIBUTION: India, Sri Lanka.

DESCRIPTION: Forehead, lores, sides of head, neck and upper breast black; feathers of breast have lighter rachis. Back brownish grey with light rachis; rump white; blackish lower tail coverts have light brown rachis. Lower parts white, except flanks, lower tail coverts and thighs, which are brownish grey with light rachis; the tail is black. The iris is brown; the upper mandible is black and the lower mandible lead grey; the feet and legs are bluish grey. Length: 4¾ in. (12 cm).

These birds can be observed in small flocks in fields of cereals and in the plains. They are not timid and visit settlements. They build a ball-shaped nest in trees, particularly in lianas and thick bushes. Clutches of 4–8 eggs are incubated for 12–13 days and the young leave the nest when 22–24 days old.

The behaviour of these birds is reminiscent of that of members of the genus *Spermestes*. Neunzig considers that the White-rumped Mannikin and the Long-tailed Grass Finch were the ancestors of the Bengalese, but Wolters-Steinbacher, in *Prachtfinken*, considers that this domestic bird is derived from the subspecies *Lonchura str. swinhoei* and *Lonchura str. subsquamicollis.*

The White-rumped Mannikin was imported into Europe as early as the seventeenth century and even bred at that period. After Bengalese were imported, and became known to be exceptionally good breeders, White-rumped Mannikins lost their popularity and were imported only occasionally. But they are still kept in India and will reproduce in the cage. In the *Avicultural Magazine*, 1934, No. 2, there is a detailed report by G. Davis of a successful attempt to breed. According to him, the birds had a preference for ripening or germinated seeds for feeding their young.

SPICE FINCH, NUTMEG MANNIKIN, *Lonchura p. punctulata* (Linnaeus)

G. Muskatfink; F. Damier Commun, Muscade; D. Muskaatfink (Pl. XXXI)

DISTRIBUTION: Java and Bali.

DESCRIPTION: Head and neck brownish red; sides of neck and lower parts lighter, and marked with even lighter lines of the rachis. Rump and light brown upper tail coverts carry a somewhat indistinct and very fine dark brown wavy pattern. Abdomen white, slightly clouded with brown towards lower tail coverts. Breast and side feathers have dark brown and black edges, producing a wavy pattern. Tail brown with grey edges on feathers. Beak lead grey, darker on top. Iris reddish brown and feet and legs bluish grey. Length 4¾ in. (12 cm). Sexes are alike.

SUBSPECIES: Ten subspecies are distinguished differing only slightly in size and colouring. Two or three of them are imported quite often, particularly the Indian Spice Finch, *Lonchura p. lineoventer*, from India, distinguished by a brown rump with clear black and white lines, yellowish brown upper tail coverts, with yellowish brown on central tail feathers and dark brown with yellowish brown ends on other tail feathers. The Chinese Spice Finch, *Lonchura p. topela*, is also regularly imported from China and Formosa. The wavy pattern is heavier and blackish grey on abdomen, and more yellow on upper tail coverts and tail. Finally, the subspecies *Lonchura p. subundulata* and *Lonchura p. fretensis* are imported from time to time from South-east Asia and Malaysia. The first is known as the Cochin China Spice Finch.

Spice Finches have been kept as cage birds for a long time and live peaceably with other species of small exotic birds

Spice Finch, *Lonchura p. punctulata*

and have a long life in captivity.

The song of the male is subdued, but he utters it as he draws up to his full height, puffing out his breast feathers and moving his head from side to side. These efforts produce no more than a feeble murmur punctuated by a few slight flute-like sounds. This rather ostentatiously delivered song is the only indication of sex. Wild Spice Finches live in open country, feeding on grass seeds and other plants. They visit settlements and can often be seen in gardens, on paths, amongst shrubs and on the ground, usually in small groups. Their nests have been found in thick bushes, in creepers on the walls of houses and in trees. They are built of blades of grass, bamboo leaves and small pieces of vegetation, and have a side entrance.

Although Spice Finches live peaceably in a mixed aviary, if they are to nest, they need a planted aviary with no other birds. The nest boxes must be hidden under ivy or by fir branches. The birds will not tolerate being disturbed on the nest.

The basis of their diet is various kinds of millet and canary seed. They also eat a good deal of green food and germinated seeds of all kinds, which are indispensable during the breeding period. They easily grow used to soft food, to bread dipped in milk, to ants' eggs and to mealworms.

In building their open quite large nest they use grass, moss, bark and leaves. If the pair use a nest box, it may be crammed with material until there is little room for the eggs. During his display, the male jumps up and down with a blade of grass in his beak, and mating follows immediately. The pair take turns to sit on the 3–7 eggs, which hatch after 13 days. The young birds fly after 3 weeks, but return to the nest at night. The juvenile moult takes a long time, and it is not until the age of about 6 months, they have their full colouring.

Genus: Spermestes

MAGPIE MANNIKIN, *Spermestes fringilloides* (Lafresnaye)
G. Riesenelsterchen; F. Spermète pie, Grande nonne, Nonnette géante; D. Reuzenekstertje   (Pl. XXX)

DISTRIBUTION: Tropical Africa.

DESCRIPTION: Head, neck, rump and upper tail coverts, black, remainder of back dark brown, with a pattern of fine lines on scapulars, which have whitish rachis. Lower parts white, with a black mark on sides of breast and a rust coloured mark on sides. Tail black, iris reddish brown; upper beak black and lower beak lead grey, feet and legs bluish grey. Length: 4¾ in. (12 cm). Sexes are alike.

These birds can be observed in pairs or small family groups in areas where there is thick grass, but especially close to rice fields. They always like to be close to water and spend the night amongst the reeds. They travel from one area to another as the seeds ripen. With their powerful beak they can easily take a husk off rice, but they feed mainly on grass seeds and other wild plants. The nest is built with straw, bark and leaves in trees alongside the fields.

In 1871, Dr. Russ mentioned this species in his *Handbuch fur Vogelliebhaber*; we can therefore assume that the birds have been imported into Europe as early as this. Later, these Mannikins were regularly imported amongst shipments of other *Spermestes*.

They keep contact with other birds of the same species by means of a gentle flutelike call, while the song of the male is somewhat melancholy and not very tuneful.

In a large inside or outside aviary, a pair will soon begin to nest. They defend their nest fiercely against any intruder even larger species. The male often does not carry out a

Magpie Mannikin, *Spermestes fringilloides*

nuptial display, but sometimes touches the beak of the female with his own, turning his neck far round. Mating probably takes place in the nest. When they have the opportunity, these birds prefer to nest in a place hidden by reeds or foliage. The first case of successful breeding was noted in 1933; B. Regge published a detailed report in *Die Gefiederte Welt*, 1933, No. 7, which we quote:

> 'The birds sat continually on the 5 eggs, all of which hatched at 13 days. From then on, they tolerated the inspection of the nest. For feeding the young, they preferred germinated seed, and especially rice still in the husk, but also took chopped mealworms and the white of a boiled egg. But the Magpie Mannikin will also raise its young when the latter food is not available . . .

The birds were as tame as Gouldian Finches. After leaving the nest, the young could fly perfectly, and did not stay on the ground like young Bengalese. More than 3 weeks after flight, the young birds were independent. The parents tolerated their presence, even after they had already begun to nest again. The second nesting produced 6 young which were successfully raised, whereupon the parents started a third brood of six young. Magpie Mannikins can also raise the young of other birds, for two Zebra Finches abandoned by their parents were raised with the six young Magpie Mannikins. Five months after the first brood, the same pair were sitting for the fourth time.'

The German breeder H. Rubner also records that he bred 40–50 young birds every year (*Die Gefiederte Welt*, 1955, p. 31).

These Spermestes are robust outdoor birds, which can live throughout the year in an outside aviary, provided they have a comfortable shelter.

BLACK AND WHITE MANNIKIN, *Spermestes b. bicolor* (Fraser)

G. Glanzelsterchen; F. Spermète bicolore, Nonnette métallique; D. Glansekstertje

DISTRIBUTION: Guinea-Bissau.
DESCRIPTION: Head and neck black with a green sheen; back and wings black, but small flight feathers bear a row of white marks. Rump, lower tail coverts and tail black, lower parts white, while there are white stripes on the black feathers of sides. Iris brown, beak lead grey, and feet and legs black. Length: about 3¾ in. (9·5 cm). Sexes are alike.
These lively birds are found mainly in clearings in the woods and on cleared land which has been brought into cultivation. As they are quite shy, they are not found in the immediate

Black and White Mannikin, *Spermestes b. bicolor*

vicinity of settlements. Outside the breeding period, they can be seen in flights of 30 or more, often accompanied by related species. They feed largely on grass seeds, but also take small insects on the ground. They nest amongst thick brushwood, in trees, and amongst creepers; the round nest has a side entrance, and 3–6 eggs are laid.
The first Black and White Mannikins were imported about 1930. In small cages, they were wild and shy, and were very aggressive to other small exotic birds. The sexes could be distinguished only by the song of the male. Several succeeded in breeding, both in an aviary and in a spacious breeding cage. Both birds sit, either in turn or together. The young birds hatch out after 13 days and are usually well cared for. While the young are being fed, the parents must have mealworms, soft food and germinated seeds. The young birds leave the nest after 3 weeks, but are still somewhat clumsy and are fed for about 10 days by their parents. Once they are independent, they must be removed, because they are pursued by the older birds, who want to start a new brood.

BLACK-BACKED MANNIKIN, *Spermestes bicolor poensis* (Fraser)

G. Gitterflügelsterchen; F. Spermète à dos noir; D. Zwartrug-Ekstertje

DISTRIBUTION: Cameroon, west and central Africa.
DESCRIPTION: Mainly black oith greenish sheen, rump feathers have fine white horizontal marks, thighs, wings and tail black. Outer tail feathers have numerous white marks at their base. Iris reddish brown; beak lead grey; feet and legs black. Length: 3½ in. (9·5 cm). The sexes are alike.
In 1888 these very lively small birds were imported for the first time. They have not often been imported to Europe since. Their way of life is similar to that of the Black and White Mannikin. They are rarely found near settlements, but small flights often go into fields of cereal crops. They feed mainly on grass seeds and small insects, which they find in abundance in clearings, on the savannah and along river banks.
Neunzig records that a pair belonging to Nagel, in Germany, nested. The first nest was built in a nest box and the second in a bush. The nests were built of blades of grass, vegetable fibre and small stalks of asparagus fern. Successful breeding did not take place until much later.
These birds cannot share accommodation with other small species, particularly not in a cage. They like to bathe and must have the opportunity of doing so. Their diet includes mixed millet seeds and small canary seed, and they must also have these seeds in the germinated state. During the breeding period, green food and mealworms are indispensable. They can winter in an unheated aviary.

Black-backed Mannikin, *Spermestes bicolor poensis*

In order to sex these birds, it is necessary to observe the male: he makes low 'Kwai-kwai' sounds, while the female has a sharper call 'ker-ker'. During his display, the male has a murmuring song, which he sings, raising his whole body, spreading his tail like a fan and wagging his head. These birds eat canary seed and various kinds of millet seeds, either dry or germinated; they need plenty of green food. In the breeding period they must be given soft food, and some pairs will accept a few mealworms and ants' eggs. They do not willingly nest in a cage, but will do so in a planted aviary, where they shelter in the bushes. The incubation period for the 4–6 eggs is 13 days; the young remain in the nest for 22 days and are independent 15 days after flight.

RUFOUS-BACKED MANNIKIN, *Spermestes bicolor nigriceps* (Cassin)

G. Braunrückenelsterchen; F. Spermète à dos brun, Nonnette métallique à dos brun; D. Bruinrug-Glansekstertje

DISTRIBUTION: East Africa.
DESCRIPTION: Head and neck black, and upper parts chest-

nut, with black, finely streaked with white, on rump and upper tail coverts. Lower parts white; the black feathers on side have broad white marks. Wings black, with grey and btown; large flight feathers carry a white check pattern, and tail black. Iris brown, beak lead grey, and feet and legs black. Length 4 in. (10 cm). Sexes are alike.

This subspecies has the same habits as the preceding species. They can be seen in grassy plains, often accompanied by

Rufous-backed Mannikin, *Spermestes bicolor nigriceps*

Weaver Birds. They feed on the ground, or hang onto stalks, pecking at the ears. They nest amongst brushwood and in trees, building a nest from blades of grass. Six to 8 eggs are laid.

They were first imported into Europe in.1895; since then, they have been imported irregularly in small numbers. In 1898, Negel of Germany recorded the first success in breeding. His pair moved into a nest box, and sat for 12 days in turn on 4 white eggs. While they were raising their young, he gave them plenty of mealworms and germinated seeds. The female does most of the incubating. The young birds flew after 16 days, and their parents continued to feed them for a further 3 weeks. From the moment when they young birds ate on their own, the parents refused mealworms. They reached their full colour 10 weeks after flight; they were then chased by their parents and had to be taken from the aviary.

This subspecies cannot tolerate the presence of other small exotic birds, for they are very aggressive. But they can be housed in the company of Cut-throats, Red-headed Finches, Weavers or Java Sparrows. They can be allowed to winter in an unheated room.

BRONZE-WINGED MANNIKIN, HOODED FINCH, *Spermestes c. cucullatus* (Swainson)

G. Kleinelsterchen; F. Sperméte à capuchon, Nonnette ordinaire; D. Ekstertje   (Pl. XXX)

DISTRIBUTION: West Africa.

DESCRIPTION: Head and neck black with green sheen. Back and wings are dark brownish grey, with a black mark with a green sheen on scapulars. The black throat has a purple sheen. Rump and upper tail coverts have blackish brown transverse pattern on a background of white clouded with brown. Lower parts white; sides of breast have black marks with a green sheen, while the greyish brown sides carry horizontal white stripes. Tail black, upper beak black and lower beak lead grey; iris brown and feet and legs black. Length: 3¾ in. (9 cm). Sexes are alike.

Outside the breeding period, these Mannikins live in small flights of about 20 in the semi-desert and savannah, often approaching settlements where they go into the fields and gardens. During the nesting period the pairs withdraw to an isolated spot amongst the brushwood or in woodland. Nests have been found close together beneath the roofs of native huts. The round or oval nest is built of blades of grass and lined with feathers, they also use abandoned nests of Weaver birds. The female lays 4–8 eggs, on which the pair take turns to sit.

In 1860 they were first imported into Europe, and Dr. Russ was the first to succeed in breeding them. They are not suitable for a cage with a mixed population as they are extremely aggressive, even attacking larger birds. These lively birds need spacious quarters although a pair may breed in a large cage. When they are in a large outside aviary, they behave less agressively, especially if they share it with larger birds; in this case they do no more than defend their nest against intruders. During the breeding period, the male can be recognised by his purring call. If they are well looked after, these birds breed and raise their young very well; a pair will often raise 4 broods in a season, or even more. The female lays 5–7 eggs, on which both birds sit for 12 days. The young birds remain in the nest for more than 3 weeks and are independent shortly after flying. The juvenile moult is complete towards the age of 6 months. In addition to the usual seeds, these birds will take mealworms, germinated seeds, bread dipped in milk and green food; these forms of food are indispensable while the young are being fed.

BIB-FINCH, AFRICAN PARSON FINCH, *Spermestes nana* (Pucheran)

G. Zwergelsterchen; F. Spermète nain, Nonnette naine; D. Dwergeskterje

DISTRIBUTION: Madagascar.

DESCRIPTION: Forehead, lores, eyebrows and bib black. Grey feathers on top of head have black rachis, while sides of head are light grey. Upper parts greyish brown, with olive green on rump and upper tail coverts. Lower parts brownish, with light rachis, whilst breast is lighter grey. Lower tail coverts black with dark yellow edging. Tail black, iris brown, upper mandible black and lower mandible bluish grey, feet and legs horn coloured. Length: 3¾ in. (9 cm). Sexes are alike.

These birds can be seen in flights on cultivated fields. They climb with agility up the stalks to peck at the ears of ripen-grain. They nest in trees or bushes, building their nest of

Bib-finch, *Spermestes nana*

blades of grass. The female lays 3–5 eggs. They have been imported since 1880, but in small numbers. Successful attempts to breed were soon recorded, but it was also found that these birds were extremely aggressive during breeding, attacking the nests of other birds in the same aviary. This may explain why these pretty birds have never been popular; moreover, they are only imported occasionally and in small numbers. The charming song of the male consists of four phrases, repeated 3 or 4 times. This song, and the display of the male, are the only way of distinguishing the sexes. The best chance of their nesting occurs if they are housed in a well planted aviary in the company of larger species. They readily use a nest box to build their domed nest, of grass, hemp and coconut fibres lined with feathers.

In the aviary, the brood is usually larger than in the wild; thus in the aviary the female will lay 6–7 eggs, which hatch after 11–12 days. The young remain in the nest more than 3 weeks, and shortly after flight, they are independent. The pair will usually start a new brood at once, before the first offspring are completely independent. The young birds already have the black bib at the time they fly, but the olive green on the rump does not appear until they are more than 6 months old; they are 2 years old before they have their complete adult colouring.

PEARL-HEADED SILVERBILL, GREY-HEADED SILVERBILL, *Odontospiza caniceps* (Reichenov)

G. Perlhalsamadine, Grauköpfiges Silberschnäbelchen; F. Amadine à cou perlé, Bec d'argent à collier perlé, Spermète à tête grise; D. Parlehalsamandine, Grijskopzilverbekje

DISTRIBUTION: East Africa.

DESCRIPTION: Top of head, forehead and chin pearl grey, and throat black; cheeks and chin bear tiny white dots. Back, breast and abdomen fawn, with a whitish anal region. Wings dark brown, while the rump and lower tail coverts white; tail dark brown. Iris brown, upper mandible greyish black and lower mandible silver grey; feet and legs dark grey. Length: 4 in. (10 cm). Sexes are alike.

At the beginning of 1962, large numbers of these birds were imported into Europe. They inhabit semi-deserts where thorn bushes grow; they feed on grass seeds and small insects. They nest in trees, building a somewhat untidy nest with grass, lined with feathers. Four to 6 eggs are laid in a clutch.

The male can be recognised by his gentle chirping song, as well as by the defensive attitude which he takes up when approached: leaning forward a little, he opens his beak and shows his tongue.

London Zoo had 4 of these birds as early as 1930. However, records of successful breeding date from the time when several experienced bird keepers had specimens in cage and aviary, i.e. from 1963. W. Langberg succeeded in Denmark, and virtually at the same time Dr. R. Burkard, in Switzerland.

Langberg had received a considerable number of these birds, and was therefore able to sex them. Different specimens turned out to have a slightly different colouring on the breast. One of the light-breasted birds fell ill, and when it died shortly afterwards, the post-mortem proved that if was a female. Langberg was thus able to sex his birds, and it was later confirmed that the birds with the darker breast were in fact males. The Silverbills were housed in an inside aviary, together with Peale's Parrot Finch, Painted Finches and Gouldian Finches. One male carried out a nuptial display recalling that of a *Spermestes*, and soon one pair had begun to build a nest. If these birds have the chance to use an old abandoned nest, they will prefer it to a nest box. A female has been known to lay eggs without going on to sit. But the two parents sat in turn on a third clutch, and the young birds were raised properly. In addition to canary seed and various kinds of millet seeds, the parents received a daily supply of germinated seeds, soft food, bread and milk, with a vitamin supplement. Mealworms were given in large quantities, and the latter were used in particular to feed the young birds. When they flew, the young birds closely resembled the Bib-Finch. Fifteen days after flight, the males were already carrying out the nuptial display, giving their low call. After a few months, it was no longer possible to tell them from their parents.

Only one pair raised the young properly, the other as their eggs or their young.

Dr. Burkard kept his birds in an outside aviary, where they showed no inclination to nest. As winter approached, he housed them in a heated inside aviary, and one of the pairs soon accepted a nest box. After they had sat for 14 days, particularly the female, the eggs hatched. The female was tolerant of examination of the nest. The newly hatched birds were almost naked, and were pink with a very small amount of down. They had no papillae at the commissures of the beak, which carried a light bluish white edging; the beak itself was pink with a black point. Thd young birds spent 34 days in the nest, and then flew awkwardly.

They continued to demand to be fed for a long time. Their head was tilted as they raised it, and their wings trembled. They began to fly somewhat better 4 days after the first attempt, but the parents still brought them back to the nest at sunset. A second and then a third brood was raised, and the young birds remained in the nest for 5 weeks, and flew well when they left. It may be that the first brood accidently left the nest somewhat too soon.

The experiences of Dr. Bukard (*Die Gefiederte Welt*, 1963, No. 10) show that these birds can raise their young well, but must be kept in a heated aviary in the winter.

Genus: Euodice

INDIAN SILVER-BILL, *Euodice malabarica malabarira* (Linnaeus) (Pl. XXX)

G. Malabarfasänchen; F. Bec de plomb; D. Loodbekje

DISTRIBUTION: Sri Lanka, Indian sub-continent, Arabia.

DESCRIPTION: Upper parts light brown in both sexes; centre of top of head carries lines of dark rachis; rump and lower tail coverts white, with black edges on outer feathers. Tail and flight feathers black. Lower parts and sides of head fawn. Iris brown, beak lead grey and feet and legs flesh coloured. Length: 4½ in. (11·5 cm).

SUBSPECIES: Several subspecies have been described, the best known being the African Silver-bill, which lives in Africa and is distinguished principally by its black rump. In Africa there are also the following subspecies: *E. m. inornata*, *E. m. orientalis* and *E. m. meridionalis*; in the two latter, the lower parts are virtually white. Some writers separate the subspecies in India and those living in Africa into separate species.

These birds can be seen in small flights in gardens, fields, meadows and are regular visitors to settlements and often nest amongst creepers on houses. The somewhat ill-constructed nest is made of grass and vegetable wool; it contains 4–6 eggs. Sometimes they make use of the abandoned nests of Weaver Birds. They feed mainly on grass seeds.

They are favourite cage birds in India, and have long ago been imported into Europe; they were successfully bred very early. Although large numbers are never imported, they are regularly found in shipments. The Indian Silver-bill is often confused with the African Silver-bill, *E. m. cantans*, and it is not possible to tell which species is involved in the cases of successful breeding mentioned in early literature. Even amongst more recent records, there are accounts which suggest that both species breed and raise their young very well.

They can be housed in a large cage, with other small exotic birds; there are no quarrels, provided there are a sufficient number of nesting boxes available. Newly imported birds must be acclimatized first; it often takes several months before a pair is formed which decides to nest. The female lays 4–6 eggs, on which both birds incubate for 11 days. The young remain in the nest for 19 days and then fly, starting to

Indian Silverbill, *Euodice malabarica malabarira*

South-western Arabia.

DESCRIPTION: Upper parts light brown; feathers on top of head have dark rachis; all upper parts carry a fine wavy pattern. Upper tail coverts and tail black. Sides of head rusty yellow, with cream-coloured lores. Flight feathers blackish brown and wing coverts white; iris reddish brown, beak bluish grey and feet and legs flesh coloured. Length: 4¼ in. (11 cm).

These birds are regularly imported, raise their young well, and are also prepared to take on the young of other species. A diet of mixed seeds is sufficient for them. They will even raise their young with germinated seeds and green food. In

African Silver-bill, *Euodice malabarica cantans*

feed themselves about 5 days later. The adults usually accept neither mealworms nor ants' eggs, even when breeding. They prefer to feed their young with millet on the ear and other germinated seeds, and have a great demand for green food. They usually ignore soft food. The nuptial display of the male is carried out with a blade of grass in his beak, and he utters a low, murmuring song.

The skin of the newly hatched young is black; they are very silent, and do not begin to beg audibly for food until they are 10 days old. After flight, they regularly return to the nest, but they are independent in about 15 days. In a breeding cage or aviary, these birds often raise as many as 4 broods in a season, and it is not unusual for a single pair to raise up to 20 young in a year.

They are frequently crossed with African Silver-bills, and the offspring are fertile; in these specimens, the feathers of the rump carry red edges.

These birds can winter in an unheated aviary and are ideal birds for the beginner.

AFRICAN SILVER-BILL, *Euodice malabarica cantans* (Gmelin)

G. Silberschnäbelchen; F. Bec d'argent; D. Zilverbekje

(Pl. XXX)

DISTRIBUTION: Northern tropical Africa, Senegal, Tanzania,

the wild, they move in small flocks along meadows, watercourses, and near settlements. They nest in thick bushes, in hedges and amongst creepers on houses. The male constantly utters his sweet, sparkling song, and to attract the female, carries out a display with a blade of grass in his beak. This display and the song of the male are the only indications of sex. They are peaceable birds, and even allow other birds in the same aviary to chase them from the nest. They are particularly suitable for cages or small aviaries, where they will live peaceably with Bengalese or other small quiet species. They prefer to nest in a nest box, which they cram with fine blades of grass, coconut fibres and vegetable wool. Both birds sit on the 3–6 eggs for 11 days. The young are very dark, are naked at birth, remain for 19 days in the nest, and then are fed for a further 2 weeks. Sometimes a pair will raise as many as 5 broods in a season.

FAMILY: PLOCEIDAE

Genus: Vidua SUBFAMILY: VIDUINAE

(This genus contains the so-called Vidurine Whydahs; non-Vidurine Whydahs are listed in the genus *Euplectes* starting on p. 200.)

QUEEN WHYDAH, *Vidua regia* (Linnaeus)

G. Konigswitwe; F. Veuve reine, Veuve royale, Veuve a quartre brins; D. Koningswida (Pl. XLI)

DISTRIBUTION: Botswana, Transvaal, Angola.

DESCRIPTION: *Male*. Upper parts black, nape bar, sides of head and under parts orange-yellow-brown. Wings black and blackish-brown with narrow brown edges. Under tail coverts and thighs black, under wing coverts white. Tail blackish-brown with white mottling on inner edges of tips. The 4 extended tail feathers are like stiff black wires with the end quarter being webbed and shaped like a canoe paddle. These extended feathers are about 8 in. (20 cm) long. Length: 12 in. (32 cm) including tail. *Female*. Upper parts brown with dark brown markings, head and neck yellowish-brown.

under parts yellowish-brown, merging into white towards middle of abdomen. Iris brown, beak, feet and legs coral-red. These birds occur mainly in very dry areas, provided there is plenty of grass. They haunt brambles and trees and fly rapidly from one group of trees to another. Flights of 10–20 are usually seen, with only one male in ornamental plumage, which indicates a polygamous way of life. They do not build nests. During the breeding season, the males fight fiercely to defend their breeding territory.

These attractive whydahs were imported at the beginning of this century, they are now regularly obtainable. The males don their ornamental plumage in November. In a large aviary they are very easy to keep together with other birds, for they are peaceable. Their song is hoarse and croaking. In their winter plumage they keep themselves very much in the background. They like bathing and, apart from seed of all kinds, eat a lot of green and sometimes mealworms and other insects.

During the winter their night accommodation must be kept free from frost. A hybrid has been produced with the Paradise Whydah, *Steganura paradisea*.

Queen Whydah, *Vidua regia*

FISCHER'S WHYDAH, *Vidua fischeri* (Reichenow)
G. Fischer Witwe, Strohwitwe; F. Veuve de Fischer;
D. Fischer's Wida   (Pl. XLIV)
DISTRIBUTION: East Africa.
DESCRIPTION: Crown buff-yellow, rump and upper tail coverts dull brown with darker stripes, remaining upper parts, head, neck, scapulars and back, all black. Under parts straw-yellow to rust-coloured-yellow. Wings and tail black and blackish-brown with the 4 middle ones buff-yellow and very long, up to 8 in. (20 cm). Length: 11 in.

Fischer's Whydah, *Vidua fischeri*

(29 cm) including tail. Iris brown, beak, feet and legs red. *Female*. Upper parts buff-brown with brown markings, under parts buff-yellow. In winter plumage, sexes are alike.

These Whydahs live in dry steppe country, often in the vicinity of deserts, where the occasional bramble grows. They are not very common and are always found in small flocks, consisting during the breeding season of a single male in ornamental plumage and a number of females.

The male executes a typical display flight, flying steeply up and down.

A number of these whydahs reached Hamburg Zoo in 1911. Since then they have been sporadically imported. The aviary must be planted with a few bushes and trees and, if possible, reeds or bamboo. As well as Violet-eared Waxbills, Cordon Bleus may also be taken into the colony. Whydahs are able to adapt rapidly and surely. The normal seed diet, a great deal of green, soft food and occasionally live insects or mealworms keep the birds in good condition. A frost-free or moderately heated winter housing is necessary.

PIN-TAILED WHYDAH, *Vidua macroura* (Pallas)
G. Dominikaner Witwe; F. Veuve dominicaine; D.
Dominikaanwida   (Pl. XLI)
DISTRIBUTION: Africa south of the Sahara.
DESCRIPTION: *Male*. Crown, lores and feathers of nape, back and scapulars black. Sides of head, a bar in nape and under

Pin-tailed Whydah, *Vidua macroura*

parts white. Chin and sides of upper breast show a black patch. Wings black with a broad, white transverse stripe, rump white, upper tail coverts black. Tail black, the 4 middle tail feathers are long and ribbon-like. Overall length: including the 8 in. (20 cm) tail is 11 in. (28 cm). Iris brown, beak red, feet and legs reddish-brown. *Female*. Has black stripes on her pale brown upper parts; over crown run two black stripes; middle is reddish-brown, as also are rump and upper tail coverts. These whydahs are very common in both inhabited and cultivated areas. In their ornamental plumage, the males execute display dances making their tails vibrate. A male is always accompanied by 6 or more females and a few young males who have not yet fully developed their colouring. Outside the breeding season, the birds gather in large flocks together with a number of finch species. One male in his ornamental plumage dominates all the others, including much larger birds. He sings his shrill, chirruping song, perched in the top of a tree or bush.

Of all whydahs this form is the most frequently imported.

When they are in their ornamental plumage, they are troublesome and chase and frighten the other inhabitants of the aviary, performing their display dance. In a spacious, well-planted aviary they can however easily be kept together with Weavers and Zebra Finches.

Breeding results have been obtained on repeated occasions in an aviary with small finches. In the mating season, the male flies over the females with whirring tail and, when the latter vibrate their wings and tail, they are ready to mate.

Genus Steganura

SUBFAMILY: PLOCEINAE

PARADISE WHYDAH, *Steganura p. paradisa* (Linnaeus) (Pl. XLI)
G. Paradieswitwe; F. Veuve de Paradis; D. Paradijswida

DISTRIBUTION: East Africa, Erytrea, Ethiopia, Sudan, Angola to South Africa.

DESCRIPTION: *Male.* Head, chin, throat down to upper breast, back, upper and under tail coverts, thighs, wing coverts and tail black. Vent area white, flights dark brown with brown edges. Nape bar, sides of neck and under parts yellow-ochre; upper breast golden-brown towards abdomen merging into paler hues. Iris dark brown, beak black and feet and legs dark horn-colour. Length: including 4 extended middle tail feathers about 16 in. (40 cm). Tail about 11 in. (28 cm) long. *Female.* Has black crown with a buff longitudinal stripe, sides of head and eyes stripe sand-coloured. Behind iris a black stripe runs to ear coverts, upper parts yellowish-brown with a black stripe in middle. Under parts white and slightly rust-coloured towards throat. Male similar to female in winter plumage but somewhat darker in the black areas.

These attractive whydahs are very common in the steppe

lands, especially in areas where there are brambles. They prefer perches in bare tree tops and males in ornamental plumage execute their steep display flights and wheeling swooping descents. The long tail prevents them from coming down to the ground and, as the males fly, they do so with difficulty and jerkily for short distances. When they perch, they allow their tail to hang down straight. As they fly, they emit soft, chirruping warbling notes. One male gathers a number of females around him. This species does not engage in nest-building; sometimes they take over abandoned weavers' nests for roosting purposes, and in the breeding season the females go industriously in search of the nests of various members of the finch race, Pytilia. They lay 1–2 eggs in the nests, which are somewhat larger than those of their hosts. The young are usually reared together with those of the Pytilia.

Breeding results have been obtained in the aviaries, when these birds have been kept together with various small finches. Their diet consists of a mixture of millets and canary seeds, with some soft food and green added. A hybrid form has been produced with the Queen Whydah, *Vidua regia.*

SUBFAMILY: BUBALORNITHINAE

BUFFALO WEAVER, *Bubalornis a. albirostris* (Vieillot) (Pl. XXXIV)
G. Büffelweber; F. Tisserin alecto; D. Buffelwever

DISTRIBUTION: North-eastern Africa, northern Uganda, north-western Kenya, northern Ethiopia.

DESCRIPTION: Main colouring black. On sides of body, the white of base of plumage penetrates through. Wings black with white edges along the flights. Iris brown; beak pinkish-white with a black spot; feet horn-coloured. Length: 8¾ in. (22 cm).

SUBSPECIES: Two other subspecies are the South African Buffalo Weaver, *B. a. niger,* and the Somali Buffalo Weaver, *B. a. intermedius.* Both forms have a red and black bill, which during the mating season shows no swelling, as with the nominate race.

Outside the breeding season, large numbers of these birds occur in and around river beds overgrown with grass, wherever cattle graze. They are also often to be seen around native huts. They run, mostly in the company of Glossy Starlings, feverishly pecking around the cattle, examining the excrement, and also pecking parasites and flies off these animals. They eat all kinds of seeds and fruits.

They nest in colonies. High up in a tree, an elaborate network of small branches and twigs is constructed, and in this the birds make their nests, twined over with blades of grass. The nests are lined with fine grass, plant fibres, hair and wool, and in them are laid 3–4 off-white eggs, with greenish-brown mottling.

These birds have been imported several times and taken into collections. They quickly become tame and do not interfere with other birds in the aviary. They scamper around busily

Buffalo Weaver, *Bubalornis a. albirostris*

and need insectivorous food, a large number of mealworms and other live food. They also eat seeds, greenstuff and all kinds of fruit. In a spacious aviary, in which a stout tree has been planted, they will build a large nest of twigs and branches. In the middle of this tangle of branches they make a round nest of hemp, blades of grass and leaves. The nest has a tunnel entrance, the mouth of which is at the upper edge of the twigs. This enables them to go in and out easily. The first breeding results were obtained at the Berlin Zoo, where a number of pairs were kept together. Two females hatched and reared 4 young. Other Buffalo Weavers continued building until the nest was 3 ft (1 m) high.

DINEMELLI'S WEAVER, WHITE-HEADED BUFFALO WEAVER, *Dinemellia d. dinemelli* (Rüppell) (Pl. XXXIV)
G. Weisskopfviehweber, Starweber; F. Dinemelli à tête blanche, Tisserin dinemelli; D. Witkop-Veewever

DISTRIBUTION: Sudan, Ethiopia.

DESCRIPTION: Head and neck white. Back brown; shoulder plumage brown with white edges to the feathers. Upper and under tail coverts red. Under parts white; thighs brown. Wings brown with a small white speculum. Tail, beak and feet dark brown. Iris brown. Sexes alike. Length: 8 in. (20 cm).

SUBSPECIES: One other subspecies has been described, which is found in the Congo, Tanganyika and Kenya: the Böhms Buffalo Weaver, *D. d. böhmi*, which does not have the white wing speculum, and has scarlet upper tail coverts.

Dinemelli's Weavers also gather together in large numbers in pasture land and steppe country, wherever cattle graze. They are very industrious and feed mainly on worms, insects and seeds. Their flight is somewhat fluttering, though not completely so. They nest in colonies in the tops of isolated trees, often using thorny twigs, which serve as a form of defence. Inside the voluminous stronghold of twigs, round nests are built from grass stalks and plant fibres, with a long tunnel entrance leading downwards. Two to 4

Dinemelli's Weaver, *Dinemellia d. dinemelli*

glossy blue-white eggs are laid; these have dark brown markings.

These birds were first imported into Hamburg in 1910. It is difficult to match a pair as there are no outward sex distinguishing marks. However, during the mating season, the male begins to court the female with all sorts of comical bowings and with outspread wings, chattering gaily. The female answers the male's declarations of love with a reserved fluttering of her wings. Sometimes the male feeds the female. The first breeding results were obtained at the Pittsburg Zoo (USA). Mr. R. A. Hawkins has given an account with photographs in the *Avicultural Magazine*, 1958, No. 2. Dinemelli's Weavers can be kept during the winter in an outside aviary, if night accommodation protected from frost is available.

SUBFAMILY: PASSERINAE

MAHALI WEAVER, WHITE-BROWED SPARROW WEAVER, *Plocepasser m. mahali* (Smith) (Pl. XXXIV)
G. Mahaliweber; F. Tisserin Mahali; D. Mahaliwever

DISTRIBUTION: Cape Province, Rhodesia, western part of Orange Free State.

DESCRIPTION: Top of head, lores, cheeks and beard stripe black. Rest of head brown. Broad eyebrow stripe, rump, upper tail coverts and all under parts white. On breast and sides of body a brown marking sometimes appears. Neck, back and lesser wing coverts brown. Rest of wings blackish-

Mahali Weaver, *Plocepasser m. mahali*

brown with white tips on feather edges. Iris reddish-brown, beak brownish-black, feet pinkish-brown. Length: 6¾ in. (17 cm). *Female*. A little smaller.

SUBSPECIES: Five other subspecies have been described, which show minor differences in colour and size. Of these the best-known in aviculture is the Black-billed Mahali Weaver Bird, *Plocepasser mahali melanorhynchus*, from southern Sudan and north Uganda, southern Ethiopia and central Kenya. The birds live the whole year through in large colonies, and fly noisily from tree to tree. In their

behaviour they resemble sparrows and their song is like that of the Yellowhammer. Nests are built in colonies high up in a tree at the ends of branches. They are pouch-shaped and made out of thin twigs and grass blades. Loose ends of grass stick out like bristles. The nests have 2 entrances underneath. During the incubation period one entrance is closed but opened again when the young are ready to fly out. The nest serves also as a roost and is used for several years. Two to 3 pinkish-white eggs are laid, covered with reddish-brown stripes.

The birds feed chiefly on all sorts of insects, which they pick up from the ground; they also eat greenstuffs and seeds. They were first kept in captivity at the Berlin Zoo in 1876. The males are very aggressive, especially in the spring, and several pairs can be kept together only in a very large aviary.

SOCIABLE WEAVER, SOCIAL WEAVER, *Philetarius s. socius* (Latham) (Pl. XXXIV)
G. Siedelweber, Siedelsperling; F. Tisserin social républicain; D. Koloniewever, Republikeinwever

DISTRIBUTION: Namibia and South Africa.

DESCRIPTION: Top of head dark grey, sides of head reddish-grey. Lores, cheeks, chin and throat patch black. Back and rump greyish-brown, neck and upper part of back dark brownish-black; feathers have light grey edges. Under parts reddish-grey, under tail coverts grey with lighter edges. Wings and tail a dull grey. Iris brown, beak grey-blue, feet brownish-flesh-colour. Length: about 5½ in. (14 cm).

In Africa these birds live in colonies, where they build a large number of nests, under a communal roof, high in an acacia or aloe tree. The nest sometimes has a diameter of about 15 ft (5 m) and a height of 7½ ft (2·5 m). The individual nests are made of grass stalks and blades; they are spherical and have a round entrance on the lower side. When a nest has been used once it is abandoned and a new nest built.

It can even happen that the tree cannot bear the weight of the number of nests built and collapses. Indeed, as many as 300 nests have been counted in one place!

It has been reported that in aviaries they have been known to appropriate old weavers' nests, and over the top of these have built a communal roof of strong stalks. They flew up from the ground and straight into the nest without first perching on the edge of it. They laid and hatched several clutches of eggs, but abandoned their young because there was not enough live food available, such as ants' eggs and mealworms. They ate all kinds of seed, especially canary seed.

Small finches, lizards and snakes often move into the old colony nests. Nests have been found which were a hundred years old. Beneath them the droppings from the birds form a thick layer. The breeding locations are often far away from drinking water. Even in the aviary, the birds drink little. A varied diet with greenstuffs, a lot of live insects and ants' eggs increases the chances of successful breeding.

These birds were first introduced into Germany in large numbers in 1907.

Sociable Weaver, *Philetarius s. socius*

CAPE SPARROW, MOSSIE, *Passer m. melanurus* (Müller) (Pl. XXXV)

G. Kapsperling; F. Moineau du cap, Moineau mélanure; D. Kaapse Mus

DISTRIBUTION: South Africa.
DESCRIPTION: *Male*. Head black. A white stripe runs from the eye across top of ear coverts to nape and sides of neck. Upper parts warm cinnamon-brown, back of neck and upper part of back a little greyer. Upper tail coverts brown. Foreneck black down as far as breast. Under parts white, greyer at sides of body. Lesser wing coverts reddish-brown; others black with white tips and broad brown edges. Wings and tail blackish-brown with pale edges. Iris brown, beak black, feet brown. Length: 5½ in. (14 cm). *Female*. Is Brownish-grey colour, where male is black; throat and upper breast grey.

Originally the Cape Sparrow inhabited dry, inhospitable steppe country, but it has become increasingly drawn towards human settlements, where food is plentiful, and may now be seen quite frequently in large towns. On the plains these birds assemble in large flocks outside the breeding season, stripping the cornfields around the farms. They strongly resemble the House Sparrow in their behaviour and in their chirruping and song. During the winter months they roam around in the company of finches and weavers

Cape Sparrow, *Passer m. melanurus*

of all kinds. Their food consists mainly of seed, greenstuff, berries, fruit and insects of all kinds. They build nests the whole year round, to sleep in as well as for laying their eggs. The nests are bottle-shaped, roomy and located in thorn bushes or trees. They have a 6 in. (15 cm) long tunnel entrance. The material used consists of thick stalks, leaves, scraps of paper and grass. The lining is made of all kinds of soft materials and feathers. Sometimes old weavers' nests are taken over. The nests are now often found under the eaves of houses. The 3–6 eggs are greyish-white speckled with brown and grey. The incubation period lasts 13 days and the young remain in the nest for at least 3 weeks.

These birds are easy to keep and will also breed. However, the young can only be reared on live food. They live peaceably with related and other species and they will survive the winter in a frost-free location.

A successful breeding was reported by D. Seth-Smith in *Avicultural Magazine*, Vol. 7, 1900–01, pp. 165–7, 215.

GREY-HEADED SPARROW, *Passer griseus diffusus* (Smith)

G. Weisskehlsperling; F. Moineau à tête grise, Moineau gris; D. Grijskopmus

DISTRIBUTION: Angola, northern Namibia, Botswana, Rhodesia, Transvaal, Orange Free State, Natal.
DESCRIPTION: *Male*. Head, neck and under parts grey. Under tail coverts and tail brownish-grey with white edges. Upper parts russet-brown, rump reddish-brown. Upper tail coverts, tail and wings brown, the feathers edged with paler brown. Flights blackish-brown edged with cinnamon.

Grey-headed Sparrow, *Passer griseus diffusus*

Iris brown, beak black, feet reddish-brown. Length: 6¼ in. (16 cm). *Female*. Somewhat paler in colour and markings.

Outside the breeding season the birds live mostly in the company of weavers and small finches, and with cordon bleus and waxbills. They are often mistaken for the female Cape Sparrow. They inhabit dry regions where thorn bushes and the rare acacias grow. They used to be shy birds, but have become increasingly attracted towards the kind of food to be found in human settlements. In cultivated fields they eat their fill of grain. They may also be found in villages and towns. In the gardens they eat all kinds of insects and weed seeds.

They build their nests in rock clefts, gaps in walls and abandoned woodpeckers' holes. For material they use strong stalks and leaves; the lining consists of soft grasses and feathers.

Grey-headed Sparrows are occasionally kept in aviaries. They are a bit troublesome when kept with smaller birds and are best with starlings or related birds.

They breed in nesting-boxes or in abandoned weavers' nests. The first breeding was achieved in 1909 by Mr. W. E. Teschemaker in England, *Avicultural Magazine*, (3), Vol. 1, 1909–10, pp. 238–9.

The birds must have a varied menu and the main diet for the young while they are being reared consists of mealworms and other live insects.

SUDAN GOLDEN SPARROW, *Passer l. luteus* (Lichtenstein)   (Pl. XXXV)
G. Braunrückengoldsperling; F. Moineau doré; D. Bruinrug-Goudmus

DISTRIBUTION: Nigeria, Sudan, Ethiopia.

DESCRIPTION: *Male.* Entire head and under parts canary-yellow. Mantle and edges of innermost flights chestnut-brown. Wing coverts have white edges. Rump yellowish and tail blackish-brown with pale edges. Iris brown; beak horn-coloured, turning black in the breeding season; feet dark flesh-colour. Length: 5¼ in. (13 cm). *Female.* Has a paler brown head, mantle and rump, and one or two black stripes on her coat. Under parts greyish-white, the feathers edged with yellow.

Sudan Golden Sparrow, *Passer l. luteus*

These birds wander in large flocks around cotton fields, over steppes and along small lakes and streams. They do not stay away from human settlements and are sometimes to be seen sitting in long lines on the edges of roofs or on walls. They chirrup like House Sparrows. At drinking places they sit in large numbers on the overhanging branches so that they bend under the birds' weight and almost reach the surface of the water. Indeed, the birds are sometimes snatched away from their perches by predatory fish. They are peaceful by nature and breed in colonies, building pouch-like nests close together in thorny bushes. The 3–4 greenish-white eggs are hatched in 10–12 days.

Sudan Golden Sparrows make good cage or aviary birds. They can be kept with smaller finches and usually breed in nest-boxes. They fill the whole of the inside with blades of grass and thin twigs, and generally provide the nest with a short tunnel entrance. They breed several times in succession, and, even when no ants' eggs or mealworms are available, they usually rear their young to a healthy size with greenstuff, soft food and soaked seed. The young leave the nest after 14 days and are then cared for by the parents for a further 2 weeks. The birds acclimatise quite well.

ARABIAN GOLDEN SPARROW, GOLDEN SPARROW, *Passer luteus euchlorus* (Bonaparte)   (Pl. XXXV)
G. Goldsperling; F. Enfant du soleil, Moineau doré; D. Goudmus

DISTRIBUTION: Southern Saudi Arabia, Yemen, southern Yemen, coastal regions of Ethiopia.

DESCRIPTION: *Male.* Main colour canary-yellow. Wing coverts white touched with yellow. Flights and tail feathers blackish-brown with white edges. Iris brown; beak black; feet flesh-coloured. Length: 5 in. (12·5 cm). *Female.* Has a pale yellow head and breast. Upper parts yellowish-grey colour and under parts white in middle, with a brown tinge on edges.

Arabian Golden Sparrow, *Passer luteus euchlorus*

These birds have a similar way of life to that of the Sudan Golden Sparrow. They have a distinctly more peaceful nature and are generally found in villages and settlements. They nest in thorny trees and bushes. The strongly-built nest is usually covered over with thorny twigs.

The first breeding results were obtained in Germany at the end of the last century by Dr. Russ. Since then they have only occasionally been imported and then not in large numbers. Neunzig reports that the young must be reared exclusively on mealworms, caterpillars, greenfly and other insects but subsequent breeding results, particularly those of Mr. B. Mullard of Camberley, England, indicate that, apart from the seed diet, only mealworms need be given as food. (*Foreign Birds*, 1956, No. 3.)

In an aviary in which lived Pekin Robins, Mozambique Yellow-fronted Canaries and Dominican Cardinals, the Arabian Golden Sparrows bred in a nesting-box rigged close to the roof, in which they had made a nest of grass, moss and cow hair. Four greyish eggs were laid. The parents ate canary seed, yellow and white millet and mealworms. When the young flew they resembled the female. About 6 weeks later there was a second clutch.

Although Arabian Golden Sparrows acclimatise well and fly around in an outside aviary even during the winter, damp chilly days are harmful and they will not remain in good condition without a night-box in the aviary. They depend a great deal on light and sunshine, and during the winter months they like to find a place under the heating lamp.

CHESTNUT SPARROW, *Passer eminebey* (Hartlaub)
G. Emins Goldsperling; F. Moineau doré d'Emin; D. Emins Mus

DISTRIBUTION: Sudan, Uganda, Kenya and Ethiopia.

DESCRIPTION: *Male.* Main colour chestnut-brown, darkest on head and neck. Flights and tail blackish-brown with brown edges; wing coverts chestnut-brown. Iris blackish-brown; back black; feet reddish-brown. Length: 4½ in. (11·5 cm). *Female.* Crown ash-grey, upper parts dull brown with black stripes. Rump and upper tail coverts reddish-brown. Under parts white.

These birds are nearly always seen in small groups, often with Ribbon Finches. They prefer to keep to the papyrus swamps, where they retire to small islands with trees and bushes. They are not particularly shy and often frequent the villages and become very tame there. They nest in trees fairly high above the ground. The nests look like those of weavers and there is some doubt as to whether the birds have built their own or have actually taken over abandoned weavers' nests and relined them with fine grass and feathers. The 3–4 eggs are a pale greenish-white colour with black and dark brown spots. Their food consists of grass and weed seeds and insects of all kinds.

Chestnut Sparrows, with Arabian Golden Sparrows, were first imported to Germany in 1913. Their requirements are similar to those of the Arabian Golden Sparrow, *Passer luteus euchlorus*.

Genus: Petronia

ROCK SPARROW, *Petronia p. petronia* (Linnaeus)

G. Steinsperling; F. Moineau soulcie, Moineau fou; D. Rotsmus

DISTRIBUTION: Central Europe, Asia Minor.

DESCRIPTION: From a distance it looks like the female House Sparrow. At close quarters a clear yellow patch on throat of male is visible, paler on female. White spots on tips of tail feathers can be seen, especially when in flight.

The Rock Sparrow nests in rock crannies on stony slopes and also in ruins. Its call is mostly a dissyllable and harsher than the House Sparrow's. Unlike similar species, it avoids the neighbourhood of human beings and is very shy. Rearing and feeding as for other species.

A successful breeding was reported in *Avicultural Magazine*, No. 3, 1896–97, pp. 28–9, by E. G. B. Meade-Waldo.

YELLOW-THROATED SPARROW, SOUTH AFRICAN ROCK SPARROW, *Petronia superciliaris* (Blyth)

(Pl. XXXV)

G. Augenbrauenkehlsperling; Afrika-Steinsperling; F. Moineau à sourcils; D. Afrikaanse Rotsmus

DISTRIBUTION: Africa, south of the Equator.

DESCRIPTION: Sexes alike. The upper parts are dark brown. Above and behind the eye runs a white stripe. The mantle shows black stripes. The under parts are yellowish-white or greyish-white. On the throat there is a small yellow spot. Length: about 6 in. (15 cm).

These birds are mostly seen in pairs in rocky regions, but in and near settlements they are sometimes in boabab trees and large euphorbias. Their food consists mostly of insects. In winter they search on the ground for grass and weed seeds. They seem to enjoy eating young green buds; they often hang from branches like tits. Their large nests, built of grass and feathers, are made in the hollow trunks of euphorbias and in the holes in rocks. The 3–4 eggs are a light bluish-white, freckled and spotted with brownish-grey. A number of pairs breed together. They are not typical birds of mountainous and rocky regions, as their name would suggest. When they come down to the ground, they do not hop but run around like starlings.

At the end of the last century they were imported for the first time into Germany and Britain; later they have appeared sporadically in Europe.

LESSER ROCK SPARROW, BUSH PETRONIA, *Petronia dentata* (Sundevall)

G. Kleiner Kehlsperling; F. Moineau denté; D. Kleine Rotsmüs

DISTRIBUTION: Sudan, Arabia and Ethiopia.

DESCRIPTION: Upper parts dark brown, crown greyish-brown. Stripe above and behind the eye rust-coloured brown; mantle rust-brown. Yellow patch on throat paler and smaller than that of Yellow-throated Sparrow, *P. superciliaris*; beak black in breeding season, otherwise horn-coloured. Eye stripe buff. Length about 4½ in. (11·5 cm).

The birds are especially found in low-lying country, mostly in pairs, both on the open fields near water and the hot lowland forests of Ethiopia. Although they are found on the rocky slopes which lead to the central plateau, they show no special preference for perching on rocky points. On the contrary they usually perch in high trees, where they also look for their food, consisting of insects of all kinds. The birds nest in the trees, in abandoned woodpeckers' holes. In the steppes country they frequently come down to the ground in order to look for grass and weed seeds.

In the same area, the Yellowish-speckled Rock Sparrow, *P. xanthocollis pyrgita*, which is distinguishable from the Bush Petronia mainly by the fact that it lacks the eyebrow stripe, has a smaller yellow throat patch and is much larger, namely about 6½ in. (16 cm). In their way of life these birds are very similar to one another.

Genus: Sporopipes

SPECKLE-FRONTED WEAVER, RED-FRONTED FINCH, *Sporopipes f. frontalis* (Daudin) (Pl. XXXV)

G. Schuppenköpfchen; F. Sénégali à front pointillé; D. Schubbenkopje

DISTRIBUTION: Senegal to Ethiopia.

DESCRIPTION: Sexes alike. Forehead, top of head and beard stripe black, flecked with white. Crown and nape of neck cinnamon-brown. Mantle and rump reddish-sand-colour. Wings and tail grey with yellowish-white edges. Sides of head and breast greyish. Rest of under parts white. Iris brown; beak, feet and legs horn-coloured. Length 4¾ in. (12 cm).

Except in the breeding season these birds are to be seen in large flocks beside waterholes in steppe and desert country where bramble bushes grow. They are sluggish birds, which are also seen in the vicinity of settlements, on the roofs of houses and huts. They are often found on the ground, where they look for their food. They roost at night in abandoned weavers' nests, sometimes 5–6 birds in one nest. In the breeding season they live in pairs, but one or two pairs may be seen living in close proximity to one another. The 4 eggs are greyish in colour, with dark brown oblong spots.

They are much more peaceable than Bearded Tits and can be kept in an aviary with small finches. They must be acclimatised with care and need a lot of warmth. Only when the days begin to get warmer can they be placed in outside aviaries. In addition to canary seed and various kinds of millet they eat ants' eggs and mealworms. They must get accustomed to mealworms so that later they can feed their young on them.

Breeding results have been achieved only a few times, presumably because of an insufficiently varied breeding diet.

Speckle-fronted Weaver, *Sporopipes f. frontalis*

A large number of insects and especially fresh ants' eggs must be available, also egg fodder and germinated seed. Both birds breed and rear the young. They must have heated accommodation in winter. To avoid breeding during the winter months the pairs must be separated. This applies to most species that are accustomed to roosting in nests.

SCALY-CROWNED WEAVER, SCALY WEAVER, SCALY-FRONTED WEAVER, *Sporopipes squamifrons* (A. Smith)

G. Schnurrbärtchen; F. Tisserin à front pointillé; D. Baardmannetje (Pl. XXXV)

DISTRIBUTION: Namibia, Botswana, northern part of the Cape Province, south-western Rhodesia, west Transvaal and western Orange Free State.

DESCRIPTION: Sexes alike. Black and white scale-like markings on top of head. Lores black and there is a black stripe

Scaly-crowned Weaver, *Sporopipes squamifrons*

on both sides of the throat. The rest of the head, the ear coverts and upper parts are ash-grey. The wing coverts, the innermost flights and the tail are black with white edges. The remaining parts of the wings dark grey. Under parts whitish-grey. Beard strip and throat white. Iris brown, beak pink, legs and feet a greyish-brown. Length: 4 in. (10 cm).

Outside the breeding season, these weavers appear in small groups in arid steppe country where thorny bushes abound. Usually they sit on the ground looking for food, which consists of grass and weed seeds. In inhabited areas, they are trusting and behave rather like ordinary sparrows. While eating they chatter constantly. Captain B. R. Horsbrugh, of South Africa, kept a large number of them in his aviary, but came to the conclusion that they did not adapt well to life in the aviary. People have had the same experience in Europe: the acclimatisation process must take place very gradually and the birds must be accustomed carefully to the diet of seed and greenstuff.

The birds breed in colonies and Captain Horsbrugh mentioned having discovered a small acacia in which there were more than 200 nests. In most of the nests there were young, and the noise they made reminded him of cicadas. (*Avicultural Magazine*, 1906, p. 224.)

In the *African Handbook of Birds*, Series 2, Vol. 2, by Praed and Grant, a diet of seeds only is mentioned. Experience has, however, shown that these birds are very fond of live insects and that they rear their young almost exclusively on insects. Many amateurs have lost clutches of young birds because they have failed to supply enough fresh ants' eggs. Aphids, white worms and mosquito larvae can also prove extremely useful for rearing purposes.

In the aviary, these birds are inclined to build a free-standing nest in a forked branch. They make an extensive structure with a nest room in the upper part which has a tunnel entrance. Other pairs seeking a nesting place are chased ferociously. They can be left to breed in an aviary with a few unpaired birds. Both parents take turns to incubate the 3–5 eggs; the female mostly during the day and both birds during the night. During the day, the female leaves the nest only for short periods to eat and drink. After 14 days the eggs hatch and the young are fed on insects into their crops. Pairs are difficult to select. The males seem to be a little larger, but this can only be seen properly when there are a number of them together. The song and the mating behaviour are the decisive means of making the distinction.

Fully successful breeding results are rare. One was reported by W. E. Teschemaker in *Avicultural Magazine*, (3), No. 4, 1912–13, pp. 362–6.

SUBFAMILY: PLOCEINAE

THICK-BILLED WEAVER, *Amblyopsiza a. albifrons* (Vigors) (Pl. XXIX)

G. Weisstirnweber, Dickschnabelweber; F. Tisserin à gros bec; D. Witvoorhoofdwever

DISTRIBUTION: South-eastern Africa.

DESCRIPTION: *Male.* Beak brownish-black and remarkably heavily formed. Forehead usually white. Rest of head, neck, mantle and breast warm brown. Rest of upper parts, including wings and tail, brownish-black. The large flights have a white speculum. Under parts dark grey. All feathers are edged with brown and white. Iris, feet and legs brownish. *Female.* Has brown upper parts with paler edge-colouring to the feathers and creamy-white under parts, with black stripes. Beak yellowish. Length: about 7¼ in. (18 cm).

SUBSPECIES: The 10 subspecies show few differences in colour and size, and occur in large tracts of country in central and southern Africa.

Thick-billed Weavers mainly inhabit marshy areas in low-lying country, where they are common. The nests are ingeniously woven between a couple of marsh reeds. They are oval and closely woven with fine blades of grass. The male performs this task alone and builds a number of nests close together. The female finishes the interior of the nest. There is a round side entrance, which, with some races, is covered over. The 3 eggs are cream-coloured with a number of reddish-brown spots.

At the beginning of this century these birds appeared in various collections in Europe and in 1936 a breeding result was reported by Mr. W. Shore-Baily in *Avicultural Magazine*, Vol.00, p. 314. The birds built a free-standing nest in a bush and the eggs hatched out in 13 days. Some time later the male pulled away the bottom part of the nest and a young bird flew out. Some time afterwards the pair began to breed again and this time, also, the young were hatched.

The birds feed on seed and insects. They can be kept during the winter in a frost-free room and they fascinate the onlooker by their interesting nest-building activity. It is advisable to plant reeds or bamboos in the outside aviary for them. In this way it is also possible to prevent their nails from growing too long as otherwise they would have to be regularly clipped.

PELZELN'S WEAVER, SLENDER-BILLED WEAVER, *Ploceus p. pelzelni* (Hartlaub)

G. Pelzelns Weber; F. Tisserin de Pelzeln, Tisserin à bec grêle; D. Pelzeln's Wever

DISTRIBUTION: Interior of north-eastern Africa around Lake Victoria.
DESCRIPTION: *Male.* Forehead, front part of crown, sides of head, ear coverts and chin black. Back of head, nape, sides of neck and under parts golden-yellow. Mantle green, wings greyish-brown with yellow edges and tail olive-brown with yellow-tinged edges. Beak black, long and narrow. *Female.* Has yellow head and throat; neck green, beak black. Length: 4¾ in. (12 cm).
SUBSPECIES: A subspecies is to be found in Ghana and northern Angola. This is the Monk Weaver, *Ploceus pelzelni monachus*, which is broadly similar to *Ploceus p. pelzini*, but has a somewhat shorter and blacker bill and has a slightly different mask.
Pelzeln's Weaver prefers to live in marshy areas or in damp forests. In one area in Uganda the birds have adapted themselves to new conditions and have built nests in all the trees of a town. Like the tits, the birds hang suspended from twigs in trees, searching for hidden insects, which constitute their main food.
They usually nest in papyrus marshes. Between the stalks of reeds they suspend long and transparent nests of grass, which they cover with a few feathers. The 2–3 eggs are pinkish-white, with brown or russet spots.

LITTLE MASKED WEAVER, ATLAS WEAVER, *Ploceus l. luteolus* (Lichtenstein)

G. Zwergmaskenweber; F. Petit tisserin masqué; D. Dwergmaskerwever

DISTRIBUTION: Senegal to Ethiopia, Cameroon and north-eastern Zaire.
DESCRIPTION: *Male.* In display plumage, forehead and sides of head, ear coverts, chin and throat; black; crown, sides of neck, upper tail coverts and under parts canary-yellow; mantle greenish-yellow and striped. Wings and tail brownish-with yellow edges. Bill black, iris reddish-brown, feet flesh-coloured. Outside the breeding season the upper parts of the male are greenish-grey, the mantle grey with brown stripes. Sides of head and under tail coverts yellowish. Remaining under parts white with a little buff colouring on breast and flanks. Length: 4¾ in. (12 cm). *Female.* Has yellow under parts. Head green, sides of head and chin pale yellow.
These weavers are sociable and frequent gardens and wooded areas. They usually gather in large flocks in fields, where they eat insects and seed of all kinds. The nests hang closely together in bramble bushes. A surprising fact is that the birds like to build their nests near wasps' nests and in some cases there are nests in trees in which wasps have also created settlements. The oblong, spout-like nests have a tunnel entrance which goes from the lower side upwards into the round nest chamber. The nests swing to and fro in the wind and a sort of fence in the exit tunnel prevents the eggs from falling out. The nests, which are made of blades of grass, are sometimes lined with hair and other soft materials. The 2–3 eggs are white.

This weaver is easily confused with Pelzeln's Weaver, *Ploceus p. pelzelni*, and Monk's Weaver, *Ploceus pelzelni monachus*, because the differences in the masks are so slight. It is a lively bird, which clambers through the twigs and branches as dexterously as a siskin. The male, in his nuptial plumage, becomes excited, and when he has built his nest he chases all the other birds away from the vicinity.
Breeding results have been obtained on several occasions. The female hatches the 4 eggs in 12 days, being relieved by

Little Masked Weaver, *Ploceus l. luteolus*

the male for short periods only. Both parents rear the young. Dr. Russ bred 3 clutches one after the other. The young take a full year before growing their display plumage. In *Bird Notes*, 1914: p. 305; 1915: p. 42, a successful breeding is reported by Mr. W. Shore-Baily.
In addition to the seed diet the birds must also be given a great many live insects and mealworms. Most weavers also eat all kinds of fruit and greenstuff.
If the birds are kept in an outside aviary all the year round, they must be provided with additional and preferably slightly heated accommodation during the winter.

SPECTACLED WEAVER, *Ploceus ocularis crocatus* (Hartlaub) (Pl. XXIX)

G. Brillenweber; F. Tisserin à lunettes; D. Brilwever
DISTRIBUTION: Cameroon to southern Sudan and southern Ethiopia, western Kenya, Tanzania, Congo, eastern and southern Zaire, Angola and Zambia.
DESCRIPTION: *Male.* Forehead and crown of adult male

Spectacled Weaver, *Ploceus ocularis crocatus*

golden-yellow. Remainder of upper parts, including wings and tail, yellowish-green. Under parts yellow, tinged with golden-brown around throat patch. Lores, a broad stripe through eye and a large throat patch, descending as far as upper breast, black. Wing coverts yellowish-green. Flights blackish-brown with greenish-yellow and white edges. Tail greenish-yellow. Iris grey; beak black; feet grey. The male does not have display plumage. Length: 6 in. (15 cm).

Female. Lacks the throat patch and the stripe from lores through the iris is narrower. Crown greenish-yellow.

These weavers do not form groups but live mainly in pairs in open country, in both low-lying and plateau areas, in tracts of land in which bramble bushes grow and in wooded areas. They are often found in the company of other birds. They live in the trees and on the ground. Their food consists largely of insects. They build their nests, which are provided with tunnel entrances, at the ends of branches or palm leaves, beside or over water. Sometimes they make two tunnels, sometimes they merely make a round opening to the nest. For nest-building they use grass, bark and leaves. The nests are often green in colour and are never lined. The 2–3 eggs are white with reddish-brown mottling. Both parents sit on the eggs alternately and are so devoted that they cannot be moved even if grabbed by the hand.

BLACK-NECKED WEAVER, *Ploceus nigricollis brachypterus* (Swainson)

G. Kurzflügelweber; F. Tisserin à cou noir; D. Zwartnek-Wever

DISTRIBUTION: Senegal to Cameroon.

DESCRIPTION: *Male*. Head and breast yellow, tinged with chestnut-brown. A stripe through the eye and the chin to the neck at the front is black. Mantle, wings and tail brownish-black. Flights and tail coverts edged with green. Rump greenish, breast down to under tail coverts golden-yellow. Bill black. No display plumage. *Female*. Has a black crown and nape. Mantle tinged with green. Eyebrow stripe golden-yellow, and under parts golden-yellow from the chin. Length: 6 in. (15 cm).

A common weaver form, inhabiting damp woods and marshes, but not found in groups. The birds are lively and clamber rapidly through the branches like tits, searching for insects which form their diet. The nests are built separately and are voluminous, sometimes 4 ft (1·20 m) high and 5¾ ft (1·80 m) wide, with a tunnel leading perpendicularly downwards, 6 ft (1·90 m) long. The entrance is 19¾ in. (50 cm) in diameter. The 2–3 eggs are whitish-blue, covered with reddish-brown, grey and blue-grey spots.

At the beginning of this century there were some Black-necked Weavers in the London and Berlin Zoos.

CAPE WEAVER, *Ploceus c. capensis* (Linnaeus)

G. Kapweber; F. Tisserin doré, Tisserin à front d'or; D. Kaapse Wever

DISTRIBUTION: Western part of Cape Province, South Africa.

DESCRIPTION: *Male*. Upper parts yellowish-green, crown olive-yellow, forehead golden-yellow, sides of head yellow. Upper tail coverts have brown stripes. Under parts yellow, sides of body suffused with green. Flights brownish-black with yellowish-green edges. Iris red; bill dark brown; feet flesh-coloured. *Female*. Has a grey-brown-olive colouring on upper parts and olive-yellow on under parts. Breast and sides brownish. In winter the male has the same colouring as the female. Length: 6¾ in. (17 cm).

Except in the breeding season these birds form large flocks together with starlings. They feed on insects, blossoms and seed. They breed in colonies. The birds are polygamous. The nests are pouch-shaped and often hang over water, but also close to houses. The males build the nests of reeds and blades of grass, and the female makes the soft lining. The 2–5 eggs are hatched in 13 days. The young fly after 17 days. These birds often appear in English collections.

The Olive Weaver, *Ploceus capensis olivaceus*, has been imported occasionally and has even been bred successfully.

As well as insects, these weavers eat fruit, including figs, pears and grapes. The birds feed their young conscientiously.

They are placid and peaceful by nature. In *Die Gefiederte Welt*, 1932, 0. 208, an extensive account appeared of a breeding experience with the Olive Weaver. One young bird was reared exclusively on ants' eggs and mealworms. Mr. A. Krabbe, in whose aviary the breeding took place, had planted a great deal of reed vegetation, and the young bird was able to find good protection in this when it flew out.

SMITH'S GOLDEN WEAVER, *Ploceus subaureus aureoflavus* Smith (Pl. XXIX)

G. Goldgelber Weber; F. Tisserin à front d'or, Tisserin jaune doré; D. Goudgele Wever

DISTRIBUTION: Eastern Kenya, eastern Tanzania, Zanzibar, Malawi and Mozambique.

DESCRIPTION: *Male*. Head and throat golden-yellow, shading off into golden-brown. Upper parts olive-yellow, upper tail coverts silvery-yellow. Under parts lighter yellow. Wings olive-brown suffused with yellow. Iris red; beak black; feet reddish flesh-colour. Length: 4¾ in. (12 cm). *Female*. Upper parts yellowish-green, under parts whitish yellow. Beak is longer.

Smith's Golden Weaver is an extremely sociable bird, which breeds in large colonies, where a great deal of noise is generated. These colonies are found in high trees, in bushes and in reed lands. The males build the nests and are probably polygamous. Locally the birds may be numerous and outside the breeding season may form enormous flocks. The nests are fixed to a single branch or twig and are made from grass in the shape of 2 balls. The 2–3 eggs are light blue in colour, sometimes with darker spots. The birds eat seed, greenstuff and insects.

They were first imported in 1898 to the Berlin Zoo and they lived there for more than 12 years. They are mentioned in literature under their old name, *Xanthopilus aureoflavus*.

MOMBASA GOLDEN WEAVER, GOLDEN PALM WEAVER, BOJER'S WEAVER, *Ploceus bojeri* (Cabanis)

G. Bojers Weber; F. Tisserin Bojer, Tisserin jaune citron; D. Bojer's Wever (Pl. XXIX)

DISTRIBUTION: Southern Somalia, Kenya.

DESCRIPTION: *Male*. Head and throat golden-yellow. A golden-red bar runs across the throat. Upper parts olive-yellow, upper tail coverts bright yellow. Under parts golden-yellow, sometimes suffused with an orange bloom. Wings olive-green with olive-brown flights, edged with yellow. Iris reddish-brown; beak black; feet and legs horn-coloured. *Female*. Upper parts dull olive-green, with brown and black stripes in the middle. Eyebrow stripe yellow; under parts whitish-yellow, tinged with brown at sides. Length: 5½ in. (14 cm).

This weaver is likely to be confused with Smith's Golden Weaver, because the birds can only be recognised by their call. They are noisy and always to be found in large groups. Their twittering resembles that of sparrows.

They nest in trees and bushes along the banks of rivers, lakes, and along the coast. The nest is shaped like an oblong ball and the opening is at an oblique angle to the base. They are made of green straws and fragments of leaves, and they are also to be found in the rushes, hanging about 3¼ ft (1 m) above the water. None of the nests found has had a tunnel entrance.

These birds were first imported into Germany in 1881. Their treatment is similar to that of other weavers.

MASKED WEAVER, *Ploceus i. intermedius* Rüppel

G. Olivgrauer Weber; F. Tisserin masqué; D. Kleine Textorwever

DISTRIBUTION: Southern Ethiopia, Sudan, Somalia, Kenya, Uganda, Rwanda, Congo, Tanzania.

DESCRIPTION: *Male*. In courtship plumage the male has a black head. The black of the chin and throat do not extend as far as upper breast. In winter plumage the crown is yellow-green, as are the remainder of the upper parts; eyebrow stripe and sides of head yellow, chin and throat and under tail coverts yellow, middle of abdomen white, bill horn-coloured and not black, as in the mating season. *Female*. Olive-green, somewhat paler yellow on under parts. Length: 5½ in. (14 cm).

SUBSPECIES: *Ploceus intermedius cabansii*, which has a golden-yellow nape and a narrow, golden-brown stripe along the rear surface of the head and throat, comes from south-west Africa, Angola, Transvaal and Zululand. It is often called Masked Weaver and confused with this subspecies. It is the Cabanis Weaver and is also only occasionally imported, but then sometimes in large numbers.

Both subspecies live in dry country and often nest near to water. They breed in colonies and seek out dead trees or trees stripped of their leaves. They also hang their nests in reeds. The building of the nests is a noisy process. The males fly up with palm leaves and long blades of grass, and are often attacked by other males. They lock together in combat and fall to the ground. In spite of the noise and fighting, the nests do get built and the males hang upside down under the nest and flutter to and fro, flapping their wings, and emitting the hoarse, staccato cries of which their song consists. This is a subsidiary part of their display. They also execute small sideways hops while sitting on a branch, singing and whirring their wings. The females, having responded to these overtures, begin to line the nest with fine grasses, mimosa leaves and hair. The eggs are blue, covered with brown dots. When the young hatch out the eggshells fall to the ground in hundreds. Under the tree where the colony live there is not only a thick layer of excreta but also a number of old and new nests which have fallen to the ground during the many fights.

These weavers were already imported to Germany in 1887 and since then breeding results have been obtained in many countries. The males are, however, particularly aggressive, not just among themselves but also towards other weavers and small finches. A separate aviary with rushes and a stout, widely branched, bare tree is suitable for these attractive and zestful birds.

BLACK-FRONTED WEAVER, NAMAQUA MASKED WEAVER, SOUTHERN MASKED WEAVER, *Ploceus v. velatus* Vieillot (Pl. XXIX)

G. Schwarzstirnweber, Maskenweber; F. Tisserin à front noir, tisserin à masque noire; D. Zwartvoorhoofd-Wever

DISTRIBUTION: Southern Angola, Rhodesia, Malawi, Zambia, Mozambique, west Transvaal, Botswana, Namibia, north-western Cape Province.

DESCRIPTION: *Male*. Narrow black bar across forehead in mating plumage. The whole area around the eye, sides of head, ear coverts, chin and throat is black. Crown saffron-yellow, nape and under parts golden-yellow; mantle yellowish-green with brown stripes; tail brownish-green. Breast suffused with orange. Iris orange, beak black, feet and legs brown. In winter plumage, upper parts striped with olive-yellow and brown: under parts yellowish-white. *Female*. Yellowish-white plumage, somewhat yellower on under parts during breeding season. Outside breeding season, she is greyer on top and paler underneath. Length: 6½ in. (16 cm).

These birds occur in large flocks in low country and in the vicinity of farmland and water. They nest, hundreds together, in high trees and they carefully strip all leaves from the branches, on which they build their nests. Apart from insects, they eat seeds and do enormous damage to rice and maize fields and are exterminated by plantation owners with chemical sprays.

SUBSPECIES: Another subspecies, *P. v. vitellinus*(Lichtenstein), originates in the area from Senegal to the Sudan. Mask black, crown, throat and nape golden-brown, remaining upper parts greenish-yellow. Under parts golden-yellow. Upper tail coverts yellow. Wings dark brown, edged with yellow; flights a brownish-olive colour and edged with yellow and greenish-yellow. Iris reddish-orange-yellow colour beak black and feet flesh-coloured. Female has dull brownish upper parts suffused with olive-yellow and has brown stripes. Under parts pale yellow, and olive-yellow appears on the head, rump and tail. The male is somewhat darker in winter plumage than the female.

A successful breeding of *P. velatus* by W. Shore Bailey was reported in *Bird Notes*, 1916: 25.

Of all weavers, *P. v. vitellinus*, is one of the best breeding birds. The male builds the pear-shaped nest in a few days from rush blades and blades of green grass and engages himself during the entire incubation period in extending and elaborating it. After display comes the actual mating, and the female vanishes immediately into the nest for a time.

The birds are noticeably tame during the breeding period and take mealworms from a human hand. The female is curious and peeps out of the bottom entrance of the nest whenever anyone comes near. The young, which hatch out after an incubation period of about 12 days, are reared more or less exclusively on mealworms. Ants' eggs are not accepted as a rule. Seed, vegetable matter and berries are also eaten. Towards the time when the young will fly out, the male helps to feed them. Often several clutches are reared in a single season. The old nest is always destroyed and replaced by a new one.

These 2 subspecies are especially peace-loving with regard to other birds, but prior to the breeding period they must be given adequate room so that other birds can leave them alone. The male effectively chase all intruders away, hissing like a snake. It appears that they are polygamous; so it is advisable to keep at least 4 females with the male.

SPOTTED-BACKED WEAVER, BLACK-HEADED WEAVER, VILLAGE WEAVER, *Ploceus c. cucullatus* (Müller)

G. Textorweber, Hausweber; F. Tisserin cap-moor, Tisserin des villages; D. Grote Textorwever (Pl. XXXII)

DISTRIBUTION: Senegal, Fernando Póo.

DESCRIPTION: Head and throat black, down to upper breast. A chestnut-brown bar runs down to the upper breast where it becomes narrower. Upper and under parts yellow, flanks and breast suffused with golden-brown. Wing coverts black with yellow tips; flights blackish-brown with greenish-

Spotted-backed Weaver, *Ploceus c. cucullatus*

Plate XLI

Paradise Whydah, *Steganura p. paradisea*

Pin-tailed Whydah, *Vidua macroura*

White-winged Whydah, *Euplectes a. albonotatus*

South African Indigo Bird, *Hypochera amauropteryx*

Queen Whydah, *Vidua regia*

Plate XLII

Red-billed Quelea, *Quelea q. quelea*   Red-headed Quelea, *Quelea erythrops*

Grenadier Weaver, *Euplectes o. orix*

Napoleon Weaver, *Euplectes a. afra*

Orange Bishop, *Euplectes orix franciscanus*

yellow edges. Tail olive-brown suffused with green. Iris bright orange-red; beak black; feet and legs brown. Length: 6–7 in. (15–17 cm). *Female*. Has olive-coloured upper parts with dark brown longitudinal stripes, under parts yellow, sides of body suffused with brown, abdomen whitish. *Males* in their winter plumage resemble females but have darker markings and are more yellow.

These birds are very common, both in dry steppe country and in inhabited areas in palm trees and along the water edges and in reed fields. The pear-shaped nests are hung on the ends of banana leaves. Sometimes more than a hundred nests hang in the same tree, along the water edge. Nests are built with numerous other weaver species in colonies. Fierce fights often take place between the males during the nest building. The voice is shrill and hoarse. As soon as a nest is ready and the male has won a female through his display, mating takes place and incubation begins; the male then starts to build another nest and tries to claim another female for it. Each male can have 4–5 females. The clutches usually consist of 2 eggs, which are hatched in 14 days. The young fly after 3 weeks. Usually, 3 clutches follow one from another.

Breeding results have been obtained several times. One was reported at the London Zoo in 1905, and again in 1913. (*L.Z. Repts.*) The birds must, however, be kept in a separate aviary. They eat seed, greenstuff, fruit, ants' eggs and mealworms. Live food is indispensable during the breeding period.

GREAT MASKED WEAVER, ABYSSINIAN BLACK-HEADED WEAVER, *Ploceus cucullatus abyssinicus* (Gmelin)

G. Larvenweber; F. Tisserin masque, Tisserin jaune masqué d'Abyssinie; D. Abessijnse Textorwever

DISTRIBUTION: Ethiopia.
DESCRIPTION: Head black, nape saffron-yellow; mantle and scapulars have black and yellow mottling; rump yellow. Wing coverts black edged with yellow. Tail yellowish-olive. Under parts yellow with saffron along the edge of the black parts. Beak black, iris reddish-brown or golden-yellow, feet and legs reddish-brown. Length: 6½ in. (17 cm). In winter plumage, the males are yellowish-olive colour on head and greyish-brown with brown stripes on back and rump; under parts are yellow and off-white. *Female*. Has a green head; mantle, scapulars and rump yellowish-green; remaining upper parts ash-grey with brown stripes. Under parts yellow with white in the middle of abdomen. Female smaller than male.

These birds occur in great flocks, mostly in low-lying country and near water. They live the whole year round in the vicinity of their breeding places. The low trees in which they nest are often weighed down with hundreds of nests. These nests are woven from leaves and blades of grass and lined with small soft leaves by the female and sometimes have a short tunnel entrance on the lower side. The birds live to a large extent on insects and weed seeds, but they still do a lot of damage on farmland and grainfields. As with starlings, colonies of these weavers make a great spectacle.
SUBSPECIES: Layard's Weaver, *P. c. nigricep* (Layard), shown in Plate XXXII is found in the same regions and in south-eastern African areas.
The black colouring on the head is more widespread and not edged with russet-yellow. Upper parts more spotted with yellow and black. Males also build more than one nest and live polygamously. These birds appear frequently in settlements and villages and even nest in them. They have the habit of suddenly flying up all together and returning to the same tree together. The birds also build roosting nests. They feed mainly on seed and grain and cause a great deal of damage in rice fields and farm lands, and all sorts of methods

are used to get rid of them.
The Yellow-headed Weaver, *P. c. spilonotus* Vigors, from South Africa, which has yellow crown and black at sides of head, throat and upper breast, has a similar way of life and builds nests in colonies; sometimes there are more than a hundred nests made of palm leaves and stiff grass in one acacia tree.
All these birds were already being kept in European zoos at the end of the last century where they also bred occasionally.

CHESTNUT WEAVER, *Ploceus r. rubiginosus* Rüppell

G. Rotbrauner Weber; F. Tisserin brun-noir, Tisserin brun; D. Roodbruine Wever   (Pl. XXXII)

DISTRIBUTION: Ethiopia, south-eastern Sudan, Somalia, north-eastern Uganda, Kenya, Tanzania.
DESCRIPTION: Head and throat black. Remaining plumage chestnut-brown. Black longitudinal stripes appear on scapulars. Wings blackish-brown with whitish-brown edges. Beak black, iris orange-yellow, feet and legs dark brown. Length: 6 i¼n. (16 cm). *Female*. Upper parts light brown and greyish-brown, with black shaft stripes on head and back. Eye stripe whitish-brown; throat white, under parts yellowish-brown, middle of abdomen white.
These weavers are found in large numbers in particular localities and they probably sometimes move to other breeding areas. They breed in colonies. When the males have built nests and acquired females, who then lay the eggs and incubate them, they leave and settle themselves in a high acacia. Meanwhile, life in the female colony is very noisy. When the young hatch out, the females go off to look for insects and other live food for them. Fully-grown birds also eat seed. They are lively and aggressive birds. Apart from the normal seed mixture, they must be given green food, insectivorous food and mealworms.

Chestnut Weaver, *Ploceus r. rubiginosus*

BENGAL WEAVER, *Ploceus manyar benghalensis* (Linnaeus)

G. Bengalenweber; F. Tisserin du Bengale; D. Bengaalse Wever

DISTRIBUTION: Bangladesh, Burma, India, Sri Lanka.
DESCRIPTION: Crown and nape orange-yellow; lores ear, coverts and cheeks blackish-brown. Upper breast and breast golden-yellow, separated by a black bar. Sides of head and throat vary sharply in colour from whitish to dark brown. Remaining under parts whitish-yellow. Back and rump brown. Upper tail coverts yellow. Beak whitish-grey, iris light brown, feet and legs flesh-coloured. Length: 5¼ in. (13 cm). *Female*. Under parts, breast bar sandy. Upper mandible whitish-yellow and lower greyish-brown. Sexes alike in winter plumage.
These weavers are very common in certain areas. The nests

are built in low bushes, and in tall grass where the grass has grown unusually high after floods. The blades of grass on which the nests are suspended are sometimes intertwined with the nest. The nest is pouch-shaped, the entrance is

Bengal Weaver, *Ploceus manyar benghalensis*

never longer than 2 in. (5 cm), and slants at an angle to the lower face. Although the birds breed in colonies, the nests are not built close together, but spaced fairly far apart. Two nests are seldom found in the same bush. The clutch consists of 2–3 eggs, which are incubated by the female alone and hatch out in 13 days. Only when the young are 10 days old does the male help with the feeding. In their nest-building and general behaviour, these birds show great similarity with the larger Baya Weavers, *P. philippinus*, which however have a yellow breast.

These weavers were already occasionally imported at the end of the last century, and they built their elegant nests in a nest-box. Dr. Russ was the first to obtain breeding results with them. Since then, breeding results in many countries have been obtained. The birds are very strong and mainly eat seed, but they need mealworms and other live food to rear their young. Green food and fruit are eaten. In the winter, they can be left in an outside aviary, provided the night shelter is free from frost. Like most others of their family, they are fairly troublesome to other birds during the breeding season.

MANYAR WEAVER, *Ploceus m. manyar* (Horsfield)
G. Manyarweber; F. Tisserin Manyar; D. Manyar-Wever

DISTRIBUTION: Java, Bali.
DESCRIPTION: Crown and back of head yellow. Mantle and wing flights dark brown, feathers edged with reddish-brown. Rump and upper tail coverts rust-yellow with black stripes; tail dark yellowish-brown edged with a paler colour. Face

Manyar Weaver, *Ploceus m. manyar*

and throat blackish-brown; upper breast and sides dull brown with black stripes. Remaining under parts greyish-white. Iris brown, black beak, feet and legs dark flesh-colour. Length: 5½ in. (14 cm). *Female.* Upper parts ash-grey with black longitudinal stripes. Sides of head blackish-grey, stripe white. Under parts white with black stripes on neck,

breast and sides of body.

In Java, these birds frequently occur in plateau lands covered with grass. They live in large flocks and breed in colonies. The pear-shaped nests are usually built at the ends of palm leaves. The stem which attaches the nest to the palm leaf is only 1 in. (2·5 cm) thick, yet so strong that the nest does not become detached during storms. The stem is 6 in. (15 cm) long, and it is at this point that the broadening out begins. This part is about 10 in. (25 cm) high and 6 in. (15 cm) wide. The nest hollow in which the eggs are laid is separated from the entrance by a high threshold. The entrance is about 4 in. (10 cm) long and 2 in. (5 cm) across and ends at the lower face of the nest. Blades and stalks of grass are used almost exclusively for the nest. The 3–4 white eggs are oblong.

Amazing stories are told of the intelligence of the males. Roosting nests have been found with small piles of loam in them. The natives say that at night the males catch fireflies or glow worms and stick them to the piles of loam in order to have light.

These birds do great damage to crops of sugar cane and rice. They breed at least twice a year.

Breeding results in aviaries have been obtained on several occasions and there have also been hybrids with the Baya Weaver, *P. manyar philippinus*.

BAYA WEAVER, *Ploceus manyar philippinus* (Linnaeus) (Pl. XXXII)
G. Bayaweber; F. Tisserin Baya; D. Bajawever

DISTRIBUTION: India, Pakistan, Sri Lanka.
DESCRIPTION: Crown golden-yellow; narrow forehead bar, lores, orbital ring, sides of head and ear coverts blackish-brown; cheeks and throat light brown, sometimes ash-grey.

Baya Weaver, *Ploceus manyar philippinus*

Upper parts yellow with black central area. Under parts and rump brown, upper tail coverts yellow. Sides of neck yellow with black stripes, upper breast and breast golden-yellow, remaining under parts buff, sides suffused with brown. Wing coverts brownish-black with pale edges. Tail brown with olive-yellow edges. Iris brown, beak horn-coloured, feet and legs flesh-coloured. Length: 5½ in. (13·5 cm). *Female.* Upper parts brown with black stripes. Under parts yellowish-white and white in the middle. There is a little ochre on breast. In winter plumage, sexes are alike, though male may be somewhat browner.

Baya Weavers prefer low-lying, dry country and the foothills of mountains. They are not found higher up than 1,650 ft (500 m). They lead a nomadic existence, mostly in large flocks. They feed on carefully grown grain crops, especially rice. They also kill a large number of harmful insects but this does not offset their destruction of crops.

They suspend a number of nests at the ends of palm leaves. These consist of three parts. The first is a 12 in. (30 cm) long stem by which the nest is attached to the palm leaf. Then follows the broad nest chamber and entrance. This hangs like an elephant's trunk below the nest. The nest is made of torn-off fragments of palm leaves and grass. The bird pecks a short tear in the base of the palm leaf and then flies away, so that the fragment strips away from the leaf. Usually, only the main arteries of the leaves are left intact. In the nest little piles of earth and loam are found, which presumably give the nest greater stability. The breeding period falls in the rainy season and the nests are therefore woven with great care and are completely watertight. The 2–4 eggs are oblong in form and are white. The female incubates alone for 14 days.

In various parts of India, Thailand, Malaysia and Indonesia, local forms of the Baya Weaver are found, which are all counted as subspecies of *P. manyar*. They show only small differences in size and colour and have only sporadically turned up in European aviaries.

These birds stand up to the climate well, must be fed on seed, green food and mealworms. They will always fascinate by their liveliness and building skill.

RED-HEADED QUELEA, RED-HEADED WEAVER,

Quelea erythrops (Hartlaub) (Pl. XLII)
G. Rotkopfweber; F. Tisserin à tête rouge, Quéléa à tête rouge; D. Roodkopwever

DISTRIBUTION: Senegal to Ethiopia, Angola, Fernando Póo, San Thomé.

DESCRIPTION: Head and throat scarlet. Throat feathers have a black base, so that the black on throat glimmers through. Upper parts striated brown. Rump and upper tail coverts somewhat paler brown. Under parts light brown, abdomen and under tail coverts frequently white. Wings blackish-brown edged with a yellowish colour. Tail brownish-black edged with light brown. Iris dark brown, beak black, legs and feed flesh-coloured. Length: 4½ in. (11 cm). *Female.* Lacks red on head and throat. Beak horn-coloured brown. The males look the same as the females when they are in eclipse plumage.

These birds were fairly regularly imported towards the end of the last century and were first brought to Berlin in 1869, where Dr. Russ had various clutches reared in his indoor aviary. They are fairly peaceable towards other finches. They only eat insects during the breeding season, apart from the seed diet of tropical finches.

RED-BILLED QUELEA, RED-BILLED WEAVER, *Quelea*

q. quelea (Linnaeus) (Pl. XLII)
G. Blutschnabelweber; F. Travailleur, Quéléa à bec rouge; D. Zwartmasker-Roodbekwever

DISTRIBUTION: Senegal.

DESCRIPTION: *Male.* Bar across forehead, sides of head and throat black. Crown, sides of neck and under parts buff, suffused with pink. Abdomen and under tail coverts white or yellowish-white. Upper parts yellowish-brown with black bars. Wings brown with pale edges. Iris brown, orbital ring orange-yellow, beak light red, feet and legs reddish flesh-colour. Length: 4½ in. (11 cm). *Female.* Brownish-grey head and under parts white. The male in eclipse plumage is similar to female, except that he always has a red beak,

while the female in eclipse plumage has a yellow beak, which colours red in the breeding season.

These birds are known for their ceaseless activity. In France they are known as the 'travailleur'—worker. In their natural habitat, they occur in incredible numbers and do enormous damage to the grain harvest, whenever they descend upon the fields like plagues of locusts. Outside the breeding season, they choose large tracts of marshland with reed fields. Nests are found in reeds or long grass. They are small thin structures made of fine grass. The 2–4 eggs are pale blue mottled with brown.

The birds live at peace in large aviaries with other small finches, but if they do not have sufficient nest-building material avaiable, they frequently pull out the tail feathers of other birds. Both birds participate in the nest building.

The incubating period is 14 days and the young fly after 3 weeks. The birds should be kept in a frost-free place during the winter. They like bathing.

Outside the breeding season, they more or less exclusively live on canary seed, millet, other seeds and green food. In the breeding season, plenty of mealworms must be made available. Although breeding results have been obtained in the aviary, this is rather exceptional; Possibly because not sufficient variety is maintained in the diet supplied. A successful breeding is reported by Rattigan in *Bird Notes*, 1911, p. 323.

MADAGASCAR WEAVER, *Foudia madagascariensis* (Linnaeus)

G. Madagascarweber; F. Foudi rouge, Foudi; D. Madagascarwever

DISTRIBUTION: Madagascar, Mauritius, Seychelles, St. Helena.

DESCRIPTION: Head, rump and under parts bright scarlet. Upper back, mantle and scapulars scarlet marked with black. Wings black with brownish-white edges, partly suffused with red. Lores and orbital ring black. Iris brown, beak black, feet and legs flesh-coloured. Length: 5 in. (13 cm). *Female.* Upper parts olive-grey with black stripes. Eye stripe and sides of head pale olive-coloured; under parts yellowish-grey.

Madagascar Weaver, *Foudia madagascariensis*

Over the ear coverts is a darker stripe. Beak greyish-horn-colour with black tip. Male in eclipse plumage is similar to female but slightly greyer on back. These birds are found everywhere in great numbers outside the wooded areas. They attack the rice fields in swarms and do a great deal of damage. They nest in acacias, tamarindas and mimosas. Unlike some weavers, they do not nest in colonies. The nests are pear-shaped and made of fine grasses. The tunnel entrance is short and appended to the side of the nest in the middle. The 4–5 pale blue eggs are laid which hatch out in 14 days, and the young leave the nest some 21 days later.

In 1869, these birds were first bred by Dr. Russ in Germany, since when they have often been imported and many amateurs have had breeding results.

In 1938, the first breeding result was obtained in England by Mr. A. Ezra, *Avicultural Magazine*, (5), No. 3, 1938, p. 220. The birds built their nest in a cypress tree; it was pear-shaped and had a side entrance. Three of the 4 eggs were fertilised, and these hatched. The young were fed with flies and mealworms by the female; seed, fruit and insectivorous food were not touched. A week after they flew, the young ate seed and insectivorous food.

Genus: Euplectes

NAPOLEON WEAVER, GOLDEN BISHOP, YELLOW-CROWNED BISHOP, *Euplectes a. afer* (Gmelin) (Pl. XLII)
G. Napoleonweber; F. Worabée; D. Napoleonwever

DISTRIBUTION: West Africa, from Senegal to Angola.
DESCRIPTION: *Male.* Upper parts and under tail coverts golden-yellow; back sometimes inclines towards a greenish shade and may have black spots. Nape feathers edged with black, and has black bar running across. Sides of head, throat, breast and abdomen black. Below the upper breast is a reddish-brown patch. Wings and tail dark brown with light brown edges. Beak black, iris yellowish-brown, feet and legs flesh-coloured. Length: 4½ in. (11 cm). *Female.* Upper parts pale brown with blackish-brown quill stripes. Under parts whitish. Upper breast and sides of body suffused with brown. Beak yellowish-horn colour. In eclipse plumage, the male is similar to female.

These birds live more or less exclusively in marshy regions, feeding on grass seed and insects. Great flocks of them are frequently seen. Since the young males are similar to the females, it is difficult to establish whether the number of males is in fact much smaller than that of females. There are, however, numerous indications which lead us to conclude that the Napoleon Weavers are polygamous. Every male builds a number of nests, both in long grass and in reeds, where they hang above water. They are made of split reed blades and coarse grass stalks, lined with fine grasses and contain 2–4 white eggs, covered with fine black dots. Their song consists of different soft, chirping and hissing sounds and is very monotonous.

In the breeding season, the males puff up their feathers so that they look like a round yellow ball. They stage harmless fights with one another but become so excited in the process that they frighten other birds. Although the birds breed in colonies, the best results are obtained in an aviary if only one or, at the most, two males are put together with 8–10 females. Fully successful breeding results have only occasionally been obtained in aviaries. The incubation period is 14 days. The female takes incubating the eggs and feeding the young entirely upon herself; the young fly after 3 weeks.

Napoleon Weaver, *Euplectes a. afer*

TAHA WEAVER, BISHOP, *Euplectes afer taha* Smith
G. Tahaweber; F. Tisserin taha; D. Tahawever

(Pl. XLIII)

DISTRIBUTION: Southern Angola, Zambia, Rhodesia, Malawi, southern Mozambique.
DESCRIPTION: *Male.* Sides of head, under parts and a broad bar across nape black: upper parts yellow. Thighs pale yellow with a brownish bloom, wing feathers have yellowish and brownish edges. Iris brown, beak black, feet and legs brown. Length: 4¼ in. (11 cm). *Female.* Dull brown upper parts with black longitudinal stripes. Under parts white suffused with a brownish colour on sides of body and upper breast; blackish-brown quill stripes. Eye stripe yellowish-white. Beak pale horn colour, feet and legs pale brown.

These birds are to be found in great flocks wherever steppes and marshes provide abundant grasslands. The males are particularly noticeable because they can raise their head and back feathers like a sort of collar, so that they look like small golden balls flying to left and right with a humming sound. They build a number of nests and gather several females around themselves. The nests are found close to the ground in tall grass, and are often covered by the grass: the

Taha Weaver, *Euplectes afer taha*

3–4 eggs are white with small black dots and mottlings. They feed mainly on grass seed of all kinds, and insects particularly in the breeding season. Their call consists of a monotone chirruping and a soft song.

These Weavers can be kept together with a number of other species quite satisfactorily in a spacious aviary, although they are somewhat wild by nature.

They were first imported to Europe in small numbers at the beginning of this century.

CRIMSON-CROWNED WEAVER, FIRE-CROWNED BISHOP, *Euplectes h. hordaceus* (Linnaeus)   (Pl. XLIII)
G. Flammenweber; F. Euplecte à couronne de feu; D. Vlammenwever

DISTRIBUTION: Senegal, Congo to Angola, Zambia, Rhodesia, Tanzania, Kenya and San Thomé.
DESCRIPTION: *Male.* Upper parts scarlet, apart from sides of head and back, which are black and reddish-brown. Under parts black, lower tail coverts yellowish-white suffused with red. Thighs yellowish-brown, feet and legs flesh-coloured. Length: 5 in. (13 cm). *Female.* Upper parts light brown with blackish-brown quill stripes or makings; under parts whitish. Eye stripe yellowish-white, lower wing coverts dark brown. Length: 4¼ in. (11 cm).

Together with the Red-billed Weavers, the Crimson-crowned Weavers form enormous flocks in order to look for their food on the wide tracts of grass lands, along streams and in marshy regions. Towards evening, they gather in high bushes along the reed fields. They are restless, noisy and shy. In the breeding season, the males carry out display flights low over the grass, puffing up their plumage and emitting their chattering song. In their first year males do not breed; later they gather a number of females around them and seek a

Crimson-crowned Weaver, *Euplectes h. hordaceus*

breeding territory of their own. The nests are pouch-shaped and built in reeds, course grass or low shrubs, secured between two upright twigs or stalks. They are made of green grass, have a domed entrance and contain 2–4 pale turquoise-blue eggs spotted here and there with violet, brown or black marks. Apart from grass seed, they eat paddy (rice) and grain of all kinds and some insects.

Nests have often been built in aviaries, and females have even laid their eggs, but breeding results have seldom been obtained.

The birds can be kept in a large aviary together with one or two of their own family and with larger finches, although they usually turn somewhat wilder during the breeding season. If the sleeping shelter is free from frost, they can be left in an outside aviary during the winter.

GRENADIER WEAVER, RED BISHOP, *Euplectes o. orix* (Linnaeus) (Pl. XLII)

G. Oryxweber, Grosser Grenadierweber; F. Oryx, Monseigneur; D. Grenadierwever

DISTRIBUTION: Southern Angola, Namibia, Botswana, Zambia, Rhodesia, South Africa and Mozambique.

DESCRIPTION: *Male.* Forehead, crown, sides of head and throat black. Back reddish-brown. Rest of head, neck, upper and under tail coverts scarlet. Remaining under parts black, thighs rust-yellow suffused with red. Wings and tail blackish-brown with pale edges. Beak black, iris dark brown, feet and legs flesh-coloured. Length: 5¾ in. (14·5 cm). *Female.* Upper parts pale brown with dark brown stripes. Eye stripe rust-coloured yellow. Under parts pale brown with dark brownish-black quill stripes. On rump and under tail coverts there are no markings. Beak sandy horn-colour.

In their extensive homeland, they occur mainly in marshy areas and grasslands alongside water. Then the crops ripen in the grainfields, they descend upon them in the company of others of their species in large swarms and do great damage. However, they eat the seeds of many weeds and grasses the whole year round. They spend their nights in the extensive reed fields. Although the birds breed in colonies, the males have their own breeding territory. They are polygamous and have four or more females each. They build their purse-shaped nests in tall reeds, using green blades of grass, of which they weave only the stalks so that the best is covered on the outside with soft tufts. Although the weaving is tough, it is very thin and the 3–4 pale blue eggs are visible. The entrance is covered over with an awning, secured to a reed stalk at a distance of about 8 in. (20 cm).

In areas where the imported Mexican Marigold has grown wild on a large scale and has formed into clumps about 26 ft (8 m) across and up to 5½ ft (1·8 m) high, the weavers have left the reed fields and started to nest in these plants. The males blow themselves up during the breeding season into round reddish-black balls, flying up and down from the tops of flowers and sometimes bouncing up and down. Fights amongst the males are part of these manifestations.

These weavers are among the most industrious nest builders, and not very troublesome to other birds in large aviaries, except during the breeding season when the males become lively and excited. In an aviary planted with shrubs or reeds where a male is housed with one or two females, one can count with certainty upon the building of nests, laying of eggs and chicks hatching.

The incubation period lasts for 14 days; the young fly after 3 weeks, and resemble the female. Sometimes 2 clutches are reared in 1 season. The males do not get their nuptial plumage and begin breeding until their third year of life.

Apart from the normal seed mixture, these weavers must have oats, wheat and, in the breeding season, maggots, mealworms and live insects. They can be left in an outside aviary all through the year provided they have a frost-free sleeping shelter.

ORANGE BISHOP, FIRE-CROWNED WEAVER, *Euplectes orix franciscanus* (Isert) (Pl. XLII)

G. Feuerweber, Orangeweber; F. Ignicolore; D. Oranjewever

DIATRIBUTION: Senegal to Sudan, Cameroon, Zaire, Uganda and Kenya.

DESCRIPTION: *Male.* Crown, sides of head and under parts black, rest of plumage orange-red. Back reddish-brown, wings blackish-brown with pale feather edges. Iris brown, beak black, feet and legs flesh-coloured. Length 4¾ in. (12 cm). *Female.* Upper parts pale brown with blackish-brown stripe markings; eye stripe yellowish-white. Under parts white, upper breast and sides of body suffused with brown. Iris brown, beak, feet and legs yellowish-horn colour. Males have somewhat heavier markings in their winter plumage than females. Orange Bishops are very numerous in their extensive homeland. The males are particularly noticeable during the breeding season. They make a whirring sound with their wings and make themselves into round feathered balls, flying up and down over the shrubs and grass areas. The males are distinctly polygamous and seek out their own breeding territory with their 4 or 5 females, and defend it ferociously against intruders. The nests are oval in shape and have a covered entrance at the upper face. The eggs are pale turquoise-blue and sometimes covered with fine brown spots. After moulting the reddish-orange often does not return to the same depth of colour, and the orange itself is often somewhat paler. This is to a large extent attributable to a one-sided seed diet. It has been found that the Orange Bishop is inclined towards a diet more usual for insect-eaters. When they are given the opportunity, they eat insectivorous food, mealworms, maggots and ants' eggs. The depth of colour of the orange-red reacts to this rapidly. The seed supplied must include canary seed, mixed millet and maw seed. In addition to the improvement in the plumage condition, the bird itself becomes livelier and sings more.

These birds have seldom bred in aviaries.

SUBSPECIES: Black-foreheaded Weaver, *E. o. nigrifrons*, from Uganda, Zaire and Tanganyika, differs from the other subspecies in that its chin, forehead and the sides of its hear are black and its throat red. In its behaviour, it is similar to the Orange Bishop.

YELLOW BISHOP, YELLOW-BACKED WEAVER, CAPE WEAVER, YELLOW-SHOULDERED WEAVER, *Euplectes c. capensis* (Linnaeus)   (Pl. XLIII)
G. Sammetweber; F. Gros bec tacheté du cap de bonne espérance; D. Geelstuitwever, Fluweelwever

DISTRIBUTION: Cape Province.
DESCRIPTION: Main colour black; scauplar wings, bottom part of back and rump bright lemon-yellow. Iris brown, beak grey and feet and legs brown. Length: 6¼ in. (16 cm). *Female.* Upper parts brown with black stripes; rump mustard-brown, scapular wings yellow with black stripes. Under parts paler brown with brown stripes. Throat, breast and abdomen yellowish-white in the middle. Beak horn-coloured.

Yellow Bishop, *Euplectes c. capensis*

Yellow Bishops are particularly common in areas with very tall grass, but never in such large numbers as the other weavers and only in certain breeding areas. The males get there slightly before the females. They execute a display dance, flying towards the females with their wings whirring and then falling to the ground. The male perches high up in the tall grass and sings with his rump feathers standing up on end. He is polygamous and tries to secure 4 or more females for himself. The nests are capacious, half roofed in and equipped at the upper face with a covered entrance. They usually hang between two stout upright stalks, low above the ground. The 4 eggs are greyish or white and covered with dark brown dots, and lie on a soft lining of fine grass tips and feathers. The incubation period lasts 14 days and the young are reared almost exclusively on insects and beetles, leaving the nest when about 3 weeks old.

RED-SHOULDERED WHYDAH, *Euplectes a. axillaris* (Smith)
G. Rotschulterwidafink; F. Veuve à épaulettes rouges; D. Roodschouderwida

DISTRIBUTION: Zambia, Rhodesia, Malawi, Mozambique, Transvaal.
DESCRIPTION: *Male.* Main colouring black, scapular wings orange-red, lesser wing and under wing coverts brown; edges of flights yellowish-brown. Beak bluish-grey. *Female.* Upper parts striped with black and yellowish-white; eye stripe yellowish-white. Under parts whitish, scapular feathers black with orange edges. Beak pale horn colour. Length: 6¼ in. (16 cm).
These birds are very common along rivers and in extensive marshes. They are noisy and fly with an undulating flight. One male is followed by 10 or more females and in the breeding season they split up into breeding groups. The nests are found in clumps of grass 12 in. (30 cm) above the ground. They are large but lightly built of grass stalks with the support stalks mostly woven into a dome across the top. The females help in the building of the nest sand incubate the 3 greenish-grey eggs alone. The male keeps

Red-shouldered Whydah, *Euplectes a. axillaris*

watch during the breeding season and will not let any intruder into his breeding territory.
These birds are shy by nature and hide away in the dense shrubbery. They seldom come to the ground or go near the other birds in the aviary. During his display, the male points his tail downwards and his feathers stand up on end, and his wings hang spread out downwards. He flies around the females in this way and utters a few notes of his grating song.
Red-shouldered Whydahs were first imported and bred at the end of the 19th century. The young were reared on mealworms, ants' eggs, egg food and canary seed mashed in water. A few live ants were thrown into the aviary every day and these were greedily snapped up. The male took no part in the feeding of the young, but protected the nests against intruders. When the young had flown, they did not return to the nest, but were fed for a further 14 days by the female.

YELLOW-BACKED WHYDAH, YELLOW-MANTLED WHYDAH, *Euplectes m. macrourus* (Gmelin) (Pl. XLIII)
G. Gelbrückenwidah, Gelbmantelwidah; F. Veuve à dos d'or, Veuve à manteau jaune; D. Geelmantel-wida, geelrug-wida

DISTRIBUTION: Senegal, Angola, Zambia, Rhodesia, Malawi, Mozambique.
DESCRIPTION: *Male.* Main colouring black. Lesser wing coverts and top part of back yellow. Wings black with feathers edged with brown. Iris brown, beak black, feet and legs greyish brown. Length: 8 in. (19 cm). *Female.* Upper parts brownish-grey with black feather stripes. Upper tail coverts brown, sides of head, upper breast and sides of body paler brown with darker longitudinal stripes. Throat and middle of abdomen whitish-yellow suffused with brown. Beak horn-coloured brown, feet and legs flesh-coloured. Male is similar to female in winter plumage, except for yellow lesser wing coverts.
These whydahs are very common in damp low-lying grassy areas and in the steppes where the grass stands tall between the sparse shrubs and low trees. The birds are active by nature and climb rapidly along the reed and grass stalks and through the branches of shrubs and bushes, seeking out the tops. The males sit there and sing, making short flights, in which they hold their bodies erect and puff up their nape feathers. When the grain ripens in the fields they descend upon it with other weavers and do a great deal of damage. They build their nests in the tall grass. The nest is built of grass stalks and the upper face entrance is covered over with protruding stalks which form a sort of awning. The 2–3 eggs are greenish with grey mottling.
Mr. W. Shore-Baily obtained the first breeding result in 1923.
Young birds only attain their colour and breeding condition in their third year. It sometimes happens that a bird in an aviary will be ready for breeding in his second year. During nest building the female brings the material, while the male

does the work. The female only makes the lining. The eggs hatch out after an incubation period of 13–14 days. For their first days of life, the young are fed almost exclusively on live insects, but after a few days the hen begins to administer egg food, bread soaked in milk and seed. It is important to keep germinated or mashed seed available. After 3 weeks the young fly. The young males can be recognised immediately by the yellow scapular patch.

Yellow-backed Whydah, *Euplectes m.macrourus*

YELLOW-SHOULDERED WHYDAH, *Euplectes macrourus macrocerus* (Lichtenstein) (Pl. XLIV)
G. Gelbschulterwidah; F. Veuve à épaulettes jaunes; D. Geelschouderwida

DISTRIBUTION: Northern Ethiopia, western Kenya.
DESCRIPTION: *Male*. Main colouring black, scapular wings yellow and the flights have lighter edges. Beak black. Tail graduated and black. *Female*. Upper parts yellowish-white with black stripes; sides of head and throat buff-coloured. Wing butt and scapular feathers yellow; under parts buff. In winter plumage the male differs from the female only by his larger size. Length: including tail 9 in. (23 cm).

These birds are seen in large numbers on the plateau lands of Eritrea, along rivers and streams and in marshy pasture lands. At eventide they retire to the extensive reed fields to roost. They fly very low over the ground and the rapid rate of their wing beats causes a buzzing noise. The male likes to get a perch on the tip of a stalk or shrub where he can make his hissing, grating song. He points his head down, lets his collar feathers stand up on end, holds his body erect and lets his wings droop down. When he flies up, he remains hovering above the same spot for a time. The males build roosting nests. The 2–4 eggs are pale blue and mottled olive-brown, which the female incubates for 13–14 days. Breeding results have only been obtained on one or two occasions. They favour the same habitats as other weavers.

WHITE-WINGED WHYDAH, *Euplectes a. albonotatus* (Cassin) (Pl. XLI)
G. Spiegelwidah; F. Veuve à ailes blanches; D. Witvleugelwida, Spiegelwida

DISTRIBUTION: Southern Tanzania, south-eastern Zaire, Zambia, Rhodesia, Malawi, Mozambique, Transvaal, Botswana and Natal.
DESCRIPTION: *Male*. Main colouring black. Base of flights, under wing coverts and major part of wing coverts white. *Females*. Mainly dull brown, upper parts mottled with

blackish-brown, under parts and eyestripe brownish-yellow, chin and breast whitish. Lesser wing coverts yellowish-white, remainder of wings and tail mottled with blackish-brown on a paler background. The tail is not very long and cut off abruptly. Length: 6¾ in. (17 cm).

These whydahs are very widespread in their homelands and are to be found especially on open grassland. The males mostly perch at the tips of stalks and utter a chattering song. They are polygamous and supervise a large breeding territory, in which they build nests for their 6–10 wives. The nests are oval, built of stalks and have a large side entrance and interior lining of fine grass tips. The 2–4 eggs are turquoise-blue and speckled with brown or grey.

They were first imported in 1870 and exhibited at the London Zoo, since when they have been imported and bred fairly frequently. Like all whydahs, these birds become quite aggressive in the breeding season and frighten other birds by flying over them suddenly with their tails outspread. Some males also build nests as soon as they have acquired their ornamental plumage. There are four subspecies.

JACKSON'S WHYDAH, *Euplectes jacksoni* (Sharpe)
G. Jackson's Widah, Leierschwanzwida; F. Veuve de Jackson; D. Jackson's Wida (Pl. XLIV)

DISTRIBUTION: Central Kenya, northern Tanzania.
DESCRIPTION: *Male*. Main colouring jet black. Lesser wing coverts yellowish-brown, greater coverts and flights blackish-brown with brown edges. Tail black, long and arched like a

Jackson's Whydah, *Euplectes jacksoni*

domestic cockerel. Iris dark brown, beak grey with light tip, feet and legs black. Length: a good 12 in. (30 cm) including tail in male. *Female*. Upper parts light brown with black shaft stripes, under parts pale buff, middle of abdomen almost white. Beak greyish horn-coloured; feet and legs greyish black.

On the extensive grassy plains of the uplands these birds are a striking but quite a common feature. The males arrange arenas, where they execute their typical display dances. During these, the female perch sometimes in a nearby clump of grass to look on. The males throw their heads back into their napes, throw up their tails rigidly, so that one or two feather tips touch the napes of their necks and, with outspread wings, make leaps of at least 19 in. (0·5 m) into the air. The arenas can be recognised by flattened grass. The male's song consists of a few low warbled notes and a series of grating trills.

The nests are generally transparent, built low in the grass and provided with a covered entrance made of green grass. They are not built near the dancing areas. The 2–4 eggs are pale blue-green and covered with brown specks.

They appeared at London Zoo as early as 1911. Amateurs report that these birds are much more peaceable than most other similar species. All whydahs and weavers only put on their ornamental plumage towards the beginning of the European winter, so that they are particularly suitable for the bird exhibitions which are held in the winter months.

GIANT WHYDAH, LONG-TAILED WHYDAH, *Euplectes p. progne* (Boddaert) (Pl. XLIV)

G. Hahnschweifwidah; F. Veuve géante, Veuve à épaulettes; D. Hanestaartwida

DISTRIBUTION: Zambia, east Africa, south to the eastern part of the Cape Province.

DESCRIPTION: *Male.* Main colouring black; scapular wings orange-red, median wing coverts white or buff. Tail long, middle quills very long. Beak bluish-white, feet and legs light brown. Length: in breeding plumage about 22 in. (55 cm), the tail extends to 16 in. (45 cm) in male. *Female.* Upper parts buff, brown and black. Scapular patch orange with black stripes. Under parts pale buff with darker stripes, under wing coverts black. These polygamous whydahs occur in flocks, consisting of 2 males and 10–20 females in marshy, grassy regions. The very striking males execute slow flights over the grass, letting their spread-out tails hang downwards.

Giant Whydah, *Euplectes p. progne*

In the breeding period, when the females incubate the eggs, the males fly to neighbouring reed fields and roost there. Although the male has 6 or more females around him, this does not mean that they all nest and rear young.

Since the beginning of the century these large, attractive whydahs have been brought to Europe and have attracted a great deal of attention in collections. They can be kept quite easily in large aviaries together with glossy starlings or other larger birds. In the breeding season, they are restless and the males dance ceaselessly above the other birds, causing confusion. In England breeding results have been obtained.

Some oats, wheat and, during the winter months, some hemp must be added to the normal seed diet. Mealworms and various insects are usually eaten; also a variety of fruits, insectivorous food and soft food. They have to spend the winter months in a frost-free sleeping shelter, although during the day they can stay in the outside aviary.

RED-NAPED WHYDAH, CRIMSON-WINGED WHYDAH, *Euplectes ardens laticauda* (Lichtenstein)

G. Rotscheitelwidah; F. Veuve à longue queue; D. Roodschedelwida (Pl. XLIII)

DISTRIBUTION: Sudan, Eritrea, Ethiopia.

DESCRIPTION: Main colouring black. A broad, scarlet bar runs along the rear of sides of head and across upper breast. Feathers of upper parts generally have narrow, brown edges. Iris brown, beak, feet and legs black. Length: 12 in. (30 cm). *Female.* Difficult to distinguish from that of the nominate race.

Red-naped Whydah, *Euplectes ardens laticauda*

The extensive steppes with sparse bushes and large marshes with grass fields in between them constitute the homeland of these very striking birds, which form small groups of isolated males and a larger number of females, frequently mingling with other whydahs forms.

Males often fight over females, who stay hidden on the ground amongst the grass. Only when the males chase one another is their flight fast and agile, otherwise they are sluggish. The song has a grating, hissing sound and they execute display flights over the grasslands.

Colonies of some 20 nests close together have been found, but the nests were always completely apart. They are woven loosely from dry or green stalks and 2–3 eggs can be seen in them.

RED-COLLARED WHYDAH, CUT-THROAT WHYDAH, *Euplectes a. ardens* (Boddaert) (Pl. XLIV)

G. Schildwidan; F. Veuve en feu, Veuve niobe; D. Schildwida

DISTRIBUTION: Uganda, south-eastern Kenya, southern Zaire, Angola, Tanzania, east Africa to the eastern Cape Province.

DESCRIPTION: *Male.* Main colouring black. A red band runs

across nape at foremost side. Wing coverts have whitish edges. The tail is long and graduated, the middle quills are the shortest. Iris brown, beak, feet and legs black. *Female*. Upper parts black and brown striped. Eye stripe buff-coloured. Under parts yellowish-white, chin and throat somewhat yellower. Beak horn-coloured yellow. In winter plumage, the male is bigger and has darker stripes on upper parts. Length: about 14 in. (35 cm) including tail.

In their homelands, these birds usually occur in the tall grass areas, spending the nights in reed fields. They do a fair amount of damage to crops. They are usually seen in groups of about 60 consisting of 5 males in ornamental plumage, some in their young plumage, and the rest females. The birds are highly polygamous; males execute typical display flights, wheeling over the waving stalks of grass and uttering their grating song. Females often move around on the ground between the grass stalks looking for fallen seeds and small insects. The nests are more or less transparent, round in shape, and the entrance is covered by protruding stalks. These whydahs were first imported to Europe at the beginning of the century. One on his own does not bother about the other birds in the aviary. A number of pairs together become restless during the breeding season when the males fight and chase other birds from their nests.

Red-Collared Whydah, *Euplectes a. ardens*

Genus: Anomalospiza

CUCKOO WEAVER, PARASITIC WEAVER, *Anomalospiza imberbis* (Cabanis) (Pl. XXIX)
G. Kuckucksweber; F. Tisserin parasitique; D. Koekoekswever

DISTRIBUTION: From Sierra Leone to Ethiopia, Transvaal and Zanzibar.

DESCRIPTION: *Male*. Has yellow forehead, sides of head and under parts. Remaining upper parts greenish-yellow with long black stripes. Wings and tail grey with greenish-yellow edges. Beak blackish. *Female*. Upper parts yellowish-brown with black stripes. Sides of head, eyebrows, chin and throat brown suffused with yellow. Remaining under parts yellowish-brown, striped with darker brown. Length: about 5¼ in. (13 cm).

Because of its appearance, which is similar to that of the canary, this bird is often wrongly classified. Cuckoo Weavers have characteristic parasitic habits; the young are not at all like their parents but resemble more the *Cisticola* species. The eggs and young have been found in the nests of song birds of the *Cisticola*, *Prinia* and *Passer* species. In one nest 2 young Cuckoo Weavers were found; the young of the host birds had been thrown out.

Except in the breeding season the birds assemble in large flocks in open country, in steppe country, cultivated fields and pasture land. They feed mainly on seeds. They are rather shy and fly on to the tops of nearby trees when approached too closely.

They were first seen at an exhibition in Berlin in 1879. It would be worth while, in view of their especially interesting way of life, to keep some of these birds with *Cisticola* species from the same native regions, so that their breeding parasitism could be studied more closely.

H. L. Sich, in *Avicultural Magazine* (4) Vol. 4, 1926, pp. 193–4, 323–4, reported a successful breeding. Sich, however, did not know that the species was parasitic, but as he appears only to have observed eggs in a nest and later the young bird emerging in a mixed collection of birds, the record may be genuine (C. J. O. Harrison 'Records of Breedings' in *Avicultural Magazine*, 78, No. 6, Nov./Dec. 1972).

Cuckoo Weaver, *Anomalospiza imberbis*

FAMILY: STURNIDAE

Mynahs and Starlings

BY H. J. BATES AND R. L. BUSENBARK

There are very few families which show as much diversity as the starlings and mynahs. Many are exceptionally beautiful birds. This group also includes the talking mynahs which are very popular.

Members of this family for the most part are very hardy, quickly adaptable to aviary life, and usually aggressive to other birds. The diet is an insectivorous mixture with rather more live food and/or raw meat than many groups. Soft fruits and berries are enjoyed by them.

Most of the birds in this family should not be kept with birds smaller than themselves because they could become dangerously aggressive to them. They can also be aggressive to larger birds which are timid or gentle by nature.

There are twenty-six genera in the family with one genus separated into a subfamily. One hundred and eleven species and numerous subspecies fit into the twenty-six genera. Two species of the genus set aside in the subfamily are Oxpeckers which are unusual birds and not regular avicultural subjects.

Starlings and mynahs are found in many parts of the world. The greatest number of species desirable for aviaries come from Africa, India, and South East Asia.

The popular names of starling, mynah, and grackle are sometimes used interchangeably and this leads to a considerable amount of confusion. Most of the smaller starlings and mynahs, especially those of the genera *Sturnus* and *Acridotheres*, spend a considerable amount of the time on the ground. Their walk is a bold swagger with long strides and frequent forward head movements. Larger mynahs of the genus *Gracula* do not walk but hop and they prefer not to spend their time on the ground. Glossy Starlings from Africa are largely arboreal and spend as little time on the ground as possible.

For all their hardiness and adaptability, most starlings and mynahs do not breed well in captivity. The Greater India Hill Mynahs and Glossy Starlings have frequently gone to nest, but total success has been particularly rare. The main drawback to success in the past has been improper diet. They need a coarse-grade insectivorous mixture, with fruits and green food. Great quantities of live foods and perhaps raw meat must be added for nesting birds. Mealworms and maggots will certainly be the main source of live foods available for aviary birds, but as many other types of live foods as possible must also be given.

Most starlings and mynahs nest in boxes. The ideal size is a cockatiel nest box. Their nests are coarse, flimsy, and somewhat carelessly put together. The birds process and soften twigs and straw working on each piece for a considerable period. They also incorporate leaves into the nest if any are available.

Genus: Aplonis

SUBFAMILY: STURNINAE

SINGING GLOSSY STARLING, *Alponis cantoroides* (Gray)

G. Inselstar; F. Stourne des îles; D. Eilandspreeuw

DISTRIBUTION: Papua-New Guinea and neighbouring islands.
DESCRIPTION: Mainly black plumage with green metallic sheen. Large wing coverts, flights, tail and vent region matt black. Irides red, beak, feet and legs black. Length: about 8 in. (20 cm).

This genus is sub-divided into 24 species living in southern Asia. In 1800 Dr. Heinroth brought back several specimens from a voyage to the Bismarck Islands; he presented them to the Berlin Zoo.

They were young specimens, which he had raised by hand. The birds which were first given a liquid mash did far better than those given a dry mash. After they had been fed by hand for a time they began to take a general mash, fruit, mealworms, pieces of raw meat and various insects. A number of young specimens were on display at an exhibition in Copenhagen, Denmark, in 1932.

In the wild, these birds live in large flights which practically always remain in the trees, where they find fruit and berries, and make a terrible uproar. They nest in colonies, the nests are built at a great height in the trees, amongst the lianas or at the end of branches; sometimes several nests touch each other. The female lays 2 light blue eggs with pointed ends and red marks; both birds sit on them for 2 weeks. The young are fed on fruit and live insects. Like all *Sturnidae*, they are somewhat aggressive; a pair must be housed on their own in the aviary, unless they are put with large species capable of defending themselves.

SHINING STARLING, SHINING CALORNIS, *Aplonis m. metallica* (Temminck)

G. Spinnenstar, Metalstar; F. Stourne métallique; D. Metaalglansspreeuw

DISTRIBUTION: The Aru Islands, the Moluccas, Papua-New Guinea and northern Queensland in Australia.
DESCRIPTION: Mainly black plumage with a green metallic sheen. Head, back and breast have a violet- or copper-coloured sheen. Young birds have greyish-black upper parts; matt black under parts with white streaks; after the first moult, under parts are generally pure white. Length: about 8 in. (20 cm).

Like the Common Starling, *Sturnus vulgaris*, this Starling has pointed feathers and a long arrow-shaped tail.

The birds fly extremely well, making cackling sounds as they fly, from which they are known in Australia as 'Whirlwind Birds'. The Indonesians call them *Burung-matta-mera*, which means 'red-eyed bird'.

These starlings form flocks of a dozen or more. They feed mainly on various kinds of fruit, including the nutmeg; they also take insects in flight. They nest in colonies, sometimes in holes in trees, but more often in a nest built like that of the Weaver Bird, that is a suspended purse-shaped nest with a side entrance. A single tree will often carry 200 of these nests, each hanging from a woven cord. The materials used include roots, vegetable fibre, often very fine, and pieces of palm leaf. The nest is 10 in. (25 cm) wide and 20 in. (50 cm) high. The pair sit in turn for 14 days on on 2–4 whitish-blue eggs.

Shining Starling *Aplonis m. metallica*

These birds are rarely found in collections. Neunzig mentions that in 1907 an English collector had some for the first time. They do not seem to have bred in captivity. These fruit eaters must be gradually accustomed to general mash, mealworms, and pieces of raw meat. They seem to be hardy if they have been carefully acclimatised, but must winter in a heated place. A pair may live with other sufficiently large species.

ASIAN GREEN STARLING, ASIATIC GLOSSY STARLING, GLOSSY CALORNIS, *Aplonis p. panayensis* (Scopoli)

G. Asiatischer Glanzstar; F. Stourne bronzé, Stourne asiatique; D. Aziatische Glansspreeuw

DISTRIBUTION: Southern China, Indonesia, Philippines.
DESCRIPTION: Plumage mainly metallic black with green and violet sheens. Lores, beak, feet and legs black. Irides bright red with a yellow orbital ring. *Female*. Smaller than male. Length: about 9 in. (22 cm).
This species is divided into 13 subspecies varying slightly in length and plumage. From time to time a single specimen or

a pair is obtained by an aviculturist, who will be delighted both by their brilliant plumage, and also by the good nature of these very intelligent birds. They are even suitable for a large cage, where they will live at peace with smaller birds. In the wild, they live in trees, where they find their food, consisting largely of fruit and various insects.
It was successfully bred in the London Zoo as reported in *Avicultural Magazine*, 63, 1957, p. 170.
The subspecies, *Aplonis p. strigata*, which comes from Thailand, was bred by F. Johansen of Denmark; in 1959, first in an inside aviary and later in an outside aviary. He gives a detailed report in the *Avicultural Magazine*, 1960, Vol 66, No. 1:

'The behaviour of these starlings is reminiscent of that of the common starling. Their song consists of melodious sounds, but also of discordant cries; they are interesting birds. They must winter in heated conditions.'

They have also been successfully bred in America.

Genus: Poeoptera

NARROW-TAILED STARLING, *Poeoptera lugubris* Bonaparte

G. Spitzshcwanzglanzstar; F. Stourne à queue pointillée; D. Spitzztaart-Glansspreeuw

DISTRIBUTION: Africa, in a diagonal belt including parts of northern Angola into Zaire and western Uganda.
DESCRIPTION: *Male*. Bright yellow eyes are in sharp contrast to the very dark plumage which would be black except for rich bluish-purple metallic reflections. Wings dark brownish with some of the feathers showing pale margins and darker tips. *Female*. Greyish with blue glosses. Tail is shorter. Concealed wing patch shows as vivid chestnut in flight. Length: a little over 9 in. (23 cm) including the long graduated tail. The longest of the narrow tail feathers are the

central pair which are about 5 in. (12 cm).
SUBSPECIES: Two other species in this genus are considerably less distinctive than the above species. Stuhlmann's Starling, *Poeoptera stuhlmanni* (formerly *Stilbopsar stuhlmanni*) is from the middle eastern area of Africa. *Male*. is quite dull compared with other Glossy Starlings because of less intense gloss. Blue and purplish glosses do occur, but they are less vivid. The tail is not long and the size is small. *Female*. Greyish with greenish glosses and some chestnut in the wing.
Kenrick's Starling, *Poeotera kenricki* (formerly *Stilbopsar kenricki*), has 2 subspecies in a very limited range in Kenya and Tanzania. It is similar to Stuhlmann's Starling except the back of male has a bronze gloss instead of blue; female also shows bronze on upper parts.

Genus: Onychognathus

RED-WINGED STARLING, *Onychognathus m. morio* (Linnaeus)

G. Rotschwingenglanzstar; F. Roupenne; D. Roodvleugel-Glansspreeuw

DISTRIBUTION: Africa, widespread areas in the east and the south and in a limited area in the central portion north of the Equator extending from Nigeria to Sudan.
DESCRIPTION: The dominant feature is the primary wing feathers which are reddish-chestnut with blackish tips. This wing shading and size are variable in different subspecies. *Male*. Very dark with purplish-blue glosses, but iridescence is not really intense. Irides dark red. *Female*. Has a greyish head and chest with bluish streaks. Length: 11–13 in. (28–33 cm), the broad tail being approximately half of this length.

The heavier beak and thicker neck make this a less attractively proportioned bird than any of the above species, but the long, broad tail adds a slight flamboyance.
There are 9 other species in this genus from various parts of Africa. Most are called Chestnut-winged Starlings. Variations are reasonably slight in colouring but beaks and tails vary considerably. The Slender-billed Chestnut-winged Starling, *Onychognathus tenuirostris*, is perhaps the most attractive in shape because of its longer, more slender tail and more shapely beak. The Bristle-crowned Starling, *Onychognathus salvadorii*, has a particularly long tail with a bristly cushion of small feathers on the forehead. The White-billed Starling, *Onychognathus albirostris*, has a much shorter tail and a white beak.

Genus: Lamprotornis

PURPLE-HEADED GLOSSY STARLING, VELVET-HEADED GLOSSY STARLING, *Lamprotornis p. purpureiceps* (J. and E. Verreaux) (Pl. XXXVI)

G. Violetkopfiger Glanzstar; F. Merle bronzé à tête pourpre; D. Purperkop-Glansspreeuw

DISTRIBUTION: Africa, from southern Nigeria in the west and Uganda in the east.

DESCRIPTION: Sexes alike. Upper head feathers velvety instead of glossy and smooth. Other areas glossy. Head, neck and chest violet-purple. Rest of colouring metallic-green with some blue shadings and a shade of copper on tail. Black spots on wing coverts feather are absent. Irides bright golden; beak, feet and legs black. Have been bred a number of times and appear to make good parents. Length: about 8½ in. (22 cm) including tail 3 in. (7·5 cm).

PURPLE GLOSSY STARLING, *Lamprotornis p. purpureus* (Müller)

G. Purperglanzstar; F. Merle bronzé pourpre; D. Purperglansspreeuw

DISTRIBUTION: Africa, above the Equator across most of the continent from Senegal in the west to Sudan, Uganda, and Kenya in the east.
DESCRIPTION: One of the most attractive of this group. Head and throat particularly vivid purple, nape bright blue. Rump blue, tail deep purple and blue. Metallic-green occurs on back and wings. Beak, feet and legs black. Irides golden-yellow. Length: 8¾ in. (22·5 cm). Have bred in captivity.

CAPE RED-SHOULDERED GLOSSY STARLING, *Lamprotornis nitens phoenicopterus* (Swainson)

G. Rotschulterglanzstar; F. Merle à épaulettes rouges; D. Roodschouder-Glansspreeuw

DISTRIBUTION: Africa, mostly in southern areas.
DESCRIPTION: Plumage metallic-green with blue and purplish reflections. Shoulder patches golden-bronze instead of red, but they sometimes have a gloss of reddish-purple. Length: about 8½ in. (22 cm).

BRONZE-TAILED GLOSSY STARLING, SHORT-TAILED GLOSSY STARLING, *Lamprotornis c. chalcurus* Nordmann

G. Senegal-Glanzstar; F. Merle métallique à queue bronzée; D. Bronsstaart-Glansspreeuw

DISTRIBUTION: Africa, from Senegal in the west to Kenya and Uganda in the east.
DESCRIPTION: Tail blue and purple shorter than the Green Glossy Starling, *L. chalybaeus*, and the purple on the abdomen is much more extensive. Ear coverts show a deeper shade of purplish-blue, otherwise same as *L. chalybaeus*, including velvety-black spots on wings.
Young birds brownish instead of blackish. Adult females a little smaller than adult males, but otherwise the same.

GREEN GLOSSY STARLING, *Lamprotornis chalybaeus*

G. Grünschwanzglanzstar, Abessinischer Stahlglanzstar; F. Merle métallique à oreilles bleues; D. Groene Glansspreeuw

DISTRIBUTION: Broad equatorial regions of Africa from eastern to western coasts and south to eastern Transvaal and northern south-west Africa.
DESCRIPTION: *Male.* Robust and shapely in appearance, tail broad and squared at the end. Feet, legs and beak black. Irides very bold and bright yellowish-orange or golden-straw-coloured. Pupil small and black, but golden iris often quite large and dominant. Plumage very dark with various metallis shades of bronzed green, blue and purple. Green predominates in most areas with blue becoming prominent on face, throat, head, nape, rump, tail and abdomen. Glossy purple also appears on the abdomen and to a limited extent on the wings. Velvety-black spots on the wing coverts. Tail blue-green. Length: about 9½ in. (24 cm). *Female.* Similar but smaller. Immature birds blackish with slight green glossiness.
Glossy Starlings are not the easiest of birds to keep. The long-tailed variety needs a very large cage, otherwise the birds will soon damage their tails. The short-tailed variety needs a great deal of space on account of its liveliness. Short-tailed Glossy Starlings will not live in constant harmony either with their own kind or with other species even of the

same size. Sudden outbursts of temper frequently occur, and may prove fatal. They will, however, not molest the larger parrakeets or such birds as the White-crested Jay Thrush, *Garrulax leucilopbus*, not the sweetest tempered of birds themselves. All Glossy Starlings must have a very large aviary at their disposal or a conservatory in which each bird has a corner to itself. These starlings bathe freely and often.

Green Glossy Starling, *Lamprotornis chalybaeus*

They have been successfully bred in captivity. Both male and female will share in building a nest from twigs and grasss in a nest-box. The eggs hatch in 14 days, and the young will remain another 4 weeks in the nest. Rearing food should consist of insectivorous food to which must be added ants' eggs, finely chopped raw meat, worms, snails, mealworms, fruit in season, and also dates, finely cut up. Germinating seeds are enjoyed.
The Lesser Blue-eared or Swainson's Glossy Starling, *Lamprotornis chloropterus*, is the same in appearance as *L. chalybaeus*, except that it is smaller. This species with 3 subspecies covers much the same range as *L. chalybaeus*, except that it is in a more southern area. Young birds are brownish instead of blackish.

SPLENDID GLOSSY STARLING, *Lamprotornis splendidus* (Vieillot)   (Pl. XXXVI)
G. Prachtglanzstar; F. Merle métallique; D. Prachtglansspreeuw   (Pl. XX)

Splendid Glossy Starling, *Lamprotornis splendidus*

DISTRIBUTION: Africa, in most of the extensive range of the species above, but in a narrower belt which is less northerly. The western range extends in a far more southerly area to include most of Angola.

DESCRIPTION: *Male.* Under parts deep reddish-purple with subordinate blue shadings; upper parts mainly deep metallic-bronze-green with subordinate bluish and purplish shadings. Blue prominent on nape, sides, rump, upper tail and under tail coverts. A large facial area is black followed by a paler spot which is nearly copper. Length: about 10 in. (25 cm). *Female.* Similar but shows more blue and less purple on undersides. Young chicks far less vivid than adults.

LONG-TAILED GLOSSY STARLING, *Lamprotornis caudatus* (Müller) (Pl. XXXIX)
G. Langschwanzglanzstar; F. Merle métallique à longue queue; D. Langstaart-glansspreeuw

DISTRIBUTION: Africa, in a broad belt across the continent above the Equator starting at Senegal down to the Ivory Coast and extending to central Sudan.

DESCRIPTION: Plumage is especially dark but still heavily glossed with green. A golden-bronze shade occurs on head

Long-tailed Glossy Starling, *Lamprotornis caudatus*

and chest, tail is purplish. Blue dominantly highlights rump and wings and serves as a subordinate accent to green in other areas. The pale brownish-yellow eye forms a bright contrast. Velvety-black spots occur on wing coverts. This species is a very handsome bird because of its tail; and it shows spectacularly in a large, high aviary. Young birds similar but far less iridescent. Length of body: about 10 in. (2·5 cm). Tail very long; feathers broad and graduated in length with central feathers the longest. In the male, these central feathers become 14 in. (35·5 cm) long. In the female, they are about 11 in. (28 cm).

RUPPELL'S LONG-TAILED GLOSSY STARLING, *Lamprotornis purpuropterus* Rüppell
G. Schweifglanzstar; F. Merle bronzé à dos poupre; D. Purperrug-Glansspreeuw

DISTRIBUTION: Eastern Africa—mostly Ethiopia but also parts of Sudan, Kenya, Uganda and the Congo; also Zanzibar.

DESCRIPTION: Similar to *L. caudatus* but tail shorter and black spots on wing coverts missing. Violet occurs on nape and rump, and back shows more blue and purple.

A first breeding is recorded in *Avicultural Magazine*, (4), 11, p. 357, 1933.

LONG-TAILED PURPLE STARLING, MEVE'S LONG-TAILED GLOSSY STARLING, *Lamprotornis mevesii* (Wahlberg) (Pl. XXXVI)
G. Mewes Glanzstar; F. Merle métallique de Meve; D. Meve's Langstaart-Glansspreeuw

DISTRIBUTION: Angola, Namibia, Botswana, southern Rhodesia and southern Nyasaland.

DESCRIPTION: Like *L. purpuroterus*, except dark blue covers neck, head and throat instead of golden-bronze; rump has a golden-bronze shade.

EMERALD STARLING, *Lamprotornis iris* (Oustalet)
G. Smaragdgrüner Glanzstar; F. Merle émeraude; D. Smaragdgroene Glansspreeuw

DISTRIBUTION: Guinea, Sierra Leone, and the Ivory Coast.

DESCRIPTION: Brilliant reddish-purple occurs sharply divided on lower chest and abdomen and on long cheek patches which start at rear of eyes and broaden down to sides of neck. Rest of plumage brilliant metallic-green with bronze glosses. Irides brownish. This is one of the most beautiful of the Glossy Starlings; but, at 7½ in. (19 cm) it is also one of the smallest.

Genus: Cinnyricinclus

WHITE-BELLIED AMETHYST STARLING, VIOLET-BACKED STARLING. *Cinnyricinclus l. leucogaster* (Boddaert) (Pl. XXXVI)
G. Amethystglanzstar; F. Merle violet à ventre blanc; D. Amethist-glansspreeuw

DISTRIBUTION: Widespread over most areas of Africa south of Senegal in the west and Sudan in the east. Migrations account for much of the distribution.

DESCRIPTION: *Male.* This rather small starling is exceptionally beautiful. All upper parts, head, and a broad bib down to chest brilliant glossy violet. Under parts below bib through under tail coverts white. Division on chest irregular and somewhat scaled. Violet colourings show slight variations in shadings ranging from reddish-purple to bluish-purple. Many of the feathers have slightly paler edges which gives a softly scaled appearance. Flights dull black which does not really detract from the dazzling appearance. Iris bright straw-yellow with sharp black pupil. Beak, feet and legs black. *Female.* Brownish above with paler edges on most of the feathers giving a scaled appearance. Under parts white heavily streaked with long spots of dark brown.

Young birds are like females. Length: 7 in. (18 cm).

Subspecies *C. l. verreauxi* in the east is well-known as Verreaux's Amethyst Starling. This species is smaller than most African starlings, and less aggressive. Not strictly as hardy as preceding members of the family, this species, and several of those following, must have a little extra care in the beginning. It is perhaps best kept with birds of its own size and disposition.

A recent breeding was by Mr. W. D. Cummings of Keston Bird Farm, England, reported in *Avicultural Magazine*, No. 2, 1959.

Genus: Spreo

SUPERB SPREO STARLING, SUPERB STARLING, *Spreo superbus* Rüppell (Pl. XXXVI)
G. Dreifarbenglanzstar; F. Spreo superbe; D. Driekleurige Glansspreeuw

DISTRIBUTION: Eastern Africa, south-eastern Sudan, southern Ethiopia, Somalia to Tanzania.

DESCRIPTION: Tail slightly rounded; and general structure almost squarish with its broad head, broad chest, and short neck. The large, powerful feet and legs, as well as the beak black. Iris metallic-straw with sharp black pupils. Glossy black with green and blue highlights cover the entire head and a large bib extending onto upper chest. Back and wings rich metallic dark green. Tail black with green and blue highlights. Velvety-blackish spots occur near the tips of wing coverts. An uneven narrow white band borders lower area of bib followed by bright chestnut which continues past thighs and legs. Under tail coverts, vent area, and under wing coverts white. Undersides of tail and flights dull black. Length: is a little over 8 in. (20 cm) including the tail of 2½ in. (6 cm). *Female.* Similar but very slightly smaller in size.

One of the most beautiful of African Glossy Starlings and so tolerant that it can be safely kept with most other birds in a communal flight. Its voice is rather loud and not particularly beautiful; which makes it unsuitable for a living-room.

Its gaudiness of plumage and tameness make this species much in demand. Another advantage is that no special diet is needed. Insectivorous food, fruit, and many mealworms with the addition of finely chopped raw meat once or twice a week is sufficient. The bird soon learns to take the mealworms from the hand. It is hardy and will breed readily in captivity. A nesting-box of the size needed for parrakeets or a little larger will be filled with any materials available. There are usually 2–3 chicks in a brood.

During breeding time these birds require a large quantity of ants' eggs and worms, together with other insects, as they will hardly touch the insectivorous food throughout this period. Large beetles will be eaten eagerly. Hatching takes 13 days.

First bred in 1924 by Mr. Ezra as recorded in *Avicultural Magazine*, Vol. 4, No. 2, 1924, p. 168. Many recent breedings have been recorded in several countries.

Superb Spreo Starling, *Spreo superbus*

HILDEBRANDT'S SPREO STARLING, SHELLEY'S SPREO STARLING, CHESTNUT-BELLIED STARLING, *Spreo hildebrandti* (Cabanis)
G. Hildebrandts Glanzstar; F. Etourneau de Hildebrandt; D. Hildebrandts Glansspreeuw

DISTRIBUTION: Eastern Africa in very limited area. The nominate race in southern Kenya and Tanzania. Shelley's Starling is found in the extreme south-eastern Sudan, southern Ethiopia, southern Somalia to eastern Kenya.

DESCRIPTION: Hildebrandt's Starling is darker than *S. superbus*. The most noticeable difference is the absence of white border below bib and white undertail coverts. This removes some of the bright contrasts. The chestnut shade also a little paler but less bright. A metallic shading of green occurs on nape; and shoulders and wing coverts are more of a metallic-blue than green.

Shelley's Starling shows a deeper shade of chestnut on under parts and a deeper purplish shading in metallic gloss of head, throat, chest, back, shoulders and wing coverts.

Both of these starlings are very rarely available for the aviculturist.

Genus: Cosmopsarus

ROYAL STARLING, GOLDEN-BREASTED STARLING, *Cosmopsarus regius* Reichenow (Pl. XXXVI)
G. Königsglanzstar; F. Spreo royal, Merle métallique royal; D. Koningsglansspreeuw

DISTRIBUTION: Eastern Africa, mostly Ethiopia and Kenya.

DESCRIPTION: Colours are vivid and heavily lustrous, and the tail is very long, slender and graduated. The dominant feature is brilliant but not iridescent golden-yellow on lower chest and remaining under parts. Other areas all dark but highly variable in iridescence. Metallic-green covers head, nape, and back, shading to purplish-blue on ear coverts, wings, rump and upper tail coverts. Tail golden-brownish in a somewhat dull shade, but it is also mixed with blue and purple. Upper chest is richly glossed with violet. Length: about 14 in. (35·5 cm) at least half is tail. Sexes are alike.

The only other member of this genus is very dull grey with greenish gloss on upper parts. In shape it is similar but all other resemblance ends there. This drab cousin is the Ashy Starling, *Cosmopsarus unicolor*, from southern Kenya and Tanzania.

Genus: Creatophora

WATTLED STARLING, LOCUST BIRD, *Creatophora cinerea* (Meuschen) (Pl. XXXIX)
G. Lappenstar; F. Martin caronculé; D. Lelspreeuw

DISTRIBUTION: All of southern Africa from Angola and eastern Africa south of Sudan.
DESCRIPTION: Wattled Starlings have no flambuoyant, bright or lustrous colours. Flight and tail feathers dull black with only a slight greenish gloss. A small bar of white occurs near base of outer primaries. Primary coverts white in male and black in female. The rest of plumage is soft pale brownish-grey. A black line on each side of throat starts at lower corners of lower mandible. Beak pale yellowish-green. In females and non-breeding males the body colouring extends over the head.
Males in breeding dress shed most of their head feathers, leaving bare yellow wattle skin. The wattles grow quickly into fleshy appendages below and above beak. Most of the wattle skin turns to black on the face, crown and throat. Yellow remains on rear of crown and facial areas behind behind eyes. Irides, feet and legs brown. Length: about 8 in. (20·3 cm).
This is one of the most unusual of all the starlings; in breeding periods the male has a striking appearance on account of the strange wattles.
Members of the species are gregarious nomads which follow locust swarms. They are protected because they consume great quantities of insects. When the insect population is plentiful the birds settle down to raise families in a hurry. When insects are sparse, the birds disperse over wide areas, and nesting activity is reduced or may cease altogether.
The nests are built close together in brushwood or on the ground and consist of a base of twigs and grasses, which is

Wattled Starling, *Creatophora cinerea*

often vaulted by a second nest built on top. The 4–5 blue eggs take 14 days to hatch. After breeding has ceased the wattles begin to dry out as the parts to which they are attached become gradually covered with feathers. Yellow on top of head of female also only becomes pronounced during the breeding season.
Wattled Starlings were first exhibited in 1885 in the Zoological Gardens, London. They cannot be counted among the most beautiful coloured birds but they are certainly among the most interesting. They seem to be friendly and unobtrusive with other birds. They can be kept in excellent condition with an insectivorous mixture, mealworms and some fruit. Their winter quarters should be heated.

Genus: Sturnus

ANDAMAN MYNAH, ANDAMAN STARLING, WHITE-HEADED STARLING, *Sturnus erythropygius adamanensis* (Tytler)
G. Andamanstar, Weisskopfstar; F. Martin à tête blanche; D. Andamanenspreeuw

DISTRIBUTION: Andaman and Nicobar Islands.
DESCRIPTION: Head, neck and under parts white, sometimes clouded with grey. Vent and lower tail coverts brownish-white. Upper parts light grey, with a whitish rump and grey upper tail coverts. Wings black, with green gloss on outer side; lower wing coverts white. Tail black, with a green sheen all main tail feathers, except middle pair, have white tips. Irides white; feet, legs and beak yellow. Length: 8 in. (20·3 cm).
These mynahs live in open woods, cultivated fields, or in meadows, and they feed on the ground. They can be seen in flights of up to 40 near settlements. They are not shy, but are lively and curious.
They were to be found in the London Zoo as early as 1885, and in the Berlin Zoo a few years later. Unlike other Sturnidae, these mynahs never panic, but always maintain the dignified behaviour which is their characteristic. They can share an aviary with other birds, but during breeding the male mounts guard near the nest, which he defends ferociously, fighting and pursuing intruders.
These birds are not difficult to keep. Their main diet consists of an insectivorous mixture, supplemented by various kinds of fruit and mealworms. Their aviary must be heated in winter. They bathe often and eagerly at all times of the year.

They are sometimes known by their former name, *Temenuchus andamanensis*.
A breeding was reported by R. Farrar in *Avicultural Magazine*, No. 7, 1901, pp. 192–6. In 1935 they bred at the Berlin Zoo. In London they have been crossed with the Malabar Mynah, *Sturnus m. malabaricus*, and young were reared.

PAGODA STARLING, BRAHMINY MYNAH, *Sturnus pagodarum* (Gmelin) (Pl. XXXVII)
G. Pagodenstar; F. Martin des Pagodes; D. Pagodespreeuw

DISTRIBUTION: Afghanistan, Nepal, India, Sri Lanka.
DESCRIPTION: A large black cap, extending down to nape, is composed of slightly elongated, slender, glossy feathers, which are partially erectile. The headdress is not a crest in the true sense of the word, but is commonly described as such. Facial areas, sides of neck, throat, and all under parts, a warm shade of pastel reddish-brown, fading to white under tail. Upper parts greyish-brown and flights blackish. Tail has white tips. Feet, legs and beak horn-coloured. Length: about 8 in. (20·3 cm). Sexes alike, except that female has shorter crest and is a little smaller.
Pagoda Starlings are common and appear in open fields and in settlements. They make slovenly nests of grass and feathers in hollows of trees, but nests have also been found in walls of houses. As well as a number of croaking noises, they can also make melodious flute-like tones, and it is well known that they have powers of mimicry. They hold their

Pagoda Starling, *Sturnus pagodarum*

In their countries of origin, Rosy Pastors are often kept as cage birds, and they can be taught to fly freely in and out. In a cage, hygiene must be strictly maintained, as the birds eat a great deal and the excreta is liquid. It is essential to cover the floor with a layer of forest soil or peat dust. Unfortunately these birds lose their beautiful rose colour unless there is an addition of colouring matter to their food. Probably the locusts provide this red colouring matter, because they are originally red, and become green only through the food they eat.

These lively and noisy birds show up better in an aviary than in a cage. They do excellently on the normal food for starlings, which consists of insectivorous food with the addition of grated carrot, all sorts of berries and mealworms.

G. H. Gurney reported a successful breeding in *Avicultural Magazine*, Vol. 4, No. 12, 1934, pp. 77, 300–1. Breeding results have been obtained on many other occasions. The birds carry straw and feathers to a nest-box, where they lay 3–4 blue eggs. While the young are being reared, great quantities of mealworms and maggots must be provided.

beaks against their breasts as they sit singing.

This intelligent bird soon becomes tame and can be allowed to fly in and out of its cage. In a cage the Pagoda behaves very quietly and does not upset the drinking or feeding troughs as do their larger relatives. As floor covering for a cage, soil from a fir wood is best, as this dissipates the acrid odour of excreta. Coarse insectivorous mixture, soaked bread, and egg food form the chief ingredients of the diet, with, of course, all kinds of fruit. Mealworms are eaten only when the birds are chicks and their skin is still soft; they much prefer maggots.

Pagoda Starlings first came to the Zoological Gardens of Amsterdam in 1853, and then were regularly imported. After careful acclimatisation they become hardy and can remain in an outside aviary in both winter and summer, provided they have access to a night shelter. They are eager to bathe, but must be prevented from doing so during severe frosts.

Breeding results have been repeatedly obtained. What is believed to be a first breeding was reported by R. Farrar in *Avicultural Magazine*, No. 7, 1901, pp. 197–9. Generally the birds accept a half-opened nest-box, in which they place some straw and feathers as a nest for their 3–4 blue eggs.

ROSY PASTOR, ROSE-COLOURED STARLING, *Sturnus roseus* (Linnaeus)   (Pl. XXXIX)
G. Rosenstar; F. Martin roselin; D. Rose-Spreeuw

DISTRIBUTION: Eastern Europe, Russia, and the Middle East in summer. India and Sri Lanka in winter. There are also nomadic occurences outside the normal range.

DESCRIPTION: A black hood covers entire head and neck and extends as a bib down onto chest. Feathers on crown form same type of crest as described for *S. pagodarum*. Wings and tail black; remainder of colouring rose, which could easily fade in captivity if a colour-holding agent is not used. Beak, feet and legs pinkish-horn. Length: 8½ in. (21·6 cm). Sexes alike, but female has shorter crest and is slightly duller in colouring.

In the years when locusts abound in the Balkan States, Rosy Pastors, in flights of several hundred, move west, and, after they have helped defeat the plague, remain to breed. Because of their work on the locusts, they are highly esteemed in Turkestan, and have been called 'Birds of God'. However, locusts are not available all through the year, and when berries, grapes and other soft fruits are ripe, the birds, in even larger numbers, visit orchards and gardens; this is *not* welcomed.

Rosy Pastor, *Sturnus roseus*

DAURIAN STARLING, *Sturnus sturnius* (Pallas)
G. Siberischer Graustar; F. Martin de la Sibérie; D. Siberische Spreeuw

DISTRIBUTION: Wide migratory range includes USSR, China, Korea, Burma, Thailand, Khmer, Laos, Vietnam, Malaysia and Indonesia.

DESCRIPTION: Glossy purple occurs on nape and on most of upper parts. Tail green. Under parts and sides of face grey. White occurs around eyes. Similar in many respects to Violet-backed Starling, the major difference being absence of chestnut on sides of neck. Sexes alike, but female lacks purple on rump. Length: 7 in. (17·8 cm).

In the spring these small, ornamental starlings emerge from their hibernating quarters in Indonesia and India and go back to their breeding territories. They seek their food mostly on the ground, but sometimes in trees. They nest in hollows of trees.

In 1916 the first specimen came into the possession of a French aviculturist, but it lived only for a short time. Its food consisted of bread and milk, pieces of raw meat, and millet seeds. Plant lice were readily accepted, but grasshoppers and fruit were refused. The bird took frequent baths. It uttered some hoarse sounds, but also some melodious couplets. Later, these starlings were imported to other countries and were kept with much success in aviaries.

Plate XLIII

Yellow-backed Whydah, *Euplectes macrourus*

Red-naped Whydah, *Euplectes a. laticauda*

Taha Weaver, *Euplectes afra taha*

Crimson-crowned Weaver, *Euplectes h. hordaceus*

Yellow Bishop, *Euplectes c. capenis*

Plate XLIV

Giant Whydah, *Euplectes p. progne*   Red-collared Whydah, *Euplectes a. ardens*

Fischer's Whydah, *Vidua fischeri*   Shiny Black Whydah, *Hypochera hypocherina*

Yellow-shouldered Whydah, *Euplectes macrourus macrocercus*

Jackson's Whydah, *Euplectes jacksoni*

They ate insectivorous food, fruit, and drank a mixture of milk, sugar, syrup and meal.

MANDARIN MYNAH, CHINESE MYNAH, *Sturnus sinensis* (Gmelin)

G. Mandarinstar; F. Martin de Chine; D. Mandarijn-spreeuw

DISTRIBUTION: China, Formosa and South-east Asia.
DESCRIPTION: Flights and tail feathers black with white on tips of tail and on wing scapulars and coverts. Beak black. Rest of plumage soft pale greyish-white.

PIED MYNAH, PIED STARLING, *Sturnus c. contra* (Linnaeus) (Pl. XXXVII)

G. Elsterstar; F. Martin pie; D. Voor-Indische Spreeuw

DISTRIBUTION: Northern India, Nepal, Assam.
DESCRIPTION: Outer tip of beak whitish-horn and base reddish. Facial mask of bare skin yellowish, and eyes surrounded by reddish skin. A large pale grey facial patch surrounds mask and extends to lower cheeks. Upper parts, remaining head colouring, chin, throat and upper chest all black, except for a long, narrow wing bar across scapulars. Remaining under parts pale grey, shading to whitish on under tail coverts. Beak and feet yellow; iris brown. Length: about 9 in. (22·9 cm). Sexes alike, except that female is smaller.

Pied Mynah, *Sturnus c. contra*

SUBSPECIES: In Indonesia there is a fairly common sub-species, *Sturnus contra jalla*, the Jalla Starling. This bird very closely resembles *S. c. contra*, but irides are yellow and there is more extensive naked skin around the eyes. As these birds chiefly feed on insects which are harmful to agri-culture, they are highly regarded and protected by the Indonesians.
In all areas where there are meadows with cattle, and in tilled fields, flights of these birds are to be found. They show a preference for worms, cockchafer grubs, beetles and insects, which they find in abundance around cattle. With their sharply pointed beaks they make openings in the ground in order to trace cockchafer grubs. Unlike other starlings, they do not nest in the hollows of trees, but prefer to seek a high palm tree and build a nest, conical in shape and bulkily built from rice stalks and grass. The tip of the cone is against the trunk of the tree and its base lies athwart and has an entrance. From early morning until late at night these birds are always busy; only in the heat of midday do they seek a sheltered spot amongst the dense green foliage. Towards their breeding season they depart in pairs and, while searching for food, the male bird will utter his mel-odious whistle, at the same time lifting his wings up and making deep bows.
The species form was first exhibited in London in 1871. Later these starlings were spasmodically imported. As cage birds they would certainly be very attractive if they did not make such a mess. They throw all their food about the cage, and, if they get the chance, they will upset the bath or drinking trough. Any cage in which they are kept must be spacious, and the food and drink containers must be firmly fixed on.
Starlings are sociable and affectionate birds and they will attach themselves to their keeper and greet him with a whistle. Their best place is in an aviary, where they live on a friendly basis with other different kinds of bird. They accept worms, maggots and insects, but not always mealworms. Their diet should include insectivorous food, pieces of raw meat, raisins and all kinds of fruit. They are hardy birds which can be kept out of doors both in winter and summer, provided they have overnight accommodation.

BLACK-NECKED STARLING, BLACK-COLLARED STARLING, *Sturnus nigricollis* (Paykull)

G. Schwarzhalsstar; F. Martin à cou noir; D. Zwarthals-Spreeuw

DISTRIBUTION: South China, Burma and Thailand.
DESCRIPTION: The large bare facial area shows two colours; reddish skin forms a slender mask before and behind eyes, with yellowish skin underneath. A broad black collar surrounds neck down to nape and upper chest. Division on chest soft and slightly blended rather than sharp. Head, a band under collar on nape, and all remaining under parts white. Upper parts black, except for white tips on tail and many of wing feathers. Rump white. Beak black; feet and legs horn-coloured. Length: about 11 in. (27·9 cm). Sexes alike, except that female is slightly smaller.
These birds are common and always in the vicinity of people. In addition to insects, they eat all kinds of remains from the table. They utter their song, which consists of the weirdest sounds, either on the ground or high in a tree, with feathers puffed out, wings hanging and beaks wide open, while their bodies are stiffly erect. This starling will often bring his beak in front of his breast and then make bowing movements. In addition to a number of scolding and murmuring sounds, he can also produce flute-like notes. A single bird soon becomes tame and imitates a number of sounds, and also learns to speak a few words. The care of this bird is the same as for other members of the family.
What may be a first breeding was reported by A. E. Hall in *Avicultural Magazine*, Vol. 76, 1970, pp. 6–8.

Genus: Leucopsar

ROTHSCHILD'S GRACKLE, BALI MYNAH, *Leucopsar rothschildi* (Stresemann)

G. Bali Star; F. Martin de Rothschild; D. Bali Spreeuw

DISTRIBUTION: Confined to the island of Bali in Indonesia.
DESCRIPTION: The heavy body, pleasing proportions, and thick graceful crest make this the most beautiful of the mynahs. The marvellous crest is composed of many slender,

1 in. (2·5 cm) long, supple white feathers, starting at forehead and extending back to lower nape. Those on back of head and upper nape are particularly long. Colouring snow-white with black on a broad tip of tail and on ends of flight feathers. Bare facial mask of blue surrounds eyes and tapers to a point on sides of neck. Thick beak bluish-grey with dull yellowish-horn on tip. Feet and legs bluish-grey. Length: about 10 in. (25·4 cm). Sexes alike, except that females are somewhat smaller and feathers of crest are about 1 in. (2·5 cm) long.

In the wild the birds congregate in flights of about 20 in the melon trees, the fruit of which they eat; as a result, they dirty their snow-white plumage. While the troop of birds eats, one bird keeps watch, and lets forth shrill cries in the event of the slightest danger.

In 1912 Dr. E. Stressemann discovered this singularly beautiful starling. It was not until 1928 that 5 specimens were sent to Europe and came into the possession of Mr. A. Ezra. Sexes looked alike, but from their behaviour the males could soon be recognised. The pairing takes place with a skipping movement, by which the crest is erected. At Mr. Ezra's home a pair were placed in a separate aviary and nested the same year on several occasions, but every time the eggs disappeared after the birds had sat on them for about a week. In 1931 one young bird was reared. In that year the female had already laid 3 eggs on 4 occasions, and these had been placed under a blackbird and a thrush. However, just when they were due to hatch, all of them came to grief. The birds were allowed to keep their fifth lay, and after about a fortnight the nest-boxes were inspected. One box contained the male bird dead and the other the female with one young bird. As she was extremely timid and would not eat if anyone was near, the mealworms were placed in a large trough in the aviary and when there was no one about the female fed them to her young.

This fine species is rare even in its wild state and could become extinct. While some protection is given to the species by a reserve within its natural habitat, a species with such a limited distribution presents a challenge to conservation workers and aviculturists to perpetuate it. It is difficult to keep in aviculture. See article by D. T. Spilsbury in *Foreign Birds*, Vol. 35, No. 5, Spet./Oct. 1969, p. 70. Some zoos have specimens and there is a long breeding report from the manager of the San Diego Zoological Gardens in the USA.

Genus: Acridotheres

COMMON MYNAH, *Acridotheres t. tristis* (Linnaeus)
G. Hirtenstar; F. Martin triste; D. Herdermaina
(Pl. XXXVII)

DISTRIBUTION: Afghanistan, India, introduced into South Africa, Australia, New Zealand and Malaysia.

DESCRIPTION: Sexes alike. There is a bare facial mask of yellowish wattle skin. A black hood extends down to mantle and upper chest. White occurs in a large wing patch, tips of tail, under tail coverts and vent area. Remaining areas bright rufous with a darker brown on wings and tail. Iris reddish; beak, feet and legs yellowish. Length: about 9 in. (22·9 cm).

SUBSPECIES: *A. t. melanosternus*, from Ceylon, is darker than the nominate race. It appears almost completely black, with the exception of one wine-red area, which lies over abdomen. The female is very much smaller.

In its habitat the Common Mynah is generally near human settlements. It is numerous in meadows where cattle graze,

Common Mynah, *Acridotheres t. tristis*

and also frequents parks and gardens. Constantly bobbing their heads, the mynahs move over the land with hasty steps, looking for food. They do not bore holes in the ground, but pick grasshoppers and insects out of the grass and sometimes off the cattle themselves. At night the birds congregate in high trees to sleep, sometimes in the centre of a village, and while gathering together they create a tre-

mendous noise. They make all kinds of remarkable sounds, which hardly ever merit the name 'song'; in doing this they touch their breasts with their beaks.

They make their nests in houses, in holes in walls and in nest-boxes which are especially hung up for them. They bring grass, stalks, feathers and fibres of plants to line the nests. Four to 5 greyish-blue eggs are laid. Young specimens, brought up by hand, become quite tame and sometime learn to speak a few words. Once they get used to a cage or an aviary they can safely be trusted to fly around. They will remain faithful to their home and will seek a regular roosting place in a high tree. This place will be fiercely defended against all intruders, no matter how large.

The birds breed successfully if they have a well-planted aviary entirely to themselves. A single specimen can live peaceably in a mixed aviary with non-related birds; a pair is intolerant of smaller birds and will soon kill them. If the aviary stands in a large garden, the birds may be allowed to fly around freely as soon as young have been hatched. One is thus freed from a great burden, for it is not easy to find sufficient living insects to feed to the birds and their young.

The first breeding result was obtained at the London Zoo in 1905 (*L.Z. Reports*, 1905). Another was reported in 1936 by R. Neunzig in Germany. The birds constructed their simple nest in a parakeet breeding box, the entrance of which was made a little larger. Five eggs were laid and 3 hatched after 15 days incubation. The female alone incubated them and left the nest every day for food. The male, however, began to carry food in as soon as the young had been hatched. All the other birds living in the aviary had to be removed after the male bird had killed some of them. After 3 weeks the first chick left the nest. It was two-thirds the size of its parents and could not fly. Its feet, however, were especially well developed, so that it could immediately clamber up into the branches. In addition to mealworms, the parents also fed it with ants' eggs.

All mynahs are inclined to panic quickly if they get frightened by anything. If one is being kept in a spacious cage, the top should be covered with stretched nylon gauze. The birds easily acclimatise themselves, and can be kept winter and summer in an outside aviary, provided they have good sleeping accommodation.

BROWN MYNAH, *Acridotheres f. fuscus* (Wagler)
G. Braunmaina; F. Martin brun; D. Bruine Maina

DISTRIBUTION: India, Burma, Malaysia, Java and the Celebes Islands.
DESCRIPTION: Head, wings and tail dusky greyish-black with darker shadings. A small tuft of feathers forms a bristly cushion on the forehead. White occurs on a large wing patch and tip of tail. Irides bright yellowish-straw; feet and legs reddish; beak horn-coloured. Length: about 9 in. (22·9 cm). Sexes alike, but female a little smaller.
In its habits the Brown Mynah is identical to the Common Mynah. It occurs more frequently in mountainous areas. Its food consists of fruit, seeds and insects. It nests in hollows of trees and in the roofs of houses.
It first appeared in the Artis Zoological Gardens, Amsterdam, in 1854, and some years later in other European collections. The first breeding result was obtained in the Zoological Gardens, Berlin, in 1893. A nest-box was used and both parents sat alternately on the 3 eggs, but only one young bird was reared.

BANK MYNAH, *Acridotheres ginginianus* (Latham)
(Pl. XXXVII)
G. Ufermaina; F. Martin de rivage; D. Oevermaina
DISTRIBUTION: India.
DESCRIPTION: This species is similar to the Common Mynah but the hood does not extend so far on nape, nor does it occur on neck, throat or chest. *Male.* Main colouring dusky-grey; rump and upper tail coverts somewhat lighter; lower

Bank Mynah, *Acridotheres ginginianus*

tail coverts yellowish-grey, and breast and middle of abdomen covered with a red sheen. Head black. Wings grey and black, with a green suffusion. Tail black with a yellowish-grey tip. Lower wing coverts yellowish-grey. Irides red; naked ring around eye reddish. Beak orange with yellow tip; legs and feet yellowish-orange. Length: 8½ in. (21·6 cm). *Female.* Smaller and duller in colour than male.

GOLDEN-CRESTED GRACKLE, GOLDEN-CRESTED MYNAH, *Ampeliceps coronatus* Blyth
G. Kronenatzel; F. Mainate couronné; D. Goudkuifmaina
DISTRIBUTION: India, Burma, Thailand, Khmer, Laos, Vietnam and northern Malaysia.
DESCRIPTION: The shape and many characteristics are similar to those of the Greater India Hill Mynah, except for head, smaller size, and the large wing patch being yellow instead of white. The rest of the plumage, except head, is black, with glossy blue and green reflections. Beak orange-horn; feet and legs yellowish-orange. Extensive bare orbital

These birds occur in large numbers, especially around railway stations. They walk busily along the platforms among passengers and their baggage, picking up remains of food. They are also to be seen on meadow lands among cattle or on refuse heaps, where they find all sorts of food, including beetles and insects which are also attracted to the refuse. They make their nests under bridges and in holes which they themselves carve out of river banks. Their eggs are laid on a nest of stalks and feathers. They walk in a typical erect attitude, with short, quick steps. When frightened, they hold themselves stiffly upright.
A first breeding was reported from the London Zoo in 1909 (*L.Z. Reports*, 1909).

CHINESE CRESTED MYNAH, CRESTED MYNAH, CHINESE JUNGLE MYNAH, *Acridotheres cristatellus* (Linnaeus)
G. Haubenmaina; F. Martin huppé; D. Kuifmaina

DISTRIBUTION: South China, Formosa, Burma, Hainan, Vietnam, Laos.
DESCRIPTION: Head black with green sheen, and a crest on forehead. Otherwise colouring is greyish-black lighter, on under parts. Under tail coverts have white tips. Wings black with brownish sheen. Tail black with fine white tips. Iris golden-yellow; beak yellow, reddish at base; feet and legs orange-yellow. Length: 10½ in. (26·7 cm). Sexes alike, except that female has smaller crest.
These birds fly in small flights, chiefly in low-lying land. They visit meadows where cattle are grazing in order to find an abundance of insects. In addition to insects, many of which they catch on the animals themselves, they eat seeds, berries and fruit. They make their nests in various hollows, not only those in trees, but also under roofs, in walls and banks. The nest is an untidy, slovenly construction of grass, straw, leaves and feathers.
Mynahs, in particular, may be allowed to fly around, not only when there are young in their nests, but also if they have first been kept for a considerable time as cage-birds and have become attached to their keepers.
In 1840 the first of these birds came to Artis Zoological Gardens, Amsterdam. They are exceptionally lively birds and during the breeding season are dangerous to all other smaller birds. Their song has a throaty sound, flute-like and chirping, now and then alternated with a couple of melodious flute-like notes.
First breeding results were obtained in London by J. Weiner. In addition to insectivorous mixture the birds eat mealworms, all sorts of fruit cut up into small pieces, and bread soaked in milk. They like to bathe and enjoy it enormously. They can be kept during the winter in an outside aviary, provided their night quarters are heated.

Genus: Ampeliceps

patch yellowish. Bright glossy yellow covers chin, throat, upper part of head down to lower nape. Black behind eyes divides the two yellow areas. A yellow crest on forehead is short and bristly. Length: about 8 in. (20·3 cm). Sexes alike, but female has shorter crest and less yellow on throat. Young birds lack golden-yellow colouring on head.
These birds occur in small groups of 8–10 in the dense woods and bushland. Their nests are difficult to find, as they breed in the hollows of very high trees. They also occur in dry regions that are less densely covered with bushes. Their main food consists of insects, which they catch on the wing. In their general behaviour they are like their relations, the mynahs. In 1905 the first specimen arrived in the Berlin

Zoological Gardens.

The care of these birds is much the same as that for mynahs. Insectivorous food, fruit and insects must be provided. Their winter quarters need warmth. They are to be recommended as cage birds, as they become very tame and soon learn to fly freely about the house.

The species is a good aviary bird and has successfully nested in captivity.

One successful breeding was recorded by W. R. Partridge in *Avicultural Magazine*, Vol. 71, 1965, pp. 129–9.

Genus: Sarcops

COLETO MYNAH, BALD-HEADED STARLING, *Sarcops c. calvus* (Linnaeus) (Pl. XXXIX)
G. Kahlkopfstar; F. Sarcops chauve; D. Kaalkopspreeuw

DISTRIBUTION: Philippine Islands, with one race in nearby Sulu Islands.

DESCRIPTION: Large bare facial patch extends back to hind-crown, lower cheeks and down to lower beak. A fine line of black borders rear area of facial skin. A narrow feathered black line runs down centre of head and across very narrow forehead. Wattle skin variable in colour, normally chalky-flesh, but frequently blushing to deep pink. During illness or cold weather all traces of pink may vanish and a feint trace of blue may occasionally show in the white. Upper parts dark silver-grey. Sides silver-grey. A large crescent of shiny silver follows on nape, extending down to upper mantle. Another large area of shiny silver starts on middle of back and extends to upper tail coverts and lower sides. The silver becomes intense on rump and upper tail coverts. Remaining plumage, except for a concealed white patch at base of wing, black, glossy in all areas except under tail coverts. Iris reddish-brown; beak, feet and legs black. Length: 11 in. (27·9 cm), including 1 in. (2·5 cm) beak and 4½ in. (11·4 cm) rounded and slender tail. Sexes alike, except that female is somewhat smaller. When resting, Coleto Mynahs frequently fluff the silver feathers on nape. These are tree-birds, which inhabit the dense woods and forests in great numbers and feed on insects and fruit. For their nests they make use of the abandoned nests of woodpeckers.

They were first imported to England in 1905, after being caught on the coast of Mindanao. A single specimen can be kept with other birds, particularly if it is a female, but a pair must be kept in a separate aviary, because all other birds are driven away as soon as the Mynahs want to start nesting. Insectivorous mixture, bread soaked in milk, with mealworms and fruit, form their daily diet. Variety should be provided by way of fruit. They show a preference for oranges and raisins. They will make a nest of hay, twigs and feathers in a breeding box for large parrots. During both winter and summer the birds can remain in an aviary. They enjoy taking baths and are always lively.

The Coleto cannot really be called beautiful, but it is handsome and very interesting in a strange way. It has a ringing bell-like call note and can be taught to talk if it is trained while still young. It has a curious ventriloquial character to its voice.

Coletos which were owned by H. J. Bates and R. L. Busenbark were easily frightened at first, but gradually gained a remarkable confidence in their aviaries. Of their own volition and with no training, they became tame enough to accept food offered by hand, even although they were already adults. One pair which they owned went to nest on an enclosed patio through which many visitors passed daily. They were removed to other quarters when they became too aggressive for the other birds. They chose a cockatiel nest-box which unfortunately was already occupied After they nearly destroyed the occupants, they selected a nail keg and spent a considerable amount of time working on both nests. Nesting material was not abundant and so they supplemented it with leaves from privet shrubs. Another coleto which they had shared an aviary with Greater India Hill and Java Hill Mynahs, and harmlessly dominated all of them.

Genus: Gracula

BY H. J. BATES AND R. L. BUSENBARK

There are two species of the genus *Gracula*. One of these species, the Hill Mynah, *G. intermedia*, has ten subspecies and it is in this species that the very popular pet, talking mynahs (or Grackles) are found.

Not many of the talking mynahs are kept as aviary birds with breeding as the goal, but they have been successfully reared in captivity a few times after many failures. Mynahs are excellent as pets or as aviary birds. Tame and talking birds continue to talk and usually remain tame after they have been put into aviaries; and they are therefore perfect as outstanding pets of great personality. If, however, they start nesting operations, they become aggressive to other birds and to their human keepers.

Young birds of all subspecies have taut, whitish, and underdeveloped wattles and no gloss on their black plumage. Beaks are pale. At about a year, the wattles are bright yellow with bulbous swellings on the nape starting to develop into long flaps. Females never develop flaps as long as the males.

CEYLON MYNAH, CEYLON GRACKLE, *Gracula ptilogenys* (Blyth)
G. Dschungelatzel; F. Mainate de Ceylon; D. Ceylon Beo

DISTRIBUTION: Sri Lanka.

DESCRIPTION: *Male.* Upper parts black with green sheen. Head black with purple sheen. Yellow wattle is confined to flap on nape; facial areas are devoid of wattle. Large flight feathers have a white spot. Tail black with purple sheen. Iris greyish-white; beak orange-red, black at the base; feet and legs yellow. Length: 9½ in. (24 cm). *Female.* Smaller, duller in colour, and yellow wattle smaller.

These birds dwell especially in wooded regions and in the forests of the humid zone as far as the mountains at heights of 6,000 ft (1,800 m) above sea level. Now and then they also occur in the dryer regions, but never in large numbers.

They are often seen in pairs. They are restless and are wide-ranging over great distances. They are fast on the wing and the beat of their wings produces a musical buzzing tone. Their food consists mainly of fruits which they find in abundance high in the trees of the dense forests. They nest in the hollows of trees, mostly very high trees.

These birds are often kept in a cage and looked upon as members of the family, in the same way as larger parrots. If sufficient attention is paid to the bird it will learn to talk well, but one must avoid giving it too much to eat, as it becomes fat and very soon gives up its talking and whistling. A domesticated bird soon learns to fly around the room, and will return to its cage when given a whistled signal. A disadvantage, however, is their liquid excretion, and so the cage has to be kept exceptionally clean.

Although the bird will eat everything it is offered, preference should be given to an insectivorous mixture, bread soaked in milk, mealworms and pieces of fruit. These birds die early if not fed correctly. They do quite well in an aviary, but become less tame and do not learn to speak, only imitating the sounds they pick up from other birds. They can winter quite well in an unheated room.

LESSER INDIAN HILL MYNAH, SOUTHERN HILL MYNAH, *Gracula religiosa indica* (Cuvier)
G. Kleiner Beo; F. Petit Mainate; D. Kleiner Beo

DISTRIBUTION: Southern India and Sri Lanka.

DESCRIPTION: Head smaller than *G. r. intermedia*; beak more slender; the wattle difference is the most notable variation. A wide separation occurs on nape, and two ends turn forward towards top of crown showing two bold U-shaped figures when seen from above. Instead of a triangular partial separation on side of face, the black feathers completely divide a small wattled area below eyes. Length: about 9½ in. (24 cm).

This subspecies is not considered to be a good talking pet. It has less ability.

These birds occur especially in the humid lowlands covered with bamboo and in forests, and on the damp mountain slopes where they congregate in colonies. The pairs or family groups wander about in the vicinity of their nests. Their flight is swift and powerful and causes a melodious buzzing note which can be heard a great distance away. Birds of a particular flight keep contact with each other by means of shrill whistling notes alternated by husky throat sounds. These birds often approached the neighbourhood of human settlements and do not seem to be shy. They have an inquisitive nature and follow with the greatest interest from a branch in a tree everything that takes place beneath them. Sometimes they will take flight with a shrill cry and return after a short flight back to their perches.

They nest as high as possible in the hollows of trees. A few leaves and straws form the layer upon which lie their 2 blue eggs, covered with brown spots.

These birds were first brought to the Artis Zoological Gardens in Amsterdam, in 1945. They have been bred by B. Bertram as reported in *Avicultural Magazine*, 75, 1969, pp. 173–6.

INDIAN MYNAH, NEPAL HILL MYNAH, ASSAM HILL MYNAH, *Gracula religiosa intermedia* (Hay)
G. Mittelbeo; F. Mainate intermédiaire, Béo intermédiaire; D. Beo

DISTRIBUTION: The hills of the southern Himalayas, northern India, Burma and southern China.

DESCRIPTION: Large wing patch white, and all other plumage black with glossy reflections of green, blue, and purple. Feet and legs yellow. Wattles yellow; beak bright orange fading to yellow on tip. Feathers on top of head are velvety

in texture. Wattles start in broad area below eyes and extend backwards covering most of lower facial area. They become narrow on nape, and two sides do not quite meet at back. Two loose flaps grow from wattle on hind crown, but these flaps are highly variable depending on age. A small triangle of velvety-black feathers interrupts wattle behind and below eye. Length: about 11 in. (28 cm) including 3¾ in. (9 cm) squared tail.

Flights of 25–30 of these birds can regularly be seen in hot and quite arid areas with patches of thick woodland. They are sedentary birds, preferring the plains. They feed mainly on fruit, but will take nectar from flowers and eat insects. They sing mostly in the morning and the evening, producing a variety of sounds, sometimes soft and gurgling, sometimes raucous, and sometimes very high pitched and flute-like. Their swift flight is accompanied by a melodious humming.

They nest in holes abandoned by woodpeckers, enlarging them and filling them with leaves, grass and feathers, as a base on which they lay 2 greenish-blue eggs, speckled with brown spots.

They seem to be even more successful at imitating sounds and words than the Lesser Indian Hill Mynah.

They were first imported to London Zoo in 1859. A few aviculturists have succeeded in reproducing this subspecies;

Indian Mynah, *Gracula religiosa intermedia*

a very varied selection of live food is essential for success. These birds must have an opportunity to bathe every day. They can winter in an unheated aviary but it is better to give them some heat in winter. Any which have become used to living in a cage should be housed in an aviary during part of the summer, in order to give them the chance of exercise and to avoid their becoming too fat. This can prevent many minor illnesses with harmful consequences, such as liver infections.

GREATER HILL MYNAH, JAVAN HILL MYNAH, NORTHERN HILL MYNAH, *Gracula r. religiosa* (Linnaeus)
G. Grosser Beo; F. Mainate religieux, Béo religieux; D. Grote Beo   (Pl. XL)

DISTRIBUTION: Malaysia, Sumatra, Java, Bali and neighbouring islands.

DESCRIPTION: Plumage is mainly black, purple sheen on head, neck, shoulders, back and abdomen, while the other parts carry a greenish sheen. Irides reddish-brown; wattles on face, yellow. Beak, orange-red with yellow point; feet and legs yellow. Length: 12 in. (30 cm).

G. r. peninsularis is also called the Greater India Hill Mynah. It is from the north-eastern peninsular area of India. It is about 1 in. (2·5 cm) smaller and beak is more slender. The wattle flaps are less broad, and the area of black feathers behind and below eyes is nearly rectangular because the opening behind eyes is broader.

Hill Mynahs live in forests, preferring rocky regions. They feed on insects and fruit. They live in pairs, nesting in holes in trees. Their voice is more distinct than that of parrots, and their repertoire is often very wide: they easily learn to imitate.

A tame bird will usually sleep in its cage, but it is easy to teach it to fly freely. It eats a great deal and rapidly dirties the cage, so it is more ritable for a large bird-room.

Most zoos possess a Hill Mynah, which forms a considerable attraction for visitors both young and old. The bird imitates the human voice so well that visitors think another human being is calling to them. When housed in a cage, the Javan Hill Mynah will struggle up to the bars if you talk to it or whistle a tune; it seems to be trying to show that it is listening carefully. The best time to teach it is in the evening, when the bird is quiet and half-asleep. To begin, one must repeat simple words and phrases, always employing the same tone.

A bird in a cage will often begin by imitating the noises or sounds which it hears frequently during the day, and to which the human beings never pay any attention. A specimen like this likes to be coaxed and to eat tasty morsels from the hand. It should be given a general insectivorous mixture, various kinds of fruit, mealworms, and from time to time a little raw meat or a young mouse.

Greater Hill Mynah, *Gracula r. religiosa*

It is difficult to distinguish the sexes, but the wattles seem to be a little smaller in the females, and their colouring is less bright.

Gracula religiosa have been bred at Keston Foreign Bird Farm, as reported in *Avicultural Magazine*, Vol. 63, 1957, pp. 160–2 and *Avicultural Magazine*, Vol 64, 1958, pp. 38–9.

FAMILY: ORIOLIDAE

Old World Orioles

Most of the Old World or true orioles show brilliant golden yellow and shiny black as their principal colouring. The name 'oriole' is from a latin word which means yellow, and it has also been applied to many yellow and black New World Icterids or Hangnests which thereby causes confusion. The two groups are not at all closely related.

There are twenty-four species of forest-dwelling Old World Orioles centred mainly in Africa and Asia, but also extending into Europe and the Australia–New Guinea areas. Some are migratory. Those eight species from Australia and New Guinea are not important in worldwide aviculture because they are never available on any commercial basis, and so they will not be described. The single species which ranges into Europe also occurs in Africa and India. When available, the export point is usually India. Two Philippine species, the Isabella Oriole and the White-lored Oriole, are too rare to become available to aviculture. There are also four species of Figbirds (*Sphecotheres*) in Australia and a few islands in that general area. These are closely related but are not available to bird fanciers.

Orioles are wonderful aviary birds and reasonably good songbirds. They are easily acclimatised to domestic diets, and the acclimatisation period is usually very short. The diet is the simple standard softbilled diet plus nectar. Orioles consume a greater percentage of fruits than most large softbills, and this acceptability of inert foods is the most important single factor in their easy acclimatisation.

Orioles are peaceful for the most part. The writers have frequently mixed them with bulbuls and tanagers which are very mild in disposition and much smaller in size. Many birds which are of similar size are, in fact, too dominant and aggressive to be included with orioles.

Most orioles are heavy-bodied with broad chests and large thick beaks. Tails are broad, squared, and medium in length. The beaks are usually a surprising shade of pink. Colours of most males are sharply divided and very intensely vivid. The pattern is usually very simple. Females are not as colourful as males. Full colour development often takes a long time.

GOLDEN ORIOLE, *Oriolus oriolus*

DISTRIBUTION: Europe, Africa, the Middle East and India.
DESCRIPTION: *Male.* This species has more yellow than most species; except for a very slight elliptical black mask surrounding the eyes, the entire head is yellow. All under parts and upper parts down to the wings are brilliant golden-yellow as also are the back, rump and upper tail coverts. The two central tail feathers are black. The bases of the other tail feathers are also black, but yellow is the predominant colour. The wings are shiny black with a yellow bar near the base and bold yellow edges to many of the inner wing feathers. The irides are dark brownish-red, the beak is pink and the feet and legs are bluish-grey. Length: about 10 in. (25 cm). *Female.* Very dull with soft olive-yellow above and darker brownish-olive-yellow on the wings and tail. Under parts are dusky olive-whitish-yellow with indistinct olive spots. The beak is dark maroon-pink. Immature birds are like females but have less soft shades and rather bolder spots.

The subspecies *kundoo* which occurs in the eastern areas of Europe and Asia as well as India is brighter yellow and has slightly more black in the eye areas. This race is popularly called the Indian Golden Oriole, and the nominate race is usually called the European Oriole.

AFRICAN GOLDEN ORIOLE, *Oriolus auratus*

DISTRIBUTION: Africa in a broad belt across the continent above the Equator for the nominate race and another broad belt from east to west north of South Africa.

DESCRIPTION: Both races are similar to *O. oriolus* and both are brighter than the European subspecies which occurs in Africa. Irides are brighter red, and the black mask area before and behind the eye is more extensive in both sexes. The yellow edges on the inner wing feathers are far more extensive and prominent in the male, and the black tail in the nominate race has yellow on the outer rims. The subspecies *notatus* has more yellow on the outer tail feathers. The female is somewhat brighter in colouring than the female of the European species, but she is still dull olive-yellow compared to the male. The dull yellowish edges to the wings are more sharply contrasting to the olive-slate which replaces the black of the male. Immature birds have bold spots on the breast and olive-grey masks to distinguish them from females.

This species, like all African orioles, is very seldom available.

BLACK-NAPED ORIOLE, *Oriolus ch. chinensis* Linnaeus (Pl. XVI)
G. Chinesischer Pirol; F. Loriot de Chine; D. Chinese Wielewaal

DISTRIBUTION: India, China, Burma, Sri Lanka, Thailand, Malaysia, Indonesia, Borneo, the Philippines, Andaman and Nicobar Islands, and many South Pacific islands.

DESCRIPTION: There are variations among the different subspecies; but, since relatively few subspecies will be available,

Black-naped Oriole, *Oriolus ch. chinensis*

only those subspecies from the export points will be described. Aviculturally, this is the most important species of the family and the most frequently available.

The handsomest race is the Philippine subspecies *chinensis*. This race appears to be bolder and a little larger in body than the other races which the writers have had.

Male. The velvety-black nape is particularly extensive covering all of the head back to the nape except the forehead. Only a relatively small crescent of bright yellow occurs across the forehead to the widely separated nostrils. The flight and shoulder feathers are velvety-black. Tail, the central feathers and the bases of the lateral feathers are black. All the remaining plumage, including all the small wing feathers to the bend of the wing and under wing coverts, is brilliant golden-yellow. The beak is thick, bold and pink in colour, the iris reddish-brown surrounded by a bare pink eye ring and the feet and legs are grey. Length: 10–11 in. (25–28 cm) including the large beak of 1¼ in. (3 cm) and the tail between 3–4 in. (7·5–10 cm). *Female.* Has dull slate in black areas and variable shades of dusky greenish-yellow in the other areas. These shades are brightest on the forehead, throat, and upper tail coverts. Under parts are slightly less bright and have slightly less of a greenish tinge. The back and wings are the duskiest with more of an olive shade. The divisions on the tail between black and yellow are not as sharp as they are in the male. The beak is darker pinkish-brown in the upper mandible.

The 2 races from Thailand are *diffusus* and *tenuirostris*. The latter is called the Slender-billed Oriole. It has a narrow black nape band continuing through the eyes and lores, a tinge of olive on the back, black and yellow on the secondary flights, and a far more slender bill than the above race. The subspecies *diffusus* has a broader black nape band than the Slender-billed Oriole, but it is not nearly as broad as in the Philippine race. The entire top of the head is yellow, and the extent of yellow in the secondary flights is about the same as in the Slender-billed subspecies. These 2 races are the most widespread members of the species and are also exported from India. The other Indian race, *invisus*, is like the Slender-billed Oriole.

The subspecies *maculatus*, from Singapore, Indonesia, and Borneo is smaller and has more black on the secondary flights than the races in India and Thailand but less than the Philippine race.

Immature birds have streaky dark spots on the under parts and olive-brown in place of the black areas. On some races the black nape is totally missing in youngsters.

INDIAN BLACK-HEADED ORIOLE, *Oriolus xanthornus*

DISTRIBUTION: India, Sri Lanka, Burma, Thailand, Sumatra, northern Malaysia, and some islands near Borneo.

DESCRIPTION: Black hood covers the head down to the mantle and forms a broad V-shaped area on the breast. Many of the black wing feathers have patches of yellow and yellow edges. The amount of yellow also varies in the different races. The beak is pink, iris dark red, and feet and legs are grey. *Female.* Patterned like males but the plumage is much duller.

Immature birds have greyish-white under parts with dark streaky spots and a greenish tinge on the upper parts. The black head shows yellowish on the forehead and dull yellowish streaks on the crown and nape. Length: 9–10 in. (23–35 cm).

FAMILY: CORVIDAE

BY H. J. BATES AND R. L. BUSENBARK

Jays, Magpies, Pies, Magpie Jays, Cissas

This large family of twenty-six genera and a hundred species contains many very colourful and fascinating birds, most of which are exceptionally hardy and long-lived. Only the cissas among the more attractive species are difficult to transfer to artificial diets. Separate instructions for these will be given under the description of the species.

The food for the other members is the simple insectivorous diet, supplemented by raw meat and live food. They also enjoy mice and small birds as a part of the diet, but these are not essential. They adapt quickly to aviary life. Most are very aggressive to related species and cannot be kept with smaller birds. Their personalities are often amusing, and with a little patience many individuals become tame. They are very intelligent and curious about everything.

Many of the members of this family have long tails, which add gracefulness to their large bodies, large heads, large thick beaks, and strong feet and legs.

In most species sexes are alike.

LANCEOLATED JAY, BLACK-THROATED JAY, *Garrulus lanceolatus* Vigors

G. Strichelhaher; F. Geai strié; D. Strepengaai

DISTRIBUTION: Himalayan Mountain Range.
DESCRIPTION: Head black; throat black with white stripes. Upper parts grey; back has red tinting. Under parts dark wine-red, greyer at upper breast, with white stripes. Wings grey and black; coverts and vent region white. Flights blackish-brown with white transverse stripes. Tail greyish-blue with black transverse stripes and a white tip, in front of which is a broad black band. Irides black; beak greenish horn-colour, with black base; feet and legs lead-grey. Length: 12 in. (30·5 cm).

Lanceolated Jay, *Garrulus lanceolatus*

Lanceolated Jays dwell in the Western Himalayas in open woods, on hills covered with undergrowth, and where groups of trees and settlements alternate. High in isolated trees the birds build nests of twigs, which they sometimes line with plant fibres and grass stalks. They eat fruit, seeds, acorns and all kinds of human food refuse which they find around the houses. They build storehouses where they keep supplies of acorns, which form their chief food during the winter months. They steal eggs and also plunder the nests of their related species in an aviary, so that they have to be kept in pairs or with large birds.

In 1897 they were kept in the Zoological Gardens of Amsterdam and London, and in 1885 in Berlin. They soon become acclimatised and can remain in an outside aviary during the winter.

Breeding results have often been obtained. Mr. D. Goodwin, of England, gives a comprehensive report on this in the *Avicultural Magazine,* No. 5, 1954. Together the birds build their nest high in a tree or bush, and the female remains sitting for 2 days before she lays her 3–4 eggs. She is fed by the male. Incubation lasts about 16 days. The female sits on

the nest alone and only leaves it to bathe and to fly around a little. After the eggs have been hatched the female becomes extremely aggressive. Both parents feed the young with large quantities of ants' eggs and mealworms. Many other insects, butterflies, caterpillars, and some red meat are also eaten. After 3 weeks the youngsters fly out of the nest. In the first few days they remain close to the nest and only start flying after about 4 days. The young resemble the older birds, but are a little paler in colour; the bill and feet are a light flesh-colour.

PILEATED JAY, PILEATED WOOD JAY, *Cyanocorax c. chrysops* (Vieillot)

G. Kappenblauwrahe, Blaunackengrünhäher; F. Pie akahé; D. Witnekgaai

DISTRIBUTION: Brazil, Bolivia, Paraguay, Uruguay, Argentina.
DESCRIPTION: Crown has a plushy cap in the form of a large tuft, longer on forehead than mid-crown and longest on hind crown. Plushy cap, face, other head areas, throat and large bib black. Bright patch above eye turquoise and cobalt; another patch below eye cobalt; a large patch near base of lower mandible purplish-cobalt. Nape frosty-turquoise shading to cobalt on mantle. This is followed by dull blackish-cobalt to upper tail coverts. Tail deeper, somewhat glossy, blackish-cobalt with bold whitish-buff ends to feathers. Upper tail coverts and under parts below bid whitish-buff with a blend of yellowish-straw-colour. Underside of tail dull black with broader pale buff ends. Broader pale ends shown from underside are on outer tail feathers only, which are tucked under central tail feathers. Tail feathers very borad. Length: 12½ in. (31·8 cm) including the 5 in. (12·7 cm) tail and the black beak of 1⅛ in. (2·8 cm).
SUBSPECIES: The Blue-bearded Jay, *C. cyanopogon*, which is strictly a Brazilian race, has long been listed as a separate species, but Peters lists it as a subspecies. In only a few respects does it resemble *C. c. chrysops*. Under parts and upper tail coverts white. Pileated or plushy cap less pronounced on forehead but becomes a long lateral crest above

Pileated Jay, *Cyanocorax c. chrysops*

the eyes, ranging from 1¼–1½ in. (3·1–3·8 cm) long. Nape greyish-white. Back greyish-brown. Spots above and below eyes similar to those of other species, but patch near lower mandible smaller and duller. Beak also a little shorter.

Other subspecies vary in colouring and in the length and quality of the plushy head feathers.

These jays are true arboreal birds. They seek human company and, if caught, become completely tame in a few days and like to be caressed, when they close their eyes. Like jackdaws, they are deliberately mischievous, and will snatch a cigarette out of one's mouth and hide it. Placed in front of a mirror, they will start preening themselves, at the same time making chirruping bird sounds, which alternate with a couple of screeches. A single bird can easily be kept in a large sleeping cage and be let loose in the house or garden during the day. The usual food consists of soaked bread, maize, hard-boiled egg, fruit and meat, but, as a member of the household, the bird learns to eat most foods and generally thrives very well on them. Naturally the bird has the opportunity to catch all sorts of insects in the garden.

Already in 1864 these birds appeared in the Zoological Gardens in London and in Amsterdam. They cannot be kept in an aviary with smaller birds.

AMERICAN BLUE JAY, *Cyanocitta c. cristata* (Linnaeus)

G. Ostliche Blauhahe; F. Geai bleu d'Amerique, Geai bleu huppé; D. Amerikaanse Blauwe Gaai

DISTRIBUTION: Canada, eastern, central and middle-western USA.

DESCRIPTION: Most upper parts, including very shapely crest, bright soft blue. Wings and tail brighter and glossier, marked with narrow black bars. Tips of tail and bold wing patches white. Facial areas, including eyebrows, chin and throat, white. A bold black band encircles back of crest, facial area and lower throat. Beak and irides black. Under parts pale greyish-white. Length: 11–12 in. (27·9–30·5 cm), including the 4 in. (10·2 cm) tail.

American Blue Jay, *Cyanocitta c. cristata*

The American Blue Jay likes to live in open woods, often in the vicinity of human habitations, in gardens and orchards. The males quarrel over a female and, especially in spring, fight each other fiercely, uttering their cry of 'cake, cake'! They can also imitate the sounds of many other birds.

They live on nuts, berries, fruits and all kinds of insects and small animals. During the breeding season they plunder the nests of other birds. After breeding, they wander in large flocks, migrating to warmer regions in the south. In April

they return to their breeding territory. They nest in hardwood and fir trees and build their nests of twigs and leaf stalks. Sometimes the inside is plastered with mud, and twigs with thorns are attached on the outside. The 3–5 eggs are incubated by the female.

STELLER'S JAY, *Cyanocitta stelleri*

DISTRIBUTION: Alaska, Canada, western USA, Mexico and Central America.

DESCRIPTION: A handsome, robust species, with dusky colouring. Head, nape, back and under parts almost to abdominal areas dark blackish-blue. Below these areas the blue becomes brighter. Wings and tail narrowly barred with black and blue, which is the same shade, but glossy. Pale streaks occur on forehead and sometimes on throat in a more diffused shade. There are whitish spots above and sometimes below the eyes. The crest is luxurious and handsome. Beak, feet and legs black. Length: about 12–13 in. (30·5–33 cm).

Both species, which are closely related, are strong and intolerant of smaller birds, and can be kept in outside aviaries in winter and summer.

HUNTING CISSA, HUNTING MAGPIE, *Cissa c. chinensis* (Boddaert)

G. Grünkitta; F. Pirolle de Chine; D. Groene Kitta

DISTRIBUTION: India, Burma, Thailand, Malaysia, Indonesia.

DESCRIPTION: Main colouring pale soft green, darker on back, wings and tail. Reddish irides surrounded by bare reddish rings. A long, slender and tapering black mask is narrow on lores, expanding round eyes and extending narrowly back to nape. Flights deep chestnut-maroon.

Hunting Cissa, *Cissa c. chinensis*

Tertiaries tipped in pale greenish-white preceded by black. This feature provides a bold pattern down the lower central upper parts when wings are folded. Tail feathers have very pale greenish-white tips preceded in all but the central pair by black bands. Beak, legs and feet bright red-orange. Length: varying among subspecies from 13–15 in. (33–38 cm) with the tail ranging from 6–8 in. (15·2–20·3 cm).

Cissas are sometimes called Green Magpies. Their beautiful green colouring may fade to an equally or even more beautiful shade of soft blue in captivity. The tail is graduated, with the central feathers longer than the progressively shorter outer feathers. A recumbent crest is occasionally partially raised.

These birds live in trees and bushes in mountainous regions, where they search mainly for insects as food, mostly not too high above the ground. They sing in loud flute-like notes, but also emit unpleasant shrill screeches. They nest in trees and build basin-shaped nests out of stalks, leaves and fibres of plants.

They were first imported in 1861 to London, and at present they do not appear often in collections.

They are somewhat difficult to acclimatise as they are almost exclusively insect-eaters and do not quickly get used to artificial food. With the help of mealworms, young mice and living insects, they do gradually learn to acclimatise; then they eat insectivorous food, pieces of fruit, all kinds of seeds, such as sunflower, hemp and oats, and now and then some minced raw meat.

HOODED RACKET-TAILED TREE PIE, MAGPIE,
Crypsirina cucullata (Jerdon) (Pl. XIII)
G. Spatelschwanzelster; F. Pie bleue de l'Himalaya; D. Himalaya Ekster

DISTRIBUTION: Burma.
DESCRIPTION: Main colouring grey; head, wings and tail black. Over the neck runs a narrow light grey stripe. Lower tail coverts silver-grey. Beak, legs and feet black. Length: 12 in. (30·5 cm).

These birds appear in small groups, particularly in hilly and mountainous regions where open land alternates with woods. They usually remain in the trees, where they search for insects, tree-frogs and berries.

They are seldom seen in collections, and this is even more true of the Black Tree Magpie, *Crypsirina temia*, from Thailand, which is almost completely black, shot with bronze. The remarkable 6¾ in. (17·1 cm) tail has two central feathers, which gradually become broder towards the end and have the shape of a racket.

Crypsirina temia also occurs frequently in Indonesia, although never in the vicinity of human habitation. The birds are lively and soon become tame. A drawback, however, is that they are pugnacious and can only be kept together with a few large birds who are well able to defend themselves.

In addition to insectivorous mixture and mealworms, they must now and then be given some raw meat. During the winter months they must remain in heated quarters.

OCCIPITAL BLUE PIE, RED-BILLED BLUE PIE, *Urocissa erythrorhyncha occipitalis* (Blyth) (Pl. XIII)
G. Rotschnabelschweifkitta; F. Pie bleue occipitale; D. Roodsnavelkitta

DISTRIBUTION: India, the Himalayas, China, Burma, Thailand and neighbouring countries.
DESCRIPTION: Dominant colouring very rich cobalt or royal-blue on upper parts, with subordinate shades of grey. Upper tail coverts have blackish tips preceded by paler greyish-blue areas. Tips of wing feathers white, preceded by narrow black bands. This feature is more prominent on the tertiaries. Long graceful tail is strikingly graduated and is the same colour as wings and back, the blue being even more intense and glossy. Broad white tips on tail feathers are preceded by black on all but central pair. Tail flares broadly in flight, and central feathers are slightly curved near the end. Undersides of tail greyish, with broad bands of white preceded by black. A black hood covers head and neck down to mantle and onto a large bib. A broad streak of very pale bluish-white starts on centre of crown and extends to mantle. This bold wide stripe has whitish spots on outer

boundaries. Under parts below bib pale off-white with a shade of grey on thighs and ventral area. Iris of male golden-brown, of female golden-yellow. Large beak, legs

Occipital Blue Pie, *Urocissa erythrorhyncha occipitalis*

and feet bright red-orange. Length: 24–26 in. (61–66 cm) including tail of 16–17 in. (40·6–43·2 cm). Sexes are similar and difficult to distinguish, especially as some of the sub-species also vary just slightly enough for the difference to be mistaken as indicating the sex.

Occipital Blue Pies are wonderful aviary birds, being hardy and easily acclimatised. The diet is the simple one used for nearly all members of this family and the birds take to it even more readily than do most sthers. Highly active and colourfully flamboyant at all times, the birds are also considerably more peaceful than most others of similar size. In 1862 Occipital Blue Pies appeared in the London Zoological Gardens, and shortly afterwards in Amsterdam and Hamburg.

YELLOW-BILLED BLUE PIE, *Urocissa flavirostris*
G. Gelbnabelschweifkitta; F. Pie bleue à bec jaune; D. Geelsnavelkitta

DISTRIBUTION: India, Tibet, Burma, Vietnam.
DESCRIPTION: Yellow bill, more black and less white on head, and apple-green body colouring (darker above) are the main distinctions of this bird from *Urocissa erythrorhyncha occipitalis*.

The Yellow-billed Blue Pie is very rarely available. Towards the end of the nineteenth century they appeared in the Zoological Gardens of Amsterdam and London, and a little later in Berlin.

The birds are hardy and tolerate the climate excellently; they can be kept in an outside aviary in both summer and winter. In addition to receiving insectivorous food and fruit, they should also have raw meat and occasionally a mouse.

CEYLON BLUE MAGPIE, *Urocissa ornata* (Wagler)
G. Blaukitta; F. Pie bleue ornée; D. Blauwe Kitta

DISTRIBUTION: Sri Lanka.

DESCRIPTION: Body colouring rich cobalt or purplish-blue on both under and upper parts. Wings black on shoulders and on median and lesser coverts; rich chestnut, with no white tips, on all remaining wing feathers. A very extensive hood in a deeper chestnut shade covers head, neck, mantle and upper breast. A bold bare eye ring is dark red. Tail blue, the most exterior feathers dark bluish-black with white tips. Beak, feet and legs deep red-orange with brownish shade. Length: 18 in. (45·7 cm).

The Ceylon Blue Magpie lives in dense and inaccessible mountain forests and humid tropical woods on the hilltops. The birds never appear in large numbers, and are rather shy. They pass most of the day in the trees, living on insects, tree-frogs, hairy caterpillars and lizards. While eating they make a few twittering sounds, but at other times their harsh screeches can constantly be heard, and during rain they are at their noisiest. Their nests are well hidden amid foliage high in the trees, and are made of twigs and lined with moss. The 3–5 eggs are whitish and covered with brown spots.

APPENDIX

NOTES ON CERTAIN SPECIES IN VOLUME 1

As already summarised on page xii, the importation into Great Britain of all species of birds is controlled by the Ministry of Agriculture, Fisheries and Food or the Department of Agriculture for Scotland. However, certain birds dealt with in Volume 1 are classed as poultry (pheasants, quails, turkeys, etc.) and so a summary of the regulations for poultry and all other captive birds is given below.

Importation of Poultry and Hatching Eggs

The Poultry and Hatching Eggs (Importation) Order 1972, as amended, regulates the importation of all species of domestic fowls, turkeys, geese, ducks, guinea fowls, pheasants, partridges and quails. These include live exotic poultry and hatching eggs and day old chicks of all the aforementioned species and are similarly subject to licensing from countries other than Northern Ireland, The Republic of Ireland, the Channel Islands and the Isle of Man. European quail are also subject to Department of Environment regulations.

The landing in Great Britain of any poultry or hatching eggs from any country outside Great Britain other than Northern Ireland, the Republic of Ireland, the Channel Islands and the Isle of Man is prohibited unless the landing is authorised by a licence in writing issued by the Minister and containing such conditions (if any) as to quarantine, movement and any other matters relative to the prevention of the introduction and spread of disease as the Minister may think necessary. Each consignment must have a certificate of freedom from disease signed by a veterinary Officer duly authorised for the purpose by the government of the exporting country, in a form approved by the U.K. Minister.

As with other import laws, failure to comply with any condition of a licence is an offence against the Diseases of Animals Acts 1950 and 1975.

Licences

Before licences can be granted the Ministry must be satisfied as to the disease situation in the exporting country. Applications for such licences are therefore treated on merit. If granted these licences will specify veterinary and strict quarantine conditions, and licences are not normally issued to allow the import of adult poultry.

BIBLIOGRAPHY

Allen, Robert Porter. *Birds of the Carribbean.* New York, 1961.

Archer, G. F. and Godman. *Birds of British Somaliland and the Gulf of Aden.* London, 1937.

Austin, Oliver L., Jr. *Birds of the world.* London, 1961.

Avon, Dennis and Tilford, Tony. *Birds of Britain and Europe.* Poole, 1975.

Balen, J. H. van. *De dierenwereld van Insulinde in woord en beeld.* Deventer.

Bannerman, David A. *Birds of Tropical West Africa.* London, 1930–51.
Birds of West and Equatorial Africa, Vols. I–II. Edinburgh, 1951–53.
Birds of the British Isles, Vols. I–XII. Edinburgh, 1958.

Barruel, Paul. *Leven en gewoonten der Vogels.* Amsterdam.

Bates, H. J. and Busenbark, R. L. *Finches and Soft-billed Birds,* Jersey City, 1963.

Bates, Marston, *The Land and Wildlife of South America.* New York, 1964.

Bates, R. S. and Lowther, E. H. N. *Breeding Birds of Kashmir.* London, 1952.

Beebe, William. *Two Bird Lovers in Mexico.* London, 1905.

Berger, A. J. *Bird Study.* London.

Berndt, Dr. Rudolf and Meise, Dr. Wilhelm. *Naturgeschichte der Vogel.* Stuttgart, 1958.

Blake, Emmet Reid. *Birds of Mexico.* Chicago, 1953.

Bond, James. *Birds of the West Indies.* London, 1961.

Boosey, Edward, J. *Foreign Bird Keeping,* London.

Booth, Ernest Sheldon. *Birds of the West.* Escondido, California, 1960.

Brooksbank, Alec. *Foreign Birds for Garden Aviaries.* London.

Brown, Vinson and Weston, Henry G. *Handbook of California Birds.* Healdsburg, California, 1965.

Buchan, James. *The Bengalese Finch.* Bristol, 1976.

Burton, John A. and Risdon, D. H. S. *The Love of Birds.* London, 1975.

Butler, Dr. A. G. *Foreign Birds for Cage and Aviary.* London.

Campbell, A. J. *Nests and Eggs of Australian Birds.* Sheffield, 1901.

Campbell, Bruce. *The Dictionary of Birds in Colour.* London, 1974.

Cave, Col. Francis O. and Macdonald, J. D. *Birds of the Sudan.* London, 1955.

Cayley, Neville W. *What Bird is That?* Sydney, 1964.

Clancey, P. A. *Birds of Natal and Zululand.* London, 1964.

Delacour, J. and Mayr, Ernst. *Birds of the Philippines.* New York, 1946.

Delapchier, L. *Les Oiseaux du Monde.* Paris, 1959.

de Schauensee, R. M. *The Birds of Colombia.* Narberth, Pennsylvania, 1964.
Birds of South America. Philadelphia, 1966.

Dodwell, G. T. *Encyclopaedia of Canaries.* New Jersey, 1976.

Doeksen, D. I. J. *Erfelijkheid en fokkerhi bij hoenders.* Zwolle, 1953.

Dorst, Jean. *The Migration of Birds.* London, 1962.

Dost, Helmuth. *Handbuch der Vogelpflege und-züchtung.* Leipzig, 1954.

du Pont, John E. *Philippine Birds.* Delaware, 1971.

Engel, Fritz Martin. *Das grosse Buch der Vogel.* München.

Etchecopar, R. D. *The Birds of North Africa.* Edinburgh, 1967.

Fehringer, Prof. Dr. Otto. *Die Vogel Mitteleuropas,* Vols. I–III. Heidelberg, 1950.

Fisher, James and Peterson, Roger Tory. *The World of Birds.* London, 1964.

Flowers, M. L. and Flowers, F. *Canaries, their Care and Breeding.* Bird Haven, Reseda, California, 1941.
Finches, their Care and Breeding. Bird Haven, Reseda, California, 1943.

Gill, Leonard. *First Guide to South African Birds.* Cape Town, 1950.

Glenister, A. G. *The Birds of the Malay Peninsula, Singapore and Penang.* London, 1951.

Gooders, John. *Birds – an Illustrated Survey.* Middlesex, 1975.

Goodwin, Derek. *Crows of the World.* London, 1976.

Gould, J. *The Birds of Australia.* London, 1840–48.

Gray, Annie P. *Bird Hybirds.* Farnham Royal, Bucks. 1958.

Gruson, Edward S. *A Checklist of the Birds of the World.* London, 1976.

Haverschmidt, F. *Birds of Surinam.* London, 1968.

Henry, G. M. *A Guide to the Birds of Ceylon.* London, 1955.

Herklots, G. A. C. *The Birds of Trinidad and Tobago.* London, 1961.

Hopkinson, Dr. E. *Records of Birds Bred in Captivity.* London, 1926.

Howard, Len. *Vogels als huisgenoten.* Amsterdam, 1953.

Hudson, W. G. *Birds of La Plata:* Vols. I and II. London, 1920.

Hvass, Hans. *Vogels der wereld.* Amsterdam, 1963.

Immelmann, Dr. Klaus. *Australian Finches in Bush and Aviary.* Sydney, 1965.

Iredale, Tom. *Birds of New Guinea*. Melbourne, 1956.

Jardine, Sir W. *The Naturalist's Library*. Edinburgh, 1834.

Jessen, Hoyrup. *Tropical Birds in Colour*. Esbjerg, 1959.

Johnson, A. W. *Birds of Chile*. Buenos Aires, 1965.

Lack, David. *Enjoying Ornithology*. London, 1965.

Land, Hugh C. *Birds of Guatemala*. Pennsylvania, 1970.

Landsborough Thomson, Sir A. *A New Dictionary of Birds*. London, 1964.

Legendre, Marcel. *Oiseaux exotiques de cage*. Paris, 1958.
Oiseaux de cage. Paris, 1952.

Lekagul, Dr. Boonsong. *Bird Guide of Thailand*. Bangkok, 1968.

Lucanus, F. v. *Zugvogel und Vogelzug*.

Low, Rosemary. *Beginner's Guide to Birdkeeping*. London, 1974.
Mynah Birds. Beckenham, 1976.

Mackworth-Praed, C. W. and Grant, Captain C. H. B. *Birds of Eastern and North Eastern Africa*. London, 1957.
Birds of the Southern Third of Africa. London, 1962.
Birds of West-Central and Western Africa. London, 1970.

Makatsch, Dr. Wolfgang. *Die Vogel der Erde*. Berlin, 1954.

Mesch, W. *Das Ziergeflügel*. Berlin, 1956.

Moncrieff, P. *New Zealand Birds*. 3rd edition. Wellington.

Newton, Prof. Alfred. *A Dictionary of Birds*. London, 1896.

Newton, Ian. *Finches*. London, 1973.

Norgaard-Olesen, E. *Tanagers*, Vol. 1. Denmark, 1973.

Norgaard-Olesen, E. *Tanagers*, Vol. 2. Denmark, 1976.

Oliver, W. R. B. *New Zealand Birds*. Wellington, 1955.

Olrog, Claes Chr. *Las Aves Argentinas*. Tucuman, 1959.

Oordt, Dr. G. J. van. *Vogeltrek*. Leiden, 1960.

Orlando, Vittorio. *Ucelli Esotici*. Udine, 1959.

Otten, H. W. *Das Bilderbuch der Vogel. Taggreife. Was-Spechte, Eulen*. Hanover, 1963.

Oude Vrielink, A. G. M. *Erfelijkheidsleer*. Zwolle, 1951.

Pearson, T. G. (Ed.). *Birds of America*. New York, 1917.

Peters, J. L. *Check-list of Birds of the World*. Cambridge, Massachusetts, 1930–1977.

Peterson, R. T. *The Birds of North America*. Amsterdam, 1964.

Peterson, R. T., Mountfort, G. and Hollom, P. A. D. *Vogelgids*. Amsterdam, 1964.
Field Guide to the Birds of Britain and Europe, London, 1958.

Pough, Richard H. *Audubon Bird Guide*. New York, 1946.

Rand, Austin L. and Gilliard, E. Thomas. *Handbook of New Guinea Birds*. London, 1967.

Ramsay, Col. Wardlaw. *The Birds of Europe and North Africa*. Edinburgh, 1923.

Restall, R. *Finches and Other Seed-eating Birds*. London, 1975.

Risdon, D. H. S. *Foreign Birds for Beginners*, London, 1953.

Robbins, Chandler S., Bruan, Bertel and Zim, Herbert S. *Birds of North America*. New York, 1966.

Roberts, Dr. Austin. *Birds of South Africa*. Kaapstad, 1958.

Rogers, C. H. *Encyclopaedia of Cage and Aviary Birds*. New York and London, 1975.
Zebra Finches. Edinburgh, 1976.
Zebra Finches. Leicester, 1976.

Rutgers, A. *Vogels in Huis en Hun Verzorging*. Utrecht, 1960.
Tropische Volierevogels, I and II. Gorssel, 1961.
De Huisvesting van Volierevogels. Utrecht, 1965.
The Handbook of Foreign Birds, Vols. 1 and 2, Poole, 1977.
Birds of Asia. London, 1969.

Salim, Ali. *Indian Hill Birds*. Bombay, 1949.
The Birds of Sikkim. Madras, 1962.
The Book of Indian Birds. Bombay, 1955.

Santos, Eurico. *Passaros do Brasil*. Rio de Janeiro, 1960.

Savino, Dr. Fernando. *Anthologie Canaricole, Vols. I–IV*. Bari, 1957.

Serventy and Whittell. *Birds of Western Australia*. Perth, 1962.

Sharland, Michael. *A Territory of Birds*. London, 1964.
Tasmanian Birds. Sydney, 1958.

Shelley, G. E. *The Birds of Egypt*. London.

Smet, G. *Canaris couleurs. Le Canari du Harz*. Les Coudreaux, Chelles, 1947.
Les Canaris. Paris, 1953.

Smythies, B. E. *The Birds of Burma*. London, 1953.
The Birds of Borneo. Edinburgh, 1960.

Soderberg, P. M. *Foreign Birds for Cage and Aviary*, Vols. I–IV.

Steinbacher, Georg. *Knaurs Vogelbuch*. München, 1957.

Steinbacher, Joachim. *Exotische Vogel in Farben*. Ravensburg, 1965.

Stepanek, O. *Birds of Field and Forest*. London.

Stevens, Lyla. *Birds of Australia in Colour*. Melbourne.

Stork, C. J. *Het Houden, Verzorgen en de Kleurkweek van Zebravinken*. Amsterdam.

Stresemann, Erwin. *Die Entwicklung der Ornithologie*. Aachen, 1951.

Stroud, Robert. *Stroud's Digest on the Diseases of Birds*. Jersey City, 1964.

Sutton, G. M. *Mexican Birds*. Norman, Oklahoma, 1951.

Taverner, P. A. *Birds of Canada*. Ottawa, 1934.

Taylor, Lady. *Introduction to the Birds of Jamaica*. London, 1955.

Thorburn, Archibald. *British Birds*. London, 1925.

Tinbergen, L. *Vogels in hun domein*. Zutphen, 1962.

Tyne, Josselyn van and Berger, Andrew J. *Fundamentals of Ornithology*. New York, 1959.

Veerkamp, H. J. *Handleiding voor de Kleurkanarie-kweker*. Zutphen, 1967.

Voous, Dr. K. H. *De Vogels van de Nederlandse Antillen*. Curacao, 1955.

Walker, G. B. R. *Coloured Canaries*. Poole, 1976.

Wallace, G. J. *Introduction to Ornithology*. London.

Werken, H. van de. *Artis dieren-encyclopedie. Vogels*. Amsterdam, 1960.

Wetmore, Alexander. *Song and Garden Birds of North America*. Washington.

Whistler, Hugh. *Popular Handbook of Indian Birds*. London, 1963.

Wildash, P. *The Birds of South Vietnam*. Tokyo, 1968.

Wilson, Edward. *Birds of the Antarctic*. London, 1967.

Woolham, F., Avon, D. and Tilford, T. *Aviary Birds in Colour*. London, 1975.

Yamashina, Yoshimano. *Birds in Japan*. Tokyo, 1961.

JOURNALS

Avicultural Magazine. Magazine of the Avicultural Society. Hertford, 1894–

Bird Notes. Journal of the Foreign Bird Club. Brighton, 1902–

British Museum Catalogues (Birds).

Cage and Aviary Birds, London.

The Emu. Journal of the Royal Society of Western Australia.

Foreign Birds. Journal of the Foreign Bird League. Wellington, Somerset, 1933–

Ibis. Journal of the British Ornithologists' Union London, 1858–

Les Oiseaux du Monde. Paris.

Bêtes et Nature. Saint-Ouen.

Die Gefiederte Welt. Pfungstadt.

Die Vogelpost. Werdohl.

L'Oiseau. Paris.

Onze Vogels. Bergen op Zoom.

Ornithophile. Udine.

Vogelkosmos. Stuttgart.

Systematische Liebersicht.

INDEX TO LATIN NAMES

INDEX TO LATIN NAMES • 231

INDEX

Tanager, Yellow-throated 111
Thrush 1, 8, 76
  Abyssinian Ground 77
  Ant 58
  Ashy Ground 77
  Black 77
  Black-throated Laughing Jay 84
  Chinese Jay 84, Pl. VI
  Dama 76
  Dhyal 81, Pl. VII
  Glossy Black 77
  Jay 2, 82, 84
  Jewel 66
  Kuhl's Ground 77
  Masked Jay 84
  Melodius Jay 83
  Orange-headed Ground 76, Pl. VII
  Pied Ground 77
  Red-capped Jay 83
  Red-legged 78, Pl. VII
  Siberian Ground 77
  Spectacled Jay 83
  Streaked Laughing Jay 83
  Striated Laughing Jay 83
  Ward's Ground 77
  White-breasted Jay 83
  White-crested Jay 82, Pl. VI
  White-masked Ground 76
  White-throated Ground 76
  White-throated Laughing Jay 83
Tit 93
Tityra 63
Tody, Broad-billed 21
Toucan 2, 43
  Ariel 50
  Baillon's 50, Pl. VIII
  Black-billed Mountain 49
  Channel-billed 50
  Cuvier's 51
  Giant 52
  Green-billed 50
  Hill 49
  Inca 51
  Keel-billed 50
  Laminated-billed 49
  Mountain 49
  Plate-billed Mountain 49
  Red-billed 51
  Short-billed 51
  Spot-billed Pl. VIII
  Sulphur 50
  Sulphur-breasted 50, Pl. VIII
  Swainson's 51
  Toco 45, 52
  White-breasted 50
  Rainbow-billed 50
  Red-breasted 50
  Red-billed 51
  Short-billed 51
  Sulphur-breasted 51
  Swainson's 45, 51
Toucanet, Aracari 46
  Baillon's 49
  Banana 50
  Blue-throated 45
  Chestnut-billed Emerald 45
  Emerald 43, 45
  Lemon-collared 48
  Red-rumped Green 45
  Spot-billed 45, 48
  Yellow-eared 48

Touraco 12, 26
Trogon 12
  Bar-tailed 14
  Black-headed Pl. I
  Ceylon 15
  Collared 14
  Cuban 12, 16, Pl. I
  Duvaucel's 16, Pl. I
  Fire 12
  Highland 14
  Indian 15, Pl. II
  Masked 14
  Narina's 15, Pl. I
  Philippine 15
  Resplendant 12
  Striped 15
  White-tailed 14
Troupial 119, 120, Pl. XIV
  Red-headed Pl. XV
  Yellow-headed Pl. XV
Tumbler, Japanese 93
Twin-spot, Brown 151
  Dybowski's 148
  Green-backed 149, Pl. XXVI
  Grey 147
  Peters' 148, Pl. XXVI
  Rosy 148
  Verreaux's 148
Twite 126
Tyrant Flycatcher 59
  Long-tailed 59
  Sulphury 60

Umbrella Bird 62, 63
  Ornate 65
  Long-wattled 65
  Pensile 65

Violet-ear 7

Warbler 5, 6
Waxbill 1, 6, 7
  Aurora 166, Pl. XXVII
  Black-capped 142
  Black-cheeked 142, Pl. XXVIII
  Black-crowned 142
  Black-headed 142
  Black-masked 144
  Blue-breasted 168, Pl. XXVI
  Blue-headed 168, Pl. XXVI
  Common 141
  Crimson-winged 140
  Dufresne's 139
  Fawn-breasted 143
  Golden-breasted 165
  Green-breasted Pl. XXI
  Grey 141
  Masked 144
  Orange-cheeked 140, Pl. XXV
  Purple-bellied 169
  Red-bellied 141
  Red-eared 141, Pl. XXV
  Red-faced 166
  Red-faced Aurora 167
  St. Helena 141, Pl. XXV

Sidney 157, Pl. XXIV
Striped 166
Sundevall's 140, Pl. XXV
Vinaceous 144
Violet-eared 169, Pl. XXVII
Yellow-bellied 140, Pl. XXV
Waxwing 75, 76
  Bohemian 76
  Cedan 75
  Eastern 76
  Japanese 76
Weaver, Abyssinian Black-headed 197
  Atlas 194
  Baya 198, Pl. XXXII
  Bengal 197
  Black-foreheaded 201
  Black-fronted 196, Pl. XXIX
  Black-headed 196
  Black-necked 195
  Blue-billed Crimson-breasted 150
  Böhms Buffalo 189
  Bojer's 195
  Buffalo 188, Pl. XXXIV
  Cabanis 196
  Cape 195, 202
  Chestnut 197, Pl. XXXII
  Congo Crested, Pl. XXXII
  Crimson-crowned 200, Pl. XLIII
  Cuckoo 205, Pl. XXIX
  Dinemelli's 189, Pl. XXXIV
  Fire-crowned 201
  Golden Palm 195
  Great Masked 197
  Grenadier 201, Pl. XLII
  Layard's 197, Pl. XXXII
  Little Masked 194
  Madagascar 199
  Manyar 198
  Masked 195
  Mombasa Golden 195, Pl. XXIX
  Monk 194
  Napoleon 200, Pl. XLII
  Namaqua Masked 196
  Olive 195
  Parasitic 205
  Pelzeln's 194
  Red-billed 199
  Red-headed 199, Pl. XXII
  Scaly 193
  Scaly-crowned 193, Pl. XXXV
  Scaly-fronted 193
  Slender-billed 194
  Smith's Golden 195, Pl. XXIX
  Sociable 189, Pl. XXXIV
  Social 189
  Somali Buffalo 188
  South African Buffalo 188, Pl. XXXIV
  Southern Masked 196
  Speckle-crowned Pl. XXXV
  Speckle-fronted 192
  Spectacled 194, Pl. XXIX
  Spotted-backed 196, Pl. XXXII
  Taha 200, Pl. XLIII
  Thick-billed 193, Pl. XXIX
  Thick-billed Forest 161
  Village 196
  White-headed Buffalo 189
  White-browed Sparrow 189
  Yellow-backed 202